PROPHECY AND GENDER IN THE HEBREW BIBLE

THE BIBLE AND WOMEN

An Encyclopaedia of Exegesis and Cultural History

Edited by Christiana de Groot, Irmtraud Fischer,
Mercedes Navarro Puerto, and Adriana Valerio

Volume 1.2: Prophecy and Gender in the Hebrew Bible

SBL PRESS

PROPHECY AND GENDER IN THE HEBREW BIBLE

Edited by
L. Juliana Claassens and Irmtraud Fischer

with the assistance of
Funlola O. Olojede

SBL PRESS

Atlanta

Copyright © 2021 by SBL Press

All rights reserved. No part of this work may be reproduced or transmitted in any form or by any means, electronic or mechanical, including photocopying and recording, or by means of any information storage or retrieval system, except as may be expressly permitted by the 1976 Copyright Act or in writing from the publisher. Requests for permission should be addressed in writing to the Rights and Permissions Office, SBL Press, 825 Houston Mill Road, Atlanta, GA 30329 USA.

Library of Congress Control Number: 2021938422

Contents

Abbreviations ix

Women in the Prophetic Books of the Hebrew Bible
    Irmtraud Fischer.. 1

Part 1. Historical Background: Prophecy and Gender in the Ancient Near East

Narrative, Story, and History in the Biblical Traditions about the
    Formation of the Israelite Monarchy (1 Samuel 9–2 Samuel 5)
    Omer Sergi 13

Cult and War: Contributions of Iconography to a Gender-Oriented
    Exegesis of Prophecy
    Silvia Schroer 47

Nonmale Prophets in Ancient Near Eastern Sources
    Martti Nissinen 75

Women and Magic Practices in the Prophets (Joshua–Malachi)
    Ora Brison 111

Part 2. Female Literary Figures and Their Social-Historical Context in the Nevi'im

Female Biblical Prophets: Visible Bodies, Audible Voices—
    Liberated Word
    Nancy C. Lee..135

Profiles of Resistant Women in the Former Prophets
    Rainer Kessler 157

Women in the War Narratives of the Prestate Period
    (Joshua–Judges)
    Michaela Bauks 173

Gendered Politics: Dynastic Roles of Women in the Narratives
    about Saul, David, and Solomon
    Ilse Müllner 193

Women at the King's Court: Their Political, Economic, and
    Religious Significance in the Accounts of the Former Prophets
    Maria Häusl 229

Part 3. Gender and Metaphor in the Latter Prophets

Daughter Zion and Babylon, the Whore: The Female
    Personification of Cities and Countries in the Prophets
    Christl M. Maier 255

The Marriage Metaphor in the Prophets: Some Gender Issues
    Marta García Fernández 277

Do the Prophets Have a Private Life? Women as Literary and
    Redactional Tools
    Benedetta Rossi 293

Between Excruciating Pain and the Promise of New Life:
    Birth Imagery in the Prophets and Trauma Hermeneutics
    L. Juliana Claassens 315

Embodied Memories: Gender-Specific Aspects of Prophecy
    as Trauma Literature
    Ruth Poser 333

Pornoprophetics Revisited, Decades Later
    Athalya Brenner-Idan 359

The Meaning of the Female Presence in Messianic Texts
    within the Corpus of the Nevi'im
        Ombretta Pettigiani 373

The Never-Ending Search for God's Feminine Side:
    Feminine Aspects in the God-Image of the Prophets
        Hanne Løland Levinson 393

Contributors 411
Ancient Sources Index 413
Modern Authors Index 431

Abbreviations

1QIsa^a	Isaiah^a
2 Esd	2 Esdras
ÄAT	Ägypten und Altes Testament
AB	Anchor Bible
ABE	Asociación Bíblica Española
ABG	Arbeiten zur Bibel und ihrer Geschichte
ABR	*Australian Biblical Review*
ABRL	Anchor Bible Reference Library
AcT	*Acta Theologica*
ADPV	Abhandlungen des Deutschen Palästina-Vereins
AfO	*Archiv für Orientforschung*
AIL	Ancient Israel and Its Literature
AIRF	Acta Instituti Romani Finlandiae
AMD	Ancient Magic and Divination
AnBib	Analecta Biblica
ANEM	Ancient Near East Monographs
ANEP	Pritchard, James B., ed. *The Ancient Near East in Pictures Relating to the Old Testament*. 2nd ed. Princeton: Princeton University Press, 1994.
ANESSup	Ancient Near Eastern Studies Supplement Series
ANET	Pritchard, James B., ed. *Ancient Near Eastern Texts Relating to the Old Testament*. 3rd ed. Princeton: Princeton University Press, 1969.
Ant.	Josephus, *Jewish Antiquities*
AOAT	Alter Orient und Altes Testament
AoF	*Altorientalische Forschungen*
AR	Acts et recherches
ARAB	Luckenbill, Daniel David. *Ancient Records of Assyria and Babylonia*. 2 vols. Chicago: University of Chicago

	Press, 1906–1907. Repr., New York: Russell & Russell, 1962.
ARMT	Archives royales de Mari, transcrite et traduite
ASOR	American Schools of Oriental Research
AT	Antico Testamento
ATD	Das Alte Testament Deutsch
ATDan	Acta Theologica Danica
ATSAT	Arbeiten zu Text und Sprache im Alten Testament
b.	Babylonian Talmud
B	Codex Vaticanus
BA	*Biblical Archaeologist*
BAH	La bibliothèque archéologique et historique
BAR	*Biblical Archaeology Review*
BASOR	*Bulletin of the American Schools of Oriental Research*
BBB	Bonner biblische Beiträge
BCAWAH	Blackwell Companions to the Ancient World: Ancient History
BDB	Brown, Francis, S. R. Driver, and Charles A. Briggs. *A Hebrew and English Lexicon of the Old Testament*
BEATAJ	Beiträge zur Erforschung des Alten Testaments und des antiken Judentums
BETL	Bibliotheca Ephemeridum Theologicarum Lovaniensium
BfT	Biblisch-feministische Texte
Bib	*Biblica*
BibEnc	Biblical Encyclopedia
BibInt	Biblical Interpretation Series
BibW	BibleWorld
BJS	Brown Judaic Studies
BK	*Bibel und Kirche*
BKAT	Biblischer Kommentar, Altes Testament
BMW	Bible in the Modern World
BN	*Biblische Notizen*
BThSt	Biblisch-Theologische Studien
BTZ	*Berliner Theologische Zeitschrift*
BW	Bible and Women
BWANT	Beiträge zur Wissenschaft vom Alten und Neuen Testament
BZ	*Biblische Zeitschrift*

BZAW	Beihefte zur Zeitschrift für die alttestamentliche Wissenschaft
ca.	circa
CBQ	*Catholic Biblical Quarterly*
CBR	*Currents in Biblical Research*
CBW	*Conversations with the Biblical World*
CCM	Colección in clave de mujer
CH	Code of Hammurabi
CoIS	Copenhagen International Series
coll.	collective
COS	Hallo, William W. *The Context of Scripture*. 3 vols. Leiden: Brill, 1997–2002.
CP	Clásicos del pensamiento
CPB	*Christlich-Pädagogische Blätter*
CurTM	*Currents in Theology and Mission*
DJD	Discoveries in the Judaean Desert
EE	Estudios y ensayos
EJP	*European Journal of Psychotraumatology*
ERHBfT	Erev-Rav-Hefte: Biblisch-feministische Texte
EstEcl	*Estudios ecclesiásticos*
ESV	English Standard Version
EUZ	Exegese in unserer Zeit
FAT	Forschungen zum Alten Testament
FB	Forschung zur Bibel
FCB	Feminist Companion to the Bible
FM	Florilegium marianum
FOTL	Forms of the Old Testament Literature
FRLANT	Forschungen zur Religion und Literatur des Alten und Neuen Testaments
GAT	Grundrisse zum Alten Testament
GTA	Göttinger Theologische Arbeiten
HALOT	Koehler, Ludwig, Walter Baumgartner, and Johann J. Stamm. *The Hebrew and Aramaic Lexicon of the Old Testament*. Translated and edited under the supervision of Mervyn E. J. Richardson. 4 vols. Leiden: Brill, 1994–1999.
HANEM	History of the Ancient Near East Monographs
HAT	Handbuch zum Alten Testament
HB	Hebrew Bible

HBAI	*Hebrew Bible and Ancient Israel*
HBS	History of Biblical Studies
HdO	Handbook of Oriental Studies
HThKAT	Herders Theologischer Kommentar zum Alten Testament
HTR	*Harvard Theological Review*
HUBP	The Hebrew University Bible Project
ICC	International Critical Commentary
IECOT	International Exegetical Commentary on the Old Testament
Inc	*Incognita*
IPIAO	Schroer, Silvia. *Die Ikonographie Palästinas/Israels und der Alte Orient: Eine Religionsgeschichte in Bildern*. 4 vols. Fribourg: Academic Press, 2005–2011; Basel: Schwabe Verlag, 2018.
ITS	*Indian Theological Studies*
JAAR	*Journal of the American Academy of Religion*
JAJSup	Journal of Ancient Judaism Supplement Series
JBL	*Journal of Biblical Literature*
JFSR	*Journal of Feminist Studies in Religion*
JH	*Jewish History*
JHS	*Journal of Hellenic Studies*
JNES	*Journal of Near Eastern Studies*
JPOS	*Journal of the Palestine Oriental Society*
JSem	*Journal of Semitics*
JSOT	*Journal for the Study of the Old Testament*
JSOTSup	Journal for the Study of the Old Testament Supplement Series
JSS	*Journal of Semitic Studies*
JTSA	*Journal of Theology for Southern Africa*
J.W.	Josephus, *Jewish War*
K	tablets in the collections of the British Museum
KAT	Kommentar zum Alten Testament
KHC	Kurzer Hand-Commentar zum Alten Testament
KST	Kohlhammer-Studienbücher Theologie
KTU	Dietrich, Manfried, Oswald Loretz, and Joaquín Sanmartín, eds. *Die keilalphabetischen Texte aus Ugarit*. Münster: Ugarit-Verlag, 2013.
l(l.)	line(s)

LAS	Leipziger altorientalistische Studien
ld	*lectio difficilior*
LHBOTS	The Library of Hebrew Bible/Old Testament Studies
LOS	Lehrbücher orientalischer Sprachen
L^s	Fragmenta Sangallensia
L^w	Codex Wirceburgensis
LXX	Septuagint
M.	tablet signature of texts from Mari
Meg.	Megillah
MN	Mémoires de NABU
MS	Monograph Series
MSL	Materials for the Sumerian Lexicon
MT	Masoretic Text
NBE	Nueva Biblia Española
NCB	New Cambridge Bible
NEB	Die Neue Echter Bibel
NICOT	New International Commentary on the Old Testament
NKJV	New King James Version
NR	*Nova Religio*
NRSV	New Revised Standard Version
NTOA	Novum Testamentum et Orbis Antiquus
OBO	Orbis Biblicus et Orientalis
OBT	Overtures to Biblical Theology
OIP	Oriental Institute Publications
OIS	Oriental Institute Seminars
OJA	*Oxford Journal of Archaeology*
OLA	Orientalia Lovaniensia Analecta
OPSNKF	Occasional Publications of the Samuel Noah Kramer Fund
ORA	Orientalische Religionen in der Antike
OT	Old Testament
OTL	Old Testament Library
OTS	Old Testament Studies
OtSt	Oudtestamentische Studien
PBA	Proceedings of the British Academy
PdÄ	Probleme der Ägyptologie
pl.	plural
POr	Pliegos de Oriente
PP	*Pastoral Psychology*

QD	Quaestiones Disputatae
RAI	Rencontre assyriologique internationale
RB	*Revue biblique*
RevScRel	*Revue des sciences religeuses*
RGRW	Religions in the Graeco-Roman World
RI	Religionspädagogik Innovativ
RP	Religion und Politik
RRBS	Recent Research in Biblical Studies
RSV	Revised Standard Version
SAA	State Archives of Assyria
SAAB	*State Archives of Assyria Bulletin*
SAAS	State Archives of Assyria Series
SAM	Sheffield Archaeological Monographs
SANER	Studies in Ancient Near Eastern Records
SBFA	Studium Biblicum Franciscanum Analecta
SBLDS	Society of Biblical Literature Dissertation Series
SBLSBS	Society of Biblical Literature Sources for Biblical Study
SBR	Studies of the Bible and Its Reception
SBS	Stuttgarter Bibelstudien
SCS	Septuagint and Cognate Studies
SEJ	*Scandinavian Evangelical e-Journal*
Sem	*Semitica*
SemeiaSt	Semeia Studies
SHANE	Studies in the History of the Ancient Near East
SRB	Studies in Rewritten Bible
SSN	Studia Semitica Neerlandica
SSS	Syria Supplement Series
ST	Serie Teologica
StBibLit	Studies in Biblical Literature
STDJ	Studies on the Texts of the Desert of Judah
SVTG	Septuaginta: Vetus Testamentum Graecum
SymS	Symposium Series
TA	Texte und Arbeiten
TA	*Tel Aviv*
TC	Texts @ Contexts
TCL	Textes cunéiformes, Musées du Louvre
TDOT	Botterweck, G. Johannes, and Helmer Ringgren, eds. *Theological Dictionary of the Old Testament*. Translated

	by John T. Willis et al. 8 vols. Grand Rapids: Eerdmans, 1974–2006.
TFE	Theologische Frauenforschung in Europa
THAT	Jenni, Ernst, ed., with assistance from Claus Westermann. *Theologisches Handwörterbuch zum Alten Testament*. 2 vols. Munich: Chr. Kaiser Verlag; Zürich; Theologischer Verlag, 1971–1976.
ThWAT	Botterweck, G. Johannes, and Helmer Ringgren, eds. *Theologisches Wörterbuch zum Alten Testament*. Stuttgart: Kohlhammer, 1970–1995.
TLOT	Ernst Jenni, ed. with assistance from Claus Westermann. *Theological Lexicon of the Old Testament*. Translated by Mark E. Biddle. 3 vols. Peabody, MA: Hendrickson, 1997.
TUAT	Otto Kaiser, ed. *Texte aus der Umwelt des Alten Testaments*. Gütersloh: Mohn, 1984–2001.
TZ	*Theologische Zeitschrift*
UF	*Ugarit-Forschungen*
VOK	Veröffentlichungen der Orientalischen Kommission
VS	Vorderasiatische Schriftdenkmäler der Staatlichen Museen zu Berlin
VT	*Vetus Testamentum*
VTSup	Supplements to Vetus Testamentum
VWGT	Veröffentlichungen der Wissenschaftlichen Gesellschaft für Theologie
UTB	Uni-Taschenbücher
WAW	Writings from the Ancient World
WMANT	Wissenschaftliche Monographien zum Alten und Neuen Testament
WO	*Die Welt des Orients*
WUB	*Welt und Umwelt der Bibel*
ZAW	*Zeitschrift für die alttestamentliche Wissenschaft*
ZBK	Zürcher Bibelkommentare
ZDPV	*Zeitschrift des deutschen Palästina-Vereins*

Women in the Prophetic Books of the Hebrew Bible

Irmtraud Fischer

Women among the prophets? Without insight from biblical studies, Christian readers, both male and female, instinctively would say no. Not only is this perception connected to the fact that the early church had a difficult relationship with its (Montanist) prophetesses or that the feminine element in prophecy, especially from the early Renaissance until the high baroque period, was represented by prophetesses from among the nations, the sibyls,[1] but it is prompted especially by the form of the Christian canon of prophecy, which relates to the later prophets exclusively. On the other hand, the Jewish notion of prophecy opens an essentially wider window for female activities in the divination of the future and the interpretation of the present.

The present volume not only traces women as subjects of prophecy in the Bible and in the ancient Near East, which was shaped by various phenomena, and investigates the complex context of prophecy and gender. It also considers the sociohistorical background against which the narratives about women in the Former Prophets are to be understood. At the same time, it attempts to highlight the significance of feminine metaphors and personifications in the prophetic books of the Bible and to understand them within the context of ancient Near Eastern iconography. In addition, the volume provides insight into innovative gender-oriented approaches to the exegesis of texts, such as interpreta-

---

1. For details, see Irmtraud Fischer, "Konstruktion, Tradition und Transformation weiblicher Prophetie," in *Tradition(en) im alten Israel: Konstruktion, Transmission und Transformation*, ed. Ruth Ebach and Martin Leuenberger, FAT 127 (Tübingen: Mohr Siebeck, 2019), 189–99. The contextualization of the patristic view of prophetesses is treated by Agnethe Siquans, *Die alttestamentlichen Prophetinnen in der patristischen Rezeption: Texte—Kontexte—Hermeneutik*, HBS 65 (Freiburg: Herder, 2011).

tive concepts from trauma studies. Before interested readers are invited to immerse themselves in the multifaceted details of the connection between women and prophecy and in the gender-relevant themes of these biblical books, some basic facts about prophecy in ancient Israel and its different reception in the Jewish and Christian Bible should be outlined.

1. The Structure of the Canon Decisively Determines the Perception of Female Prophets

Anyone who reads the prophetic books in the Christian canon may well form the impression that exclusively men were active in this profession. All the so-called books of the biblical prophets were handed down under masculine names. Not a single prophetess can be found who is mentioned by name. The few references to female prophets have been either overlooked (e.g., Ezek 13:17–23; Joel 3:1) or pushed out of consciousness due to inadequate interpretation, as in the case of the prophetess to whom the prophet Isaiah went and who (consequently) bore him a son with a descriptive name (Isa 8:3) and who therefore was perceived exclusively by her role as the wife of a prophet.

But prophecy is only a part of the substantially larger prophetic canon of the Hebrew Bible. The Hebrew Bible presents the books of Joshua to 2 Kings not, as the Christian Old Testament does, as historical books but rather as prophecy. This inscribed hermeneutics has a considerable effect on the understanding of the books: they are not understood as historical narrative but rather as narratives of the prophetically conducted history of God and his people. This means that the truth of these books should not be sought in the historical but rather in the theological sphere. The arrangement of the canon of the Hebrew Bible also has a great impact on the emergence of the visibility of female prophets as well as of those significant women who, in this narrative of the history of Israel and Judah, had a decisive influence on political events. Anyone who reads the prophetic canon in this form encounters a woman as the first and the last prophetic figure in the Former Prophets. Two women designated as prophetesses, Deborah and Huldah, begin and conclude the series of great prophet(esse)s in, so to speak, an *inclusio*, such that with every mention of the grammatically masculine plural form, נביאים, "prophets," the term *prophetess* also must be read. For, on the one hand, Hebrew has no gender-neutral plural, and, on the other hand, the stylistic device of *inclu-*

sio indicates that what is valid for the first and the last member of a chain has validity also for all the other members.[2]

2. Significance of the Canonical Structure for Understanding Prophecy

Not only the scope of the prophetic canon but also the arrangement of its parts is different in the Jewish and the Christian Bible.[3] By placing prophecy at the end of the Old Testament canon and by understanding prophecy as a foretelling of the Messiah who would emerge in the New Testament, Christianity reads its two Testaments as contiguous. Thus not only Malachi's proclamation of the returning Elijah (Mal 3:23–24) formed a golden thread between prophecy and the gospels (with reference to John the Baptist in Matt 11:14; 17:10–13; Luke 1:17; with reference to Jesus in Matt 16:14; Mark 6:15; 8:28; Luke 9:19) but also all the texts from the prophetic books that at that time were understood messianically. Ombretta Pettigiani studies such texts in this volume with a special focus on the significance of the women in them. Klaus Koch called this theological linkage of both Testaments, often accompanied by an anti-Jewish accent and produced by the end position of prophecy, a "prophetic connection theory."[4] A view that takes both parts of the Christian Bible together is today a legitimate reception of biblical prophecy only if the texts are allowed to retain their original significance within the framework of the Hebrew Bible. The Jewish arrangement of the canon is, however, not simply irrelevant to Christians, as certain theological structures that emerge from the tripartite division of

---

2. This inclusion was addressed for the first time by Klara Butting, *Prophetinnen gefragt: Die Bedeutung der Prophetinnen im Kanon aus Tora und Prophetie*, ERHBfT 3 (Wittingen: Erev-Rav, 2001), 165–67. On the translation of the Hebrew masculine plural form into languages with gender-neutral forms, see Irmtraud Fischer, "Zwischen Kahlschlag, Durchforstung und neuer Pflanzung: Zu einigen Aspekten Feministischer Exegese und ihrer Relevanz für eine Theologie des Alten Testaments," in *Theologie und Exegese des Alten Testaments/der Hebräischen Bibel: Zwischenbilanz und Zukunftsperspektiven*, ed. Bernd Janowski, SBS 200 (Stuttgart: Katholisches Bibelwerk, 2005), 41–72.

3. See further details in Irmtraud Fischer, *Gotteskünderinnen: Zu einer geschlechterfairen Deutung des Phänomens der Prophetie und der Prophetinnen in der Hebräischen Bibel* (Stuttgart: Kohlhammer, 2002).

4. See on this point Klaus Koch, *The Rediscovery of Apocalyptic: A Polemical Work on a Neglected Area of Biblical Studies and Its Damaging Effects on Theology and Philosophy* (London: SCM, 1972), 35–46.

the Hebrew Bible and that are laid out probably for redactional reasons are no longer discernible as binding and meaningful in the reduced Christian prophetic canon.[5]

The key text to understanding prophecy in the Hebrew Bible is found in the Torah, in the law of prophecy in Deut 18:9–22. As the last of the Deuteronomistic laws on the administration of various offices (Deut 16:17–18:22), it defines the leadership skills necessary for a fruitful life in the promised land, beginning with the phrase "when you enter the land" (18:9; see 17:14). After the introduction, which warns against adopting the practices of the peoples of the land, the phenomenon of prophecy as divining the future and interpreting the present is first defined in terms of what it is not.[6] The mere fact that all cited means of communicating with a deity are listed in the law of prophecy shows that (at least) until the claim of monolatry in Deuteronomy such practices were understood in the context of prophecy. As Martti Nissinen also demonstrates for the ancient Near East, prophecy was by no means seen only in terms of the proclamation of the word. Some of the practices enumerated in Deut 18:10–14 can be found also in other passages in the Hebrew Bible (2 Kgs 21:6), but it is not possible, based on the sketchy information provided, to identify their precise procedures and rites. The essay by Ora Brison probes possible traces of such practices in the narrative texts of the Hebrew Bible. Many of these, such as using a drinking cup for divinatory purposes (see Gen 44:5–16), are also found in nonincriminating texts. Others, such as necromancy or passing children through fire, are strictly rejected. But these practices are also mentioned in narratives that take on a substantially different significance when read in connection with Deut 18:9–22. Thus the necromancy practiced by the woman from Endor who uses this practice to divine the future, by which she brings up the true prophet Samuel from the land of the dead after Saul's oath to YHWH (1 Sam 28:10), must be seen in the context of the practices forbidden in the Deuteronomistic laws concerning public offices, the so-called *Ämtergesetze*. The woman from Endor should therefore not be designated a witch in this intertextual reading but rather a

---

5. For example, the understanding of prophecy as an actualization of the Torah, which is portrayed in terms of imagery similar to that used in Wisdom. Sirach 24:23–33 is to be recognized here certainly as the endpoint of this development. See further details in Irmtraud Fischer, *Gotteslehrerinnen: Weise Frauen und Frau Weisheit im Alten Testament* (Stuttgart: Kohlhammer, 2006), 204–9.

6. See details in Fischer with a summary table of the Old Testament references to these practices (*Gotteskünderinnen*, 43–51; table on 58).

false prophetess in the sense of Deut 18:11, although she obviously practices her profession within the cult of Israel's deity, otherwise the oath offered to YHWH would make no sense.

Following this first part that declares the listed practices to be illegal, the law of prophecy in Deut 18:14b–22 defines what constitutes true prophecy in Israel and how one can recognize it. The reception of the word is stated (vv. 18–22; see also Jer 18:18) as the criterion par excellence. This word is meant to be heard (Deut 18:15, 19). The institution of prophecy as a mediatory office between God and the people takes place according to this law, in the theologically highly significant scene that follows the reception of the Decalogue on Horeb (Deut 18:15–18, with reference to 5:22–33). After the divine manifestation on the mountain, the people demand that they not risk any further direct encounter with YHWH. God grants this request and appoints Moses as the prophetic intermediary who, from the time of this event, takes over communication between God and his people. Consequently, the law of prophecy sees any form of prophecy in the light of succession to Moses: God will raise up a prophetically gifted person like him when needed (Deut 18:15, 18). The prophetic office is then the only one that individuals can neither occupy by their own choice nor pass on to the next generation—for the arrogation of the reception of the prophetic word without a previous divine initiative convicts a person of practicing false prophecy, which, according to Ezek 13:17, is committed also by women.

3. Prophetesses as Mediators between God and the People and as Bearers of Divine Messages

In his essay, Nissinen shows that prophecy in the ancient Near East existed already much earlier than in Israel and that it was always a gender-inclusive phenomenon. Women as well as men, and even transsexual and intersexual persons, are found in the entire ancient Near Eastern context among those who acted as mediators between the human and the divine worlds. The evidence, as far as it is known to us,[7] of Neo-Assyrian prophecy, which historically stands closest to biblical prophecy, shows a clear prevalence of prophetesses.

---

7. This connection has been established also by Hermann Spieckermann, *Juda unter Assur in der Sargonidenzeit*, FRLANT 129 (Göttingen: Vandenhoeck & Ruprecht, 1982), 302.

The first named prophetess of the Hebrew Bible is in the Torah. This is Miriam, who is designated a נביאה, "prophetess," in Exod 15:20. Narratively, this text stands before the encounter of the people with God on Mount Horeb, several chapters before the institution of the prophetic office as portrayed in Deut 5 and 18.[8] The other prophetesses—Deborah, Huldah, the prophetess to whom Isaiah goes, and Noadiah—are highlighted in the chapter by Nancy Lee, who also poses the interesting question of whether one can detect prophetic words uttered by women by means of their peculiar linguistic expressions like those that appear, for example, in songs ascribed to women. The significance of the wives of the prophets in the Latter Prophets—for example, Gomer, the wife of Hosea; the wife of Ezekiel; and the prophetess to whom Isaiah goes—and the meaning of Jeremiah's celibacy are investigated in the essay by Benedetta Rossi, who is extremely skeptical about the evidence of traces of a private life of the biblical prophets.

4. Political Roles of Women in the Narrated History of Israel

The books of the Former Prophets narrate a continuous story of the life of the people of God in the promised land from their entry into the land under the leadership of Joshua to their involuntary departure from it into exile in Babylon. This part of the Bible is shaped by world-engendering narratives[9] that outline the identity of Israel as an organized nation settling in the land from Dan to Beersheba. Omer Sergi concludes, on the basis of historical-archeological evidence from the Iron Age, that the beginning of the story in the land must have taken place differently from how it is presented in the biblical narratives and that originally the name "Israel" was not limited to the Northern Kingdom, just as it was used again with a broader application in the period after its decline.

---

8. A detailed essay that considers the evidence from prophecy is devoted to Miriam in Mercedes García Bachmann, "Miriam, Primordial Political Figure in the Exodus," in *Torah*, ed. Irmtraud Fischer, Mercedes Navarro Puerto, and Andrea Taschl-Erber, BW 1.1 (Atlanta: Society of Biblical Literature, 2011), 329–74.

9. On this concept, see Nelson Goodman, *Ways of Worldmaking* (Indianapolis: Hackett, 1978); on its application in Old Testament exegesis, see Irmtraud Fischer, "Menschheitsfamilie—Erzelternfamilie—Königsfamilie: Familien als Protagonistinnen von Welt erzeugenden Erzählungen," *BK* 70 (2015): 190–97.

The stories that take place during the period of the Iron Age tell again and again of strong women who decisively influenced political events.[10] Michaela Bauks examines female figures of the so-called prestate period, of whom the books of Joshua and Judges speak. A large part of these books consists of narratives about battles and wars, in which women step in "if need (of a man) be" and produce a good outcome. Given that a patriarchal order is assumed in ancient Near Eastern societies and that the art of war was practiced exclusively by men, the texts that present women as especially independent and as determinedly active in the community are surprising. With reference to the same corpus, Rainer Kessler focuses specifically on the diverse profiles of what he describes as resistant women. Women are portrayed as victims of sexual violence, as leaders of their community, as supporters of future victors. Women may abuse their power, or they may fight for their rights. This diversity in roles is important, as the narratives of the Former Prophets do not reduce the portrait to one single image of the resistant woman.

In her chapter on women in war and in the cult, Silvia Schroer considers the corresponding iconographic evidence and looks into the religious history of the changing significance of the cult of the goddess in the transition period from the Bronze to the Iron Age. In addition, she relates the biblical texts that suggest the veneration of female deities to the visual material from Eretz Israel of the same periods. Her essay is also relevant for understanding feminine metaphors and the verbal imagery in biblical texts. Three other essays in this volume similarly address this subject matter. Christl Maier highlights the phenomenon of female personification of cities and countries that is found in numerous prophetic texts and discusses the gender-specific implications of such linguistic constructions. Marta García Fernández devotes her discussion to the marital imagery that, in many prophetic texts, portrays the illustrious but also thorny relationship between Israel's deity and the people. This metaphorical language, the feminine aspect of which also represents men, has gender-specific effects on gender roles and gender constructions. Hanne Løland Levinson's essay focuses on the metaphorical language for God in the prophetic literature and reflects on what has changed and not changed since biblical scholars started the search for the feminine side of God.

---

10. On the useful distinction between narrated time, in which the story is set, and narrating time, in which the story is told, see Paul Ricoeur, *Zeit und Erzählung 3: Die erzählte Zeit*, Übergänge 18.3 (Munich: Fink, 1991).

The great significance of female characters in the texts that tell of the founding of a dynastic monarchy over three generations is investigated by Ilse Müllner. The many women around David who help him in his ascension to power and in the legitimation of his rule and who support him as diplomats but also are in need of his help, such as his daughter Tamar, are anchored in his family circle in spite of the political context of royal dominion. Although queens appear in these texts, in particular in their genealogical-dynastic function as the mothers of future kings, and intervene in the succession to the throne, several other references to the economic and religious significance of women at royal courts are found in 1–2 Kings. The essay by Maria Häusl focuses on these female figures and references to their economic-political independence or even their offices.

When read together, these individual essays, which illustrate various aspects of the life of women in ancient Israel at the time of the origins of the biblical texts, result in a multifaceted and colorful picture that clearly refutes the often-enunciated view that women had nothing to say or to contribute to decision making in patriarchal societies, that they were economically dependent on their fathers or husbands and played neither a political nor a cultic role. However, most of the stories only provide an insight into the lives of the upper class or at least into the socioeconomic life context of well-to-do people (see the diptych of gender-specific threatening speech in Isa 3:1–15; 3:16–4:1).[11] Among the underprivileged classes of the society, the male members also had little say in decision-making processes. If they were absent as husbands, brothers, or sons, then their work and their social responsibility in these social classes quickly had to be taken over by women. A chapter on the complex nature of these gender-specific problems that are addressed by the prophetic social critique in many biblical books (see Hos 4:12–14; Mic 2:8–11; Mal 2:10–16) would have certainly enriched the present volume even more.

5. Recent Approaches

A relatively new approach to the violent texts of prophecy is trauma hermeneutics, which helps to illuminate many dark texts in the Hebrew

---

11. See details in Irmtraud Fischer, "Isaiah: The Book of Female Metaphors," in *Feminist Biblical Interpretation: A Compendium of Critical Commentary on the Books of the Bible and Related Literature*, ed. Luise Schottroff and Marie-Theres Wacker (Grand Rapids: Eerdmans, 2012), 306–18.

Bible with its gender-conscious slant. It can read disconcerting circumstances, such as the cruelest threats of divine punishment in prophetic texts or the escalation of fantasies of vengeance, against the background of the experience of traumatized people and can make research in transgenerational trauma fruitful for Old Testament exegesis. Through this hermeneutics, Juliana Claassens investigates texts in biblical prophecy that employ aspects of the birth process, such as the inescapability of labor pains, as a metaphor for violent political upheavals. Ruth Poser probes the connection between trauma and gender in prophetic texts in the context of the hermeneutical premise of postcolonial studies. She argues that the explanation, which is associated with the idea of theodicy, that God consciously wanted to punish his people through the victory of their enemies (and by no means was too weak to effect salvation!) reflects a strategy for coping that leads away from the experience of total impotence insofar as the people themselves were responsible for the catastrophe, which can thus be avoided in the future by a different behavior. Finally, Athalya Brenner-Idan revisits decades later what she described as pornoprophetic passages (Jer 2; 5; Ezek 16; 23; Hos 1–3) in the context of, for example, the #MeToo movement and recent developments in terms of gender theory.

This volume offers a multifaceted insight into the portrayal of female life within prophetic contexts. It correlates biblical texts with historical-archaeological and iconographic material from the ancient Near East and reads, with a fair regard for gender, the numerous metaphorical texts that see the people as female and illustrate what happens to it with images from female biology. It thus offers a compendium compatible with historical reception as well as a hermeneutical background for conceptions that continue to be influential today.

Bibliography

Bachmann, Mercedes García. "Miriam, Primordial Political Figure in the Exodus." Pages 329–74 in *Torah*. Edited by Irmtraud Fischer, Mercedes Navarro Puerto, and Andrea Taschl-Erber. BW 1.1. Atlanta: Society of Biblical Literature, 2011.

Butting, Klara. *Prophetinnen gefragt: Die Bedeutung der Prophetinnen im Kanon aus Tora und Prophetie*. ERHBfT 3. Wittingen: Erev-Rav, 2001.

Fischer, Irmtraud. *Gotteskünderinnen: Zu einer geschlechtsfairen Deutung des Phänomens der Prophetie und der Prophetinnen in der Hebräischen Bibel*. Stuttgart: Kohlhammer, 2002.

———. *Gotteslehrerinnen: Weise Frauen und Frau Weisheit im Alten Testament*. Stuttgart: Kohlhammer, 2006.

———. "Isaiah: The Book of Female Metaphors." Pages 303–18 in *Feminist Biblical Interpretation: A Compendium of Critical Commentary on the Books of the Bible and Related Literature*. Edited by Luise Schottroff and Marie-Theres Wacker. Grand Rapids: Eerdmans, 2012.

———. "Konstruktion, Tradition und Transformation weiblicher Prophetie." Pages 181–204 in *Tradition(en) im alten Israel: Konstruktion, Transmission und Transformation*. Edited by Ruth Ebach and Martin Leuenberger. FAT 127. Tübingen: Mohr Siebeck, 2019.

———. "Menschheitsfamilie—Erzelternfamilie—Königsfamilie: Familien als Protagonistinnen von Welt erzeugenden Erzählungen." *BK* 70 (2015): 190–97.

———. "Zwischen Kahlschlag, Durchforstung und neuer Pflanzung: Zu einigen Aspekten Feministischer Exegese und ihrer Relevanz für eine Theologie des Alten Testaments." Pages 41–72 in *Theologie und Exegese des Alten Testaments/der Hebräischen Bibel: Zwischenbilanz und Zukunftsperspektiven*. Edited by Bernd Janowski. SBS 200. Stuttgart: Katholisches Bibelwerk, 2005.

Goodman, Nelson. *Ways of Worldmaking*. Indianapolis: Hackett, 1978.

Koch, Klaus. *The Rediscovery of Apocalyptic: A Polemical Work on a Neglected Area of Biblical Studies and Its Damaging Effects on Theology and Philosophy*. London: SCM, 1972

Ricoeur, Paul. *Zeit und Erzählung 3: Die erzählte Zeit*. Übergänge 18.3. Munich: Fink, 1991.

Siquans, Agnethe. *Die alttestamentlichen Prophetinnen in der patristischen Rezeption: Texte—Kontexte—Hermeneutik*. HBS 65. Freiburg: Herder, 2011.

Spieckermann, Hermann. *Juda unter Assur in der Sargonidenzeit*. FRLANT 129. Göttingen: Vandenhoeck & Ruprecht, 1982.

Part 1
Historical Background:
Prophecy and Gender in the Ancient Near East

Narrative, Story, and History in the Biblical Traditions about the Formation of the Israelite Monarchy (1 Samuel 9–2 Samuel 5)

Omer Sergi

1. Introduction

The traditions about the formation of the Israelite monarchy that are embedded within 1 Sam 9–2 Sam 5 tell about Saul, the first king of the Israelites, who failed to establish dynastic monarchy. He was followed by his rival, David, who succeeded precisely where Saul failed. David established a long-lasting dynastic monarchy and brought the Israelites and the Judahites under his rule. Although this story line forms a rather unified narrative (at least in its theme and plot), with many links tying together the different accounts embedded in it,[1] the conventional wisdom that rules contemporary scholarship on the matter is that these traditions stem from two distinct sources, each of different origin: a northern Israelite tradition about Saul (usually identified as 1 Sam 9–14), which tells about the rise and fall of the first Israelite king; and a Judahite collection of stories about David's rise, which presents David as Saul's legitimate successor (1 Sam 16–2 Sam 5). It is assumed that the northern Israelite traditions about Saul arrived in Judah only after the fall of Samaria in 720 BCE and stimulated the composition of the stories about David's rise, which are dated, accordingly, to the seventh century BCE. It is further assumed that these stories created the first literary link between Saul the Israelite and David the Judahite in order to present Judah as the political and cultural

---

1. Walter Dietrich and Thomas Nauman, "The David–Saul Narrative," in *Reconsidering Israel and Judah: Recent Studies on the Deuteronomistic History*, ed. Gary N. Knoppers and J. Gordon McConville (Winona Lake, IN: Eisenbrauns, 2000), 276–318.

successor of the former kingdom of Israel.[2] In other words, it is argued that the stories about David's rise connect two formerly unrelated literary protagonists—the first king of Israel (Saul) and the first king of Judah (David)—in order to present the house of David (Judah) as the rightful successor to the house of Saul (Israel).

At the heart of this hypothesis lies the assumption that the stories in 1 Sam 16–2 Sam 5 are actually an allegory to the histories of Israel and Judah. This assumption, however, is the result of historical, and not literary, observation. Historically, it is quite clear today that the kingdoms of Israel and Judah were never united within one political entity under the rule of the house of David from Jerusalem (see below). It is therefore assumed that any portrayal of the first kings of Judah (David) as the heir of the first king of Israel (Saul) could only reflect a Judahite wishful thinking and not an accurate political reality. The main problem with this assumption is that both the early Saul traditions and the stories about David's rise are well embedded in the social and political realia of southern Canaan in the early Iron Age (below); therefore, there is no real reason to read them as allegories. Rather, we should at least try to read them for what they are—an attempt to portray the rise of the Israelite monarchy. In this study, I aim to do exactly that, and accordingly, following a brief review of the historical context in which the formation of Israel and Judah should be

---

2. For example, Walter Dietrich and Stefan Münger, "Die Herrschaft Sauls und der Norden Israels," in *Saxa Loquentur: Studien zu Archäologie Palästinas/Israels, Festschrift für Volkmar Fritz zum 65. Geburtstag*, ed. Cornelius G. den Hertog, Ulrich Hübner, and Stefan Münger, AOAT 302 (Münster: Ugarit-Verlag, 2003), 39–54; Reinhard G. Kratz, *The Composition of the Narrative Books of the Old Testament* (London: T&T Clark, 2005), 181–82; Israel Finkelstein, "The Last Labayu: King Saul and the Expansion of the First North Israelite Entity," in *Essays on Ancient Israel in Its Near Eastern Context: A Tribute to Nadav Na'aman*, ed. Yaira Amit et al. (Winona Lake, IN: Eisenbrauns, 2006), 171–88; Kratz, "Saul, Benjamin and the Emergence of Biblical Israel: An Alternative View," *ZAW* 123 (2011): 348–67; Walter Dietrich, *The Early Monarchy in Israel: The Tenth Century BCE*, BibEnc 3 (Atlanta: Society of Biblical Literature, 2007), 247–48, 304–8; Otto Kaiser, "Der historische und biblische König Saul (Teil I)," *ZAW* 122 (2010): 524–26; Kaiser, "Der historische und biblische König Saul (Teil II)," *ZAW* 123 (2011): 1–14; Jacob L. Wright, *David, King of Israel, and Caleb in Biblical Memory* (Cambridge: Cambridge University Press, 2014), 39–50, 141–46; Hannes Bezzel, *Saul: Israels König in Tradition, Redaktion und früher Rezeption*, FAT 97 (Tübingen: Mohr Siebeck, 2015), 228–34; but see Nadav Na'aman, "Saul, Benjamin and the Emergence of Biblical Israel," *ZAW* 121 (2009): 211–24, 335–49, who challenged this perception.

seen, I shall summarize the archaeological remains that may attest to the nature of the formation of these two kingdoms. This historical and archaeological discussion will be the basis for examining the historical context, the origins, and meaning of the biblical traditions about the formation of the Israelite monarchy in 1 Sam 9–2 Sam 5.[3]

---

3. The assumption that a great united monarchy was a political entity that included both Israel and Judah under the centralized rule of the house of David from Jerusalem was based on the description of David's kingdom in the so-called succession narrative (2 Sam 13–20; 1 Kgs 1–2) and on the stories about the Solomonic kingdom and its breakup (1 Kgs 3–12). Already during the late eighties and the early nineties of the last century, scholars had begun to doubt the historicity of these narratives, pointing to the lack of any extrabiblical evidence for the existence of a great united monarchy. Biblical scholars emphasized, consequently, the gap between the rather late date of the biblical narratives (not before the eighth century BCE, and for many scholars even much later; see below) and the early reality they yearn to depict (the tenth century BCE). The archaeological explorations of the past thirty years followed, bringing the reconstruction of a great united monarchy to its final end. From an archaeological point of view, it became clear that the northern Samaria Hills were much more densely settled compared to the regions of Judah and Jerusalem, and, accordingly, they exhibit faster accumulation of wealth, which enabled the development of complex social structure and political centralization. Furthermore, based on growing archaeological knowledge in the fields of relative and absolute chronologies, it became clear that monumental buildings in northern Israel, which were traditionally dated to the mid-tenth century BCE and attributed to Solomon, were actually erected in the ninth century BCE, and they are now almost commonly attributed to the Omride dynasty. This new dating went hand-in-hand with historical sources indicating the priority of the kingdom of Israel, especially during the Omride reign. The archaeological picture from Jerusalem and Judah supported this conclusion, indicating the gradual growth of Judah mainly during the second half of the ninth century BCE, and much after Israel was established as a significant territorial kingdom. In light of all the above, the historicity of a great united monarchy, as depicted in 2 Sam 13–2 Kgs 12, could not be maintained, and scholarly interest is focused today on the formation of Israel and Judah as separated entities, and on the formation of the biblical traditions regarding the united monarchy and their origin. For the summary of archaeological evidence and the state of research on the great united monarchy, see Israel Finkelstein, "A Great United Monarchy? Archaeological and Historical Perspectives," in *One God—One Cult—One Nation*, ed. Reinhard G. Kratz and Hermann Spieckermann, BZAW 405 (Berlin: de Gruyter, 2010), 3–28. For state formation in Judah, see Omer Sergi, "Judah's Expansion in Historical Context," *TA* 40 (2013): 226–46; Sergi, "The Emergence of Judah as a Political Entity between Jerusalem and Benjamin," *ZDPV* 133 (2017): 1–23; and further below. For the formation of Israel, see below. For recent discussion of the biblical traditions regarding the united monarchy, see Nadav Na'aman, "Memories of Monarchical Israel

2. Historical Context: State Formation in the Early Iron Age Levant

The early Iron Age saw the reformation of political organization throughout the Levant when, following the demise of the Hittite and Egyptian political domination, new kin-based territorial polities ruled by local dynasties emerged on the scene.[4] It was the demise of the Late Bronze Age social structure with its ruling elites—related to the former city-state system and to the regional powers (Egyptian and Hittites)—that allowed the rise of new elites, of different origin, who found its legitimacy in a different social structure.[5] As these new, rising elites managed to grow in strength, they were engaged in a relentless effort to expand their political hegemonies beyond their core communities, thus integrating different territories, communities, and political formations under their centralized rule.[6] This is the social and political context in which we should understand the rise of Israel and Judah. Coming to reconstruct state formation in Israel and Judah, we should first ask when a new elite rose to power and over whom it first established its political hegemony. A brief review of the archaeological finds from the central Canaanite hill country may shed light on these questions.

---

in the Narrative of David's Wars with Israel's Neighbours," *HBAI* 6 (2017): 308–28; Sergi, "The United Monarchy and the Kingdom of Jeroboam II in the Story of Absalom and Sheba's Revolts," *HBAI* 6 (2017): 329–53, with further literature.

4. Trevor R. Bryce, *The World of the Neo-Hittite Kingdoms: A Political and Military History* (Oxford: Oxford University Press, 2012), 202–4; Helen Sader, "History," in *The Aramaeans in Ancient Syria*, ed. Herbert Niehr, HdO 106 (Leiden: Brill, 2014), 11–13.

5. For example, Glenn M. Schwartz, "The Origins of the Aramaeans in Syria and Northern Mesopotamia: Research Problems and Potential Strategies," in *To the Euphrates and Beyond: Archaeological Studies in Honor of Maurits N. van Loon*, ed. Odette M. C. Haex, Hans H. Curvers, and Peter M. M. G. Akkermans (Rotterdam: CRC, 1989), 275–91; Guy Bunnens, "Syria in the Iron Age: Problems and Definitions," in *Essays on Syria in the Iron Age*, ed. Guy Bunnens, ANESSup 7 (Leuven: Peeters, 2000), 3–19; Stefania Mazzoni, "Syria and the Periodization of the Iron Age: A Cross-Cultural Perspective," in Bunnens, *Essays on Syria*, 31–59; Bryce, *World of the Neo-Hittite Kingdoms*, 163–65, 202–4.

6. On state formation in the early Iron Age Levant, see Omer Sergi and Izaak de Hulster, "Some Historical and Methodological Considerations Regarding the Question of Political, Social and Cultural Interaction between Aram and Israel in the Early Iron Age," in *In Search of Aram and Israel: Politics, Culture and the Question of Identity*, ed. Omer Sergi, Manfred Oeming, and Izaak de Hulster, ORA 20 (Tübingen: Mohr Siebeck, 2016), 1–14, with additional literature.

3. The Formation of Israel and Judah in the Central Canaanite Hill Country: Archaeological Perspective

The central Canaanite hill country may be divided into two major geographical units—the Samaria Hills to the north and the Judean Hills to the south. The Samaria Hills stretch from the Jezreel Valley in the north to the highlands of Shiloh/Bethel in the south, and it forms the most suitable part for habitation in the hill country. To the south, the Judean Hills, between Jerusalem and the Beersheba Valley, have desert-fringe areas to both the east and south. The central range is relatively flat but rocky and steep in its western flank. The area north of Jerusalem, the Benjamin Plateau, between Jerusalem and Bethel, with its desert fringe, is relatively amenable to habitation and hence makes an intermediate zone between the more hospitable Samaria Hills to the north and the less convenient Judean Hills to the south.[7]

A massive sedentarization process characterizes the central Canaanite highlands during the Iron I (late twelfth–early tenth centuries BCE).[8] It is almost universally agreed today that the settlement pattern (throughout the Early Bronze Age I–Iron Age I), the architectural layout, and the material remains of the recently settled population all reflect the sedentarization of mobile pastoralist groups that shifted from subsistence economy based mainly on animal husbandry to an agropastoral mode of life. That means that the Iron I settlers in the hill country were the indigenous mobile pastoral population of the Samaria and Judean Hills, and if so, they were not only well acquainted with the regions in which they chose to settle but were also an integral part of the highlands' social structure.[9] Most of the

---

7. Israel Finkelstein, "The Great Transformation: The 'Conquest' of the Highlands Frontiers and the Rise of the Territorial States," in *The Archaeology of Society in the Holy Land*, ed. Thomas Levy (London: Leicester University Press, 1995), 353.

8. For the current state of research regarding the absolute chronology of the early Iron Age (based on a large body of radiocarbon measurements), see Sharen Lee, Christopher Bronk Ramsey, and Amihai Mazar, "Iron Age Chronology in Israel: Results from Modeling with a Trapezoidal Bayesian Framework," *Radiocarbon* 55 (2013): 731–40; Michael B. Toffolo et al., "Absolute Chronology of Megiddo, Israel in the Late Bronze and Iron Ages: High Resolution Radiocarbon Dating," *Radiocarbon* 56 (2014): 221–44.

9. For example, Israel Finkelstein, *The Archaeology of the Israelite Settlement* (Jerusalem: Israel Exploration Society, 1988); Finkelstein, "Great Transformation," 349–65; Finkelstein, "Ethnicity and the Origin of the Iron I Settlers in the Highlands of Canaan:

newly founded settlements clustered in the Samaria Hills, between the Jezreel Valley and Shiloh.[10] The hilly terrain south of Shiloh, all the way to Bethel (some 20 km south of Shiloh), was only sparsely settled (compared to the region to its north) during the Iron I and even more so in the Iron IIA. The next cluster of settlements is concentrated in the Benjamin Plateau, between Bethel in the north and Jerusalem in the south.[11] Noteworthy is that settlement expansion into the hilly terrain of the Shechem and the Shiloh regions demonstrates clear spatial continuity between the northern and southern Samaria Hills, while no such continuity exists south of Shiloh or south of Jerusalem. This leaves the southern cluster of settlements (in the Benjamin Plateau) rather isolated.

Shechem (Tell Balaṭah) was the most important political and economic center in the Samaria Hills throughout the second millennium, BCE as is demonstrated by textual sources (Egyptian execration texts, el-Amarna archive) and archaeological remains. From the Middle Bronze II–III to the Iron I (with a short hiatus in the Late Bronze I), Shechem was a well-fortified highland stronghold with sanctuaries built on its summit.[12]

Can the Real Israelites Stand Up?," *BA* 59 (1996): 198–212; Baruch Rosen, "Economy and Subsistence," in *Shiloh: The Archaeology of a Biblical Site*, ed. Israel Finkelstein, MS 10 (Tel Aviv: Institute of Archaeology, 1993), 362–67; and for Transjordan, see Evelin J. Van Der Steen, *Tribes and People in Transition: The Central East Jordan Valley in the Late Bronze Age and Early Iron Ages; A Study of the Sources* (Leuven: Peeters, 2004); Benjamin Porter, *Complex Communities: The Archaeology of Early Iron Age Central Transjordan* (Tucson: University of Arizona Press, 2013).

10. Finkelstein, "Great Transformation," 349–65; Adam Zertal, *The Shechem Syncline*, vol. 1 of *The Manasseh Hill Country Survey*, CHANE 21.1 (Leiden: Brill, 2004); Zertal, *The Eastern Valleys and the Fringe of the Desert*, vol. 2 of *The Manasseh Hill Country Survey*, CHANE 21.2 (Leiden: Brill, 2008); Adam Zertal and Nivi Mirkam, *From Nahal Iron to Nahal Shechem*, vol. 3 of *The Manasseh Hill Country Survey*, CHANE 21.3 (Leiden: Brill, 2016); Yuval Gadot, "The Iron I in the Samaria Highlands: A Nomad Settlement Wave or Urban Expansion?," in *Rethinking Israel: Studies in the History and Archaeology of Ancient Israel in Honor of Israel Finkelstein*, ed. Oded Lipschits, Yuval Gadot, and Matthew J. Adams (Winona Lake, IN: Eisenbrauns, 2017), 103–14.

11. Finkelstein, *Archaeology of the Israelite Settlement*, 188–92, 198–99, 201–2; Israel Finkelstein and Zvi Lederman, *Highlands of Many Cultures: The Southern Samaria Survey; The Sites*, MS 14 (Tel-Aviv: Institute of Archaeology, 1997), 949–51; Sergi, "Emergence of Judah," 1–23.

12. Edward F. Campbell, *Shechem III: The Stratigraphy and Architecture of Shechem/Tell Balâṭah*, vol. 1, *Text*, ASOR 6 (Boston: American Schools of Oriental

Shechem demonstrates clear and organic continuity in the transition from the Late Bronze Age to the Iron I,[13] but it was utterly destroyed at the end of that period, namely, in the early tenth century BCE.[14] The city was only sparsely settled throughout the Iron IIA (tenth–ninth centuries BCE),[15] and during that period the political and economic weight shifted first to Tell el-Farʿah north, identified with biblical Tirzah,[16] and then to Samaria. Sometime during the end of the tenth or the early ninth century BCE, Tirzah rapidly developed from a rather poor settlement (stratum VIIa) to a rich urban center exhibiting social hierarchy, cultic activity, and long-distance trade (stratum VIIb). It was utterly destroyed shortly after, probably still within the first half of the ninth century BCE, and was abandoned throughout the ninth century BCE.[17]

Following the destruction of Tirzah in the early ninth century BCE, the power balance shifted back to the heartland of Samaria, where a palatial compound was lavishly built on what was previously an agricultural estate that had no preceding urban or monumental tradition.[18] It manifested the accumulation of wealth and consequently also political power in the hands of newly emerged elites, the Omride dynasty, with which

---

Research, 2002); Israel Finkelstein, "Shechem in the Late Bronze and the Iron I," in *Timelines: Studies in Honor of Manfred Bietak*, ed. Ernst Czerny et al., OLA 149 (Leuven: Peeters, 2006), 349–56.

13. Campbell, *Shechem III*, 210–33; Finkelstein, "Shechem in the Late Bronze," 352.

14. The excavators dated the destruction to the twelfth century BCE (Campbell, *Shechem III*, 230–33), but the small Iron I assemblage published contains also vessels representing the end of the Iron I (Finkelstein, "Shechem in the Late Bronze," 352).

15. The published data do not confirm when exactly in the Iron Age Shechem flourished again—whether in the late Iron IIA or later, in the early Iron IIB (Campbell, *Shechem III*, 235–70). In either case, it seems that throughout most of the tenth century and probably some parts of the ninth century, Shechem was not a major player in the region.

16. William F. Albright, "The Site of Tirzah and the Topography of Western Manasseh," *JPOS* 11 (1931): 241–51.

17. See Assaf Kleiman, "Comments on the Archaeology and History of Tell el-Farʿah North (Biblical Tirzah) in the Iron IIA," *Sem* 60 (2018): 85–104.

18. For a discussion of the stratigraphy of the palatial compound in Samaria and related literature, see Omer Sergi and Yuval Gadot, "Omride Palatial Architecture as Symbol in Action: Between State Formation, Obliteration and Heritage," *JNES* 76 (2017): 105–6.

the palace on the Samaria hilltop is exclusively identified (1 Kgs 16:24).[19] Assuming that the rich agricultural estate preceding the erection of the Omride palace in Samaria was the family's estate, it reflects the wealth that accumulated in the hands of the Omrides prior to their rise to power.[20]

By the early ninth century BCE, from their seat in the heartland of Samaria, the Omrides extended their political hegemony over vast territories that inhabited different social groups, as is also clear from biblical and extrabiblical sources.[21] The extension of Omride political hegemony was marked in the landscape by the erection of royal compounds on the western (Megiddo VA–IVB) and eastern (Jezreel) edges of the Jezreel Valley. A new fortified town was erected in the Hulah Valley (Hazor X–IX), on the ruins of what was once the royal capital of one of the strongest polities in second-millennium BCE Canaan. All these buildings manifested the power and wealth of the highland dynasty and served as the locale for integrating local elites into the web of the newly established Omride hegemony.[22] The Omrides extended their political hegemony

---

19. For example, Israel Finkelstein, "Omride Architecture," *ZDPV* 116 (2000): 114–38; Finkelstein, *The Forgotten Kingdom: The Archaeology and History of Northern Israel*, ANEM 5 (Atlanta: Society of Biblical Literature, 2013), 85–94; H. Michael Niemann, "Core Israel in the Highlands and Its Periphery: Megiddo, the Jezreel Valley and the Galilee in the Eleventh–Eighth Century BCE," in *Megiddo IV: The 1998–2002 Seasons*, ed. Israel Finkelstein, David Ussishkin, and Baruch Halpern, MS 24 (Tel Aviv: Institute of Archaeology, 2006), 821–42; Niemann, "Royal Samaria—Capital or Residence? Or: The Foundation of the City of Samaria by Sargon II," in *Ahab Agonistes: The Rise and Fall of the Omri Dynasty*, ed. Lester L. Grabbe, LHBOTS 421 (London: T&T Clark, 2007), 184–207.

20. Sergi and Gadot, "Omride Palatial Architecture," 109. For the archaeological remains of the agricultural estate that preceded the building of the palace in Samaria (Building Period 0), see Lawrence E. Stager, "Shemer's Estate," *BASOR* 277/278 (1990): 93–107; Norma Franklin, "Samaria: From the Bedrock to the Omride Palace," *Levant* 36 (2004): 190–94.

21. Nadav Na'aman, "The Northern Kingdom in the Late Tenth–Ninth Centuries BCE," in *Understanding the History of Ancient Israel*, ed. Hugh G. M. Williamson, PBA 143 (Oxford: Oxford University Press, 2007), 399–418; Israel Finkelstein, "Stages in the Territorial Expansion of the Northern Kingdom," *VT* 61 (2011): 227–42; Finkelstein, *Forgotten Kingdom*, 83–112; Daniel Fleming, *The Legacy of Israel in Judah's Bible: History, Politics and the Reinscribing of Tradition* (Cambridge: Cambridge University Press, 2012), 28–90.

22. Niemann, "Core Israel," 821–42; Sergi and Gadot, "Omride Palatial Architecture," 108–10.

also to the more arid and less sedentary regions of the plains of Moab by establishing patronage relationship with local leaders of mobile pastoral groups (see 2 Kgs 3:4), and by erecting forts on the main trade routes that crossed the region.[23]

The dramatic shifts in power balance in the northern Samaria Hills, from Shechem to Tirzah and to Samaria, had little or no effect on the political formation in the south, around Jerusalem. Jerusalem was the seat of local ruling elites as early as the second millennium BCE,[24] and yet, monumental architecture in the city of David appeared—for the first time since the Middle Bronze Age—only in the early Iron Age, with the erection of the stepped-stone structure on the eastern slopes of the ridge. It is almost unanimously agreed that the foundations of this structure were laid no earlier than the mid-late Iron I, namely, in the mid-eleventh or early tenth century BCE.[25] The stepped-stone structure, which stood out in the rural landscape surrounding Jerusalem, marked it as a highland stronghold, the seat of local ruling elites. It seems, therefore, that by the end of the eleventh/early tenth century BCE, a centralized political rule was established in Jerusalem, with a developing hierarchical social structure. In order to explain this social change, one must shift the view from Jerusalem to its surroundings.

Throughout the fourteenth–twelfth centuries BCE, Jerusalem ruled over a rather barren land inhabited mainly by pastoral nomads, while to its

---

23. Israel Finkelstein and Oded Lipschits, "Omride Architecture in Moab: Jahatz and Atharot," *ZDPV* 126 (2010): 29–42.

24. Nadav Na'aman, "Canaanite Jerusalem and Its Central Hill Country Neighbors in the Second Millennium BCE," *UF* 24 (1992): 257–91.

25. A collared-rim jar found in situ on a floor of a structure buried immediately below the stone terrace of the stepped stone structure, together with pottery sherds retrieved from within the stone terraces, dates its construction to the late Iron I or the very early Iron IIA. See also Margaret L. Steiner, *The Settlement in the Bronze and Iron Ages*, vol. 3 of *Excavations by Kathleen M. Kenyon in Jerusalem 1961–1967*, CoIS 9 (London: Sheffield Academic, 2001), 24–28, figs. 4.3–4.6; 29–36; fig. 4.16; Jane Cahill, "Jerusalem at the Time of the United Monarchy: The Archaeological Evidence," in *Jerusalem in Bible and Archaeology: The First Temple Period*, ed. Andrew G. Vaughn and Anne E. Killbrew (Atlanta: Society of Biblical Literature, 2003), 13–80, esp. 46–51; Amihai Mazar, "Jerusalem in the Tenth Century B.C.E.: The Glass Half Full," in Amit et al., *Essays on Ancient Israel*, 255–72. For a recent and updated discussion of the stepped-stone structure, its construction and date, see Sergi, "Emergence of Judah," 2–5.

south there were some sedentary settlements.²⁶ Massive sedentarization characterizes the eleventh century BCE in the Benjamin Plateau, when for the first time since the Middle Bronze Age settlements were founded north of Jerusalem, while to its south their number did not increase critically.²⁷ Hence, if the stepped-stone structure reflects the establishment of political power, it was mainly in order to impose political authority over the settlers north of Jerusalem; they were the only inhabitants who could provide the kings of Jerusalem with the required (human and financial) resources as well as the political motivation to erect it.

As demonstrated above, the cluster of settlements north of Jerusalem was rather isolated, as the region north of Bethel and south of Jerusalem was only sparsely settled in the Iron I–IIA. Jerusalem—at the southern end of this cluster—was the seat of local rulers since the second millennium BCE, and by the late eleventh/early tenth century BCE, the stepped-stone structure differentiated it from the rural settlements in its vicinity. Thus, in the absence of territorial continuity and vis-à-vis the long-standing political status of Jerusalem, it is difficult to believe that Shechem could have established its political hegemony over rural settlements located some 30–40 km to its south, especially when Jerusalem's political status was reaffirmed with the erection of the stepped-stone structure. It should be concluded, therefore, that by the early tenth century BCE, the Benjamin Plateau was politically affiliated with Jerusalem, whose political hegemony probably extended between Bethlehem/Beth-zur in the south and Bethel in the north. The erection of the stepped-stone structure marks, therefore, the early emergence of a polity ruled from Jerusalem, and evidently Benjamin was part of this polity from its early beginnings. Throughout the Iron IIA the power and strength of Jerusalem grew steadily,²⁸ reflecting the accumu-

---

26. For the region north of Jerusalem, see Israel Finkelstein, "The Sociopolitical Organization of the Central Hill Country in the Second Millennium BCE," in *Biblical Archaeology Today, 1990: Proceedings of the Second International Congress on Biblical Archaeology; Supplement; Pre-Congress Symposium: Population, Production and Power, Jerusalem, June 1990*, ed. Avraham Biran and Joseph Aviram (Jerusalem: Israel Exploration Society, 1993), 116–23. For the region south of Jerusalem and further literature, see the summary in Sergi, "Emergence of Judah," 5–8.

27. For recent discussion of the archaeological evidence from Benjamin in the Iron I–IIA, based on both excavations and surveys and further literature, see Sergi, "Emergence of Judah," 8–12.

28. Joe Uziel and Nahshon Szanton, "Recent Excavations near the Gihon Spring and Their Reflection on the Character of Iron II Jerusalem," *TA* 42 (2015): 233–50;

lation of economic and consequently also political wealth in the hands of the ruling dynasty in Jerusalem—the house of David. It was not until the fall of the Omride dynasty in the second half of the ninth century that the Davidic kings in Jerusalem extended their hegemony from the Judean Hills to the Judahite lowlands in the west and to the Beersheba and Arad valleys in the south.[29]

Last, it is important to note the difference between the political formations in the Samaria Hills vis-à-vis those that occurred in the Jerusalem–Benjamin region. Power balance in the north shifted, culminating in territorial expansion and the formation of the Omride polity—the kingdom of Israel; the south experienced what seems to have been a rather organic process of centralization of power in the hands of the ruling elites in Jerusalem, culminating in the formation of the territorial polity ruled by the house of David—the kingdom of Judah. Throughout that time, the highlands between Bethel (and later Mizpah) in the south and Shiloh (and even Shechem) in the north were devoid of any political center,[30] and thus it is hard to imagine that the political developments in the north had any influence on the centralization of power in the south. It is evident, therefore, that Israel and Judah developed separately, side by side, throughout the tenth–ninth centuries BCE, and while the political formation of Israel was marked by struggles and shifting political alliances, that of Judah was marked by centralization of power in the hands of the Davidic ruling family, residing in Jerusalem.

With this in mind, I will now examine the biblical traditions embedded in the book of Samuel regarding the formation of the early Israelite monarchy.

Uziel and Szanton, "New Evidence of Jerusalem's Urban Development in the Ninth Century BCE," in Lipschits, Gadot, and Adams, *Rethinking Israel*, 429–39; Joe Uziel and Yuval Gadot, "The Monumentality of Iron Age Jerusalem prior to the Eighth Century BCE," *TA* 44 (2017): 123–40.

29. See Aren Maeir, Louise Hitchcock, and Liora Horwitz, "On the Constitution and Transformation of Philistine Identity," *OJA* 32 (2013): 1–38; Sergi, "Judah's Expansion," 226–46; Gunnar Lehmann and H. Michael Niemmann, "When Did the Shephelah Become Judahite?," *TA* 41 (2014): 77–94.

30. Shiloh, which during the Iron I was a highland stronghold with a sanctuary built on its summit, was the regional center of southern Samaria, but the site was destroyed by the mid-Iron I. See Israel Finkelstein, "The History and Archaeology of Shiloh from the Middle Bronze Age II to Iron Age II," in *Shiloh: The Archaeology of a Biblical Site*, ed. Israel Finkelstein, MS 10 (Tel Aviv: Institute of Archaeology, 1993), 371–93.

4. Saul: The First King of the Israelites

The early Saul traditions are usually identified as 1 Sam 9–14. It is almost unanimously agreed that the beginning of these traditions may be found in 1 Sam 9:1–10:16, in the legendary tale about the young Benjaminite, the son of a wealthy patriarchal and rural elite, who goes to look for his father's asses. On his way, he meets a man of God, who tells him that he is about to perform a great deed.[31] Since Julius Wellhausen, it has been accepted that this story continues in 1 Sam 11:1–15 (excluding 1 Sam 10:17–27 as a secondary, exilic, or even postexilic expansion) where the words of the man of God are fulfilled.[32] Saul leads a successful military campaign to Jabesh-gilead and liberates the Jabeshites from Ammonite subjugation.[33] One point of dispute is whether the successful battle against the Ammo-

---

31. The reconstructions of the original core and literary growth of the story in 1 Sam 9:1–10:16 are mostly based on the work of Ludwig Schmidt. See Schmidt, *Menschlicher Erfolg und Jahwes Initiative: Studies zu Tradition, Interpretation und Historie in Überlieferungen von Gideon, Saul und David*, WMANT 38 (Neukirchen-Vluyn: Neukirchener Verlag, 1970), 58–102; and see, for instance, Fritz Stolz, *Das erste und zweite Buch Samuel*, ZBK 9 (Zürich: Theologischer Verlag, 1981), 62–70; Anthony F. Campbell, *1 Samuel*, FOTL 8 (Grand Rapids: Eerdmans, 2003), 106–8; Walter Dietrich, *Samuel VIII/1, 5*, BKAT (Neukirchen-Vluyn: Neukirchener Verlag, 2008), 288–400; Bezzel, *Saul*, 149–79. For other reconstructions, assuming a more unified narrative with only minor redactional interventions, see, for instance, P. Kyle McCarter, *I Samuel: A New Translation with Introduction, Notes and Commentary*, AB 8 (New Haven: Doubleday, 1980), 166–88; Nadav Na'aman, "The Pre-Deuteronomistic Story of King Saul and Its Historical Significance," *CBQ* 54 (1990): 638–58; Graeme Auld, *I and II Samuel: A Commentary*, OTL (Louisville: Westminster John Knox, 2011), 98–111.

32. For example, Schmidt, *Menschlicher Erfolg*, 79–80; McCarter, *I Samuel*, 26–27, 184–88, 194–96, 205–7; Stolz, *Erste und zweite Buch Samuel*, 19–20; Na'aman, "Pre-Deuteronomistic Story," 644; Campbell, *1 Samuel*, 88–89, 115–16, 128–29; Kratz, *Composition of the Narrative Books*, 171–72; Kaiser, "Historische und biblische König Saul (Teil I)," 533–38; Bezzel, *Saul*, 151–79, 196–204. See also Julius Wellhausen, *Die Composition des Hexateuchs und der historischen Bücher des Alten Testament* (Berlin: de Gruyter, 1889), 240–43.

33. Yet, some scholars argue that the original continuation of the story in 1 Sam 9:1–10:16 was in the stories about the wars of Saul and Jonathan with the Philistines in 1 Sam 13–14. See, for example, Hans J. Stoebe, *Das Erste Buch Samuelis*, KAT 8.2 (Gutersloh: Gutersloher Verlagshaus, 1973), 64–66; Dietrich, *Early Monarchy in Israel*, 268–69; Auld, *I and II Samuel*, 126. Indeed, the story of Saul's meeting with the man of God anticipates the wars with the Philistines (1 Sam 10:5a). However, 1 Sam 13–14

nites leads to Saul's coronation in Gilgal in 1 Sam 11:15, or whether the note about the coronation was only later added to the original narrative.[34] I opt for the former, not only because it makes the perfect conclusion to the heroic tale of the young Benjaminite but also because Saul's kingship is anticipated already in the story of his meeting with the man of God. As argued by Diana Edelman, asses were conceived as a royal animal (see 1 Kgs 1:33, 39), and Saul's search for them implies his search for kingship.[35] The coronation in Gilgal places Saul in the geographical and political point of departure for the stories of Saul and Jonathan's wars with the Philistines in 1 Sam 13–14. These stories presuppose Saul's kingship and should be regarded as the direct continuation of 1 Sam 11:1–15.[36] They form a collection of anecdotes and heroic tales that were weaved together because they share the theme of war with the Philistines, but it is mostly agreed that they belong to the early layer of the Saul traditions.[37]

---

already presupposes the kingship of Saul, who is enthroned over Israel only as a result of his victory over the Ammonites; see further details below.

34. For the former, see Schmidt, *Menschlicher Erfolg*, 79–80; Na'aman, "Pre-Deuteronomistic Story," 642–43; Kaiser, "Historische und biblische König Saul (Teil I)," 538–40. For the latter, see, e.g., Bezzel, *Saul*, 196–97, 200–201.

35. Diana Edelman, "The Deuteronomist's Story of King Saul: Narrative Art or Editorial Product?," in *Pentateuchal and Deuteronomistic Studies: Papers Read at the Thirteenth IOSOT Congress Leuven 1989*, ed. Christianus Brekelmans and Johan Lust (Leuven: Peeters, 1990), 208–14; Edelman, "Saul Ben Kish, King of Israel, as a 'Young Hero'?," in *Le jeune héros: Recherche sur la formation et la diffusion d'un theme littéraire au Proch-Orient ancient*, ed. Jean M. Durand, Thomas Römer, and Michael Langlois, OBO 250 (Göttingen: Vandenhoeck & Ruprecht, 2011), 161–83.

36. Na'aman, "Pre-Deuteronomistic Story," 645–49.

37. E.g., Stoebe, *Erste Buch Samuelis*, 64–66; McCarter, *I Samuel*, 26–27; Na'aman, "Pre-Deuteronomistic Story," 645–47; Marsha C. White, "The History of Saul's Rise: Saulide State Propaganda in 1 Samuel 1–14," in *"A Wise Discerning Mind": Essays in Honor of Burke O. Long*, ed. Saul M. Olyan and Robert C. Culley, BJS 325 (Providence: Brown University Press, 2000), 271–92; White, "Saul and Jonathan in 1 Samuel 1 and 14," in *Saul in Story and Tradition*, ed. Carl S. Ehrlich and Marsha C. White, FAT 47 (Tübingen: Mohr Siebeck, 2006), 119–38; Kratz, *Composition of the Narrative Books*, 171–74; Dietrich, *Early Monarchy in Israel*, 268–69; Auld, *I and II Samuel*, 126. On the weaving together, see, for example, Stoebe, *Erste Buch Samuelis*, 63–64, 240–62; McCarter, *I Samuel*, 26–27; Stolz, *Erste und zweite Buch Samuel*, 82–83. For different reconstructions of the literary growth of these stories, see: David Jobling, "Saul's Fall and Jonathan's Rise: Tradition and Redaction in 1 Sam 14:1–46," *JBL* 95 (1976): 367–76; Stolz, *Erste und zweite Buch Samuel*, 87–96; Kaiser, "Historische und biblische König Saul (Teil II)," 1–6; Campbell, *1 Samuel*, 134–50; Bezzel,

Eventually, in the battle with the Philistines on Mount Gilboa, Saul and his sons meet their death. According to the account in 1 Sam 31:1–13, the victorious Philistines pin the bodies of Saul and his sons to the walls of Beit Shean, but the Jabeshites, in a bold action, rescue the bodies, bring them to Jabesh-gilead, burn them, bury the bones, and mourn seven days. The question is, of course, whether the account of Saul's death in the Gilboa was part of the early Saul traditions. Indeed, some scholars have excluded it, arguing that the bulk of the early Saul traditions is embedded only within 1 Sam 1–14, probably with an ending in 1 Sam 14:46–52.[38] However, the war with the Philistines, the main theme in 1 Sam 13–14, covers also 1 Sam 31:1–13. Neither narrative mentions David; instead, both focus on Saul and his sons. Furthermore, this report brings the early Saul traditions to their perfect literary conclusion: Saul came to the throne by rescuing the people of Jabesh-gilead, and when he dies they repay him by salvaging his body.[39] Hence, there is no reason to assume that the report about the death and burial of Saul and his sons in 1 Sam 31:1–13 was somehow distinct from the stories about the wars of Saul and Jonathan with the Philistines in 1 Sam 13–14.[40] Accordingly, the entire theme of wars with the Philistines may be counted with the early Saul traditions. What we have here, therefore, is a collection of early narratives

---

Saul, 208–28. For an approach viewing the stories in 1 Sam 13–14 as a more unified literary work, see McCarter, *I Samuel*, 224–52; Na'aman, "Pre-Deuteronomistic Story," 645–47. There is a scholarly consensus, however, that the rejection of Saul in 1 Sam 13:7b–15 and the story of the altar in 1 Sam 14:32–35 are secondary expansions; see, for instance, Wellhausen, *Composition des Hexateuchs*, 240–46; McCarter, *I Samuel*, 230; Stolz, *Erste und zweite Buch Samuel*, 82; Campbell, *1 Samuel*, 110–15; Auld, *I and II Samuel*, 115–16; Kaiser, "Historische und biblische König Saul (Teil II)," 1–6, 9–11; Bezzel, *Saul*, 214.

38. White, "History of Saul's Rise," 271–92; Kratz, *Composition of the Narrative Books*, 171–74; Bezzel, *Saul*, 115–48.

39. Wright, *David, King of Israel*, 67.

40. Bezzel has convincingly demonstrated that many literary connections that bind 1 Sam 13–14 with 1 Sam 31, although he argues that the theme of war with the Philistines in 1 Sam 1–4; 13–14; 31 should be considered as a late Judahite expansion of the old Israelite Saul traditions (in 1 Sam 9–10:16, 11, 14:46–51), dated by him to after the fall of Samaria in 720 BCE (*Saul*, 229–34; see also 179–94). However, these stories hardly reflect any of the geographical, political, or religious realia of the late eighth and the seventh centuries BCE (below). Thus, they seem to be much earlier than assumed by Bezzel, and if so, they may be counted with the early Saul traditions.

embedded within 1 Sam 9–14, 31, telling the story of the rise and fall of a heroic king.[41]

It is almost taken for granted that the early Saul traditions as sketched above are of north Israelite origin and that they could not have arrived in Judah before the fall of Samaria.[42] However, these traditions hardly reflect any of the geographical or political reality of the kingdom of Israel. Their geographical scope is restricted to the area north of Jerusalem, in the Benjamin region and the southernmost parts of the Ephraim hill country, with only one excursion to the Gilead. The entire hill country north of Bethel, which was the heart of the kingdom of Israel, is completely absent. Nothing in these stories even implies a north Israelite perspective: the main political centers of Israel (Shechem, Tirzah, Samaria), the importance of the cult place in Bethel, the Israelite royal cities in the northern valleys, and the Israelite cult centers in the Gilead, most notably Penuel, are all completely absent from the narrative.[43] Furthermore, there is not even a hint of the Israelite history—its involvement with northern Levantine polities, the fierce relations with Aram-Damascus, or its constant effort (and success) to expand northward.

Saul's military excursion to the Gilead is often viewed as a reflection of Israelite territorial and political interest in the region.[44] Indeed, at least some parts of the Gilead were affiliated with Israel for certain periods during the ninth and eighth centuries BCE.[45] However, as far as we can judge, the Israelite interest in the Gilead was mainly in the Jabbok passage (which was

---

41. Edelman, "Deuteronomist's Story of King Saul," 207–20; Edelman, "Saul ben Kish," 161–83.

42. See note 2 AQ: Please confirm cross-reference. above; see also Schmidt, *Menschlicher Erfolg*, 79–80; Hans J. Grønbæk, *Die Geschichte vom Aufstieg Davids (1 Sam. 15–2 Sam. 5): Tradition und Komposition*, ATDan 10 (Copenhagen: Prostant Apud Munksgaard, 1971), 267–69.

43. Mahanaim is mentioned as the capital of Saul's heir, Ishbaal (2 Sam 3:8), but this is not part of the so-called early Saul traditions. Rather, it is part of what is assumed to be a Judahite composition (see also Na'aman, "Saul, Benjamin," 346–48).

44. See Dietrich and Münger, "Herrschaft Sauls," 41–46; Finkelstein, "Last Labayu," 178–80; Finkelstein, "Saul, Benjamin," 353–55; Wright, *David, King of Israel*, 66–74.

45. On the political affiliation of the Gilead in the ninth and eighth centuries BCE, see Omer Sergi, "The Gilead between Aram and Israel: Political Borders, Cultural Interaction and the Question of Jacob and the Israelite Identity," in Sergi, Oeming, and de Hulster, *In Search of Aram*, 333–37.

on the route to Shechem; see 1 Kgs 12:25). This region and the sites located along it—Penuel, Mahanaim, and Sukkoth—play a prominent role in what is often viewed as Israelite literature; the pre-Priestly Jacob cycle, considered by many to be the origin myth of the northern Israelite kingdom,[46] attributes the foundation of these sites to the eponymic ancestor of Israel. They are also important to the story of Gideon's pursuit of the Midianites (Judg 8:4–21), which is considered to be a part of an Israelite collection of heroic tales.[47]

None of these sites, so prominent in Israelite literature, is mentioned in the early Saul traditions. In fact, Saul goes to war in Jabesh-gilead, a toponym mainly referred to in the narratives related to Saul (1 Sam 11:1, 3, 5, 9–11; 31:13; 2 Sam 2:4–5; 21:12; see 1 Chr 10:12).[48] Jabesh-gilead is never mentioned in relation to Israel,[49] not even in the town list of the northern tribes. Furthermore, as correctly observed, cremation is not an Israelite practice, and by ascribing it to the people of Jabesh-gilead (1 Sam 31:12) the author probably intended to mark them as non-Israelites.[50] Thus, the role of the Gilead and its residents in the early Saul traditions could hardly reflect the Israelite point of view.

A look at the geopolitical picture of the early Saul traditions seems to reflect a Jerusalemite point of view. Saul's sphere of influence is mainly in

---

46. See Albert de Pury, "The Jacob Story and the Beginning of the Formation of the Pentateuch," in *A Farewell to the Yahwist? The Composition of the Pentateuch in Recent European Interpretation*, ed. Thomas B. Dozeman and Konrad Schmid, SymS 34 (Atlanta: Society of Biblical Literature, 2006), 51–72; Jeremy M. Hutton, "Mahanaim, Penuel, and Transhumance Routes: Observations on Genesis 32–33 and Judges 8," *JNES* 65 (2006): 161–78; Erhard Blum, "The Jacob Tradition," in *The Book of Genesis: Composition, Reception and Interpretation*, ed. Craig E. Evans, Joel N. Lohr, and David L. Petersen (Leiden: Brill, 2012), 181–211; Israel Finkelstein and Thomas Römer, "Comments on the Historical Background of the Jacob Narrative in Genesis," *ZAW* 126 (2014): 317–38; Sergi, "Gilead between Aram," 333–54.

47. See Walter Groß, *Richter*, HThkAT (Freiburg: Herder, 2009), 367–89, 473–74, with further literature. On the role of the Jabbok outlet in Judg 8:4–21, see Sergi, "Gilead between Aram," 346–49.

48. Jabesh-gilead is also mentioned in the story of the outrage at Gibeah (Judg 21), which is dated to the late postexilic period (Groß, *Richter*, 821–22, with previous literature). Jabesh-gilead is identified at Tell el-Maqlūb. See Martin Noth, "Jabes-Gilead," *ZDPV* 69 (1953): 28–41; Erasmus Gaß, *Die Ortsnamen des Richterbuchs in historischer und redaktioneller Perspektive*, ADPV 35 (Wiesbaden: Harrassowitz, 2005), 504–9, with earlier literature.

49. Contra Auld, *I and II Samuel*, 121, who calls it "Israelite city."

50. Wright, *David, King of Israel*, 66–68.

Benjamin and the southern Ephraim hill country, regions that according to the narrative were transgressed by the Philistines, who were the inhabitants of the Judahite Shephelah (1 Sam 13:20; 14:31). The Philistines are depicted as warriors who raided and plundered the rural society in the Benjamin region; they seem to be wealthier (mastering specialized productions; see 1 Sam 13:19–22) and are considered the stronger and more aggressive side in the conflict (1 Sam 13:5–6, 14, 17–18). The Israelites, on the other hand, are depicted as a rural society, residing in the hill country and its foothills, dependent on Philistine metal production, and in need of defending themselves from Philistine aggressiveness. These characteristics draw the line between the more urban societies of southwestern Canaan and the rural societies of the Benjamin–Jerusalem region prior to the Iron IIB, and probably even prior to the fall of Gath in the last third of the ninth century BCE.

The limited geographical scope of these stories is telling: 1 Sam 13–14 contains a detailed topographical description of a small territory north of Jerusalem. Clearly, its authors were well acquainted with the Benjamin region, while the lower regions of Canaan—the northern valleys or the Shephelah (west of Judah)—were less known to them, as may also be deduced from the odd appearance of the Philistines in the Jezreel Valley (1 Sam 31:1, 10). While the archaeological phenomenon of the Philistines is mostly restricted to southwest Canaan in the Iron I, the Jezreel Valley during this period, and before it came under Israelite rule, maintained its former (Late Bronze Age) social and political structure of city-states and palace economy.[51] There is no reason to assume that the local towns in the Jezreel Valley were somehow affiliated with the Philistines, as suggested by Dietrich and Münger.[52] Israel Finkelstein's suggestion that the memory of the Philistines in the Jezreel Valley (and especially in Beit Shean) reflects the Egyptian rule during the Late Bronze Age is similarly improbable.[53] As far as we can judge, the pre-Israelite Jezreel Valley was conceived in Israelite historical memory as Canaanite (see Judg 4–5) and not as Philistine or Egyptian. Clearly, the author of the Saul story was not well acquainted with the political or social composite of the pre-Israelite Jezreel Valley. The Philistines, on the other hand, were the archenemy of the kingdom of Judah, as is also clear from the

---

51. Finkelstein, *Forgotten Kingdom*, 27–36. On the archaeological phenomenon of the Philistines, see Maeir, Hitchcock, and Horwitz, "Constitution and Transformation," 1–38.

52. Dietrich and Münger, "Herrschaft Sauls," 48.

53. Finkelstein, "Last Labayu," 182–83.

important role they played in the stories about the early Davidic monarchy.[54] Indeed, throughout the formative period of the Judahite monarchy, Gath was the strongest polity to its west.[55] Only a narrator from Jerusalem, being remote from the Jezreel Valley, would assume that Saul met in the Jezreel Valley the same enemies he met in Benjamin, namely, the Philistines.

Last, from an archaeological point of view the inhabitants of the Benjamin region were affiliated with the Jerusalemite political hegemony as early as the tenth century BCE. Thus, if the memory of a Benjaminite hero was kept and recorded somewhere, it would have been in the scribal school of Jerusalem. This is also the best explanation for the complete absence of any trace of Israelite geography, politics, or concerns within these early traditions, which rather reflect the political realia, problems, and interests of Judah. Yet, Judah and Jerusalem are not mentioned in these early traditions, which present Saul as the first king of the Israelites (below). Could it be that the memory of an Israelite king was preserved in Jerusalem? Before answering that question, I shall briefly comment on the historical context of the stories about David's rise.

5. David the Second King of the Israelites?

The stories about David's rise in 1 Sam 16–2 Sam 5 include many different narrative strands that were quite loosely redacted together by a pre-Deuteronomistic scribe (namely, before they were integrated into the books of Samuel). These traditions tell about David's service in Saul's court (1 Sam 16:14–23, 17–19), David's flight from Saul (1 Sam 20–26), his consequent service of the king of Gath (1 Sam 27–2 Sam 1) until the death of Saul (1 Sam 31–2 Sam 1), and David's coronation, first over Judah (2 Sam 2:1–4) and later over Israel (2 Sam 5:1–3). Of course, the extent and literary growth of this composition is disputed, but for the purpose of this study, suffice it to stress that in spite of the mosaic nature of the stories about David's rise, it is painted with a unifying royal, pro-Davidic ideology, meaning that its authors were not mere compilers.[56]

---

54. Omer Sergi, "State Formation, Religion and Collective Identity in the Southern Levant," *HBAI* 4 (2015): 64–75.

55. Sergi, "Judah's Expansion," 226–46; Lehmann and Niemmann, "When Did the Shephelah," 77–94.

56. For further discussion and for different reconstructions of the sources and redactions within this composition, see, for instance, Artur Weiser, "Die Legitimation

Quite similar to the early Saul traditions, the geographical scope of the stories about David's rise is restricted to the southern Canaanite hill country and its foothills, while the Philistines control the western Shephelah. Accordingly, David was quite independent (as a leader of a warriors' band) whenever he operated in the Judean hill country and its foothills (1 Sam 23–26; 2 Sam 5), but he was at the service of the king of Gath whenever he crossed to the west or the south (see 1 Sam 27; 29–30). This geopolitical scenario is further highlighted by the importance of Gath in these stories (1 Sam 17:4, 23, 52; 21:11, 13; 27:2–4, 11). Gath reached its zenith during the tenth–ninth centuries BCE, when it became by far the biggest and the most prosperous city in southern Canaan. However, it was utterly destroyed in the last third of the ninth century and never regained its former power.[57] The stories in 1 Sam 16–2 Sam 5, like those in 1 Sam 9–14 are therefore consistent with the social and political reality in southern Canaan during the tenth–ninth centuries BCE and prior to the Judahite expansion to the Shephelah, as is also confirmed by the fact that all these traditions fail to mention Lachish—the main royal Judahite town in the Shephelah from the second half of the ninth century BCE.[58]

In light of all the above, the stories of David's rise cannot be dated much later than the early eighth century BCE, which means that they were composed long before the fall of Samaria. Since both the early Saul traditions and the stories about David's rise are well acquainted with the geopoliti-

---

des Königs Davids: zur Eigenart und Entstehung der sogen. Geschichte von Davids Aufsteig," *VT* 16 (1966): 325–54; Grønbaek, *Geschichte vom Aufstieg Davids*; Stolz, *Erste und zweite Buch Samuel*, 17–18; Kratz, *Composition of the Narrative Books*, 177–81. Timmo Veijola assigned the composition of the history of David's rise to the Deuteronomistic scribes. See Veijola, *Die ewige Dynastie: David und die Entstehung seiner Dynastie nach der deutronomistischen Darstellung* (Helsinki: Suomalainen Tiedeakatemia, 1975); see also John Van Seters, *The Biblical Saga of King David* (Winona Lake, IN: Eisenbrauns, 2009). However, this view never gained much scholarly consensus (Dietrich, *Early Monarchy in Israel*, 245–46). For a critical review of past research, see Dietrich, *Early Monarchy in Israel*, 240–55.

57. Aren M. Maeir, "The Tell eṣ-Ṣafi/Gath Archaeological Project 1996–2010: Introduction, Overview and Synopsis of Results," in *Tell eṣ-Ṣafi/Gath I: The 1996–2005 Seasons*, part 1, *Text*, ed. Aren M. Maeir, ÄAT 69 (Wiesbaden: Harrassowitz, 2012), 26–49.

58. Sergi, "Judah's Expansion," 226–46; Nadav Na'aman, "The Kingdom of Judah in the Ninth Century BCE: Text Analysis versus Archaeological Research," *TA* 40 (2013): 247–76; Lehmann and Niemmann, "When Did the Shephelah," 77–94.

cal settings in southern Canaan—between Benjamin and the Judean hill country in the east, and the Judahite Shephelah in the west—they probably reflect a Judahite (or, better, Jerusalemite) and not an Israelite point of view. If so, it seems that they were composed close to each other,[59] no later than the early eighth century BCE. The remaining question is why David, who is considered the founder of the kingdom of Judah, was portrayed as the successor of the first king of Israel long before the fall of Samaria. The key to this problem lies in the answer to the question, What is the nature of Israelite identity assumed by the narrators of the traditions about the early Israelite monarchy?

6. Israel as a Kinship Identity in the Traditions about the Formation of the Israelite Monarchy

As demonstrated above, both the early Saul traditions and the stories of David's rise are well embedded in the social and political realia of southern Canaan in the Iron IIA. It is in this context that we should explore the historical meaning of their attempt to portray the rise of the monarchy. The stories of Saul's wars with the Philistines in 1 Sam 13–14 presuppose his kingship over Israel, or, at the least, commemorate him as Israel's military leader and liberator (see 1 Sam 11:15; 14:47). The name *Israel* is mentioned fourteen times in 1 Sam 13–14. In most of these cases, it clearly refers to a group of people. Namely, Israel in 1 Sam 13–14 is a designation for a kinship group and not a territorial polity. The text identifies the Israelites as a composite clan/tribal society settled in the Benjamin Plateau and in the southern Ephraim hill country (1 Sam 13:4–6, 20; 14:22–24), between Gibeah in the south (or even Bethlehem; see 1 Sam 17:2) and Bethel in the north. The name also reflects the complex nature of Israel as a kinship group, consisting of different clans (such as the Benjaminites) that were brought together under a more encompassing Israelite kinship identity. Being a Benjaminite (1 Sam 9:1), Saul was also considered an Israelite, and thus the early Saul traditions tell the story of the rise and fall of a Benjaminite who came to rule the Israelites. In other words, the story never portrayed Saul as the king of Israel, relating to the northern polity formed by the Omrides far to the north, in the region of Shechem and Samaria.

---

59. See Nadav Na'aman, "The Scope of the Pre-Deuteronomistic Saul-David Story Cycle," in *From Nomadism to Monarchy: Thirty Years Update*, ed. Ido Koch, Omer Sergi, and Oded Lipschits (Tübingen: Mohr Siebeck, forthcoming).

Rather, it tells how Saul came to rule his kinsmen Israelites residing in the Benjamin Plateau.

This calls for a clear distinction between Israel as a political identity, namely, the territorial polity that bore this name from the time of the Omride rule and onward; and Israel as a social identity, the name of a kinship group. The name Israel was used to identify a kinship group (in the Merneptah stela, late thirteenth century BCE) long before it was used to designate the Northern Kingdom,[60] as in the other three occurrences of this name outside the Hebrew Bible: in the Mesha inscription, the Kurkh monolith, and the Dan inscription (all dated to the mid-second half of the ninth century BCE). Moreover, in one of these occurrences, that is, in the Assyrian Kurkh monolith (852 BCE), it is applied to Ahab, who is identified as Israelite (KUR.*syrʿalāya*) and not as the king of Israel (as Omri and Joram are identified in the contemporaneous Mesha stela and Dan inscription, respectively). It is clear, therefore, that the name Israel had (at least initially) a kinship association. The question then is how the designation of a kinship group was later applied to a political entity. This question is highlighted by the fact that Israel was not the only name used to refer to the northern kingdom, which was also named (by the Assyrians) "the house of Omri." After all, the occurrences of the name Israel in historical sources are related almost exclusively to the time of the Omride rule, and this fact alone casts doubt on the assumption that Israel was only or mainly a political identity, the name of a territorial polity and nothing more.

Kinship was in essence the most dominant social ideology in ancient Near Eastern societies.[61] Kinship relations were formulated in order to legitimize membership in a group, and they were utilized in order to stretch time and space, and to enable the conception of common identity with unknown others.[62] Kinship relations appear to maintain their essential integrity over long periods of time and even under different political formations. Thus, for instance, the ruling elite in Ebla or Mari was able to maintain its tribal

---

60. See the summary in Michael G. Hasel, *Domination and Resistance: Egyptian Military Activity in the Southern Levant, ca. 1300–1185 B.C.*, PdÄ 11 (Leiden: Brill, 1998), 170–204.

61. Ann Porter, *Mobile Pastoralism and the Formation of Near Eastern Civilization: Weaving Together Society* (Cambridge: Cambridge University Press, 2012), 12–37.

62. Porter, *Mobile Pastoralism*, 57–58, 326; Porter, *Complex Communities*, 56–57. On the purpose of kinship relations, see Van Der Steen, *Tribes and People*, 126–30, with further literature.

identity, related to kin, even when residing in a wealthy urban center.[63] Similarly, and closer to the Saul and David stories, the Mesha inscription presents Mesha as "king of Moab, the Dibonite." Ernst Knauf notes that Mesha did not identify himself as a Moabite, after the name of the territorial polity he formed and ruled—but as a Dibonite, probably his kinship identity, of the social group with which he was affiliated.[64] There is therefore no real dichotomy between social and political identity, as they both represent identities that are current. That means Israel was first and foremost a kinship identity, even when the name Israel was given to the polity ruled by the Omrides.[65] Moreover, since extrabiblical sources from the Iron Age identify Israel exclusively with the Omrides, it may be argued that the Omrides were affiliated with a kinship group named Israel, which eventually gave its name to the polity they ruled. That, however, does not mean that all the Israelites lived within the boundaries of the Omride polity, and evidently at least the early Saul traditions identify Israelites also in the region of Benjamin, far to the south from the Omride's core community in Samaria.

Similar portrayal of Israel as a kinship group residing in the region of Jerusalem and Benjamin also characterizes the stories of David's rise and especially of his service in Saul's court (1 Sam 18–19; see 2 Sam 5:1–2). Inna Willi-Plein shows how these stories presuppose an early monarchic political landscape, in which establishing political hegemony was done through marriage and personal alliances (see 1 Sam 17:58; 18:2, 17).[66] She

---

63. Daniel Fleming, "Kinship of City and Tribe Conjoined: Zimri-Lim at Mari," in *Nomads, Tribes and the States in the Ancient Near East: Cross-Disciplinary Perspectives*, ed. Jeffrey Szuchman, OIS 5 (Chicago: University of Chicago Press, 2009), 227–40; Ann Porter, "Beyond Dimorphism: Ideologies and Materialities of Kinship as Time-Space Distanciation," in Szuchman, *Nomads, Tribes and the States*, 201–25; Porter, *Mobile Pastoralism*, 240.

64. Eveline J. Van Der Steen and Klaas A. D. Smelik, "King Mesha and the Tribe of Dibon," *JSOT* 32 (2007): 139–62. See Ernst A. Knauf, "The Cultural Impact of Secondary State Formation: The Cases of Edomites and Moabites," in *Early Edom and Moab: The Beginning of Iron Age in Southern Jordan*, ed. Pioter Bienkowski, SAM 7 (Sheffield: Equinox, 1992), 47–54.

65. For recent studies of the nature of Israel as a kinship identity and its historical significance, see Fleming, *Legacy of Israel*; Kristin Weingart, *Stämmevolk—Staatvolk—Gottesvolk? Studien zur Verwendungs des Israels-Namens im Alten Testament*, FAT 2/68 (Tübingen: Mohr Siebeck, 2014), esp. 171–286, 340–60.

66. Inna Willi-Plein, "I Sam. 18–19 und die Davidshausgeschichte," in *David und Saul im Widerstreit—Diachronie und Synchronie im Wettstreit: Beiträge zur Auslegung*

therefore argues that these stories portray the establishment of kingship over Israel, while Israel refers to a group of people and not to the territorial polity.[67] That means that the story of David's rise, like the traditions about Saul, tells of his rise as the king of the Israelites. Thus, David is presented as the successor of Saul, not as an allegory to hypothetical wishes of late monarchic Judah, but simply because both Saul and David tried to establish their hegemony over the same group of people—the Israelites residing in the Jerusalem-Benjamin highlands. Of course, the house of David was the ruling dynasty of Judah, whose royal seat was in Jerusalem. This, however, does not mean that David's kinship identity was Judahite (just as Mesha king of Moab was not a Moabite but a Dibonite). Nowhere in the stories of his rise to kingship is David identified as a Judahite. Quite the contrary, in 1 Sam 17:12 it is stated that his family originated from an Ephratite clan (thus, Israelite) that settled in Bethlehem,[68] and throughout the stories of his rise, David is explicitly identified as Israelite at least three more times (1 Sam 18:18; 27:12; 2 Sam 5:1).

This picture, according to which at least some of the inhabitants in the region of Jerusalem were Israelites, concurs with the one portrayed in the early Saul traditions. Furthermore, also like the early Saul traditions, the stories about David's rise attest to the complex nature of Israel as a kinship group consisting of different clans (Saul the Benjaminite, David the Ephratite). Assuming an Israelite origin for David may also explain why his coronation over the people of Judah (2 Sam 2:1–4) is not taken for granted; not only does David inquire of YHWH before advancing to Hebron (an action he otherwise takes only before battles; see 1 Sam 23:2, 4; 30:8; 2 Sam 5:19, 23–24), but prior to his arrival he bribes the Judahite leaders, sending them booty he took from the Amalekites (1 Sam 30:26). His coronation over Israel, on the other hand (2 Sam 5:1–3), seems to be much more natural, as the Israelites themselves declare David their king on account of his being their kinsman and because of his previous service in the court of Saul, the former king of Israel (2 Sam 5:1–2).

---

des ersten Samuelbuches, ed. Walter Dietrich, OBO 206 (Fribourg: Academic Press, 2004), 148–53, 156–59.

67. Willi-Plein, "I Sam. 18–19," 161–68.

68. For a recent study of the Ephratites' settlements, see Nadav Na'aman, "The Settlements of the Ephratites in Bethlehem and the Location of Rachel's Tomb," *RB* 121 (2014): 516–29.

Therefore, it may be concluded that according to both the early Saul traditions and the stories of David's rise, Saul and David were affiliated with the kinship group named Israel, which consisted of several clans that settled north (Benjaminite clans) and south (Ephratite clans) of Jerusalem. Besides Israelite clans, this region was inhabited also by Judahites and Jebusite clans (e.g., 2 Sam 2:1–4; 5:6),[69] and eventually, as demonstrated in the archaeological discussion, all these clans came under the political hegemony of the house of David, whose seat was established in Jerusalem.

7. Conclusion: The Biblical Traditions about the Formation of the Israelite Monarchy in Historical Perspective

The stories of the formation of the Israelite monarchy in 1 Sam 9–2 Sam 5 portray the attempt by two local leaders to establish a dynastic monarchy over a group of people, identified by the authors as Israelites. Israel in these traditions is the designation for a kinship group, and thus it denoted a social and not a political identity, one that is ascribed to a group of people, in this case the clans inhabiting the Jerusalem and Benjamin regions. The name Israel in 1 Sam 9–2 Sam 5 does not refer to the territorial polity known by this name from the time of the Omride rule and onward. Moreover, these stories reflect nothing of the geopolitical configuration of the Northern Kingdom, as they are well embedded in the social and political realia of southern Canaan in the early Iron Age, and especially in the core territory of Judah. Hence, the stories about the rise of David in 1 Sam 16–2 Sam 5 should not be read as an allegory for an assumed late monarchic Judahite wish to inherit the northern kingdom of Israel. They should be read for what they are—a story of the rise of Israelite monarchy.

In this sense, it is important to remember that these traditions are a literary product of intellectual elites that should be dated to the period after the formation of the territorial kingdom centered on Jerusalem (second half of the ninth century BCE). The conceptualization of Israel as a kinship group residing north and south of Jerusalem is, therefore, the one ascribed to the population of the region by scribes servicing the ruling dynasty in Jerusalem, with its constant need to form politically and socially unified structure under centralized rule. That being said, these traditions concur

---

69. See Nadav Na'aman, "Jebusites and Jabeshites in the Saul and David Story Cycle," *Bib* 95 (2015): 481–97.

well with the archaeological picture portrayed above, according to which the Iron IIA saw the growth of Jerusalem as the main political center among the rather isolated cluster of rural settlements between Jerusalem and Bethel. In this state of affairs, it was the ruling dynasty in Jerusalem, the house of David, that reclaimed Israel as its kinship affiliation, and accordingly the core community on which it established its rule was consequently seen as Israelite.

What, then, may be said regarding the historicity of the traditions about the formation of the Israelite monarchy in the book of Samuel? Indeed, there can be little doubt that they were composed much later than the events they depict, and to a large extent they may even be regarded as legendary. However, as these traditions are well embedded in the political and social realia of southern Canaan in the early Iron Age, they preserve, at least in their essence (but not in their details), an authentic memory regarding the formation of Judah. Both Saul and David are portrayed as newly formed ruling elites, rising to power among their own kinsmen, the so-called Israelites, by means of agricultural wealth, military skills, and familial relationships. This depiction correlates well with the way we understand the social evolution that generated state formation in the Iron Age Levant. In this regard, the early traditions about Saul and David preserve the memory of a struggle for power in the early monarchic period. The rise of dynastic monarchy in Jerusalem was the result of a struggle between two Israelite ruling families that attempted to establish their political hegemony over their own fellow Israelites who settled in the regions north and south of Jerusalem.

Bibliography

Albright, William F. "The Site of Tirzah and the Topography of Western Manasseh." *JPOS* 11 (1931): 241–51.

Auld, Graeme. *I and II Samuel: A Commentary*. OTL. Louisville: Westminster John Knox, 2011.

Bezzel, Hannes. *Saul: Israels König in Tradition, Redaktion und früher Rezeption*. FAT 97. Tübingen: Mohr Siebeck, 2015.

Blum, Erhard. "The Jacob Tradition." Pages 181–211 in *The Book of Genesis: Composition, Reception and Interpretation*. Edited by Craig E. Evans, Joel N. Petersen, and David L. Petersen. Leiden: Brill, 2012.

Bryce, Trevor R. *The World of the Neo-Hittite Kingdoms: A Political and Military History*. Oxford: Oxford University Press, 2012.

Bunnens, Guy. "Syria in the Iron Age Problems and Definitions." Pages 3–19 in *Essays on Syria in the Iron Age*. ANESSup 7. Edited by Guy Bunnens. Leuven: Peeters, 2000.

Cahill, Jane. "Jerusalem at the Time of the United Monarchy: The Archaeological Evidence." Pages 13–80 in *Jerusalem in Bible and Archaeology: The First Temple Period*. Edited by Andrew G. Vaughn and Anne E. Killbrew. Atlanta: Society of Biblical Literature, 2003.

Campbell, Anthony F. *1 Samuel*. FOTL 8. Grand Rapids: Eerdmans, 2003.

Campbell, Edward F. *Shechem III: The Stratigraphy and Architecture of Shechem/Tell Balâṭah*. Vol. 1, *Text*. ASOR 6. Boston: American Schools of Oriental Research, 2002.

Dietrich, Walter. *The Early Monarchy in Israel: The Tenth Century BCE*. BibEnc 3. Atlanta: Society of Biblical Literature, 2007.

———. *Samuel VIII/1, 5*. BKAT. Neukirchen-Vluyn: Neukirchener Verlag, 2008.

Dietrich, Walter, and Stefan Münger. "Die Herrschaft Sauls und der Norden Israels." Pages 39–54 in *Saxa Loquentur: Studien zu Archäologie Palästinas/Israels. Festschrift für Volkmar Fritz zum 65. Geburtstag*. Edited by Cornelius G. den Hertog, Ulrich Hübner, and Stefan Münger. AOAT 302. Münster: Ugarit-Verlag, 2003.

Dietrich, Walter, and Thomas Nauman. "The David–Saul Narrative." Pages 276–318 in *Reconsidering Israel and Judah: Recent Studies on the Deuteronomistic History*. Edited by Gary N. Knoppers and J. Gordon McConville. Winona Lake, IN: Eisenbrauns, 2000.

Edelman, Diana. "The Deuteronomist's Story of King Saul: Narrative Art or Editorial Product?" Pages 207–20 in *Pentateuchal and Deuteronomistic Studies: Papers Read at the Thirteenth IOSOT Congress Leuven 1989*. Edited by Christianus Brekelmans and Johan Lust. Leuven: Peeters, 1990.

———. "Saul Ben Kish, King of Israel, as a 'Young Hero'?" Pages 161–83 in *Le jeune héros: Recherche sur la formation et la diffusion d'un theme littéraire au Proch-Orient ancien*. Edited by Jean M. Durand, Thomas Römer, and Michael Langlois. OBO 250. Göttingen: Vandenhoeck & Ruprecht, 2011.

Finkelstein, Israel. *The Archaeology of the Israelite Settlement*. Jerusalem: Israel Exploration Society, 1988.

———. "Ethnicity and the Origin of the Iron I Settlers in the Highlands of Canaan: Can the Real Israelites Stand Up?" *BA* 59 (1996): 198–212.

———. *The Forgotten Kingdom: The Archaeology and History of Northern Israel*. ANEM 5. Atlanta: Society of Biblical Literature, 2013.

———. "The Great Transformation: The 'Conquest' of the Highlands Frontiers and the Rise of the Territorial States." Pages 349–65 in *The Archaeology of Society in the Holy Land*. Edited by Thomas Levy. London: Leicester University Press, 1995.

———. "A Great United Monarchy? Archaeological and Historical Perspectives." Pages 3–28 in *One God—One Cult—One Nation*. Edited by Reinhard G. Kratz and Hermann Spieckermann. BZAW 405. Berlin: de Gruyter, 2010.

———. "The History and Archaeology of Shiloh from the Middle Bronze Age II to Iron Age II." Pages 371–93 in *Shiloh: The Archaeology of a Biblical Site*. Edited by Israel Finkelstein. MS 10. Tel Aviv: Institute of Archaeology, 1993.

———. "The Last Labayu: King Saul and the Expansion of the First North Israelite Entity." Pages 171–88 in *Essays on Ancient Israel in Its Near Eastern Context: A Tribute to Nadav Na'aman*. Edited by Yaira Amit, Ehud Ben-Zvi, Israel Finkelstein, and Oded Lipschits. Winona Lake, IN: Eisenbrauns, 2006.

———. "Omride Architecture." *ZDPV* 116 (2000):114–38.

———. "Shechem in the Late Bronze and the Iron I." Pages 349–35 in *Timelines: Studies in Honor of Manfred Bietak*. Vol. 2. Edited by Ernst Czerny, Irmgard Hein, Hermann Hunger, Dagmar Melman, and Angela Schwab. OLA 149. Leuven: Peeters, 2006.

———. "The Sociopolitical Organization of the Central Hill Country in the Second Millennium BCE." Pages 110–31 in *Biblical Archaeology Today, 1990: Proceedings of the Second International Congress on Biblical Archaeology*. Supplement, *Pre-Congress Symposium: Population, Production and Power, Jerusalem, June 1990*. Edited by Avraham Biran and Joseph Aviram. Jerusalem: Israel Exploration Society, 1993.

———. "Stages in the Territorial Expansion of the Northern Kingdom." *VT* 61 (2011): 227–42.

Finkelstein, Israel, and Zvi Lederman. *Highlands of Many Cultures: The Southern Samaria Survey; The Sites*. MS 14. Tel-Aviv: Institute of Archaeology, 1997.

Finkelstein, Israel, and Oded Lipschits. "Omride Architecture in Moab: Jahatz and Atharot." *ZDPV* 126 (2010): 29–42.

Finkelstein, Israel, and Thomas Römer. "Comments on the Historical Background of the Jacob Narrative in Genesis." *ZAW* 126 (2014): 317–38.

Fleming, Daniel. "Kinship of City and Tribe Conjoined: Zimri-Lim at Mari." Pages 227–40 in *Nomads, Tribes and the States in the Ancient Near East: Cross-Disciplinary Perspectives*. Edited by Jeffrey Szuchman. OIS 5. Chicago: University of Chicago Press, 2009.

———. *The Legacy of Israel in Judah's Bible: History, Politics and the Reinscribing of Tradition*. Cambridge: Cambridge University Press, 2012.

Franklin, Norma. "Samaria: From the Bedrock to the Omride Palace." *Levant* 36 (2004): 189–202.

Gadot, Yuval. "The Iron I in the Samaria Highlands: A Nomad Settlement Wave or Urban Expansion?" Pages 103–14 in *Rethinking Israel: Studies in the History and Archaeology of Ancient Israel in Honor of Israel Finkelstein*. Edited by Oded Lipschits, Yuval Gadot, and Matthew J. Adams. Winona Lake, IN: Eisenbrauns, 2017.

Gaß, Erasmus. *Die Ortsnamen des Richterbuchs in historischer und redaktioneller Perspektive*. ADPV 35. Wiesbaden: Harrassowitz, 2005.

Grønbæk, Hans J. *Die Geschichte vom Aufstieg Davids (1 Sam. 15–2 Sam. 5): Tradition und Komposition*. ATDan 10. Copenhagen: Prostant Apud Munksgaard, 1971.

Groß, Walter. *Richter*. HThkAT. Freiburg: Herder, 2009.

Hasel, Michael G. *Domination and Resistance: Egyptian Military Activity in the Southern Levant, ca. 1300–1185 B.C.* PdÄ 11. Leiden: Brill, 1998.

Hutton, Jeremy M. "Mahanaim, Penuel, and Transhumance Routes: Observations on Genesis 32–33 and Judges 8." *JNES* 65 (2006): 161–78.

Jobling, David. "Saul's Fall and Jonathan's Rise: Tradition and Redaction in 1 Sam 14:1–46." *JBL* 95 (1976): 367–76.

Kaiser, Otto. "Der historische und biblische König Saul (Teil I)." *ZAW* 122 (2010): 520–45.

———. "Der historische und biblische König Saul (Teil II)." *ZAW* 123 (2011): 1–14.

Kleiman, Assaf. "Comments on the Archaeology and History of Tell el-Far'ah North (Biblical Tirzah) in the Iron IIA." *Sem* 60 (2018): 85–104.

Knauf, Ernst A. "The Cultural Impact of Secondary State Formation: The Cases of Edomites and Moabites." Pages 47–54 in *Early Edom and Moab: The Beginning of Iron Age in Southern Jordan*. Edited by Pioter Bienkowski. SAM 7. Sheffield: Equinox, 1992.

Kratz, Reinhard G. *The Composition of the Narrative Books of the Old Testament*. London: T&T Clark, 2005.

———. "Saul, Benjamin and the Emergence of Biblical Israel: An Alternative View." *ZAW* 123 (2011): 348–67.

Lee, Sharen, Christopher Bronk Ramsey, and Amihai Mazar. "Iron Age Chronology in Israel: Results from Modeling with a Trapezoidal Bayesian Framework." *Radiocarbon* 55 (2013): 731–40.

Lehmann, Gunnar, and H. Michael Niemmann. "When Did the Shephelah Become Judahite?" *TA* 41 (2014): 77–94.

Maeir, Aren M. "The Tell eṣ-Ṣafi/Gath Archaeological Project 1996–2010: Introduction, Overview and Synopsis of Results." Pages 26–49 in *Tell eṣ-Ṣafi/Gath I: The 1996–2005 Seasons. Part 1, Text*. Edited by Aren M. Maeir. ÄAT 69. Wiesbaden: Harrassowitz, 2012.

Maeir, Aren, Louise Hitchcock, and Liora Horwitz. "On the Constitution and Transformation of Philistine Identity." *OJA* 32 (2013): 1–38.

Mazar, Amihai. "Jerusalem in the Tenth Century B.C.E.: The Glass Half Full." Pages 255–72 in *Essays on Ancient Israel in Its Near Eastern Context: A Tribute to Nadav Na'aman*. Edited by Yaira Amit, Ehud Ben-Zvi, Israel Finkelstein, and Oded Lipschits. Winona Lake, IN: Eisenbrauns, 2006.

Mazzoni, Stefania. "Syria and the Periodization of the Iron Age: A Cross-Cultural Perspective." Pages 31–59 in *Essays on Syria in the Iron Age*. Edited by Guy Bunnens. ANESSup 7. Leuven: Peeters, 2000.

McCarter, P. Kyle. *I Samuel: A New Translation with Introduction, Notes and Commentary*. AB 8. New Haven: Doubleday, 1980.

Na'aman, Nadav. "Canaanite Jerusalem and Its Central Hill Country Neighbors in the Second Millennium BCE." *UF* 24 (1992): 257–91.

———. "Jebusites and Jabeshites in the Saul and David Story Cycle." *Bib* 95 (2015): 481–97.

———. "The Kingdom of Judah in the Ninth Century BCE: Text Analysis versus Archaeological Research." *TA* 40 (2013): 247–76.

———. "Memories of Monarchical Israel in the Narrative of David's Wars with Israel's Neighbours." *HBAI* 6 (2017): 308–28.

———. "The Northern Kingdom in the Late Tenth–Ninth Centuries BCE." Pages 399–418 in *Understanding the History of Ancient Israel*. Edited by Hugh G. M. Williamson. PBA 143. Oxford: Oxford University Press, 2007.

———. "The Pre-Deuteronomistic Story of King Saul and Its Historical Significance." *CBQ* 54 (1990): 638–58.

———. "Saul, Benjamin and the Emergence of Biblical Israel." *ZAW* 121 (2009): 211–24, 335–49.

———. "The Scope of the Pre-Deuteronomistic Saul-David Story Cycle." In *From Nomadism to Monarchy: Thirty Years Update*. Edited by Ido Koch, Omer Sergi, and Oded Lipschits. Tübingen: Mohr Siebeck, forthcoming.

———. "The Settlements of the Ephratites in Bethlehem and the Location of Rachel's Tomb." *RB* 121 (2014): 516–29.

Niemann, H. Michael. "Core Israel in the Highlands and Its Periphery: Megiddo, the Jezreel Valley and the Galilee in the Eleventh–Eighth Century BCE." Pages 821–42 in *Megiddo IV: The 1998–2002 Seasons*. Edited by Israel Finkelstein, David Ussishkin, and Baruch Halpern. MS 24. Tel Aviv: Institute of Archaeology, 2006.

———. "Royal Samaria—Capital or Residence? Or: The Foundation of the City of Samaria by Sargon II." Pages 184–207 in *Ahab Agonistes: The Rise and Fall of the Omri Dynasty*. Edited by Lester L. Grabbe. LHBOTS 421. London: T&T Clark, 2007.

Noth, Martin. "Jabes-Gilead." *ZDPV* 69 (1953): 28–41.

Porter, Ann. "Beyond Dimorphism: Ideologies and Materialities of Kinship as Time-Space Distanciation." Pages 201–25 in *Nomads, Tribes and the States in the Ancient Near East: Cross-Disciplinary Perspectives*. Edited by Jeffrey Szuchman. OIS 5. Chicago: University of Chicago Press, 2009.

———. *Mobile Pastoralism and the Formation of Near Eastern Civilization: Weaving Together Society*. Cambridge: Cambridge University Press, 2012.

Porter, Benjamin. *Complex Communities: The Archaeology of Early Iron Age Central Transjordan*. Tucson: University of Arizona Press, 2013.

Pury, Albert de. "The Jacob Story and the Beginning of the Formation of the Pentateuch." Pages 51–72 in *A Farewell to the Yahwist? The Composition of the Pentateuch in Recent European Interpretation*. Edited by Thomas B. Dozeman and Konrad Schmid. SymS 34. Atlanta: Society of Biblical Literature, 2006.

Rosen, Baruch. "Economy and Subsistence." Pages 362–67 in *Shiloh: The Archaeology of a Biblical Site*. Edited by Israel Finkelstein. MS 10. Tel Aviv: Institute of Archaeology, 1993.

Sader, Helen. "History." Pages 11–36 in *The Aramaeans in Ancient Syria*. Edited by Herbert Niehr. HdO 106. Leiden: Brill, 2014.

Schmidt, Ludwig. *Menschlicher Erfolg und Jahwes Initiative: Studies zu Tradition, Interpretation und Historie in Überlieferungen von Gideon, Saul und David.* WMANT 38. Neukirchen-Vluyn: Neukirchener Verlag, 1970.

Schwartz, Glenn M. "The Origins of the Aramaeans in Syria and Northern Mesopotamia: Research Problems and Potential Strategies." Pages 275–91 in *To the Euphrates and Beyond: Archaeological Studies in Honor of Maurits N. van Loon.* Edited by Odette M. C. Haex, Hans H. Curvers, and Peter M. M. G. Akkermans. Rotterdam: CRC, 1989.

Sergi, Omer. "The Emergence of Judah as a Political Entity between Jerusalem and Benjamin." *ZDPV* 133 (2017): 1–23.

———. "The Gilead between Aram and Israel: Political Borders, Cultural Interaction and the Question of Jacob and the Israelite Identity." Pages 333–54 in *In Search of Aram and Israel: Politics, Culture and the Question of Identity.* Edited by Omer Sergi, Manfred Oeming, and Izaak de Hulster. ORA 20. Tübingen: Mohr Siebeck, 2016.

———. "Judah's Expansion in Historical Context." *TA* 40 (2013): 226–46.

———. "State Formation, Religion and Collective Identity in the Southern Levant." *HBAI* 4 (2015): 56–77.

———. "The United Monarchy and the Kingdom of Jeroboam II in the Story of Absalom and Sheba's Revolts." *HBAI* 6 (2017): 329–53.

Sergi, Omer, and Izaak de Hulster. "Some Historical and Methodological Considerations Regarding the Question of Political, Social and Cultural Interaction between Aram and Israel in the Early Iron Age." Pages 1–14 in *Search of Aram and Israel: Politics, Culture and the Question of Identity.* Edited by Omer Sergi, Manfred Oeming and Izaak de Hulster. ORA 20. Tübingen: Mohr Siebeck, 2016.

Sergi, Omer, and Yuval Gadot. "Omride Palatial Architecture as Symbol in Action: Between State Formation, Obliteration and Heritage." *JNES* 76 (2017): 103–11.

Stager, Lawrence E. "Shemer's Estate." *BASOR* 277/278 (1990): 93–107.

Steiner, Margaret L. *The Settlement in the Bronze and Iron Ages.* Vol. 3 of *Excavations by Kathleen M. Kenyon in Jerusalem 1961–1967.* CoIS 9. London: Sheffield Academic, 2001.

Stoebe, Hans J. *Das Erste Buch Samuelis.* KAT 8.2. Gutersloh: Gutersloher Verlagshaus, 1973.

Stolz, Fritz. *Das erste und zweite Buch Samuel.* ZBK 9. Zürich: Theologischer Verlag, 1981.

Toffolo, Michael B., Eran Arie, Mario A. S. Martin, Elisabetta Boaretto, and Israel Finkelstein. "Absolute Chronology of Megiddo, Israel in the Late Bronze and Iron Ages: High Resolution Radiocarbon Dating." *Radiocarbon* 56 (2014): 221–44.

Uziel, Joe, and Yuval Gadot. "The Monumentality of Iron Age Jerusalem prior to the Eighth Century BCE." *TA* 44 (2017): 123–40.

Uziel, Joe, and Nahshon Szanton. "New Evidence of Jerusalem's Urban Development in the Ninth Century BCE." Pages 429–39 in *Rethinking Israel: Studies in the History and Archaeology of Ancient Israel in Honor of Israel Finkelstein*. Edited by Oded Lipschits, Yuval Gadot, and Matthew J. Adams. Winona Lake, IN: Eisenbrauns, 2017.

———. "Recent Excavations near the Gihon Spring and Their Reflection on the Character of Iron II Jerusalem." *TA* 42 (2015): 233–50.

Van Der Steen, Evelin J. *Tribes and People in Transition: The Central East Jordan Valley in the Late Bronze Age and Early Iron Ages; A Study of the Sources*. Leuven: Peeters, 2004.

Van Der Steen, Eveline J., and Klaas A. D. Smelik. "King Mesha and the Tribe of Dibon." *JSOT* 32 (2007): 139–62.

Van Seters, John. *The Biblical Saga of King David*. Winona Lake, IN: Eisenbrauns, 2009.

Veijola, Timmo. *Die ewige Dynastie: David und die Entstehung seiner Dynastie nach der deutronomistischen Darstellung*. Helsinki: Suomalainen Tiedeakatemia, 1975.

Weingart, Kristin. *Stämmevolk – Staatvolk – Gottesvolk? Studien zur Verwendungs des Israels-Namens im Alten Testament*. FAT 2/68. Tübingen: Mohr Siebeck, 2014.

Weiser, Artur. "Die Legitimation des Königs Davids: zur Eigenart und Entstehung der sogen. Geschichte von Davids Aufsteig." *VT* 16 (1966): 325–54.

Wellhausen, Julius. *Die Composition des Hexateuchs und der historischen Bücher des Alten Testament*. Berlin: de Gruyter, 1889.

White, Marsha C. "The History of Saul's Rise: Saulide State Propaganda in 1 Samuel 1–14." Pages 271–92 in *"A Wise Discerning Mind": Essays in Honor of Burke O. Long*. Edited by Saul M. Olyan and Robert C. Culley. BJS 325. Providence: Brown University Press, 2000.

———. "Saul and Jonathan in 1 Samuel 1 and 14." Pages 119–38 in *Saul in Story and Tradition*. Edited by Carl S. Ehrlich and Marsha C. White. FAT 47. Tübingen: Mohr Siebeck, 2006.

Willi-Plein, Inna. "I Sam. 18–19 und die Davidshausgeschichte." Pages 138–71 in *David und Saul im Widerstreit—Diachronie und Synchronie im Wettstreit: Beiträge zur Auslegung des ersten Samuelbuches*. Edited by Walter Dietrich. OBO 206. Fribourg: Academic Press, 2004.

Wright, Jacob L. *David, King of Israel, and Caleb in Biblical Memory*. Cambridge: Cambridge University Press, 2014.

Zertal, Adam. *The Shechem Syncline*. Vol. 1 of *The Manasseh Hill Country Survey*. CHANE 21.1. Leiden: Brill, 2004.

———. *The Eastern Valleys and the Fringe of the Desert*. Vol. 2 of *The Manasseh Hill Country Survey*. CHANE 21.2. Leiden: Brill, 2008.

Zertal, Adam, and Nivi Mirkam. *From Nahal Iron to Nahal Shechem*. Vol. 3 of *The Manasseh Hill Country Survey*. CHANE 21.3. Leiden: Brill, 2016.

Cult and War: Contributions of Iconography to a Gender-Oriented Exegesis of Prophecy

Silvia Schroer

1. Introduction

On the contribution of iconography to a feminist or gender-related exegesis of the Nevi'im, only a brief overview of existing research and of selected relationships between texts and images will be possible here.¹ This is all the more so in view of the especially extensive, multifaceted, and—in terms of literary genre—heterogeneous body of texts. Text-image relationships

---

Most of the illustration credits refer to the cursory catalogue numbers of the completed four-volume work: Silvia Schroer, *Die Ikonographie Palästinas/Israels und der Alte Orient: Eine Religionsgeschichte in Bildern*, 4 vols. (Fribourg: Academic Press, 2005–2011; Basel: Schwabe Verlag, 2018). These volumes are suitable for a more detailed analysis of individual images and of the thematic stories that are merely sketched out in the present essay.

1. In two volumes on the Torah and the Ketuvim, I have attempted to demonstrate—cursorily in the one case, using the example of selected texts; in the other case, combined with thematically oriented text groups—how the knowledge of the ancient Near Eastern images and their symbolism contributes to a gender-oriented exegesis. The content of the introductions to these earlier works is not to be recapitulated here; for this reason, consulting them additionally is to be recommended. See Silvia Schroer, "Ancient Near Eastern Pictures as Keys to Biblical Texts," in *Torah*, ed. Irmtraud Fischer, Mercedes Navarro Puerto, and Andrea Taschl-Erber, BW 1.1 (Atlanta: Society of Biblical Literature, 2011), 31–60; Schroer, "Ancient Near Eastern Pictures as Keys to Biblical Metaphors," in *The Writings and Later Wisdom Books*, ed. Christl M. Maier and Nuria Calduch-Benages, BW 1.3 (Atlanta: Society of Biblical Literature, 2014), 129–64; see also Schroer, "Genderforschung, altorientalische Kunst und biblische Texte," *HBAI* 5 (2016): 132–50.

can be formed already in the primary sources when, for example, reliefs are mentioned and described in a biblical text (Ezek 8:7–11; 23:14–15). But they also can result from historical and iconographical research; that is, they can be produced or reconstructed and can demonstrate connections between different primary sources. Relationships between texts and images, and the act of putting texts and images in relation to one another, lead to reflections, to refractions, and to hermeneutically valuable lighting effects. Placing a text and an image in parallel or in contrast to each other is potentially enlightening for the understanding of both, far beyond a mere illustration. This is because texts are not captions for images, and images are not illustrations for a text. Such ascriptions fall far too short.

In the following, a selection of relevant themes is gathered into two larger complexes. In the early as well as later prophecy, there are, in terms of content, two centers of gravity that are often woven together. The one revolves around the cult, the other around war. In both cases, gender plays a central role.

2. Traces of the Cult of the Goddesses and the Outlawing of the Goddess: Iconography as a Contribution of Religious History to Gender Research and as Pièce de Résistance

In the Nevi'im, a sometimes subtle but also open conflict about women and the cult, women and religious or ritual tasks, and the goddesses or their representatives is perceptible. In terms of method, iconographic sources as a backdrop contrary to the biblical portrayals help to uncover the underlying constellations or associations, especially the polemical ones, in their originally positive evaluation. Texts and images thereby can complement one another in terms of their informative content, but also can contradict or stand in tension to one another. The relationships are not always equally close, as the following examples will show.

2.1. The Polemic against the Indigenous Goddess of Vegetation and Her Cult

The biblical polemic against the Asherah and the cult under the green trees is a reaction against the traditional rooting and presence of the branch or earth goddess in Palestine/Israel since the Chalcolithic period, but especially since the Middle Bronze Age. The distorting prophetic—and often probably Deuteronomistic—portrayal of the veneration of the goddesses is aimed at the local Canaanite goddess (fig. 2.1), who is erotic and nurturing, a "mother of all living things."[2] Occasionally, closer relationships between biblical texts and images can be detected. In particular, the prophetic critique of the cult under the green trees is characterized by a sexualized language, which seems to correspond to the erotic stripe of many a representation of dance and the tree cult (fig. 2.2).[3] The positive assessment of the connection of eroticism and vegetation in iconography stands in stark contrast to prophetic texts that paint these in distinctively negative colors:

Fig. 2.1. Scarab from Aphek (seventeenth/sixteenth century BCE). In the midst of branches stands a naked goddess whose pubic triangle is highlighted by a leaf-like engraving. The power that makes the plants thrive is thus closely linked with eroticism. Source: *IPIAO* 2, no. 411.

---

2. Such, according to Gen 3:20, is the honorary title of the first created woman. On the multifaceted connections between biblical texts and the images of goddesses, see Othmar Keel and Silvia Schroer, *Eva—Mutter alles Lebendigen: Frauen- und Göttinnenidole aus dem Alten Orient* (Fribourg: Universitätsverlag; Göttingen: Vandenhoeck & Ruprecht, 2010). Here I cannot recapitulate the complex discussions about gender-relevant and, above all, maternal images of God in Hos 4 and 11. See Martti Nissinen, *Prophetie, Redaktion und Fortschreibung im Hoseabuch: Studien zum Werdegang eines Prophetenbuches im Lichte von Hos 4 und 11*, AOAT 231 (Neukirchen-Vluyn: Neukirchener Verlag, 1991), 269–98; Marie-Theres Wacker, "Gott Vater, Gott Mutter— und weiter? Exegese und Genderforschung im Disput über biblische Gottes-Bilder am Beispiel von Hosea 11," in *Geschlechter bilden: Perspektiven für einen geschlechterbewussten Religionsunterricht*, ed. Andrea Qualbrink, Annebelle Pithan, and Mariele Wischer (Gütersloh: Gütersloher Verlagshaus, 2011), 136–57.

3. See Silvia Schroer, "Die Zweiggöttin in Palästina/Israel: Von der Mittelbronze IIB-Zeit bis zu Jesus Sirach," in *Jerusalem: Texte—Bilder—Steine; Zum 100. Geburtstag von Hildi und Othmar Keel-Leu*, ed. Max Küchler and Christoph Uehlinger, NTOA 6 (Fribourg: Universitätsverlag; Göttingen: Vandenhoeck & Ruprecht, 1987), 201–25.

Fig. 2.2. Scarab from trade (seventeenth/sixteenth century BCE). A woman leans forward in a dancing movement with a branch in her hand. The pose can be understood in terms of its parallels as a call for coitus. Dance in the cult has a clearly sexual component here. Source: *IPIAO* 2, no. 492.

Indeed, upon every high hill
   and under every green tree
   you lie as a whore. (Jer 2:20)

She [Israel] went up on every high hill and under every green tree and whored there. (Jer 3:6)

Indeed, you will be ashamed because of the large trees you take pleasure in and blush because of the gardens that please you. (Isa 1:29)

you who burn hot for the great trees under every green tree (Isa 57:5)[4]

It is important for history of religion as well as theological gender research to confront polemical texts with the iconographic evidence in order to understand and to question the biased prophetic-Deuteronomistic diction. The voice of the group of biblical writers does not represent the voice of religion in the land, but rather it is a dissenting voice that, anchored in the tradition of scriptural prophecy, is patriarchal.

2.2. Women and Men at the Entrances to the Holy Districts and Spaces

In the cult, as well as in the context of violent, warlike confrontations, the entrances to buildings or cities—that is, windows, doors, and gates—play a significant role.

    Basic social-geographical approaches assume that spaces are constructions whose quality and significance may be altered by the presence of

---

4. All biblical translations are mine.

human beings, and, conversely, human beings and their significance may also experience alterations through spaces.⁵ A gender-specific question derived from this approach relates to the place of women or men in the interpretive arts and in biblical texts and the cultural or redactional intentions behind such placement. What roles do women or men play at the sensitive entrances of buildings or cities? What do they do there? Thresholds and doors distinguish boundary and transitional zones between the street and familial space (house), between defenselessness and shelter, between the profane and the holy. Boundaries and transitions require special means of protection. In these sensitive zones calamity-deterring symbols, but also cultic items, are found in ancient Israel. Thus, a stela of the moon god was found in a small cultic high place (במה) at the gate in et-Tell north of the Sea of Gennesaret.⁶ By the gates to the court of the Jerusalem temple, likewise, according to Ezekiel, there was a cult figure, the "idol of jealousy" (Ezek 8:3–6), and it was possibly here that women practiced a ritual bewailing of Tammuz (Ezek 8:14).⁷ For Ezekiel, the veneration of the "idol of jealousy" and the bewailing of Tammuz are idolatry. The participants presumably would have seen this differently, but we are told only Ezekiel's view of the matter.

Casting a glance back to the early Israelite period, 1 Sam 2:22 speaks about women serving at the entrance of the tent of meeting: "Eli had grown very old. And again and again he heard about all the things his sons were doing to Israel and that they slept with the women who served at the entrance to the tent of meeting."⁸ The sexual promiscuity of Eli's sons distracts from the question of what the task of the women at the entrance

---

5. See the overview by Ilse Müllner and Yvonne Sophie Thöne, "Von Mutterhäusern, Landestöchtern und Stadtfrauen. Raum und Geschlecht im Alten Testament," *lectio difficilior* 1 (2012), https://tinyurl.com/SBL6016a. The spacing approach has been applied by Maier also in the context of prophetic metaphors about Zion. See Christl M. Maier, *Daughter Zion, Mother Zion: Gender, Space and the Sacred in Ancient Israel* (Minneapolis: Fortress, 2008).

6. See Monika Bernett and Othmar Keel, *Mond, Stier und Kult am Stadttor: Die Stele von Betsaida (et-Tell)*, OBO 161 (Fribourg: Universitätsverlag; Göttingen: Vandenhoeck & Ruprecht, 1998).

7. See Othmar Keel, *Die Geschichte Jerusalems und die Entstehung des Monotheismus* (Göttingen: Vandenhoeck & Ruprecht, 2007), 704–5, 708–9; Keel, *Jerusalem and the One God: A Religious History* (Minneapolis: Fortress, 2017), 123–24.

8. See Schroer, "Ancient Near Eastern Pictures as Keys to Biblical Texts," 53–54, on Exod 38:8 and the mirrors of the women serving at the entrance to the tent of meeting.

to the sanctuary actually was. Were they there to invite men to have sexual intercourse with them? Or did they, as temple servants, have an administrative office? Here, iconography can provide some clues to understand this puzzling information about women in the service of the sanctuary of YHWH.

Numerous clay models and cultic pedestals from Syria from the third century BCE have doorway and window openings at which women stand, in most cases naked and depicted erotically.[9] In the early Iron Age IIA, there are a larger number of small clay houses from Jordan and Phoenicia that show women at entrances (fig. 2.3). These small clay houses were intended to be small chapels. They are not models depicting a temple but rather transportable mini-shrines, in which a small cult figure could be placed. In cases where the female figures are modeled in more detail, the support of the breasts, but also a scarf on the head and body, is emphasized, and in many cases the women hold a drum or, more seldom, also wear an ankle bracelet. Sometimes guardian lions are found next to the women. In place of the naked women, palmettes or pillars also appear.

An important key to understanding the significance of these models is provided by the much older, famous image of the temple of Ishtar that was found in the palace of Mari (fig. 2.4). In this very richly detailed image, we see two protective Lama goddesses in the Old Babylonian and Old Syrian form of presentation as well as hybrid beings who guard the temple precinct on both sides. The basic configuration of the guarding of the entrance to the sanctuary by goddesses and/or (female) guardians is constant. The twin figures on each side of the entrance of the Iron Age temple model are, like the Lama goddesses, female guards. They protect what is most holy inside the shrine, probably a small (no longer extant) cult figure. Eroticism and, occasionally, the beating of the drum are connected with these female

---

9. See Silvia Schroer, "Frauenkörper als architektonische Elemente: Zum Hintergrund von Ps 114,12," in *Bilder als Quellen/Images as Sources: Studies on Ancient Near Eastern Artefacts and the Bible Inspired by the Work of Othmar Keel*, ed. Susanne Bickel et al., OBO (Fribourg: Universitätsverlag; Göttingen: Vandenhoeck & Ruprecht, 2007), 425–50; Schroer, "Ancient Near Eastern Pictures as Keys to Biblical Metaphors," 154–56; Schroer, "The Iconography of the Shrine Models of Khirbet Qeiyafa," in *Khirbet Qeiyafa in the Shephelah: Papers Presented at a Colloquium of the Swiss Society for Ancient Near Eastern Studies Held at the University of Bern, September 6, 2014*, ed. Silvia Schroer and Stefan Münger, OBO 282 (Fribourg: Universitätsverlag; Göttingen: Vandenhoeck & Ruprecht, 2017), 137–58.

Fig. 2.3. Pottery model, probably from Jordan (tenth/ninth century BCE). The entrance of the small shrine is flanked by naked women, each with a beautiful headscarf, foot and arm rings, perhaps belt jewelry, and a hand drum in the arm. Lions also guard the entrance. Several busts of drummers can be found in the capitals and in the tympanon. Source: *IPIAO* 4, no. 1193.

guardians. The link with the drum suggests an erotic, sacred dance.[10] The female figures are turned toward the observer; their effect is of erotic temptation. Here, the puzzling coupling of service at the door with the charge of sexual services by the women at the sanctuary made in 1 Sam 2:22 perhaps shows a parallel. Still, the background of the connection of eroticism and the role of the guardian remains unclear, especially since the biblical text sounds cliché.

Conspicuously, women who beat the drum disappear in the biblical tradition from the cultic contexts, in which they appear in art. The context in the literature is in most cases that of joyful events and victory celebrations, to which circle-type dances belong (see below). Thus, the passage through the Red Sea is celebrated by the prophetess Miriam and the women with dance and the sound of drums (Exod 15:20). Men returning home from war, such as Jephthah, are greeted by women with singing and drumming (Judg 11:34; 1 Sam 18:6–7).[11] The cultic connection, a procession to the holy shrine, is only still recognizable in Ps 68:24–26: "Your

---

10. The subject of women with drums in Iron Age iconography has been treated repeatedly. See Sarit Paz, *Drums, Women, and Goddesses: Drumming and Gender in Iron Age II Israel*, OBO 232 (Fribourg: Universitätsverlag; Göttingen: Vandenhoeck & Ruprecht, 2007).

11. See Thomas Staubli, *Musik in biblischer Zeit und orientalisches Musikerbe* (Stuttgart: Katholisches Bibelwerk, 2007), 13–17; Keel and Schroer, *Eva*, 179.

Fig. 2.4. Colored mural painting from the palace of Mari (1800 BCE). The picture was placed to the right of the entrance to the throne room and shows the temple of Ishtar, where the ruler of Mari and the goddess Ishtar meet. The temple stands in a large park that includes stylized trees and date palms. Two men each climb up the slender trunks (harvest or pollination?). A white dove soars from the preserved palm crown on the right. In addition to the hybrid creatures, two goddesses, left and right, with raised hands, guard the temple. Source: *IPIAO* 2, no. 434.

entry was seen, God, the entry of my God, my King, into the sanctuary. The singers preceded, then the string players, and in the midst the young women, beating the hand drum. In groups they praised God, YHWH from Israel's fountain."

In the postexilic cult (see the books of Chronicles), drums no longer appear, presumably a result of their old connection with erotic dance and women, which was unpopular in certain circles.[12] It is possible that women were banned from making music with the drum in the sanctuary and from serving as gatekeepers. In 2 Chr 23:19 and in many other passages in Chronicles, as well as in Ezra and Nehemiah, the "gatekeepers of the Temple of YHWH" are mentioned. There must have been a large number of such temple gatekeepers, who probably were temple person-

---

12. The erotic dance still has purely negative connotations also for the gospel writers (see Mark 6:22; Matt 14:6 on the dance performed by Herodias).

nel with fixed tasks.[13] Singers and other professionals belonging to the team of these gatekeepers are mentioned. They certainly did not stand at the gate the whole day, but rather had other tasks, for example, administration of financial contributions (2 Kgs 22:4), ensuring security and looking after the temple and its furnishings, and perhaps participating in the sacrifices. They appear not to have had a high position, even though they are designated with terms such as חיל and ראשי הגבורים. According to Ezek 44:9–11, the unemployed Levites are posted as "punishment" to such offices as service personnel.

2.3. The Continued Life of Goddesses in Feminine Literary Types

In many of the feminine characters in biblical literature, the ancient Near Eastern goddesses live on in various facets.[14] Thus, the warrior women Jael and Deborah take up literally the legacy of warrior goddesses such as Ishtar, Anat, Astarte, and special manifestations of Qedeshet, which circulated in the Late Bronze Age. The figure of Judith also can be classified in this series.[15] Some of the goddesses mentioned appear on a horse (figs. 2.5–6); they even ride at a time when horses were used normally only as draft animals for chariots. Sex appeal and martial power are combined in these goddess types. It is not said of Jael and Deborah that they rode, just as masculine warriors infrequently rode horses at the end of the second millennium in Palestine/Israel. Since the third millennium, it was the ass that was ridden in the region, which is definitely prestigious but is never associated with war. Art depicts men riding asses, but not women, while the biblical texts mention women from the well-situated classes who ride on asses, such as Abigail or the great woman from Shunem. The images help to identify typologies (bellicose goddess—female warrior) and influences. The differences between images and texts is thereby remarkable: goddesses ride on a horse, not on an ass; only men—in nonwarlike contexts—are represented as riding on an ass; the biblical texts do not recognize riding

---

13. On the significance of the gatekeepers, see John Wesley Wright, "Guarding the Gates: 1 Chronicles 26.1–19 and the Roles of Gatekeepers in Chronicles," *JSOT* 48 (1990): 69–81.

14. See on this the massive fundamental work by Urs Winter, *Frau und Göttin: Exegetische und ikonographische Studien zum weiblichen Gottesbild im Alten Israel und in dessen Umwelt*, OBO 53 (Fribourg: Universitätsverlag, 1983).

15. Winter, *Frau und Göttin*, 644–48; see also Keel and Schroer, *Eva*, 138–41.

Fig. 2.5. Scarab from trade (fifteenth–twelfth century BCE). A war goddess with an Egyptianizing Atef crown on horseback jumps high over a fallen man. She swings a wooden weapon in her raised right hand. Source: *IPIAO* 3, no. 876.

Fig. 2.6. Lachish gold foil (thirteenth/twelfth century BCE). The goddess on the horse appears much less warlike than the armored horse. She wears a lush crown and holds lotus flowers in her hands. Source: *IPIAO* 3, no. 869.

on horses, independent of sex, in the preexilic period, while riding on asses is mentioned in several instances of daily life.[16]

2.4. The Cult of the Queen of Heaven

The very widely documented iconographic astralization wave in the religious notions of the seventh century BCE illuminates the background of

---

16. See details in Silvia Schroer, "Gender und Ikonographie—aus der Sicht einer feministischen Bibelwissenschaftlerin," in *Images and Gender: Contributions to the Hermeneutics of Reading Ancient Art*, ed. Silvia Schroer, OBO 220 (Fribourg: Universitätsverlag; Göttingen: Vandenhoeck & Ruprecht, 2006), 107–24.

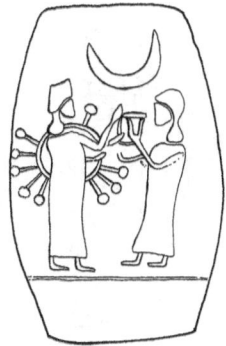

Fig. 2.7. Engraved agate bead from Dor (seventh century BCE). Under a crescent moon, a devotee with a gift stands in front of the goddess Ishtar, who is marked by a radiant nimbus. Source: *IPIAO* 4, no. 1874.

the veneration of the Queen of Heaven, who is spoken of in Jer 7 and 44. Historically, these texts refer to the sixth century BCE; the cults mentioned, however, are older.[17] A series of stamp seals from Palestine/Israel confirms the knowledge of Ishtar in her uranian form, as she was venerated in accord with Assyrian influence (fig. 2.7).

These seals are likely to have entered the country through Assyrian officials; they are thus not to be construed as direct products of the religious ideas that were widespread in the land. There are sometimes surprising relationships between images and biblical texts, for example, the familial reverence for the Queen of Heaven (fig. 2.8). Since we possess no other source than the Jeremiah texts on the cult of the Queen of Heaven in the seventh/sixth century BCE in Judah, the pictorial material represents a valuable supplement to our knowledge. Neither in the Neo-Assyrian representations nor in the biblical texts does the goddess or her cult bear erotic hallmarks. As a uranian goddess, she is a remote goddess, but her appearance is at the same time martial, and the men and women who venerate her expect from her and the cult divine blessing in the form of nourishment, peace, and protection against hunger and war (Jer 44:15–19). Nevertheless, many questions remain unanswered, for example, whether in Palestine/Israel the title "Queen of Heaven" was ascribed to the local vegetation goddess Asherah.

---

17. See, in particular, Winter, *Frau und Göttin*, 561–76.

Fig. 2.8. New Assyrian cylinder seal from northern Mesopotamia (seventh century BCE). The Queen of Heaven receives a family of four. The parents and two children come to her in a small procession, astral symbols above them. The unusual scene recalls that Jeremiah describes the cult for the Queen of Heaven as a cult of the whole family. Source: *IPIAO* 4, no. 1876.

3. Sexualized Masculinity and Femininity in the Context of Battle and War

Long passages in the books of the Former as well as the Latter Prophets deal with warlike events or make reference to situations of political conflict that have the potential for war. Emphatic masculinity, but also missing, robbed, or destroyed masculinity, belongs to the language of war. Masculinity is manifested here in clothing, armament, body posture, gestures, and the markedly masculine body and its sexual parts, including hair. Those men who are defeated or conquered are portrayed in the Egyptian as well as Near Eastern visual conception as denuded figures, and their sexual parts often are clearly visible (figs. 2.9–10). Enemies are grabbed by a shock of hair. The capture or killing of a warrior is aimed also at his sexual parts. Collections of penises as trophies of war are known to us from biblical texts (1 Sam 18:25–27; 2 Sam 3:14) and from reliefs in the temple of Ramesses III in Medinet Habu.[18] The masculinity of men engaged in the acts of war is frequently emphasized openly or subtly in ancient Near Eastern art, as Cynthia Chapman has shown in her work.[19]

---

18. See Harold Hayden Nelson et al., *Medinet Habu 1: Earlier Historical Records of Ramses III*, OIP 8 (Chicago: University of Chicago Press, 1930), 22–23.

19. Cynthia R. Chapman, *The Gendered Language of Warfare in the Israelite-Assyrian Encounter* (Winona Lake, IN: Eisenbrauns, 2004); Chapman, "Sculpted

Cult and War 59

Fig 2.9. Siltstone palette, probably from Abydos in Egypt (around 3000 BCE). A lion representing the Egyptian ruler devours a naked, bearded man. Other men are already lying on the battlefield, some tied up and the prey of scavenging birds. Others are tied to the banners of the victors. The genitals of the vanquished are always clearly visible. Source: *IPIAO* 1, no. 128.

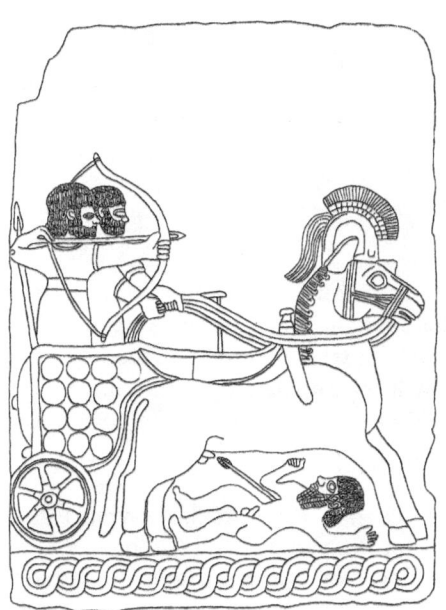

Fig. 2.10. Basalt orthostat from Carchemish on the Syrian-Turkish border (tenth century BCE). In a chariot, a driver and an archer go into battle. Under the vehicle or the horse lies a warrior hit by the arrow on his back. He is naked, his gender clearly marked. Source: *IPIAO* 4, no. 1345.

3.1. Fighting Heroes in Ancient Near Eastern Art and in Biblical Literature

From the third millennium BCE onward, fighting heroes are portrayed first of all as naked, whereby their naked bodies express power and superiority (fig. 2.11).[20] The curly-haired heroes of early Near Eastern iconography, which are not gods but are still superhuman beings, are the prototypes of a Samson or a Hercules. Samson is described in the book of Judges as a lion slayer (Judg 14:5–9) and as a dangerous warhorse who causes bloodbaths in his life and even in his death (14:19; 15:15; 16:30). His masculinity resides in the overabundant strength of his muscles and in his hair. This masculinity manifests itself in battles (against animals and human beings) as well as in his relationships with women, which, at the same time, bring disaster on him. In the lap of a woman (16:19), the muscle man is robbed of his locks and thus of his masculine power. Blinded, fettered, and forced to labor at the mill—work that usually was done by cattle or asses—the hero is turned into a pitiable, dependent creature. Only in his act of suicide does he appear one last time as an invincible man.

Fig. 2.11. Akkadian cylinder seal, in the British Museum, London (last third of the third millennium BCE). Six-armed heroes fight with a raised bull and a lion. The heroes are naked except for a strap, and their strength is despite the schematic representation recognizable in terms of their leg muscles. Source: Othmar Keel, *Das Recht der Bilder gesehen zu werden*, OBO 122 (Fribourg: Universitätsverlag; Göttingen: Vandenhoeck & Ruprecht, 1992), fig. 3.

Warriors: Sexuality and the Sacred in the Depiction of Warfare in the Assyrian Palace Reliefs and in Ezekiel 23:14–17," Id (2007), https://tinyurl.com/SBL6016b.

20. Julia M. Asher-Greve and Deborah Sweeney, "On Nakedness, Nudity, and Gender in Egyptian and Mesopotamian Art," in Schroer, *Images and Gender*, 126–76.

3.2. The Sex Appeal of Well-Built Warriors

How much masculine sexuality and sexualized body language manifest in texts as well as in visual representations is found in the much-discussed chapter 23 of Ezekiel. The chapter about the political whoring by the sisters Oholah and Oholibah—representing Samaria and Judah—with the Assyrians and Babylonians is rich in prophetic polemic.[21] In several verses (Ezek 23:5–7, 12, 23), Samaria and Judah are seen as being extremely fascinated by the powerful figures of Assyria and Babylonia, but especially by their warriors and horsemen. The repeated description of these men as בחורי חמד is, like the entire graphic context of Ezek 23, sexually charged. They are attractive, desirable young men who deeply captivate the officials in Samaria and Judah. Their sex appeal lies in their well-formed appearance, which leads to a notable political alliance with the major powers. The charming warriors and powerful people, after whom the officials in Samaria and Judah run, will directly, in the view of the prophet, turn against Oholah and Oholibah. The proud sisters will be humiliated completely.[22] Ezekiel's polemic reflects quite well the Neo-Assyrian self-portrayal, particularly in regard to the well-built, potent horsemen. Assyrian reliefs and wall paintings (fig. 2.12) emphasize the stateliness of the warriors and high functionaries by emphasizing clothing, armament, and the conspicuous warriors' legs (see the dissociation from them in Ps 147:10; Jdt 9:11). Although Ezek 23:14–16 refers to images of Babylonians, for which we do not have any iconographic sources, the verses about the wall reliefs portraying the decorative warriors[23] can be included here:

> But she went even further with her harlotries: She saw men—a relief on the wall, images of Chaldeans, carved in red paint, girded with a belt on their hips, headdresses hanging down from their heads, all of them had the appearance of excellent fighters, a portrayal of the Babylonians,

---

21. On the connection between Ezek 16 and 23, see Winter, *Frau und Göttin*, 607–13; Silvia Schroer, *In Israel gab es Bilder: Alttestamentliche Nachrichten von darstellender Kunst*, OBO 74 (Fribourg: Universitätsverlag; Göttingen: Vandenhoeck & Ruprecht, 1987), 179–80; Keel, *Geschichte Jerusalems*, 718–77.

22. The proud sitting, that is, enthronement, of women in biblical texts is associated conspicuously often with prostitution (Jer 3:2; Ezek 23:41; Prov 9:14).

23. Schroer, *In Israel gab es Bilder*, 180–87.

Fig. 2.12. Detail of a wall painting from Til Barsip (eighth century BCE). An Assyrian warrior in full armor attacks the crouching man in front of him, wearing only a shirt. Source: Othmar Keel, *The Symbolism of the Biblical World: Ancient Near Eastern Iconography and the Book of Psalms* (Winona Lake, IN: Eisenbrauns, 1997), fig. 133.

whose land of birth is Chaldea. And when her eyes saw their appearance, she desired[24] them, and she sent messengers to them in Chaldea.

3.3. Death through Violence

Normal dying, with the exception of the Egyptian death rituals, in which those who have died or the dead are portrayed in their mummified form while lying in state, is not a theme in iconography. The death that is portrayed is the death of men caused by sovereign or martial violence.[25] Death in one's own ranks is never portrayed; it is always the death of enemies. These appear bound, stripped bare, thrown down, in chaotic piles, lying on the stomach or on the back, under the foot of their conqueror, pierced by a weapon, dropping or falling to the ground, grabbed by the hair,

---

24. The Hebrew עגב is not only negative (in German, "schmachten nach" or "yearn for"); a שיר עגבה is also a song of longing.

25. See Angelika Berlejung, "Bilder von Toten – Bilder für die Lebenden," in *Tod und Jenseits im alten Israel und in seiner Umwelt*, ed. Angelika Berlejung and Bernd Janowski, FAT 64 (Tübingen: Mohr Siebeck, 2009), 199–253.

impaled, and beheaded. Their nakedness, the sexual parts exposed to the view of the observer, is degrading. The practice of violence is not reserved quite exclusively for men. In the Near East, goddesses are also portrayed in the act of killing enemies, although very seldom.[26] The killing of men by women with their own hands is a rare exception in the ancient Israelite literature (see above).

Violence against women does not belong to the repertoire of themes in the ancient Near Eastern iconography. As an exception, the assault carried out by Assyrian troops against nomadic women in their tent is portrayed on one of Assurbanipal's (668–627 BCE) reliefs. The subject here is perhaps rape, or the killing of pregnant women (fig. 2.13). In Neo-Assyrian art, though, women appear otherwise only as deported women, sometimes alongside men, children, and livestock (Lachish reliefs), sometimes also in columns separated according to sex, such as on the Balawat bronze gates from the time of Shalmaneser III (858–824 BCE). The humiliation of women, as of men, is not depicted by fettering, divestiture of clothing, and complete nudity, but rather by loosened hair, exposed breasts, and, not uncommonly, by the lifting of the hems of the skirt (fig. 2.14). The loosening of the hair and the ripping of the outer garments belong to mourning rituals. Portraying the complete denuding of the female prisoners of war did not correspond to convention, yet it is suggested by the gathering up of the skirt. The lifting of the hem is to be interpreted as a partial exposure of the genitals, an indication that the women had to be sexually available to the victors. Alfred Jeremias initially connected the motif of Neo-Assyrian art with Isa 47:3; Jer 13:22, 26; Ezek 23:29; Mic 4:11; and Nah 3:5.[27]

Long passages of the biblical texts reflect the gender signs in iconography: violence by men against men is the norm. They differ starkly from each other, however, in one respect: violence against women is a theme in biblical literature, found frequently even in a critical refraction of the theme. The texts in this case are less stereotypical than the images, which completely disregard entire realms of reality.

---

26. See *IPIAO* 2, nos. 518, 520, 522.

27. See Gerlinde Baumann, *Love and Violence: Marriage as Metaphor for the Relationship between YHWH and Israel in the Prophetic Books* (Collegeville, MN: Liturgical Press, 2003), 79–81.

Fig. 2.13. Relief from the palace of Assurbanipal in Nineveh (668–627 BCE). Assyrian soldiers massacre nomads and nomad women in their tents. Source: Keel, Küchler, and Uehlinger. *Geographisch-geschichtliche Landeskunde*, fig. 105.

Fig. 2.14. Bronze fitting of a gate wing from Balawat in Iraq, in the time of Shalmaneser III (858–824 BCE). From a conquered and ablaze city, Assyrian soldiers are leading the population away—naked men with their hands tied behind their backs, and women lifting or opening their skirts with one hand. Source: Keel, *The Symbolism of the Biblical World*, fig. 136.

3.4. Proud Cities and Their Destruction

Cities and countries, against the background of ancient Near Eastern traditions, are personified as feminine in the Nevi'im.[28] The protective, beautiful city on a hill is linked symbolically with nurturing mothers, splendidly adorned women, goddesses, and female rulers (fig. 2.15). Biblical figures such as the woman from Abel Beth-Maacah (2 Sam 20),[29] who negotiates with David's commander from the city (wall), or the personified wisdom in Prov 1 and 8 also can be assigned to this symbolic field. The city is the epitome of security and prideful self-confidence. This image, however, has another side. The siege, or even the destruction, of a city is of existential significance to the inhabitants and traumatizes them.[30] Lamenting women standing on the city walls are an emblem of its catastrophe.[31] In prophetic texts as well as in Assyrian reliefs, the motif becomes effective as a threatening image (Jer 9). When Neo-Assyrian war iconography portrays lamenting women standing on the city walls (fig. 2.16), then, it reenacts the power relationships between the victorious Assyrians and the conquered cities and their fate—men fall in a hopeless battle; and to the population, often represented by women, there remains only lament.[32]

In these images and in the biblical texts, the women's lament becomes a daunting picture of a threat, but in the Bible it is directed against Judah and Jerusalem, that is, inwardly and not against an external enemy. The destroyed city is represented then as a powerless, desperate woman. She thus becomes the counterimage to the proud city with its walls and battlements. The conquering and razing of cities, which so often is portrayed in Neo-Assyrian art as a high point of the imperial military campaigns,

---

28. See the essay by Christl Maier in this volume.

29. See Silvia Schroer, "Die weise Frau auf der Stadtmauer von Abel-bet-Maacha (2 Sam 20,14–22)," in *Seitenblicke: Literarische und historische Studien zu Nebenfiguren im zweiten Samuelbuch*, ed. Walter Dietrich, OBO 249 (Fribourg: Universitätsverlag; Göttingen: Vandenhoeck & Ruprecht, 2011), 394–411.

30. See the essay by Ruth Poser in this volume.

31. See Silvia Schroer, "Biblische Klagetraditionen zwischen Ritual und Literatur: Eine genderbezogene Skizze," in *Klagetraditionen: Form und Funktion der Klage in den Kulturen der Antike*, ed. Margaret Jaques, OBO 251 (Fribourg: Universitätsverlag; Göttingen: Vandenhoeck & Ruprecht, 2011), 83–102.

32. See Silvia Schroer, "Trauerriten und Totenklage im Alten Israel: Frauenmacht und Machtkonflikte," in Berlejung and Janowski, *Tod und Jenseits*, 299–321; see the different essays in Jaques, *Klagetraditionen*.

Fig. 2.15. Detail from a relief of Assurbanipal in Nineveh (668–627 BCE). The queen Assursharrat—the name means "Assur is ruler"—is represented in a ceremony in honor of the king in her regalia, to whom a mural crown diadem belongs. Source: Keel, *Deine Blicke sind Tauben*, fig. 8.

Fig. 2.16. Bronze fitting of a gate wing from Balawat in Iraq, in the time of Shalmaneser III (858–824 BCE). Assyrian warriors conquer a city with weapons and a ladder or ramp. On their battlements stand wailing women. Out of the burning city, the population, bound men and women, are deported in a long procession, under guard of soldiers. Source: Silvia Schroer, "Biblische Klagetraditionen zwischen Ritual und Literatur: Eine genderbezogene Skizze," fig. 3.

appear as brutal, masculine acts. Assyrian warriors, frequently outsized, approach the city's defenses with battering rams, ladders, or ramps. They encircle it, break its foundations, set them on fire, and kill the defenders who fall from the walls (figs. 2.17–18).

Fig. 2.17. Bronze fitting of a gate from Balawat in Iraq, in the time of Shalmaneser III (858–824 BCE). The Assyrian artillery attacks the city of Parga with a battering ram. At the same time, the soldiers aim at the defenders on the city battlements. Victims are already falling from the wall. Source: *IPIAO* 4, no. 1683.

Fig. 2.18. Relief of Tiglath-pileser III from Nimrud (745–727 BCE). The Assyrian invaders are oversized, as well as the battering ram that conquers a city on a mountain. On the other side are warriors who enter the city by means of a ramp or ladder. The defenders of the city are stabbed and thrown from the wall, beheaded by soldiers, and impaled for punishment and deterrence. Unarmed persons are shown to be pleading on the battlements. The defeated are mostly undressed and their genitals recognizable. Source: Keel, *The Symbolism of the Biblical World*, fig. 132.

3.5. Women at the Entrances and Windows of Living Quarters and Palaces

Women in biblical literature are to be encountered not infrequently at the entrances of their tents or houses. It is striking how frequently in the narratives these scenes are embedded in the context of war and political conflicts, and how serious the consequences of these encounters and confrontations are. It is almost always a matter of life and death.[33] Jael guides Sisera into her tent (Judg 4:17–22). Jephthah's daughter comes out of the door of her house in order to receive her father, returning home from the battle, with drums and dance and to celebrate him as victor (Judg 11:34). Rahab and Michal help men to flee—out the window (Josh 2:15; 1 Sam 19:12). As different as these two stories are, what connects them is that both women stand under the portent of perilous conflicts and that, as helpers in escape, both also commit treason. Rahab betrays her city, and Michal sides with David against her father, Saul. The window here has something of the character of a back door. It is not normal to climb through a window, and only thieves or death itself enter from outside through the window (Jer 9:21). Astonishingly often, women from the upper class tarry before the palace windows, for example, the mother of Sisera (Judg 5:28–30), Michal (2 Sam 6:16), and Jezebel (2 Kgs 9:30). The situations described are all different, but all these women are, so to say, on guard in their houses, and the situation has to do in most cases with life and death.

Sisera's mother waits at the window for the return of her son from war. It is an anxious waiting. Michal observes from the palace how her husband, as leader of the cult completely rooted in the Canaanite tradition, dances erotically while bringing the ark of YHWH into the temple. Her observance is aloof, indeed even full of contempt for what the king does. Michal represents a tradition, or circles, in Israel that did not value eroticism in the cult. Whether she historically advocated something similar is more than doubtful. She is needed in the story as a counterfigure, for here David is in the right. The look through the window of the palace at the cultic events in the public realm is attentive. The daughter of the king as well as the wife of the king remains at a distance; but she sees everything, and her devastating commentary shows that women in such a position

---

33. This is true also of narratives that we cannot discuss further here. The raped concubine of the Levite lies, according to Judg 19:27, half-dead on the threshold of the house. After raping her, Amnon throws his half-sister Tamar out through the door and thereby seals her fate (2 Sam 13:17–20).

can exercise power and that her observance and judgments are feared. The same is true for Jezebel, whose appearance in the palace window is a last, provocative confrontation with Jehu.

For a long time, women at the palace window have been associated with the motif of the woman at the window, which appears frequently in the Levantine-Syrian ivory carvings (fig. 2.19). The tablets found in the great hoards that come from the looting campaigns carried out by Assyrian rulers decorate the furnishings at the royal courts. The women look from out of an open window, or over a balustrade, with recessed frames. This indicates quite clearly the architecture of a palace. Windows did not play such an important role in temple buildings in general. The women themselves are distinguished as rich, beautiful women from their hairstyles and jewelry. Frequently, they wear a *taw*, or a tiara on the forehead, possibly the sign of their affiliation with a deity. Iconographically, they join the tradition of the goddesses with a friendly, full-faced look. This frontality, though, requires investigation. The position of the expensive, small badges in the interior decoration, on pieces of furniture or as wall paneling, is perhaps an indication of an apotropaic function.

Fig. 2.19. Ivory plaque from Arslantash in northern Syria (ninth/eighth century BCE). In a palace window with recessed frames, above a balustrade with capitals, the head of a woman appears on the front, on the forehead of whom a diadem or adornment in the form of a plaque is attached. Source: *IPIAO* 4, no. 1558.

4. Conclusion

In the context of antiquity, the cult secured the well-being and peace of a country and its population on behalf of the divinity. The neglect of the cult therefore endangered the vital, life-giving social, political, and even cosmic order. Violence and war occur today just as in the most distressing events of human experience and history. As such, according to ancient Near Eastern cultures, they are also an expression of broken relationships between the divinity/divinities and human beings, cities, and peoples. Gender plays a role in the intricate connection of cult and war with gods, goddesses, men, and women. Iconographic evidence can help in sharpening the understanding of gender in texts.

Bibliography

Asher-Greve, Julia M., and Deborah Sweeney. "On Nakedness, Nudity, and Gender in Egyptian and Mesopotamian Art." Pages 126–76 in *Images and Gender: Contributions to the Hermeneutics of Reading Ancient Art*. Edited by Silvia Schroer. OBO 220. Fribourg: Universitätsverlag; Göttingen: Vandenhoeck & Ruprecht, 2006.

Baumann, Gerlinde. *Love and Violence: Marriage as Metaphor for the Relationship between YHWH and Israel in the Prophetic Book*. Collegeville, MN: Liturgical Press, 2003.

Berlejung, Angelika. "Bilder von Toten—Bilder für die Lebenden." Pages 199–253 in *Tod und Jenseits im alten Israel und in seiner Umwelt*. Edited by Angelika Berlejung and Bernd Janowski. FAT 64. Tübingen: Mohr Siebeck, 2009.

Bernett, Monika, and Othmar Keel. *Mond, Stier und Kult am Stadttor: Die Stele von Betsaida (et-Tell); Unter Mitarbeit von Stefan Münger*. OBO 161. Fribourg: Universitätsverlag; Göttingen: Vandenhoeck & Ruprecht, 1998.

Chapman, Cynthia R. *The Gendered Language of Warfare in the Israelite-Assyrian Encounter*. Winona Lake, IN: Eisenbrauns, 2004.

———. "Sculpted Warriors: Sexuality and the Sacred in the Depiction of Warfare in the Assyrian Palace Reliefs and in Ezekiel 23:14–17." *Id* 1 (2007): https://tinyurl.com/SBL6016b.

Jaques, Margaret, ed. *Klagetraditionen: Form und Funktion der Klage in den Kulturen der Antike*. OBO 251. Fribourg: Universitätsverlag; Göttingen: Vandenhoeck & Ruprecht, 2011.

Keel, Othmar. *Deine Blicke sind Tauben: Zur Metaphorik des Hohen Liedes*. SBS 114/115. Stuttgart: Verlag Katholisches Bibelwerk, 1984.

———. *Die Geschichte Jerusalems und die Entstehung des Monotheismus*. Göttingen: Vandenhoeck & Ruprecht, 2007.

———. *Jerusalem and the One God: A Religious History*. Minneapolis: Fortress, 2017.

———. *Das Recht der Bilder gesehen zu werden*. OBO 122. Fribourg: Universitätsverlag; Göttingen: Vandenhoeck & Ruprecht, 1992.

———. *The Symbolism of the Biblical World: Ancient Near Eastern Iconography and the Book of Psalms*. Winona Lake, IN: Eisenbrauns, 1997.

Keel, Othmar, Max Küchler, and Christoph Uehlinger. *Geographisch-geschichtliche Landeskunde*. Vol. 1 of Orte und Landschaften der Bibel: Ein Handbuch und Studien-Reiseführer zum Heiligen Land. 5 vols. Benziger: Vandenhoeck & Ruprecht, 1982.

Keel, Othmar, and Silvia Schroer. *Eva—Mutter alles Lebendigen: Frauen- und Göttinnenidole aus dem Alten Orient*. Fribourg: Universitätsverlag; Göttingen: Vandenhoeck & Ruprecht, 2010.

Maier, Christl M. *Daughter Zion, Mother Zion: Gender, Space and the Sacred in Ancient Israel*. Minneapolis: Fortress, 2008.

Muellner, Ilse, and Sophie Thöne. "Von Mütterhäusern, Landestöchtern und Stadtfrauen. Raum und Geschlecht im Alten Testament." *lectio difficilior* 1 (2012): https://tinyurl.com/SBL6016a.

Nelson, Harold Hayden, et al. *Medinet Habu I: Earlier Historical Records of Ramses III*. OIP 8. Chicago: University of Chicago Press, 1930.

Nissinen, Martti. *Prophetie, Redaktion und Fortschreibung im Hoseabuch: Studien zum Werdegang eines Prophetenbuches im Lichte von Hos 4 und 11*. AOAT 231. Neukirchen-Vluyn: Neukirchener Verlag, 1991.

Paz, Sarit. *Drums, Women, and Goddesses: Drumming and Gender in Iron Age II Israel*. OBO 232. Fribourg: Universitätsverlag; Göttingen: Vandenhoeck & Ruprecht, 2007.

Schroer, Silvia. "Ancient Near Eastern Pictures as Keys to Biblical Metaphors." Pages 129–64 in *The Writings and Later Wisdom Books*. Edited by Christl M. Maier and Nuria Calduch-Benages. BW 1.3. Atlanta: Society of Biblical Literature, 2014.

———. "Ancient Near Eastern Pictures as Keys to Biblical Texts." Pages 31–60 in *Torah*. Edited by Irmtraud Fischer, Mercedes Navarro Puerto, and Andrea Taschl-Erber. BW 1.1. Atlanta: Society of Biblical Literature, 2011.

———. "Biblische Klagetraditionen zwischen Ritual und Literatur: Eine genderbezogene Skizze." Pages 83–102 in *Klagetraditionen: Form und Funktion der Klage in den Kulturen der Antike*. Edited by Margaret Jaques. OBO 251. Fribourg: Universitätsverlag; Göttingen: Vandenhoeck & Ruprecht, 2011.

———. *Die Ikonographie Palästinas/Israels und der Alte Orient: Eine Religionsgeschichte in Bildern*. IPIAO 1–4. Fribourg: Academic Press, 2005–2011.

———. "Die weise Frau auf der Stadtmauer von Abel-bet-Maacha (2 Sam 20,14–22)." Pages 394–411 in *Seitenblicke: Literarische und historische Studien zu Nebenfiguren im zweiten Samuelbuch*. Edited by Walter

Dietrich. OBO 249. Fribourg: Universitätsverlag; Göttingen: Vandenhoeck & Ruprecht, 2011.

———. "Die Zweiggöttin in Palästina/Israel. Von der Mittelbronze IIB-Zeit bis zu Jesus Sirach." Pages 201–25 in *Jerusalem: Texte—Bilder—Steine; Zum 100. Geburtstag von Hildi und Othmar Keel-Leu*. Edited by Max Küchler and Christoph Uehlinger. NTOA 6. Fribourg: Universitätsverlag; Göttingen: Vandenhoeck & Ruprecht, 1987.

———. "Frauenkörper als architektonische Elemente. Zum Hintergrund von Ps 114,12." Pages 425–50 in *Bilder als Quellen/Images as Sources: Studies on Ancient Near Eastern Artefacts and the Bible Inspired by the Work of Othmar Keel*. Edited by Susanne Bickel, Silvia Schroer, René Schurte, and Christophe Uehlinger. OBO. Fribourg: Universitätsverlag; Göttingen: Vandenhoeck & Ruprecht, 2007.

———. "Gender und Ikonographie—Aus der Sicht einer feministischen Bibelwissenschaftlerin." Pages 107–24 in *Images and Gender: Contributions to the Hermeneutics of Reading Ancient Art*. Edited by Silvia Schroer. OBO 220. Fribourg: Universitätsverlag; Göttingen: Vandenhoeck & Ruprecht, 2006.

———. "Genderforschung, altorientalische Kunst und biblische Texte." *HBAI* 5 (2016): 132–50.

———. "The Iconography of the Shrine Models of Khirbet Qeiyafa." Pages 137–58 in *Khirbet Qeiyafa in the Shephelah: Papers Presented at a Colloquium of the Swiss Society for Ancient Near Eastern Studies Held at the University of Bern, September 6, 2014*. Edited by Silvia Schroer and Stefan Münger. OBO 282. Fribourg: Universitätsverlag; Göttingen: Vandenhoeck & Ruprecht, 2017.

———. *In Israel gab es Bilder: Alttestamentliche Nachrichten von darstellender Kunst*. OBO 74. Fribourg: Universitätsverlag; Göttingen: Vandenhoeck & Ruprecht, 1987.

———. "Trauerriten und Totenklage im Alten Israel. Frauenmacht und Machtkonflikte." Pages 299–321 in *Tod und Jenseits im alten Israel und in seiner Umwelt*. Edited by Angelika Berlejung and Bernd Janowski. FAT 64. Tübingen: Mohr Siebeck, 2009.

Staubli, Thomas. *Musik in biblischer Zeit und orientalisches Musikerbe*. Stuttgart: Katholisches Bibelwerk, 2007.

Wacker, Marie-Theres. "Gott Vater, Gott Mutter—und weiter? Exegese und Genderforschung im Disput über biblische Gottes-Bilder am Beispiel von Hosea 11." Pages 136–57 in *Geschlechter bilden: Perspektiven für einen geschlechterbewußten Religionsunterricht*. Edited by Andrea

Qualbrink, Annebelle Pithan, and Mariele Wischer. Gütersloh: Gütersloher Verlagshaus, 2011.

Winter, Urs. *Frau und Göttin: Exegetische und ikonographische Studien zum weiblichen Gottesbild im Alten Israel und in dessen Umwelt*. OBO 53. Fribourg: Universitätsverlag, 1983.

Wright, John Wesley. "Guarding the Gates: 1 Chronicles 26.1–19 and the Roles of Gatekeepers in Chronicles." *JSOT* 48 (1990): 69–81.

Nonmale Prophets in Ancient Near Eastern Sources

Martti Nissinen

1. Nonmale Prophecy in the Ancient Near East

Prophecy was, and remains, a gender-inclusive phenomenon. Both women and men, even trans- or intersexed persons, can be found among people who act as intermediaries between the human and the divine worlds. According to anthropological and textual evidence, this is true of modern times as well as of the distant past.[1] Among different types of religious agency, prophecy appears to be the least gender specific, typically not discriminating between the subjects of prophetic activity on the basis of gender. Without claiming that this has been true always and everywhere, this non-gender-specific pattern occurs often enough in the sources to make it a distinct feature of prophetic divination.

What can we know, then, about ancient prophecy, and how can we know it? To study the prophetic phenomenon in the ancient Near East, one has to be content with the fact that the sources documenting ancient prophecy are few and far between. Besides the Hebrew Bible, most of the available texts documenting prophecy derive from two sources—Old Babylonian Mari and the Neo-Assyrian Nineveh; other than these, we have only scattered texts from different times and places, giving only a

---

1. For anthropological evidence, see Lester L. Grabbe, "'Her Outdoors: An Anthropological Perspective on Female Prophets and Prophecy," in *Prophets Male and Female: Gender and Prophecy in the Hebrew Bible, the Eastern Mediterranean, and the Ancient Near East*, ed. Jonathan Stökl and Corrine L. Carvalho, AIL 15 (Atlanta: Society of Biblical Literature, 2013), 11–25; Kirsi Stjerna, "Finnish Sleep-Preachers: An Example of Women's Spiritual Power," *NR* 5 (2001): 102–20; Thomas W. Overholt, *Prophecy in Cross-Cultural Perspective: A Sourcebook for Biblical Researchers*, SBLSBS 17 (Atlanta: Scholars Press, 1986).

very restricted view of prophecy in other historical contexts.² Written by scribes other than the prophets themselves, the texts are always secondary to the prophetic performances. They represent different genres, each of which paints but a narrow and genre-specific view of the prophets and the historical scene of their activity. On the other hand, the wide variety of genres also makes it possible to view prophets and prophecy from different angles. In addition, the temporal range and geographical distribution of the sources demonstrate the permanence of the prophetic phenomenon as a part of ancient Near Eastern divination through millennia. The gender aspect of prophetic activity varies according to culture-specific patterns and preconditions.

This essay, based on original sources and an increasing number of studies in nonmale prophetic activity in the ancient Near East,³ aims at a full inventory of female and other nonmale subjects of prophetic activity in ancient Near Eastern sources. The evidence can be divided into three sets of sources: (1) Old Babylonian texts, mostly from the eighteenth-century BCE kingdom of Mari; (2) Assyrian texts, predominantly from the seventh-century BCE archives of Nineveh; and (3) the Hebrew Bible,

---

2. The available evidence is collected in Martti Nissinen, *Prophets and Prophecy in the Ancient Near East*, 2nd ed., WAW 41 (Atlanta: SBL Press, 2019). In what follows, numbers with an asterisk (*) refer to the texts included in this collection; see the list in appendix 1.

3. For example, Susan Ackerman, "Why Is Miriam Also among the Prophets (And Is Zipporah among the Priests?)," *JBL* 121 (2002): 47–80; Irmtraud Fischer, *Gotteskünderinnen: Zu einer geschlechtsfairen Deutung des Phänomens der Prophetie und der Prophetinnen in der Hebräischen Bibel* (Stuttgart: Kohlhammer, 2002); Wilda C. Gafney, *Daughters of Miriam: Women Prophets in Ancient Israel* (Minneapolis: Fortress, 2008); Hugh G. M. Williamson, "Prophetesses in the Hebrew Bible," in *Prophecy and Prophets in Ancient Israel: Proceedings of the Oxford Old Testament Seminar*, ed. John Day, LHBOTS 531 (London: T&T Clark, 2010), 65–80; Jonathan Stökl, "Female Prophets in the Ancient Near East," in Day, *Prophecy and Prophets*, 47–61; Stökl, "Gender 'Ambiguity' in Ancient Near Eastern Prophecy: A Reassessment of the Data behind a Popular Theory," in Stökl and Carvalho, *Prophets Male and Female*, 59–80; Hanna Tervanotko, "Speaking in Dreams: The Figure of Miriam and Prophecy," in Stökl and Carvalho, *Prophets Male and Female*, 147–68; Esther J. Hamori, "Childless Female Diviners in the Bible and Beyond," in Stökl and Carvalho, *Prophets Male and Female*, 161–91; Hamori, *Women's Divination in Biblical Literature: Prophecy, Necromancy, and Other Arts of Knowledge*, ABRL (New Haven: Yale University Press, 2015); Martti Nissinen, *Ancient Prophecy: Near Eastern, Biblical, and Greek Perspectives* (Oxford: Oxford University Press, 2017), 297–325.

the pertinent passages of which are difficult to date but presumably derive from eighth through fourth centuries BCE.

Other ancient documents of prophecy from the Near East, written in languages other than Akkadian or Hebrew,[4] do not mention nonmale prophets. However, female prophecy was a permanent feature of Greek oracular practice in later periods, represented by the well-known female prophets of Apollo at Delphi and Didyma, as well as the priestesses of Dodona.[5] Even the New Testament acknowledges female prophecy, and female prophets played a prominent role in early Montanism.[6] Although Greek-language sources fall out of the scope of this article, it is important to recognize that nonmale prophecy is not typical of Near Eastern cultures but belongs to a wider eastern Mediterranean tradition.

Concerning genre, the main part of the Old Babylonian evidence consists of circa twenty letters belonging to the correspondence of King Zimri-Lim of Mari, plus a couple of administrative documents from Mari and Larsa, a text pertaining to the ritual of Ishtar at Mari, and a lexical list. The Assyrian documents comprise a dozen of written oracles attributed to nonmale prophets, half a dozen letters to King Esarhaddon of Assyria, and a few Middle Assyrian and Neo-Assyrian administrative documents, omen texts, and lexical lists.[7] The narrative texts of the Hebrew Bible mention four women in the books of Exodus, Judges, 2 Kings, 2 Chronicles, and Nehemiah, as well as an anonymous female prophet in the book of Isaiah, and an anonymous group of women who are said to prophesy in the book of Ezekiel. The historical information obtainable from the available source texts is essentially related to the textual genre. The written

---

4. That is, the Zakkur stela (*137), the Deir Alla inscription (*138), the Amman Citadel inscription (*136), the Til Barsip stela (*143), and the Lachish Letters (*139–41).

5. For the female prophets of Apollo, see, e.g., Lisa Maurizio, "Anthropology and Spirit Possession: A Reconsideration of the Pythia's Role at Delphi," *JHS* 115 (1995): 69–86; Michael A. Flower, *The Seer in Ancient Greece* (Berkeley: University of California Press, 2008), 211–39; Antti Lampinen, "Θεῷ μεμελημένε Φοίβῳ: Oracular Functionaries at Claros and Didyma in the Imperial Period," in *Studies in Ancient Oracle and Divination*, ed. Mika Kajava, AIRF 40 (Rome: Institutum Romanum Finlandiae, 2013), 49–88; Nissinen, *Ancient Prophecy*, 25–27, 130–37, 191–200, 224–42.

6. See Antti Marjanen, "Female Prophets among Montanists," in in Stökl and Carvalho, *Prophets Male and Female*, 127–43. The female prophet Anna is mentioned in Luke 2:36–38, and the daughters of Philip are said to have the gift of prophecy (Acts 21:9).

7. See the list of sources in appendix 1.

oracles as well as the royal correspondence from Mari and Assyria provide primary evidence documenting the recording of prophetic performances according to the preference and interpretation of contemporary writers. The administrative and ritual texts provide firsthand evidence of the presence of (nonmale) prophets in Mesopotamian temples, and the lexical lists indicate how (nonmale) prophets were associated with socioreligious groups. The biblical passages mentioning nonmale subjects of prophetic activity are embedded in secondary literary contexts and, therefore, are historically more distant from the circumstances to which they refer. They can be read as documents of interpretation and alleged impact of prophetic activity set in the more or less distant past, in some cases even yielding valuable historical information.

Nonmale persons involved in prophetic activity can be recognized in the sources in two ways. First, the Akkadian and Hebrew languages use certain specific designations for prophetic activity and its practitioners. Second, even without carrying any prophetic or other title, people can be acknowledged as subjects of prophetic activity if they do what prophets do, that is, transmit divine messages without using inductive methods.[8]

2. Nonmale Prophets in Old Babylonian Sources

2.1. *Muḫḫūtum* and *Āpiltum*

The Old Babylonian texts written in the Akkadian language have two different designations used exclusively of female prophets. Both correspond to a masculine noun used of male prophets. The most common among them is derived from the verb *maḫû*, denoting frenzied behavior. The Old Babylonian form *muḫḫūtum* appears in a lexical list as an equivalent of the Sumerian mí-lú-gub-ba; this entry follows the corresponding male designation *muḫḫûm*, Sumerian lú-gub-ba (*120). Both entries appear in the vicinity of designations of male and female people with ecstatic behavior (*zabbu*, *zabbatu*). The other designation, *āpiltum*, is the feminine equiva-

---

8. For the definition of prophecy as noninductive (or nontechnical) method of divination, that is, acquiring divine knowledge, see Manfred Weippert, *Götterwort in Menschenmund: Studien zur Prophetie in Assyrien, Israel und Juda*, FRLANT 252 (Göttingen: Vandenhoeck & Ruprecht, 2014), 231–32; Jonathan Stökl, *Prophecy in the Ancient Near East: A Philological and Sociological Comparison*, CHANE 56 (Leiden: Brill, 2012), 7–11; Nissinen, *Ancient Prophecy*, 19–23.

lent of the much more common *āpilum*, derived from the verb *apālum* and denoting something like "interpreter" or "spokesperson."⁹

The women carrying the title *muḫḫūtum* are without exception presented as prophets of female deities. A ritual text pertaining to the ritual of Ishtar, a major annual celebration of the city of Mari, mentions female prophets (pl. *muḫḫātum*) among the performers of the ritual (*52).¹⁰ An anonymous woman is listed among recipients of silver in a document from the Babylonian city of Larsa from the time of King Rim-Sin I (early eighteenth century BCE). This woman, designated as a *muḫḫūtum* (MÍ.LÚ.GUB.BA) of Inanna of Zabala, receives half a shekel of silver (*135g). Another, poorly known manifestation of Ishtar, Ishtar of Bišra, also speaks through a *muḫ*[*ḫūtum*]. This is reported by Ḫammi-šagiš to his father, the official Šu-nuḫra-Ḫalu. Judged from the few words that have been preserved, the divine message is about divine protection (*50b).¹¹

The rest of the women carrying the title *muḫḫūtum* are affiliated with Annunitum, an Ishtar-like goddess who had a prominent temple at Mari.¹² Annu-tabni, a *muḫḫūtum* of Annunitum, is awarded with some pieces of clothing by the court official Mukannišum in an administrative document from Mari (*58, ll. 6–10): "One *uṭublum* garment of second quality and two woven turbans for Annu-tabni, female prophet of Annunitum."

Two letters from Mari may refer to one and the same *muḫḫūtum*. The official Baḫdi-Lim tells about the hair and the garment fringe of a *muḫḫūtum* brought to him by Aḫum, a priest of the temple of Annunitum in the city of Mari (*11). A prophet's hair and a fringe of a garment

---

9. See Paolo Merlo, "*Āpilum* of Mari: A Reappraisal," *UF* 36 (2004): 323–32; Stökl, *Prophecy in the Ancient Near East*, 43.

10. Another text pertaining to the same ritual mentions a male prophet in a similar role (*51).

11. See Dominique Charpin, "Prophéties et rêves 'censurés' dans les archives royales de Mari," in *Comment devient-on prophète? Actes du colloque organisé par le Collège de France, Paris, les 4–5 avril 2011*, ed. Jean-Marie Durand, Thomas Römer, and Micaël Bürki, OBO 265 (Fribourg: Academic Press; Göttingen: Vandenhoeck & Ruprecht, 2014), 23–33. Ištar of Bišra appears also in *42. For this deity, see Jean-Marie Durand, "La religion à l'époque amorrite d'après les archives de Mari," in *Ebla, Mari*, vol. 1 of *Mythologie et religion des sémites occidentaux*, ed. Gregorio del Olmo Lete, OLA 162 (Leuven: Peeters, 2008), 249, 270, 288.

12. For Annunitum, see Spencer L. Allen, *The Splintered Divine: A Study of Ištar, Baal, and Yahweh Divine Names and Divine Multiplicity in the Ancient Near East*, SANER 5 (Berlin: de Gruyter, 2015), 192–97.

were sometimes attached to the letter to represent the prophet when the trustworthiness of the prophetic words was tested against another method of divination.[13] Baḫdi-Lim also attaches the "tablet of Aḫum," which may in fact be the letter in which Aḫum himself reports two oracles delivered by Ḫubatum, the *muḫḫūtum*, relating to Zimri-Lim's victory over the Yaminite tribes (*10).[14] Addu-duri, Zimri-Lim's mother, writes to the king about an ominous dream of her own, also quoting an anonymous *muḫḫūtum* who had arisen in the temple of Annunitum and delivered the goddess's warning against going on campaign (*42, ll. 21–26):

> Another matter: a female prophet arose in the temple of Annunitum and spoke: "Zimri-Lim, do not go on campaign! Stay in Mari, and I shall continue to answer."

Addu-duri, too, attaches a hair and a fringe of a garment—not of the prophet, however, but of her own. (*42)

The other designation, *āpiltum*, is attested only twice. One woman bearing this title is introduced by her name: Inib-šina, sister of King Zimri-Lim, reports an oracle pronounced by Innibana the *āpiltum*. The wording of the divine message is badly damaged, but it seems to warn the king about moving and acting too freely when his enemies are "circling about his borders" (*14). The other occurrence of the word is in the letter of Nur-Sîn, Zimri-Lim's representative in the kingdom of Aleppo. Nur-Sîn does not refer to any particular person but refers to prophets as an undefined group (*1, ll. 34–45):

> Previously, when I was still residing in Mari, I would convey every word spoken by a male or female prophet [*āpilum u āpiltum*] to my lord. Now, living in another land, would I not communicate to my lord what I hear and what they tell me? Should anything ever not be in order, let not my lord say: "Why have you not communicated to me the word which the prophet [*āpilum*] spoke to you when he was demanding your area?" Herewith I communicate it to my lord. My lord should know this.

---

13. See Esther J. Hamori, "*Gender and the Verification* of Prophecy at Mari," *WO* 42 (2012): 1–22.

14. For Zimri-Lim's wars against the Yaminites, see Dominique Charpin and Nele Ziegler, *Florilegium marianum 5: Mari et le Proche-Orient à l'époque amorrite, Essai d'histoire politique*, MN 6 (Paris: SEPOA, 2003), 190–91, 194–95.

Nur-Sîn thus wants to convince the king about his constant alertness to divine messages. The impersonal way the prophets are mentioned as a male-female assembly tells nothing specific about the female prophets but rather places them on a par with the male ones. In the same letter, Nur-Sîn quotes a male *āpilum* and an oracle pronounced by "prophets" (*āpilū*), which can be understood as a gender-inclusive reference.

The difference between the two designations, *muḫḫūtum* and *āpiltum*, is far from clear. The available evidence may suggest that the role of the male *muḫḫûm* was more temple-bound, while the male *āpilum* was more mobile and could be employed by the royal court.[15] The rareness of the word *āpiltum* makes it difficult to know whether such a distinction can be made between the corresponding feminine designations as well. Nevertheless, it is remarkable that neither of these two cases gives the female prophets any affiliation with a specific temple.

2.2. Women with Other than Prophetic Titles

Nonmale persons acting as prophets may sometimes carry titles that are not specifically prophetic and may refer to a different role. In the letters of Mari, divine words are transmitted by a woman with the title *qammatum*. This title is used three times, probably referring to one and the same anonymous woman (*7, *9, *13). She is called "*qammatum* of Dagan of Terqa," which associates her with Dagan and probably also with the major temple of this deity in the city of Terqa. The meaning of the title itself is unclear and does not necessarily denote a prophetic function. The message of the *qammatum* was directed against making peace between the kingdoms of Mari and Eshnunna, and it is referred to by three different letter writers, each quoting the proverb-like saying "beneath straw water runs" (*šapal tibnim mû illakū*) but otherwise giving a different wording to the oracle.[16] Both Inib-šina, the king's sister, and Sammetar, his high official, tell about the *qammatum* having come to them with her message. Both writers may refer

---

15. See Durand, "La religion à l'époque amorrite," 420–23, 445–50; Stökl, *Prophecy in the Ancient Near East*, 43–49.

16. The letters are written by Inib-šina (*7, ll. 11–19), Sammetar (*9, ll. 41–50), and Kanisan (*12, ll. 7–16), who, in fact, quotes the oracle as words of a male prophet (*muḫḫûm*). This discrepancy may be due to the chain of communication—Kanisan writes what he has heard from his father, who, for his part, had heard about the oracle from others; hence, Kanisan did not necessarily know who the actual speaker was.

to the same two-step event, since Sammetar is said to reward the woman with a garment and a nose ring, after which she "delivered her instructions in the temple of Belet-ekallim to the high pr[iestess In]ib-šina" (*9, ll. 51–54). Whatever these instructions (*wu"urtum*) may have been, and whatever the social position of the *qammatum* was, all this indicates that the divine word she transmitted was given serious consideration.

In addition to people introduced in texts with prophetic and other designations, female persons may appear as fulfilling a prophetic function without carrying any specific title. This is especially true of the letters from Mari, which report several divine messages transmitted by women whose role was not specifically prophetic. A dream of a woman without title may be reported,[17] or the female sender of a letter reports her own dream. Zunana reports to the king a revelation of Dagan in a dream concerning her servant girl (*37), and Addu-duri, Zimri-Lim's mother, reports two ominous dreams of her own, both concerning the safety of Zimri-Lim (*42, *43). Some letter writers give an account of divine messages mediated by ordinary women. Kibri-Dagan tells about an anonymous "woman, a spouse of a free man" (*ištēn awīltum aššat awīlim*) who claims to have been sent by Dagan with a soothing message to Zimri-Lim predicting the fall of Hammurabi, king of Babylon (*20, ll. 11–2′): "Dagan has sent me. Write to your lord that he should not be anxious, and [neither] should the la[nd] be anxious. [Ha]mmurabi, [king o]f Babylon [...... is ru]shing to his complete undoing."

Queen Šibtu writes about the performance of Aḫatum, the servant girl (*ṣuḫartum*) of Dagan-malik in the temple of Annunitum, which had been reported to her by Aḫum, the priest of the temple. The girl had gone into a trance and delivered an oracle, in which the deity (presumably Annunitum) promises to deliver Zimri-Lim's enemy into his hand in spite of his negligence toward the deity (*24).

2.3. *Assinnu*

One well-attested designation used of persons involved in prophetic activity is *assinnu*, which is known throughout the entire period of cuneiform writing, from the third through the first millennium BCE.[18] Together with

---

17. That is, *41, the vision of Kakka-lidi, and *36, the dream of Ayala, an otherwise unknown woman.

18. The Sumerian equivalent is used already in Ur III period texts, and the latest occurrences of *assinnu* are to be found in texts belonging to the Arsacid period. See

another designation *kurgarrû*, the title *assinnu* is used of ritual performers closely affiliated with the worship of the goddess Ishtar. They can be found performing in ritual dramas such as battle scenes, in purification rites, and in sickness rituals. They are mentioned receiving food rations together with male and female prophets in texts from the Middle Assyrian city of Kar-Tukulti-Ninurta (*123). This evidence does not present prophesying as the main occupation of the *assinnu*, even though persons thus designated could assume the prophetic role at least at Mari, as we shall shortly see. In lexical lists, the *assinnu* as well as the *kurgarrû* are regularly associated with prophets and other ecstatics, as well as people with various cultic functions, especially those related to lament and magic.[19] If the socioreligious location of the *assinnu* with that of prophets was as close as the lexical associations suggest, this may explain their involvement in the transmission of divine messages.

Why, then, should the *assinnu* be discussed in the context of nonmale prophetic agency? This is because the *assinnu*, without being a woman, does not fulfill the expectations of the traditional male performance either. The translations of the word include "cult homosexual" and "male cult prostitute," and depending on the underlying gender theory (or the lack thereof), *assinnu*s have also been characterized as transvestites, hermaphrodites, and third-gender persons. The gender-ambivalent characteristics of the *assinnu* have also been contested.[20] While the sources are not informative enough to reveal any details of the sexual performance of the *assinnu*, there are consistent hints through the source material from different places and periods that the behavior of the *assinnu* as sexual beings was somehow nonstandard and related to Ishtar's power of transgressing and transforming gender. *Assinnu*s do not seem to have assumed the conventional male agency and function in the society but are presented as people whose masculinity was turned into femininity by Ishtar herself.[21]

Saana Svärd and Martti Nissinen, "(Re)constructing the Image of the Assinnu," in *Studying Gender in the Ancient Near East*, ed. Saana Svärd and Agnès Garcia Ventura (University Park, PA: Eisenbrauns, 2018), 373–411.

19. See *124, *126; for more examples, see Svärd and Nissinen, "(Re)constructing the Image."

20. Ilona Zsolnay, "The Misconstrued Role of the Assinnu in Ancient Near Eastern Prophecy," in Stökl and Carvalho, *Prophets Male and Female*, 81–99; see also Stökl, "Gender 'Ambiguity.'"

21. Thus the Epic of Erra 4:52–59; see Ilan Peled, "*Assinnu* and *kurgarrû* Revisited," *JNES* 73 (2014): 287–88.

Two persons carrying the title *assinnu* are known by name in the documents from Mari: Ili-ḫaznaya and Šelebum, both mentioned in an outlay of silver to the temple of Annunitum (*65b). Queen Šibtu reports to Zimri-Lim, her husband, about a message Ili-ḫaznaya, *assinnu* of Annunitum, transmitted in the temple of Annunitum. Almost the whole message is cut off, but what is left of it suggests that it concerned Babylon and its king Hammurabi (*22). The letters concerning Šelebum, the other *assinnu*, are better preserved. Inib-šina, Zimri-Lim's sister, refers to her previous message concerning an oracle delivered by Šelebum without quoting it, but since she goes on to report the above-quoted oracle of the *qammatum* concerning the peace with Ešnunna, one could assume that Šelebum had transmitted a divine word with related content. One of the letters of Šibtu is all about Šelebum, who had gone into trance in the temple of Annunitum and pronounced the following oracle (*23, ll. 7–22):

> Thus says Annunitum: Zimri-Lim, you will be tested in a revolt! Protect yourself! Let your most favored servants whom you love surround you, and make them stay there to protect you! Do not go around on your own! As regards the people who would tes[t you]: those pe[ople] I deli[ver up] into your hands.

As much as Šelebum's services may have been appreciated by the king through the royal women, he himself gives a murky picture of his life. The writer of a letter (the names of the writer and the addressee are cut off) reports about Šelebum having come to him/her, complaining about his inadequate living conditions, eating porridge and living "amidst an abundance of shit and piss" (*8). The way he refers to his insufficient nourishment ("*idatum*-beer has been taken from Annunitum") gives the impression that he depended on the provisions of the temple.

3. Nonmale Prophets in Assyrian Sources

3.1. *Maḫḫūtu*

The Assyrian word *maḫḫūtu* corresponds linguistically to the Old Babylonian *muḫḫūtum* but has a different sociolingustic profile. A Neo-Assyrian lexical list presents the word as an equivalent of the Sumerian mí-al-è-dè (*125, l. 119). Even here, *maḫḫūtu* is grouped together with the male lú-al-è-dè = *maḫḫû* and the male and female ecstatics (*zabbu, zabbatu*); hence, the list follows the Old Babylonian lexical tradition, probably also corresponding to contemporary socioreligious practice. This may be deduced from the association of prophets and ecstatics in the ritual text pertaining to the ritual of Ishtar and Dumuzi, performed on the twenty-eighth and twenty-ninth day of the month of Tammuz to a person seized by spirits or evil things. The ritual is performed in the presence of certain personnel, including a male and a female prophet (*maḫḫû, maḫḫūtu*) and a male and a female ecstatic (*zabbu, zabbatu*; *118, l. 31).

In omen literature, *maḫḫūtu* is used three times in a quite interesting manner. The strong presence of prophets in a city, whether male or female, is introduced as an unfavorable omen in the series of city omens Šumma ālu (*129, ll. 101–2): "If there are many male prophets [*maḫḫû*] in a city, the city will fall. If there are many female prophets [*maḫḫātu*] in a city, the city will fall." The omen list is structured like the lexical lists, grouping together diviners (prophets, dreamers, haruspices, etc.), cultic performers (musicians, dancers, *kurgarrû*), and people with different kinds of disabilities, such as limping men and women, mad men and women, people with skin diseases, deaf and blind persons, and cripples. It is difficult to explain the logic of the omen list, according to which the city is well if there are many mad people, red-skinned persons, and dancers, while prophets, like most other groups, including wise men, musicians, and haruspices, appear as unfavorable omens. The only thing that diviners, cultic performers, and disabled people seem to share is their liminal position between the human and divine worlds, either as intermediaries or as carriers of god-given signs on their bodies. In the birth omens of the series Šumma izbu, the idea is easier to grasp (*127): "If an anomaly's right ear is cropped and inflated with wind: female prophets will seize the land. If an anomaly's left ear is cropped and inflated with wind: the same happens to the land of the enemy."[22] The idea here seems to be based on the left-right dichotomy.[23] The left side usually indicates a negative value; hence, the presence of female prophets in their own country would be a favorable omen (right ear), while their appearance in the enemy's country (left ear) would be unfavorable for their own country. This logic could be applied even to the city omens, if the ominous "city" in them is a city belonging to an enemy.

---

22. The commentary to this omen (*128) clarifies that the word *maḫḫātu* means "possessed people" (*šēḫu*).

23. See Ann K. Guinan, "Left/Right Symbolism in Mesopotamian Divination," *SAAB* 10 (1996): 5–10.

In the above-mentioned texts—lexical lists, ritual texts, and omens— the word *maḫḫūtu* is used in a generic sense. In two administrative documents, this word is used to refer to specific individuals, both times in plural and without mentioning personal names. In a long Middle Assyrian list of food rations from Kar-Tukulti-Ninurta, barley is delivered to temple officials to be distributed among the temple personnel (*123): "Ten homers four seah five liters for Aššur-apla-iddina on the second day for the food rations of the male and female prophets [*maḫḫu'ē maḫḫu'āte*] and the *assinnu*s of the Ishtar temple." This text without doubt refers to persons who actually functioned in the temple of Ishtar in the Middle Assyrian capital. It also indicates that the association of prophets with *assinnu*s, which can be found many times in lexical lists, has a counterpart in the structure of the temple communities. The presence of female prophets in a major Assyrian temple becomes evident also in the Neo-Assyrian list of expenditures for ceremonies in the temple of Ešarra, that is, the temple of the Assyrian principal god Ashur in the city of Assur (*110):

> The expenditure for the divine council: [The c]onfectioner tak[es] 1 seah of honey, 5 liters of oil and 4 seahs [5 liters of sesame. The bakers take] 10 homers of barley for bread and 5 homers of wheat for *qa*[*dūtu*]-bread. The brewers tak[e] 1 homer 5 liters (of barley) for the presence of the prophetesses. Total: 1 seah 4 liters of honey, 5 liters of oil, 4 seahs 5 liters of sesame, [11 homers 5 seahs of barley], 5 homers of wheat. All this [is the expenditure for the divine council].

This text is dated to the time of Adad-nirari III (year 809 BCE) and relates to various different cultic occasions in Ešarra. The ceremony in which the prophets are involved is the celebration of the divine council, which makes sense with regard to the intermediary function of the prophets. Since no male prophets are mentioned in this text pertaining to a specific ceremony, it may be concluded that only female prophets participated in it.

The use of *maḫḫūtu* in extant Neo-Assyrian texts is rather genre specific, since it is found only in lexical and omen texts and in administrative documents. Unless new evidence gives reasons to conclude otherwise, the indication is that *maḫḫūtu* was not the word for a female prophet used in Neo-Assyrian vernacular but was rather an official and literary designation.

3.2. Raggintu

The designation of a female prophet that belonged to Neo-Assyrian colloquial speech seems to have been *raggintu* rather than *maḫḫūtu*. Female prophets are called *raggintu* both in letters and in written oracles,[24] but not in literary texts or administrative documents. This word and its male equivalent, *raggimu*, are derived from the verb *ragāmu*, which means shouting and proclaiming. *Raggintu* is an exclusively Neo-Assyrian word[25] and can be understood as the standard title of a female prophet in this period.

Only two or three women carrying the title *raggintu* in the texts are known by their names. A poorly preserved tablet contains a fragmentary prophecy to Assurbanipal pronounced by Dunnaša-amur "the prophetess who pro[phesied ...]" (*95). The title is written logographically as MÍ.GUB.BA, the pronunciation of which is (and was) up to the reader but most probably should be read as *raggintu*.[26] Two other cases are clearer. An oracle report from the time of Assurbanipal is ascribed to the *raggintu* Mullissu-kabtat, whose name serves as the colophon in the very beginning of the tablet (*92). The tablet contains one or more prophecies of Mullissu,[27] that is, Ishtar of Nineveh, addressed to Assurbanipal, who still appears to be the crown prince of Assyria, living in the Palace of Succession. The oracle assures the kingship of Assurbanipal of the goddess's support, his authority over his own courtiers and the kings of other countries, and the motherly care executed by the goddess (*92, ll. r. 6–11):

> You whose mother is Mullissu, fear not! You whose nurse is the Lady of Arbela, fear not! Like a nurse I will carry you on my hip. I will put you, a pomegranate, between my breasts. At night I will be awake and guard

---

24. Letters: *105, *109, *111; written oracles: 92, 95.

25. The male word *raggimu* is also Neo-Assyrian, with the exception of one occurrence in a Late Babylonian lexical list (*135q).

26. Thus Simo Parpola, *Assyrian Prophecies*, SAA 9 (Helsinki: Helsinki University Press, 1997), xlvi; see also Stökl, who prefers to read the logogram as *maḫḫūtu* (*Prophecy in the Ancient Near East*, 152). The same woman is the speaker of *94; the title is broken, but she is probably introduced as [a woman of Arbe]la ([*mar'at Arba*]il).

27. The first part of the text (ll. 2–11) may be quoted from an earlier oracle; see Weippert, *Götterwort in Menschenmund*, 120–21.

you; throughout the day I will give you milk, at dawn I will hush you. Fear not, my calf whom I rear!

Another *raggintu* is named Mullissu-abu-uṣri, whose prophecy is the subject matter of a letter written to the king (Esarhaddon) by Adad-aḫu-iddina, a temple administrator probably functioning in the temple of Ešarra in the city of Assur. He says that Mullissu-abu-uṣri, who had earlier conveyed the king's clothes to "the land of Akkad," had prophesied that even the throne should also be sent away (*111, ll. 11-r. 9):"The throne from the temple […] Let the throne go! I will catch the enemies of my king with it!" The temple administrator is reluctant to rely on this prophecy and promises to act according to what the king orders. It is possible that both the king's clothes and the throne were meant to be used in the substitute's king ritual that took place on the occasion of the lunar eclipse in the newly reestablished cult site of Akkad in the month of Tebet (X), 671 BCE.[28] Mar-Issar, Esarhaddon's emissary in Babylonia, gives an account of the burial of Damqî, the substitute king, mentioning even the performances of a *raggintu* on this occasion (*109 ll. 22-r. 4): "[I] have heard that, before rituals, a female prophet had prophesied [*raggintu tartugum*], saying to Damqî, the son of the chief administrator: 'You will take over the kingship!' [Moreover], the female prophet had spoken to him in the assembly of the country: 'I have revealed the thieving polecat of my lord and placed it in your hands.'" The reception of divine words sounding like royal oracles (the name of the deity is not mentioned) would have served as proof of the real kingship of the substitute king.

Anonymous *raggintu*s are mentioned by the astrologer Bel-ušezib, who writes to Esarhaddon soon after his rise to power, complaining about not having been treated according to his merits by the newly enthroned king. He wonders why the king had summoned male and female prophets (*raggimānu raggimātu*), but not Bel-ušezib, who had told the omens of kingship to Esarhaddon and looked after his interests during the civil war, even if his own life was threatened (*105, ll. 7-21).[29] Bel-ušezib's

---

28. For references to this occasion and the letter, see Simo Parpola, *Letters of Assyrian Scholars to the Kings Esarhaddon and Assurbanipal, Part 2: Commentary and Appendices*, AOAT 5.2 (Kevelaer: Butzon & Bercker; Neukirchen-Vluyn: Neukirchener Verlag, 1983), 176–77, 270–72; Martti Nissinen, *References to Prophecy in Neo-Assyrian Sources*, SAAS 7 (Helsinki: Neo-Assyrian Text Corpus Project, 1998), 68–77.

29. For this letter, see Nissinen, *References to Prophecy*, 89–95.

choice of words indicates that the renowned astrologer was demoralized about the king's favor toward people who in his eyes appeared as second-rank diviners.

3.3. Women without Title or with Other Titles Than the Prophetic

Prophetic titles are not used for all who appear involved in prophetic activity in Neo-Assyrian sources. In some cases, the title of the prophet whose words are quoted is cut off, as in the fragmentary letter of Nabû-reši-išši, who says a female person "prophesied" (*tarrugum*), but her name and title, if originally mentioned, have not been preserved (*113, l. r. 7).

Most Neo-Assyrian prophetic oracles name the prophet without, however, giving her or him any specific prophetic title. The two collections of prophetic oracles, State Archives of Assyria 9, tablets 1 and 2, include sixteen individual oracles pronounced by ten different prophets whose names have been preserved. Five of them are presented as women (Sinqiša-amur, a woman from Arbela; Remut-Allati from Dara-aḫuya; Issar-beli-da"ini, a female votary of the king; Aḫat-abiša, a woman from Arbela; and Urkittu-šarrat, a woman from Calah), two are presented as men (La-dagil-ili, a man from Arbela; [Nabû]-ḫussanni, a man from Assur), and in three cases the gender is not clear; we shall discuss these cases below. The colophons of the individual oracles included in the collections follow a certain pattern, indicating the name, the place of origin, and the gender of the prophet, such as: "By the mouth of Aḫat-abiša, a woman from Arbela" (*ša pî Aḫāt-abiša mar'at Arbail*). The prophetic title is left unmentioned, as if it were found superfluous in a colophon attached to a prophetic oracle. One could reasonably argue that these women were the same people who were called *raggintu* by contemporary Assyrians.

Nonmale persons acting as prophets sometimes carry titles that refer to a role that is not specifically prophetic. In Neo-Assyrian sources, there are a couple of cases where the prophetic word has been pronounced by a *šēlūtu*, a female votary belonging to the temple community.[30] This role does not as such entail prophetic activity. The votaries were women who were given to temples. Some of them were daughters or wives of high-ranking men; others are presented as the property of the temple. The cases are too few to define the agency of the *šēlūtu* more precisely, but the

---

30. See Saana Svärd, *Women's Roles in the Neo-Assyrian Era: Female Agency in the Empire* (Saarbrücken: VDM, 2008), 79–80.

prophetic function of two votaries, Issar-beli-da"ini and the anonymous woman mentioned in a fragment of a letter, indicates that women belonging to temple communities could assume a prophetic role even without being "officially" labeled as prophets (*74, *114).

We have seen that the letters from Mari sometimes quote divine messages received by ordinary women. This is not common in Neo-Assyrian texts; in fact, only one such letter can be quoted, written by Nabû-reḫtu-uṣur, who reports a conspiracy to Esarhaddon. He tells about a slave girl (*amtu*) of Bel-aḫu-uṣur, who had pronounced an oracle of Nusku concerning Sasî, the person whom Nabû-reḫtu-uṣur believed to be among the main insurrectionists (*115, ll. r. 2–5):

> A slave girl of Bel-aḫu-uṣur […] upon […] on the ou[tski]rts of H[arran]; since Sivan she has been enraptured and speaks a good word about him: "This is the word of Nusku: the kingship is for Sasî! I will destroy the name and seed of Sennacherib!"[31]

Even though an oracle like this was probably considered pseudo-prophecy by Nabû-reḫtu-uṣur, he nevertheless feels obliged to report it and recommends the case to be examined by performing a ritual on the slave girl's account.

3.4. Prophets of Unclear Gender

The *assinnu*s, whose gender role was different from the conventional male performance, are known also from Neo-Assyrian sources. They are attested in different types of texts—not only in lexical lists and omen texts but also in administrative and literary texts as well as in texts referring to rituals and cultic actions.[32] These documents demonstrate that the *assinnu*s belonged to the Neo-Assyrian society, especially to communities worshiping Ishtar.

---

31. See Nissinen, *References to Prophecy*, 108–53, and see also the discussion in Steven W. Holloway, *Aššur Is King! Aššur Is King! Religion in the Exercise of Power in the Neo-Assyrian Empire*, CHANE 10 (Leiden: Brill, 2003), 336–37, 410–14; Eckart Frahm, "Hochverrat in Assur," in *Assur-Forschungen: Arbeiten aus der Forschungsstelle "Edition literarischer Keilschrifttexte aus Assur" der Heidelberger Akademie der Wissenschaften*, ed. Stefan M. Maul and Nils P. Heeßel (Wiesbaden: Harrassowitz, 2010), 89–137.

32. See the appendix of Svärd and Nissinen, "(Re)constructing the Image."

As already mentioned above, the *assinnu*s are listed together with male and female prophets receiving food rations in the Middle Assyrian administrative text from Kar-Tukulti-Ninurta. No Neo-Assyrian document presenting an *assinnu* functioning as a prophet is known so far. However, there are three cases, all in the collection of ten oracles to Esarhaddon from the year 673 BCE (SAA 9.1) indicating that the gender of the prophet was not clear to the scribe who wrote the tablet. In the first case, the feminine determinative indicating the gender of Issar-la-tašiyaṭ has been erased and replaced by a masculine one by the scribe (*68). This may simply be an error of the scribe, who has corrected his own mistake; if not, it may reflect the uncertainty of the scribe about the gender of the prophet.

In two other cases, the same scribe has knowingly given ambiguous information on the gender of the prophet. The prophet Bayâ is introduced as "a man" from Arbela whose name nevertheless has a feminine determinative (*71: MÍ.*ba-ia-a* DUMU URU.*arba-il*).³³ The name of Ilussa-amur has a feminine determinative, but the domicile is given with a masculine gentilic *Libbālā[yu]* instead of *Libbālītu* (*72: MÍ.DINGIR-*sa—a-mu[ur]* URU.ŠÀ—URU-*a*-[*a*]). The problem regarding the gender of these persons has been interpreted to mean that they belong to a "third gender" or undefinable sex group. Since this cannot be shown by gender-specific determinatives, it has been indicated by using intentionally contradictory designations.³⁴

Some scholars have warned against laying too much weight on these three cases, either explaining all of them as scribal errors or suspecting that they are resting on "modern reconstruction of gender ambiguity."³⁵ In my view, the way this professional scribe writes the names (at least in the cases of Bayâ and Ilussa-amur) is ambiguous enough to reflect the ambiguity confronted by the scribe himself. This, of course, does not turn all prophets into gender-ambiguous persons, but it increases the probability that such persons, like the *assinnu*, could assume the prophetic function.

---

33. The same prophet is probably the speaker in *79 as well, but the determinative is cut off (see Parpola, *Assyrian Prophecies*, il).

34. Parpola, *Assyrian Prophecies*, il–l; Saana Teppo, "Sacred Marriage and the Devotees of Ištar," in *Sacred Marriages: The Divine-Human Sexual Metaphor from Sumer to Early Christianity*, ed. Martti Nissinen and Risto Uro (Winona Lake, IN: Eisenbrauns, 2008), 75–92.

35. Thus Stökl, "Gender 'Ambiguity,'" 78. Weippert interprets the incongruities as scribal errors (*Götterwort in Menschenmund*, 187–88).

4. Female Prophets in the Hebrew Bible

Biblical Hebrew has only one designation for a female prophet. The word *nəbîʾâ* is the female equivalent of the standard Hebrew word for a male prophet, *nābîʾ*. This feminine word occurs six times in the Hebrew Bible (Exod 15:20; Judg 4:4; 2 Kgs 22:14; Isa 8:3; Neh 6:14; 2 Chr 34:22); in addition, the verb *hitnabbêʾ*, used of prophesying, is used of women who "prophesy [*mitnabbəʾôt*] out of their own hearts" in Ezek 13:17.[36]

Beginning with the last of the female prophets in biblical chronology, Nehemiah mentions in his memoir Noadiah the *nəbîʾâ* and "the rest of the prophets who wanted to make me afraid" (Neh 6:14) together with his archenemies Tobiah and Sanballat.[37] Nothing more is said about this woman, but it is noteworthy that she is the only prophet presented as a contemporary in Ezra-Nehemiah; all other prophets are figures of the past.[38] Earlier in the same chapter, Nehemiah claims to have been accused of setting up prophets to proclaim him king of Jerusalem, which he vehemently denies and regards as pure intimidation (Neh 6:5–9). The text gives the impression that there was prophetic activity in Jerusalem that was not favorable to Nehemiah's mission, with Noadiah being the leader of the oppositional group of prophets. Noadiah and the other prophets, perhaps both male and female, may be taken as continuing the prophetic tradition in Jerusalem, the legitimacy of which was called into question during the reorganization of the worship of the Second Temple. Nothing is said about Noadiah's prophetic activity, but her role is presented as emphatically political.

---

36. Unless otherwise stated, biblical quotations follow the NRSV.
37. On Noadiah, see Robert P. Carroll, "Coopting the Prophets: Nehemiah and Noadiah," in *Priests, Prophets and Scribes: Essays on the Formation and Heritage of Second Temple Judaism in Honour of Joseph Blenkinsopp*, ed. Eugene Ulrich et al., JSOTSup 149 (Sheffield: Sheffield Academic, 1992), 87–99; Fischer, *Gotteskünderinnen*, 255–73; Martti Nissinen, "The Dubious Image of Prophecy," in *Prophets, Prophecy, and Prophetic Texts in Second Temple Judaism*, ed. Michael H. Floyd and Robert D. Haak, LHBOTS 427 (London: T&T Clark, 2006), 30–35; Gafney, *Daughters of Miriam*, 111–14; Williamson, "Prophetesses in the Hebrew Bible," 65–67; Hamori, *Women's Divination*, 186–88.
38. Haggai and Zechariah in Ezra 5:1–2; 6:14 and anonymous prophets in the past in Ezra 9:11; Neh 9:26, 30, 32. In the LXX, Noadiah is presented as a male character (2 Esd 16:14: τῷ Νωαδια τῷ προφήτῃ).

The female prophet mentioned in the book of Isaiah collaborates with the prophet Isaiah,[39] who is told by God to take a tablet and write on it the name Maher-shalal-hash-baz. Isaiah says that he "went to the prophetess [wā-'eqrab 'el-han-nəbî'â], and she conceived and bore a son," who is then given the name that was written on the tablet; the ominous name "Pillage hastens, looting speeds" predicts that "the wealth of Damascus and the spoil of Samaria will be carried away by the king of Assyria" (Isa 8:1–4). The mother of the child is anonymous, but her designation bears a definite article. The woman is not called Isaiah's wife; what matters more than the marital configuration is that the woman who gives birth to the child with the God-given ominous name is actually called a prophet in the narrative set in the mouth of Isaiah. She is not presented as speaking divine words;[40] giving birth to the child is her oracle. Unlike Gomer, the woman who bears children with likewise portentous names for the prophet Hosea (Hos 1:2–9), she is recognized as a prophet, and her agency is on equal terms with that of Isaiah. She participates in the ominous chain of events, including the inscription of the name by Isaiah, the sexual intercourse between the two, the parturition of the son by herself, and the fulfillment of the prophecy by God. The female prophet is first and foremost a narrative character. The text hardly reveals anything about the family life of historical prophets, but it demonstrates the (gendered) use of prophecy in a religiopolitical narrative.

Another religio-political narrative employing a female prophet is 2 Kgs 22:3–20, which tells about the "book of the law" (*sefer hat-tôrâ*) found during the restoration works in the temple of Jerusalem. Hilkiah the high priest and Shaphan the scribe bring the scroll to the notice of King Josiah, who sends them together with three royal officials to inquire from God about the scroll. The men go to Huldah, the wife of Shallum, keeper of the wardrobe, and she delivers an oracle to Josiah, which says that God's wrath has kindled against Jerusalem and its temple, and he will bring a disaster

---

39. On this female prophet see, e.g., Ernst Axel Knauf, "Vom Prophetinnenwort zum Prophetenbuch: Jesaja 8,3f im Kontext von Jesaja 6,1–8,16," *lectio difficilior* 2 (2000), https://tinyurl.com/SBL6016c; Fischer, *Gotteskünderinnen*, 189–220; Gafney, *Daughters of Miriam*, 103–7; Williamson, "Prophetesses in the Hebrew Bible," 74–76; Hamori, *Women's Divination*, 160–66.

40. Unless Isa 8:3–4 is not an oracle originally spoken by her, as suggested by Knauf ("Vom Prophetinnenwort zum Prophetenbuch").

on them. Josiah himself, however, will not see the disaster but will be gathered to his ancestors in peace.⁴¹

Whether or not Huldah is a historical character, in the world of the narrative she is a central agent in the event that, according to 2 Kgs 22–23, eventually leads to a religious reform carried out by Josiah; in 2 Chr 34 the reform precedes Huldah's oracle. In both narratives, the most authoritative delegation representing both the temple and the royal court is sent to Huldah, even though there were other prophets in Jerusalem (see 2 Kgs 23:2). She carries the title *nəbîʾâ* but is presented through her husband's profession, which may create a link between her and the temple or court, depending on whose wardrobe Shallum is keeping. That she lives in the new quarter of Jerusalem may be mentioned to create a certain distance between her and the temple and court institutions. The words pronounced by Huldah have a distinct Deuteronomistic character, and the whole story can be seen as fulfilling the Deuteronomic ideals about a king who consults and observes the Torah (Deut 17:18–20), mediated by a prophet raised up by God (Deut 18:15–22).⁴² Obviously, such a role could be attributed to a woman, and it is noteworthy that both the first and the last prophets mentioned in Joshua–Kings, that is, Deborah and Huldah, are women.

Deborah, who features in the narrative of the book of Judges (Judg 4–5), is a different figure from her prophetic colleagues.⁴³ She bears the

---

41. On Huldah, see, e.g., Lowell K. Handy, "The Role of Huldah in Josiah's Cult Reform," *ZAW* 106 (1994): 40–53; Renita J. Weems, "Huldah, the Prophet: Reading a (Deuteronomistic) Woman's Identity," in *A God So Near: Essays on Old Testament Theology in Honor of Patrick D. Miller*, ed. Brent A. Strawn and Nancy R. Bowen (Winona Lake, IN: Eisenbrauns, 2003), 321–39; Fischer, *Gotteskünderinnen*, 158–88; Gafney, *Daughters of Miriam*, 94–103; Williamson, "Prophetesses in the Hebrew Bible," 68–72; Hamori, *Women's Divination*, 148–59; Blaženka Scheuer, "Huldah: A Cunning Career Woman?," in *Prophecy and Prophets in Stories: Papers Read at the Fifth Meeting of the Edinburgh Prophecy Network*, ed. Bob Becking and Hans M. Barstad, OTS 65 (Leiden: Brill, 2015), 104–23.

42. For the similarity between Huldah's oracle and the book of Jeremiah, see Thomas Römer, "From Prophet to Scribe: Jeremiah, Huldah, and the Invention of the Book," in *Writing the Bible: Scribes, Scribalism, and Script*, ed. Philip R. Davies and Thomas Römer, BibW (Durham, NC: Acumen, 2013), 86–96; for the role of Huldah as a follower of Moses, see Fischer, *Gotteskünderinnen*, 182–85.

43. On Deborah, see, e.g., Fischer, *Gotteskünderinnen*, 109–30; Gafney, *Daughters of Miriam*, 85–93; Yaakov S. Kupitz and Katell Berthelot, "Deborah and the Delphic Pythia: A New Interpretation of Judges 4:4–5," in *Images and Prophecy in the Ancient Eastern Mediterranean*, ed. Martti Nissinen and Charles E. Carter, FRLANT 233 (Göt-

title ’iššâ nəbî’â (Judg 4:4), and she indeed pronounces divine words that sound like royal oracles of victory: "Up! For this is the day in which the LORD has given Sisera into your hand. The Lord is indeed going out before you" (Judg 4:14; see 4:6). Deborah's agency, however, is not limited to mediating divine messages, since she also acts as a judge. The first thing that is said about her is that she "used to sit under the palm of Deborah between Ramah and Bethel in the hill country of Ephraim; and the Israelites came up to her for judgment" (Judg 4:5). The role of judge, to be sure, can be understood as another divinatory function, invoking the image of the Delphic Pythia sitting on her tripod.[44] At the same time, it highlights Deborah's position as one of the judges who led the people of Israel before the establishment of the monarchy. Deborah's leadership is also of military nature, as she plays a crucial role in the war between Barak and Jabin, king of Canaan, and his commander Sisera. It deserves attention that she is called "a mother in Israel" in this military context (Judg 5:7), which may highlight her divinatory role as the mediator of divine knowledge, comparable to that of Ishtar, who in some prophetic oracles has a maternal image. In addition, she is also presented as a musician, intoning a song of victory together with Barak: "Awake, awake, Deborah! Awake, awake, utter a song!" (Judg 5:12).

The multiple roles of Deborah are interesting from the point of view of both prophecy and gender. Her divinatory role goes beyond the conventional functions of prophecy, especially when it comes to military leadership. On the other hand, both judging and music can be understood as means of divine-human communication. The way Deborah combines divinatory and leadership functions can be compared to the equally manifold job descriptions of Moses and Samuel.[45] In the biblical narrative, such an amalgamation of divinatory roles seems to belong to the time when there was no king—as well as no prophets of the conventional type. On the other hand, Deborah is but another example of a formidable female figure in Joshua–Kings. The narrative in Judg 4, indeed, rests on the action of two powerful women, Deborah and Jael.[46]

---

tingen: Vandenhoeck & Ruprecht, 2009), 95–124; Williamson, "Prophetesses in the Hebrew Bible," 72–74; Hamori, *Women's Divination*, 82–93.

44. See Kupitz and Berthelot, "Deborah and the Delphic Pythia."
45. Hamori, *Women's Divination*, 88–89.
46. See Ora Brison, "Jael, *'eshet heber* the Kenite: A Diviner?," in *Joshua and Judges*, ed. Athalya Brenner and Gale A. Yee, TC (Minneapolis: Fortress, 2013), 139–60.

The first woman called prophet in the Hebrew Bible is Miriam, the sister of Aaron.[47] She is first introduced after the troops of Pharaoh have drowned in the sea and the Israelites have marched on dry ground to the other side. Miriam bears the title *nəbîʾâ*, but what she does is take up a drum and sing to the people a song of victory: "Sing to the LORD, for he has triumphed gloriously; horse and rider he has thrown into the sea" (Exod 15:21). While music is undeniably a way of divine-human communication, one may ask whether this song is enough to qualify Miriam as a prophet, but there is another text that clearly implies that she was recognized as such. Numbers 12 tells about a conflict between Miriam and Moses, and the story is essentially about prophetic authority. Miriam and Aaron oppose the marriage of Moses and come to him asking, "Has the LORD spoken only through Moses? Has he not spoken through us also?" (Num 12:2)—as if to remind the reader of Mic 6:4, where Moses, Aaron, and Miriam appear together as the ones who lead the people out of Egypt.[48] Miriam (but not Aaron) is punished with a disease for questioning the authority of Moses. Miriam's prophetic role is not denied; what matters more is the authority of Moses, to whom God speaks face to face and who is, therefore, superior to any other prophet (Num 12:6–8). The narrative indicates that Miriam is "remembered in connection to her role as a prophet, if in a deeply conflicted fashion."[49] The remembrance of Miriam as involved in divine-human communication continues in Hellenistic Jewish literature in works such as Visions of Amram and Pseudo-Philo.[50]

Finally, a group of women is presented in Ezek 13:17–23 as "the daughters of your people, who prophesy out of their own imagination" (13:17: *bənôt ʿammakā ham-mitnabbəʾôt mil-libbəhen*). Ezekiel is told to prophesy

---

47. On Miriam, see, e.g., Ursula Rapp, *Mirjam: Eine feministisch-rhetorische Lektüre der Mirjamtexte in der hebräischen Bibel*, BZAW 317 (Berlin: de Gruyter, 2002); Susan Ackerman, "Why Is Miriam"; Rainer Kessler, "Miriam and the Prophecy of the Persian Period," in *Prophets and Daniel*, ed. Athalya Brenner, FCB 2/8 (Sheffield: Sheffield Academic, 2001), 77–86; Fischer, *Gotteskünderinnen*, 64–94; Gafney, *Daughters of Miriam*, 76–85; Tervanotko, "Speaking in Dreams"; Hamori, *Women's Divination*, 61–81.

48. Therefore, Kessler reads Num 12 as a countertext to Mic 6:4 ("Miriam and the Prophecy"). Rapp suggests that the advocacy of Miriam's prophetic role goes back to the same circles of the Persian period that even Noadiah represented (*Mirjam*, 178–93).

49. Hamori, *Women's Divination*, 81.

50. See Tervanotko, "Speaking in Dreams."

(*nibbāʾ*) to them, pronouncing divine condemnation on the practice of these women, described as sewing bands on wrists and making veils for the heads in order to entrap human lives. Despite the difficulties in translating the Hebrew vocabulary, the activity designated as "prophesying" (*hitnabbēʾ*) does not seem to refer to the transmission of divine words, as in the case of the just-condemned male prophets (13:1–16), but rather to a different kind of divination. Entrapping "lives" (*nəpāšôt*) has been interpreted, for instance, as necromancy.[51] In the concluding verse the women are supposed to hear that they will no longer "see false visions or practice divination" (13:23: *šāwʾ lōʾ teḥĕzênâ wə-qesem lōʾ tiqsamnâ ʿôd*), which complements the image of the women with two more divinatory terms. The divinatory agency of the women condemned in Ezek 13 is described in seemingly precise but vague terms—perhaps intentionally as a part of enemy rhetoric relying on negative stereotypes.[52]

What matters from the point of view of prophecy in Ezek 13:17–23 is that the use of the verbal root *nbʾ* overlaps with other divinatory vocabulary in the description of the activity of the women. This challenges our customary definition of prophecy and makes the women operate at the crossroads of prophecy and other kinds of divination—or, perhaps, at the interface of divination and magic, if divination is understood as acquisition of superhuman knowledge, while magic is supposed to bring about a change in the patient's life, in this case, the *nəpāšôt* manipulated by the women.

5. Comparison

The survey of nonmale subjects of prophetic activity demonstrates the presence and impact of women and people with unconventional gender performance in all major source materials of ancient Near Eastern prophecy. Space permits only a brief comparison of the sources by way of conclusion.[53]

---

51. Thus Hamori, *Women's Divination*, 167–83, and Jonathan Stökl, "The מתנבאות of Ezekiel 13 Reconsidered," *JBL* 132 (2013): 61–76. Bowen associates the activity of the women with medical and ritual aspects of childbirth. See Nancy R. Bowen, "The Daughters of Your People: Female Prophets in Ezekiel 13:17–23," *JBL* 118 (1999): 417–33.
52. I am indebted to Patrik Jansson regarding this perspective.
53. For a more profound analysis, see Nissinen, *Ancient Prophecy*, 297–325, 346–48.

Female prophets feature most prominently in Neo-Assyrian texts, in which two-thirds of the prophets known to us are women. This reflects the strong connection of prophecy with the worship of Ishtar, the goddess who disclosed the secrets of gods to humans. Even though the prophets of Ishtar are not exclusively women, virtually all nonmale prophets speak her words—that is, as far as the divine speaker is discernable.[54] Nonmale prophets have a strong presence even in the documents from Mari, but their share in these sources is about one-third. All but three nonmale subjects of prophetic activity in Mari documents, as far as we know, are connected with Annunitum or Ishtar, while male prophets at Mari appear to speak the words of both male and female deities. While there is no universal gender correspondence between prophets and deities, the correlation between female deities and nonmale prophets is palpable both at Mari and in Assyria.

In both Assyrian and Old Babylonian sources, nonmale prophets not only pronounce words of female deities but also are somehow linked to their temples. The only female prophet known from Old Babylonian sources other than Mari documents is the anonymous *muḫḫūtum* affiliated with the temple of Inanna in Zabala, which was one of the major Babylonian centers of her worship. In the kingdom of Mari, all women bearing the title *muḫḫūtum* as well as the two *assinnus* pronounce the words of Annunitum or Ishtar or perform in their temples. The case with the only known *āpiltum* is unclear because of the damage to the tablet. It is noteworthy that none of the three women who mediate the words of Dagan, that is, the *qammatum* from Terqa, Zunana, and the "spouse of a free man," bear a standard prophetic title, and neither does Kakka-lidi, whose vision in the temple of the male god Itur-Mer is reported by Queen Šibtu (*41).

In Assyria, the link between nonmale prophets and the goddess Ishtar, either in the form of Ishtar of Arbela or Mullissu, is ubiquitous. Egašankalamma, her temple in Arbela, is the most important center of Neo-Assyrian prophecy in the sources known to us.[55] Female prophets can

---

54. The divine speaker may be Ishtar or one of her manifestations, among whom I count even Annunitum. Exceptions to this rule include the *qammatum* of Dagan of Terqa (*7, *9); Zunana, who reports the revelation of Dagan in her dream (*37); Kakka-lidi, who had a vision of Itur-Mer (*41); and the slave-girl in the region of Harran, who spoke the words of Nusku (*115).

55. See Martti Nissinen, "Ištar of Arbela," in *Arbela Antiqua, actes du colloque*

also be found in Ešarra, the temple of Assur in the city of Assur, where the divine council was celebrated in the presence of female prophets (*110), and which is the probable base of Mullissu-abu-uṣri (*111) and Ilussa-amur (*72). One woman, Urkittu-šarrat, comes from Calah, where there was a prominent temple of Ishtar, there called the Lady of Kidmuri. The only nonmale prophets mediating words of male deities are the slave-girl who speaks the words of Nusku on the outskirts of Harran (*115) and Bayâ, who speaks in the name of Bel and Nabû as well as Ishtar (*71).

In addition to the strong link between female deities and nonmale prophets, it is typical of the letters from Mari that the words spoken by nonmale prophets are reported to Zimri-Lim by women who are closest to him—his wife, Šibtu, his sister Inib-šina, and his mother, Addu-duri.[56] Even male characters quote words of female prophets in the Mari correspondence, but reports of performances of male prophets written by women are very few.[57] This suggests a closer connection between the royal women of Mari and nonmale prophets than male ones. In Assyrian letters, all references to nonmale prophets were written by males.[58] This, of course, is due to the lack of female writers in Assyrian correspondence and tells nothing about the relationship between prophets and women. That Naqia, the queen mother, is addressed in many extant prophetic oracles suggests a strong link between her and the prophets of Ishtar of Arbela.[59]

The divinatory agency of nonmale prophets is related to political and religious institutions and their authority. Deriving from royal archives, the two main corpora of sources strongly focus on royal concerns; especially in Assyria, the prophets, regardless of their gender, appear as orthodox

---

international d'Erbil (7–10 avril 2014) Arbèles antique – Histoire d'Erbil pré-islamique, ed. Frédéric Alpi et al., BAH 218 (Beirut: Presses de l'Ifpo, 2020), 129–55.

56. Šibtu: *17, *22, *23, *24, *41; Inib-šina: *7, *14; Addu-duri: *35, *42; see also Zunana (*37), Šimatum (*44), and Timlû (*45), who report their own dreams.

57. Addu-duri (*5, *43) and Šibtu (*17, *18, *21). Male characters quoting words of female prophets include Nur-Sîn (*1), Sammetar (*9), Aḫum (*10), Baḫdi-Lim (*11), Kibri-Dagan (*20), Itur-Asdu (*27), and Ḫammi-šagiš (*50b).

58. Bel-ušezib (*105), Mar-Issar (*109), Nabû-reši-išši (*113), and Nabu-reḫtu-uṣur (*115).

59. Oracles addressed to Naqia include *74 (probably Ishtar of Arbela, female votary Issar-bel-da''ini), *75 (Ishtar of Arbela, female prophet Aḫat-abiša), *78 (goddesses of Esaggil, male prophet [Nabû]-ḫussanni), *83 (Ishtar of Uruk, unknown prophet), and *90 (Ishtar of Arbela, unknown prophet).

proclaimers of state ideology.⁶⁰ In this respect, the agency of nonmale prophets is not different from that of male prophets. Direct contacts between rulers and prophets, whether male or nonmale, are not reported, but this does not exclude the possibility that the ruler witnessed prophetic performances, for instance in rituals, such as the ritual of Ishtar at Mari. However, the king was typically not approached by the prophets themselves. The words spoken by nonmale prophets are without exception brought to the king's notice by his officials, temple administrators, or family members.

In all the Mesopotamian source material, it is clear that nonmale prophets had an established position in temple communities. As mediators of divine knowledge, nonmale prophets enjoyed the same appreciation as male ones—at least in theory, since the words mediated by prophets, regardless of their person and gender, were divine words.⁶¹ In practical terms, however, a certain gender bias becomes evident in the divinatory practice at Mari, where the messages transmitted by nonmale prophets were more often checked against another method of divination using the hair and the fringe of the garment attached to the letter by the writer.⁶²

What makes the sources from the Levant different in terms of gender from those from Mari and Assyria is the prevalence of male prophets. Nonmale prophets are only known from the Hebrew Bible, where the share of women among prophets mentioned by name is only about one-tenth. The drastically smaller number of female prophets in the Hebrew Bible compared with Mari or, especially, Assyria, may go back to historical circumstances, since all the few Levantine texts at our disposal represent the male god/male prophet pattern. However, the meager amount of sources prevents definitive conclusions concerning the gender ratio of Levantine prophets. Defining the socioreligious status of female prophets in "ancient Israel," whether in the monarchical or postmonarchical period, is equally difficult based on the available texts.

The Hebrew Bible does not yield a coherent presentation of female prophets. The biblical presentation shares some important features with the patterns known from cuneiform sources. The position of Huldah in

---

60. See Parpola, *Assyrian Prophecies*, xxxvi–xliv.

61. For discussion of the religious agency of women, see Nissinen, *Ancient Prophecy*, 304–14.

62. See Hamori, "Gender and the Verification of Prophecy at Mari"; for a comparable case in Assyrian texts, see *115.

particular is well comparable to her Mesopotamian colleagues in relation to kings and religiopolitical power.[63] None of the female prophets of the Hebrew Bible are presented as being employed by either the temple or the royal court, but the temple of Jerusalem provides itself as the natural base of Noadiah, and perhaps the same can be said of Huldah, especially if the occupation of her husband is understood as being affiliated with the temple. The conflict between Miriam and Moses in Num 12 as well as the laconic reference to Noadiah by Nehemiah may reflect power struggles in the Persian period, implying a relatively strong claim of women to religious authority.

On the other hand, some female subjects of prophetic activity in the Hebrew Bible appear in roles that do not conform very well to the image of nonmale prophecy in the cuneiform sources. The distribution of divinatory roles and the interface of divination and magic are far less absolute than they appear to be in Mesopotamian tradition. Biblical diviners—women in particular—may mediate divine words, but they also engage in other activities. This raises the question of which of them should be labeled as prophets nonetheless.[64] The women accused of "prophesying out of their own hearts" in Ezek 13:17–23 are described in terms of divination or magic rather differently from what is usually understood as prophecy. Some narrative characters, such as Deborah and Miriam, assume multiple divinatory and leadership roles that, because of their legendary nature, are difficult to identify with any kind of historical practice. For this reason, it is also difficult to know exactly how prophetic divination in Judah or Yehud differed from that documented in the sources from Mari and Assyria.

Knowledge of ancient prophecy comes to us through several filters created partly by chance and partly by some ancient scribes and archivists who long ago determined what we see today. In the case of the Hebrew Bible, due to the long process of textual transmission, the distance between the text and the historical divinatory practice is significantly larger than in the cuneiform sources. In the Hebrew Bible, female prophets appear in

---

63. See, e.g., Handy, "Role of Huldah."
64. See Hamori, who discusses also Rebekah, Rachel, Hannah, the necromancer of En-Dor, the "wise woman" of 2 Sam 14 and 20, and the women in the vision of Joel 3 (*Women's Divination*). See also Fischer, who includes the women mentioned in Exod 38:8, the woman of En-Dor, and the women of Joel 3 (*Gotteskünderinnen*); and Gafney, on the women of Joel 3 and the daughters of Heman in 1 Chr 25:5–6 (*Daughters of Miriam*).

narratives embedded in contexts that dissociate the prophetic figures from their historical environments, unless the prophets are narrative characters from the beginning. The image of biblical prophecy is the construct of biblical writers who may have had ideological reasons for diminishing the role of women without, however, erasing it altogether. The ideological bias, however, is not typical of the Hebrew Bible alone. The selection of the prophecies that were written down and preserved for posterity was far from being a bias-free process. The Assyrian construct of prophecy reflects the royal ideology propagated in temples of Ishtar, and this may partly explain the prevalence of the nonmale prophets of Ishtar in the extant Assyrian sources. The ancient Near Eastern sources, thus, provide us with authentic but biased glimpses into the ancient divinatory practice, without ever showing the full picture. Much remains undisclosed, but it is clear that prophecy was not just a man's profession.

Bibliography

Ackerman, Susan. "Why Is Miriam Also among the Prophets (And Is Zipporah among the Priests?)." *JBL* 121 (2002): 47–80.

Allen, Spencer L. *The Splintered Divine: A Study of Ištar, Baal, and Yahweh Divine Names and Divine Multiplicity in the Ancient Near East*. SANER 5. Berlin: de Gruyter, 2015.

Bowen, Nancy R. "The Daughters of Your People: Female Prophets in Ezekiel 13:17–23." *JBL* 118 (1999): 417–33.

Brison, Ora. "Jael, *'eshet heber* the Kenite: A Diviner?" Pages 139–60 in *Joshua and Judges*. Edited by Athalya Brenner and Gale A. Yee. TC. Minneapolis: Fortress, 2013.

Carroll, Robert P. "Coopting the Prophets: Nehemiah and Noadiah." Pages 87–99 in *Priests, Prophets and Scribes: Essays on the Formation and Heritage of Second Temple Judaism in Honour of Joseph Blenkinsopp*. Edited by Eugene Ulrich, Robert P. Carroll, John W. Wright, and Philip R. Davies. JSOTSup 149. Sheffield: Sheffield Academic, 1992.

Charpin, Dominique. "Prophéties et rêves 'censurés' dans les archives royales de Mari." Pages 23–33 in *Comment devient-on prophète? Actes du colloque organisé par le Collège de France, Paris, les 4–5 avril 2011*. Edited by Jean-Marie Durand, Thomas Römer, and Micaël Bürki. OBO 265. Fribourg: Academic Press; Göttingen: Vandenhoeck & Ruprecht, 2014.

Charpin, Dominique, and Nele Ziegler. *Florilegium marianum 5: Mari et le Proche-Orient à l'époque amorrite, Essai d'histoire politique.* MN 6. Paris: SEPOA, 2003.

Civil, Miguel, Benno Landsberger, Erica Reiner. *The Series* lú = ša *and Related Texts.* MSL 12. Rome: Pontificium Institutum Biblicum, 1969.

De Zorzi, Nicla. *La serie teratomantica Šumma izbu: Testo, tradizione, orizzonti culturali.* HANEM 15. Padova: S.A.R.G.O.N., 2014.

Durand, Jean-Marie. *Archives épistolaires de Mari I/1.* ARMT 26. Paris: Editions Recherche sur les Civilisations, 1988.

———. *Florilegium Marianum 7: Le Culte d'Addu d'Alep et l'affaire d'Alaḫtum.* MN 8. Paris: SEPOA, 2002.

———. "La guerre ou la paix? Réflexions sur les implications politiques d'une prophétie." Pages 251–72 in *Leggo! Studies Presented to Frederick Mario Fales on the Occasion of His 65th Birthday.* Edited by Giovanni B. Lanfranchi, Daniele Morandi Bonacossi, Cinzia Pappi, and Simonetta Ponchia. LAS 2. Wiesbaden: Harrassowitz, 2012.

———. "La religion à l'époque amorrite d'après les archives de Mari." Pages 163–631 in *Ebla, Mari.* Vol. 1 of *Mythologie et religion des sémites occidentaux.* Edited by Gregorio del Olmo Lete. OLA 162. Leuven: Peeters, 2008.

Durand, Jean-Marie, and Michaël Guichard. "Les rituels de Mari." Pages 19–78 in *Florilegium Marianum 3: Recueil d'études à la mémoire de Marie-Thérèse Barrelet.* Edited by Dominique Charpin and Jean-Marie Durand. MN 4. Paris: SEPOA, 1997.

Dyckhoff, Christian. *Belegmaterial.* Vol. 2 of *Das Haushaltsbuch des Balamunamḫe.* München: Ludwig-Maximilians-Universität München, 1999.

Farber, Walter. *Beschwörungsrituale an Ištar und Dumuzi:* Attī Ištar ša ḫarmaša Dumuzi. VOK 30. Wiesbaden: Harrassowitz, 1977.

Fischer, Irmtraud. *Gotteskünderinnen: Zu einer geschlechtsfairen Deutung des Phänomens der Prophetie und der Prophetinnen in der Hebräischen Bibel.* Stuttgart: Kohlhammer, 2002.

Flower, Michael A. *The Seer in Ancient Greece.* Berkeley: University of California Press, 2008.

Frahm, Eckart. "Hochverrat in Assur." Pages 89–137 in *Assur-Forschungen: Arbeiten aus der Forschungsstelle "Edition literarischer Keilschrifttexte aus Assur" der Heidelberger Akademie der Wissenschaften.* Edited by Stefan M. Maul and Nils P. Heeßel. Wiesbaden: Harrassowitz, 2010.

Freedman, Sally M. *If a City Is Set on a Height: The Akkadian Omen Series Šumma Ālu ina Mēlê Šakin*. Vol. 1. OPSNKF 17. Philadelphia: University of Pennsylvania Museum, 1998.

Freydank, Helmut. "Zwei Verpflegungstexte aus Kār-Tukultī-Ninurta." *AoF* 1 (1974): 55–89.

Gafney, Wilda C. *Daughters of Miriam: Women Prophets in Ancient Israel*. Minneapolis: Fortress, 2008.

Grabbe, Lester L. "'Her Outdoors: An Anthropological Perspective on Female Prophets and Prophecy." Pages 11–25 in *Prophets Male and Female: Gender and Prophecy in the Hebrew Bible, the Eastern Mediterranean, and the Ancient Near East*. Edited by Jonathan Stökl and Corrine L. Carvalho. AIL 15. Atlanta: Society of Biblical Literature, 2013.

Guinan, Ann K. "Left/Right Symbolism in Mesopotamian Divination." *SAAB* 10 (1996): 5–10.

Hamori, Esther J. "Childless Female Diviners in the Bible and Beyond." Pages 161–91 in *Prophets Male and Female: Gender and Prophecy in the Hebrew Bible, the Eastern Mediterranean, and the Ancient Near East*. Edited by Jonathan Stökl and Corrine L. Carvalho. AIL 15. Atlanta: Society of Biblical Literature, 2013.

———. "Gender and the Verification of Prophecy at Mari." *WO* 42 (2012): 1–22.

———. *Women's Divination in Biblical Literature: Prophecy, Necromancy, and Other Arts of Knowledge*. ABRL. New Haven: Yale University Press, 2015.

Handy, Lowell K. "The Role of Huldah in Josiah's Cult Reform." *ZAW* 106 (1994): 40–53.

Holloway, Steven W. *Aššur Is King! Aššur Is King! Religion in the Exercise of Power in the Neo-Assyrian Empire*. CHANE 10. Leiden: Brill, 2003.

Kessler, Rainer. "Miriam and the Prophecy of the Persian Period." Pages 77–86 in *Prophets and Daniel*. Edited by Athalya Brenner. FCB 2/8. Sheffield: Sheffield Academic, 2001.

Knauf, Ernst Axel. "Vom Prophetinnenwort zum Prophetenbuch: Jesaja 8, 3f im Kontext von Jesaja 6, 1–8, 16." *lD* 2 (2000). https://tinyurl.com/SBL6016c.

Kupitz, Yaakov S., and Katell Berthelot. "Deborah and the Delphic Pythia: A New Interpretation of Judges 4:4–5." Pages 95–124 in *Images and Prophecy in the Ancient Eastern Mediterranean*. Edited by Martti Nissinen and Charles E. Carter. FRLANT 233. Göttingen: Vandenhoeck & Ruprecht, 2009.

Kupper, Jean-Robert. *Documents administratifs de la salle 135 du Palais de Mari*. 2 vols. ARMT 22. Paris: Editions Recherche sur les Civilisations, 1983.

Lampinen, Antti. "Θεῷ μεμελημένε Φοίβῳ: Oracular Functionaries at Claros and Didyma in the Imperial Period." Pages 49–88 in *Studies in Ancient Oracle and Divination*. Edited by Mika Kajava. AIRF 40. Rome: Institutum Romanum Finlandiae, 2013.

Marjanen, Antti. "Female Prophets among Montanists." Pages 127–43 in *Prophets Male and Female: Gender and Prophecy in the Hebrew Bible, the Eastern Mediterranean and the Ancient Near East*. Edited by Jonathan Stökl and Corrine L. Carvalho. AIL 15. Atlanta: Society of Biblical Literature, 2013.

Maurizio, Lisa. "Anthropology and Spirit Possession: A Reconsideration of the Pythia's Role at Delphi." *JHS* 115 (1995): 69–86.

Merlo, Paolo. "*Āpilum* of Mari: A Reappraisal." *UF* 36 (2004): 323–32.

Nissinen, Martti. *Ancient Prophecy: Near Eastern, Biblical, and Greek Perspectives*. Oxford: Oxford University Press, 2017.

———. "The Dubious Image of Prophecy." Pages 26–41 in *Prophets, Prophecy, and Prophetic Texts in Second Temple Judaism*. Edited by Michael H. Floyd and Robert D. Haak. LHBOTS 427. London: T&T Clark, 2006.

———. "Ištar of Arbela." Pages 129–55 in *Arbela Antiqua, actes du colloque international d'Erbil (7–10 avril 2014) Arbèles antique – Histoire d'Erbil pré-islamique*. Edited by Frédéric Alpi, Zidan Bradosty, Jessica Giraud, John MacGinnis, and Raija Mattila. BAH 218. Beirut: Presses de l'Ifpo, 2020.

———. *Prophets and Prophecy in the Ancient Near East*. 2nd ed. WAW 41. Atlanta: SBL Press, 2019.

———. *References to Prophecy in Neo-Assyrian Sources*. SAAS 7. Helsinki: Neo-Assyrian Text Corpus Project, 1998.

Overholt, Thomas W. *Prophecy in Cross-Cultural Perspective: A Sourcebook for Biblical Researchers*. SBLSBS 17. Atlanta: Scholars Press, 1986.

Parpola, Simo. *Letters of Assyrian Scholars to the Kings Esarhaddon and Assurbanipal, Part 2: Commentary and Appendices*. AOAT 5.2. Kevelaer: Butzon & Bercker; Neukirchen-Vluyn: Neukirchener Verlag, 1983.

Peled, Ilan. "*Assinnu* and *kurgarrû* Revisited." *JNES* 73 (2014): 283–97.

Rapp, Ursula. *Mirjam: Eine feministisch-rhetorische Lektüre der Mirjamtexte in der hebräischen Bibel*. BZAW 317. Berlin: de Gruyter, 2002.

Römer, Thomas. "From Prophet to Scribe: Jeremiah, Huldah, and the Invention of the Book." Pages 86–96 in *Writing the Bible: Scribes, Scribalism, and Script*. Edited by Philip R. Davies and Thomas Römer. BibW. Durham, NC: Acumen, 2013.

Scheuer, Blaženka. "Huldah: A Cunning Career Woman?" Pages 104–23 in *Prophecy and Prophets in Stories: Papers Read at the Fifth Meeting of the Edinburgh Prophecy Network*. Edited by Bob Becking and Hans M. Barstad. OTS 65. Leiden: Brill, 2015.

Stjerna, Kirsi. "Finnish Sleep-Preachers: An Example of Women's Spiritual Power." *NR* 5 (2001): 102–20.

Stökl, Jonathan. "Female Prophets in the Ancient Near East." Pages 47–61 in *Prophecy and Prophets in Ancient Israel: Proceedings of the Oxford Old Testament Seminar*. Edited by John Day. LHBOTS 531. London: T&T Clark, 2010.

———. "Gender 'Ambiguity' in Ancient Near Eastern Prophecy: A Reassessment of the Data behind a Popular Theory." Pages 59–80 in *Prophets Male and Female: Gender and Prophecy in the Hebrew Bible, the Eastern Mediterranean and the Ancient Near East*. Edited by Jonathan Stökl and Corrine L. Carvalho. AIL 15. Atlanta: Society of Biblical Literature, 2013.

———. *Prophecy in the Ancient Near East: A Philological and Sociological Comparison*. CHANE 56. Leiden: Brill, 2012.

———. "The מתנבאות of Ezekiel 13 Reconsidered." *JBL* 132 (2013): 61–76.

Svärd, Saana. *Women's Roles in the Neo-Assyrian Era: Female Agency in the Empire*. Saarbrücken: VDM, 2008.

Svärd, Saana, and Martti Nissinen. "(Re)constructing the Image of the Assinnu." Pages 373–411 in *Studying Gender in the Ancient Near East*. Edited by Saana Svärd and Agnès Garcia Ventura. University Park, PA: Eisenbrauns, 2018.

Teppo, Saana. "Sacred Marriage and the Devotees of Ištar." Pages 75–92 in *Sacred Marriages: The Divine-Human Sexual Metaphor from Sumer to Early Christianity*. Edited by Martti Nissinen and Risto Uro. Winona Lake, IN: Eisenbrauns, 2008.

Tervanotko, Hanna. "Speaking in Dreams: The Figure of Miriam and Prophecy." Pages 147–68 in *Prophets Male and Female: Gender and Prophecy in the Hebrew Bible, the Eastern Mediterranean and the Ancient Near East*. Edited by Jonathan Stökl and Corrine L. Carvalho. AIL 15. Atlanta: Society of Biblical Literature, 2013.

Weems, Renita J. "Huldah, the Prophet: Reading a (Deuteronomistic) Woman's Identity." Pages 321–39 in *A God So Near: Essays on Old Testament Theology in Honor of Patrick D. Miller*. Edited by Brent A. Strawn and Nancy R. Bowen. Winona Lake, IN: Eisenbrauns, 2003.

Weippert, Manfred. *Götterwort in Menschenmund: Studien zur Prophetie in Assyrien, Israel und Juda*. FRLANT 252. Göttingen: Vandenhoeck & Ruprecht, 2014.

Williamson, Hugh G. M. "Prophetesses in the Hebrew Bible." Pages 65–80 in *Prophecy and Prophets in Ancient Israel: Proceedings of the Oxford Old Testament Seminar*. Edited by John Day. LHBOTS 531. London: T&T Clark, 2010.

Zsolnay, Ilona. "The Misconstrued Role of the Assinnu in Ancient Near Eastern Prophecy." Pages 81–99 in *Prophets Male and Female: Gender and Prophecy in the Hebrew Bible, the Eastern Mediterranean and the Ancient Near East*. Edited by Jonathan Stökl and Corrine L. Carvalho. AIL 15. Atlanta: Society of Biblical Literature, 2013.

Appendix:
List of Ancient Near Eastern Texts Mentioning Nonmale Prophets

Numbering follows Martti Nissinen, *Prophets and Prophecy in the Ancient Near East*, 2nd ed., WAW 41 (Atlanta: SBL Press, 2019).

Old Babylonian

*1	FM 7 39 (Durand 2002, 134–35)	*āpilum u āpiltum*
*7	ARMT 26 197 (Durand 1988, 424)	Šelebum the *assinnu*; *qammatum*
*8	ARMT 26 198 (Durand 1988, 425)	Šelebum the *assinnu*
*9	ARMT 26 199 (Durand 2012)	*qammatum*
*10	ARMT 26 200 (Durand 1988, 429–30)	Ḫubatum the *muḫḫūtum*
*11	ARMT 26 201 (Durand 1988, 430)	(Ḫubatum?) the *muḫḫūtum*
*13	ARMT 26 203 (Durand 1988, 431–32)	*qammatum*
*14	ARMT 26 204 (Durand 1988, 432–33)	Innibana the *āpiltum*
*17	ARMT 26 207 (Durand 1988, 435–37)	male and female persons

108   Martti Nissinen

*20	ARMT 26 210 (Durand 1988, 439–40)	a woman, spouse of a free man
*22	ARMT 26 212 (Durand 1988, 440–41)	Ili-ḫaznaya the *assinnu*
*23	ARMT 26 213 (Durand 1988, 441–42)	Šelebum the *assinnu*
*24	ARMT 26 214 (Durand 1988, 442–43)	Aḫatum the servant girl
*35	ARMT 26 227 (Durand 1988, 467)	[...-b]ila'u
*36	ARMT 26 229 (Durand 1988, 468–69)	Ayala
*37	ARMT 26 232 (Durand 1988, 471–72)	Zunana
*41	ARMT 26 236 (Durand 1988, 477–78)	Kakka-lidi
*42	ARMT 26 237 (Durand 1988, 478–79)	Addu-duri; *muḫḫūtum*
*44	ARMT 26 239 (Durand 1988, 480–81)	Šimatum
*45	ARMT 26 240 (Durand 1988, 481–82)	Timlû
*50b	M. 7160 (Charpin 2014, 32)	*muḫ*[*ḫūtum*] of Ishtar of Bišra
*52	FM 3 3 (Durand and Guichard 1997)	*muḫḫâtum* (pl.)
*58	ARMT 22 326 (Kupper 1983, 510–13)	Annu-tabni the *muḫḫūtum*
*65b	M. 11299 (Durand 1988, 399)	Šelebum and Ili-ḫaznaya
*120	MSL 12 5.22 (Civil et al. 1969,158)	mí-lú-gub-ba = *muḫḫūt*[*um*]
*135g	TCL 10 39 (Dyckhoff 1999, 39–43)	mí-lú-gub-ba of Inanna of Zabala

Assyrian

*68	SAA 9 1.1	Issar-la-tašiyaṭ, a man (?) of Arbela
*69	SAA 9 1.2	Sinqiša-amur, a woman of Arbela
*70	SAA 9 1.3	Remut-allati, a woman of Dara-aḫuya
*71	SAA 9 1.4	woman Bayâ, a man of Arbela

*72	SAA 9 1.5	woman Ilussa-amur, a man of Assur
*74	SAA 9 1.7	Issar-beli-da"ini, a female votary
*75	SAA 9 1.8	Aḫat-abiša, a woman of Arbela
*79	SAA 9 2.2	[woman Bay]â, a man of Arbela
*81	SAA 9 2.4	Urkittu-šarrat, a woman of Calah
*92	SAA 9 7	Mullissu-kabtat, the *raggintu*
*94	SAA 9 9	Dunnaša-amur, a woman of Arbela
*95	SAA 9 10	Dunnaša-amur, the mí-gub-ba
*105	SAA 10 109	*raggimānu, raggimātu*
*109	SAA 10 352	*raggintu*
*110	SAA 12 69	*maḫḫātu*
*113	SAA 13 144	NN
*114	SAA 13 148	NN, a female votary
*115	SAA 16 59	slave girl
*118	K 2001+ (Farber 1977, 128–55)	*maḫḫû, maḫḫūtu*
*123	VS 19 1 (Freydank 1974, 58–73)	*maḫḫû, maḫḫātu, assinnu*
*125	MSL 12 4.222 (Civil et al. 1969, 132)	*maḫḫû, maḫḫūtu*
*127	Šumma izbu xi (De Zorzi 2014, 642)	*maḫḫātu*
*128	Šumma izbu Comm. (De Zorzi 2014, 640)	*maḫḫātu, maḫḫû*
*129	Šumma ālu i (Freedman 1998, 32–35)	*maḫḫû, maḫḫātu*

Women and Magic Practices in the Prophets (Joshua–Malachi)

Ora Brison

In m. Avot 2:7, it is said: "Most women engage in sorcery."

1. Magic and Divination in the Bible

This essay examines the presentation of magic, divination and gender in the books of the Prophets (Joshua–Malachi). The discussion focuses on two categories: (1) the imagery of women in the Bible who engaged in or are associated with magic and divination and (2) the employment of the female metaphor to personify sinful cities and countries portrayed as sorceresses and whores by the prophets.[1]

The Hebrew Bible abounds with evidence of extensive magical and divinatory activities in ancient biblical societies. Magic was practiced in the realm of official religion and in unofficial cult, similar to other reli-

---

1. On magic, divination, and their practitioners in the Bible and the ancient Near East, see Michael Fishbane, "Studies in Biblical Magic: Origins, Uses and Transformations of Terminology and Literary Form" (PhD diss., Brandeis University, 1971); Ann Jeffers, *Magic and Divination in Ancient Palestine and Syria*, SHANE 8 (Leiden: Brill, 1996); Fredrick Cryer, *Divination in Ancient Israel and Its Near Eastern Environment: A Socio-historical Investigation*, JSOTSup 142 (Sheffield: JSOT Press, 1994); Lester L. Grabbe, *Priests, Prophets, Diviners, Sages: A Socio-historical Study of Religious Specialists in Ancient Israel* (Valley Forge, PA: Trinity Press International, 1995); Jean Bottéro, *Religion in Ancient Mesopotamia*, trans. Teresa Lavender-Fagan (Chicago: University of Chicago Press, 1998), 170–202; Tzvi Abusch, *Mesopotamian Witchcraft: Toward a History and Understanding of Babylonian Witchcraft Beliefs and Literature*, AMD 5 (Leiden: Brill, 2002); Rüdiger Schmitt, *Magie im Alten Testament* (Münster: Ugarit-Verlag, 2004). On early Jewish magic, see Gideon Bohak, *Ancient Jewish Magic: A History* (Cambridge: Cambridge University Press, 2008).

gious systems in the ancient Near East. However, magical and divinatory practices differ from one society to another and must be studied and understood in their specific context.² The biblical texts present a dialectical discourse of denial and acceptance, and of ambivalent and contradictory attitudes and viewpoints toward these practices and their practitioners (men and women alike). Officially, the Bible emphatically and continually condemns and forbids praxes of magic, divination, sorcery and witchcraft. At the same time, it is quite clear, says Athalya Brenner-Idan, that neither magic nor divination is forbidden per se. The proscription itself is testimony to the continuation of magic and divination in the cultural substrata of ancient Israel.³

Deuteronomy 18:10–11 presents the most comprehensive list of magic and divination practitioners and practices.⁴ However, due to the scarcity of pertinent information in the biblical texts, there is no consensus by premodern or modern commentators regarding the meaning and purpose of most of the magical and divinatory practices and devices referred to in these verses. Interpretations of these practices have often been based on extrabiblical parallels. The boundaries between various magical and divinatory practices, prophecies, interpretation of dreams, necromancy, and so on are not always clear and definable.⁵ Nonetheless, there is agreement among scholars that the use of certain roots such as כשף (to practice divination; BDB, 506), קסם (to practice sorcery; BDB, 890), and נחש (to

---

2. Theodore J. Lewis, *Cults of the Dead in Ancient Israel and Ugarit*, HSM 39 (Atlanta: Scholars Press, 1989), 104; Karel van der Toorn, *Family Religion in Babylonia, Syria, and Israel*, SHANE 7 (Leiden: Brill, 1996), 206–35; Jeffers, *Magic and Divination*, 2–24; Rüdiger Schmitt, "Theories Regarding Witchcraft Accusations and the Hebrew Bible," in *Essays in Social Theory and the Study of Israelite Religion: Essays in Retrospect and Prospect*, ed. Saul M. Olyan (Atlanta: Society of Biblical Literature, 2012), 182.

3. See Athalya Brenner-Idan, *The Israelite Woman: Social Role and Literary Type in Biblical Narrative* (London: Bloomsbury T&T Clark, 2014), 68. Fishbane argues that the biblical editing and reduction process removed many of the original references to magic (*Studies in Biblical Magic*, 38–43).

4. We find smaller lists in Exod 7:11; 2 Kgs 21:6; Jer 27:9.

5. Irmtraud Fischer suggests that the term *prophecy* before Deut 18 included various divinatory practices. See Fischer, *Gotteskünderinnen: Zu einer geschlechterfairen Deutung des Phänomens der Prophetie und der Prophetinnen in der Hebräischen Bibel* (Stuttgart: Kohlhammer, 2002), 44–49.

practice divination; BDB, 638; e.g., 2 Chr 33:6), generally denotes magical praxes denounced in the codes of law.⁶

Deuteronomy 18:14–15 states that in the land of Canaan, the prophets (empowered by God) would replace the various types of diviners and sorcerers. This statement demonstrates the similarity between these two groups of intermediaries. Indeed, biblical stories show that prophets were consulted on the same matters as diviners and sorcerers, and that prophets also performed miracles and magical acts similar to those of foreign sorcerers⁷ (e.g., Moses in Exod 7:10; Samuel in 1 Sam 9:19–20; Elijah in 1 Kgs 17:10–16, 18–24; etc.). Priests and Levites also engaged in divination, employing the Urim and Thummim (Num 27:18–23; 1 Sam 14:41–2) as well as the ephod (Judg 17–18). None of them are censured or condemned for the magical activities. In other words, the Bible never indicates that these practices are ineffective. Jacob Milgrom suggests, "Most syncretistic forms of magic and divination did not meet the opposition of prevailing spiritual leadership, priestly and prophetic alike, because the latter did not regard them—or were unaware of them—as possible threats to the covenant faith."⁸

What appears to determine the biblical attitudes toward these practices as being either legitimate or illegitimate is their source of authority and the acceptability of the intermediaries performing the magical and divinatory acts, whether or not they were empowered by Yahweh.⁹ When magic and divination are associated with foreign pagan cults—which is often the case—they are described in negative terms discrediting these cults, which are frequently labeled as harlotry (e.g., Num 25:1–2; Nah 3:4).

---

6. Unless otherwise noted, biblical quotations are from the NKJV translation of the Hebrew Bible.

7. See, for example, Martti Nissinen, "Prophecy and Omen Divination: Two Sides of the Same Coin," in *Divination and Interpretation of Signs in the Ancient World*, ed. Amar Annus, OIS 6 (Chicago: University of Chicago Press, 2010), 341–51; Grabbe, *Priests, Prophets, Diviners, Sages*, 130.

8. Jacob Milgrom, "Magic, Monotheism and the Sin of Moses," in *The Quest for the Kingdom of God: Studies in Honor of George E. Mendenhall*, ed. Herbert B. Huffmon, Frank A. Spina, and Albert R. W. Green (Winona Lake, IN: Eisenbrauns, 1983), 262–63.

9. Many scholars say that it is quite evident in various laws and decrees, as well as in many references in biblical stories condemning magical practices, that these are regarded as aspects of idolatry and foreign customs (Jeffers, *Magic and Divination*; Cryer, *Divination*; Grabbe, *Priests, Prophets, Diviners, Sages*).

2. Magic and Women in the Bible

The relationship between magic, divination, and gender in the Hebrew Bible is significant for understanding the feminine paradigm in ancient Israel, especially since in biblical Israelite societies, women were excluded from officiating in Yahweh's cult as priestesses or as female Levites.[10] In effect, there are no feminine nouns for these cultic functions in biblical Hebrew. The only religious, cultic, or spiritual role that was acceptable for a woman to perform was that of a prophetess. It is worth emphasizing that, compared to the thousand references to male prophets in the Hebrew Bible, only five prophetesses are mentioned.

Only four specific terms are used to describe women associated with prophecy, magic, and divination, that is, *prophetess, sorceress, medium,* and *soothsayer*. Furthermore, only few occurrences in the Prophets describe individual women/specialists associated with magic and divination: the prophetesses Deborah (Judg 4–5) and Huldah (2 Kgs 22:14–20), the medium of Endor (1 Sam 28:7–20), a group of prophesying women (Ezek 13:17–23), and Jael, אשת חבר the Kenite (Judg 4–5), who might be described as a woman associated with magic and divination.[11] Queen Jezebel is also accused of practicing sorcery.

The image of women associated with prophecy, magic, and divination takes on a different persona in prophetic writings describing the relationship between Yahweh and the metaphorical sinful cities personified as women.

The formulae of most legal laws and prohibitions against magic, as well as the recurrent accusations and condemnations against those who engage in false prophecies or magical practices, are written in the masculine form, either singular or plural.[12] Nonetheless, it is the image of a female figure, a sorceress (מכשפה), that was chosen by the prophets as a metaphor for the personification of sinful foreign cities.

---

10. On magic and women in the Bible, see Ann Louise Fritschel, "Women and Magic in the Hebrew Bible" (PhD diss., Emory University, 2003); Esther J. Hamori, *Women's Divination in Biblical Literature: Prophecy, Necromancy, and Other Arts of Knowledge* (New Haven: Yale University Press, 2015).

11. For this interpretation, see Ora Brison, "Jael, 'eshet heber the Kenite: A Diviner?," in *Joshua and Judges*, ed. Athalya Brenner and Gale A. Yee, TC (Minneapolis: Fortress, 2013), 139–60. See further under 3.1.3.

12. They, in all likelihood, pertain to members of both sexes.

2.1. Women, Laws, and Prohibitions against Magic

Although the books of the Pentateuch are beyond the scope of this essay, two laws relating to women/specialists associated with magic in Exod 22:17 (v. 18 in some English versions) and Lev 20:27 relate to this study. Both laws are written in the singular form. The law in Leviticus includes both sexes and is mentioned distinctly among laws against magical and divinatory practices: "A man or a woman who is a medium, or who has familiar spirits, shall surely be put to death; they shall stone them with stones. Their blood shall be upon them." However, the law written in Exodus is the only one in the feminine singular form that refers specifically to a sorceress.[13]

2.2 The Law of the Sorceress (Exod 22:17 [18])

The apodictic law known as the law of the sorceress, "You shall not permit a sorceress to live" (מכשפה לא תחיה; Exod 22:18), is the first biblical reference to a law concerning magic.[14] Though no biblical explanation is provided for the term מכשפה (sorceress) or for her expertise, the etymology of the term derives from the root כשף, interpreted as "practicing sorcery/witchcraft." The מכשפה is generally interpreted as a female diviner, a medium, a magician or a soothsayer, based on its use in Ugaritic and Akkadian texts. The masculine singular form, מכשף (sorcerer), appears in the list of magic in Deut 18:10–11, and in the plural form מכשפים (sorcerers) in Exod 7:11; Mal 3:5; and Dan 2:2.[15] Nahmanides notes that the connection between sex and sorcery is implied by the literary context of the law of the sorceress. It follows two other laws that have

---

13. The Targum Onqelos uses the masculine singular form in its translation, and the LXX employs the masculine plural form.

14. For a comprehensive study of the subject, see Yitschak Sefati and Jacob Klein, "The Law of the Sorceress (Exod 22:17[18]) in Light of Biblical and Mesopotamian Parallels," in *Sefer Moshe: The Moshe Weinfeld Jubilee Volume; Studies in the Bible and the Ancient Near East, Qumran, and Post-biblical Judaism*, ed. Chaim Cohen, Avi Hurvitz, and Shalom M. Paul (Winona Lake, IN: Eisenbrauns, 2004), 171–90. A series of laws, decrees, and regulations were added to the Decalogue and set within the narrative of the Sinai covenant.

15. BDB, 506; see also Jeffers, *Magic and Divination*, 65–70; Hamori, *Women's Divination*, 24–29.

sexual connotations—the seducer of a virgin (Exod 22:15) and bestiality (Exod 22:16).[16]

Does the emphasis on the gender of the sorceress indicate a historical reality in which more women than men were involved in magic? Was the phenomenon of female sorceresses so widespread in the Israelite society that it was essential at the time these texts were written to denounce or oppose them with a special law? Is this an indication that might explain the Mishnah's attitude toward magic and gender? These are some of the questions to be discussed in what follows.[17]

3. Female Imagery Associated with Magic

Four categories in the Prophets (Joshua–Malachi) portray female imagery associated with magic, divination, and prophecy. In the first category are two officially Yahwistically authorized prophetesses, namely, Deborah (Judg 4–5) and Huldah (2 Kgs 22:12–20; also 2 Chr 34:20–28). Another prophetess is mentioned in Isa 8:3 who is described as having a sign-child.[18] As there is an article about female prophecy in this volume, this topic will not be discussed in this essay. The second category is composed of specific but nameless women/experts associated with practices of magic and divination: the medium of Endor (1 Sam 28); a group of women—the prophesying women in Ezek (13:17–23); and one named woman/expert—Jael אשת חבר the Kenite in Judg 4–5.[19] In the third category is a single woman—Queen Jezebel in 2 Kgs 9:22. She is accused of sorcery and harlotry, although her connection to magic is not specified.

---

16. Nahmanides, *Commentary on the Torah: Exodus* (New York: Shilo, 1973); see also Sefati and Klein, *Law of the Sorceress*, 173–77.

17. See discussion on gender in the different sociopolitical settings in Michelle Zimbalist Rosaldo, "Women, Culture and Society: A Theoretical Overview, " in *Women, Culture and Society*, ed. Michelle Zimbalist Rosaldo and Louise Lamphere (Stanford: Stanford University Press, 1974), 17–42; Carol L. Meyers, *Rediscovering Eve: Ancient Israelite Women in Context* (New York: Oxford University Press, 2013); Meyers, "From Household to House of Yahweh: Women's Religious Culture in Ancient Israel," in *Congress Volume Basel*, ed. André Lemaire, VTSup 92 (Leiden: Brill, 2001), 277–303.

18. For further details on Isa 8: 3, see Fischer, *Gotteskünderinnen*, 214,16–18; Wilda G. Gafney, *Daughters of Miriam: Women Prophets in Ancient Israel* (Minneapolis: Fortress, 2008); Hamori, *Women's Divination*, 160–66.

19. On this interpretation, see Brison, "Jael, 'eshet heber the Kenite"; see further under 3.1.3.

The imagery of personified sinful cities—Jerusalem (Isa 57:3), Babylon (Isa 47:1–15), and Nineveh (Nah 3)—metaphorically portrayed as sorceresses makes up the fourth category.

3.1. Images of Women/Experts Practicing Magic

The stories of the medium of Endor, the prophesying women in Ezek 13, and Jael אשת חבר the Kenite fall into this category: women/experts practicing magic. Their accounts provide the reader with a rare glance into the modus operandi, technique, and devices of magical and divinatory practices in biblical Israel.

3.1.1. The Medium of Endor (1 Samuel 28:3–25)

In 1 Sam 28:3–25, King Saul encounters the medium אשת בעלת־אוב of Endor. Saul, facing war with the Philistines, after failing to obtain divine knowledge and guidance through numerous legitimate channels of communication, seeks the help of a female necromancer.

Necromancy and other cults of the dead are prohibited and punishable by death in ancient Israel. The story begins with a deliberate reference to Saul himself having "put the mediums and the spiritists out of the land" (1 Sam 28:3). It is therefore surprising that the author exceptionally chose to preserve a story about necromancy rather than to censor it, and that he does not attempt to discredit the effectiveness of the practice.[20]

The story offers some insight about the woman/medium. She is an acknowledged expert in an established site known to people who wish to consult the dead; she owns property, namely, a house in which she practices necromancy and, most likely, she gets paid for her services.[21] Her professional skills are reflected in the value of her practice, her verbal skills, eloquence, persuasiveness, and her authoritative yet empathic attitude toward the customer. The lavish food (a fatted calf) she offers Saul demonstrates her favorable economic status. This narrative provides the reader with a rare glance into one of the most extraordinary and sup-

---

20. The prophet Samuel, who has accused Saul of using magical practices in the past (1 Sam 15:23), does not comment on the necromancy séance, nor does he accuse the medium of sorcery.

21. The evidence that prophets and diviners get paid for oracles and other magical practices rendered can be seen in 1 Sam 9:7; Ezek 13:19; Mic 3:11.

pressed magical practices in biblical Israel—the raising of the dead (העלאה באוב) and communicating with them.

The importance of the medium's story is that it presents official and legal prophecy and illegal magic on the same continuum. That communication with the supernatural realm can be achieved by both intermediaries, male and female—the prophet and the woman/medium—indicates that the boundaries between the practices are blurred, both thematically and terminologically.[22]

3.1.2. The Prophesying Women in Ezekiel (Ezekiel 13:17–23)

Ezekiel considered himself a true prophet, a messenger of Yahweh, and opposed all other intermediaries, calling them false male prophets using the masculine plural form (13:1–16).[23] He does not call the women prophetesses[24] but instead refers to them as "the daughters of your people, who prophesy out of their own heart" (13:17). He accuses them of deceiving the people who consulted them by using sorceries and lies (שוא וקסם כזב), asserting that they did not receive messages from God, nor did they possess real divine authority. Therefore, they were illegitimate and religiously sinful women-intermediaries who took the name of Yahweh in vain. Ezekiel accuses them of performing a type of divination intended to capture people's souls by using magical techniques and devices (מספחות, כסתות), interpreted as tying magical knots and using various kinds of cloths, veils, and bands.[25] As there is no clear consensus as to what type of magic is being described in this passage, several different interpretations exist.

---

22. Consider, for example, the use of the verbs שאל (*qal*) and דרש (*qal*), which usually relate to consulting a supernatural power (1 Sam 28:7; 1 Chr 10:13), and the use of the root קסם (to practice sorcery), which often refers to idolatry (1 Sam 28:8). For further study on this encounter, see Uriel Simon, "A Balanced Story: The Stern Prophet and the Kind Witch," *Prooftexts* 8 (1988): 159–71; Ora Brison, "The Medium of En-dor (אשת בעלת אוב) and the Phenomenon of Divination in the Twenty-First Century Israel," in *Samuel and Kings*, ed. Athalya Brenner and Archie C. C. Lee, TC (London: Bloomsbury T&T Clark, 2017), 124–47. For another approach see Fischer, *Gotteskünderinnen*, 147–54.

23. For a comprehensive study on the prophesying women in Ezekiel, see Nancy R. Bowen, "The Daughters of Your People: Female Prophets in Ezekiel 13:17–23," *JBL* 118 (1999): 417–33.

24. Like other females/prophets (Miriam, Deborah, or Huldah).

25. Many scholars link כסתות to the Akkadian verb *kasû*, "to bind," used to describe magical binding. See, e.g. Saggs, *External Souls*, 5; Walther Zimmerli, *Ezekiel*

The majority of commentators, for example Moshe Greenberg, interpret the prophesying women as witches or sorceresses, whereas Jo Ann Scurlock and Nancy Bowen propose that they were specialists associated with consultations concerning pregnancy and childbirth.²⁶ They maintain that Ezekiel's descriptions are based on the Mesopotamian corpus of incantations known as Maqlû. This corpus of antiwitchcraft incantations and rituals comprises a plethora of health rituals, childbirth rituals, and so on. Karel van der Toorn argues, on the basis of Ugaritic and Mesopotamian parallels, that these prophesying women practiced necromancy and divination.²⁷ Henry Saggs, Maijo Korpel, and Esther Hamori identify the women's activities as necromancy based mainly on the recurrent references to לצודד נפשות, interpreted as catching/hunting "souls," "life force," or "spirits of the dead."²⁸ Walther Zimmerli is one of the scholars who suggests that these women are prophetesses rather than sorceresses, whose actions go beyond the prophetic into the realm of magic.²⁹

Ezekiel's detailed descriptions of the prophesying women's techniques and devices suggest his firsthand knowledge that offers the readers insight into the *materia magica* used at that time.

Both the story of the medium and Ezekiel's prophesying women seem to be associated with the cult of the dead. Ezekiel's opposition to these women's magical practices reflects the persistent struggle of Yahwist prophets against syncretism and infiltration of Mesopotamian cultic elements into Israelite religion.

I: Chapters 1–24, trans. Ronald E. Clements, Hermeneia (Philadelphia: Fortress, 1979), 413; see also Fishbane, *Studies in Biblical Magic*, 56–58, 81–89.

26. Moshe Greenberg, *Ezekiel 1–20*, AB (New York: Doubleday, 1983), 240; Jo Ann Scurlock, "Baby-Snatching Demons, Restless Souls and the Dangers of Childbirth: Medio-Magical Means of Dealing with Some of the Perils of Motherhood in Ancient Mesopotamia," *Inc* 2 (1991): 135–83; Bowen, *Daughters of Your People*, 421; see also Abusch, *Mesopotamian Witchcraft*.

27. Karel van der Toorn, *From Her Cradle to Her Grave: The Role of Religion in the Life of the Israelite and Babylonian Woman*, trans. Sara J. Denning-Bolle (Sheffield: JSOT Press, 1994), 123.

28. Henry W. F. Saggs, "External Souls in the Old Testament," *JSS* 19 (1974): 6; Maijo C. A. Korpel, "Avian Spirits in Ugarit and Ezekiel 13," in *Ugarit, Religion and Culture*, ed. Nicolas Wyatt, Wilfred G. E. Watson, and Jeffrey B. Lloyd (Münster: Ugarit-Verlag, 1996), 102–5; Hamori, *Women's Divination*, 167–83.

29. Zimmerli, *Ezekiel I*, 296–97; see also Fritschel, *Women and Magic*, 132.

3.1.3. Jael, *'eshet heber* the Kenite (Judges 4–5)

Another identifiable/named woman/expert in the first category is Jael the Kenite (אשת חבר). Elsewhere I suggest that her story provides various indications that she probably practiced magic and may have been known during that period (Judg 5:6) as an intermediary between the human and the supernatural realms, a diviner.[30] Sisera, the commander of the Canaanite army, after his defeat in the war against the Israelite's army, flees to Jael's tent seeking an audience with a magic practitioner in order to receive a divine message about his destiny. The imagery, settings, and dialogues in Jael's tent share many similar thematic and parallels with Saul's encounter with the medium of Endor (1 Sam 28:3–25).

With regard to Jael's description as אשת חבר, syntax analysis shows that in Hebrew, אשת joined with an apposition in a construct form can be descriptive, such as אשת כסילות ("woman of folly"; Prov 9:13) or אשת־חיל ("woman of valor"; Prov 31:10). Following the *Hebrew and Aramaic Lexicon of the Old Testament*, such constructs may indicate occupation or public office, in parallel to the masculine noun formation איש־אלהים ("man of G-d"; 1 Sam 2:27) and איש כהן ("man of priest[hood] = priest"; Lev 21:9).[31] Therefore, אשת חבר can be considered in relation to אשת בעלת־אוב, a medium (1 Sam 28), a woman-expert, one who "binds magic knots" (deriving from the common Semitic root חבר, "to tie, bind," also mentioned in Deut 18:11; Isa 47:9; Ps 58:6).[32]

Jael's confident behavior; the use of different materials and unique artifacts such as "a lordly bowl" (ספל אדירים) and curds (חמאה); and the use of the verb הקריבה, "offered" (Judg 5:25), associated in the Bible with offerings, along with several other indications, means that this story might be interpreted as a session of divination or necromancy, or perhaps an incubation/dream séance.[33]

---

30. Brison, "Jael, *'eshet heber* the Kenite"; see also Susan Ackerman, *Warrior, Dancer, Seductress, Queen: Women in Judges and Biblical Israel*, ABRL (New York: Doubleday, 1998), 96–101.

31. *HALOT*, 43–44.

32. BDB, 287–88; see also Fishbane, *Studies in Biblical Magic*, 52–56; Jeffers, *Magic and Divination*, 31–35.

33. For more about this interpretation see Brison, "Jael, *'eshet heber* the Kenite." On female diviner/necromancer and dream interpreter in Mesopotamia, see van der Toorn, *From Her Cradle*, 124–28.

3.2. Jezebel (2 Kings 9:22)

In the third category, we find a prominent female figure, Jezebel queen of Israel, whose image has become synonymous with the ultimate wicked woman and sorceress.[34] The daughter of King Ethbaal of Sidon and Tyre (1 Kgs 16:31), the princess Jezebel married King Ahab of Israel. As a worshiper of the Canaanite gods Baal and Asherah, Jezebel was probably responsible for the building of a temple for Baal in the capital Samaria. Her cultic/religious activities are described in 1 Kgs 18:19, which mentions the "four hundred fifty prophets of Baal, and the four hundred prophets of Asherah, who eat at Jezebel's table."

Jezebel was powerful, aggressive, and intelligent, and had a special authoritative status and influence in Ahab's court as his reigning partner and as regent after the death of his sons.[35] The biblical text presents her as an active and cruel adversary of Israel's true God, his believers, and his prophets. She persecutes Yahweh's prophets almost to the point of total extinction (1 Kgs 18:4, 13), and the prophet Elijah is forced to hide from her, fearing for his life. Jehu, a commander in Ahab's army, carries out a coup against the house of Ahab with the blessings of the prophets Elijah and Elisha. Upon meeting with Joram, king of Israel and Jezebel's son, Jehu refers to Jezebel:

> Now it happened, when Joram saw Jehu, that he said, "Is it peace, Jehu?" So he answered, "What peace, as long as the harlotries of your mother Jezebel and her witchcraft are so many?" (2 Kgs 9:22)
> ויהי כראות יהורם את־יהוא ויאמר השלום יהוא ויאמר מה השלום־עד־זנוני איזבל אמך וכשפיה הרבים

As noted by Rüdiger Schmitt, Jehu's accusation of Queen Jezebel with many "sorceries" is the only occurrence in the Hebrew Bible of a specific woman being accused of practicing witchcraft in the Deuteronomistic History.[36] Having said that, nothing in the text suggests that Jezebel was

---

34. On Jezebel, see Patricia Dutcher-Walls, *Jezebel: Portraits of a Queen* (Collegeville, MN: Liturgical Press, 2004).

35. For Jezebel as a reigning queen, see Irmtraud Fischer, *Gotteslehrerinnen: Weise Frauen und Frau Weisheit im Alten Testament* (Stuttgart: Kohlhammer, 2006), 127–30.

36. Schmitt, *Social Theory*, 187.

unfaithful to her husband, Ahab, or that she was associated with magic and sorceries.

Brenner-Idan maintains that Jehu's portrayal of Jezebel as a sorceress and a whore probably refers to the queen's role as patroness of the Baal fertility cult.[37] Jehu's words, according to Patricia Dutcher-Walls, characterize Jezebel as the source of all evil that must be purged from Israel.[38] Adjectives such as *malicious, arrogant, conniving, wicked*, and *demonic* have been used throughout history to describe Jezebel. Her portrayal in Rev 2:20 as a false prophetess, "Jezebel, who calls herself a prophetess," marks her as the archetype of the sexually dangerous seductress, an evil woman. In contemporary dictionaries, *Jezebel* has been coined as a term synonymous with negative female figures—a promiscuous woman and a whore, according to the Merriam-Webster Dictionary, and, in the Cambridge Dictionary, as an immoral woman who deceives people in order to get what she wants.

Jezebel is the first woman in the Prophets accused of harlotry and sorcery. The link between gender, magic, and harlotry is portrayed in Jezebel's story and image, and plays an important role in expounding the female/sorceress metaphor in the prophecies of Isaiah, Ezekiel, Jeremiah, and Micah.

3.3. The Female/Sorceress/Harlot Metaphor

The fourth category presents the use of multivalent, negative, and derogatory female imagery by a number of prophets using the female/sorceress metaphor in their polemic against sinful cities.[39] These metaphorical

---

37. Brenner-Idan, *Israelite Woman*, 22–27. The claim that a woman could act in a priestly capacity— especially a foreign woman who worshiped foreign gods— was probably considered by those who wrote and edited these stories as inconceivable. Within the patriarchal structure of Israelite/Judean society, this kind of appointment had no legitimacy or validity whatsoever.

38. Dutcher-Walls, *Jezebel*, 75.

39. See, for example, Peggy L. Day, "The Personification of Cities as Female in the Hebrew Bible: The Thesis of Aloysius Fitzgerald, F.S.C.," in *Reading from This Place: Social Location and Biblical Interpretation in Global Perspectives*, ed. Fernando F. Segovia and Mary Ann Tolbert (Minneapolis: Fortress, 1995), 2:283–302; Stéphanie Anthonioz, "Cities of Glory and Cities of Pride: Concepts, Gender, and Images of Cities in Mesopotamia and in Ancient Israel," in *Memory and the City in Ancient Israel*, ed. Diana V. Edelman and Ehud Ben Zvi (Winona Lake, IN: Eisenbrauns, 2014), 21–42.

prophecies follow another biblical metaphor used for describing the relationship between Yahweh and Israel as husband and wife—the marriage metaphor (e.g., Jer 2:2; Hos 2:18–22).[40]

Isaiah and Nahum use the female metaphor to the extreme by presenting sinful cities (Babylon, Nineveh) as female, thus emphasizing the link between magic, harlotry, and gender.[41] Isaiah personifies Babylon (Isa 47:1–15; 57:3–13) and also Judea (Isa 37:21; 47:1) as female, and Nahum personifies Nineveh (Nah 3:4). The prophet Micah (Mic 5:11–13) also uses the feminine form to describe Judea's association with magic, paralleling idolatry with sorcery. The prophets condemn these feminized, personified cities, denoting them as sorceresses and whores, thus associating magic with harlotry. Although the biblical author employs the verb לזנות, "to whore after," deriving from the root זנה, also when referring to men, says Hamori, men are "only" accused of idolatry rather than sorcery (e.g., Exod 34:15–16; Lev 17:7; 20:5–6; Deut 31:16; Judg 2:17; 8:27; etc.).[42] The prophets not only use the verb זנה in the sense of prostitution/harlotry in descriptions employing the female metaphor; they also apply degrading, insulting, humiliating, and even pornographic language and imagery.

The prophetic female metaphor shows five predominant stereotypical characteristics: (1) independent behavior in the public sphere, (2) foreign origin, (3) association with harlotry and/or sexual promiscuity (4) association with idolatry, and (5) association with magic. Some or all of these characteristics are often attributed to the negative biblical female images.

I propose that the negative and almost demonic representation of Jezebel, accused of and linked to magic and harlotry, might have been used as the role model for the female metaphor employed in theses prophetic texts. The following are examples employed by the prophet Isaiah to describe the sorceress metaphor in two prophecies: against the personified Babylon (Isa 47:9–13) and the faithless Israelite people (Isa 57:3).

---

40. See, for example, Julie Galambush, *Jerusalem in the Book of Ezekiel: The City as Yahweh's Wife*, SBLDS 130 (Atlanta: Scholars Press, 1992).

41. Whoring as a metaphor for apostasy is an established rhetorical device in the prophetic literature (Jer 2:20; 3:1–13; Hos 2:4, 4:12–13); see Brenner-Idan (*Israelite Women*, 80).

42. Hamori, *Women's Divination*, 210.

3.3.1. Isaiah 57:3: Soothsayer/Conjurer/Necromancer?

> But as for you, come closer, You sons of a sorceress, You offspring of an adulterer and a harlot! (Isa 57:3 NJPS)
> ואתם קרבו־הנה בני עננה זרע מנאף ותזנה

Isaiah uses the metaphor for the faithless people of Israel, describing them as offspring of a sorceress (sons of עננה), children of a mother who is a whore and of a father who is an adulterer. No scholarly consensus has been reached with regard to the etymology of the term עננה.[43] Most commentators agree that the term מעונן in the masculine form (Deut 18:10; Isa 2:6) refers to a sorcerer and a diviner practicing a foreign type of divination. In the plural form, the term עננים/מעוננים is parallel to different types of sorcerers and diviners, as seen in Jer 27:9.

The accusation "sons of עננה" is part of a prophetic text that includes descriptions and imagery associated with the cult of the dead (Isa 57:9). The root ענ has overtones of raising spirits of the dead, probably suggesting that עננה is also linked with these practices, and hence עננה could be translated "conjurer." This woman/sorceress/harlot metaphor is extended throughout this passage, in which Isaiah blames the personified city for sorcery, harlotry, and idolatry.

3.3.2. Isaiah 47:1–15: Babylon

> They shall come upon you in their fullness
> Because of the multitude of your sorceries,
> For the great abundance of your enchantments. (Isa 47:9)
> באו עליך ברב כשפיך בעצמת חבריך מאד

> Stand now with your enchantments
> And the multitude of your sorceries. (Isa 47:12)
> עמדי־נא בחבריך וברב כשפיך באשר יגעת מנעוריך

---

43. Lewis suggests that the most appealing proposed possible etymology comes from Arabic meaning "to appear (to or before)"; "to take shape, to form, arise, spring up" (*Cults of the Dead*, 251 n. 49). Also, Cross maintains that "in Arabic the meaning of the verb 'to appear' and the nouns in the sense 'apparition, phenomenon' are most easily explained as denominative, i.e., secondarily derived from the meaning 'cloud' cloud bank." See Frank M. Cross, *Canaanite Myth and Hebrew Epic* (Cambridge: Harvard University Press, 1973), 165–66 n. 86; see also 153 n. 30.

In his prophecy against the personified Babylon, Isa 47:1–15 applies all the negative characteristics employed by the female metaphor for describing Babylon: an independent royal woman (vv. 1–5), a foreigner (vv. 1–5), a sorceress (vv. 12–15), and a harlot (vv. 2–3). He condemns her independent behavior using humiliating graphic descriptions of her nakedness, emphasizing her foreign origin and her promiscuity, blaming her for sorceries and witchcraft, mocking her idolatry, and says she consults with all types of magicians and diviners who will not save her:

> The scanners of heaven, the star-gazers,
> Who announce, month by month,
> Whatever will come upon you. (Isa 47:13 NJPS)
> יעמדו־נא ויושיעך הברו (הברי) שמים החזים בכוכבים מודיעים לחדשים מאשר יבאו עליך

3.3.3. Nahum 3:4: Nineveh

The prophet Nahum also addresses his prophecy to the personified city of Nineveh utilizing the female metaphor. Nahum denounces Nineveh:

> Because of the countless harlotries of the harlot,
> The winsome mistress of sorcery,
> Who ensnared nations with her harlotries
> And peoples with her sorcery. (Nah 3:4 NJPS)
> מרב זנוני זונה טובת חן בעלת כשפים המכרת גוים בזנוניה ומשפחות בכשפיה

Nineveh's seductive yet destructive political and commercial policies are identified here as a harlot's sexual allure and the illegitimate power of a sorceress. Nineveh's punishment will be similar to the punishment of the whore and the adulteress, which is mainly humiliation by presenting her naked in the public sphere. That kind of humiliation is also expressed in Isa 47:2–3; Jer 13:26; Ezek 16:37; and Hos 2:5, 12.[44]

3.3.4. Micah 5:12–14: Judah

Micah's prophecy is addressed to the people of Judea, accusing them of sorceries and idolatry:

---

44. Karolien Vermeulen, "The Body of Nineveh: The Conceptual Image of the City in Nahum 2–3," *JHS* 17 (2017): 1–17.

> I will cut off sorceries from your hand,
> And you shall have no soothsayers;
> Your carved images I will also cut off,
> And your sacred pillars from your midst;
> You shall no more worship the work of your hands;
> I will pluck your wooden images from your midst;
> Thus I will destroy your cities.
> והכרתי כשפים מידך ומעוננים לא יהיו־לך והכרתי פסיליך ומצבותיך מקרבך ולא־תשתחוה עוד למעשה ידיך ונתשתי אשיריך מקרבך והשמדתי עריך

The prophet Micah also uses the metaphor of a female sorceress to describe the sins of Judea, but does not accuse her of harlotry. Here, the connection to idolatry is clearly pronounced.

The personified sinful cities are turned in the hand of God into passive objects on which he decrees the punishment of destruction, humiliation, and death. The prophets employ this female imagery as a rhetorical means by which they delegitimize magic practices and present magic functionaries and users negatively.[45] The use of the female sorceress/harlot metaphor is characterized by the objectification of the female figure.[46] The similarity between the imagery of Jezebel's humiliating punishment and that of the sinful cities suggests a link between gender, magic, and harlotry. It also enhances the previously proposed role of the figure of Jezebel in expounding the female sorceress metaphor in Joshua–Malachi.

4. Conclusion

This essay examined the subject of gender and magic in the books of the Prophets (Joshua–Malachi). Three stories describe the active participation of female intermediaries in the communication between humans and the supernatural realm—the medium of Endor, the prophesying women in Ezekiel, and Jael the Kenite, אשת חבר. The biblical writings that pertain to these women show that despite the differences between the women's characters and stories, they share some common features. The women are all authoritative; they demonstrate rhetorical excellence and professional abilities and practice in the public space. These women are portrayed in various nontraditional roles and positions in patriarchal, traditional

---

45. Galambush, *Jerusalem in the Book of Ezekiel*, 38.
46. Fritschel, *Women and Magic*, 171.

societies, in the sense that they are exceptional in the canonical books. Nonetheless, they should not be considered unique or anomalous, as some commentators suggest, given that stories about women in traditional roles in the domestic sphere—such as mothers and wives—are also few when compared to stories about men. There is a consensus among commentators that the Hebrew Bible was written *by* men *for* men; stories centering on women are almost always secondary to stories about men. The texts present ambivalent and contradictory attitudes toward women engaging in or associated with magic and divination. In some of them, women are accused of sorcery, as in the case of the prophesying women in Ezekiel. In others, they are portrayed as nonthreatening, and therefore tolerated, such as the medium of Endor; in some texts, they are respected and acknowledged, such as the prophetesses Deborah and Huldah. On rare occasions, they are even blessed, as in the case of Jael. Queen Jezebel is portrayed as a sorceress, but there is no description of her magical activities.

Michelle Rosaldo suggests that the bias and negative attitude toward these women stem from the patriarchal worldview, perceiving women in nontraditional roles and positions as a threat to the social order.[47] Irmtraud Fischer points out that neither of the sage females in the Bible is presented as a mother.[48] Hamori says that women engaged in magical, prophetic, or divinatory activities are presented as childless.[49] One may assume that these women were portrayed that way in order to separate them from the stereotypical family-oriented, patriarchal wife and mother—hence, the ideal female figure.

The multivalent female metaphor used in the prophets' descriptions of the sins of the personified cities of Jerusalem, Babylon, and Nineveh correlates with the predominant prejudicial feminine characteristics also employed in describing Jezebel. The graphic—and at times even pornographic—expressions and descriptions used for these personifications were probably intended to demean and dishonor a real and powerful enemy, represented as a helpless woman, in the same way that Jezebel's fall from power to disgrace culminates in the obscene description of her death. The strategy behind this literary structural device—the female metaphor—was probably intended to arouse the interest, imagination,

---

47. See Rosaldo, *Women, Culture and Society*, 17–42; see also Meyers, *Rediscovering Eve*.

48. Fischer, *Gotteslehrerinnen*, 16–17.

49. Hamori, *Women's Divination*, 219–21.

fantasies, fears, and satisfaction of the readers and audience. Using female metaphors to describe the cities of their enemies demonstrates the objectification of women and their inferior social status in these ancient biblical societies.

The stories about gender and magic present the active practice by women in the biblical era as intermediaries between the human world and the supernatural realm. They also indicate the political, social, gender, and religious concerns underlying the choice of negative female metaphors that cater to the patriarchal ideology regarding the place of women in biblical societies as well as the stereotypification of women/gender and magic.

The deep-seated metaphoric correlation between gender and magic, sex, harlotry, and idolatry in the Prophets continued to gain propensity in the postbiblical era. Women were accused of being associated with the world of magic, and in the rabbinic literary corpus there are numerous discussions about women and sorcery, which attribute sorcery predominantly to women.[50] For example, b. Sanh. 67a in reference to the law of the sorceress states, "[Thou shalt not suffer] a witch [to live]: this applies to both man and woman. If so, why is a [female] witch stated?—Because mostly women engage in witchcraft." The account in Mishnah Sanhedrin 6:4 and in the y, Sanh. 6:6 also describes the hanging of eighty witches of Ashkelon by Simeon Ben Shetach, the head of the Sanhedrin during the reign of Alexander Jannaeus (ca. 103–76 BCE).[51]

I suggest that this biased approach expressed in the Mishnah and the Talmud—in addition to the existing social patriarchal discrimination against women—was a factor in strengthening the linkage between gender and magic in the Judeo-Christian world throughout the Middle Ages.

Bibliography

Abusch, Tzvi. *Mesopotamian Witchcraft: Toward a History and Understanding of Babylonian Witchcraft Beliefs and Literature.* AMD 5. Leiden: Brill, 2002.

Ackerman, Susan. *Warrior, Dancer, Seductress, Queen: Women in Judges and Biblical Israel.* ABRL. New York: Doubleday, 1998.

---

50. Sefati and Klein, *Law of the Sorceress*, 176 n. 18, 189.

51. For more on the subject, see Simcha Fishbane, "'Most Women Engage in Sorcery': An Analysis of Sorceresses in the Babylonian Talmud," *JH* 7 (1993): 27–42.

Anthonioz, Stéphanie. "Cities of Glory and Cities of Pride: Concepts, Gender, and Images of Cities in Mesopotamia and in Ancient Israel." Pages 21–42 in *Memory and the City in Ancient Israel*. Edited by Diana V. Edelman and Ehud Ben Zvi. Winona Lake, IN: Eisenbrauns, 2014.

Bohak, Gideon. *Ancient Jewish Magic: A History*. Cambridge: Cambridge University Press, 2008.

Bottéro, Jean. *Religion in Ancient Mesopotamia*. Translated by Teresa Lavender-Fagan. Chicago: University of Chicago Press, 1998.

Bowen, Nancy R. "The Daughters of Your People: Female Prophets in Ezekiel 13:17–23." *JBL* 118 (1999): 417–33.

Brenner-Idan, Athalya. *The Israelite Woman: Social Role and Literary Type in Biblical Narrative*. London: Bloomsbury T&T Clark, 2014.

Brison, Ora. "Jael, *'eshet heber* the Kenite: A Diviner?" Pages 139–60 in *Joshua and Judges*. TC. Edited by Athalya Brenner and Gale A. Yee. Minneapolis: Fortress, 2013.

———. "The Medium of En-dor (אשת בעלת אוב) and the Phenomenon of Divination in the Twenty-First Century Israel." Pages 124–47 in *Samuel and Kings*. Edited by Athalya Brenner and Archie C. C. Lee. TC. London: Bloomsbury T&T Clark, 2017.

Cross, Frank M. *Canaanite Myth and Hebrew Epic*. Cambridge: Harvard University Press, 1973.

Cryer, Fredrick. *Divination in Ancient Israel and Its Near Eastern Environment: A Socio-historical Investigation*. JSOTSup 142. Sheffield: JSOT Press, 1994.

Day, Peggy L. "The Personification of Cities as Female in the Hebrew Bible: The Thesis of Aloysius Fitzgerald, F.S.C." Pages 283–302 in *Reading from This Place: Social Location and Biblical Interpretation in Global Perspectives*. Vol. 2. Edited by Fernando F. Segovia and Mary Ann Tolbert. Minneapolis: Fortress, 1995.

Dutcher-Walls, Patricia. *Jezebel: Portraits of a Queen*. Collegeville, MN: Liturgical Press, 2004.

Fischer, Irmtraud. *Gotteskünderinnen: Zu einer geschlechtsfairen Deutung des Phänomens der Prophetie und der Prophetinnen in der Hebräischen Bibel*. Stuttgart: Kohlhammer, 2002.

———. *Gotteslehrerinnen: Weise Frauen und Frau Weisheit im Alten Testament*. Stuttgart: Kohlhammer, 2006.

Fishbane, Michael. "Studies in Biblical Magic: Origins, Uses and Transformations of Terminology and Literary Form." PhD diss., Brandeis University, 1971.

Fishbane, Simcha. "'Most Women Engage in Sorcery': An Analysis of Sorceresses in the Babylonian Talmud." *JH* 7 (1993): 27–42.

Fritschel, Ann L. "Women and Magic in the Hebrew Bible." PhD diss., Emory University, 2003.

Gafney, Wilda G. *Daughters of Miriam: Women Prophets in Ancient Israel*. Minneapolis: Fortress, 2008.

Galambush, Julie. *Jerusalem in the Book of Ezekiel: The City as Yahweh's Wife*. SBLDS 130. Atlanta: Scholars Press, 1992.

Grabbe, Lester L. *Priests, Prophets, Diviners, Sages: A Socio-historical Study of Religious Specialists in Ancient Israel*. Valley Forge, PA: Trinity Press International, 1995.

Greenberg, Moshe. *Ezekiel 1–20*. AB. New York: Doubleday, 1983.

Hamori, Esther J. *Women's Divination in Biblical Literature: Prophecy, Necromancy, and Other Arts of Knowledge*. New Haven: Yale University Press, 2015.

Jeffers, Ann. *Magic and Divination in Ancient Palestine and Syria*. SHANE 8. Leiden: Brill, 1996.

Korpel, Maijo C. A. "Avian Spirits in Ugarit and Ezekiel 13." Pages 99–113 in *Ugarit, Religion and Culture*. Edited by Nick Wyatt, Wilfred G. E. Watson, and Jeffrey B. Lloyd. Münster: Ugarit-Verlag, 1996.

Lewis, Theodore J. *Cults of the Dead in Ancient Israel and Ugarit*. HSM 39. Atlanta: Scholars Press, 1989.

Meyers, Carol L. "From Household to House of Yahweh: Women's Religious Culture in Ancient Israel." Pages 277–303 in *Congress Volume Basel*. Edited by André Lemaire. VTSup 92. Leiden: Brill, 2001.

———. *Rediscovering Eve: Ancient Israelite Women in Context*. New York: Oxford University Press, 2013.

Milgrom, Jacob. "Magic, Monotheism and the Sin of Moses." Pages 251–63 in *The Quest for the Kingdom of God: Studies in Honor of George E. Mendenhall*. Edited by Herbert B. Huffmon, Frank A. Spina, and Alberto R. W. Green. Winona Lake, IN: Eisenbrauns, 1983.

Nahmanides. *Commentary on the Torah: Exodus*. New York: Shilo, 1973.

Nissinen, Martti. "Prophecy and Omen Divination: Two Sides of the Same Coin." Pages 341–51 in *Divination and Interpretation of Signs in the Ancient World*. Edited by Amar Annus. OIS 6. Chicago: Chicago University Press, 2010.

Rosaldo, Michelle Zimbalist. "Women, Culture and Society: A Theoretical Overview." Pages 17–42 in *Women, Culture and Society*. Edited by

Michelle Zimbalist Rosaldo and Louise Lamphere. Stanford: Stanford University Press, 1974.

Saggs, Henry W. F. "External Souls in the Old Testament." *JSS* 19 (1974): 1–12.

Schmitt, Rüdiger. *Magie im Alten Testament*. Münster: Ugarit-Verlag, 2004.

———. "Theories Regarding Witchcraft Accusations and the Hebrew Bible." Pages 181–94 in *Essays in Social Theory and the Study of Israelite Religion: Retrospect and Prospect*. Edited by Saul M. Olyan. Atlanta: Society of Biblical Literature, 2012.

Scurlock, Jo Ann. "Baby-Snatching Demons, Restless Souls and the Dangers of Childbirth: Medio-Magical Means of Dealing with Some of the Perils of Motherhood in Ancient Mesopotamia." *Inc* 2 (1991): 135–83.

Sefati, Yitscha, and Jacob Klein. "The Law of the Sorceress (Exod 22:17[18]) in Light of Biblical and Mesopotamian Parallels." Pages 171–90 in *Sefer Moshe: The Moshe Weinfeld Jubilee Volume; Studies in the Bible and the Ancient Near East, Qumran, and Post-biblical Judaism*. Edited by Chaim Cohen, Avi Hurvitz, and Shalom M. Paul. Winona Lake, IN: Eisenbrauns, 2004.

Simon, Uriel. "A Balanced Story: The Stern Prophet and the Kind Witch." *Prooftexts* 8 (1988): 159–71.

Toorn, Karel van der. *Family Religion in Babylonia, Syria, and Israel*. SHANE 7. Leiden: Brill, 1996.

———. *From Her Cradle to Her Grave: The Role of Religion in the Life of the Israelite and Babylonian Woman*. Translated by Sara J. Denning-Bolle. Sheffield: JSOT Press, 1994.

Vermeulen, Karolien. "The Body of Nineveh: The Conceptual Image of the City in Nahum 2–3." *JHS* 17 (2017): 1–17.

Zimmerli, Walther. *Ezekiel I: Chapters 1–24*. Translated by Ronald E. Clements. Hermeneia. Philadelphia: Fortress, 1979.

Part 2

Female Literary Figures and
Their Social-Historical Context in the Nevi'im

Female Biblical Prophets: Visible Bodies, Audible Voices—Liberated Word

Nancy C. Lee

1. Introduction

Although female biblical prophets were recognized within Israelite culture and religious practice, this fact is not widely known by members of faith communities today or in the larger world due to a neglect in the history of scholarship, biblical study, and preaching. No biblical books are named after female prophets, but they are named after numerous male prophets. However, the collectors and canonizers of biblical texts did record for posterity five named female prophets (Miriam, Deborah, Huldah, Noadiah, and Anna).[1] They also recognized other unnamed female prophets,[2] such as *hannĕvî'â*, "the female prophet" in Isa 8:3 who was the partner of Isaiah. Three of these female prophets—*hannĕvî'â*, Deborah, and Huldah—appear in the Nevi'im section of the Hebrew Bible.[3] This essay focuses on these three women and considers the possibility that

---

1. See Mercedes García Bachmann, "Miriam, Primordial Political Figure in the Exodus," in *Torah*, ed. Irmtraud Fischer and Mercedes Navarro Puerto, BW 1 (Atlanta: Society of Biblical Literature, 2011), 329–74. Noadiah is mentioned in Neh 6:14 and Anna in Luke 2:36–38.

2. Because Hebrew masculine plural nouns (e.g., "prophets") may refer to a mixed-gender group, some texts probably include women.

3. Postbiblical Judaism identified more female prophets, a total of seven, including Sarah, Hannah, Abigail, and Esther. The Talmud did not include Noadiah. Also Mary, Jesus's mother, is regarded as a prophet by some Islamic traditions. See Amira El Azhary Sonbol, *Beyond The Exotic: Women's Histories In Islamic Societies* (Syracuse, NY: Syracuse University Press, 2005), 402 n. 7.

oracles by some unnamed female prophets may also be embedded in prophetic books.[4]

The Bible uses the same Hebrew root term for a male prophet (*nāvî'*) or a female prophet (*nevî'â*). Other terms for prophetic figures also appear, such as "seer" (*ro'eh*) or "visionary" (*ḥozeh*)—who have access to the divine through visions, while others receive dreams.[5] Although biblical texts do not use these terms for the named female prophets, this does not mean that women were not active in this form of prophecy.[6]

Scholars in recent years have broadened the meaning of biblical prophets. Like their counterparts in other cultures, biblical prophets practiced various forms of divination even though the expression of lyrical, divine oracles became the dominant, most visible form in Scripture.[7] Some texts prohibit the practices of other cultures (e.g., Lev 20:27; Deut 18:9–14), including consulting the dead, or necromancy. Ironically, in 1 Sam 28, a desperate King Saul seeks out a medium in Israel—the woman of Endor—to divine (*q-s-m*) and contact a spirit, namely, the late Samuel, for his prophetic guidance. A long history of the erroneous and negative view of the woman of Endor as a witch is corrected both by the text itself, which also presents her favorably, and by recent interpreters.[8]

---

4. Rainer Kessler, "Miriam and the Prophecy of the Persian Period," in *A Feminist Companion to Prophets and Daniel*, ed. Athalya Brenner, FCB 2/8 (London: Sheffield Academic, 2001), 85–86; Klara Butting, *Prophetinnen Gefragt: Die Bedeutung der Prophetinnen im Kanon aus Tora und Prophetie*, BfT 3 (Knesebeck: Erev-Rav, 2001), 9; Nancy C. Lee, *Hannevi'ah and Hannah: Hearing Women Biblical Prophets in a Women's Lyrical Tradition* (Eugene, OR: Wipf & Stock, 2015).

5. For example, Miriam in postbiblical Jewish tradition (Meg. 14a; Sotah 12b).

6. In 1 Chr 25:1–7, the sons and daughters of Heman (a "visionary") prophesy with music. See Wilda Gafney, *Daughters of Miriam: Women Prophets in Ancient Israel* (Minneapolis: Fortress, 2008), 30.

7. In this volume, see Ora Brison, "Women and Magic Practices in the Prophets (Joshua–Malachi)," and Martti Nissenen, "Nonmale Prophets in Ancient Near Eastern Sources." See also Esther Hamori, *Women's Divination in Biblical Literature: Prophecy, Necromancy, and Other Arts of Knowledge* (New Haven: Yale University Press, 2015), 105–11.

8. On this and the technical vocabulary, see Hamori, *Women's Divination*, 105–11. Fischer considers the medium a "prophetess" because (in relation to Deut 18:9–14) she mediates Samuel's prophecy of YHWH, does not lead anyone to worship other gods, is not criticized by Samuel or YHWH, and provides a ritual meal (like Elisha in 1 Kgs 19:21). See Irmtraud Fischer, *Gotteskünderinnen: Zu einer Geschlechtsfairen Deutung des Phänomens der Prophetie und der Prophetinnen in der Hebräischen Bibel*

2. Visible Bodies, Audible Voices

Female prophets in the Bible are visible, as depicted by narrators and by headings to their lyrical performances, yet their voices are barely audible. Many believe that the actual contributions of female prophets were greater than the biblical representations suggest. The unnamed female prophet associated with the prophet Isaiah, called *hannĕvî'â*, illustrates this point. The text infers that she is Isaiah's wife, and they have a child (Isa 8:3-4), named by YHWH, but nowhere in the book is her speech directly quoted. Texts of First Isaiah are prime territory for searching for this female prophet's unattributed speech. Her experience of having a child is paralleled by the famous passage just before it (Isa 7:14). There Isaiah speaks to King Ahaz: "The Lord himself will give you a sign. Look, the young woman is with child and shall bear a son, and shall name him Immanuel."[9] Thus, YHWH is associated with the bearing of children by both women.

To discern words of *hannĕvî'â*, perhaps we only need to examine further the text in Isa 8:18. After the description of the child born to Isaiah and *hannĕvî'â* (Isa 8:3-4), a voice says: "See, I and the children whom the LORD has given me are signs and portents in Israel from the LORD of hosts, who dwells on Mount Zion." The person speaking about the children from the Lord can easily be interpreted as *hannĕvî'â*, the mother of the child. It is not Isaiah who is the sign, but the woman and the child together serve as the sign. As Isaiah himself tells Ahaz, *the woman bearing the child* is the sign to you from God. If the declaration in Isa 8:18 is *hannĕvî'â's*, and just before it, Isaiah apparently says to a group, presumably his prophet followers: "Bind up the testimony, seal the teaching among my disciples. I will wait for the LORD, who is hiding his face from the house of Jacob, and I will hope in him" (vv. 16-17), then it is logical that *hannĕvî'â* would respond immediately with what she as prophet and mother had waited and hoped for from God—this child.

(Stuttgart: Kohlhammer, 2002), 141-45, 154. Brison suggests that the medium giving Saul a ritual meal, as Samuel did earlier (1 Sam 9:19-24), shows that their work is on a continuum. See Ora Brison, "The Medium of En-dor (אשת בעלת אוב) and the Phenomenon of Divination in Twenty-First Century Israel," in *Samuel, Kings, and Chronicles*, ed. Athalya Brenner and Archie C. C. Lee, TC (London: Bloomsbury T&T Clark, 2016), 128.

9. Unless otherwise stated, biblical translations are from the NRSV.

3. Women Composing as Subjects versus Constructing Women as Objects

In the past thirty years, attention to female prophets in the Bible and in the ancient Near East has finally emerged due to the groundbreaking efforts of scholars who have tried to correct the very long neglect of the subject for nearly all of the postbiblical period. From early studies on biblical women's sociocultural and religious roles, and focused studies on individual female prophets, to the first books fully treating female biblical prophets,[10] it is clear that understanding of the subject is growing.

A significant amount of work in recent years has focused on how male prophets constructed women as personae or metaphors within their rhetoric. Assessing female biblical prophets, on the other hand, requires consideration of the agency of women as *acting, speaking subjects*.[11] The analysis below will consider female prophets as described in narrative and poetic texts in the Nevi'im. One way to examine the contributions of female prophets is to take seriously any relationship between their prophetic rhetoric and women's lyrical composition of other genres.[12]

Anthropologically, in oral traditional cultures, a composer was a performer, and shared techniques would have been passed down through the generations. Carol Meyers relates this phenomenon to women's practice:

---

10. For early studies on biblical women's sociocultural and religious roles, see Athalya Brenner, *The Israelite Woman: Social Role and Literary Type in Biblical Narrative* (Sheffield: Sheffield Academic, 1985); Carol Meyers, *Discovering Eve: Ancient Israelite Women in Context* (Oxford: Oxford University Press, 1988). For focused studies on individual female prophets, see Rita J. Burns, *Has the Lord Indeed Spoken Only through Moses? A Study of the Biblical Portrait of Miriam*, SBLDS 84 (Atlanta: Scholars Press, 1987); Fokkelien van Dijk-Hemmes, "Mothers and a Mediator in the Song of Deborah," in *A Feminist Companion to Judges*, ed. Athalya Brenner, FCB 4 (Sheffield: JSOT Press, 1993), 110–14. For the first books fully treating female biblical prophets, see Butting, *Prophetinnen Gefrag*; Fischer, *Gotteskünderinnen*.

11. Shlomo D. Goitein, "Women as Creators of Biblical Genres," *Prooftexts* 8 (1988): 3; Eunice B. Poethig, "The Victory Song Tradition of the Women of Israel" (PhD diss., Union Theological Seminary, 1985); Athalya Brenner and Fokkelien van Dijk-Hemmes, *On Gendering Texts: Female and Male Voices in the Hebrew Bible*, BibInt 1 (Leiden: Brill, 1993), 62–71.

12. Gafney, *Daughters of Miriam*, 25, 30, draws attention to the musical dimension of biblical prophecy.

Women with greater expertise become mentors to others, probably younger women or their own daughters or daughters-in-law ... transmitting their skills to others.... This would also have been true for women's expertise in areas such as midwifery, prophecy, sagacity, musical performance, and lamenting the dead that have not left traces in the archaeological record but are known from passages in the Hebrew Bible.[13]

Groups of women in Israelite communities experienced one another's performances of different genres in their own Hebrew language. An example of a particular composing technique in the Hebrew language, relevant to female prophets, is the use of triplet consonantal sound repetition pattern,[14] consistently found in voices attributed to women. In the Nevi'im, the excerpt from Hannah's prayer-song of praise/thanks below illustrates the use of triplet soundplays:[15]

[*female*]	
My heart exults IN *YHWH*!	ʿālaṣ libbî baYHWH
My strength arches high IN *YHWH*!	rāmâh qarnî baYHWH
My speech is amplified	raḥav pî
above my enemies,	ʿal-ʾôyəvay
BECAUSE	KÎ
I rejoice	śāmaḥtî
in your salvation.	bîšûʿātekā
NO one (is) holy like YHWH,	ʾÊN-qādôš kaYHWH
INDEED!	KÎ
NO ONE besides you!	ʾÊN biltekā
and NO rock	wəʾÊN ṣûr
like our GOD.	kēʾlōhēnû
(1 Sam 2:1–2 my trans.)	

---

13. Carol Meyers, "Archaeology: A Window to the Lives of Israelite Women," in Fischer and Navarro Puerto, *Torah*, 105.

14. Because Hebrew consonants necessarily begin syllables, this triplet repetition also repeats syllables (and creates internal rhyme and/or tripled words). In the Song of Songs, the female voice consistently employs triplet soundplays, and the male voice uses doublet soundplays.

15. The inclusion of Hannah is not to suggest that the Bible calls her a prophet but to focus on women's attributed lyrics. Hamori's caution against regarding figures as prophets simply because they sing songs or offer lyrical prayers is helpful (*Women's Divination*, 98–99, 103).

The pattern can be seen in the translation, to the left, and in the Hebrew sound transliteration, to the right.[16] The triplet soundplays are pervasive throughout the first nine verses of the song. On the other hand, a song in this genre attributed to a male voice—David (2 Sam 22:1–51)—exhibits pervasive *doublet* soundplays throughout, a pattern consistently found also in lyrics attributed to male prophets.[17]

This suggested gendered usage of sound patterns as a technique for lyrical composition and performance, across genres, does not restrict creative style and does not determine the content of an oracle or song, nor does it essentialize the contributions of women or men. It was simply an oral traditional vehicle in the culture.

4. Liberated Word

4.1. Deborah

The female prophet about whom the most details are recorded in the Bible is Deborah. Her story and represented voice in a song of victory/thanksgiving appear in Judg 4:1–5:31.[18] The narrative (Judg 4:4–5) characterizes her thus: "And Deborah—a woman, a prophet, a woman of *lappîdôth* [literally 'flames']—she was judging Israel at that time. She was sitting under the palm of Deborah between Ramah and Bethel in the hill country of Ephraim, and the Israelites came up to her for judgment" (my translation). Recent commentators suggest that *lappîdôth* be translated as "woman of flames"[19] rather than "wife of Lappidoth," since the latter term appears nowhere else as a name but as a noun. Perhaps the phrase relates

---

16. What appear to be doublet repetitions above (*kî, kî*, and *bîšû'āteka, biltekā*) are actually part of triplet soundplays completed in the very next verse (1 Sam 2:3; Lee, *Hannevi'ah and Hannah*, 18–21).

17. For example, in First Isaiah and Micah; see also the triplet sound pattern in the woman's implied voice in the song of the vineyard in Isa 5 and in other Isaiah texs (Lee, *Hannevi'ah and Hannah*, 3–43).

18. The setting of the story is in premonarchic times, ca. 1200–1020 BCE.

19. The Babylonian Talmud relates לפידות to fire (noted in Gafney, *Daughters of Miriam*, 188 n. 42). The Talmud says she was a prophet and used to make wicks for the sanctuary and hence was called "woman of flames" (b. Meg. 14a). For a critique of reception history that only translates the term as "wife of Lappidoth," see Mieke Bal, *Death and Dissymmetry: The Politics of Coherence in the Book of Judges* (Chicago: University of Chicago Press, 1988), 209, 252.

to Deborah's divine inspiration as prophet, since prophets often were associated with fire.[20] She is also the only woman in the Bible described as a judge.

In two seminal works on female prophets, Klara Butting notes that Deborah was the first prophet to appear in the Nevi'im after Miriam, while Irmtraud Fischer suggests that the biblical canon intended to present Deborah as both the successor to Moses and the one to carry on Miriam's prophetic role.[21] Thus, Deborah is given a very important place in Israelite history and Scripture.

The narrative of Judg 4 depicts a situation in which the Israelites are in need again of a leader to rescue them from their enemy, the Canaanite king Jabin, whose cruel commander Sisera has oppressed them for twenty years (4:1–3). Therefore, Deborah as prophet summons a militia commander from among the Israelites—Barak. As was typical especially of earlier seer-like prophets, Deborah gives an oracle to Barak about military strategy to accomplish assured victory. She states, "The LORD, the God of Israel, commands you, 'Go take position at Mount Tabor'" (4:6).

Barak's characterization, by his response to her delivery of the oracle to him, has been interpreted in different ways. He says to Deborah, "If you will go with me, I will go; but if you will not go with me, I will not go." Some interpret Barak as faithful and wise to insist that Deborah go with him, since she has God's guidance and can invoke divine help. Others interpret Barak as fearful and resistant, not simply obeying the command of God. In the former reading, Barak respects the authority of the female prophet and depends on her for help. In the latter reading, Barak doubts either himself or the female prophet, or both, and hence fails to promptly obey the command. Both readings are countercultural for an androcentric culture.

The unfolding narrative sheds more light on how to interpret Barak, for soon after Deborah's first response to his request—that she will surely go with him—she makes a significant change in the first oracle. Whereas she first announced that YHWH would deliver the enemy into Barak's hand, now the oracle becomes, "nevertheless, the road on which you are going will not lead to your glory, for the LORD will sell Sisera into the hand of a woman" (4:9).

---

20. For example, Moses (Exod 3:1–5), Isaiah (Isa 6:6–7), Jeremiah (Jer 20:9), and Ezekiel (Ezek 1:4, 27).

21. Butting, *Prophetinnen gefragt*, 100; Fischer, *Gotteskünderinnen*, 123–24.

Therefore, Barak dutifully musters the troops, and Deborah goes with him onto the battle scene, which is hardly described. While some commentators suggest that Deborah was also a warrior, the text does not describe her fighting. The narrative (4:12–17) shows YHWH intervening to help Barak defeat Sisera's troops, and the once-invincible Sisera himself climbs down from his chariot and runs away. The countercultural narrative continues as Sisera, now the cowardly, weary warrior, escapes from the battle scene. The narrator follows a retreating Sisera, who is now invited into the tent of Jael, his ally's wife (4:17–21).[22] The horrific fate of Sisera that next unfolds at the hand of Jael, who kills him by driving a tent-peg into his head while he is asleep or unguarded (5:26), thus fulfills Deborah's (revised) oracle. None too soon, Barak comes running onto the scene chasing Sisera, only to be invited also by Jael into her tent, where he finds his defeated enemy already dead. Now both men are deprived of honor by this woman, or rather, by these women.

The victory song by Deborah and Barak that follows in Judg 5 essentially recounts the same events in the narrative, with some variation. Some commentators suggest that since the song includes Deborah as singer, then the narrative must have been the male account, produced by a male author. Perhaps an unstated assumption is behind this, that all biblical narratives are composed by men; this is problematic, since men are portrayed also as singing songs of praise/thanks, and there is no reason to assume that women could not also be storytellers in the culture.

We have seen how the narrative portrays the prophet Deborah; the song in Judg 5 does not disagree but adds to her portrait with subtle complexity, both by the lyrics represented as her voice and by how others speak of her. Often with poetic songs or oracles in the Bible, it is necessary to discern where speaking voices change, usually indicated only indirectly by changes in who is addressed, grammatical forms, and shifts in focus. The shifts in speakers, female and male, in Judg 5 are as follows: 5:2–6 (female), 5:7 (male), 5:8 (female), 5:9–12a (male), 5:12b (female), 5:13–19 (male), 5:20–31ab (female), 5:31c (male). Triplet and doublet soundplay patterns follow gender.

---

22. On the possibility of Jael being a diviner, see Ora Brison, "Jael, *'eshet heber* the Kenite: A Diviner?," in *Joshua and Judges*, ed. Athalya Brenner and Gale A. Yee, TC (Minneapolis: Fortress, 2013), 139–60.

The feminine singular verb in Judg 5:1 suggests that Deborah opens the song. Verses 2–6 are replete with triplet soundplays:

[*female*]

When LOCKS were LONG in ISRAEL, when the people freely offered themselves,	biphrōaʻ pōrʻôt bəYIŚRĀʼĒL bəhitnaddēv ʻām
bless YHWH! **hear**, O kings; **give** EAR, O PRINCES;	bārăkû YHWH šimʻû məlāKîm haʼĂZîNû rōZəNîm

I,   TO YHWH,
I,
I will sing!
I will MAKE MELODY TO YHWH,
               GOD of ISRAEL.
(Judg 5:2–3 my trans.)
	ʼĀNŌKî LAYHWH
	ʼĀNŌKî
	ʼāšîrâ
	ʼĂzammēr LAYHWH
	        ʼĔlōhê YIŚRĀʼĒL

Deborah begins to sing about the people volunteering for battle. She follows with three imperative verbs, the first a call for everyone to bless YHWH, who is the focus of her song, not unexpected from a prophet after the people have been saved by God in fulfillment of her prophecy. She repeats the term *YHWH* three times. Then, three times with the repetition of an "a" sound, she repeats her intention to sing unto YHWH. With a fourth initial "a" term ("I will make melody"), she completes a triplet soundplay with the "z" sound begun earlier, to emphasize the line: "Give ear, O princes.... I will make melody."

As intermediary with the deity, Deborah directly addresses YHWH in verses 4–6 and pictures YHWH's theophany and arrival on the scene, as at Sinai. She then shifts attention to the people's needs, the difficulty they had in passing through the land, presumably because of the enemy. Indeed, she says, travel by road had ceased "in days of Jael."

Just here, a male voice (understood to be Barak) interjects (v. 7) and employs four doublet soundplays to say that "deliverance" had also "ceased," "until you arose Deborah, arose a mother in Israel." *Mother* was likely used as a figurative title of respect for a female prophet, just as Elijah is called "father" by Elisha (2 Kgs 2:12).²³ Apparently Barak continues the singing from verses 9–12a, as he expresses exuberant gratitude to those who volunteered to fight, rather ironic and sanguine, since we know from the narrative that he did not initially willingly go to battle. Yet, he summons all the voices around to help recount the victory (vv. 10–11). He interrupts himself to appeal repeatedly to Deborah to "awake" and "sing," presumably to join in the retelling of his/their victory (v. 12a).²⁴

A call and response between Barak and Deborah ensues, as she responds to his appeal. With one line, ironically, she does not sing to recount this warrior's victory but calls him to "Get up, Barak, lead away [šăvēh] your captives [ševyəkā] , O son of Abinoam [ʾăvînōʿam]" (v. 12b, my translation). After what could be interpreted as her ironic dismissal, she falls silent, and Barak himself proceeds with the singing in verse 13, now recounting by himself those who marched down "for me" against the enemy. This is further irony, because the male warrior cannot get the female prophet to sing about him, for his honor and glory.²⁵

Another voice (understood to be male, using doublet soundplays) enjoins Barak's singing and describes the response of the Israelite tribes to the call to fight, referring to Deborah and Barak in third person (vv. 13–18). One can imagine the women standing around listening to the song unfold this way, knowing who the song *should* be about—Jael.

Meanwhile, Deborah, who knows how the victory was really won, turns away from the men's singing in order to describe instead (in vv. 20–22) other hidden battlefronts. With a striking series of twelve triplet soundplays, Deborah sings of a conscious, responsive Nature: the sky and

---

23. Jo Ann Hackett, "In the Days of Jael: Reclaiming the History of Women in Ancient Israel," in *Immaculate and Powerful: The Female in Sacred Image and Social Reality*, ed. Clarissa W. Atkinson, Constance H. Buchanan, and Margaret R. Miles (Boston: Beacon, 1985), 28.

24. Barak employs more than ten doublet soundplays in four verses (Lee, *Hannevi'ah and Hannah*, 88–111).

25. Poethig argues that the women's victory-song tradition was probably "a self-conscious women's movement aware of the social implications of the [songs] for women.... The theology is revolutionary because it extols liberation from the oppressive monarchies of the [ancient Near East]. It is doubly revolutionary because it was used by women to celebrate the victories won by women. In the later years of ... the exile, prophetic poets used Victory Song imagery to herald the new exodus of a redeemed people" (*Victory Song Tradition*, 8).

stars supplying a downpour of water;[26] the hurried motion of the little Wadi Kishon racing like a warrior, caused to surge by a force beyond itself, doing its part to take down the enemy chariots clogged in mud. Deborah sings of what no man had been able to do. Her lyrics are a countercultural statement, a defiant decision not to sing a victory song for male warriors but for YHWH—and for a woman.[27]

Deborah shifts the song-scene to the tent of Jael (with more triplet soundplays) and sings of what transpired there. Numerous commentators rightly discuss the ethical problem involved in the prophet's lyrics, which glorify one who took such a horrific action.[28] The problem is not resolved; it is perhaps tempered by Deborah's final lyrics, which imagine Sisera's mother ironically waiting for his return from battle, putting words in her mouth that he must be taking conquered women (likely raped) and bringing the spoil home to her.[29]

The lyrics of Judg 5 suggest a tradition of highly skilled women's composition, in spite of some repulsive content from the violent stories. The text suggests that Deborah follows in the footsteps of Miriam to compose and perform a song that innovates the victory song tradition, even transforms it from the male warrior-glorification culture into a praise song honoring YHWH. Their lyrics render instead the worldview of prophets in which God's power ends oppression. This gifted lyricizing is no small matter and surely confirms why these female prophets were remembered, elevated among others, and given a legacy.

The triplet sound pattern in the female voice of the song raises the question of whether the narrative of Judg 4 may also contain a similar pattern. Did women compose the story? Scholars have suggested that biblical narratives likely arose from oral epic or storytelling, such that the

---

26. Deborah's lyrics resonate with Canaanite myths of the warrior goddess Anat. See Susan Ackerman, *Warrior, Dancer, Seductress, Queen: Women in Judges and Biblical Israel* (New York: Doubleday, 1998), 27–88.

27. The song is an expression of resistance (Butting, *Prophetinnen gefragt*, 119; Poethig, *Victory Song Tradition*, 8).

28. Danna Nolan Fewell and David M. Gunn, "Controlling Perspectives: Women, Men, and the Authority of Violence in Judges 4 and 5," *JAAR* 58 (1990): 389–411.

29. Women are referred to as "wombs." Exum finds that women are being co-opted to serve male ideology in these lyrics. See Cheryl Exum, "Feminist Criticism: Whose Interests Are Being Served?," in *Judges and Method: New Approaches in Biblical Studies*, ed. Gale A. Yee (Minneapolis: Fortress, 1995), 65–90.

boundary is blurred between prose and poetry.³⁰ Even the opening of 4:1–3 is structured by triplet soundplays: three times *bənê yiśrā'ēl*; three times *YHWH*; and *wə'ēhûd, wəhû', wəhû'* ("Ehud ... and he ... and he"), the latter referring to Sisera's power in contrast to the dead Ehud. With a shift of focus to Deborah, the storyteller continues with at least ten triplet soundplays in just two verses:

[female narrator]		
Now **DEBORAH**,	a **WOMAN**	ûDəVÔRÂ 'iššâ
a **prophet**,	a **WOMAN** of flames,	nəvî'â 'ēšet lappîdôt
SHE was	**JUDGING**	**HÎ'** šōphəṭâ
	ISRAEL	'et-**YIŚRĀ'ĒL**
		bā'ēt
at **THAT**	**TIME.**	ha**HÎ'**
	SHE was **sitting** under the Palm	wə**HÎ'** yôševet taḥat-tōmer
of **DEBORAH, BETWEEN** **RAMAH**		**DəVÔRÂ BÊN** **H**A**R**āmâ
	AND Bethel	ûVÊN bêt-'ēl
	in the **HILLS** of Ephraim	bəhar 'ephrāyim
	and the **PEOPLE** of **ISRAEL**	wayya'ălû
	would **come up**	'ēlêhā
	to her	**B**ə**NÊ** **YIŚRĀ'ĒL**
	for **JUSTICE**.	lammišpāṭ
	(Judg 4:4–5 my trans.)	

Triplet soundplays are with *Dəvôrâ, nəvî'â* (a prophet), *Dəvôrâ*; with "a woman, a woman of flames, judging" (*'iššâ, 'ēšet lappîdôt, šōphəṭâ*); with "she, at that time, she" (*hî', hahî', hî'*); with "judging, sitting, for justice" (*šōphəṭâ, yôševet, mišpāṭ*). The storyteller continues using triplet soundplays throughout Judg 4.

What does this analysis suggest about female prophets in Israel? First, their rhetorical utterances are not isolated from the larger community of women and a tradition of women's professional composition.³¹ Second, female prophets could have their allies in the community of women, which appears to have produced a complementary story to the female prophet's

---

30. Susan Niditch, *Judges*, OTL (Louisville: Westminster John Knox, 2008), 14–18.

31. One may discern alternating triplet and doublet soundplays by antiphonal voices in the Song of the Sea in Exod 15 (Lee, *Hannevi'ah and Hannah*, 59–87).

song lyrics. Moreover, female prophets could have allies among men, who included them in the canon.

This leads to two additional questions: (1) Did female prophets utter judgment and salvation oracles as male prophets did? (2) If a triplet sound pattern is a kind of signature of women's composition, can it be used to locate female prophets' *unattributed* voices embedded in specific prophetic books? With these points in mind, we turn to the female prophet Huldah and her judgment oracle, and to the prophetic books of Micah and Second Isaiah.

4.2. Huldah

While Deborah appears near the beginning of the Former Prophets, the female prophet Huldah appears near the end of this corpus in one biblical setting in 2 Kgs 22:14–20, recounted in 2 Chr 34:22–28.[32] Huldah is identified as "wife of Shallum." She is said to be living, or seated (the verb can mean either—perhaps suggesting an official role for this female prophet) in the Mishneh or the Second Quarter of Jerusalem.

The setting is the late seventh century BCE when the high priest, Hilkiah, is said to find a scroll or book of the law in the temple. He and the scribe, Shaphan, need additional guidance about the book, as does the king of Judah. Therefore, Josiah sends his officials to inquire of a prophet about the words of the scroll.[33] Scholars regard the scroll as an edition of Deuteronomy, including its warnings about severe punishment for non-Yahwistic practice.

Interestingly, the narrative of 2 Kgs 22:3–20 does not say that the king sent the officials to Huldah by name, but her first reply to them is ironic, "Tell the man who sent you to me" (v. 15b)—not "Josiah," not "the king," but "the man." Huldah clearly speaks as one with authority (even above the king, as prophets called kings to account). Perhaps Huldah regards

---

32. A difference is that the Chronicler had Josiah destroy non-Yahwistic worship sites before finding the scroll; in 2 Kings, he destroys them afterward. This significant placement of the two female prophets in the former prophets is noted by Butting, *Prophetinnen Gefragt*, 99–100, and Fischer, *Gotteskünderinnen*, 185.

33. Hamori notes that even the religious officials needed a higher spiritual authority, a diviner (Huldah), with access to divine knowledge to validate the scroll. Huldah is the first person in the Bible to canonize a text: "It may be Josiah's reform, but it is Huldah's canon" (Hamori, *Women's Divination*, 152–53).

him as just another man in the kingdom, who is not to exalt himself above others (as stipulated in Deut 17:20, the very text that calls for the king to keep this book). In all this, the 2 Kings text, and likely the Deuteronomistic school, portray Huldah as standing in the tradition of Moses.[34] As was Deborah, Huldah is simply regarded with respect, that is, as God's prophet having authority.

On the other hand, the reception history about Huldah (beginning with the Talmud) belies the question of why she, a female prophet, is consulted by the king, and not the male prophet Jeremiah, her contemporary. One explanation was that Jeremiah was not available, as he was visiting the exiles, or, since women are more compassionate, the king purposefully consulted Huldah, hoping her response might be less harsh (see b. Meg. 14b). Contemporary commentators, perhaps sexist, continue to ask why Huldah was consulted, rather than simply accept her prophetic authority given straightforwardly by the Bible.

Of greater importance, though, is that here one finds the first attributed instance of a female prophet uttering a judgment oracle—in fact, two oracles.[35] The text of 2 Kgs 22:15b–20c includes Huldah's judgment oracle against the kingdom of Judah, and second, an oracle about the fate of King Josiah.

Though printed as prose, Huldah's oracles are lyrical. Her first utterance is marked by fourteen words, every one of which participates in four overlapping triplet soundplays. The emphases of the soundplays (v. 15) are to arrest the attention of the king: *kō-ʾāmar, ʾimrû, kō ʾāmar* (thus says the Lord/tell the man/thus says the Lord); *lāʾîš, ʾăšer-šālaḥ* (the man who sent); *ʾĕlōhê, ʾetkem, ʾēlāy* (God/you/to me). Huldah's next utterance (v. 16) announces the punishment, made emphatic by four more triplet soundplays: *mēvîʾ, māqôm, melek* (I am bringing/place/king); *rāʿâ, divrê, qārāʾ* (disaster/words/read); *ʾel, ʿal, kol* (against/upon/all); *hammāqôm, hazzeh, hassēpher* (the place/this/the book). Then Huldah utters God's words, indicting Judah, punctuated by ten triplet soundplays: *taḥat, wayqaṭ, ḥāmāt* (because/they offer/my anger); *ăzāvûnî, hakʿîsēnî, ḥămātî* (they abandoned me/they vex me/my anger); *lēʾlōhîm ʾăḥērîm, yĕdêhem* (to other gods/their hands).

---

34. Kessler, "Miriam and the Prophecy," 81, citing U. Rüterswörden (1995).

35. That is, unless one interprets Deborah's second oracle to Barak as a judgment oracle.

In Huldah's second oracle (vv. 18–20), God exonerates Josiah, since the king heard the words of the book, humbled himself regarding the wrongs, and aimed to remedy the situation. Again, YHWH utters a key triplet soundplay to Josiah about his contrite response: *šāmāʿtā, bəšomʿăkā, ʾānōkî šāmaʿtî* (you heard/when you heard/so I have heard you). Then, as if to demarcate the verdict to the king, YHWH interrupts the dominant pattern with doublets: "Behold, I will gather you [*hinnî ʾōsiphkā*] to your ancestors [*ʿal-ʾăvōtêkā*], and you shall be gathered [*wəneʾĕsaphtā*] to your grave [*ʾel-qivrōtêkā*] in peace" (v. 20a).[36]

4.3. False Prophets in Ezekiel 13:17–23

The prophet Ezekiel expresses oracles condemning both male and female false prophets. He opens Ezek 13 by indicting male prophets who "prophesy out of their own imagination … follow their own spirit" (vv. 2–3) and utter "falsehood" and "lying divinations" [*q-s-m*]; he says that "YHWH has not sent them" (v. 6) and that they "whitewash" the people's deed (v. 10). Ezekiel equally critiques female prophets ("the daughters of your people") who "prophesy out of their own imagination" (v. 17), who will no longer "see false visions or practice divination [*q-s-m*]" (v. 23). Their obscure practices are indicted because they also put people's lives at risk (vv. 18–22).[37]

---

36. Since Josiah later died in battle (2 Kgs 23:29–30), part of the prophecy was incorrect, though he did not see Jerusalem's destruction. Hamori suggests that the seeming mistake in Huldah's oracle was cleaned up by the Chronicler's later modification of Josiah's death—adding Neco's (divine) warning to Josiah to leave the battle, moving Josiah's death from Megiddo to Jerusalem, adding that he was buried with his fathers (Hamori, *Women's Divination*, 154–59).

37. Traditional interpreters often simply condemned the women in Ezek 13 as practicing outlawed sorcery or magic. Some recent interpreters disregard or temper Ezekiel's negative polemic and rather see the women positively as prophets. See, e.g., Nancy R. Bowen, "The Daughters of Your People: Female Prophets in Ezekiel 13:17–23," *JBL* 118 (1999): 417–33. Jonathan Stökl regards the women positively, but as technical diviners, not prophets. See Stökl, "The מתנבאות in Ezekiel 13 Reconsidered," *JBL* 132 (2013): 61–76. Lapsley notes the false female prophets also victimize the people for their own economic gain. See Jacqueline E. Lapsley, "Ezekiel," in *Women's Bible Commentary*, ed. Carol A. Newsom, Sharon H. Ringe, and Jacqueline E. Lapsley, 3rd ed. (Louisville: Westminster John Knox, 2012), 287.

4.4. Female Prophets in the Book of Micah and in Second Isaiah?

Scholars increasingly suggest that female prophets' utterances may be embedded in the prophetic books. The challenge has been how to find or discern them. One of the texts under consideration is Mic 7:1–10, because it includes a woman's voice (vv. 8–10).[38] Most commentators regard the woman as a personification of the city of Jerusalem. However, since no references to a city are found in close proximity, some scholars have suggested the possibility of a female prophet here.[39] That another female prophet might be active in the eighth century is not surprising, as Micah of Moresheth (in Judah, not too far from Jerusalem) was a contemporary of Isaiah, who partnered with *hannĕvî'â*. Moreover, Mic 6:4 refers in a very egalitarian way to the legacy of Miriam by name, along with Moses and Aaron, as prophetic leaders of the past. Are there any other indications in the Mic 7 text of the presence of a female prophet than a gendered voice?

The voice that opens Mic 7 expresses a personal lament, "Woe is me! For I am like the gatherer of summer fruit [*qayiṣ*] … (but) there is no cluster to eat!" The term *gatherer* is a feminine participle in the LXX. The imagery echoes God's question to another prophet, Amos: "What do you see?" He answers, "*qayiṣ*"—a basket of summer fruit. In a wordplay, God responds, "the *qēṣ* ['end'] has come upon my people Israel" (Amos 8:1–2).

The voice in Mic 7 goes on to describe the rampant violence and corruption of officials, of broken trust in all human relationships, including women's.[40] Triplet soundplays permeate her lines. In verse 4 she says: "the day of your sentinels … has come." In numerous biblical texts, the term "sentinel" (*məṣappeh*, from "to watch," *ṣāpāh*) is a metaphor for a prophet (Hos 9:8; Isa 21:6; 52:8; Jer 6:17; Ezek 3:17; 33:1–6; Hab 2:1). The prophet was God's sentinel, holding watch over a city or nation, often bringing dire news to warn the people. It is highly significant, then, that this same voice in verse 7 next uses this verb to refer to her action: "But I, for the Lord, I

---

38. The authorship and context of Mic 6 and 7 are inconclusive; some scholars think they originate from the time of Micah; some others argue that they are from a later period.

39. Gruber also laments "the tendency to ignore female voices by turning them into personifications." See Mayer I. Gruber, "Women's Voices in the Book of Micah," *lectio difficilior* 1 (2007): https://tinyurl.com/SBL6016d; Lee, *Hannevi'ah and Hannah*, 35–56.

40. Gruber notes her "gender-matched synonymous parallelism" in 7:5–6 ("Women's Voices").

will *watch* (as a sentinel) [*'ăṣappeh*]." That this is a female speaker is further corroborated by the feminine grammar in the lines where she quotes her enemy as speaking against her in verse 10.[41]

A number of scholars have suggested that a female prophet or prophets are possibly embedded in Isa 40–66.[42] Those responsible for these chapters, which are dated to the exilic period or later, long after Isaiah of the eighth century, are anonymous. Moreover, several texts contain strikingly unusual female imagery for God, such as God as mother.[43] A key text considered by some scholars as possibly including the voice of a female prophet is Isa 40, with its feminine noun *məbaśśeret* ("herald of good tidings;" 40:9).[44] As with the Mic 7 text, traditional interpretation has regarded her as a personification of Zion/Jerusalem, thus the usual translation:

> Get you up to a high mountain
> O Zion, herald of good tidings [*məbaśśeret*];
> lift up your voice with strength,
> O Jerusalem, herald of good tidings,
> lift it up, do not fear;
> say to the cities of Judah,
> "Here is your God!" (40:9)

It is important to consider the literary context of Isa 40:9. Just before it, the response of another discouraged prophetic voice in verses 6–7, when

---

41. Thus, Gruber's assessment of a persecuted female prophet is on target here ("Women's Voices").

42. See James Newsome, *The Hebrew Prophets* (Atlanta: John Knox, 1984), 142; Bebb Wheeler Stone, "Second Isaiah: Prophet to Patriarchy," *JSOT* 56 (1992): 85–99; Steve McEvenue, "Who Was Second Isaiah?," in *Studies in the Book of Isaiah: Festschrift Willem A. M. Beuken* (Leuven: Leuven University Press, 1997), 213–22; Lee, *Hannevi'ah and Hannah*, 156–82.

43. For the idea that Isa 42:14–16 and 49:13–21 were composed possibly by female prophets, see Lee, "Women's Voices," 178–81. In this volume, see Hanne Løland Levinson, "The Never-Ending Search for God's Feminine Side: Feminine Aspects in the God-Image of the Prophets."

44. For recent comments, see John Goldingay and David Payne, *A Critical and Exegetical Commentary on Isaiah 40–55*, ICC (London: T&T Clark, 2006), 44–49; Lena-Sofia Tiemeyer, *For the Comfort of Zion: The Geographical and Theological Location of Isaiah 40–55*, VTSup 139 (Leiden: Brill, 2011), 17–18, 29–30, 279–85; Lee, *Hannevi'ah and Hannah*, 156–68.

asked to cry out, says, "What shall I cry? All flesh is grass that withers, because the breath of YHWH has blown against it." This discouraged voice expresses futility after God's destroying punishment. It is to this discouraged voice that the voice of verse 9 says (retranslating): "Upon a lofty mountain, go up, O woman-herald to Zion; raise with power your voice, O woman-herald to Jerusalem—raise it, have no fear; announce to the cities of Judah: See your God!" This prophetic voice encourages a discouraged prophet, in this reading, to announce an oracle of salvation that God is here, bringing home the exiles, restoring the city and nation. These texts open the possibility of a female prophet called on to announce an oracle of salvation after decades of trauma and near hopelessness.

5. Conclusion: Female Prophets—Past, Present, and Future (Joel 2:28–29)

Usually dated to the Second Temple period (fifth century) in Jerusalem, Joel's oracles include a call to lament (Joel 1);[45] announcement of the day of the Lord, a call to return to the Lord, a salvation oracle (Joel 2); and judgments against the nations (Joel 3). Beyond the present salvation, God promises a remarkable action and continued affirmation of female prophets along with men:

> Then afterward
>   I will pour out my spirit on all flesh;
> your sons and your daughters shall prophesy,
>   your old men shall dream dreams,
> and your young men shall see visions.
>   Even on the male and female slaves,
> in those days, I will pour out my spirit. (Joel 2:28–29)

Notably, Luke cites this text in Peter's speech to explain the outpouring of inspired words by the people in his first-century portrayal of Pentecost (Acts 2:17–18).

In conclusion, as this review shows, in biblical times, female prophets—recognized also as having the highest calling by God to society—were well-attested in the Nevi'im and in all sections of the Bible.

---

45. Claassens notes that the practice of lament, in this case, from the traumas of a devastating locust plague, drought, and the ever-present threat of war, relied especially on women's leadership. See L. Juliana Claassens, "Joel," in Newsom, Ringe, and Lapsley, *Women's Bible Commentary*, 310. Joel is identified as the son of Pethuel (Joel 1:1).

Bibliography

Ackerman, Susan. *Warrior, Dancer, Seductress, Queen: Women in Judges and Biblical Israel.* New York: Doubleday, 1998.

Bachmann, Mercedes García. "Miriam, Primordial Political Figure in the Exodus." Pages 329–74 in *Torah.* Vol. 1 of *The Bible and Women: An Encyclopaedia of Exegesis and Cultural History.* Edited by Irmtraud Fischer and Mercedes Navarro Puerto. Atlanta: Society of Biblical Literature, 2011.

Bal, Mieke. *Death and Dissymmetry: The Politics of Coherence in the Book of Judges.* Chicago: University of Chicago Press, 1988.

Bowen, Nancy R. "The Daughters of Your People: Female Prophets in Ezekiel 13:17–23." *JBL* 118 (1999): 417–33.

Brenner, Athalya. *The Israelite Woman: Social Role and Literary Type in Biblical Narrative.* Sheffield: Sheffield Academic, 1985.

Brenner, Athalya, and Fokkelien van Dijk-Hemmes. *On Gendering Texts: Female and Male Voices in the Hebrew Bible.* BibInt 1. Leiden: Brill, 1993.

Brison, Ora. "Jael, *'eshet heber* the Kenite: A Diviner?" Pages 139–60 in *Joshua and Judges.* Edited by Athalya Brenner and Gale A. Yee. TC. Minneapolis: Fortress, 2013.

———. "The Medium of En-dor (אשת בעלת אוב) and the Phenomenon of Divination in Twenty-First Century Israel." Pages 124–47 in *Samuel, Kings, and Chronicles.* Edited by Athalya Brenner and Archie C. C. Lee. TC. London: Bloomsbury T&T Clark, 2016.

Burns, Rita J. *Has the Lord Indeed Spoken Only through Moses? A Study of the Biblical Portrait of Miriam.* SBLDS 84. Atlanta: Scholars Press, 1987.

Butting, Klara. *Prophetinnen Gefragt: Die Bedeutung der Prophetinnen im Kanon aus Tora und Prophetie.* BfT 3. Knesebeck: Erev-Rav, 2001.

Claassens, L. Juliana. "Joel." Pages 309–11 in *Women's Bible Commentary.* 3rd ed. Edited by Carol A. Newsom, Sharon H. Ringe, and Jacqueline E. Lapsley. Louisville: Westminster John Knox, 2012.

Dijk-Hemmes, Fokkelien van. "Mothers and a Mediator in the Song of Deborah." Pages 110–14 in *A Feminist Companion to Judges.* Edited by Athalya Brenner. FCB 4. Sheffield: JSOT Press, 1993.

El Azhary Sonbol, Amira. *Beyond the Exotic: Women's Histories in Islamic Societies.* Syracuse, NY: Syracuse University Press, 2005.

Exum, J. Cheryl. "Feminist Criticism: Whose Interests Are Being Served?" Pages 65–90 in *Judges and Method: New Approaches in Biblical Studies*. Edited by Gale A. Yee. Minneapolis: Fortress, 1995.

Fewell, Danna Nolan, and David M. Gunn. "Controlling Perspectives: Women, Men, and the Authority of Violence in Judges 4 and 5." *JAAR* 58 (1990): 389–411.

Fischer, Irmtraud. *Gotteskünderinnen: Zu einer Geschlechterfairen Deutung des Phänomens der Prophetie und der Prophetinnen in der Hebräischen Bibel*. Stuttgart: Kohlhammer, 2002.

Gafney, Wilda. *Daughters of Miriam: Women Prophets in Ancient Israel*. Minneapolis: Fortress, 2008.

Goitein, Shlomo D. "Women as Creators of Biblical Genres." *Prooftexts* 8 (1988): 1–33.

Goldingay, John, and David Payne. *A Critical and Exegetical Commentary on Isaiah 40–55*. ICC. London: T&T Clark, 2006.

Gruber, Mayer. "Women's Voices in the Book of Micah." *Id* 1 (2007). https://tinyurl.com/SBL6016d.

Hackett, Jo Ann. "In the Days of Jael: Reclaiming the History of Women in Ancient Israel." Pages 15–38 in *Immaculate and Powerful: The Female in Sacred Image and Social Reality*. Edited by Clarissa W. Atkinson, Constance H. Buchanan, and Margaret R. Miles. Boston: Beacon, 1985.

Hamori, Esther. *Women's Divination in Biblical Literature: Prophecy, Necromancy, and Other Arts of Knowledge*. New Haven: Yale University Press, 2015.

Kessler, Rainer. "Miriam and the Prophecy of the Persian Period." Pages 64–72 in *A Feminist Companion to Prophets and Daniel*. Edited by Athalya Brenner. FCB 2/8. London: Sheffield Academic, 2001.

Lapsley, Jacqueline E. "Ezekiel." Pages 283–92 in *Women's Bible Commentary*. Edited by Carol A. Newsom, Sharon H. Ringe, and Jacqueline E. Lapsley. 3rd ed. Louisville: Westminster John Knox, 2012.

Lee, Nancy C. *Hannevi'ah and Hannah: Hearing Women Biblical Prophets in a Women's Lyrical Tradition*. Eugene, OR: Wipf & Stock, 2015.

McEvenue, Steve. "Who Was Second Isaiah?" Pages 213–22 in *Studies in the Book of Isaiah: Festschrift Willem A. M. Beuken*. Leuven: Leuven University Press, 1997.

Meyers, Carol. "Archaeology: A Window to the Lives of Israelite Women." Pages 61–108 in *Torah*. Edited by Irmtraud Fischer and Mercedes Navarro Puerto. BW 1. Atlanta: Society of Biblical Literature, 2011.

———. *Discovering Eve: Ancient Israelite Women in Context.* Oxford: Oxford University Press, 1988.
Newsome, James. *The Hebrew Prophets.* Atlanta: John Knox, 1984.
Niditch, Susan. *Judges.* OTL. Louisville: Westminster John Knox, 2008.
Poethig, Eunice B. "The Victory Song Tradition of the Women of Israel." PhD diss., Union Theological Seminary, 1985.
Stökl, Jonathan. "The מתנבאות in Ezekiel 13 Reconsidered." *JBL* 132 (2013): 61–76.
Stone, Bebb Wheeler. "Second Isaiah: Prophet to Patriarchy." *JSOT* 56 (1992): 85–99.
Tiemeyer, Lena-Sofia. *For the Comfort of Zion: The Geographical and Theological Location of Isaiah 40–55.* VTSup 139. Leiden: Brill, 2011.

Profiles of Resistant Women in the Former Prophets

Rainer Kessler

1. Introduction

In the texts of the Former Prophets, we encounter, as is well known, many female figures. A not inconsiderable number of them are distinguished by the fact that one can assign to them the attribute *resistant*. Accordingly, there is no need to justify talking about resistant women in the Former Prophets in the series The Bible and Women.

But, why do I not speak simply about resistant women in the Former Prophets? What is meant by *profiles* of resistant women? At this point, I already anticipate the outcome of my study. The point is that there is not just one type of female resistance in the Former Prophets, but rather a variety of types. One also could speak of silhouettes, as Uta Schmidt has done in her narratological study of the portrayal of women in the books of Kings.[1] Whether we speak of silhouettes or of profiles, what is always meant is that the individual narratives can be grouped or clustered according to certain common features in the characterization of the women in question.

Altogether, I have identified five such profiles. But, since profiles of this kind, or silhouettes/clusters, do not have any sharp contours, fluent transitions between them exist, and other groupings would also certainly be conceivable.

---

1. Uta Schmidt, *Zentrale Randfiguren: Strukturen der Darstellung von Frauen in den Erzählungen der Königebücher* (Gütersloh: Chr. Kaiser; Gütersloher Verlagshaus, 2003).

2. Women as Victims of Sexual Violence

The books of the Former Prophets contain several narratives in which women become the victims of patriarchal power structures. They experience what befalls them in various feminine roles. Jephthah's daughter (Judg 11:29–40) remains nameless and, as the daughter of her father, becomes a victim. That she shows any resistance toward her father, who in the end offers her up as a burnt sacrifice (vv. 31, 39), is not reported.[2] Rather, her speech sounds as if she consents to it. Cheryl Exum comments succinctly, "The daughter submits to the authority of the father."[3] Nevertheless, the portrayal shows that Jephthah's daughter, in spite of her fundamental submission to the authority of her father, increasingly seizes the initiative and thus, in spite of her namelessness, develops into the main character in the narrative.[4] Even if the daughter "always remains a victim," she is "drawn as the real heroine of the narrative."[5] For this reason, Walter Groß describes this narrative as "one of the narratives about a strong woman that accumulate astonishingly in the Book of Judges,"[6] although the woman in it becomes the victim.

The wife of the Levite, who is handed over to the rapists by her husband in the Benjaminite Gibeah, is raped until she is (almost?) dead,[7] and subsequently is dismembered by her husband (Judg 19), is likewise nameless and portrayed as a concubine—אשה פילגש, or only פילגש (vv. 1–2, 9–10, 24–25, 27, 29)—of her master, אדון (vv. 26–27). Throughout the whole narrative, she is depicted as an object of male negotiations.[8]

---

2. See Phyllis Trible, *Texts of Terror: Literary-Feminist Readings of Biblical Narratives* (Philadelphia: Fortress, 1985), 102.

3. J. Cheryl Exum, "Murder They Wrote: Ideology and the Manipulation of Female Presence in Biblical Narrative," in *Telling Queen Michal's Story: An Experiment in Comparative Interpretation*, ed. David J. A. Clines and Tamara Cohn Eskenazi, JSOTSup 119 (Sheffield: JSOT Press, 1991), 181.

4. See Walter Groß, *Richter*, HThKAT (Freiburg: Herder, 2009), 603, 610.

5. Michaela Bauks, *Jephtas Tochter: Traditions-, religions- und rezeptionsgeschichtliche Studien zu Richter 11,29–40*, FAT 71 (Tübingen: Mohr Siebeck, 2010), 21, 59.

6. Groß, *Richter*, 610.

7. The formulation in the Hebrew text leaves open the question whether the woman was already dead after the continued rape. It is first of all the Greek text that clarifies matters by declaring that the woman was dead (see Trible, *Texts of Terror*, 79).

8. See Groß: "From (24) 25 on, everything is designed to make the mute concubine more and more comprehensively the mere object of negotiations carried out by the men; the endpoint in v. 29 is also the low point of this development" (*Richter*, 844).

Whether she was resistant or acquiescent in her actions when thrown to her rapists, we do not know.

The narrative about the rape in Gibeah opens with the sentence: "In those days, when there was no king in Israel" (v. 1). This is intended to suggest that only a king can provide law and order. The monarchy emerges—and now rape takes place within the royal family itself, in the narrative about the rape of Tamar by her half-brother Amnon (2 Sam 13). Here, the victim offers resistance, though not bodily, since she then would have been physically subdued. But she attempts to dissuade the offender to desist from his act with words. Also, after the act, she makes a suggestion that, to be sure, would not have been able to undo the deed, but at least would have prevented the complete social annihilation of the victim. Ilse Müllner remarks correctly in her article "Tamar," in the *Wissenschaftlichem Bibellexikon im Internet*, that "Tamar's verbal resistance is, in comparison with other narratives about sexual violence, extraordinary." Here she refers to the rape of Dinah in Gen 34 and the narrative from Judg 19 just mentioned above: "Therein, she is portrayed as a clever and farsighted woman whose arguments are supported by the narrative community. Thus, the suggestion of marriage made to Amnon also is to be taken seriously."[9] Of course, we know from the narrative that Tamar is not heard.

Thus we have three women who as victims offer no resistance, about whose possible resistance we hear nothing, or whose verbal resistance remains unsuccessful. This is the first profile identified here.

3. Wicked Women

In contrast to the figures considered above, two other women can also be identified as victims, but they offer fierce resistance. These two women are Queen Jezebel and Queen Athaliah. Jezebel, the daughter of the Phoenician king of Sidon, is married to Ahab, the king of Israel (1 Kgs 16:31). The tradition portrays her from the beginning as a wicked woman. She murders the prophetesses and prophets of YHWH (1 Kgs 18:4, 13; 2 Kgs 9:7), supports the prophets of Baal and Asherah (1 Kgs 18:19), and persecutes the prophet Elijah (1 Kgs 19:1–2). She organizes, on behalf of her husband,

---

9. Ilse Müllner, "Tamar," in *Das wissenschaftliche Bibellexikon im Internet* (2009), https://tinyurl.com/SBL6016e. On the narrative about Tamar and Amnon as a whole, see Ilse Müllner, *Gewalt im Hause Davids: Die Erzählung von Tamar und Amnon (2 Sam 13,1–22)*, HBS 13 (Freiburg: Herder, 1997).

the judicial murder of the honorable vineyard owner Naboth (1 Kgs 21). She also incites King Ahab to commit every wicked act (1 Kgs 21:25).

After the officer Jehu revolts against the governing royal house of the Omrides, he orders that Jezebel be murdered (2 Kgs 9:30–37). In Schmidt's narratological analysis, she is described as the silhouette of a "powerful woman."[10] When her murderer, Jehu, appears in Jezreel, Jezebel faces him proudly and courageously. Unlike the kings of Israel and Judah, who fled before Jehu and who were murdered as they fled (2 Kgs 9:20–29), Jezebel looks her enemy in the eye. With the only words allowed her by the narrator, she accuses Jehu of being a murderer. By comparing him with the murderer Zimri, who shortly afterward is himself killed (1 Kgs 16:8–20), she depicts Jehu at the same time as a loser. Although she becomes a victim because she succumbs in the power struggle with Jehu, and her corpse is eaten by dogs, she dies as a proud, courageous, and resistant woman.

Nevertheless, Jezebel does not stand a chance in the narrative. She is portrayed from the beginning as wicked, and the narrative about her murder is told in such a way that she is finally to blame for her own death. Schmidt points out that the negative interpretations of Jezebel's conduct ensue at the point where she paints her face and adorns her head.[11] She compares Jezebel with the depiction of various feminine figures that represent cities and shows that "the painting of her face and her efforts to make herself beautiful becomes sexually motivated and so becomes a reprehensible act, through which she makes herself guilty of the violent murder committed by Jehu."[12]

Her sister-in-law Athaliah, who is married to the king of Judah and assumes the throne after his murder by Jehu (2 Kgs 8:26; 11), suffers a fate similar to that of Jezebel, not only in the narrated reality but also in the manner of the narration. She also is portrayed from the beginning as the wicked woman who plots the murder of all the eligible heirs to the throne. She, too, is overthrown in a rebellion, conducted this time not by the military but rather by the priests. She, too, is murdered by the rebels and also does not surrender passively to her fate. But in the narrative, as in the case of Jezebel, not a single tear is shed over Athaliah. The narrative ends with the words, "So all the people of the land rejoiced; and the city was quiet

---

10. Schmidt, *Zentrale Randfiguren*, 138–96.
11. Schmidt, *Zentrale Randfiguren*, 146.
12. Schmidt, *Zentrale Randfiguren*, 148.

after Athaliah had been killed with the sword at the king's house" (2 Kgs 11:20 RSV).

In Jezebel and Athaliah, therefore, we encounter two women who also become victims, but who strongly resist their fate. In the narrative, they are described from the beginning as wicked. Theirs, in the end, is a futile attempt to resist the fate that, according to the narrative strategy, rightly befalls them.

4. Women Who Support Future Victors

In contrast to Jezebel and Athaliah, three other women, whom I place under a third profile, are valued positively for their resistance. They all resist a government that at the time exercises power over them. At the same time, they take sides with an important figure who later usurped the old authority.

The first example is Rahab from Jericho. The king of Jericho learns that Israelite scouts have spent the night in her house and demands that she deliver up these men (Josh 2:1–3). She, however, hides the men, lies to the king's messengers, and sends the pursuers on a false trail (vv. 4–7). In this way, she mounts resistance against the authority to which she is subject. She justifies her behavior toward the Israelite spies by pointing out that YHWH has already given them the land in any case, and no one could resist that fact (vv. 9–11). Her real concern, however, is different, as the term that introduces her speech ועתה ("and now") in verse 12 shows. Rahab seeks guarantee that she and her family will be spared after the anticipated conquest of Jericho (vv. 12–13).[13] The men promise her safety, and Rahab helps them to escape from Jericho. When Jericho is captured later and all the city's substance is dedicated to destruction (the so-called ban), Rahab with her family is spared. Thus, she is said to live in the midst of Israel "to this day" (Josh 6:25). In the genealogy of Jesus in Matt 1, she is described as the mother of Boaz, the husband of Ruth, and in essence the great-great-grandmother of King David (Matt 1:6–7).

---

13. See José Luis Sicre, *Josué*, NBE (Estella: Editorial Verbo Divino, 2002), 113: "En el fondo, la confesión de fe es una extensa introducción a lo que realmente pretende Rajab: salir con vida ella y su familia (vv. 12–13)" ("Basically, the confession of faith is a detailed introduction to what Rahab really wants: that she and her family escape with their lives").

In spite of this positive afterlife, it should be noted that Rahab, as a non-Israelite, is a woman who already foresees who the victors will be and aligns herself with them in order to save her skin. This point can be considered critically from a postcolonial perspective. In this regard, Musa Dube speaks about "collaboration with the colonizer." Thus, the positive assessment of Rahab by the narrative voice suggests that Rahab does not have power over her own story, which is written by the oppressors in order to highlight Rahab's concern and to justify their conquest of her land. In Dube's words: "Rahab's story is not her own—it is written by her oppressors to project their own agendas as well as to validate the conquest."[14]

A second example of this type of resistance is found in Michal, the daughter of Saul, who becomes David's wife (1 Sam 18:27). When her father decides to have David killed, Michal helps him to flee. She then lies first to the messengers of her father, Saul, who have come to arrest David, and then to her father by claiming that her husband has used violence to force her to act in the way she has done (1 Sam 19:11–17).

One can argue about Michal's motives. The narrative says explicitly that Michal loves David (1 Sam 18:20; see v. 28) and for this reason desires to marry him. This is the only place in the Hebrew Bible where a woman desires to marry a man.[15] But she is not alone in her love for David. Jonathan also loves David as much as he does his own life (v. 1), and all of Israel and Judah love David (v. 16). It is the love for a future victor. From chapters 15 and 16, where Saul is first rejected and David is then anointed, it is clear that Saul's time has run out. It is thus at least not inopportune that Michal takes the side of David, the future ruler, against her father, the ruling king.

As far as the emotional side of the love relationship goes, one must also say that Michal is treated rather shabbily by David. After his flight from Saul's court, he meets, of course secretly, with Saul's son Jonathan (ch. 20), but not with his wife Michal. Although he later brings back Michal, who in the meantime is now married to another man (1 Sam 25:44), it is not out of love for her. Rather, it is to demonstrate his claim to power over the family of Saul (2 Sam 3:12–16). After these things, the final rift between Michal and David occurs quickly (2 Sam 6:16, 20–23).

---

14. Musa W. Dube, *Postcolonial Feminist Interpretation of the Bible* (Saint Louis, MO: Chalice, 2000), 142–43.

15. See Robert Alter, "Characterization and the Art of Reticence (from *The Art of Biblical Narrative*)," in Clines and Eskenazi, *Telling Queen Michal's Story*, 68.

Here it is important to observe the narrative subtlety in how Michal is described through the men who have authority over her. She is the "daughter of Saul" before her marriage with David (1 Sam 18:20, 27). Afterward, she is called "his wife," that is, David's wife. But since the marriage is practically not functional from David's side after his flight, we read that Saul hands over "his daughter Michal, the wife of David" to another man (1 Sam 25:44). When David reclaims her for political reasons, he calls her at first "the daughter of Saul" (2 Sam 3:13), but then, in order to underscore his claim, "my wife" (v. 14). However, when the final rift occurs, Michal again is called the "daughter of Saul" by the narrative voice (6:16, 20). At the point when David finally rejects her, she still remains the daughter of the king whom she once opposed. In the words of David Clines: "Michal is not behaving as David's wife ... but as his opponent; she is acting like a true daughter of Saul, and the narrator has spelled this out by writing 'Michal, daughter of Saul' in two places where her criticism of David is expressed."[16]

The third example also tells of a woman who places herself early on the side of David. This woman is Abigail, the wife of Nabal (1 Sam 25:3), who challenges David and provokes him to undertake a violent reaction. In order to avoid a bloodbath, she goes out to David's men without telling her husband about it (v. 19). In a speech directed at David, she distances herself from her husband, calls him a blockhead, and claims to have known nothing about David's earlier delegation (v. 25). She announces to David in a prophetic manner—long before the famous prophecy by Nathan (2 Sam 7)[17]—that YHWH will prepare an enduring house, that is, a lasting dynasty for him (1 Sam 25:28). Consequently, David desists from his plans of revenge. Once back at home, Abigail reports what happened to her husband Nabal, who collapses and dies (vv. 36–38). The way is then free for Abigail to become the wife of the future king and founder of the dynasty (vv. 39–42).

Unlike the case of Michal, there is no report of a rift between Abigail and David. Abigail continues to be mentioned as one of the wives of

---

16. David J. A. Clines, "X, X *ben* Y, *ben* Y: Personal Names in Hebrew Narrative Style," in Clines and Eskenazi, *Telling Queen Michal's Story*, 128.

17. The link between the dynastic promises made to David by Abigail and by Nathan has been treated in detail by Irmtraud Fischer. See Fischer, *Gotteslehrerinnen: Weise Frauen und Frau Weisheit im Alten Testament* (Stuttgart: Kohlhammer, 2006), 31–36.

David (1 Sam 27:3; 30:5; 2 Sam 2:2). That she plays no further role in the story could be because her son Chileab, whom she had for David (2 Sam 3:3), died early.[18] In any case, he, unlike other sons of David, as well as his mother, is no longer mentioned.

The discussion above has focused on three women who offer resistance—Rahab to her king, Michal to her father, Abigail to her husband. It is reasonable to bring together in one profile the three women who, at an early stage, already place themselves on the side of future victors. The fate of these women is different in each case. Rahab is saved along with her family, Michal's relationship with David breaks down, and Abigail is lost in history. As important as each of their roles is in the narrated story, all of them still act in their own interest. They are not leadership figures in their communities. This leads us to the next profile.

5. Women as Leaders of Their Community

Other women who offer resistance do this in the interest of their communities. The judge Deborah falls in this category (Judg 4–5). Following the plot of the book of Judges, she appears when her people are in great crisis. The crisis was caused by the Canaanite king Jabin and his military commander Sisera. Deborah, who is introduced as a prophetess and a judge, organizes the armed resistance. She calls on the Naphtalite Barak to marshal an army and marches with him to the scene of the events (Judg 4:1–9). Irmtraud Fischer demonstrates how, in this scene, Barak "is presented from the beginning as dependent upon her (scil. Deborah)." He objects to being called to be the leader of the troops and will agree only if Deborah comes along. Thus, "Deborah has the discursive dominance in regard to Barak." His decision depends on the prophetess. Therefore, the latter informs him that the credit of the victory will in the end be given to a woman (4:9), which means reference already is made to Jael, to whom we will return shortly. Before the battle, Deborah announces the victory (v. 14). Therefore, she assumes in a certain sense the leadership of the battle;[19]

---

18. Alternatively, Fischer, *Gotteslehrerinnen*, 26, argues "that the narrative was inserted into the context only later and for this reason no longer could be more closely connected with the course of action."

19. Irmtraud Fischer, *Gotteskünderinnen: Zu einer geschlechterfairen Deutung des Phänomens der Prophetie und der Prophetinnen in der Hebräischen Bibel* (Stuttgart: Kohlhammer, 2002), 113, 115.

so does the narrative report in chapter 4. In the subsequent song, Deborah praises herself as a "mother in Israel." Her presence ends the time of need in Israel (5:6–7).

While Deborah makes her appearance solely as a leader of the tribes of Israel, it is somewhat different in the case of Jael, whose narrative is woven into that about Jabin and Sisera. She is a part of the overall story insofar as she kills the fleeing commander Sisera. But she also is designated explicitly as the wife of a Kenite, that is, as a non-Israelite woman (4:17; 5:24). According to Judg 4:17, a peace treaty exists between the house of her husband, Heber, and King Jabin. In that Jael kills Jabin's military commander, she can be assigned, on the one hand, to the profile of resistant women who, at the right time, place themselves on the side of the victors. In this, she resembles Rahab in a certain sense. On the other hand, the conclusion of Deborah's song contains clear allusions to the fact that Jael, with her killing of Sisera, escapes rape and abduction[20]—one should note here the expression that Sisera fell "between her feet" (5:27), and the expectation of Sisera's mother that the victorious men would bring home mothers' laps as spoil (5:30). Then, Jael would have belonged to the first profile of women as victims and would lend it a completely different course. She then would be a woman who avoided being a victim, which would have been her fate, by killing the offender. In any case, Jael is one of the resistant women here who cannot be assigned to just a single profile.

Likewise, two women are mentioned in warlike contexts who remain unnamed and, for this reason, are designated according to their places of origin. The first is the woman of Thebez (Judg 9:50–57). In the siege against her city, Thebez, by Abimelech of Shechem, all the people flee to a fortified tower. When Abimelech comes up close to the tower in order to set it on fire, this courageous woman crushes the skull of the attacker with a millstone that she throws down on him. The incident became so legendary that it was still recalled in David's time (2 Sam 11:21).

Less heroic, but definitely wise in the interest of her community, is the conduct of the woman from Abel Beth-Maacah (2 Sam 20:14–22). Her city, too, is besieged because a rebel, who already has been defeated, takes refuge in it. The wise woman (v. 16), however, does not throw down a millstone. Rather, she persuades her community to behead the man in flight

---

20. On the erotic foundation of the Jael-Sisera episode, see Yair Zakovitch, "Sisseras Tod," *ZAW* 93 (1981): 364–74.

and to throw his head over the wall, whereupon the siege is lifted. That may not be very pleasant, but it is effective, and it saves the city from siege and destruction.[21]

Among the women who offer resistance in the interest of their community, Delilah also should be counted. Her resistance, to be sure, is directed against the Israelite hero Samson, for which reason she, as a Philistine woman, does not come off well in the narrative (Judg 16:4–22). She is suspected of acting only in order to rake in the enormous sum of money offered to her (16:5, 18). But, evidently, she is the only one among the Philistine people who is in a position to conquer the hero. Her resistance is successful, even if also not permanent.

The large number of women who singlehandedly offer resistance in the interest of their communities is remarkable. The narrative course in the Former Prophets cannot be imagined without them. Yet, their profile covers a broad spectrum—from the prophetess, judge, and "mother in Israel" Deborah to the Philistine woman Delilah. In brief, I would like to lift up two women from this broad spectrum whom I would like to assign to a profile called "Women Fighting for Their Rights."

6. Women Fighting for Their Rights

The books of Samuel are framed by two narratives in which resistant women play a central role. These are the Hannah and Rizpah narratives.

One can ask, To what extent Hannah is a resistant woman? She does not ward off any rape, she does not act in the interest of the community, and she does not engage in any combat operations. Nevertheless, she is resistant because she does not resign herself to fate. She fights for her rights and stands against every form of obstacle. She fights against, in the sense of the title of a well-known opera, *The Power of Fate* (*La forza del destino*). In the opening of the narrative, it is mentioned three times that

---

21. Silvia Schroer shows that moral reservations toward the woman are to be found only in Christian exegesis and that "Jewish exegesis has viewed the woman from Abel consistently in a fully positive way." In addition, she notes, "The biblical authors clearly have depicted the woman from Abel positively." See Schroer, "Die weise Frau auf der Stadtmauer von Abel-bet-Maacha (2 Sam 20,14–22)," in *Seitenblicke: Literarische und historische Studien zu Nebenfiguren im zweiten Samuelbuch*, ed. Walter Dietrich, OBO 249 (Fribourg: Academic Press; Göttingen: Vandenhoeck & Ruprecht, 2011), 394–95.

she is childless (1 Sam 1:2, 5–6). She must endure the insults of her husband's second wife, who does have children (v. 6). Her husband loves and comforts her, saying, "Am I not better for you than ten sons?" (v. 8), but this means nothing to her. When she seizes the initiative and prays in the temple, the priest thinks she is drunk (vv. 12–15).

In my view, Hannah is belittled by the translators of the Bible. To Eli's charge that she is drunk, she replies: "No, my lord, I am a אשה קשת־רוח" (v. 15). This means, literally, "a woman hard and firm in the spirit." The Vulgate renders this as a "mulier infelix nimis," a "very unhappy woman." In Luther's translation of 1545, she is "an anguished woman," and in the King James Version "a woman of sorrowful spirit." The NRSV reads "a woman deeply troubled." Why should a woman who is hard or firm in the spirit be regarded as sorrowful, distraught, or unhappy? However, Oswald Loretz suggested an alternative rendering, "an intensely courageous woman," in 1959.[22] In the German *Bibel in gerechter Sprache* (Bible in Fair-Minded Language), Uta Schmidt and I translate Hannah's statement as, "I am a strong-willed woman."

Hannah wins the fight against the power of fate because God takes her side. She bears one son, Samuel, and after that three other sons and two daughters (1 Sam 2:21). Shortly after the birth of Samuel, she sings her song (2:1–10), which is in every sense a song of resistance. It sings about the God who overturns circumstances. Here the singer uses her own experience as the starting point but soon goes beyond this: "Even the barren woman gives birth seven times over, and the woman with many children withers away" (v. 5). Hannah's experience is that even an apparently barren woman can conceive a child; the fact that seven children are born is not true, either at the time Hannah sings—she has only one at this point—or later, when she bears only five more children (v. 21). Hannah's song is about more than her personal fate. It is about the divinity that reverses everything that human beings consider normal and expected. The song begins with the "bows of the mighty" that break, while those who falter gird themselves with strength (v. 4). It further refers to the fat and the hungry and, in particular, to those who have many children and those who are barren (v. 5). This God YHWH can cause the death of those who apparently are full of life and can bring human beings into the sphere of life from the sphere of death—referring to sickness, misery, and social

---

22. Oswald Loretz, "Weitere ugaritisch-hebräische Parallelen," *BZ* 3 (1959): 293–94.

isolation (v. 6). This God also overturns the apparently firmly established social order by making the poor rich and the rich poor, by lifting up people who search for something to eat from the scrap heap (so can v. 8 be translated, arguably).

In her resistance against the power of fate, against the apparently firmly established orders of the world, Hannah becomes finally a prophetess. For, in the last verse of her song, she entreats God on behalf of the future king. She does so at a time when her son Samuel, who later will anoint kings Saul and David, has just been born. As is generally known, what we have here is the model for the Magnificat of Mary in the Gospel of Luke. In it, also, the subject is the future king, the Anointed One, the Messiah, or Christ. And, following the Song of Hannah, Christ's mother likewise sings about the overthrow of all apparently unchangeable orders by the God of Israel.

The second woman, whose story is narrated at the end of the books of Samuel, also fights for her rights. But while in Hannah's case the question is about her right to children, or about the life of her children, which fate appears to dispute, Rizpah fights for the right of seven executed persons to be buried properly. Two of them are her own children, fathered by Saul, and the other five are Saul's grandchildren from one of his daughters.[23] The power of fate is here embodied by David, who infers from a divine oracle that he should surrender Saul's progeny to the Gibeonites, who will kill them. The corpses are not buried but rather are exposed to the wild animals. In this manner, David violates the commandment, read in canonical sequence, in Deut 21:22–23, which stipulates that those who are executed must be buried on the same day. Only Rizpah's relentless vigil over the dead instructs David—Rizpah becomes in a certain sense David's teacher of the torah, as Luise Metzler has noted.[24]

As in Hannah's case, Rizpah overcomes the power that she confronts, in this case the power of the ruler, because God takes her side. Metzler, in my opinion, has shown convincingly that the water that falls from heaven (v. 10) is in no way the rain that ends the famine—as such, it would occur much too early in the narrative, as has been seen repeatedly. The rain, as in other passages, is a divine demonstration of the power with which God intervenes in favor of those who belong to him. Metzler writes: "Together

---

23. See the MT of 2 Sam 21:8.

24. Luise Metzler, *Das Recht Gestorbener: Rizpa als Toralehrerin für David*, TF 28 (Berlin: LIT, 2015).

with Rizpah, YHWH protests with blows like those delivered during the liberation from Egypt. No life-saving, famine-ending rain falls from Heaven…. The hunger has not passed. It threatens to become much worse because of the rainstorm, if human beings are not buried." In the rain," says Metzler, "the solidarity of YHWH with Rizpah and with those who have been killed" is shown.[25] Only when those executed are buried does God let himself be "entreated" (v. 14).

In Hannah and Rizpah, at the beginning and the end of the books of Samuel, we encounter two women who act ostensibly in their own interest, or on behalf of their children. By so doing, they not only call into question seemingly immutable orders and power relationships, but they also bring God over to their side and, therefore, prevail.

7. Conclusion

The Former Prophets contain several narratives about resistant women. The narratives are not about only one type of resistant women. Rather—and this is the first finding of the reading of the texts—the narratives account for approximately five profiles or silhouettes or clusters. My initial task was to identify these profiles.

Second, I would like to state that these profiles, and the individual narratives that find expression in them, reflect the scope of the *conditio humana*. Women can become victims and more or less resign themselves to this fate. They can obtain power and then fail. They can already anticipate who will win in history and can profit more, but also less, from this intuition. They can commit themselves under more or less pleasant circumstances relating to their community. They can also stand up for their rights and those of their children, thereby bringing God to their side. All of this is possible, and the narratives do not reduce the portrait to one single image of the resistant woman.

Third, one should ask a question that so far I have touched on only marginally. Where is God in all this? It is striking that in none of the narratives discussed above does God play even the tiniest of roles. This is true of practically all the figures in the first four clusters. Women in resistance do not need God to act. It is not that they are godless. But in their concrete actions, God does not appear, except in the cases of Hannah and Rizpah.

---

25. Metzler, *Recht Gestorbener*, 320–21.

With these two, the decisive turn of events occurs when God takes their side. Their resistance is presumably the most difficult, because it is directed not at human beings, but rather at a supposedly divine law. Hannah is childless because "YHWH had closed her womb," as the text says (1 Sam 1:5–6). And David, in the case of the execution of the seven descendants of Saul, appeals to a divine oracle (2 Sam 21:1). Only God can take a stance against God. For this reason, the resistance of Hannah and Rizpah, in my view, is most radical. They offer resistance to a power that apparently is hostile to life, and through their resistance, they provoke the God who responds to life. For me, they are the most important mothers in the faith.

Bibliography

Alter, Robert. "Characterization and the Art of Reticence (from *The Art of Biblical Narrative*)." Pages 64–73 in *Telling Queen Michal's Story: An Experiment in Comparative Interpretation*. Edited by David J. A. Clines and Tamara Cohn Eskenazi. JSOTSup 119. Sheffield: JSOT Press, 1991.

Bauks, Michaela. *Jephtas Tochter: Traditions-, Religions- und rezeptionsgeschichtliche Studien zu Richter 11,29–40*. FAT 71. Tübingen: Mohr Siebeck, 2010.

Clines, David J. A. "X, X *ben* Y, *ben* Y: Personal Names in Hebrew Narrative Style." Pages 124–28 in *Telling Queen Michal's Story: An Experiment in Comparative Interpretation*. Edited by David J. A. Clines and Tamara Cohn Eskenazi. JSOTSup 119. Sheffield: JSOT Press, 1991.

Dube, Musa W. *Postcolonial Feminist Interpretation of the Bible*. Saint Louis: Chalice, 2000.

Exum, J. Cheryl. "Murder They Wrote: Ideology and the Manipulation of Female Presence in Biblical Narrative." Pages 176–98 in *Telling Queen Michal's Story: An Experiment in Comparative Interpretation*. Edited by David J. A. Clines and Tamara Cohn Eskenazi. JSOTSup 119. Sheffield: JSOT Press, 1991.

Fischer, Irmtraud. *Gotteskünderinnen: Zu einer geschlechterfairen Deutung des Phänomens der Prophetie und der Prophetinnen in der Hebräischen Bibel*. Stuttgart: Kohlhammer, 2002.

———. *Gotteslehrerinnen: Weise Frauen und Frau Weisheit im Alten Testament*. Stuttgart: Kohlhammer, 2006.

Groß, Walter. *Richter*. HThKAT. Freiburg: Herder, 2009.

Loretz, Oswald. "Weitere ugaritisch-hebräische Parallelen." *BZ* 3 (1959): 290–94.
Metzler, Luise. *Das Recht Gestorbener: Rizpa als Toralehrerin für David.* TF 28. Berlin: LIT, 2015.
Müllner, Ilse. *Gewalt im Hause Davids: Die Erzählung von Tamar und Amnon (2 Sam 13,1–22).* HBS 13. Freiburg: Herder, 1997.
———. "Tamar." In *Das wissenschaftliche Bibellexikon im Internet.* Edited by Michaela Bauks and Klaus Koenen. 2009. https://tinyurl.com/SBL6016e.
Schmidt, Uta. *Zentrale Randfiguren: Strukturen der Darstellung von Frauen in den Erzählungen der Königebücher.* Gütersloh: Chr. Kaiser; Gütersloher Verlagshaus, 2003.
Schroer, Silvia. "Die weise Frau auf der Stadtmauer von Abel-bet-Maacha (2 Sam 20,14–22)." Pages 394–411 in *Seitenblicke: Literarische und historische Studien zu Nebenfiguren im zweiten Samuelbuch.* Edited by Walter Dietrich. OBO 249. Fribourg: Academic Press; Göttingen: Vandenhoeck & Ruprecht, 2011.
Sicre, José Luis. *Josué.* NBE. Estella: Editorial Verbo Divino, 2002.
Trible, Phyllis. *Texts of Terror: Literary-Feminist Readings of Biblical Narratives.* Philadelphia: Fortress, 1985.
Zakovitch, Yair. "Sisseras Tod." *ZAW* 93 (1981): 364–74.

Women in the War Narratives of the Prestate Period (Joshua–Judges)

Michaela Bauks

1. Introduction

A study of the female characters in the books of Joshua and Judges shows that women in war narratives in most instances are contextualized and appear either as victims of war, war heroines, or, sometimes, both. The following remarks are limited to characters that fall into the category of victims of war. Yet, I would like to at least mention the feminine figures that are analyzed in literary terms. In the book of Joshua, we encounter women who are mentioned by name, such as Rahab (Josh 2; 6) and Achsah, Caleb's daughter (Josh 15:13–19 // Judg 1:10–15; 1 Chr 2:49), as well as the five daughters of Zelophehad, listed by name at least in Num 26:33 (see 27:1–11; 36:11; Josh 17:3–4). In the book of Judges, Deborah and Jael as well as Delilah are also mentioned by name (Judg 4–5; 16), whereas those without names include the daughter of Jephthah (Judg 11), the wife of Manoah and the mother of Samson (Judg 14), the mother of Micah the Ephraimite (Judg 17), and the wife of the Levite (Judg 19), as well as several other young women from Jabesh and Shiloh who are abducted by the Benjaminites (Judg 21). Several episodes attract attention by virtue of their relatively striking intertextual connections with texts from the Torah, for example, the accounts about Zelophehad's daughters or the narrative about the wife of the Levite, which shows clear parallels with Gen 19.

The following remarks on female victims of war in the book of Judges focus on the role of women in three vow narratives (Judg 1; 11; 20–21), which in addition contain allusions to the *ḥerem* (ban) or the consecration to war.

2. The Achsah Episode (Judges 1:10–15; see Joshua 15:13–19)

Judah went against the Canaanites [coll.] who lived in Hebron (the name of Hebron was formerly Kiriath-arba); and they defeated Sheshai and Ahiman and Talmai.

From there they [coll.] went against the inhabitants of Debir (the name of Debir was formerly Kiriath-sepher). Then Caleb said, "Whoever attacks Kiriath-sepher and takes it, I will give him my daughter Achsah as wife." And Othniel son of Kenaz, Caleb's younger brother, took it; and he gave him his daughter Achsah as wife. When she came to him, she urged him to ask her father for a field. As she dismounted from her donkey, Caleb said to her, "What do you wish?" She said to him, "Give me a present; because you have set me in the land of the Negev, give me also water springs [NRSV: Gulloth-mayim; or: since you have given me the land of Negev, then give me also water springs]." So Caleb gave her the upper springs and the lower springs [NRSV: Upper Gulloth and Lower Gulloth].

The descendants of the Kenite, Moses's father-in-law, went up with the people of Judah from the city of palms into the wilderness of Judah, which lies in the Negev near Arad. Then they [coll.] went and settled [coll.] with the people. Judah went with his brother Simeon, and they defeated the Canaanites [coll.] who inhabited Zephath, and devoted it to destruction. So the city was called Hormah [see Num 21:3]. Judah took Gaza with its territory, Ashkelon with its territory, and Ekron with its territory. The LORD was with Judah, and he took possession of the hill country, but could not drive out the inhabitants of the plain, because they had chariots of iron. Hebron was given to Caleb, as Moses had said; and he drove out from it the three sons of Anak. (Judg 1:10–20)[1]

The Achsah episode is embedded in a description of Judah's war against the Canaanite cities of Jerusalem, Hebron, and Debir.[2] Judges 1:1–2:5,

---

1. The English translation of the biblical text follows, with modification, the NRSV. The original version of this essay uses the Neue Zürcher Bibel.
2. On this episode, see J. Alberto Soggin, *Judges*, OTL (Philadelphia: Westminster, 1981), 25–26; Corinne Lanoir, *Femmes fatales, filles rebelles: Figures féminines dans le livre des Juges*, AR (Geneva: Labor et Fides, 2005), 119–23; Mareike Rake, *"Juda wird aufsteigen!" Untersuchungen zum ersten Kapitel des Richterbuches*, BZAW 367 (Berlin: de Gruyter, 2006), 80–81; Renate Jost, "Achsas Quellen: Feministisch-sozialgeschichtliche Überlegungen zu Josua 15,15–20/Ri 1,12–15," in *"Ihr Völker alle, klatscht in die Hände!" Festschrift für Erhard S. Gerstenberger zum 65. Geburtstag*, ed. Rainer Kessler et al., EUZ 3 (Münster: Ugarit-Verlag, 1997), 110–25; Jost, *Gender*,

which is an introduction to the book, forms a kind of secondary résumé of the conquest stories told in the book of Joshua. At the same time, though, it clearly sets itself apart from these stories by focusing primarily on the conquests by Judah (1:1–20) or the house of Joseph (1:22–36). The list is composed in the form of a negative catalogue of possessions (לֹא הוֹרִישׁוֹ, for example, 1:21 and passim; exception: 1:19).[3] It is remarkable that the Achsah narrative also occurs almost verbatim in Josh 15:15–19 and that the concern in both contexts is the legitimation of Caleb's acquisition of Hebron in the Judean hill country as his own inheritance (Josh 15:13–14; Judg 1:20). If one ignores the mention of Othniel (see Judg 3:7–11),[4] then the section corresponds, in addition, to the narratives about the spying out of the land in Num 13–14 (see Deut 1:22–40), to which also Josh 11:21–22, in a notice about the ban against the Anakim in Hebron and Debir, refers. Joshua 14:6–15, furthermore, offers a report about the gift of the land of Hebron to Caleb by Joshua.[5] Following also in Judg 1:17 is the notice of a ban against the city of Hormah (mentioned in Num 14:45; Deut 1:44), which presumably was located in the Negev in the area of Arad and whose name already alludes to the theme of annihilation (חרם).[6]

The book of Judges, thus, for all intents and purposes does not begin before Judg 2:6, with the notice of Joshua's death (2:6–9; see Josh 15:15–19), while older material is found in the list of the minor rulers in Judg

---

Sexualität und Macht in der Anthropologie des Richterbuches, BWANT 164 (Stuttgart: Kohlhammer, 2006), 75–76; Katrin Brockmüller, "Achsa," in *Das wissenschaftliche Bibellexikon im Internet* (2017), https://tinyurl.com/SBL6016f.

3. However this is not traced to an old list, but rather is a new, not exactly reconstructible creation. For further discussion, see Walter Groß, *Richter*, HThKAT (Freiburg: Herder, 2009), 113–18.

4. The passage on the first deliverer Othniel (מוֹשִׁיעַ) is presumably an addition supplied by the Deuteronomistic redaction in reference to the program of the regency period in Judg 2:11–12c, 14–16, 18–19, and to other Deuteronomistic framework formulas (see Ehud-Jephthah and Samson with older Northern Kingdom traditions). Thus, it is striking that in 3:7a, as in the program (2:11) and in 10:6, the sin formula aims at the cult of foreign gods.

5. See Groß, *Richter*, 109.

6. On the complicated topographical reconstruction of this city, whose name really means "rock crevice," see, Groß, who views Hormah as Simeon's allotted portion (see Judg 1:3, 17; Josh 19:4; 1 Chr 4:30; Groß, *Richter*, 136–37).

3:12–12:15.[7] The Achsah episode itself is likely to represent a secondary addition from the book of Joshua that, right at the beginning of the book, places a woman, the daughter of Caleb, at the center. In this episode, Caleb promises, "Whoever attacks Kiriath-sepher and takes it, I will give him my daughter Achsah as wife." In Josh 15:12, Caleb becomes the conqueror of the cities of Hormah and Debir, and whereas Judah's share is thematized only in Josh 15:20–63, the situation in Judg 1:10–15 is presented differently: here Judah initiates the military campaign in which Caleb is subordinate.

Interestingly, in both texts, almost literally congruent, the role of the daughter is clearly emphasized. Here it is a matter of an implicit vow of war by Caleb (Judg 1:12), who selects Achsah as the prize in the case of victory and who finally gives her away to the first deliverer, Othniel. In the subsequent passage, the matter at hand is the bride price or the paternal dowry. If one understands the formulation in 1:15 chiastically, or as a shortened parallelism in the sense of "If you already have given [+ to me] the land in Negev, then give me water springs, too,"[8] then the matter here is the dowry of the father presented to his daughter. The comparison of the textual history with the LXX is remarkable. Such a comparison reveals that in the MT the daughter is the one who demands a gift from her father. She asks for a field (v. 14) and for water springs (גלות מים) as a gift of blessing (ברכה), arguing that since she is moving to the Negev, she needs water, which Caleb also grants her (v. 15).

> And when she came to him, *she urged him* to ask her father for the field. And she dismounted from the donkey, and Caleb spoke to her: What do you wish? (Judg 1:14 MT)

> And it happened as she came (to him) that *he pressed her* to ask her father for the piece of land, and (so) *she muttered upon her mount and called* down from her mount: *You gave me away into the southern*

---

7. See detailed arguments in Groß (*Richter*, 182–95). Susan Niditch assumes a basic text influenced by Deuteronomy, whose program introduces each of the individual stories of the Judges (Judg 3–16), in which unspecified "epic-bardic voices," as in Judg 5, for example, have been incorporated and which later were supplemented by a humanistic-influenced framework text (Judg 1; 17–21). See Niditch, *Judges*, OTL (Louisville: Westminster John Knox, 2008), 8–11.

8. See Groß, *Richter*, 127–34.

country! And Caleb said to her: What do you wish [is on your heart] then? (Judg 1:14 LXX A)

And it happened as she arrived that *Gothoniel* pressed *her* to ask her father for a piece of land, and (*so*) *she muttered and called* down from her mount: *You gave me away into the southern country!* And Caleb said to her: What do you [is on your heart] then? (Judg 1:14 LXX B)

And it happened at Achsah's entry that *she counseled with him* and said: I will ask my father for a field. And she called from her donkey. And Caleb said to her: What do you wish? (Josh 15:18 LXX)

The two variants of Judg 1:14 (LXX A and B), handed down from the Greek Septuagint, confirm a subject whose sex has been changed, since her husband, Othniel, urges her to ask her father for land and not the reverse. In Josh 15:18 LXX, there is a heavily harmonized version of the course of events that makes for a finer literary text, while the Hebrew version represents, as *lectio difficilior*, the more original variant.

The problem in terms of content is that Achsah in the MT version commissions her husband, but this does not cause him to actually carry out the deal. On the contrary, she directs her request to her father personally in a course of action reduced to a minimum. The triad—(1) subornation (סות; see Job 2:3; 1 Chr 21:1; 2 Chr 18:2), (2) the stretch of travel on the donkey, and (3) the father's question—allows the younger translations to take advantage of a wider space for explication ("filling the gap"), which the three LXX translations use creatively. On the one hand, Judges LXX reads, instead of the verb צנח, "dismount," the verb צוח, "mutter" (καὶ ἐγόγγυζεν, "she muttered"; see Isa 42:11), and adds a second verb (καὶ ἔκραξεν, "and called").[9] Joshua LXX, on the other hand, adds a paraphrase with συμβουλεύομαι (to counsel with) that does not suggest a different basic text, but rather more of a cultural correction or update. In the Hellenistic period, in particular, it was quite possible that the bride negotiated her own dowry.[10]

---

9. LXX A and B expand the MT and translate it as "and so she muttered [upon her mount] and called down from her mount" (version A, long form).

10. See Cornelius den Hertog, "Jesus: Josue/Das Buch Josua," in *Genesis bis Makkabäer*, vol. 1 of *Septuaginta Deutsch: Erläuterungen und Kommentare zum griechischen Alten Testament*, ed. Martin Karrer and Wolfgang Kraus (Stuttgart: Deutsche Bibelgesellschaft, 2009), 643; Cor de Vos, *Das Los Judas: Über Entstehung und Ziele der*

Judges 1:14 points to Achsah's relationship with her father. According to the MT, she dismounts from her donkey, evincing respect, and approaches her father (see Abigail and David in 1 Sam 25:23, Rebekah and Isaac in Gen 24:64, or Anat before El in the Ugaritic Baal epic in *KTU* 1.3, vv. 19–34).[11] The verb צנח, however, is a rare and etymologically unclear verb that is translated, for example, by Alberto Soggin and Mieke Bal as "she clapped her hand," and is found also in the context of Jael's murder of Sisera in Judg 4:21, where it is used in the sense of "penetration" of the tent pole into the body.[12] In this respect, it is no surprise when the LXX translates it as καὶ ἐγόγγυζεν ("she muttered") or καὶ ἐβόησεν ("she called") in Josh 15:18. The LXX could not apprehend the meaning of the word[13] and even inserted into the text a new meaning, another clear upgrading of the daughter's self-confidence that is not discernible in this way in the MT. In place of respect for the father, there is now a clear demand, which the father grants her.

The Achsah episode in its Hebrew version tells of war, of a vow, and of its positively termed outcome. Originally, the issue of the notice probably was an etiology of the Kenite Caleb and his possession of land in the Transjordan-Edomite region (Josh 15).[14] In the new context of the opening of the book of Judges, however, the concern is the creation of a new constellation of persons that effects the integration of a foreign tribe into the people of Israel, thanks to Achsah's marriage to Othniel, the first deliverer. Consequently, a very prominent position is assigned to the daughter. While the deliverer Othniel conquers Debir and receives the daughter as the prize for victory, it is, in the final analysis, the daughter with her purposeful action who claims the land and the springs in the Negev for herself.[15] A notice of annihilation (חרם) that refers not to Caleb and his daughter but rather to Judah's brother Simeon follows in Judg 1:16–17.

Landbeschreibung in Josua 15, VTSup 95 (Leiden: Brill, 2003), 21–22; Dominique Barthélemy, *Josué, Juges, Ruth, Samuel, Rois, Chroniques, Esdras, Néhémie, Esther*, vol. 1 of *Critique textuelle de l'Ancien Testament*, OBO 50 (Fribourg: Academic Press; Göttingen: Vandenhoeck & Ruprecht, 1982), 35–36.

11. See Niditch, *Judges*, 40–41.

12. Soggin, *Judges*, 67; Mieke Bal, *Death and Dissymmetry: The Politics of Coherence in the Book of Judges* (Chicago: University of Chicago Press, 1988), 156. For further suggestions on the idea of an acoustic interjection, see Lanoir, *Femmes fatales, filles rebelles*, 135–36.

13. Barthélemy, *Critique textuelle*, 36.

14. See Groß, *Richter*, 130–32.

15. So also Groß, *Richter*, 134–35.

Near Arad, Simeon executes the ban over the city of Hormah, which, as announced in verse 3, becomes his "allotted share" (גורל). The war vow and the ban are found in closest proximity to each other, but are disassociated from the episode featuring Caleb and his daughter Achsah.

The narrative is of great interest also in the context of the book of Judges. In comparison to other female figures, Achsah is in many respects an exception. As one female foreigner among others (see Rahab in Josh 2; 6), she has a redemptive function in the preservation of the collective. Further, as one of the women mentioned by name in the book of Judges, she is especially distinguished (see Jael, Deborah, Delilah). In addition, she is assigned a positively drawn fate that clearly distinguishes her from other women, such as Jephthah's daughter or the wife of the Levite. While Caleb equips her for the rest of her life, the other two are dependent on either father or husband and are condemned to death. In the basic outline of the book of Judges, the three narratives mark the beginning, the center, and the end. Corinne Lanoir has characterized the Achsah narrative as ironic insofar as it creates a positive antithesis to the constantly progressing decline that is described in the narrative course of the book. From it emerges a critical view of war and heroism.[16] Therefore, the story in Judg 1 can be interpreted, as does Susan Niditch, as a commentary on the contingency of power, because unexpected people, such as a daughter, obtain control over it. Power, in Achsah's case, is negotiated twice by a man and a woman—between the father and the daughter and between the married couple themselves.[17] In the Achsah episode, the daughter proves to be strong-willed. In line with the case of the daughters of Zelophehad in Num 27:1–11, 36; Josh 16:1–6, it is about the right to receive the father's portion of the land and, in this way, represent a certain tribe.[18]

The narrative of the contingency of power sketched out by Niditch is also valid for other narratives in the book of Judges. It serves as a structural principle for the interpretation of each narrative.

---

16. See Lanoir, *Femmes fatales, filles rebelles*, 145–46.

17. "A comment on the serendipitous nature of power and on the capacity of unexpected ones to take control. In this case [of Achsah], power is negotiated between men and women, fathers and daughters, and wives and husbands" (Niditch, *Judges*, 41).

18. The issue is the introduction of the right of inheritance for the daughter when there are no surviving male descendants. See Ulrike Bechmann, "Zelofhad," in *Das wissenschaftliche Bibellexikon im Internet* (2011), https://tinyurl.com/SBL6016g.

3. Jephthah's Sacrificial Vow and the Consequences for His Daughter (Judg 11:30–40)

The Jephthah cycle is also set in the context of war. For the first time it deals first of all with a war of the Gileadites (or of the association of tribes called Israel) with the Transjordan tribes, not only with the Ammonites (10:6–7; 17–11:11), but also with Philistines (10:6–7) and with the otherwise allied Ephraimites (12:1–4, 6). The kings of Edom and Moab, whose land Jephthah is not allowed to cross during his campaign, are mentioned also (11:17–18, 25). The Amorites (10:8; 11:19–24) finally attack him, and their defeat extends the borders of Israel. The war by Chemosh is contrasted with the war by YHWH and is decided by YHWH in favor of Israel (vv. 23–24) or, as in the song of Heshbon (Num 21:23–30), it was brought about by Chemosh himself against his own people (see the Mesha stela, vv. 4–5: "for Chemosh was angry with his land [Moab]").[19] In preparation for the battle against Ammon (Judg 11:27), the divine spirit comes upon Jephthah (v. 29), and he makes his fateful vow to sacrifice to the Lord: "And Jephthah made a vow to the LORD, and said, 'If you will give the Ammonites into my hand, then whoever comes out of the doors of my house to meet me, when I return victorious from the Ammonites, shall be the Lord's, to be offered up by me as a burnt offering'" (11:30–31). The development of the plot of the narrative is well-known. The valiant warrior (גבור חיל; Judg 11:1) must sacrifice his only daughter when she comes to meet him, for "there was his daughter coming out to meet him with timbrels and with dancing" (v. 34). Interestingly, the narrative consists of three different rites de passage: verse 34 suggests a triumphal procession in which, as in various texts of the Hebrew Bible, women with musical instruments come out dancing to meet the warriors.[20] Texts such as the possibly very old antiphon in Exod 15:1, 21 and in 1 Sam 18:6 are evidence

---

19. See Groß, *Richter*, 592–93. On the translation, see Hans-Peter Müller, "Die Inschrift des Königs Mesa von Moab," *TUAT* 1:647.

20. See Jack Sasson, *Judges 1–12: A New Translation with Introduction and Commentary*, AB 6D (New Haven: Yale University Press, 2014), 439; Sarit Paz, *Drums, Women, and Goddesses: Drumming and Gender in Iron Age II Israel*, OBO 232 (Fribourg: Academic Press; Göttingen: Vandenhoeck & Ruprecht, 2007), 83; Michaela Bauks, "Physical Attributes of Memorials: Could the Tomb of Jephthah and the Dietary Restrictions of Tekufot Give an Insight into the Intention of Judges 11:29–40?," in *Gender and Social Norms in Ancient Israel, Early Judaism and Christianity: Texts and Material Culture in Eastern Mediterranean Context*, ed. Michaela Bauks, Katharina

that drum playing was a professional activity by women,[21] the setting of which in group contexts—for example, in war rituals as well as in funeral and lamentation rituals—played a large role.

Niditch demonstrates that the vow of sacrifice should be seen as part of the *preparation* for war, similar to what is presented in Num 21:2–3. The preparation entails that the prize to be awarded in the case of victory, or the item of sacrifice to God, also is determined in the course of the ban pronounced on the conquered city, which here, as in Judg 1:17, is called Hormah:

> When the Canaanite, the king of Arad, who lived in the Negev, heard that Israel was coming by the way of Atharim, he fought against Israel and took some of them captive. Then Israel made a vow to the LORD and said, "If you will indeed give this people into our hands, then we will utterly destroy their towns." The LORD listened to the voice of Israel, and handed over the Canaanites; and they utterly destroyed them and their towns; so the place was called Hormah. (Num 21:1–3)

Dolores Kamrada suggests that the Hebrew noun חרם should be understood in two ways: first as a ban imposed on the enemies that includes death, as found in the book of Joshua (for example, Josh 6) or on the Mesha stela, and second as an act of consecration that is to be assessed positively (see 2 Kgs 4:23; Judg 11:35–36). In both cases, a human life is consecrated in return for military victory, and the action that is carried out in the context of war is irreversible but forms the nonredeemable consequence of a vow. Since Jephthah does not surrender the Ammonite enemies, but rather his own daughter, then, what we have here is a positive consecration to the deity, which is intended to serve the interest of the people of Israel. This idea is perhaps also the basis for Lev 27:28,[22] where killing is presumed: "Nothing that a person owns that has been devoted to destruction for the LORD, be it human or animal, or inherited landholding, may

---

Galor, and Judith Hartenstein, JAJSup (Göttingen: Vandenhoeck & Ruprecht, 2019), 235–54.

21. Paz says that the "Old Testament affirms the tradition of women drummers in a variety of genres (narrative, prophesy, and psalm)" (*Drums, Women, and Goddesses*, 85). See Esther J. Hamori, *Women's Divination in Biblical Literature: Prophecy, Necromancy, and Other Arts of Knowledge* (New Haven: Yale University Press, 2015), 63–65. On the antiphon in Exod 15:1, 21, see Sasson, *Judges*, 439.

22. See Thomas Hieke, *Levitikus 16–27*, HThKAT (Freiburg: Herder, 2014), 1125–28.

be sold or redeemed; every devoted thing is most holy to the Lord. No humans who have been devoted to destruction can be ransomed; they shall be put to death" (Lev 27:28–29). The presumed institution of the offering of the daughter in Judg 11, where the concept חרם itself does not appear, explains, according to Kamrada, why a human sacrifice could not occur in the Deuteronomistic revision of the book of Judges.[23] The offering, in her opinion, was not carried out as a sacrifice but rather as a consecration of the daughter in the temple. This interpretation is theoretically possible and has been suggested frequently, by virtue of the open formulation in verse 39 that "he did with her according to the vow he had made." But Lev 27:29 contradicts this.[24]

As in the case of Achsah, a daughter here must also pay the price in the course of war. She, too, must serve as a kind of prize for victory in the course of a war vow, but this time not for a human war hero through marriage but rather for God as the authority facilitating the victory. Jephthah's daughter understands the situation and accepts it (Judg 11:36),[25] but also makes a request that in turn launches a kind of rite de passage, and it is granted by the father. She institutes a third ritual that is performed in her memory:

> And she said to her father, "Let this thing be done for me: Grant me two months, so that I may go and wander on the mountains, and bewail my virginity, my companions and I." "Go," he said and sent her away for two months. So she departed, she and her companions, and bewailed her virginity on the mountains. At the end of two months, she returned to her father, who did with her according to the vow he had made. She had never slept with a man. So there arose an Israelite custom that for four days every year the daughters of Israel would go out to lament the daughter of Jephthah the Gileadite. (vv. 37–40)

---

23. See, for example, Groß, who assumes a pre-Deuteronomistic vow narrative in Judg 11:30–40, which was edited Deuteronomistically (*Richter*, 616–18).

24. See Dolores G. Kannada, *Heroines, Heroes, and Deity: Three Narratives of the Biblical Heroic Tradition*, LHBOTS 613 (London: Oxford University Press, 2016), 63–65, with the bibliography.

25. It is remarkable that, by accepting her fate, the daughter once again actively intervenes in this narrative as the agent sustaining the action: "She said to him, 'My father, if you have opened your mouth to the Lord, do to me according to what has gone out of your mouth, now that the Lord has given you vengeance against your enemies, the Ammonites'" (11:36).

If one understands Judg 11 as an implicit חרם narrative, then the following lines of interpretation emerge for the institution of war. The concept of חרם is discussed as[26]

- sacrifice
- consecration or assignment to a deity
- taboo with a renunciation of prey
- separation from what is incompatible or foreign
- selective destruction or appropriation of the enemies' resources
- assertion of a divine idea of order
- self-differentiation from the foreign as a symbol of obedience to God
- literary sublimation of violence
- thank offering for the deity

The concept of חרם originally had a communicative function. It implied the "relinquishing of property as a thank offering to the deity for a conferred victory, whereby the offering can be pledged before the battle, but also can be consecrated after the subsequent victory."[27] Thus, it originally functioned as sacrifice or consecration, which, in the course of the Deuteronomistic theologizing, became a only practice of elimination that carried with it the separation of one's own identity. Assuming an implicit חרם reference in Judg 11, a (thank) offering function would apply to the act. This means, however, that the application does not, as Kamrada assumes, fit into the typically Deuteronomistic scheme of separation. Rather, it probably reflects the older concept of an offering.

In the broader context of the narrative in Judges, the concept obtains its tragic connotation through the fact that—in contrast to the life-affirming Achsah episode—the vow at least means the end of the social relationships, if not the physical end of the daughter. The formulation in verse 39 leaves this alternative open. According to Niditch, the ritual of remembrance intends to accentuate her willingness to be a sacrifice for the people as an identity-endowing measure in the context of the acquisition of the

---

26. See Rüdiger Schmitt, *Der "Heilige Krieg" im Pentateuch und im Deuteronomistischen Geschichtswerk: Studien zur Forschungs-, Rezeptions- und Religionsgeschichte von Krieg und Bann im Alten Testament*, AOAT 381 (Münster: Ugarit-Verlag, 2011), 59.

27. Schmitt, *"Heilige Krieg" im Pentateuch*, 60.

land.²⁸ The narrative reveals another aspect of the relationship between the sexes in an androcentric society. In contrast to Judg 1, Judg 11 lacks any form of irony. The text targets a misguided father-daughter relationship in which the daughter, who remains nameless, is given no freedom to make her own decision. The rite de passage in Judg 1 leads into marriage and the integration of the daughter into Israel, but in Judg 11 leads to her exclusion. Nonetheless, Jephthah's daughter also does not remain passive but rather takes her fate into her own hands, within the framework set for her, and acts in a convincing and self-confident manner. In the Jephthah cycle, the daughter finally becomes the real actor, that is, the strong and self-confident heroine.²⁹ In contrast, the father—at least in this episode—is characterized in an almost tragic manner as a victim of his own vow.³⁰

4. War, Sacrifice, and the Vow in Judges 19–21

In the so-called appendix to the narratives in Judges (Judg 17–21), there is an extensive narrative unit (Judg 19–21) that offers two "texts of terror" at once.³¹ The first narrative takes an individual perspective. At first glance, it focuses on the unstable plight of a traveling man in foreign territory, but beyond this it portrays the theme of the precarious situation of women in the context of gender relationships. From an anthropological perspective Judg 19 discusses both the lack of respect for women and the obligation of hospitality. However, the episode marks the occasion for a conflict among the tribes of Israel (Judg 20) that is resolved in Judg 21 collectively by means of the trading of women in times of war and restoration. Both nar-

---

28. For Niditch, "a tale of war that helps to shape Israelite concepts of their foundation in the land also becomes the origin myth that establishes a life-shaping ritual for young women and their families" (*Judges*, 134–35).

29. Michael Sjöberg, *Wrestling with Textual Violence: The Jephthah Narrative in Antiquity and Modernity*, BMW 4 (Sheffield: Sheffield Phoenix, 2006), 26.

30. LXX A emphasizes that the daughter confronts the father and actively approaches him (11:35), while LXX B remains closer to the MT and underlines the dismay on the part of the father. See Michaela Bauks, *Jephtas Tochter: Traditions-, religions- und rezeptionsgeschichtliche Studien zu Richter 11, 29–40*, FAT 71 (Tübingen: Mohr Siebeck, 2010), 6, with n. 18.

31. This is the title of the collection of essays by Phyllis Trible, *Texts of Terror: Literary-Feminist Readings of Biblical Narratives* (Philadelphia: Fortress, 1984).

ratives, in 19:1 and 21:25, are framed by and intertwined with each other by the statement "in those days, there was no king in Israel."[32]

The background of the events in Judg 19 is that a nameless concubine (פלגש) is unfaithful to her husband, a Levite (זנה + על; vv. 1–2), and returns to her family. Her husband follows her, and that is the beginning of the inexorable downward movement of the narrative.

What is striking in terms of form is the special spatial composition, hence one of the guiding concepts of יצא (vv. 22–27), "bring out" (*qal*) or "let bring out" (*hiphil*). When the man finally "comes back" (בוא), his wife is (possibly almost) dead and, in order to incite the other tribes, is cut into pieces, which are finally sent to the tribes to foment war.[33] The guiding concept conveys the impression that the act of leaving the house means entering into an unprotected outside area in danger of death. In the end, the salvation of the man comes at the cost of the woman's life.

The division of the narrative parts is also striking. While the stay with the father-in-law is narrated at length (Judg 19:3–9), most aspects of the journey remain astonishingly underreported, for example, the relationship of the couple. On their way back, the couple's place for the night in Gibeah becomes an experience of crisis, as the residents of Gibeah demand the male guest as sexual object (vv. 23–30). The host attempts to counter this by offering the attackers his own daughter and the concubine in order to save the man. Niditch surmises that this has nothing to do with homosexuality, but rather with a sexual ethics, in which the victim is put into subjection, taken possession of, and brought into an unequal relationship of power. A comparable pattern of behavior is found in Gen 19:5 on the occasion of Lot's encounter with the Sodomites, or in Judg 5:27 in regard to Jael's handling of Sisera.[34] The guest in Judg 19 hands over the rebellious concubine as a substitute who, within the social hierarchy, is inferior to the male guest or the foreigner. Nevertheless, the boundaries between victim and offender are vaguely drawn and are shaped by errors,

---

32. See, in this regard, Groß, *Richter*, 811–12.

33. On the status of the wife when the man comes back, see Trible, *Texts of Terror*, 79; see also below.

34. This is "less about views of homosexuality … than about a larger theme in sexual ethics in which one partner subdues, owns, and holds unequal power over the other" (Niditch, *Judges*, 193, with reference to Trible, *Texts of Terror*, 105–39). Groß further refers, along with Gen 19, to the semantic parallels with Tamar's rape by Ammon in 2 Sam 13:12–18 (*Richter*, 835–39).

for example, the wrong decision about where to stay for the night.[35] The Levite as victim escapes from danger by surrendering his wife as a victim, and thereby he becomes a perpetrator. At the end of the night, he lifts the rape victim onto his donkey and brings her back home in order to send her mutilated body parts to the tribes as a demonstration of what was done to him.[36] The woman is "semiotized" by the Levite and reduced to a message.[37] The death of the concubine is not even mentioned explicitly, and it cannot be concluded necessarily that she was still alive when dissected by her husband. The narrator, though, is not concerned about excluding this possibility or describing the situation with clarity, which further contributes to the reification of the woman.[38] However, this gap is apprehended and explicated by LXX A+B.[39]

The episode is not a typical war narrative but forms the basis for igniting a fresh war. Following the euphemized report of the Levite to the tribes (Judg 20:4–7), Gibeah's attack and a war against Benjamin (20:8–26) ensue, which puts Israel's unity to the test. The war leads to the order to annihilate Benjamin, an act which is described as a whole burnt offering to heaven (vv. 40, 48). Nevertheless, six hundred men survive (v. 47), who become the motor for the third part of the narrative: women are to be chosen for

---

35. See Ilse Müllner, "Tödliche Differenzen: Sexuelle Gewalt als Gewalt gegen Andere in Ri 19," in *Von der Wurzel getragen: Christlich-feministische Exegese in Auseinandersetzung mit dem Antijudaismus*, ed. Luise Schottroff and Marie-Theres Wacker, BibInt 17 (Leiden: Brill, 1996), 88–92. I thank Irmtraud Fischer for this bibliographic reference.

36. Herein, one can see the travesty of the custom connected with calling out military forces, as it is discussed in relation to the cutting up of a herd of oxen by Saul in 1 Sam 11:7 (see, on this custom, an instance from the kingdom of Mari, eighteenth century BCE, ARM 2.48): Gibeah-Saul seeks to compel the tribes of Israel to provide military aid to Jabesh-gilead against the Ammonites, which the Benjaminites, however, evade. On the numerous parallels in Judg 6–8; 11; 19–21, see Walter Dietrich, *1 Samuel 1–12*, BKAT 8.1 (Neukirchen-Vluyn: Neukirchener Verlag, 2011), 488–90; Groß, *Richter*, 814–19.

37. Müllner, "Tödliche Differenzen," 88. The procedure of dissection is associated with her desexualization, in that the Levite in this way assures himself of his masculinity (see Müllner, "Tödliche Differenzen," 96).

38. See, for example, Trible, *Texts of Terror*, 80; on the whole, Groß, *Richter*, 844–45.

39. Müllner points out that the clarification by the diction in LXX that the woman was dead before she was dissected aims especially at the exculpation of the Levite and softens the perpetrator-victim relationship by describing him without exception as a victim ("Tödliche Differenzen," 93).

them who, as compensation, seal the process of transition from enmity to reconciliation on the political level, and who help to restore the unity of the tribes of Israel. There is no reflection on an anthropological level on the damage done.

Again, in the third narrative, the focus is on the survival of Israel in the aftermath of the military confrontations, as well as on the acquisition of land and the retention of areas of settlement. The female figures and their well-being clearly call attention to the increasing limits and the depths involved in the search for land. The concept of חרם, which appears explicitly as a verb in *hiphil* only in the post-Deuteronomistic-dated passages in Judg 1:17 and 21:11 (in reference to Jabesh), is encountered in substance also in the phrase "strike a city with the edge of the sword [לפי חרב]," and then to set it ablaze (Judg 20:37) so that its flame rises to the heavens as a burnt offering (20:40), suggesting an act of sacrifice or consecration. The phrase is found frequently outside the book of Judges in parallel with חרם in other Deuteronomistically tinged texts (see Deut 13:16; Josh 6:21; 10:28–39; 11:11–14). It runs through broad narratives in the book of Judges, in which the burning of a city is reported (Judg 1:8, באש שלח; 4:16 + "no one was left"; 18:27, שרף באש; 20:48 שלח באש). In Judg 1:25, the massacre of the population is explicitly excluded, but the prophecy implicitly says that the exception is the rule and that such a killing actually befits the campaigns of conquest.

The narrative in Judg 20–21 reports a twofold consecration—on the one hand, חרם as a consecration to destruction of disloyal tribes, and on the other hand, the appropriation of, or trade in, women for the purpose of conflict resolution within the association of tribes. This occurs in three variations:

1. In view of the crime (נבלה) perpetrated against the wife of the Levite in Gibeah, the Israelites swear, as a sanction against the Benjaminites who show no solidarity, that they will never give their daughters to them in marriage (21:1–5). Thus, the Benjaminites lose their share in the group, and the number of marriageable women on the market is reduced for them.

2. When, after the quasi-genocide of the population of Benjamin, the Israelites have compassion for the surviving men (21:6, 15 נחם *hiphil*), they search for alternatives, that is, a solution compatible with their vow. Thus, they give them four hundred young women of marriageable age whom they have spared from the enforcement of a second ban, namely, against the city of Jabesh because of the noncompliance with the levy of troops (21:10–14).

3. The last variant changes the vow to deprive the Benjaminites of their daughters and instead places it in a new perspective (21:15–23): they prompt the Benjaminites to abduct a number of young women corresponding to their needs during the course of the annual wine festival in Shiloh (v. 21).[40]

What is also special about this third major narrative is the coexistence of a vow, חרם, and those women chosen by proactive men as an "offering." Although the guilt of the city of Gibeah rises to the heavens in a burnt offering (20:38–40), and Jabesh, the city, which refuses to help, is punished with the vow of annihilation, in both actions people are spared—in the first case men (Judg 20:47) and in the second case young women (21:12), a fact that contradicts the Deuteronomistic provision for the extermination of YHWH's own adherents in Deut 13:13–19. In the end, Israel designates the spared portion of the population as belonging to the rest and in this way is able to resolve the problem of finding women for the refugees of the twelfth tribe. The declared goal of the action is that Benjamin can return to its inheritance, rebuild the cities, and live in them (Judg 20:23). In this situation, too, the women are an objectified commodity. But in the violence occasionally perpetrated against men, portrayed as sexualized, the blending of the boundaries between perpetrator and victim becomes clear, so that a clear pattern of male offenders and female victims is not discernible.[41] In contrast to Judg 1 and 11, here, no heroic figures are discernible, neither among the women nor among the men.

In this narrative, the idea of sacrifice or of offering has assumed such an independent existence that the women are not meant for YHWH, but quite profanely serve as a means to an end, that is, for the purpose of preserving tribal unity. The intentional sparing of a portion of the population (the marriageable women) is, in other passages, sanctioned as an offense against YHWH that cannot be recompensed (see 1 Sam 14:39, 44). In con-

---

40. On the hidden rite de passage behind this, see Niditch, *Judges*, 210–11. Groß characterizes the scene as fantastic, that is, as unhistorical, and he claims that the goal of the abduction of the women lies in the fact that the pledged vow is not broken and that everyone continues to live "once again in peace at those locations intended for them by JHWH" (*Richter*, 876).

41. See Müllner, "Tödliche Differenzen," 94–95. She points out that it is precisely the omission of his own sexual coercion in the report by the Levite to the tribes (20:5) that lets his humiliation through feminization become discernible (see Lev 18:25; Deut 22:5).

trast, the virgins in the campaign of retribution against Midian (חרם is lacking) in Num 31 are designated as spoils of war:

> Moses said to them, "Have you allowed all the women to live? These women here, on Balaam's advice, made the Israelites act treacherously against the LORD in the affair of Peor, so that the plague came among the congregation of the LORD. Now therefore, kill every male among the little ones, and kill every woman who has known a man by sleeping with him. But all the young girls who have not known a man by sleeping with him, keep alive for yourselves." (Num 31:15–18)

The continued existence of the escaped Benjaminites who are to be subjected to the ban is not revised. The חרם thus no longer fits into the structure supported by religious arguments outlined above. Neither the aspect of sacrifice to God, nor the attempt at separation, nor that of renouncing cultural or religious unity plays a role here. The issue here is the profane implementation of an institution of war, the mechanistic course of which is explained merely by the stereotypical reference to the period as that in which the people were without a king and thus also without law (see the framing in Judg 19:1 and 21:25).

5. Conclusion: Women in War

Niditch interprets the story in Judg 1 as a commentary on the contingency of power and on the possibility that unexpected people obtain control over it. And, in fact, it is Achsah who obtains control over land and water and, at the same time, effects the alliance of the Kenites with Israel through her marriage. The narrative portrays in terse, ironic language how she negotiates the point of intersection between her father and her husband. The narrative sketched out by Niditch finds variations in two further narratives in the book of Judges that illustrate the downward spiral that is characteristic for the book of Judges as a whole. Jephthah's daughter is characterized as an active figure who makes an inescapable situation her own by shaping it herself. She is not speechless but negotiates with her father. Nonetheless, her activity leads to self-abandonment and death in favor of the collective as a consequence of the positive outcome of the war. In the outline of the book, she assumes a middle position. In contrast, no activity is conceded to the wife of the Levite at the end of the book of Judges—apart from the terse note about her departure from her husband's house. She is literally sacrificed to preserve her husband's life, and finally she functions as the cause of war. The daughters from Jabesh (21:13–14) and the daughters from Shiloh (21:20–24), who survive the conscription of troops, also are reified. Women become commodities or objects that serve as an ethical example that leads to war among the tribes or, in the end, serves to reunify Israel. The surrender of the women corresponds to the needs of the men or of the collective. Their personal perspective is ignored, thereby underlining their passive status as mere objects of negotiation. Women in Judg 19–21 remain speechless and incapable of acting. While Achsah receives land and gets a portion of the inheritance, the young women are given as compensation to the Benjaminites, so that the men can return to their inheritance and, once again, take up their life in the tribe.

If the outline of the book of Judges is seen from the perspective that the end is a witness to the decline of Israel, then this decline in the texts examined can also be described as a story of the redefinition of the status of women. Their status seems to undergo an increasing devaluation, from being reduced to a prize or a war *offering*, to being the *victim* of war, and finally to being a commodity for reparation. Since the text here at Judg 1 as well as Judg (17–)19–21 has to do with redactional insertions, a creative intent becomes apparent that, in a prominent way, demonstrates a moral decline with the concrete treatment of women in situations of war.

Bibliography

Bal, Mieke. *Death and Dissymmetry: The Politics of Coherence in the Book of Judges*. Chicago: University of Chicago Press, 1988.

Barthélemy, Dominique. *Josué, Juges, Ruth, Samuél, Rois, Chroniques, Esdras, Néhémie, Esther*. Vol. 1 of *Critique textuelle de l'Ancien Testament*. OBO 50. Fribourg: Academic Press; Göttingen: Vandenhoeck & Ruprecht, 1982.

Bauks, Michaela. *Jephtas Tochter: Traditions-, religions- und rezeptionsgeschichtliche Studien zu Richter 11, 29–40*. FAT 71. Tübingen: Mohr Siebeck, 2010.

———. "Physical Attributes of Memorials: Could the Tomb of Jephthah and the Dietary Restrictions of Tekufot Give an Insight into the Intention of Judges 11:29–40?" Pages 235–54 in *Gender and Social Norms in Ancient Israel, Early Judaism and Christianity: Texts and Material Culture in Eastern Mediterranean Context*. Edited by Michaela Bauks, Katharina Galor, and Judith Hartenstein. JAJSup. Göttingen: Vandenhoeck & Ruprecht, 2019.

Bechmann, Ulrike. "Zelofhad." *Das wissenschaftliche Bibellexikon im Internet*. Edited by Michaela Bauks and Klaus Koenen. 2011. https://tinyurl.com/SBL6016g.

Brockmüller, Katrin. "Achsa." *Das wissenschaftliche Bibellexikon im Internet*. 2017. Edited by Michaela Bauks and Klaus Koenen. https://tinyurl.com/SBL6016f.

Dietrich, Walter. *1 Samuel 1–12*. BKAT 8.1. Neukirchen-Vluyn: Neukirchener Verlag, 2011.

Groß, Walter. *Richter*. HThKAT. Freiburg: Herder, 2009.

Hamori, Esther J. *Women's Divination in Biblical Literature: Prophecy, Necromancy, and Other Arts of Knowledge*. New Haven: Yale University Press, 2015.

Hertog, Cornelis den. "Jesus: Josue/Das Buch Josua." Pages 605–56 in *Genesis bis Makkabäer*. Vol. 1 of *Sepuaginta Deutsch: Erläuterungen und Kommentare zum griechischen Alten Testament*. Stuttgart: Deutsche Bibelgesellschaft, 2009.

Hieke, Thomas. *Levitikus 16–27*. HThKAT. Freiburg: Herder, 2014.

Jost, Renate, R. "Achsas Quellen: Feministisch-sozialgeschichtliche Überlegungen zu Josua 15,15–20/Ri 1,12–15." Pages 110–25 in *"Ihr Völker alle, klatscht in die Hände!" Festschrift für Erhard S. Gerstenberger zum 65. Geburtstag*. Edited by Rainer Kessler, Kerstin Ulrich, Milton Schwantes, and Gary Stansell. EUZ 3. Münster: Ugarit-Verlag, 1997.

———. *Gender, Sexualität und Macht in der Anthropologie des Richterbuches*. BWANT 164. Stuttgart: Kohlhammer, 2006.

Kamrada, Dolores. *Heroines, Heroes, and Deity*. LHBOTS 613. London: Oxford University Press, 2016.

Lanoir, Corinne. *Femmes fatales, filles rebelles: Figures Féminines dans le livre des Juges*. AR. Geneva: Labor et Fides, 2005.

Müller, Hans-Peter. "Die Inschrift des Königs Mesa von Moab." *TUAT* 1:646–50.

Müllner, Ilse. "Tödliche Differenzen. Sexuelle Gewalt als Gewalt gegen Andere in Ri 19." Pages 81–100 in *Von der Wurzel getragen: Christlich-feministische Exegese in Auseinandersetzung mit dem Antijudaismus*. Edited by Luise Schottroff and Marie-Theres Wacker. BibInt 17. Leiden: Brill, 1996.

Niditch, Susan. *Judges*. OTL. Louisville: Westminster John Knox, 2008.

Paz, Sarit. *Drums, Women, and Goddesses: Drumming and Gender in Iron Age II Israel*. OBO 232. Fribourg: Academic Press; Göttingen: Vandenhoeck & Ruprecht, 2007.

Rake, Mareike. *"Juda wird aufsteigen!" Untersuchungen zum ersten Kapitel des Richterbuches*. BZAW 367. Berlin: de Gruyter, 2006.

Sasson, Jack. *Judges 1–12: A New Translation with Introduction and Commentary*. AB 6D. New Haven: Yale University Press, 2014.

Schmitt, Rüdiger. *Der "Heilige Krieg" im Pentateuch und im Deuteronomistischen Geschichtswerk: Studien zur Forschungs-, Rezeptions- und Religionsgeschichte von Krieg und Bann im Alten Testament*. AOAT 381. Münster: Ugarit-Verlag, 2011.

Sjöberg, Michael. *Wrestling with Textual Violence: The Jephthah Narrative in Antiquity and Modernity*. BMW 4. Sheffield: Sheffield Phoenix, 2006.

Soggin, J. Alberto. *Judges*. OTL. Philadelphia: Westminster, 1981.

Trible, Phyllis. *Texts of Terror: Literary-Feminist Readings of Biblical Narratives*. Philadelphia: Fortress, 1984.

Vos, Cor de. *Das Los Judas: Über Entstehung und Ziele der Landbeschreibung in Josua 15*. VTSup 95. Leiden: Brill, 2003.

Gendered Politics: Dynastic Roles of Women in the Narratives about Saul, David, and Solomon

Ilse Müllner

1. Women as Focus of Attention

Women assume very different roles in the narratives about Saul, David, and Solomon. These narratives locate some of their functions in the context of the family, as daughters, wives, mothers, and sisters. These family roles assumed by women deserve special attention in view of the narratives considered here because the theme of family becomes the focus of the narrative community. Also in the books of Samuel, not only are women active in the family context, but wives are at the same time economically active and are shrewd politicians (Abigail), daughters are insurgents (Michal), and wives are religious subjects (the wives of Solomon). Describing women in family roles thus does not mean reducing them to merely daughters, wives, and mothers. "Motherhood or Death"—this alternative describes only very inadequately the construction of women in the Samuel books.[1] Even though the feminist critique that stresses the patriarchal context of the texts and shows that broad areas of women's life in ancient Israel remain ignored is true, the complexity and diversity of female figures and their assumed social roles in the narrated world are yet to be observed, even within this patriarchal framework.[2]

---

1. Lai Ling Elizabeth Ngan, "Class Privileges in Patriarchal Society: Women in First and Second Samuel," in *Biblical Books*, vol. 1 of *Feminist Interpretation of the Hebrew Bible in Retrospect*, ed. Susanne Scholz, RRBS 5 (Sheffield: Sheffield Phoenix, 2013), 110, following Karla G. Shargent.

2. See Andreas Kunz, *Die Frauen und der König David: Studien zur Figuration von Frauen in den Davidserzählungen*, ABG 8 (Leipzig: Evangelische Verlagsanstalt,

The books of Samuel relate the transition from a decentralized political structure to a monarchy in Israel, whereas in the books of the Kings this political structure is established and differentiated on a broader level. The focus of the narratives describing the emergence of the monarchy has a series of implications for the roles of women in the narrated world and thus also for the conception of gender. Along with Genesis, the Samuel books comprise those texts in the Bible in which female characters are developed most densely and most intensively. The very frequent presence of women figures in these narratives corresponds with the special functions of the family, on the one hand, in the narrated world and, on the other, in that world in which the narrative receives its present shape. In the narrated world, not just the monarchy but more precisely the dynasty is established. The family therefore becomes the location of state policy.[3] The interest in the events not only within the Davidic family and at Solomon's court but also in the families of Samuel, Eli, and Saul does not feed on a lust for a glimpse into the private affairs of strange people—such a juxtaposition of the political and the private would be completely anachronistic. Here, the issue is power politics and state policy. The quite special fusion of one single family with government power is rendered problematic repeatedly in the narratives, so that the focus on family policy must be seen in close connection with the establishment of dynastic rule.

The reference to the world in which the narrative originated is considerably more complex. The positioning of the books of Samuel and Kings in literary history is—like most of the biblical texts—not consensual. Agreement exists merely in regard to the fact that sources are used and that these were combined in the course of a multistep process to become a large narrative. The position that, with the incorporation of the material in a Deuteronomistic work of history, there is a point of culmination that points to the early postexilic period is at least widespread.[4] If one thus dis-

---

2004), 11, which emphasizes the plurality of the presentations of women in the David narratives.

3. On this, see Ilse Müllner, *Gewalt im Hause Davids: Die Erzählung von Tamar und Amnon (2 Sam 13,1–22)*, HBS 13 (Freiburg: Herder, 1997), 119–42.

4. See Georg Braulik, "Theorien über das deuteronomistische Geschichtswerk (DtrG) im Wandel der Forschung," in *Einleitung in das Alte Testament*, ed. Erich Zenger and Christian Frevel, KST 1 (Stuttgart: Kohlhammer, 2016), 229–54, with a detailed bibliography. For the Samuel books in the Deuteronomistic History, see in particular Walter Dietrich, *Die Samuelbücher im deuteronomistischen Geschichtswerk: Studien zu den Geschichtsüberlieferungen des Alten Testaments 2*, BWANT 201 (Stutt-

regards the later additions,[5] then, one is directed to the later monarchical period and—more spaciously—to the postexilic period for the historical location of the narrative complex. While for the first named epoch one can assume, on the basis of the dynastic structures, a proximity between the narrated world and the period of the origin of the narrative, the family theme in the postexilic epoch is connoted quite differently. Here, one must assume a substitution of the state institutions through family structures—family presents a reference point that is intended to contribute toward compensating for the loss of the monarchy. The narratives in Genesis about the ancestral parents, with which the "history of the people [is told] as the history of a family," find resonance here.[6] The books of Samuel, with their ambivalent representation of the origins of the Davidic dynasty, encounter a new environment that, on the one hand, perceives family as a central social entity and, on the other, has to grapple with the loss of the monarchy.

The observation that the narrated female figures remain underdeveloped is not tenable:[7] first of all because only a few of the masculine figures also are designated as round characters, who, for instance, go through a development within the narrated world, or through whom the narrative voice grants male and female readers an insight into their cognitive world and thereby also their emotional inner world. In addition, the categorization of figures as flat or round is controversial because the logical criteria used to establish these designations are unclear. And the assessment connected with them frequently does not do justice to the genre-oriented needs of narrative.[8] If, therefore, access to the thoughts or emotions of female figures such as Bathsheba escapes male and female readers, or if they lament the figures' "fragmentation," as in the case of Michal, then, not only the category of gender but also the entanglement of biblical narrative

---

gart: Kohlhammer, 2012); Cynthia Edenburg and Juha Pakkala, eds., *Is Samuel among the Deuteronomists? Current Views on the Place of Samuel in a Deuteronomistic History*, AIL 16 (Atlanta: Society of Biblical Literature, 2013).

5. See here the articles in Uwe Becker and Hannes Bezzel, eds., *Rereading the Relecture: The Question of (Post)Chronistic Influence in the Latest Redactions of the Books of Samuel*, FAT 2/66 (Tübingen: Mohr Siebeck, 2014).

6. Irmtraud Fischer, *Gottesstreiterinnen: Biblische Erzählungen über die Anfänge Israels* (Stuttgart: Kohlhammer, 1995). All translations from German are mine.

7. See Ngan, "Class Privileges," 111.

8. See Fotis Jannidis, "Character," in *Living Handbook of Narratology*, ed. Peter Hühn et al. (2013), https://tinyurl.com/SBL6016h.

conventions with a series of categories of social differentiation must be considered. To these categories belong, along with gender, the place within the social order (class), the ethnic affiliation (ethnicity), and physical factors such as age or disability (body). An intersectional approach attempts to discover the trail through the complex and, according to the material in each case, various determinations of the relationships among these individual social categories.[9]

Narrative attentiveness and social status are connected here in the most intimate manner. If biblical narratives are significant to establishing identity in the productive literary epochs of biblical Israel and to contributing to the creation and the interpretation of a world as well as of individuals in a society,[10] then the narrative characters have a central function in this process. The characters and their configuration offer readers an anchor in developing their own concepts of interpreting the world in resonance with their own experiences.[11] The fact that, in ancient Israel, questions of identity were not so much individual questions but have to do with collective processes should be emphasized in line with the concept of a constellative anthropology, which has become well established in biblical studies and which, again, must be taken into consideration in the analysis of the characters.[12]

---

9. On the concept of intersectionality and its reception in biblical studies, see the articles in Ute E. Eisen, Christine Gerber, and Angela Standhartinger, eds., *Doing Gender—Doing Religion: Fallstudien zur Intersektionalität im frühen Judentum, Christentum und Islam*, WMANT 302 (Tübingen: Mohr Siebeck, 2013); see also Nele Spiering-Schomborg, *"Man kann sich nicht entscheiden, als was man geboren wird": Exodus 1 im Horizont von Intersektionalität und empirischer Bibeldidaktik*, RI 19 (Stuttgart: Kohlhammer, 2017), 16–37. See also the essay by Maria Häusl in this volume.

10. See Irmtraud Fischer, "Die Bibel als Welt erzeugende Erzählung," in *Kultur—Wissen—Narration: Perspektiven transdisziplinärer Erzählforschung für die Kulturwissenschaften*, ed. Alexandra Strohmaier (Bielefeld: Transcript, 2013), 381–97.

11. The concept of resonance is developed by Hartmut Rosa, *Resonanz: Eine Soziologie der Weltbeziehung* (Berlin: Suhrkamp, 2016). He does this also in reference to the treatment of literary texts. Here, he relies on the study of empathy by Fritz Breithaupt, which shows that mirroring and empathetic effects arise also when human beings read fictional literature (Rosa, *Resonanz*, 267). See Fritz Breithaupt, *Kulturen der Empathie* (Frankfurt: Suhrkamp, 2009).

12. See Bernd Janowski, "Konstellative Anthropologie: Zum Begriff der Person im Alten Testament," in *Biblische Anthropologie: Neue Einsichten aus dem Alten Testament*, ed. Christian Frevel, QD 237 (Freiburg: Herder, 2010), 64–87. On the concept of the constellative analysis of figures, see Ilse Müllner, "Die Samuelbücher—Gott in

2. Can Sovereignty Be Equitable?

Societies evolve systems of rule that structure societal power and, in constant negotiation processes, continue to stabilize them anew. Power cuts across various societal spheres, for example, the military, religion, and economics.[13] Societal power is concentrated in these spheres where a monarchy is established and is made hereditary as a dynasty. The text of 1 Samuel–2 Kings tells of such negotiation processes on the part of a dynastic monarchy, which, however, is characterized as thoroughly unstable and is examined critically in its concrete forms. With this ambivalent representation of monarchy, 1 Samuel–2 Kings positions itself between the two poles of the divinization of royal sovereignty and the radical rejection of human sovereignty in favor of the concept of the royal dominion of God.[14]

The theme of succession in sovereignty intensifies in the concept of the house. The question is not restricted to the Davidic house but begins already in the first chapters of 1 Samuel, where the subject is the failure of the sons of Eli. The condemnation of the Elides in 1 Sam 2:30–36 assumes a dynastic promise made by God to this family of priests (1 Sam 2:30–31). The first promise of a dynasty thus does not concern a royal dynasty but rather a priestly family. The conduct of the Elides, however, does not correspond to the ethical demands of YHWH, who then rejects this priestly dynasty. A central theme of the Deuteronomistic History, namely, the question of the

---

Menschen, Tieren und Dingen erzählen," in *Gott als Figur: Narratologische Analysen biblischer Texte und ihrer Adaptionen*, ed. Ute E. Eisen and Ilse Müllner, HBS 82 (Freiburg: Herder, 2016), 90–94.

13. See Saana Svärd, *Women and Power in Neo-Assyrian Palaces*, SAAS 23 (Winona Lake, IN: Eisenbrauns, 2015), 28–29, as well as Mosheh Halbertal and Stephen Holmes, *The Beginning of Politics: Power in the Biblical Book of Samuel* (Princeton: Princeton University Press, 2017), passim, which, however, does not mention religion in this connection, but rather defines political power as "the powers to draft and the powers to tax" (5).

14. See the major themes in the two Samuel books by Halbertal and Holmes, *Beginning*. On the function of such an ambivalent representation of sovereignty, see Ilse Müllner, "Die Samuelbücher als Werk Politischer Theologie," in *Thesaurus in vasis fictilibus: "Schatz in zerbrechlichen Gefäßen" (2 Kor 4,7); Festschrift für Bischof Heinz-Josef Algermissen zum 75. Geburtstag*, ed. Bernd Willmes and Christoph Gregor Müller (Freiburg: Herder, 2018), 284–95. A short but very instructive survey of research on this issue is given by Sara Kipfer, *Der bedrohte David: Eine exegetische und rezeptionsgeschichtliche Studie zu 1 Sam 16–1 Kön 2*, SBR 3 (Berlin: de Gruyter, 2015), 45–49.

retraction of the promise in the light of massive transgressions, is concretized in terms of the failure of a dynastic concept already at the beginning of the Samuel books. The literary parallels between 1 Sam 2:12–36 and the promise of a dynasty made to David in 2 Sam 7 support this view.[15]

Also, at the end of the Samuel books, there is a failed dynasty, or a royal house that has not even attained the form that could last for generations. Saul's last offspring are murdered in 2 Sam 21 and thrown to the animals. The confrontation centering on the dynastic factor at the beginning and the end of the Samuel books is embedded in narratives in which women play a central as well as a resistant role.[16] Hannah and Rizpah represent the beginning and the end—of the Samuel books as well as of life. Hannah agonizes before God to become a mother. Rizpah takes a stand for her own sons and the sons of a daughter of Saul, and sees to it that they are interred properly after David orders their execution. In the first three chapters of the Samuel books, as well as in 2 Sam 21, the focus is on houses, that is, dynasties that fail. Hannah bears Samuel, who, a few years later, will proclaim the downfall of the house of Eli (1 Sam 3), embrace the new institution of the monarchy, and thus be the figure behind the replacement of the Elides. Rizpah embodies the end of the house of Saul, which, as a house of bloodguiltiness (בית הדמים, 2 Sam 21:1), loses its last offspring. The failure to establish a dominion that spans the generations stands thus at the beginning and at the end of the Samuel books; the matter is the object of the most violent confrontations. From the very beginning, the struggle for social power is carried out also in the realm of family life. The great interest in sexuality throughout the narratives must be seen in this regard.[17]

3. The House: Concentration of Social Power

The concept of house (בית) encompasses several meanings. It designates the material building and, in a combined construction, can be more

---

15. Examples include the imparting of God's message through a prophet or a man of God, the reference to Egypt, the central position accorded to the term בית, the promise of a house that endures.

16. See the article by Rainer Kessler in this volume.

17. See, on this point, but with a different focus (honor and shame), Ken Stone, *Sex, Honor and Power in the Deuteronomistic History: A Narratological and Anthropological Analysis*, JSOTSup 234 (Sheffield: Sheffield Academic, 1996).

closely defined as the house of a king (palace) or the house of a deity (temple). The attribution of a house to a person is based, to be sure, on this material-local meaning, but it also goes beyond this in that the house also comprises its male and female inhabitants and so can stand metonymically for the people, that is, for those who live in that household. Last, the house, completely detached from the material connotation yet metonymically connected to it, also denotes the family.

The narrative community definitely is conscious of this multiplicity of connotations, as the various usages of the term *house* in 2 Samuel show. YHWH rejects David's request to build a temple (בית) for YHWH (7:5); instead, YHWH promises to build a house for David (v. 11) by establishing his family as a dynasty. Thus, David's successor Solomon can complete the temple building project, that is, build a house for YHWH (v. 13), without it being a detriment to David—although building a temple was actually one of the tasks of an ancient Near Eastern king.[18]

Because of the concept of dynasty, which in the ancient Near Eastern environment already was established for a considerably longer period than in biblical Israel, the ruling arrangement is extended intergenerationally beyond the current period of rule in each case. In 2 Sam 7, the permanence (עולם) is emphasized eight times,[19] showing that the view that the dynasty would transcend generations refers essentially to the establishment of the Davidic monarchy. Therefore, progeny becomes a power factor, to which the lists repeatedly offered in 1–2 Samuel of royal wives, sons, and daughters refer. The wives of Saul as well as of David are mentioned by name in these listings (1 Sam 14:47; 2 Sam 3:3–5; 5:13–16). The sons stand at the center of these agnatically arranged lists, but where daughters play a role in the narrative they, too, are mentioned by name, such as Merab and Michal in the list in 1 Sam 14.

The family as narratively developed here is an essential element of social organization both synchronically and diachronically. Synchronically, relationally based structures suggest cohesion and proximity or distance to the center of power in reference to royal sovereignty. Whoever stands in a familial relationship to the king frequently is awarded a special position, also in the context of the court. But other social centers of power and competence also are structured on the family, for example,

---

18. See Müllner, "Werk Politischer Theologie," 90–91 (and for further literature).
19. עד־עולם: 7:13, 16 (2x), 24, 25, 26; לעולם: 7:29 (2x).

priestly service. The narratives around the first three kings do not stand alone regarding their focus on the family. Broad passages of the biblical narrations make recourse to the family and place it in the context of the narrative interpretation of the world.

According to Irmtraud Fischer, the Bible represents the beginnings of defining epochs by using the form of family narratives, since, in the genealogical thought of the ancient Near East, what was true for the founding generations is true for all the progeny. Common origin is assuring in times of crisis and has an identity-forming and identity-strengthening effect where social groups are (or must be) formed anew.[20]

4. Royal Women

Not all the individual female figures or all the groups of women that are mentioned in 1 Samuel–2 Kings can be discussed here. Those who are selected here are women who exert an especially strong influence in the sphere of dynastic politics, as outlined in the narratives about Saul, David, and Solomon. The women of the royal families therefore receive preferential treatment in the following analysis. That this does not reflect the whole picture or represent all the women must be emphasized. Nonfamilial forms of political influence are likewise the object of the narratives. Women are religious authorities (1 Sam 28—the woman from Endor), or they intervene actively in political and military events through their sagacious speech (2 Sam 14—the woman from Tekoa; 2 Sam 20—the woman from Abel Beth-Maacah).[21] They are formative in the expression of political opinions (1 Sam 18:7; 21:12; 29:5—"Saul has slain his thousands, and David his ten thousands"). The queen of Sheba endorses Solomon's reputation as the wisest of all kings (1 Kgs 10). The sequence can be continued. In the present context, though, the concern is the role of women in the establishment of dynastic rule. Thus, the familial roles of women, to which also motherhood belongs, is the focus of this study. As the examples mentioned above clearly show, this does not, of course, mean that women

---

20. Irmtraud Fischer, "Menschheitsfamilie—Erzelternfamilie—Königsfamilie: Familien als Protagonistinnen von Welt erzeugenden Erzählungen," *BK* 4 (2015): 190–97.

21. For details, see Kunz, *Frauen*, 245–80; 353–55. He speaks about the "type of woman preventing violence."

appear in the narratives only as mothers, or that their social status could be determined exclusively on the basis of motherhood.

The role of the royal mother in particular is considered to be of great significance because the royal mother stands for the synchronic as well as the diachronic aspect of dynastic cohesion. On the one hand, she lives first of all in special proximity to the king, whose wife she is. As such, she has political influence and perhaps also assumes her own position of economic power. This economic power is documented repeatedly in the Neo-Assyrian Empire texts: the queen administers her own household, including issues of land ownership and other economic resources.[22] Such evidence is lacking in respect of the Israelite and Judaic monarchy. This could be due to the disparity of sources, since there is no evidence in Israel and Judah of administrative documents on the same scale as those documented for the Mesopotamian royal courts. However, the lack of such evidence in the literary texts of the Bible does not imply the lack of such a social practice.[23] A connection between the special position of an individual woman among the king's women and the succession to the throne is not to be assumed—the literary development of the succession theme within 1 Samuel–2 Kings denounces the privileged position of a son on the basis of his descent from a certain woman. But the royal mother also represents diachronically the intergenerational aspect. She does this, on the one hand, by symbolically representing the embodiment of the parentage of the then-ruling son and, through this, of the connecting line between the old and the new king. On the other hand, the royal mother is also in reality in a position of power because she establishes the continuity between the royal generations with her knowledge and her influence. The influence exerted by Bathsheba in 1 Kgs 2 points in this direction.

4.1. Michal

As a daughter of Saul and a wife of David, Michal is placed in a position of extreme tension that is expressed narratively, not in the least through its fragmentation.[24] Her figure appears like a hidden, interwoven thread

---

22. See Svärd, *Women and Power*, 61–74.

23. Maria Häusl in this volume presents another view of the matter.

24. See the title of the publication by J. Cheryl Exum, *Fragmented Women: Feminist (Sub)versions of Biblical Narratives*, JSOTSup 163 (Sheffield: Sheffield Academic, 1993). On the figure of Michal, see also the articles in David J. A. Clines and Tamara

at the nodal points in David's biography, where she lends her own color to the events in which the future king is brought into focus. The passages in 1 Sam 18; 19; 25:44; 2 Sam 3:13–16; 6:16–23 tell about Michal. She bestrides the stage of the narrated world with drum beating and trumpet sounding, and leaves it again, but in hardly a perceptive way. Michal's first action is her love for David (1 Sam 18:20). This is not only improper in the indirect context of the incipient hostility between Michal's father, Saul, and his young rival David, but it is also unique in the biblical context. With the exception of the poetic female in the Song of Songs, there is no other woman in the Hebrew Bible who is presented as a subject of love for a man. Michal's narrated end, on the other hand, is quiet and, in view of narrative time, enormously slow: "But, as for Michal, the daughter of Saul, she had no child to the day of her death" (2 Sam 6:23).[25] The whole of the rest of Michal's life is summarized with this note. Nonetheless, at the margins of the representation, there remains fuzziness. Her mention by name along with her sister Merab in the list of Saul's children (1 Sam 14:49–51) is highly unusual, since in such lists (as in the genealogical lists in Genesis), the sons are named, but not the daughters. More remarkable, however, is the mysterious ascription in the MT of 2 Sam 21:8 of Saul's remaining progeny to the supposedly childless Michal, whereas, according to the text of the Greek Septuagint, Merab's (not Michal's) children are killed.[26]

Within this framework, individual scenes are narrated in which Michal refers to David. She loves him and is given to him as wife by Saul (1 Sam 18); she cunningly helps David to flee from Saul (1 Sam 19); and she criticizes him for his behavior, which she deems not appropriate for a king (2 Sam 6). Michal's position between the first two kings of Israel is marked syntactically by her designation as the "wife of David" or the "daughter of Saul." "Michal, the wife of David" acts in 1 Sam 19 against Saul; in 2 Sam 6, it is "Michal, the daughter of Saul" who criticizes her royal husband.

Michal embodies the house of Saul, whose dynasty is not destined to continue. To David, she is attractive from the very beginning as a daughter

---

Cohn Eskenazi, eds., *Telling Queen Michal's Story: An Experiment in Comparative Interpretation*, JSOTSup 119 (Sheffield: JSOT Press, 1991).

25. Unless otherwise indicated, all biblical translations are mine.

26. Frank Moore Cross et al. reconstruct the text to read "Merab," in agreement with the LXX; the passage in the manuscript is, unfortunately, illegible. See Cross et al., *Qumran Cave 4.XII: 1–2 Samuel*, DJD 17 (Oxford: Clarendon, 2005), 178.

of the ruling king. Between Saul and David, the issue is whether David should become the "son-in-law of the king." With its frequent occurrence in 1 Sam 18:18, 2, 23, 26, and 27, the word חתן is a key word in this narrative about the beginning of the marriage between Michal and David. Michal at first represents the social position that David needs to achieve on his path to royal power, and which Saul attempts to prevent by demanding a bride price that comes only at the risk of David's life. However, as Saul gives her in marriage to another man, Paltiel, and, in 2 Sam 3, David takes her back, the game of power continues with Michal as pledge.

Michal, however, does not stand alone in this tension between the two men, but is also joined by Jonathan in her precarious position between her father and her beloved husband. Jonathan's friendship with David in many respects takes a turn that differs from that of Michal's love, and the social embedding of these relationships is also, of course, entirely different.[27] Notwithstanding, there are also clear parallels between the two figures of Michal and Jonathan, and their actions in 1 Sam 18–19 are connected in the closest way. Saul's two children love David and, in this, stand paradigmatically for the whole of Israel and Judah (1 Sam 18). The relationships of both to David are formalized—in the case of Jonathan through the conclusion of a covenant, and in the case of Michal through marriage. Both help to protect David when he flees from their father, Saul. However, both children of Saul fail—Jonathan dies in battle beside his father, while Michal remains childless.

Michal's criticism of David's conduct and her childlessness, presented as a consequence in the narrative (2 Sam 6:16, 20–23), is one scene that represents David's conflict with the house of Saul. David returns "in order to bless *his* house" (לברך את־ביתו). His answer to

---

27. On the relationship between David and Jonathan, see especially James E. Harding, *The Love of David and Jonathan: Ideology, Text, Reception* (Sheffield: Equinox, 2013); Thomas Römer, "Homosexualität in der Hebräischen Bibel: Einige Überlegungen zu Leviticus 18 und 20, Genesis 19 und der David-Jonathan-Erzählung," in *Was ist der Mensch, dass du seiner gedenkst? (Psalm 8,5): Aspekte einer theologischen Anthropologie; Festschrift für Bernd Janowski zum 65. Geburtstag*, ed. Michaela Bauks, Kathrin Liess, and Peter Riede (Neukirchen-Vluyn: Neukirchener Verlag, 2008), 435–54; Jonathan Y. Rowe, *Sons or Lovers: An Interpretation of David and Jonathan's Friendship*, LHBOTS 575 (London: T&T Clark, 2012); Gary Stansell, "David und seine Freunde: Sozialwissenschaftliche Betrachtung der David-Jonathan-Freundschaft," in *Alte Texte in neuen Kontexten: Wo steht die sozialwissenschaftliche Bibelexegese*, ed. Wolfgang Stegemann and Richard E. DeMaris (Stuttgart: Kohlhammer, 2015), 53–84.

Michal's allegation that he did not conduct himself in a way befitting a king pushes the political dimension of this encounter to the surface (2 Sam 6:21): "Before YHWH, who chose me—above your father and his house—to appoint me ruler over the people of YHWH, over Israel, before YHWH I have danced!" As a figure, Michal symbolizes the tension between autonomy and subjection. In her love for David, she is unique; in her commitment to this man against her own father, which causes her to employ deception, she relates to the matriarch Rachel, who, with the aid of an idol, outwits her father (Gen 31:19–35). Michal embodies the house of Saul, his progeny, which does not form a dynastic line, and she is a central element of the narrative plot.[28] Jonathan's death and the disability of his son Merib-Baal (see 2 Sam 9) also aligns with the report on Michal's childlessness. That Michal embodies the failure of Saul's dynasty could be a key to the mention of her name in the MT of 2 Sam 21:8. Michal in that text, therefore, symbolizes the end of the house of Saul—and in this narrative, too.

4.2. Abigail

Abigail stands in a series of female figures who, through their rhetoric and sagacious action, influence the narrated events and therefore can be interpreted in the context of Wisdom.[29] The narrative begins in 1 Sam 25 with the death of Samuel—the role of the prophet is thus vacant at this point when David encounters Abigail. An incident precedes this encounter that places both of the male characters—David and Nabal, Abigail's husband—in a bad light. David had demanded material support in exchange for the protective services that he claimed to have provided. Nabal, whose name, "idiot" or also "criminal," like the name of other figures in the Hebrew Bible underlies his behavior, refused, however, to provide for David's men, which caused David to contemplate violent action against Nabal and his house. At this point, Abigail intervenes, makes amends regarding the matter with highly artful rhetoric, and thereby saves her house. Abigail's

---

28. See the reconstruction of the reference to the history of the house of David by Ina Willi-Plein, "1 Sam 18–19 und die Davidshausgeschichte," in *Davidshaus und Prophetie: Studien zu den Nebiim*, ed. Ina Willi-Plein, BThSt 127 (Neukirchen-Vluyn: Neukirchener Verlag, 2012), 34–35.

29. See Irmtraud Fischer, *Gotteslehrerinnen: Weise Frauen und Frau Weisheit im Alten Testament* (Stuttgart: Kohlhammer, 2006), 22–38.

speech is characterized by ancient Near Eastern conventions of courtesy—her self-designation as "handmaiden" (אמה, NRSV "servant") has nothing to do with submission but rather within the framework of conventional speech is an appropriate expression in the encounter with an unfamiliar or a higher-placed counterpart. Although David at this point in the narrative does not yet hold the office of king (the readers, of course, have knowledge of the secret anointing in 1 Sam 16, but the other figures do not), Abigail indeed treats him as the future ruler. Her effort in deescalating the threatening act of violence by David and his men connects Abigail with a prophetic promise made to David:

> For YHWH will certainly erect for my lord an enduring house because my lord is fighting the battles of YHWH.... When then YHWH has done all the good for my lord that he has promised to you, and has appointed him to be the ruler over Israel, then the fact that you have shed blood without cause and that my lord has helped himself will cause you no grief and no troubled heart. (1 Sam 25:28–31)

As motivation for refraining from the planned violence, David should do everything to preserve his power-packed future, which could be damaged by such a violent course of action. In terms of the confrontation between the two characters, this argument is an uncommonly clever move. In view of the greater things that await David, which Abigail places before him as an assured future, it is obvious that he needs to abstain from acting on impulse. Abigail's utterance can be qualified as prophetic speech. She opens his eyes to the consequences of his actions. In addition, she reminds David of the theological dimension of his action.

> The speech of this woman is so convincing that David indeed reacts in accord with her conceptions. Through Abigail, he becomes ready to grasp the theological dimension of his actions. So, he begins his speech with an encomium to JHWH, who has sent Abigail to him, and with praise of her incisive intellect, which has saved him from doing wrong and, thereby, from taking bloodguilt upon himself (v. 32f).[30]

But also in terms of the narrative and thus in the communication between the text and the readers, Abigail assumes a prophetic role. She is the figure who—long before Nathan, but with a literal prereference to Nathan's

---

30. Fischer, *Gotteslehrerinnen*, 35.

prophecy in 2 Sam 7[31]—promises David a house that will endure. Therewith, Abigail initiates the narrated events leading to the dynastic future and provides these events with their place in the grand narrative of the Deuteronomic history.

That Abigail becomes David's wife after the death of her husband Nabal is certainly not the main point of the narrative, but does stand in the context of Davidic marriage policy, as presented in 1–2 Samuel. In the further course of the narrative, she is mentioned two other times within the framework of the lists of David's wives (2 Sam 2:2; 3:3). It is interesting that, through the words affixed to her name, אשת נבל, the wife of Nabal, the story in 1 Sam 25 is recalled.

4.3. Bathsheba

Bathsheba's story is not told in a single textual context but is divided into two main blocks. In 2 Sam 11–12, the subject is the frequently cited and interpreted encounter between David and Bathsheba, the killing of Uriah, and the death of the firstborn child, as well as the further consequences of David's misconduct for his family. In 1 Kgs 1–2, Bathsheba is introduced first as wife of the aging king and then as royal mother who uses her political connections to guarantee the succession to the throne for her son. The two sections of the text depict Bathsheba in very different situations and contexts, which are definitely full of tension. The connection between these two sections also constitutes part of the central points of this discussion.

Often, the question of Bathsheba's complicity in David's lustful encounter with her (2 Sam 11) is linked to 1 Kgs 1, and it is insinuated that Bathsheba, as calculating and power-conscious, showed herself naked to the king in order to secure a position in David's court. The premises of such an argument must be questioned. First, the guilt of Bathsheba is not a theme of the text, and, second, the desire to fill the gaps in 2 Sam 11 with 1 Kgs 1–2 is questionable. If literary or other artistic receptions of the David-Bathsheba-Uriah narrative draw such lines of connection and develop their characters through these gaps, then, that is quite an

---

31. Note 1 Sam 25:28 // 2 Sam 7:16. See Christa Schäfer-Lichtenberger, "Frauen im Gespräch mit David: Deuteronomistische Zwischenrufe?," in *Die Samuelbücher und die Deuteronomisten*, ed. Christa Schäfer-Lichtenberger, BWANT 188 (Stuttgart: Kohlhammer, 2010), 143.

appropriate procedure within the framework of artistic processes.³² In the exegetical task, however, the perspective is just as much a different one as are the questions asked. Here the concern is to ascertain the potential meaning of the text,³³ and then the plots of both texts must be analyzed independently of each other, in order, as a second step, to investigate the possible overall picture of the character. Scholarly literature on the moral integrity of Bathsheba, of course, would be incomplete without the nonacademic reception the analysis of this character. Obviously, powerful female characters arouse the moral judgment of both male and female exegetes. Comparable statements are made in scholarly appraisals of ancient Near Eastern literature about Naqi'a, the wife of the Assyrian king Sennacherib and the mother of Esarhaddon, who can be considered the best-documented queen and royal mother of the Neo-Assyrian Empire.³⁴

Writing in 1926, Leonhard Rost characterized Bathsheba as "a not very significant woman who only lends an all-too-willing ear to his orders,"³⁵ but in today's context this statement would be considered an incomprehensible and almost strange conclusion. Bathsheba is one of the main characters in the narrative by virtue of her unique position as the wife of David and the mother of Solomon and the fact that she assumes an influential position in both courts. Bathsheba is viewed in the history of interpretation as the woman who is seen—David espies her from the roof of his palace, desires her, has her brought to him, and sleeps with her. He does this knowing that she is the wife of Uriah, one of his commanders, who at this point is fighting one of the king's wars. That, at this time, David does not go to war like the other kings and does not besiege the city of Rabbah with his soldiers but rather remains in Jerusalem (2 Sam 11:1), is already the first indication that he shirks his responsibility as king. David has Bathsheba brought to him in order to have sexual intercourse with her. It is unclear from the

---

32. See Andrea Fischer, *Dramen zu "David, Batseba und Urija" (2 Sam 11): Zur Rezeption hebräischer Erzählkunst in Literatur und Theater—Paul Alberti (1904), Martha Hellmuth (1906) und Emil Bernhard (1919)*, EUZ 27 (Münster: LIT, 2018).

33. See Andrea Fischer, *Königsmacht, Begehren, Ehebruch und Mord—Die Erzählung von "David, Batseba und Urija" (2 Sam 11): Narratologische Analysen*, EUZ 26 (Münster: LIT, 2018).

34. See Svärd, *Women and Power*, 54–61.

35. Leonhard Rost, *Die Überlieferung von der Thronnachfolge Davids*, BWANT 42 (Stuttgart: Kohlhammer, 1926), 87. That Rost characterizes her as "not very significant" (*nicht allzu bedeutend*) twice within two pages could be interpreted almost as a forced belittlement of this female figure (86–87).

narrative whether this is a case of rape or consensual sex; that is, whether Bathsheba also desires David and plans the social encounter in advance, which then leaves room for repeated speculation. Bathsheba's feelings, her motivation, and indeed even her actions, remain blank spaces in the narrative. Only the announcement of her pregnancy (2 Sam 11:5) and her act of mourning the death of her husband (2 Sam 11:26), as well as the birth of her first child and then of Solomon (2 Sam 11:27; 12:24), are enumerated as Bathsheba's activities. Neither in regard to David's desire nor in the context of the death of her first child is insight granted into the inner world of this character. David is the focus of interest, and his confrontation with Uriah constitutes the bulk of the narrative in 2 Sam 11.[36]

The narrative voice's judgment of David's action is clear and is pronounced with the highest narrative authority: "The thing that David did was evil in the eyes of YHWH" (2 Sam 11:27). David's dealing with Bathsheba and Uriah causes a breach in the narrated world. From this point, David's power as king as well as his own well-being and that of the members of his family is threatened. Nathan's parable and his subsequent prophecy about David's house express this change (2 Sam 12). Like Saul, who acted against the command of YHWH (1 Sam 13–15), David, too, transgresses YHWH's commandment and thus conducts himself like one of the kings against which 1 Sam 8 warns. But in contrast to Saul, who loses his royal dignity because of his transgression, David keeps his, and the promise of the Davidic dynasty is also not invalidated. First, however, David's conduct toward Bathsheba and Uriah will have those consequences in the narrated world that Nathan pronounces in 2 Sam 12. Second, the story will continue to be told, since it belongs to the canonic chronicle of the memoirs of David, and it casts a negative light on him. "For David did what was right in the sight of YHWH. He did not turn aside from any command all the days of his life—except in the case of Uriah the Hittite" (1 Kgs 15:5). In this short summary of events Uriah is mentioned, but not Bathsheba.

This ambivalence remains inscribed also in the figure of Bathsheba. In the political logic of the narrative, Bathsheba, in the context of David's marriage policy, embodies the Jerusalem upper class. She represents, in addition, the stability of the dynasty as the mother of the successor to the

---

36. All the more astounding is the fact that the Luther translation from 2016 still renders "David und Batseba" as the heading for 2 Sam 11, while the German *Einheitsübersetzung* from 2017 has the title "David, Batseba und Urija."

throne and later king, Solomon. But the offense against Bathsheba and Uriah is also what secures the breach in the image of David. The death of the first child from Bathsheba is commonly interpreted against this background. The child who came from David's union with Bathsheba—a union that "was evil in the sight of YHWH"—cannot enter into the line of succession to the throne. In spite of the offense, the story continues *with* David and his dynasty, and Bathsheba, of all people, becomes a first royal mother at the birth of the Judaic dynasty.

She is depicted in this role more clearly in 1 Kgs 1–2; 1 Kgs 1:11–31 tells how Bathsheba, in agreement with the prophet Nathan, intervenes in the events surrounding the succession to the throne as the aging King David loses more and more of his political (and sexual) power. Bathsheba—following Nathan's counsel—refers to a promise that David once gave her, which is that Solomon should sit on the throne after him. At the same time, she reports to David that Adonijah already has declared himself as king and organized a feast, to which he did not invite Solomon (1 Kgs 1:19; according to the narrative voice, Nathan, Benaiah, and the "mighty men," הגבורים, also were not invited; 1 Kgs 1:10). As arranged, Nathan joins her and confirms Adonijah's deed to David and demands a clear statement about the succession. David responds to this intervention just as Nathan had foreseen; he confirms Solomon as his successor.

As in the case of 2 Sam 11, many exegetes, in their interpretation of 1 Kgs 1, approach the figure of Bathsheba as well as of Nathan with a hermeneutics of suspicion. First, it is said that Adonijah had not yet become king, as Nathan "suggests."[37] Second, "David's pledge in regard to Solomon (13d–f)" is said to be "contrived" since "for him as well as for Bathsheba and Solomon … everything is at stake now at the latest."[38] But this negative interpretation of the characters of Nathan and Bathsheba is only one among several possibilities. Syntactically, it is quite possible to read the הלוא in 1 Kgs 1:11 not as an indication of a rhetorical question but rather as an introduction to a statement: "Nathan's words in v. 11 are not to be understood as a suggestion, but rather as a summary of events. The news about Adonijah being king represents a re-narrated reality."[39]

---

37. Georg Hentschel, *1 Könige*, NEB 10 (Würzburg: Echter, 1984), 21.
38. Ernst Axel Knauf, *1 Könige 1–14*, HThKAT (Vienna: Herder, 2016), 130.
39. Till Magnus Steiner, *Salomo als Nachfolger Davids: Die Dynastieverheissung in 2 Sam 7,11b–16 und ihre Rezeption in 1 Kön 1–11*, BBB 181 (Göttingen: V&R Unipress, 2017), 146–47.

The question about the pledge also cannot be so clearly explained. "The context pointedly leaves it unclear whether this pledge is invented ad hoc, in order to move the age-worn king toward a re-thinking of, and intervention in, the succession to the throne that now has become acute through accomplished facts, or whether David actually has selected Solomon for the monarchy."[40] Many interpreters allege that Nathan, together with Bathsheba, fabricated the promise; but the interpretation as a rectifying, analeptic narrative is possible also in the sense that David's promise, which he had made long before, comes into play only now.[41] In any case, it is indisputable that Bathsheba and Nathan openly act in their own interest by forcing David in the direction of an action they believe is advantageous. But their arguments—Adonijah's self-styled declaration of himself as king and David's promise—must not be condemned yet as fabrications and lies.

After David's death, Bathsheba once again intervenes, this time, however, in favor of Adonijah, who asks her to help persuade Solomon to give him Abishag the Shunammite as his wife. Solomon interprets this wish as a renewed effort on Adonijah's part to secure the royal power and consequently has his rival murdered (1 Kgs 2:13–25). In this passage, too, the text leaves the reader wondering whether the royal mother is involved in a scheme or simply passes on Adonijah's request without any ulterior motives. Stefan Heym's chronicler Etan stops at the same conundrum as the interpreters of the books of Samuel and the Kings: "Had she been just the helpless soldier's wife coerced to quench the fire in the bowels of the King, or was she the moving spirit of the crimes which followed upon the original sin, using her body and the fruit of her womb to beguile the King until it was her son that sat on the throne…?"[42] The figure of Bathsheba, as portrayed in 1 Kgs 1–2, is more interesting than the question of her

---

40. Irmtraud Fischer, "Salomo und die Frauen," in *Das Manna fällt auch heute noch: Beiträge zur Geschichte und Theologie des Alten, Ersten Testaments; Festschrift für Erich Zenger*, ed. Frank-Lothar Hossfeld and Ludger Schwienhorst-Schönberger, HBS 44 (Freiburg: Herder, 2004), 220.

41. See Steiner, *Salomo als Nachfolger Davids*, 147.

42. Stefan Heym, *The King David Report: A Novel* (New York: G. P. Putnam's Sons, 1973), 174. See the further details in Andrea Fischer, "Opfer oder Intrigantin: Zur mehrdeutigen Darstellung der biblischen Figur Batsebas in 2 Sam 11 und in literarischen Rezeptionen," in *Das Buch in den Büchern: Wechselwirkungen von Bibel und Literatur*, ed. Andrea Polaschegg and Daniel Weidner (Paderborn: Fink, 2012), 69–84.

guilt and the polarization of victim and schemer might suggest. Bathsheba is the first woman in the biblical narrative whose role is significant for understanding the ancient Near Eastern court. The royal mother assumes a special position in the Hebrew Bible as well as in other ancient Near Eastern courts. In 1 Kgs 2, this position is described significantly by the deeds performed by Solomon when Bathsheba comes to him: "Bathsheba came to King Solomon to speak with him because of Adonijah. The king arose to meet her. He bowed before her [וישתחו לה], sat on his throne, and set up a throne for the mother of the king. Then she sat to his right" (1 Kgs 2:19).

Bathsheba, therefore, is the only woman in the Hebrew Bible before whom a person performs *proskynesis* (וישתחו). That it is the king who does this shows the status that Bathsheba has as royal mother. In addition, Solomon sets up a throne for her. However—and here the narrative is very precise—this attestation of honor is not bestowed on the person. The mention of the personal name is lacking; Bathsheba is referred to by her title, mother of the king. That Solomon performs *proskynesis* before Bathsheba and sets up a throne indicates that only because of her enthronement through Solomon is this function thus installed, and that Bathsheba acts and is distinguished in her role.

4.4. Tamar

In response to Nathan's pronouncement that evil will rise against David from within his own house (2 Sam 12), the first act of violence within the family occurs. Tamar is raped by her brother Amnon. In reaction to this, Absalom, another son of David, murders his brother (2 Sam 13).

In the narrative of the rape of Tamar, several levels of power are interwoven and overlap with each other reciprocally.[43] First, there is the most obvious level of the sexualized power of a man, Amnon, against a woman, Tamar, which is the form of expression and a part of that power that permeates gender relationships. But that is only one part of the violent action that moves within complex family and political structures. As a brother, Amnon also has power over his sister; interfamilial structures within the framework of a patriarchal order are thus so conceived. Amnon can demand from his sister that she prepare a restorative meal

---

43. On this narrative, see Müllner, *Gewalt im Hause Davids*.

for him, and in this he is supported by his father David. Absalom, who silences his sister and in return gives her a place in his house (2 Sam 13:20), also has a share in this power. David's power over Tamar and over his sons Amnon and Absalom also is taken for granted. The narrative of the act of Absalom's revenge at the shearing of the sheep subsequent to the first act of violence (2 Sam 13:23–27) makes this clear. It becomes obvious already at this point that the dimension of political rule also plays a role when sons are successors to the throne and potential rivals in the struggle for royal power. Through his murder of Amnon, because of the act of violence perpetrated against Tamar, Absalom attains first place in the succession to the throne. Interfamilial conflict situations are here insoluble, and power-political confrontations merge. This is a hallmark of the narratives about David from the beginning to their end, from Michal to Abishag—sexuality, family structures, and royal power intertwine. The entanglement of the various aspects and levels in which the permanent processes in the negotiation of social power take place shows that a simplified pattern of the power of men over women is not sufficient for understanding the social processes reflected in these narratives. Men as well as women find themselves in different familial, hierarchical, and ethnic positions so that they have access to social power also on the basis of their other social involvements.

What does this mean for understanding the figure of Tamar? First of all, it is important to recognize how distinctively Tamar is portrayed in this single narrative in which she appears. In particular, her impressive speech, with which she attempts to prevent Amnon's threatening act of violence, characterizes her as a wise woman who is conscious of the danger and who exhausts every means of resistance. Tamar is the only victim of acts of sexual violence in the Bible whom the narrator gives a voice. Her rhetoric is marked by a high level of self-consciousness and a consciousness of her belonging to Israel as a community with ethical values: "Such a thing is not done in Israel!" (2 Sam 13:12). Therefore, she not only qualifies her brother as a criminal (נבל, v. 13) but also places him outside Israel. Tamar's status as a daughter of the king contains enormous potential for her further biography,[44] a potential that is abruptly destroyed through the act of

---

44. See April D. Westbrook, *"And He Will Take Your Daughters …": Woman Story in the Ethical Evaluation of Monarchy in the David Narrative*, LHBOTS 610 (London: T&T Clark, 2015), 147.

violence. "And Tamar was desolate and lived in the house of her brother Absalom" (ותשם בית אבשלום אחיה, 2 Sam 13:20).

The act of violence against Tamar also is not to be interpreted only in the context of gender and family relationships, but rather also as part of the struggle for political rule. Tamar is attractive to Amnon precisely because, as a daughter of the king, she belongs to David's sphere of control. With this critical sexual transgression, Amnon affects not only Tamar herself but also his father, whose power as paterfamilias he thereby calls into question. Amnon's assault is also directed against the authority of the king, just as Absalom's act of violence is directed not only against his brother but also against his rivals in the struggle for the succession to the throne. "Because the monarchy occurs within an overarching patriarchal context, female characters also become visible indicators of power shifts through their objectification. In this paradigm, males may demonstrate power over each other by controlling the sexuality of women within their kinship groups."[45] This description of the power configurations can be used as a heuristic tool in reading 1 Samuel–2 Kings; it applies, however, especially to the narrative of Tamar and Amnon, and also to the ten wives of David, who are commandeered sexually by Absalom.

4.5. The Ten Wives of David

According to 2 Sam 16:20–23, men use women as weapons in their struggle for royal power. There also a king's son takes over women who belong to David's household. Ten women, as narrated in 2 Sam 15:16—and the counselor Ahithophel again takes up the theme in 2 Sam 16:21—are left behind in Jerusalem "in order to guard [שמר] the house" when David flees before Absalom. Therefore, as a metonym for the house, they are exposed and endangered at the same time. They symbolize the vulnerability of this house and lose their physical integrity as well as their social status (2 Sam 20:3): "The overt vulnerability of these women to the political machinations of both David and Absalom displays the magnitude of abusive lust for power that exists intrinsically within a monarchy. Here again, the text continues the pattern of portraying female characters in

---

45. Westbrook, *"And He Will Take,"* 26.

order to reveal dramatically the high human cost of kingship."[46] Absalom sleeps with these women "in the sight of all Israel" (2 Sam 16:21), and by virtue of this act David's humiliation takes on a public character: Israel should see that Absalom assumes the role of the king and supplants David—politically and sexually. This public disruption of the house of David is already a part of Nathan's prophecy in 2 Sam 12:12.

From the biblical and other ancient Near Eastern sources, one certainly will not be able to speak here of a ritual that combines the sexual usurpation of the harem with the seizure of power. Such notions, as well as generally the idea of a harem at ancient Near Eastern courts, make use of Western orientalistic clichés.[47] The presence of women in ancient Near Eastern courts is multifarious; they discharge many functions, of which only a part has to do with sexuality.[48] In the event of a change of power, all those belonging to the court, both men and women, are affected; the control of power changes. In the transition from Saul to David, for example, several functionaries, both men and women, seek a new position—the conduct of Abner as narrated in 2 Sam 3, also in regard to Saul's concubine Rizpah, is an example, just as is Adonijah's request to Solomon to *give* him Abishag as wife (1 Kgs 2).

Here, in my opinion, lies the key to understanding the narrative about Absalom and the concubines belonging to his father David: the sexual act by Absalom is neither a ritual, nor does it appear to be a ceremony to mark the transition of power (otherwise Ahithophel's counsel would not have been necessary). Nonetheless, Absalom's act is a sign that everyone understands. Absalom assumes the place of his father; his sexual power here becomes the sign of his political power.

---

46. Westbrook, *"And He Will Take,"* 190.

47. For a critique of the harem as distinguished from the court (and characterized by idleness and boredom), see Elna K. Solvang, *A Woman's Place Is in the House: Royal Women of Judah and Their Involvement in the House of David*, JSOTSup 349 (London: Sheffield Academic, 2003), 51–71; Svärd, *Women and Power*, 109–20, and the article by Maria Häusl in this volume.

48. See Sarah C. Melville, "Royal Women and the Exercise of Power in the Ancient Near East," in *A Companion to the Ancient Near East*, ed. Daniel C. Snell, BCAWAH (Malden, MA: Blackwell, 2005), 219–28; Solvang, *Woman's Place*; Svärd, *Women and Power*.

4.6. Rizpah

Rizpah is mentioned in the context of Ishbaal's assumption of power after the death of Saul. She is the object of a reproach made by the new but powerless king to the powerful and experienced commander Abner (2 Sam 3:7). Ishbaal interprets Abner's sexual relationship with Rizpah as an attack on his kingship.[49]

More prominent than this scene, however, is that in 2 Sam 21, in which Rizpah plays a very remarkable and active role. Martin Buber compares her with Antigone.[50] Rizpah performs the vigil for the bodies of those progeny of Saul (from Merab or Michal; see above) whom David had caused to be killed under the condition of the prohibition of their burial. In spite of the danger of losing her life, Rizpah protects the exposed bodies of the dead against desecration by animals over a period of several months (2 Sam 21:10).[51] Even David is impressed with this and finally lets the corpses of the dead Saulides be buried with the bones of Saul and Jonathan.

Rizpah's vigil brings about the resolution of several guilt relationships. This is expressed in the narrative theology of the books of Samuel by the onset of the long-overdue rain. David's guilt in not granting an appropriate place to Saul, the dead "anointed of YHWH," and Saul's guilt regarding the Gibeonites are expiated. Rizpah's resistance can be understood from this perspective of a constellative anthropology,[52] not only as an act in the narrative world but, above and beyond this, as a resistance that includes

---

49. Erin E. Fleming, "Casting Aspersions, Writing a Kingdom: Sexual Slander and Political Rhetoric in 2 Sam 3:6–11, 2 Sam 6:16; 20–23, and 1 Kgs 2:13–25," *VT* 67 (2017): 414–31, establishes a connection with two other scenes, in which sexually connoted conduct is interpreted negatively in a political context.

50. Martin Buber, "Weisheit und Tat der Frauen," in *Kampf um Israel: Reden und Schriften (1921–1932)* (Berlin: Schocken, 1933), 114. On the similarity between Antigone and Rizpah, see Friedhelm Hartenstein, "Solidarität mit den Toten und Herrschaftsordnung: 2 Samuel 21, 1–14 und 2 Samuel 24 im Vergleich mit dem Antigone-Mythos," in Bauks, Liess, and Riede, *Was ist der Mensch*, 123–43.

51. Johannes Schnocks, "Ehrenvolle Bestattung als soziale Auferstehung: Anthropologische und theologische Dimensionen der Rizpaerzählung (2 Sam 21)," in *Sterben über den Tod hinaus: Politische, soziale und religiöse Ausgrenzung in vormodernen Gesellschaften*, ed. Claudia Garnier and Johannes Schnocks, RP 3 (Würzburg: Ergon-Verlag, 2012), 213.

52. Schnocks, "Ehrenvolle Bestattung als soziale Auferstehung," draws on this approach in interpreting the Rizpah narrative.

those functions that the royal women assume in the Samuel books. If it is true that they are understood as special representatives of the house, of the dynasty, then with her act Rizpah indeed makes sure that the house of Saul, which was completely obliterated with the murder of the last Saulide progeny (with the exception of Merib-Baal), remains present in the middle of Israel on the symbolic level: "Rizpa lives her life in nothing less than a superhuman manner in that she is taken up completely in the configuration of her situation. She is here really a sister of Antigone. As one of Saul's concubines, she does not permit the annihilatiion of her family beyond death."[53]

4.7. Abishag of Shunem

Abishag of Shunem is linked to the end of David's political and sexual power. She is given to the aged David to be סכנת for him. The word signifies an administrative office at the court, but the exact scope of duties remains undetermined.[54] The other terms used for Abishag's function also indicate an office; the mention of her place of origin recalls "high-ranking women at the king's court."[55] In the present text, though, several sexual connotations are evoked. The beauty of the young woman is emphasized twice; she is intended to lie in his bosom (בחיקך); and, finally, the narrative declares, "The king did not know her" (1 Kgs 1:4). David's lack of sexual potency is made the subject here, directly, before his son Adonijah appears with his claim to the kingship.

The connection of the claim to the kingship with the desire to have Abishag of Shunem as his wife becomes Adonijah's undoing. He approaches the royal mother, Bathsheba, with the request to intervene with Solomon on his behalf so that the latter might give him Abishag as his wife. Evidently, Abishag has been transferred after David's death to the area of control belonging to the next king, from whom Adonijah now can request for her. But the intervention fails—whether Bathsheba honestly

---

53. Schnocks, "Ehrenvolle Bestattung als soziale Auferstehung," 217.

54. See Maria Häusl, *Abischag und Batscheba: Frauen am Königshof und die Thronfolge Davids im Zeugnis der Texte 1 Kön 1 und 2*, ATSAT 41 (St. Ottilien: EOS, 1993), 242. In this context and with etymological evidence, Häusl has claimed that here it is a designation for a function. The usual translation of "to nurse" introduces a gender prejudice that is not supported by the text.

55. Häusl, *Abischag und Batscheba*, 239.

intervenes here or this is a part of her plot is not answered by the text (see above). Adonijah is one of those, in a series of Solomon's enemies, who are murdered in the context of his accession to power.

In the course of these events, the link between sexuality and the politics of power is clearly present, but here we find the negation of that link. David, in blatant contrast to the story of his life as narrated up to this point, is characterized by nonaction in the whole passage. Abishag of Shunem thus stands for the king's loss of power, which expresses itself in his lack of sexual potency.

4.8. Women around Solomon

The combination of marriage policy and power politics is continued also under Solomon. Here, however, in contrast to the narratives about Saul and David, individual women appear exclusively as prominent figures who are not the wives of the king—the royal mother, Bathsheba; the two women who prompt Solomon to make his famous judgment; and the queen of Sheba. "What is important, apparently, are not the individual female figures who might characterize Solomon's government in a way that they did for his father David, but rather the *great number* of the women and their *origin* in all the neighboring nations (11:1–3)."[56] Nevertheless, the women of the king are relevant also during Solomon's reign. First, there is the "daughter of the Pharaoh" (בת־פרעה), whom Solomon marries. She is mentioned four times in 1 Kings and produces a most highly ambivalent connection to Egypt. Solomon first does in foreign policy what his father had done in domestic policy. He becomes the son-in-law (חתן) of a king, in this case, the Pharaoh, and thereby secures his power (1 Kgs 3:1). In other historical contexts of the ancient Near East also, the significance of royal marriage policy can be documented, "as royal marriages were an important diplomatic tool."[57]

The context of the statements about the Pharaoh's daughter, however, suggests that this point should be considered critically. In 1 Kgs 3:1; 7:8; and 9:24, the subject is Solomon's building activities. The Solomonic splendor arises by virtue of the king's orientation in Egypt, regarding those structures of slavery that a king must avoid, according to Deut 17:16. The

---

56. Fischer, "Salomo und die Frauen," 237.
57. Svärd, *Women and Power*, 88.

references to Solomon's chariots and horsemen and to the abundance of silver and the horses from Egypt (1 Kgs 10:26–29) show the same tendency.

This critical tendency becomes explicit where the text speaks of the "many other foreign women" (נשים נכריות רבות, 1 Kgs 11:1) whom Solomon loves. Here also a violation of the Deuteronomic law of kings can be recognized, which the narrative further develops. The condition of Solomon in old age is linked with his falling away from YHWH and his embrace of other deities, that is, from the perspective of the Deuteronomic portrayal of history, of the original sin. According to 1 Kgs 11, it is precisely the women who come from various lands and neighboring nations, and who bring their own deities and religious practices with them, who push Solomon in this direction. This line of argumentation is taken up again in the polemics against marriages with non-Judaic women in Neh 13:26. Solomon's women, the daughter of Pharaoh as well as the large number of women who are named only in the plural, are connoted negatively: "Solomon's women are to be understood not only as a large harem that distinguishes a powerful oriental ruler; they figure colorfully also as a part of that sterotypical-misogynous metaphor that illustrates the offense against JHWH's claim to exclusivity together with the feminine ability to seduce men to adopt foreign gods."[58] The women who appear as Solomon's counterparts are shown in a less linear way, but with their own individual profile. These are, first of all, his mother, Bathsheba, who quite clearly follows her own interests (see above), and the two women who, as catalysts, provoke a judgment from Solomon's wisdom (1 Kgs 3). They are portrayed also negatively and serve as the background against which Solomon's positive qualities emerge all the more clearly. The queen of Sheba also is, in the context of the narrative, a highly significant female figure since with her "evaluation visit" she confirms Solomon's reputation.[59]

5. Women and Power

Older publications "treated women as an isolated category, separate from general history, that is, male history."[60] Saana Svärd reviews studies on the

---

58. Fischer, "Salomo und die Frauen," 238.
59. Fischer, "Menschheitsfamilie—Erzelternfamilie—Königsfamilie," 196.
60. Svärd, *Women and Power*, 8. On the figure of Rizpah, see also Elisabeth C. Miescher, *"Und Rizpa nahm den Sack": Trauer als Widerstand; Eine kaum bekannte Heldin der hebräischen Bibel*, Bibelstudien 2 (Vienna: LIT, 2008); Georg Hentschel,

subject of women from the ancient Near Eastern studies, but this is true also for the field of Old Testament studies. The challenge that textual passages such as the narratives about the ancestors in Genesis and the books of Samuel pose for gender-oriented studies is the great presence that women have in these narrative works. Within the framework of a patriarchal historiography and narrative culture, the sheer quantity is striking and requires explanation. While traditional approaches often relegate female characters and related narratives to the sphere of irrelevance, feminist-oriented scholars, in particular, search for hermeneutical keys with which they can analyze the narratives about women as an integral part of each textual episode.[61]

In recent decades, a series of attempts to interpret the books of Samuel consider the high presence of women in the historiography of these books. These approaches vary and focus on the literary portrayal as well as the narrated world or the original world of the text. Both female and male exegetes agree about the political significance of the portrayals of women. The issue is not to reconstruct separate stories about women but rather to understand the female figures in the social context of the narrated world and/or of the world of the origins of the text. It seems logical that, in the narratives in which women play an important role, the point is not about private issues but rather investigating the political function of these stories:

> Even if we characterize them as "court history," they do not constitute a traditional tabloid press. Neither for the author nor for the addressees he has in view, the question really is not whether and why David was a womanizer. Rather, the issue is that these women's stories apparently offer insight into the developments in the monarchy. Nevertheless, modern readers must search for this key much more carefully than the original addressees.[62]

"Die Auslieferung der Sauliden und Rizpas Wache (2 Sam 21,1–14) ," in *Seitenblicke: Literarische und historische Studien zu Nebenfiguren im zweiten Samuelbuch*, ed. Walter Dietrich, OBO 249 (Fribourg: Academic Press, 2011), 168–87; Luise Metzler, *Das Recht Gestorbener: Rizpa als Toralehrerin für David*, TFE 28 (Berlin: LIT, 2015).

61. See the very pointed formulation of the title of the article by Irmtraud Fischer, "Den Frauen der Kochtopf—den Männern die hohe Politik? [The Cooking Pot for the Women—High Politics for the Men?] Zum Klischee der Geschlechterrollen in der Bibelauslegung am Beispiel der Erzeltern-Erzählungen," *CPB* 108 (1995): 134–38.

62. Ina Willi-Plein, "Frauen um David: Beobachtungen zur Davidshausgeschichte," in *Meilenstein: Festschrift für Herbert Donner*, ed. Manfred Weippert and Stefan Timm, ÄAT 30 (Wiesbaden: Harrassowitz, 1995), 352.

The range of interpretive approaches is broad. It extends from the literary-historical location of extensive portions of the existing text about a group of women authors gathered around Bathsheba, to the interpretation of the women as factors in safeguarding David's power in the various areas of governance, to the determination of the relationship between family and politics as an allegory, and to understanding women as symbolic of the people of Israel.[63] All of these approaches, however, leave some questions unanswered.

Insights from historical anthropology, especially as developed in the last fifteen years, can help to build bridges here. Constellative anthropology points out several aspects of the Hebraic image of the human being that are unusual for contemporary modern thinking. The historicization of basic anthropological concepts such as body, love, family, or progeny often proves to be a difficult enterprise because the historical view calls into question contemporary concepts that are such a matter of course that they appear to be decreed by nature. Notions of marriage, the private sphere, and love show their socially constructed face when we confront them with the reading of dated ancient Near Eastern texts, whereas even a glimpse into the pre-nineteenth-century Europe would suffice to demonstrate the historical development of concepts that are dominant today.

Using the constellative concept of the person, Bernd Janowski shows, "What we distinguish as the personal identity of the human [rests] upon the complex interaction of body image and social structure.... Personal identity accordingly comes about not through a 'rationality' steering the perception of the self and the exterior world, but rather through configurations, or constellations."[64] Individuality in antiquity is also not conceived as a singularity, but rather, it is associated with social involvement and positioning: "The claim by older research that power accrues to women at the king's court exclusively on the basis of their status as part of the family and only in the form of personal power, but not in the form of participa-

---

63. Ferdinand Ahuis, *Das "Großreich" Davids und die Rolle der Frauen: Eine Untersuchung zur Erzählung von der Nachfolge auf dem Thron Davids (2. Sam *10–20: 1. Kön *1–2) und ihrer Trägerinnengruppe*, BThSt 83 (Neukirchen-Vluyn: Neukirchener Verlag, 2007), 105–18; Willi-Plein, "Frauen um David"; Joel Rosenberg, *King and Kin: Political Allegory in the Hebrew Bible* (Bloomington: Indiana University Press, 1986); Westbrook, *"And He Will Take."*

64. Janowski, "Konstellative Anthropologie," 66–67.

tion in hierarchical power, is to be rejected for this reason."[65] Such a point of view could come about only when the relationship between family and political rule was only inadequately determined and when, with the bourgeois' view that is typical of the modern age, women were assigned to the sphere of the family. But the ruling power exercised by men also is tied to their family role when a king's *son* inherits the official title. Male as well as female members of the court are described repeatedly in the narrative literature by reference to their family relationships in regard to the king or also among themselves (for example, 2 Sam 13:3: Jonadab as the nephew of David; the "sons of Zeruiah" who, in 1 Chr 2:16, also are connected to David through kinship). In this way, the great significance of family relationships is made clear narratively. Such significance is, to be sure, not specifically gender bound, but through the focus on the family it enables the high narrative presence of women in the narratives about the kings.

The dynastic monarchy is a social sphere in which women and men exercise power. Women's "participation in power" *also* is determined by their reproductive functions but is not limited to them.[66] That Solomon builds a house for the daughter of the Pharaoh points to the existence of an independent economy that also benefited not only some of the king's wives but also the king's mother at the Jewish court, as data from the Assyrian Empire also suggests.[67] Royal power does not confine itself to the individual ruler but is wrapped up in a political as well as military, economic, and religious power network, in which women assume various positions.

Such an image of royal power that emanates more from intertwined structures than from the image of a pyramid arose first in the social context of the Judaic dynasty.[68] The royal period, with its very ambivalent political experience, is the original context in which a majority of the stories examined here were narrated. But the central position of the family in the context of the establishment of royal power, as outlined in these narratives,

---

65. Maria Häusl, "Women at the King's Court," 232 in this volume. See the essays in Jürgen Van Oorschot and Andreas Wagner, eds., *Individualität und Selbstreflexion in den Literaturen des Alten Testaments*, VWGT 48 (Leipzig: Evangelische Verlagsanstalt, 2017), esp. Bernd Janowski, "Persönlichkeitszeichen: Ein Beitrag zum Personverständnis des Alten Testaments," 315–40, and Sara Kipfer, "David—'Individualität' einer literarischen Figur in 1 Sam 16–1 Kön 2," 149–81, esp. 149–57.

66. Willi-Plein, "Frauen," 361.

67. Solvang, *Woman's Place*, 16–71; Svärd, *Women and Power*, 61–74.

68. Svärd, following Michel Foucault, speaks of heterarchic power in contrast to hierarchy (*Women and Power*, passim).

is also compatible with the postexilic period. This offers the possibility of appreciating the emerging monarchy positively and, at the same time, presenting the critical sides of the monarchy as being there from the very beginning and thus as necessary to the institution.

In addition, the postexilic period, with its focus on the family as the frame of reference for Judaic identity and with the possibilities of reading the narratives through a democratic lens, represents a new space in which those stories find resonance as the family is foregrounded—even though the subjects are the privileged families of the first kings. The process of democratizing the royal figures depicts them as characters with whom all of Israel and Judah can narratively identify and is part of the narrative strategy used in the postexilic, kingless period.[69] This strategy is not only to be reconstructed implicitly—based on potential historical resonance in the books of Samuel and the Kings—but shows itself explicitly in the Davidization of the Psalter, especially in the thirteen biographical headings,[70] which can be considered an invitation to all who pray to make David's voice their own. They follow the same line as the opening of the royal family narrative, with which both male and female readers can identify. This represents *one* possible way of positively using the memory of the monarchy in the postexilic period and also one possible way of keeping it alive.

Bibliography

Ahuis, Ferdinand. *Das "Großreich" Davids und die Rolle der Frauen: Eine Untersuchung zur Erzählung von der Nachfolge auf dem Thron Davids (2. Sam *10–20: 1. Kön *1–2) und ihrer Trägerinnengruppe.* BThSt 83. Neukirchen-Vluyn: Neukirchener Verlag, 2007.

---

69. This postexilic movement that maintains the dynastic concept along with the democratization of the royal family in an epoch that no longer knows a king becomes visible, for example, in the Chronicles. "In this sense, the 'House of David' is nothing other than a special case of the speech in the Chronicles of בית אבות characterized above. If one wishes to speak of a 'dynasty,' then the Israel of the Chronicles is full of such 'democratized' dynasties." See Thomas Willi, "Gibt es in der Chronik eine 'Dynastie Davids'? Ein Beitrag zur Semantik von בית," in "*... der seine Lust hat am Wort des Herrn!" Festschrift für Ernst Jenni zum 80. Geburtstag*, ed. Jürg Luchsinger, Hans P. Mathys, and Markus Saur, AOAT 336 (Münster: Ugarit-Verlag, 2007), 402–3.

70. See Ilse Müllner, "Gottesdeuter und Musiktherapeut: David und die Psalmen," *WUB* 4 (2016): 34–39.

Becker, Uwe, and Hannes Bezzel, eds. *Rereading the Relecture: The Question of (Post)Chronistic Influence in the Latest Redactions of the Books of Samuel.* FAT 2/66. Tübingen: Mohr Siebeck, 2014.

Braulik, Georg. "Theorien über das deuteronomistische Geschichtswerk (DtrG) im Wandel der Forschung." Pages 229–54 in *Einleitung in das Alte Testament.* Edited by Erich Zenger and Christian Frevel. KST 1. Stuttgart: Kohlhammer, 2016.

Breithaupt, Fritz. *Kulturen der Empathie.* Frankfurt: Suhrkamp, 2009.

Buber, Martin. "Weisheit und Tat der Frauen." Pages 107–14 in *Kampf um Israel: Reden und Schriften (1921–1932).* Berlin: Schocken, 1933.

Clines, David J. A., and Tamara Cohn Eskenazi, eds. *Telling Queen Michal's Story: An Experiment in Comparative Interpretation.* JSOTSup 19. Sheffield: JSOT Press, 1991.

Cross, Frank Moore, Donald W. Parry, Richard J. Saley, and Eugene Ulrich. *Qumran Cave 4.XII: 1–2 Samuel.* DJD 17. Oxford: Clarendon, 2005.

Dietrich, Walter. *Die Samuelbücher im deuteronomistischen Geschichtswerk: Studien zu den Geschichtsüberlieferungen des Alten Testaments 2.* BWANT 201. Stuttgart: Kohlhammer, 2012.

Edenburg, Cynthia, and Juha Pakkala, eds. *Is Samuel among the Deuteronomists? Current Views on the Place of Samuel in a Deuteronomistic History.* AIL 16. Atlanta: Society of Biblical Literature, 2013.

Eisen, Ute E., Christine Gerber, and Angela Standhartinger, eds. *Doing Gender—Doing Religion: Fallstudien zur Intersektionalität im frühen Judentum, Christentum und Islam.* WMANT 302. Tübingen: Mohr Siebeck, 2013.

Exum, J. Cheryl. *Fragmented Women: Feminist (Sub)versions of Biblical Narratives.* JSOTSup 163. Sheffield: Sheffield Academic, 1993.

Fischer, Andrea. *Dramen zu "David, Batseba und Urija" (2 Sam 11): Zur Rezeption hebräischer Erzählkunst in Literatur und Theater—Paul Alberti (1904), Martha Hellmuth (1906) und Emil Bernhard (1919).* EUZ 27. Münster: LIT, 2018.

———. *Königsmacht, Begehren, Ehebruch und Mord—Die Erzählung von "David, Batseba und Urija" (2 Sam 11): Narratologische Analysen.* EUZ 26. Münster: LIT, 2018.

———. "Opfer oder Intrigantin: Zur mehrdeutigen Darstellung der biblischen Figur Batsebas in 2 Sam 11 und in literarischen Rezeptionen." Pages 69–84 in *Das Buch in den Büchern: Wechselwirkungen von Bibel und Literatur.* Edited by Andrea Polaschegg and Daniel Weidner. Paderborn: Fink, 2012.

Fischer, Irmtraud. "Den Frauen der Kochtopf—den Männern die hohe Politik? Zum Klischee der Geschlechterrollen in der Bibelauslegung am Beispiel der Erzeltern-Erzählungen." *CPB* 108 (1995): 134–38.

———. "Die Bibel als Welt erzeugende Erzählung." Pages 381–97 in *Kultur—Wissen—Narration: Perspektiven transdisziplinärer Erzählforschung für die Kulturwissenschaften*. Edited by Alexandra Strohmaier. Bielefeld: Transcript, 2013.

———. *Gotteslehrerinnen: Weise Frauen und Frau Weisheit im Alten Testament*. Stuttgart: Kohlhammer, 2006.

———. *Gottesstreiterinnen: Biblische Erzählungen über die Anfänge Israels*. Stuttgart: Kohlhammer, 1995.

———. "Menschheitsfamilie—Erzelternfamilie—Königsfamilie: Familien als Protagonistinnen von Welt erzeugenden Erzählungen." *BK* 4 (2015): 190–97.

———. "Salomo und die Frauen." Pages 218–43 in *Das Manna fällt auch heute noch: Beiträge zur Geschichte und Theologie des Alten, Ersten Testaments; Festschrift für Erich Zenger*. Edited Frank-Lothar Hossfeld and Ludger Schwienhorst-Schönberger. HBS 44. Freiburg: Herder, 2004.

Fleming, Erin E. "Casting Aspersions, Writing a Kingdom: Sexual Slander and Political Rhetoric in 2 Sam 3:6–11, 2 Sam 6:16; 20–23, and 1 Kgs 2:13–25." *VT* 67 (2017): 414–31.

Halbertal, Mosheh, and Stephen Holmes. *The Beginning of Politics: Power in the Biblical Book of Samuel*. Princeton: Princeton University Press, 2017.

Harding, James E. *The Love of David and Jonathan: Ideology, Text, Reception*. Sheffield: Equinox, 2013.

Hartenstein, Friedhelm. "Solidarität mit den Toten und Herrschaftsordnung: 2 Samuel 21, 1–14 und 2 Samuel 24 im Vergleich mit dem Antigone-Mythos." Pages 123–43 in *Was ist der Mensch, dass du seiner gedenkst? (Psalm 8,5): Aspekte einer theologischen Anthropologie; Festschrift für Bernd Janowsk zum 65. Geburtstagi*. Edited by Michaela Bauks, Kathrin Liess, and Peter Riede. Neukirchen-Vluyn: Neukirchener Verlag, 2008.

Häusl, Maria. *Abischag und Batscheba: Frauen am Königshof und die Thronfolge Davids im Zeugnis der Texte 1 Kön 1 und 2*. ATSAT 41. St. Ottilien: EOS, 1993.

Hentschel, Georg. *1 Könige*. NEB. Würzburg: Echter, 1984.

———. "Die Auslieferung der Sauliden und Rizpas Wache (2 Sam 21,1–14)." Pages 168–87 in *Seitenblicke: Literarische und historische Studien zu Nebenfiguren im zweiten Samuelbuch*. Edited by Walter Dietrich. OBO 249. Fribourg: Academic Press, 2011.

Heym, Stefan. *The King David Report: A Novel*. New York: G. P. Putnam's Sons, 1973.

Jannidis, Fotis. "Art: Character." In *Living Handbook of Narratology*. Edited by Peter Hühn, Jan Christoph Meister, John Pier, and Wolf Schmid. 2013. https://tinyurl.com/SBL6016h.

Janowski, Bernd. "Konstellative Anthropologie: Zum Begriff der Person im Alten Testament." Pages 64–87 in *Biblische Anthropologie: Neue Einsichten aus dem Alten Testament*. Edited by Christian Frevel. QD 237. Freiburg: Herder, 2010.

———. "Persönlichkeitszeichen: Ein Beitrag zum Personverständnis des Alten Testaments." Pages 315–40 in *Individualität und Selbstreflexion in den Literaturen des Alten Testaments*. Edited by Jürgen Van Oorschot and Andreas Wagner. VWGT 48. Leipzig: Evangelische Verlagsanstalt, 2017.

Kipfer, Sara. "David —'Individualität' einer literarischen Figur in 1 Sam 16–1 Kön 2." Pages 149–81 in *Individualität und Selbstreflexion in den Literaturen des Alten Testaments*. Edited by Jürgen van Oorschot and Andreas Wagner. VWGT 48. Leipzig: Evangelische Verlagsanstalt, 2017.

———. *Der bedrohte David: Eine exegetische und rezeptionsgeschichtliche Studie zu 1 Sam 16–1 Kön 2*. SBR 3. Berlin: de Gruyter, 2015.

Knauf, Ernst Axel. *1 Könige 1–14*. HThKAT. Vienna: Herder, 2016.

Kunz, Andreas. *Die Frauen und der König David: Studien zur Figuration von Frauen in den Davidserzählungen*. ABG 8. Leipzig: Evangelische Verlagsanstalt, 2004.

Melville, Sarah C. "Royal Women and the Exercise of Power in the Ancient Near East." Pages 219–28 in *A Companion to the Ancient Near East*. Edited by Daniel C. Snell. BCAWAH. Malden, MA: Blackwell, 2005.

Metzler, Luise. *Das Recht Gestorbener: Rizpa als Toralehrerin für David*. TFE 28. Berlin: LIT, 2015.

Miescher, Elisabeth C. *"Und Rizpa nahm den Sack": Trauer als Widerstand; Eine kaum bekannte Heldin der hebräischen Bibel*. Bibelstudien 2. Vienna: LIT, 2008.

Müllner, Ilse. *Gewalt im Hause Davids: Die Erzählung von Tamar und Amnon (2 Sam 13, 1–22)*. HBS 13. Freiburg: Herder, 1997.

———. "Die Samuelbücher—Gott in Menschen, Tieren und Dingen erzählen." Pages 88–123 in *Gott als Figur: Narratologische Analysen biblischer Texte und ihrer Adaptionen*. Edited by Ute E. Eisen and Ilse Müllner. HBS 82. Freiburg: Herder, 2016.

———. "Gottesdeuter und Musiktherapeut: David und die Psalmen." *WUB* 4 (2016): 34–39.

———. "Die Samuelbücher als Werk Politischer Theologie." Pages 279–97 in *Thesaurusin vasis fictilibus: "Schatz in zerbrechlichen Gefäßen" (2 Kor 4, 7); Festschrift für Bischof Heinz-Josef Algermissen zum 75. Geburtstag*. Edited by Bernd Willmes and Christoph Gregor Müller. Freiburg: Herder, 2018.

Ngan, Lai Ling Elizabeth. "Class Privileges in Patriarchal Society: Women in First and Second Samuel." Pages 110–34 in *Biblical Books*. Vol. 1 of *Feminist Interpretation of the Hebrew Bible in Retrospect*. Edited by Susanne Scholz. RRBS 5. Sheffield: Sheffield Phoenix, 2013.

Römer, Thomas. "Homosexualität in der Hebräischen Bibel: Einige Überlegungen zu Leviticus 18 und 20, Genesis 19 und der David-Jonathan-Erzählung." Pages 435–54 in *Was ist der Mensch, dass du seiner gedenkst? (Psalm 8,5): Aspekte einer theologischen Anthropologie; Festschrift Bernd Janowski zum 65. Geburtstag*. Edited by Michaela Bauks, Kathrin Liess, and Peter Riede. Neukirchen-Vluyn: Neukirchener-Verlag, 2008.

Rosa, Hartmut. *Resonanz: Eine Soziologie der Weltbeziehung*. Berlin: Suhrkamp, 2016.

Rosenberg, Joel. *King and Kin: Political Allegory in the Hebrew Bible*. Bloomington: Indiana University Press, 1986.

Rost, Leonhard. *Die Überlieferung von der Thronnachfolge Davids*. BWANT 42. Stuttgart: Kohlhammer, 1926.

Rowe, Jonathan Y. *Sons or Lovers: An Interpretation of David and Jonathan's Friendship*. LHBOTS 575. London: T&T Clark, 2012.

Schäfer-Lichtenberger, Christa. "Frauen im Gespräch mit David: Deuteronomistische Zwischenrufe?" Pages 132–56 in *Die Samuelbücher und die Deuteronomisten*. Edited by Christa Schäfer-Lichtenberger. BWANT 188. Stuttgart: Kohlhammer, 2010.

Schnocks, Johannes. "Ehrenvolle Bestattung als sozial Auferstehung: Anthropologische und theologische Dimensionen der Rizpaerzählung (2 Sam 21)." Pages 206–18 in *Sterben über den Tod hinaus: Politische, soziale und religiöse Ausgrenzung in vormodernen Gesell-*

schaften. Edited by Claudia Garnier and Johannes Schnocks. RP 3. Würzburg: Ergon-Verlag, 2012.

Solvang, Elna K. *A Woman's Place is in the House: Royal Women of Judah and Their Involvement in the House of David*. JSOTSup 349. London: Sheffield Academic, 2003.

Spiering-Schomborg, Nele. "*Man kann sich nicht entscheiden, als was man geboren wird*": *Exodus 1 im Horizont von Intersektionalität und empirischer Bibeldidaktik*. RI 19. Stuttgart: Kohlhammer, 2017.

Stansell, Gary. "David und seine Freunde: Sozialwissenschaftliche Betrachtung der David-Jonathan-Freundschaft." Pages 53–84 in *Alte Texte in neuen Kontexten: Wo steht die sozialwissenschaftliche Bibelexegese*. Edited by Wolfgang Stegemann and Richard E. DeMaris. Stuttgart: Kohlhammer, 2015.

Steiner, Till Magnus. *Salomo als Nachfolger Davids: Die Dynastieverheissung in 2 Sam 7, 11b–16 und ihre Rezeption in 1 Kön 1–11*. BBB 181. Göttingen: V&R Unipress, 2017.

Stone, Ken. *Sex, Honor and Power in the Deuteronomistic History: A Narratological and Anthropological Analysis*. JSOTSup 234. Sheffield: Sheffield Academic, 1996.

Svärd, Saana. *Women and Power in Neo-Assyrian Palaces*. SAAS 23. Winona Lake, IN: Eisenbrauns, 2015.

Van Oorschot, Jürgen, and Andreas Wagner, eds. *Individualität und Selbstreflexion in den Literaturen des Alten Testaments*. VWGT 48. Leipzig: Evangelische Verlagsanstalt, 2017.

Westbrook, April D. "*And He Will Take Your Daughters …*": *Woman Story in the Ethical Evaluation of Monarchy in the David Narrative*. LHBOTS 610. London: Bloomsbury T&T Clark, 2015.

Willi, Thomas. "Gibt es in der Chronik eine 'Dynastie Davids'? Ein Beitrag zur Semantik von בית." "Pages 393–404 in "*… der seine Lust hat am Wort des Herrn!*": *Festschrift für Ernst Jenni zum 80. Geburtstag*. Edited by Jürg Luchsinger, Hans P. Mathys, and Markus Saur. AOAT 336. Münster: Ugarit-Verlag, 2007.

Willi-Plein, Ina. "1 Sam 18–19 und die Davidshausgeschichte." Pages 3–47 in *Davidshaus und Prophetie: Studien zu den Nebiim*. Edited by Ina Willi-Plein. BThSt 127. Neukirchen-Vluyn: Neukirchener, 2012.

———. "Frauen um David. Beobachtungen zur Davidshausgeschichte." Pages 349–61 in *Meilenstein: Festschrift für Herbert Donner*. Edited by Manfred Weippert and Stefan Timm. ÄAT 30. Wiesbaden: Harrassowitz, 1995.

Women at the King's Court:
Their Political, Economic, and Religious Significance in the Accounts of the Former Prophets

Maria Häusl

1. Introduction

Feminist exegesis began, as did historical women's studies, with studies of great biblical women.[1] It therefore uncovered the stereotypes associated with these female figures, stereotypes that reinforced research conducted from androcentric perspectives. However, the scope was soon expanded to uncover all the women in the Bible, including especially the queens and the queen mothers, who became an initial subject of feminist exegesis.[2]

The translation of this article was funded by the Technical University of Dresden, School of Humanities and Social Science. The funding is provided by the Excellence Initiative of the German Federal and State Governments.

1. See Luise Schottroff, Silvia Schroer, and Marie-Theres Wacker, *Feministische Exegese: Forschungserträge zur Bibel aus der Perspektive von Frauen* (Darmstadt: Wissenschaftliche Buchgesellschaft, 1995), 25–26.

2. See Schottroff, Schroer, and Wacker, *Feministische Exegese*, 29–33. My dissertation belongs to this phase: Maria Häusl, *Abischag und Batscheba: Frauen am Königshof und die Thronfolge Davids im Zeugnis der Texte 1 Kön 1 und 2*, ATSAT 41 (Sankt Ottilien: EOS-Verlag, 1993). Saana Svärd describes this strategy as the first wave in ancient Near Eastern studies. See Svärd, *Women and Power in Neo-Assyrian Palaces*, SAAS 23 (Helsinki: Neo-Assyrian Text Corpus Project, 2015), 8. On the queens and queen mothers specifically, see Georg Molin, "Die Stellung der Gebira im Staate Juda," *TZ* 10.3 (1954): 161–75; Herbert Donner, "Art und Herkunft des Amtes der Königinmutter im Alten Testament," in *Aufsätze zum Alten Testament aus vier Jahrzehnten*, ed. Herbert Donner, BZAW 224 (Berlin: de Gruyter, 1994): 1–24; Ihromi, "Die Königinmutter und der 'Amm Ha'arez im Reich Juda," *VT* 24 (1974): 421–29; Niels-Erik A. Andreasen, "The Role of the Queen Mother in Israelite Society," *CBQ* 45 (1983):

Investigated in this phase were the social status of these women and the office of queen mother in a power structure described as a patriarchate. In contrast to this older feminist research, the sources from parallel ancient Near Eastern cultures have been made more accessible today, the category of gender is no longer isolated but rather seen as intersectionally interlaced, and the exercise of power is described in a more nuanced way. For this reason, this article will begin with a short description of the monarchy in Israel and of the forms of participation as well as the exercise of power there. Further, the women at the king's court, their status, and their roles in the royal administration will be examined.

2. The Monarchy in Israel

A developed statehood seems to have emerged in the northern kingdom of Israel for the first time in the ninth century BCE:

> There emerges politically [for the first time] a centrally organized institutional rule with the power of sanction, a bureaucracy, a military, a judicial organization, a system of taxation and duties, public or publicly-financed buildings, state economic action, and an increasingly centralized state religion, as well sociologically the formation of a more clearly stratified society.[3]

Christian Frevel thus names the most important aspects of a centrally exercised power. This centralized power is symbolized and represented

---

179–94; Zafrira Ben-Barak, "The Queen Consort and the Struggle for Succession to the Throne," in *La femme dans le Proche-Orient antique: Compte rendu de la XXXIIIe Rencontre Assyriologique Internationale*, ed. Jean-Marie Durand, RAI 33 (Paris: Éditions Recherche sur les Civilisations, 1987), 33–40; Ben-Barak, "The Status and Right of the Gebîra," *JBL* 110 (1991): 23–34; Susan Ackerman, "The Queen Mother and the Cult in Israel," *JBL* 112 (1993): 385–401; Ktizah Spanier, "The Queen Mother in the Judean Royal Court: Maacah—A Case Study," in *A Feminist Companion to Samuel and Kings*, ed. Athalya Brenner, FCB 5 (Sheffield: Sheffield Academic, 1994); Renate Jost, *Frauen, Männer und die Himmelskönigin: Exegetische Studien* (Gütersloh: Gütersloher Verlagshaus, 1995), 137–46; Jost, "Königin (AT)," in *Das wissenschaftliche Bibellexikon im Internet* (2012), https://tinyurl.com/SBL6016i; Jost, "Königinmutter," in *Das wissenschaftliche Bibellexikon im Internet* (2008), https://tinyurl.com/SBL6016j; Anna Christine Kiesow, *Löwinnen von Juda: Frauen als Subjekte politischer Macht in der judäischen Königszeit* (Münster: LIT, 2000).

3. See Christian Frevel, *Geschichte Israels* (Stuttgart: Kohlhammer, 2016), 95.

ultimately by the king, but is exercised also by various groups. We know about various officials, the military, and the royal family. The exercise of power by members of the royal family is not exclusively founded here on the basis of the family relationship with the king. Going back to the family relationship-based chiefdom as the precursor of the monarchy in Israel, family members possess institutional power that they exercise through the assumption of tasks in the administration in the central cult[4] or in the symbolic order. More importantly, in the case of the dynastic form of rule, the "members of the royal family … participate in political rule; the familial status in the case of Gebirah (mother of the Judean king), son of the king, and daughter of the king begins to approximate an official title."[5]

Thus, in order to be able to describe the power of women at the king's court, it is important to consider all the areas in which centralized royal authority is exercised—military affairs, politics, legal organization, administration, the systems of taxation and duties, economics, state religion, and symbolic power.[6] Offices are not the sole objects of inquiry, but along with the hierarchical power that accrues to women on the basis of their status or of a function in the areas mentioned above, heterarchically exercised power also is to be considered, which, according to Saana Svärd, is expressed in "reciprocal power, petition, negotiation, resistance, persuasion" and "nets of communication."[7]

---

4. See the seal of Jezebel from the ninth century BCE; from the eighth century on, the seals with the titles "Son of the King" or "Daughter of the King."

5. See Ilse Müllner and Carsten Jochum-Bortfeld, "Königtum," in *Sozialgeschichtliches Wörterbuch zur Bibel*, ed. Frank Crüsemann et al. (Gütersloh: Gütersloher Verlagshaus, 2009), 302.

6. Elna K. Solvang mentions "access, industry, cult, service to the kingdom" and "dynasty." See Solvang, *A Woman's Place Is in the House: Royal Women of Judah and Their Involvement in the House of David*, JSOTSup 349 (London: Sheffield Academic, 2003).

7. See Svärd, *Women and Power*, 147–69; Svärd, "Women, Power and Heterarchy in the Neo-Assyrian Palaces," in *Organization, Representation, and Symbols of Power in the Ancient Near East: Proceedings of the Fifty-Fourth Rencontre Assyriologique Internationale*, ed. Gernot Wilhelm (Winona Lake, IN: Eisenbrauns, 2012), 507–18; Janet Levy, "Gender, Heterarchy, and Hierarchy," in *Handbook of Gender in Archaeology*, ed. Sarah M. Nelson (Lanham, MD: AltaMira, 2006), 219–46. In the area of Old Testament exegesis, Carol L. Meyers has taken up the concept positively in order to avoid the term *patriarchate* in referring to the Israelite society before the formation of the state. See Meyers, *Rediscovering Eve: Ancient Israelite Women in Context* (Oxford: Oxford University Press, 2013); Meyers, "Was Ancient Israel a Patriarchal Society?," *JBL* 133 (2014): 8–27. A critical position in this regard is expressed by Athalya Brenner,

The claim by older research that power accrues to women at the king's court exclusively on the basis of their status as part of the family and only in the form of personal power, but not in the form of participation in hierarchical power, is to be rejected for this reason. However, there remains the problem that, because of the scant body of source material and the negative assessment of the rule exercised by women found in several texts, it is hardly possible to distinguish between the personal exercise of power, which can be successful and skillful but also problematic, and the institutional power that is bestowed on women.

3. On the Sources

When it comes to the reconstruction of the royal court and its structure as well as the exercise of power and the influence of women at the king's court, the Old Testament texts must be regarded as the chief sources, although we do not focus here on primary sources. In addition to these, reference can be made to only a few archaeological findings, such as seals and images.

Seals or seal impressions document individual names that can be interpreted as names of royal women.[8] Thus, the seal of Queen Jezebel ([*l*ʾ]*YZBL*) most probably can be identified.[9] For the Judean queen mother Meshullemet (*MŠWLMT*) and Jehoaddin, the daughter of Uriahu (*YHWʾDN bt ʾRYHW*), the identification is uncertain.[10]

In addition, the seal findings confirm the title that we know from Old Testament texts about the royal context. Thus, along with twenty-four seals

---

"Does the 'Twist' Point to Heterarchy? A Response to Beverly Bow and George Nickelsburg," in *A Feminist Companion to Tobit and Judith*, ed. Athalya Brenner and Helen Efthimiadis-Keith, FCB 20 (London: Bloomsbury, 2015), 64–66.

8. See details of the seals belonging to women in Kiesow, *Löwinnen von Juda*, 51–63; Hennie J. Marsman, *Women in Ugarit and Israel*, OtSt 49 (Leiden: Brill, 2003), 643–59; Marjo C. A. Korpel, "Seals of Jezebel and Other Women in Authority," *JSem* 15 (2006): 349–71.

9. That the seal is most probably that of Queen Jezebel is justified by Korpel based on the extraordinary size of the seal, the Egypto-Phoenician iconography, and the reconstruction of the inscription as [*l*ʾ]*YZBL*. See Marjo C. A. Korpel, "Fit for a Queen: Jezebel's Royal Seal," *BAR* 34 (2008): 32–37; Korpel, "Seals of Jezebel," 358–62.

10. See Kiesow, *Löwinnen von Juda*, 56. Korpel refers beyond this to the seal of the ʾ*LDLH*, that is, probably of Aramaic/Amorite origin ("Seals of Jezebel," 363). According to Korpel, this could be the name of an Aramaic/Amorite princess who was a queen in Israel.

with "X, Son of the King," we find also the seal impression for "Noyah, Daughter of the King" (*NWYH bt hmlk*).¹¹ The title *'mt X / hmlk*, "Maidservant of X/of the King," is to be analyzed as a respected function and as the feminine counterpart of *'bd X / hmlk*, "Servant of X/of the King." Shulamit uses this designation of function in the sixth century BCE. She is a maidservant of Elnathan, the governor.¹² Along with these the seals of other women also are known; however, they give no indication of a function in the royal court. But the seals, or the seal impressions, clearly show that these women were economically active, possibly led their own households, and were able to conclude legal transactions.

Various representations of queens from Egypt and Mesopotamia, as we know them, are missing from materials from Palestine. The only pertinent iconographical motif that can be mentioned is that of the woman in the window. Ellen Rehm has shown that this is not to be interpreted as an indication or even as proof of the existence of a woman's palace or a harem.¹³ Instead, one must refer to the narrative about Jezebel, who appears to her enemy at the window in her royal regalia (2 Kgs 9:30, 31). Both images of

---

11. See Marsman, *Women in Ugarit and Israel*, 645; Korpel, "Seals of Jezebel," 356. See also Thomas Staubli, "Geschlechtertrennung und Männersphären im Alten Israel," *ld* 1 (2008), https://tinyurl.com/SBL6016k: "The seals for women in Judah, however, represent at maximum 3.5 percent of the total known stock, with declining tendency toward the end of the Judean monarchy; in Amman, where rural traditions had a still greater influence, the share of seals for women is, more conspicuously, two times as high." The seal impression of *M'DNH bt hmlk*, "Maadana, Daughter of the King," with the unusual representation of a *kinnor*, "harp," in the meantime, has been exposed as a forgery. See Yossi Maurey and Amir S. Fink, "Putting the Seal on Ma'adana: A Case of Forgery and Its Ramifications," in *Alphabets, Texts and Artifacts in the Ancient Near East: Studies Presented to Benjamin Sass*, ed. Israel Finkelstein, Thomas Römer, and Christian Robin (Paris: Van Dieren Éditeu, 2016), 255–69.

12. See also the seal, labeled as Ammonite, of *'LYH 'št / 'mt ḤNN'L* (ca. 600 BCE). Whether this inscription from the seventh century BCE, which only recently became known, is a forgery is a subject of controversy: [*m'*]*mt. hmlk. mn'rth. nblym. yyn. Yršlmh*[*m'*], "from the maidservant of the King, from Na'arat, jars with wine, to Jerusalem." See the critical analysis of this view: Christopher Rollston, "The King of Judah, Jars of Wine, and the City of Jerusalem: The Jerusalem Papyrus and the Forged Words on It," Bible History Daily (25 October 2017), https://tinyurl.com/SBL6016l.

13. Ellen Rehm, "Abschied von der Heiligen Hure: Zum Bildmotiv der 'Frau am Fenster' in der phönizisch-nordsyrischen Elfenbeinschnitzkunst," *UF* 35 (2003): 487–519; Sophie Kauz, "Frauenräume im Alten Testament am Beispiel der Siedlung," *ld* 2 (2009), https://tinyurl.com/SBL6016m.

Jezebel at the window and the woman at the window represent dominion in the palace, as well as protection and defense.[14]

Epigraphical sources such as contracts, correspondence, or lists from which the political, social, economic, and cultural activities of women at the king's court could be reconstructed, do not exist in the case of Palestine.[15] Here we rely on inferences from ancient Near Eastern texts and on the comparison with those texts. The comparison with Neo-Assyrian sources helps us to understand better the structure of the rule by kings.[16] The administrative texts of the Neo-Assyrian royal court give us an indication of the functions and activities of women at the king's court. The Neo-Assyrian (and other ancient Near Eastern) sources enable us to formulate hypotheses for Israel and to revise the image conceived by the historians and exegetes of the nineteenth and twentieth centuries, who proceeded from the idea of life in the harem and of the institutional powerlessness of women.

4. Harem: Space for Living and Working?

Until the 1990s, it was, of course, presumed that a harem existed also at the ancient Near Eastern royal court.[17] The ancient Near Eastern as well as the Old Testament texts about women at the king's court were read through these lenses.[18] The probe into the concept of harem goes back to nineteenth-century European scholars who described the circumstances at the Ottoman court from a perspective marked by orientalism.[19] A harem was understood to be an isolated area of the palace that was inhabited only by the wives of the ruler and their attendants and that was not accessible to

---

14. Rehm, "Abschied von der Heiligen Hure," 500–503.

15. On the recently published inscription that doubts the authenticity of the reference to the "maidservant of the king" within the framework of wine deliveries to Jerusalem, see above.

16. Of course, the relationships at a well-established, centuries-old, and large royal court such as that of the Neo-Assyrian Empire are not transferrable in toto to the small kingdoms in Judah and Israel.

17. Especially well known is Ernst Weidner, "Hof- und Harems-Erlasse assyrischer Könige aus dem 2. Jahrtausend v. Chr.," *AfO* 17 (1954/1956): 257–93.

18. See Solvang, *Woman's Place*, 52–57.

19. Solvang shows that the description of the Ottoman circumstances also is incorrect and influenced by androcentric and Eurocentric prejudices (*Woman's Place*, 58–62).

other men besides the ruler. The women were not allowed to leave this residential area, were shielded from the world (through eunuchs), and were deprived of every sort of active influence from the world, so that their lives, without any role or employment, were marked by idleness and boredom. Additionally, the topos of "harem intrigues" was formed in order to describe the nagging hostility among the women, their courting of the favor of the king, and the assurance won through unfair means of the succession to the throne for one of their own sons.[20]

In the meantime, it has been shown in ancient Near Eastern studies as well as in Old Testament exegesis that the concept of the harem and the notions described above are unsuitable for understanding the living environments and the spheres of influence of women in the ancient Near Eastern royal courts.[21] The rejection of the existence of a harem in the sense of such a way of life experienced by women at the king's court is based on the following arguments: In the Hebrew as well as in other ancient Near Eastern languages, there is no special word used for a harem.[22] A spatial separation of living quarters for men and women in the palace is presumed only in the Esther narrative, in which the "women's wing" is called בית הנשים, "house of the women," an idiom that is documented only in the book of Esther (Esth 2:3, 9, 11, 13, 14). The mention of eunuchs (סריסים) also is interpreted as an indication of isolated living quarters for women. Their task is said to be guarding the women's living area. Such a task by the eunuchs, however, can be discerned only in the book of Esther, where the eunuch Hegai is described also as שמר הנשים, "guard of the women"

---

20. See Solvang, *Woman's Place*, 58–62.

21. See Solvang, *Woman's Place*, 51–71.

22. Solvang demonstrates the circular argumentation of, for example, Abraham Malamat (Solvang, *Woman's Place*, 52–56). See Malamat, "Is There a Word for the Royal Harem in the Bible? The Inside Story," in *Pomegranates and Golden Bells: Studies in Biblical, Jewish, and Near Eastern Ritual, Law, and Literature in Honor of Jacob Milgrom*, ed. David Pearson Wright and Jacob Milgrom (Winona Lake, IN: Eisenbrauns, 1995), 785–87. Malamat already assumes the existence of a separated living area for women at the king's court and inquires only about the Hebrew word for it. An interpretation of the Hebrew *hapax legomenon* הרמון in Amos 4:3 as "harem" is improbable. For פנימה, which literally means "in it, within" and, according to Malamat, designates the living area of the women in the "house of the king," the meaning "the interior (of a building)" is rather to be assumed in 2 Kgs 7:11–12 and Ps 45:14–15. Nevertheless, there is absolutely no indication that we are dealing here with a living area for women. It is more probable that the reference is to the living quarters of the king.

(Esth 2:3, 8, 14, 15). The mere existence of eunuchs at the king's court is not enough reason to assume the existence of a women's wing, since סריס in general refers to a castrated man with the status of an official.[23]

In addition, the text of 2 Sam 20:3, which reports that the ten concubines of David are accommodated in their own building complex and live there together, is deemed an indication of a living area designated especially for women. However, that the women are confined there cannot be inferred with certainty because ויתנם בית משמרת, "He brought them to a 'guardhouse,'" in 2 Sam 20:3 says only that David commands that his concubines be brought into a house. Whether בית משמרת is to be interpreted as a name or as an indicator of the function of the house remains just as much an open question as the semantics of משמרת, which may mean "protection" or "guarding." When the concubines are qualified eventually as צררות, a derivation of the participle is possible from צרר I, "bind together," as well as from צרר II, "besetting": "Whether 2 Sam 20:3f is to be assigned to ṢRR 'surround—confine' is not certain. With reference to Lev 18:18, a meaning of 'besetting' also would be conceivable."[24] In the context of 2 Sam 20:3, a meaning such as "the one beset," in parallel with the term "a life in widowhood," is not improbable. On the basis of 2 Sam 20:3, though, one cannot conclude that all the royal women regularly lived in a separate residential area. The daughter of Pharaoh, Solomon's wife, dwells in her own house according to 1 Kgs 7:8; 9:24. These notes clearly contradict the idea of an isolated living area for all the women in the palace.[25] In the case of ancient Near Eastern palace complexes, it is increasingly doubtful whether a convincing archaeological proof of a separate residential area for women can be produced.[26]

---

23. See Ilse Müllner and Carsten Jochum-Bortfeld, "Eunuch," in *Sozialgeschichtliches Wörterbuch zur Bibel*, ed. Frank Crüsemann et al. (Gütersloh: Gütersloher Verlagshaus, 2009), 128–29. With reference to 1 Sam 8:14–15; 2 Kgs 9:32; 20:18; 24:12, Staubli arrives at a different verdict concerning the existence of a women's wing and is of the opinion that spatial separation of the sexes was a phenomenon of the upper classes that was implemented to the disadvantage of the woman and her appearance in public ("Geschlechtertrennung und Männersphären").

24. Maria Häusl, *Bedecken—Verdecken—Verstecken: Studie zur Valenz althebräischer Verben*, ATSAT 59 (Sankt Ottilien: EOS-Verlag, 1997), 101–2.

25. See Kiesow, *Löwinnen von Juda*, 77–78.

26. See Svärd, *Women and Power*, 109–20; Solvang, *Woman's Place*, 62–64. Staubli, however, refers to Egyptian images that prove the spatial separation of the sexes ("Geschlechtertrennung und Männersphären").

The indications of a strictly separated living area for men and women thus are far less clear than was for a long time assumed. That there were separate living areas in various palaces should not be denied. However, it is arguable that in every palace there *must* have been a residential area for women, and that *all* the women of the palace, or *all* the wives of the king, in fact lived in such quarters. Along with (in some cases) the separation of the living areas of women and men in palaces, there are also other forms of housing, as the independent household management by the daughter of Pharaoh shows. The assumption that separate housing based on gender might have limited women's freedom of movement or reduced their political or economic influence and that women were inactive or even insignificant should therefore be rejected:

> In conclusion, the "place" of royal women in the ancient Near East is complex and dynamic. Wherever they reside they are engaged in the functions of the royal house. From their individual positions in the hierarchy of women and collectively as an organizational network of women, they participate in shaping and preserving the royal house and extending its work domestically and internationally.[27]

5. Women in Administration at the King's Court

We have only a few references to the status of women in the administration of the royal court in Israel.[28] The female attendants at the court include female slaves (Eccl 2:7), bakers, cooks, ointment blenders (1 Sam 8:13), and nannies/wet nurses (2 Sam 4:4; 2 Kgs 11:2; 2 Chr 22:11). Quite uncertain is whether the functions of the female scribe and the female gazelle-catcher existed at the preexilic royal court.[29] To female singers and musicians, on the other hand, fell a higher status, since they are named

---

27. Solvang, *Woman's Place*, 67.
28. See Kiesow, *Löwinnen von Juda*, 84–95.
29. The assumption of these two functions can rest only on the two names הספרת, Soferet, and פכרת הצביים, Pochereth-hazzebaim, in the postexilic list in Ezra 2:55, 57. One cannot determine based on the morphology of the names whether the two names, used in the list as "family names," refer to an individual female role (female scribe, female gazelle-catcher) or to a group (guild of scribes, guild of gazelle-catchers). See Hans Rechenmacher, *Althebräische Personennamen*, LOS 2/1 (Münster: Ugarit-Verlag, 2012), 73–74. The explicit mention of female singers along with male singers in Ezra 2:65, however, could speak in favor of the designations of these female roles.

regularly along with other highly placed social groups (see 2 Sam 19:36; 2 Chr 35:25; Amos 8:3; Jer 38:22; Eccl 2:8; *ANET*, 288).

If we take the masculine descriptions of roles at the king's court that are known to us as a starting point, then, the designations בת המלך, "daughter of the king,"[30] אמת המלך, "maidservant of the king," and סכנת, "female administrator," are probable designations of female roles. The daughters are mentioned repeatedly as a separate group (Ps 45:9, 10; Jer 41:10; 43:6); they are recognizable, according to 2 Sam 13:18, by their clothing. Explicitly designated as daughter of the king are Jezebel, Merab, Michal, Tamar, Jehosheba, and Noyah (1 Sam 14:49; 2 Sam 13; 1 Kgs 9:24; 2 Kgs 11:2 // 2 Chr 22:11).[31] The Old Testament texts, in addition, recognize women who have considerable influence in decision making at the royal court by virtue of their activities. The prophetess Huldah (2 Kgs 22:14–20) and the "wise woman" of Tekoa (2 Sam 14:1–24) are probably not members of the royal court but rather possess socially established roles.[32]

That סכנת presumably designates a high administrative office at the king's court is suggested first by the masculine counterpart סכן in Isa 22:15,[33] which is clarified by אשר על הבית "the 'one set' over the house" and which refers to a "head of the palace." It is important to point out also the linguistic and factual proximity to the Neo-Assyrian *šakintu*, which is very well-documented in the Neo-Assyrian sources. Svärd (neé Teppo) analyzed the entire Neo-Assyrian material for the first time in 2007 and demonstrated that *šakintu* refers to the chief female administrator of the household of a queen.[34] She presides over the household, carries the whole

---

30. See Udo Rüterswörden, "Verwaltung," in *Das wissenschaftliche Bibellexikon im Internet* (2013), https://tinyurl.com/SBL6016n. Solvang, *Woman's Place*, 78: "These terms [wife of the king, mother of the king, daughter of the king] function as positional titles, indicating the individual's position within the structure and functions of the royal family."

31. On the seal impression, see above.

32. On Huldah, see Irmtraud Fischer, *Gotteskünderinnen: Zu einer geschlechterfairen Deutung des Phänomens der Prophetie und der Prophetinnen in der Hebräischen Bibel* (Stuttgart: Kohlhammer, 2002), 158–88. On the wise woman of Tekoa, see Silvia Schroer, "Weise Frauen und Ratgeberinnen in Israel: Literarische und historische Vorbilder der personifizierten Chokmah," *BN* 51 (1990): 41–60.

33. See Häusl, *Abischag und Batscheba*, 239–42—then, independently of Häusl, Kiesow, *Löwinnen von Juda*, 85–87.

34. Saana Teppo, "The Role and the Duties of the Neo-Assyrian Sakintu in the Light of the Archival Evidence," *SAAB* 16 (2007): 257–72.

economic responsibility, and executes legal transactions. She could be married, but a familial relationship to the king cannot be verified.

In the short passage of 1 Kgs 1:1–4, in which Abishag of Shunem is introduced at the king's court, we learn nothing about the tasks of the סכנת.[35] As in the case of David's introduction to Saul's court in 1 Sam 16:14–21, not only is Abishag's activity on behalf of the sick king described in 1 Kgs 1:1–4, but her role in the court is subsequently established. Abishag is described as a סכנת, a "female administrator" (1 Kgs 1:4), while David is described as a נשא כלים, an "armor bearer" (1 Sam 16:21). Both functions have nothing to do with the services each undertakes for the ill king. The parallels between the introductions of David and Abishag at the king's court make it possible to distinguish between Abishag's personal task and her institutional links. The structural power that is associated with her role as סכנת may not be blurred here by her personal task.[36] The analogy with the position of the *šakintu* at the Neo-Assyrian court as female administrator of the household of the queen, and the event in which Adonijah submits his request to marry Abishag of Shunem to the mother of the king, Bathsheba (1 Kgs 2:17), could indicate that Abishag as סכנת could marry and is directly subordinate to the king's mother.

6. Women of the King

The general term נשים, "women," denotes not only the wives of the king but also all the women with status and influence at the royal court,[37] just as the Neo-Assyrian term *sekretu/sekretus* refers to a number of various groups of women at the king's court: "concubines, women from the households of defeated kings, women related to the king, and without male guard-

---

35. See the excellent literary analysis by Barbara Suchanek-Seitz, *So tut man nicht in Israel: Kommunikation und Interaktion zwischen Frauen und Männern in der Erzählung von der Thronnachfolge Davids*, EUZ 17 (Berlin: LIT, 2006), 127.

36. See Häusl, *Abischag und Batscheba*, 239–42; Kiesow, *Löwinnen von Juda*, 85–87. Suchanek-Seitz and Müller misunderstand the institutional integration of Abishag as a סכנת. See Suchanek-Seitz, *So tut man nicht*, 83–84; Monika Cornelia Müller, "The Households of the Queen and Queen Mother in Neo-Assyrian and Biblical Sources," in *My Spirit at Rest in the North Country*, ed. Hermann Michael Niemann and Matthias Augustin, BEATAJ 57 (Frankfurt: Lang, 2011), 258–62.

37. So also Kiesow, *Löwinnen von Juda*, 80: "But, feminine family members or female court personnel also appear to be able to be subsumed under the expression 'women of the king.'"

ians, companions of foreign princesses, and, of course, valuable female hostages—to name just a few groups. In other words, *sekretu* meant any woman living in the palace, who was not the queen."[38] The term נשים, "the women (of the king)," occurs frequently in the context of conquests, that is, where a dynasty or the rule of a king is endangered. In order to weaken a ruling royal house, tribute payments in the form of partial deportations are imposed (1 Kgs 20:3; 5–7; Jer 38:22–23; 2 Chr 21:12–19; see also 2 Sam 19:6; 12:8, 11; *ANET*, 288).[39] The deportation of the entire royal house means the end of the king's rule. If one assumes a hierarchical sequence of those persons taken into exile in 2 Kgs 24:15, then, the "women of the king" should be regarded as a very high-ranking group, since they are mentioned directly after the king and the mother of the king but before the eunuchs.

With respect to many of the kings, the number of their wives is often mentioned, which shows that polygyny is taken for granted and, in the cases of Saul, David, Solomon, and Rehoboam, wives are distinguished from concubines (פילגשים).[40] Many of the wives are mentioned by name either because they appear as protagonists in the narratives or because they are integrated into genealogies. Thus, we know of women who share David as a husband (2 Sam 3:2–5) namely, Ahinoam, Abigail, Maacah, Haggit, Abital, Eglah, Michal, and last Bathsheba.[41] An unnamed daughter of a pharaoh is mentioned as the wife of Solomon (1 Kgs 3:1; 7:8; 9:16, 24; 11:1; 2 Chr 8:11). To Solomon also is attributed a large number

---

38. Svärd, *Women and Power*, 107–8.

39. Hezekiah must offer his daughter, his women (*sekretus*), and his male and female singers as tribute.

40. On the concept of פילגש, see Jost, "Königinnen." On polygyny, see Corinna Friedl, *Polygynie in Mesopotamien und Israel*, AOAT 277 (Münster: Ugarit-Verlag, 2000). Critique of polygyny by the kings is found in Prov 31:3–5; Deut 17:16–20.

41. The first six wives are listed in 2 Sam 3:2–5 // 1 Chr 3:1–4; see also 2 Sam 5:13–15 // 1 Chr 3:5–9; 14:3. Ahinoam comes from Jezreel and is the mother of Ammon. Abigail is the widow of Nabal from Carmel and the mother of Caleb (1 Sam 25). Maacah is the daughter of King Talmai of Geshur and the mother of Absalom. Haggit is the mother of Adonijah (see also 1 Kgs 1–2). Abital is the mother of Shephatiah. Eglah is the mother of Ithream. Michal is the daughter of Saul and is also mentioned as the wife of Palti (1 Sam 25:44) and of Adriel (2 Sam 21:8; see 1 Sam 14:49; 18:20–29; 19:11–17; 2 Sam 3:13–14; 6:16–23; 1 Chr 15:29). Bathsheba is the daughter of Ammiel, the wife of Uriah the Hittite, and the mother of Solomon (2 Sam 11:3; 12:24; 1 Kgs 1:11–31; 2:13–19; 1 Chr 3:5; Ps 51:2).

of wives and concubines from different lands, a motif that is associated with great ancient Near Eastern rulers (1 Kgs 11:1–4; see also Neh 13:26). Other royal wives who are mentioned explicitly are Maacah, the daughter of Absalom, and Mahalath, Jerimoth's daughter, both of whom are the wives of Rehoboam (2 Chr 11:18–21). Jezebel, the daughter of Ethbaal, the king of Tyre, is married to Ahab, the king of Israel (1 Kgs 16:31; 18:4–19; 19:1; 21:5–25; 2 Kgs 9:7–37). Athaliah, the daughter of Ahab,[42] is described in 2 Kgs 8:18 as the wife of Joram of Judah, even though her name is not mentioned explicitly. The wives of Abijah (2 Chr 13:21) and the wife of Joash (2 Chr 24:3) are also unnamed. Last, Rizpah, the daughter of Aiah and the concubine of Saul, who teaches David to act according to the Torah (2 Sam 3:7; 21:8–11),[43] comes to mind, as well as the already mentioned group of David's ten concubines, whose fate is reported in 2 Sam 15:14; 16:21, 22; 20:3.

In the Neo-Assyrian context, one of the wives of the king holds the office of *segallu*, queen. According to Svärd, the queen possesses great hierarchical power, by which she operates with the help of her household in the political as well as the economic sphere.[44] Such a high position by the wife of the king cannot be established in the Israelite context. What is conspicuous, rather, is that in the Old Testament texts, the titles or designations of status such as שגל, "queen," מלכה, "queen," שרה, "female ruler," גבירה, "female ruler," are used, of course, for foreign royal women, but hardly in reference to wives of Israelite kings. Thus, in Neh 2:6, the queen at the Persian court is designated as שגל.[45] The term שגל, "queen," is also found once in Ps 45:10 as the designation of the status of the future royal wife. The term שרה, "female ruler," in Isa 49:23 and in 1 Kgs 11:3 describes the status of foreign ruling women or (foreign) chief wives. No woman from either the Judean nor Israelite royal house is designated as מלכה, "queen," not even Jezebel, who governed together with her husband, Ahab, and at the time of her son Joram, or Athaliah, who was the ruling "queen" in Judah (2 Kgs 11). Only women at foreign royal courts are designated as מלכה, for example, the queen of Sheba and Vashti, the queen at the Persian

---

42. In 2 Kgs 8:26, Athaliah is designated as the daughter of Omri.
43. See the study by Luise Metzler, *Das Recht Gestorbener: Rizpa als Toralehrerin für David*, TFE 28 (Münster: LIT, 2015).
44. See Svärd, *Women and Power*, 177–223.
45. שגל is a loanword from Akkadian that corresponds to the Neo-Assyrian *segallu*.

court in the book of Esther.⁴⁶ Last, the designation גבירה is used chiefly for the mother of the king.

7. Mother of the King

The mother of the king, on the other hand, appears to possess a higher status and to exercise important functions. Thus, the designation גבירה, which in its fundamental meaning designates a woman with male and female servants,⁴⁷ is used as a title of sovereignty and/or a designation of status chiefly for the mother of the king, but seldom for foreign queens. In 1 Kgs 11:19, Tahpenes, the wife of Pharaoh and thus a foreign queen, is designated as גבירה. It is uncertain to which woman the term גבירה refers in the statement, "We have come down for the welfare of the sons of the king and the sons of the גבירה" in 2 Kgs 10:13, according to Anna Kiesow. If one assumes that "the king" refers to King Joram, who has already been murdered by Jehu, then, גבירה could mean either his otherwise-unknown wife or, more probably, the royal mother, Jezebel, who rules with him.⁴⁸ In any case, it becomes clear in parallels between king and גבירה that a higher status is conferred on her, for example, in Jer 13:18 and 29:2, where the king and גבירה appear together. In 13:18, both lose their crowns, and in 29:2, they head the list of the deported (Judean) elites.⁴⁹ In 22:26 also, the mother of the king is mentioned together with the king in the same situation of deportation. The text of 1 Kgs 15:13 (see 2 Chr 15:16) relates that the king's mother, Maacah, is removed from her rank as גבירה by King Asa.

The parallelism between Jer 29:2 and 22:26 as well as the note about Maacah's dismissal from office show that גבירה refers to the king's mother in the Judean context. In prophetic texts, we read about the "mother of the princes" only in the lament in Ezek 19. She is compared here with a lioness and with a vine.⁵⁰ The term *lioness* is used as a metaphor to denote

---

46. Solvang, *Woman's Place*, 72.

47. See Solvang, *Woman's Place*, 73. גבירה is primarily a term of relationship used to designate the rule of a woman over her attendants or slaves, both male and female, as in Gen 16:4, 8–9; 1 Kgs 5:3; Isa 24:2; Ps 123:2; Prov 30:23; in a metaphorical sense, it is used also to describe the city of Babel personified as a queen in Isa 47:5, 7. For details on גבירה, see Kiesow, *Löwinnen von Juda*, 96–134.

48. See Kiesow, *Löwinnen von Juda*, 111–13.

49. In Jer 24:1, however, the גבירה remains unmentioned.

50. In line with Kiesow, I assume that the term *mother* in the text of Ezek 19 should not be understood as a "dynasty."

royal rule. In the narrative context, only Bathsheba is designated explicitly as a "mother of the king" (1 Kgs 2:19). Bathsheba sits on the throne, and her son, King Solomon, bows down before her. A dialogue, then, ensues between the king and the "mother of the king." In this situation, Bathsheba exercises institutional power as she first listens to Adonijah's request to marry Abishag of Shunem and then communicates this request to Solomon (1 Kgs 2:18–22). To impute stupidity or a reprehensible intention to her in this situation is to avail oneself of clichés and disregard the fact that it is Solomon who, in 1 Kgs 2, is depicted negatively:

> The marriage of the king's brother Adonijah with Abishag of Shunem can be understood fundamentally as a part of the marriage policy of the royal house [or, better, of the "mother of the king"], which had as its goal the binding of the families living on the land to the royal house. Solomon, on the other hand, sees in this marriage a dangerous concentration of power within the court in the hands of his brother Adonijah and the *sokint* Abishag.... In the context of the murders of Adonijah, Joab and Schimei in 1 Kgs 2:12–46*, the rejection of Bathsheba's counsel by Solomon appears to be a curtailment of her influence in favor of the centralization of power in the hands of Solomon. From Bathsheba's support of Adonijah, though, it can be concluded, that she wants to see power distributed among members of the royal family and desires to bind social groups to the king [or to herself] through her marriage policy.[51]

In the formula used for presenting the Judean kings, the mother of the king is mentioned always, except in two instances.[52]

---

51. Häusl, *Abischag und Batscheba*, 298–99. Suchanek-Seitz views Bathsheba's position and intentions in a similar way: "The sincerity of Bathsheba's interest in helping Adonijah find a wife, on the other hand, often has been doubted. Many exegetes have implied that she wanted to provoke the vehement reaction of her son with her action and, thus, to send Adonijah to his death. I am of the opinion, however, that Bathsheba simply no longer judges Adonijah as dangerous and trusts his assertion that he recognizes Solomon as king.... To draw the erstwhile rival over to her side would have been a sign of good court politics in my opinion and would have minimized, without the shedding of blood, the danger of a renewed claim to the throne" (*So tut man nicht*, 138–39).

52. See, for details, Kiesow, *Löwinnen von Juda*, 135–85, and, more concisely, Jost, "Königinmutter."

Mother of the King	King	Text Passage	Comments
Naamah — Origin: Ammon	Rehoboam	1 Kgs 14:21, 31	
Maacah Daughter of Absalom Origin: —	Abijah	1 Kgs 15:2	In 2 Chr 11:20–22, the wife of Rehoboam and the mother of Abijah
Maacah Daughter of Absalom Origin: —	Asa	1 Kgs 15:10	Loses her status as גבירה (1 Kgs 15:13 // 2 Chr 15:16)
Azuba Daughter of Shilhi Origin: —	Jehoshaphat	1 Kgs 22:42	
—	Joram	2 Kgs 8:17–18 // 2 Chr 21:6	Instead, Joram is said to be married to a daughter of Ahab
Athaliah Daughter of Omri Origin: —	Ahaziah	2 Kgs 8:26 // 2 Chr 22:2	Designated as a daughter of Ahab in 2 Kgs 8:18 // 2 Chr 21:6
	Queen Athaliah	2 Kgs 11	
Zibiah — Origin: Beersheba	Jehoash	2 Kgs 12:2	
Jehoaddin — Origin: Jerusalem	Amaziah	2 Kgs 14:2	Seal YHW‘DN bt ’RYHW possibly belongs to her
Jecholiah — Origin: Jerusalem	Azariah/Uzziah	2 Kgs 15:2	
Jerusha Daughter of Zadok Origin: —	Jotham	2 Kgs 15:33	
—	Ahaz	2 Kgs 16:2	

Abi/Abijah	Hezekiah	2 Kgs 18:2 // 2 Chr 29:1	
Daughter of Zechariah			
Origin: —			
Hephzibah	Manasseh	2 Kgs 21:1	
—			
Origin: —			
Meshullemeth	Amon	2 Kgs 21:19	Seal *MŠWLMT* possibly belongs to her
Daughter of Haruz			
Origin: Jotbah			
Jedidah	Josiah	2 Kgs 22:1	
Daughter of Adaiah			
Origin: Bozkat			
Hamutal	Jehoahaz (Shallum)	2 Kgs 23:31	See also Ezek 19
Daughter of Jeremiah			
Origin: Libnah			
Zebidah	Jehoakim (Eliakim)	2 Kgs 23:36	
Daughter of Pedaiah			
Origin: Rumah			
Nehushta	Jehoiachin	2 Kgs 24:8	See also 2 Kgs 24:12, 15; Jer 29:2; 13:18; 22:26
Daughter of Elnathan			
Origin: Jerusalem			
Hamutal	Zedekiah (Mattaniah)	2 Kgs 24:18	See also Ezek 19
Daughter of Jeremiah			
Origin: Libnah			

If the naming of the "mother of the king" is missing only in the cases of two Judean kings, then, they probably remain unnamed only in unusual circumstances, for the title "mother of the king" obviously belongs to a stable monarchy. Whereas we cannot say why the mother of the king is unnamed in the case of Ahaz (but see, perhaps, Isa 3:12), an explanation is possible in the case of Joram. It is mentioned that Joram is married to a daughter of Ahab from the northern kingdom of Israel, more precisely to the royal mother Athaliah, denoted afterward with his son as a daughter of Omri. The Deuteronomists justify the negative assessment of Joram by means of this marriage and with it also throw a negative light on Athaliah. What attracts further attention in the naming of the king's mother is that their names often appear with their place of origin, which is not in every case the land of Judah. Thus, Naamah comes from Ammon, Athaliah from the northern kingdom of Israel, and Zebidah and possibly also Meshullemeth from the area of the former Northern Kingdom.

The patronyms provide indications of the social position of the women and of their families of origin. Maacah, as the daughter of Absalom,[53] appears to come from the house of David, Jerusha possibly from the priestly caste of the Zadokites, and Nehushta from the influential Jerusalem family of Elnathan, the son of Achbor (see Jer 26:22; 36:12; 2 Kgs 22:12, 14). Further statements about individual mothers of the king are possible,[54] which allow conclusions about the status of the king's mother. Hamutal appears twice as "mother of the king," namely, under Jehoahaz and Zedekiah, while between them, under Jehoakim and Jehoiachin, Zibiah and Nehushat have the status of the "mother of the king." The lament in Ezek 19 refers most probably to Hamutal, who is there described as a mother of lions with two lion cubs.[55] Maacah, beyond the same status during the rule of Abijah, is also "mother of the king" and גבירה under Asa. If it is true that Asa is the son of Abijah, as 1 Kgs 15:8 and 1 Chr 3:10 report, then Maacah retains her position as "mother of the king" under her grandson until she is dismissed from her office as גבירה because she erected a statue for Asherah.

Another mother of the king, or a new גבירה under Asa, however, is not mentioned. Athaliah, who occupies office as mother of the king under her son Ahaziah, assumes the entire executive power for a period of seven years after the murder of her son. She remains, as a daughter of Ahab/Omri, closely bound to the Omride ruling house in Samaria but comes under pressure when, with Jehu, the Nimshiites come to power in Samaria. "The Judean landed gentry thereupon pursues the overthrow of Queen Athaliah—perhaps even with the active support of the Nimshiites from

---

53. On the spelling of the name Absalom/Abishalom, see Rechenmacher, *Althebräische Personennamen*, 58.

54. See Kiesow, *Löwinnen von Juda*, 141.

55. Kiesow, *Löwinnen von Juda*, 168–76.

Samaria."[56] The Old Testament texts name Jehosheba, the daughter of the king, and the priest Jehoiada as protagonists of the rebellion.

The few statements on the גבירה and on the mother of the king in the Old Testament do not allow us to construct a comprehensive image. But the fact that the highest rank next to the king is ascribed to the mother of the king is shown by the texts and is supported by parallels with the Hittite as well as the Ugaritic monarchy.[57]

8. Power of Royal Women

The power of royal women, whether as the mother or the wife of the king, is based on the woman's family of origin, the political and social significance of her marriage, her economic resources, her education, the symbolic power that comes with status, and her personality. These aspects apply also in modified forms to the daughter of the king and to high-ranking women in the administration. Subsequently, the areas of politics and symbolic power and of the centralized state religion, as well as the economy and administration, will be addressed further in the summary.

8.1. Politics and Symbolic Power

The various titles, the naming of groups (of women), and the narratives about the actions of individual women show that structural power is bestowed on royal women in Judah and in Israel, which enables them to function at the very top of the royal hierarchy.

The high political status of the mother of the king in Judah, which is expressed in the designation as גבירה, "female ruler," is shown by the fact that the mother of the king is always mentioned in reports about the accession to the throne of a new king, and she is regularly named together with the king when the monarchy in Judah is threatened by prospective usurpers. The political status of the mother of the king becomes clear, additionally, in the symbols of power and obeisance. Bathsheba sits on a throne, and Solomon bows down before her. The king and the גבירה wear a crown. Jezebel confronts the usurper Jehu in her royal regalia (2 Kgs 9:32). Furthermore, a mother of the king can retain her political

---

56. Frevel, *Geschichte Israels*, 291.
57. See Jost, "Königinmutter."

power beyond the death of her royal son, as Maacah and Athalia prove, for Athalia herself takes over the government, while Maacah continues to hold office as גבירה. Hamutal is, with interruption, גבירה under two kings—both certainly her sons. While we gain at least some insight into the exercise of power by the mother of the king—Bathsheba, Maacah, Hamutal, and especially Athaliah—this is not possible in the case of the other mothers of the king.

However, we can observe other forms of the exercise of power by women at the king's court. If political alliances (whether regional or international) concluded through marriage become and remain fruitful, then an important role falls to the women as mediators, and they must assert their authority at the royal court of their husband as well as also in the sphere of influence of their families of origin, as in the cases of Jezebel, Athaliah, and the daughter of Pharaoh. The daughter of the king Jehosheba participates in a leading role in the alliance that leads to the overthrow of Athaliah. The influence of Bathsheba, who, together with the prophet Nathan, establishes the accession to the throne of her son Solomon (1 Kgs 1), should be seen as heterarchical power. Michal and Rizpah likewise exercise heterarchical power when they offer resistance to each of the kings who rule in their times (1 Sam 19; 2 Sam 6). The advisory function of the wise woman of Tekoa and of the prophetess Huldah should be viewed also as heterarchical power. In contrast to the cliché of the "palace or harem intrigue," the accession to the throne is, according to the texts, not the most important sphere of the women in the politics of the king's court. The assumption that the seizure of the harem of the preceding king was a well-established means of the assumption of power or the safeguarding of the claims to rule also is false. The rape of the ten concubines by Absalom is presented distinctly as an act of violence and a scandal.

8.2. Central State Cult

Jezebel is criticized for continuing the religious traditions of her Phoenician homeland in the state cult of the northern kingdom of Israel (1 Kgs 16:31–34; 18:4). These "false" religious practices during the reign of her husband, Ahab, and her son Joram are attributed to her (2 Kgs 9:22). These also are connected with Athaliah, who, during the reign of her husband, Joram, the reign of her son Ahaziah, and her own reign, continues Omride politics in Judah (2 Kgs 8:18, 26).

That the mother of the king plays an important role in the state cult is shown especially in the case of Maacah, who is removed from her office of גבירה because she authorized that an image for Asherah be erected (1 Kgs 15:13). Neo-Assyrian texts show that the household of the queen is responsible for the production of textiles (in the temple).[58] Thus, it would be worth considering whether the weaving in the temple, criticized in 2 Kgs 23:7, occurs under the supervision of the גבירה.

8.3. Economy

The daughter of Pharaoh clearly confirms the economic power of royal women, for she and not the future son-in-law, Solomon, receives the city of Gezer from Pharaoh as a (bridal) gift (1 Kgs 9:16), with which the basis for her economic activities is established, which are documented for other women by their seals. In addition, the daughter of Pharaoh dwells in her own house and thus presides over her own household. It is conceivable that Abishag of Shunem is the administrator of this household, although this is nowhere on record. Nonetheless, this would correspond to the status and the function of the *šakintu* in the court of the Neo-Assyrian king.

Bibliography

Ackerman, Susan. "The Queen Mother and the Cult in Israel." *JBL* 112 (1993): 385–401.
Andreasen, Niels-Erik A. "The Role of the Queen Mother in Israelite Society." *CBQ* 45 (1983): 179–94.
Ben-Barak, Zafrira. "The Queen Consort and the Struggle for Succession to the Throne." Pages 33–40 in *La femme dans le Proche-Orient antique: Compte rendu de la XXXIIIe Rencontre Assyriologique Internationale*. Edited by Jean-Marie Durand. RAI 33. Paris: Éditions Recherche sur les Civilisations, 1987.
———. "The Status and Right of the Gebîra." *JBL* 110 (1991): 23–34.
Brenner, Athalya. "Does the 'Twist' Point to Heterarchy? A Response to Beverly Bow and George Nickelsburg." Pages 64–66 in *A Feminist Companion to Tobit and Judith*. Edited by Athalya Brenner and Helen Efthimiadis-Keith. FCB 20. London: Bloomsbury, 2015.

---

58. See Svärd, *Women and Power*, 100–102.

Donner, Herbert. "Art und Herkunft des Amtes der Königinmutter im Alten Testament." Pages 1–24 in *Aufsätze zum Alten Testament aus vier Jahrzehnten*. Edited by Herbert Donner. BZAW 224. Berlin: de Gruyter, 1994.

Fischer, Irmtraud. *Gotteskünderinnen: Zu einer geschlechterfairen Deutung des Phänomens der Prophetie und der Prophetinnen in der Hebräischen Bibel*. Stuttgart: Kohlhammer, 2002.

Frevel, Christian. *Geschichte Israels*. Stuttgart: Kohlhammer, 2016.

Friedl, Corinna. *Polygynie in Mesopotamien und Israel*. AOAT 277. Münster: Ugarit-Verlag, 2000.

Häusl, Maria. *Abischag und Batscheba: Frauen am Königshof und die Thronfolge Davids im Zeugnis der Texte 1 Kön 1 und 2*. ATSAT 41. Sankt Ottilien: EOS-Verlag, 1993.

———. *Bedecken—Verdecken—Verstecken: Studie zur Valenz althebräischer Verben*. ATSAT 59. Sankt Ottilien: EOS-Verlag, 1997.

Ihromi. "Die Königinmutter und der 'Amm Ha'arez im Reich Juda." *VT* 24 (1974): 421–29.

Jost, Renate. *Frauen, Männer und die Himmelskönigin: Exegetische Studien*. Gütersloh: Gütersloher Verlagshaus, 1995.

———. "Königin (AT)." In *Das wissenschaftliche Bibellexikon im Internet*. Edited by Michaela Bauks and Klaus Koenen. 2012. https://tinyurl.com/SBL6016i.

———. "Königinmutter." In *Das wissenschaftliche Bibellexikon im Internet*. Edited by Michaela Bauks and Klaus Koenen. 2008. https://tinyurl.com/SBL6016j.

Kauz, Sophie. "Frauenräume im Alten Testament am Beispiel der Siedlung." *ld* 2 (2009). https://tinyurl.com/SBL6016m.

Kiesow, Anna Christine. *Löwinnen von Juda: Frauen als Subjekte politischer Macht in der judäischen Königszeit*. Münster: LIT, 2000.

Korpel, Marjo C. A. "Fit for a Queen: Jezebel's Royal Seal." *BAR* 34 (2008): 32–37.

———. "Seals of Jezebel and Other Women in Authority." *JSem* 15 (2006): 349–71.

Levy, Janet. "Gender, Heterarchy, and Hierarchy." Pages 219–46 in *Handbook of Gender in Archaeology*. Edited by Sarah M. Nelson. Lanham, MD: AltaMira, 2006.

Malamat, Abraham. "Is There a Word for the Royal Harem in the Bible? The Inside Story." Pages 785–87 in *Pomegranates and Golden Bells: Studies in Biblical, Jewish, and Near Eastern Ritual, Law, and Literature in Honor of Jacob Milgrom*. Edited by David Pearson Wright and Jacob Milgrom. Winona Lake, IN: Eisenbrauns, 1995.

Marsman, Hennie J. *Women in Ugarit and Israel*. OtSt 49. Leiden: Brill, 2003.

Maurey, Yossi, and Amir S. Fink. "Putting the Seal on Ma'adana. A Case of Forgery and Its Ramifications." Pages 255–69 in *Alphabets, Texts and Artifacts in the Ancient Near East: Studies Presented to Benjamin Sass*. Edited by Israel Finkelstein, Thomas Römer, and Christian Robin. Paris: Van Dieren Éditeu, 2016.

Metzler, Luise. *Das Recht Gestorbener: Rizpa als Toralehrerin für David*. TFE 28. Münster: LIT, 2015.

Meyers, Carol L. *Rediscovering Eve: Ancient Israelite Women in Context*. Oxford: Oxford University Press, 2013.

———. "Was Ancient Israel a Patriarchal Society?" *JBL* 133 (2014): 8–27.

Molin, Georg. "Die Stellung der Gebira im Staate Juda." *TZ* 10.3 (1954): 161–75.

Müller, Monika Cornelia. "The Households of the Queen and Queen Mother in Neo-Assyrian and Biblical Sources." Pages 241–63 in *My Spirit at Rest in the North Country*. Edited by Hermann Michael Niemann and Matthias Augustin. BEATAJ 57. Frankfurt: Lang, 2011.

Müllner, Ilse, and Carsten Jochum-Bortfeld. "Eunuch." Pages 128–29 in *Sozialgeschichtliches Wörterbuch zur Bibel*. Edited by Frank Crüsemann, Kristian Hungar, Claudia Janssen, Rainer Kessler, and Luise Schottroff. Gütersloh: Gütersloher Verlagshaus, 2009.

———. "Königtum." Pages 301–6 in *Sozialgeschichtliches Wörterbuch zur Bibel*. Edited by Frank Crüsemann, Kristian Hungar, Claudia Janssen, Rainer Kessler, and Luise Schottroff. Gütersloh: Gütersloher Verlagshaus, 2009.

Rechenmacher, Hans. *Althebräische Personennamen*. LOS 2/1. Münster: Ugarit-Verlag, 2012.

Rehm, Ellen. "Abschied von der Heiligen Hure. Zum Bildmotiv der 'Frau am Fenster' in der phönizisch-nordsyrischen Elfenbeinschnitzkunst." *UF* 35 (2003): 487–519.

Rollston, Christopher. "The King of Judah, Jars of Wine, and the City of Jerusalem. The Jerusalem Papyrus and the Forged Words on It." Bible History Daily. 25 October 2017. https://tinyurl.com/SBL6016l.

Rüterswörden, Udo. "Verwaltung." *Das wissenschaftliche Bibellexikon im Internet*. Edited by Michaela Bauks and Klaus Koenen. 2013. https://tinyurl.com/SBL6016n.

Schottroff, Luise, Silvia Schroer, and Marie-Theres Wacker. *Feministische Exegese: Forschungserträge zur Bibel aus der Perspektive von Frauen.* Darmstadt: Wissenschaftliche Buchgesellschaft, 1995.

Schroer, Silvia. "Weise Frauen und Ratgeberinnen in Israel: Literarische und historische Vorbilder der personifizierten Chokmah." *BN* 51 (1990): 41–60.

Solvang, Elna K. *A Woman's Place Is in the House: Royal Women of Judah and Their Involvement in the House of David.* JSOTSup 349. London: Sheffield Academic, 2003.

Spanier, Ktizah. "The Queen Mother in the Judean Royal Court: Maacah—A Case Study." Pages 186–95 in *A Feminist Companion to Samuel and Kings.* Edited by Athalya Brenner. FCB 5. Sheffield: Sheffield Academic, 1994.

Staubli, Thomas. "Geschlechtertrennung und Männersphären im Alten Israel." *ld* 1 (2008). https://tinyurl.com/SBL6016k.

Suchanek-Weitz, Barbara. *So tut man nicht in Israel: Kommunikation und Interaktion zwischen Frauen und Männern in der Erzählung von der Thronnachfolge Davids.* EUZ 17. Berlin: LIT, 2006.

Svärd, Saana. *Women and Power in Neo-Assyrian Palaces.* SAAS 23. Helsinki: Neo-Assyrian Text Corpus Project, 2015.

———. "Women, Power and Heterarchy in the Neo-Assyrian Palaces." Pages 507–18 in *Organization, Representation, and Symbols of Power in the Ancient Near East: Proceedings of the Fifty-Fourth Rencontre Assyriologique Internationale.* Edited by Gernot Wilhelm. Winona Lake, IN: Eisenbrauns, 2012.

Teppo, Saana. "The Role and the Duties of the Neo-Assyrian Sakintu in the Light of the Archival Evidence." *SAAB* 16 (2007): 257–72.

Weidner, Ernst. "Hof- und Harems-Erlasse assyrischer Könige aus dem 2. Jahrtausend v. Chr." *AfO* 17 (1954/1956): 257–93.

Part 3
Gender and Metaphor in the Latter Prophets

Daughter Zion and Babylon, the Whore: The Female Personification of Cities and Countries in the Prophets

Christl M. Maier

1. Introduction

In many Christian congregations, the hymn "Zion's Daughter, O Rejoice," intoned every year during Advent, presents Zion as a young woman awaiting the Messiah, David's son.[1] Even those who spurn Christian religion understand Babylon, the whore, as a symbol of the metropolis, the confusing and perverse city, the reception history of which is traced from the book of Revelation in the New Testament to this day, as an internationally acclaimed Babylon exhibition in Berlin in 2008 demonstrated.[2] Both Zion and Babylon are almost proverbial of a judgmental reception of female roles in the Bible. Both figures originally personify a city, which features as the addressee of massive oracles

---

1. See the English version in Oswald G. Hardwig, *The Wartburg Hymnal* (Chicago: Wartburg, 1918), 85. Around 1820, German Protestant theologian Friedrich Heinrich Ranke used a composition of Georg Frideric Handel and wrote the first strophe of this hymn according to the text of Zech 9:9. The other two strophes describe the peaceful kingdom of Jesus Christ. See Anne Gidion, "Tochter Zion, freue dich—EG 13," in *Kirche klingt: 77 Lieder für das Kirchenjahr*, ed. Jochen Arnold and Klaus-Martin Bresgott (Hannover: Lutherisches Verlagshaus, 2011), 291–93. In 1982, the vocal group Boney M. used the English text for their single "Zion's Daughter."

2. See *Babylon—Mythos und Wahrheit: Eine Ausstellung der Staatlichen Museen zu Berlin, des Musée du Louvre und der Réunion des Musées Nationaux, Paris und des British Museum, London; Pergamonmuseum, Museumsinsel, 26. Juni–5. Oktober 2008* (München: Hirmer, 2008). The term *whore* is used intentionally throughout this article in lieu of the more neutral terms *prostitute* or *sex worker* because the Hebrew word זונה carries a pejorative and polemical overtone in the respective biblical texts.

of doom and only a few oracles of salvation in prophetic texts of the Hebrew Bible. The role models based on this personification are, however, not exclusive, as Zion/Jerusalem is also portrayed as an unfaithful wife and Babylon, the whore, is also named "daughter," like the capital cities of Israel's neighbors and the land of Judah. This essay aims at clarifying the sociocultural background of the female personification of cities and countries, delineating their contemporary reception and interpreting some relevant texts from a feminist perspective.

2. The Personification of Cities and Countries

Personification is a stylistic device used to describe a group of people or a territory as a homogenous figure that acts, talks, has a personality, and thus may be held responsible for its deeds. Personification is a subcategory of metaphor. According to the theories of Max Black, Ivor Richards, and Paul Ricoeur, a metaphor creates new meaning by linking two concepts or ideas, thus merging a reader's connotations and associations of the two subjects.[3] The images generated in readers of a metaphorical statement are culture specific and time bound, although some of these associations remain constant for longer periods of time.

The metaphorical statement "the city is a woman" is based on the idea that a city has female characteristics. Providing vital resources such as food, shelter, and habitation for humans, the city is like a mother who cares for her children. Moreover, a city may be desired, conquered, protected, and governed.[4] It is obvious that linking "female" to "feeding, protective" and "male" to "conquering, strong, governing" conveys a hierarchical idea of two sexes that are diametrically opposed and generate distinct gender roles. This binary concept of sex and gender has been effective to date and has been challenged only in the last few decades.

---

3. See Max Black, *Models and Metaphors: Studies in Language and Philosophy* (Ithaca, NY: Cornell University Press, 1962), 40–45; Ivor A. Richards, *The Philosophy of Rhetoric* (New York: Oxford University Press, 1993); Paul Ricoeur, *The Rule of Metaphor: Multi-disciplinary Studies of the Creation of Meaning in Language*, trans. Robert Czerny (Toronto: University of Toronto Press, 1977).

4. See Sigrid Weigel, *Topographien der Geschlechter: Kulturgeschichtliche Studien zur Literatur* (Reinbek bei Hamburg: Rowohlt, 1990), 149–79; Christl M. Maier, *Daughter Zion, Mother Zion: Gender, Space, and the Sacred in Ancient Israel* (Minneapolis: Fortress, 2008), 60–74.

The female personification of cities is extant in many Hebrew Bible texts and can be traced back to at least three ancient Near Eastern precursors. In the West Semitic tradition, a city is female both grammatically and symbolically, attested by the use of feminine verbal forms and suffixes as well as feminine titles such as "mistress" or "lady" (for instance, the Lady of Byblos). In Hebrew, the term עיר, "city," is also grammatically feminine.

Second, the analogy of the roles of woman and city as protective, feeding, and conquered by a (male) enemy is also attested in an icon, the mural crown. In Neo-Assyrian iconography, this crown is depicted as a city wall with towers and symbolizes the city. Since the mid-ninth century BCE, the mural crown adorns royal heads, among them the wife of King Assurbanipal.[5] Her name, Ashur-sharrat, means "(the city of) Ashur is queen." In Greek culture, the female personified city is known since the sixth century BCE, the most famous example being Athena, daughter of Zeus, the father of the gods.[6] In Hellenistic and Roman times, Phoenician cities were depicted either as a sculpted female figure (Antioch on the Orontes) or as a female head with a mural crown on coins (Sidon, Seleucia), which represents either the city goddess or Tyche, the personified fate of the city.[7] In Roman times, both concepts are connected in the personification of the city of Rome. In Byzantine art, the mural crown returns due to the description of the heavenly Jerusalem with twelve gates in Rev 21:10–23, while the crowned female head is now Mary's.[8] In the famous wall paintings of the synagogue of Dura-Europos (Syria) from the third century CE, Queen Esther wears a huge mural crown. The Phoenician tradition of coin imagery was taken up in Italian stamps of the 1950s to the 1970s, in which the crowned female head represents the Italian republic.

The third precursor of the personified city is the city-lament genre, which reaches back to the third millennium BCE and profusely deplores

---

5. See fig. 3.15 in Silvia Schroer's essay in this volume.
6. See Maier, *Daughter Zion, Mother Zion*, 71. On the female personified city generally, see Marion Meyer, "Anthropomorphe Bilder von Städten in der altgriechischen Kultur," in *Prophetie in Israel: Beiträge des Symposiums "Das Alte Testament und die Kultur der Moderne" anlässlich des 100. Geburtstags Gerhard von Rads*, ed. Irmtraud Fischer, Konrad Schmid, and Hugh G. M. Williamson (Münster: LIT, 2003), 169.
7. Maier, *Daughter Zion, Mother Zion*, 64–69.
8. See Ingrid Ehrensperger-Katz, "Stadt, Städte," in *Lexikon der christlichen Ikonographie*, ed. Engelbert Kirschbaum (Freiburg: Herder, 1972), 4:198.

the destruction of Sumerian cities. The lament's speaker is often the goddess of the city or its main temple, as well as the building. This form of lament has been preserved in the second and first millennia in Assyrian liturgies for temple renovations and in the biblical book of Lamentations.[9] The conquered city in Lam 1–2 stands for her inhabitants, with her maltreated body representing their destruction and wounds.[10]

Against this traditional-historical background, the personification of Samaria and Jerusalem but also of Babylon, Tyre, and Sidon in prophetic texts comprises a stylistic means of identifying a city with its population. The female personification of a country as a delimited territory is analogous, even if it is mentioned only rarely in the Hebrew Bible. Actions and emotions are attributed to the personified figure, with the effect that the relation between the space and its population as well as between the collective and a deity appears as a personal relationship.

In the Hebrew Bible, cities and countries are personified with the title בת, "daughter," which, as an honorary title, sometimes is accompanied by בתולה, "young, marriageable woman," and in this combination signifies the city's juvenile beauty and attractiveness. "Daughter Zion" is the most frequently used title, used twenty-six times (2 Kgs 19:21; Ps 9:15; Isa 1:8; 10:32; 16:1; 37:22; 52:2; 62:11; Jer 4:31; 6:2, 23; Lam 1:6; 2:1, 4, 8, 10, 13, 18; 4:22; Mic 1:13; 4:8, 10, 13; Zeph 3:14; Zech 2:14; 9:9), sometimes parallel to "Daughter Jerusalem" (2 Kgs 19:21; Isa 37:22; Lam 2:13, 15; Mic 4:8; Zeph 3:14; Zech 9:9). Also non-Israelite cities such as Tyre (Ps 45:13),[11] Sidon (Isa 23:12), Dibon (Jer 48:18), and Babylon (see Ps 137:8; Isa 47:1, 5 [parallel to "Daughter Chaldea"]; Jer 50:42; 51:33; Zech 2:11) occasionally are referred to as "daughter." The title בתולה is combined with "daughter" with regard to Zion/Jerusalem (2 Kgs 19:21 // Isa 37:22), but also to Sidon (Isa 23:12), Babylon (Isa 47:1), and Judah

---

9. See Marc Wischnowsky, *Tochter Zion: Aufnahme und Überwindung der Stadtklage in den Prophetenschriften des Alten Testaments*, WMANT 89 (Neukirchen-Vluyn: Neukirchener, 2001), 18–42, 90–100.

10. See Christl M. Maier, "Body Space as Public Space: Jerusalem's Wounded Body in Lamentations," in *Constructions of Space 2: The Biblical City and Other Imagined Spaces*, ed. Jon L. Berquist and Claudia V. Camp, LHBOTS 490 (New York: T&T Clark, 2008), 119–38.

11. See also "Daughter Tarshish" (Isa 23:10), a city in southern Spain that was a trading partner of the Phoenician cities. The legendary ships of Tarshish (1 Kgs 10:22; Ps 48:8; Isa 2:16; 23:1) were probably solid merchant ships able to cruise the entire Mediterranean Sea.

(Lam 1:15). As a stand-alone title, it is used for Israel only; in Amos 5:2, it most probably refers to Israel's capital city Samaria,[12] in Jer 18:13 to the people, and in the oracles of salvation in Jer 31:4, 21 to a group of survivors in the land.

The designation בת־עמי, "Daughter, my people," which replicates the title "Daughter Zion," explicitly personifies the people as a female counterpart to YHWH in Isa 22:4; Jer 3–9; and Lam 2–4.[13] In contrast, one can hardly discern whether the title "daughter" for Judah (Lam 2:2, 5), Egypt (Jer 46:11, 19, 24), and Edom (Lam 4:21, 22) points to the territory or its respective population. Apparently, the personification merges the country and its inhabitants into one figure.

3. Feminist Interpretations of the Personified City

According to this use of titles, prophetic texts do not portray a city as a woman per se, but in a particular female role (daughter, wife, widow, etc.). These roles are time bound and thus fulfill a limited function related to a particular epoch and culture. In antiquity, a woman is socially and economically dependent on a man. As a daughter, she is subject to her father, who has to protect her from sexual contacts with any man until her wedding; as a wife and mother, she depends on her husband, who has to care for her and her children; as a widow, she is at the mercy of either an adult son or any male relative who takes care of her. This social dependency of women emerges from society's patriarchal system. In the metaphor, the female figure signifies the dependency of the collective—the population of a city or a country—on the deity mostly depicted as male. Prophetic Hebrew texts portray YHWH as sole guarantor of survival. He protects and feeds the city as daughter or wife. If she, that is, her population, turns away from him, he may punish her, stop caring for her, divorce her, and even kill her. The destruction is sometimes even imagined as sexual violence against the female city. Such sexually explicit and violent images are used especially in texts that accuse her of committing adultery with foreign rulers or deities.

This androcentric notion of gender relations and the use of sexually explicit images rightly offend and irritate contemporary readers. In their

---

12. See Wischnowsky, *Tochter Zion*, 17–18, 53–58.
13. My interpretation of בת־עמי as an appositional genitive is argued in Maier, *Daughter Zion, Mother Zion*, 61–62.

cultural conditioning, these ideas appear inappropriate to describe the relationship between God and humans for a present-day audience. Therefore, Cheryl Exum proposes a threefold strategy for interpreting texts that portray female sexuality negatively and apply images of sexual violence against a female figure.[14] First, Exum calls attention to the differing claims these texts make on their male and female readers. Second, "exposing pornography for what it is" leads to its evaluation as misogynist.[15] Third, Exum aims at searching for competing discourses, especially for women's suppressed points of view and their muted voices in these texts. Such critical interpretation leads one to question these metaphors and to uncover their potential effect of glorifying violence.

In my view, however, Exum's strategy is too limited because she focuses only on today's reception of the metaphor and disregards its historical dimension. Therefore, I follow Gerlinde Baumann's approach to both *explain* and *interpret* these biblical metaphors.[16] In her reading strategy, *explaining* means to reveal the cultural and social-historical background of a metaphor at the time of its emergence, whereas *interpreting* seeks to expound the metaphor's significance for contemporary readers and their estimated associations. The goal is not to condone misogynist metaphors but to explicate why they were used and to what rhetoric effect they were used in a given text. In the following, this approach will be demonstrated with regard to some texts that are relevant to this topic.

---

14. See J. Cheryl Exum, "The Ethics of Biblical Violence against Women," in *The Bible in Ethics: The Second Sheffield Colloquium*, ed. John W. Rogerson, M. Daniel Carroll R., and Margaret Davies, JSOTSup 207 (Sheffield: Sheffield Academic, 1995), 265–69.

15. Exum, "Ethics of Biblical Violence," 266. The same move is argued by Athalya Brenner, Fokkelien van Dijk-Hemmes, and Mary E. Shields. See Brenner and von Dijk-Hemmes, *On Gendering Texts: Female and Male Voices in the Hebrew Bible*, BibInt 1 (Leiden: Brill, 1993), 167–93; Mary E. Shields, *Circumscribing the Prostitute: The Rhetorics of Intertextuality, Metaphor and Gender in Jeremiah 3.1–4.4*, JSOTSup 387 (London: T&T Clark, 2004), 158–60. For the discourse on pornography, see also Christl M. Maier, "Feminist Interpretation of the Prophets," in *The Oxford Handbook of Prophets*, ed. Carolyn J. Sharp (Oxford: Oxford University Press, 2016), 470–74.

16. See Gerlinde Baumann, *Love and Violence: Marriage as Metaphor for the Relationship between YHWH and Israel in the Prophetic Books*, trans. Linda M. Maloney (Collegeville, MN: Liturgical Press, 2003), 33–35.

4. Examples of Prophetic Personifications of Cities

4.1. Daughter Zion/Jerusalem

The name Zion refers to the southeastern ridge from which the settlement of Jerusalem emerged; today, it is located south of the medieval wall of the old city.[17] From a military perspective, this ridge, between two deep valleys, was well protected. In biblical texts, Zion is also used for the entire eastern hill including the temple precinct until early Byzantine time, when the name erroneously became attached to the southwestern hill.[18] In prophetic texts, the names Zion and Jerusalem are often used synonymously. The personified figure Zion/Jerusalem plays many female roles. She is characterized as daughter, YHWH's spouse, "whore," mother, widow, and queen. Probably the earliest text that designates Jerusalem as daughter is Isa 1:7–8:

> Your country—a desolation, your cities—burned by fire;
> Your land—in your presence, foreigners devour it;
> [It is a desolation like an overthrow by foreigners.][19]
> And Daughter Zion is left like a booth in a vineyard,
> Like an overnight shelter in a field of cucumbers [like a besieged city].

The prophet here laments the country's devastation by the enemy, which comes to a halt just before the capital Jerusalem. Daughter Zion is compared to a makeshift hut made from vines and leaves in a vineyard or a cucumber field, which may be quite a suitable shelter for a summer night but totally insufficient to withstand a military assault. With this metaphor,

---

17. See Eckart Otto, "ציון," *TDOT* 12:342–43. In 2 Sam 5:7, according to Otto, "the stronghold/fortress of Zion," the late Bronze Age acropolis on the southeastern ridge, is identified with the city of David. Based on this rendering, Otto claims that ציון originally denoted a mountain ridge that was dry, in contrast to valleys. Its location generated the sense of "military defense" and originally was the name of the fortress only and, later, of the whole southeastern spur.

18. This location reaches back to Flavius Josephus's identification of the hill conquered by David with the "upper agora" on the southwestern hill. See Josephus, *J.W.* 5.137, 142–145; *Ant.* 7.61–62. Starting in early Byzantine time, this was the Christian tradition of Zion's location, which was falsified by Charles Warren's excavations on the southeastern hill in 1867–1880 (see Otto, "ציון," 343).

19. The phrases in brackets are most probably later additions. Unless otherwise indicated, all biblical translations are mine.

the prophet Isaiah describes the highly precarious condition of Jerusalem. He most probably points to Jerusalem's situation in 701 BCE, when the Neo-Assyrian king Sennacherib had conquered most of Judah's rural towns and threatened its capital.[20] Later, the Judeans explained that Sennacherib did not conquer and presumably did not even besiege Jerusalem because of the intervention of their God in favor of his chosen city. Isaiah 36–39 and 2 Kgs 18–20 transmit a story in which Isaiah announces God's support for the Judean king Hezekiah and portrays Daughter Zion as a proud and confident young woman:[21]

> This is the word that YHWH has spoken concerning him [= Sennacherib]:
> She despises you, she scorns you—Young woman, Daughter Zion;
> Behind your back, Daughter Jerusalem wags her head.
> Whom have you mocked and reviled?
> Against whom have you raised your voice and lifted your eyes on high?
> Against the Holy One of Israel! (Isa 37:22–23)

According to this prophecy, Daughter Zion feels protected by her God and thus mocks Sennacherib's envoy, who demands Hezekiah's surrender. The title בתולה entails a sexual connotation—the foreign conqueror is unable to subdue the female city because God is his true adversary. The story further relates that a divine messenger strikes thousands of soldiers in the Assyrian camp, thus forcing Sennacherib to withdraw. Its basic layer in Isa 36–39, with the portrait of Jerusalem as a self-assured young woman who relies on her father's protection, probably did not emerge at the time of the Assyrian threat but at the earliest in the second half of the seventh century,

---

20. See John A. Emerton, "The Historical Background of Isaiah 1:4–9," in *Studies on the Language and Literature of the Bible: Selected Works of J. A. Emerton*, ed. Graham Davies and Robert P. Gordon, VTSup 165 (Leiden: Brill, 2015), 537–47; Konrad Schmid, *Jesaja 1–23*, ZBK 19.1 (Zürich: Theologischer Verlag, 2011), 50. According to Schmid, the wording of Isa 1:4–9 is so vague that the text may also include later war scenarios. In his palace in Nineveh, Sennacherib had his victories depicted on ceiling-high wall reliefs, among them the conquest of the Judean city Lachish (see *ANEP* 371–73). This campaign is also documented in a royal inscription (see *COS* 2:302–3).

21. The daughter as a symbol of attractiveness, desire, and pride is discussed by Irmtraud Fischer, "Isaiah: The Book of Female Metaphors," in *Feminist Biblical Interpretation: A Compendium of Critical Commentary on the Books of the Bible and Related Literature*, ed. Luise Schottroff and Marie-Theres Wacker (Grand Rapids: Eerdmans, 2012), 310–11.

when the power of the Neo-Assyrian Empire was dwindling and the kingdom of Judah experienced a peaceful and prosperous phase.[22]

Jerusalem's personification, in the context of the lament in Isa 1, aims at demonstrating the need for the protection of the capital and its inhabitants, whereas the mocking song of Isa 37 looks back at the city's rescue and emphasizes Jerusalem's pride and inviolability. This father-daughter or God-city relationship has not received any feminist critique, probably because the need for and the importance of protection carry positive connotations.[23] In Isa 1–39, the destruction of Daughter Zion is mentioned only once in a lament (22:4) without further description, but tacitly assumed in the message of salvation that begins in chapter 40. In the latter part of the book, she is named daughter one more time (52:2), and further portrayed as an abandoned or a divorced wife (49:14, 21; 54:6) and as a barren, bereaved mother (49:21; 54:1, 4; see 51:17–20, 23), to whom the prophet announces the return of her children.[24]

In the book of Jeremiah, however, the prophet announces to Daughter Zion her destruction by a foe from the north, the Babylonians, who succeeded the Assyrian power. Jeremiah warns the personified city with impressive words (4:14–18, 30–31; 6:1–8) and portrays Jerusalem as a site of oppression and violence, her inhabitants as self-assured and unreasonable (5:1–6). This accusation against the city and its upper class is condensed in 13:20–27, where she is characterized as a "whoring" wife, whose behavior God brutally punishes:

[20] Lift up your eyes and see:[25] They come from the north.
Where is the flock that was given you, your beautiful sheep?

---

22. See Otto Kaiser, *Der Prophet Jesaja: Kapitel 13–39*, ATD 18 (Göttingen: Vandenhoeck & Ruprecht, 1973), 292, 305. For a survey of recent theses on the development of Isa 36–39, see Willem A. M. Beuken, *Jesaja 28–39*, HThKAT (Freiburg: Herder, 2010), 354–58.

23. Only Fischer mentions both negative and positive aspects of the daughter image ("Isaiah," 319–21).

24. Fischer also emphasizes that the oracles of salvation portray God not as father or husband, but as mother (Isa 49:15; see "Isaiah," 312).

25. My translation follows the *ketiv*, i.e., the Hebrew consonantal text, and the LXX, both of which identify the single female figure with Jerusalem. The *qere*, i.e., the vocalized Hebrew text, reads a plural form and thus aligns the address with Jer 13:18, where the king and the queen mother are mentioned; the Latin, Aramaic and Syrian translations follow the *qere*.

²¹ What will you say when he sets as head over you
those whom you have trained to be your intimates?
Will not pangs take hold of you, like those of a woman in labor?
²² And if you say in your heart, "Why have these things come upon me?"
It is for the greatness of your iniquity that your skirts are lifted up
and your heels are violated.
²³ Can an Ethiopian change his skin color?
Or a leopard its spots?
Then also you can do good who are accustomed to do evil.
²⁴ I will scatter them like chaff driven by the wind from the desert.
²⁵ This is your (feminine) lot, the portion I have measured out to you,
saying of YHWH,
because you have forgotten me and trusted in lies.
²⁶ I myself have lifted up your skirts over your face,
so that your shame was seen.
²⁷ Your adulteries and your neighing, your shameless "whoring"
on the hills, in the countryside—I have seen your abominations.
Woe to you, O Jerusalem! You will not be cleansed—for how long?

(Jer 13:20–27)

This passage stands out from its context by addressing a single female figure, which only at the end is identified with Jerusalem (v. 27). On the one hand, the announced calamity is described as imminent (vv. 20–21, 24); on the other hand, it has already happened (vv. 22, 26). According to verse 25, disaster struck because the addressee had forgotten YHWH and trusted in lies. Speaking of repeated acts of adultery (in Hebrew נאף) and "whoring" (זנות), verse 27 portrays the figure as an unfaithful wife. Although the term *whoring* points to prostitution and thus sociologically to a relationship that is different from adultery, the passage connects, like Hos 1–3, both transgressions in order to heighten the offence. The Hebrew term שקוצים (v. 27), "abominations," constantly refers to images and statutes of other deities (see 1 Kgs 11:5, 7; 2 Kgs 23:24; Isa 66:3; Jer 4:1; 7:30; Ezek 5:11; 7:20; Dan 11:31). Besides the veneration of foreign deities, Jer 13 also points to alliances with other rulers, which in verse 21 are called אלפים, "intimates."[26] The comparison with a dark-skinned man from Cush, that is, Ethiopia, and a spotted beast of prey emphasizes that the addressee is considered unchangeable and incorrigible.[27]

---

26. The term denotes both the heads of a tribe (see Gen 36; 1 Chr 1; Zech 12:5–6) and a childhood friend or lover (Prov 2:17; Jer 3:4).

27. For a critique of the negative portrayal of colored skin and its inherent bias

In the declaration of punishment, images of the female figure and the city overlap. On the one hand, the impending doom is categorized as military threat by foreign powers (v. 21), on the other hand as chastisement by God (vv. 24, 26). The metaphor of a woman in labor who writhes in anguish and pain is often employed in prophetic texts as a reaction to the danger of war (see Isa 13:8; Jer 6:24; 30:6; 49:24; 50:43; Mic 4:9–10).[28] The military threat is described as public exposure and rape of the "unfaithful" wife. The lifting of the skirts (Jer 13:22, 26) exposes the female lower body; the heels serve as euphemism for the genitals that are violated. In metaphorical language, the unfaithful "wife" is humiliated and raped by her former lovers, and even her furious "husband" publicly exposes her body. In social-historical terms, this means that the city of Jerusalem, which has turned away from her God to other deities and political powers, is conquered and destroyed.

Feminist interpreters often criticize texts such as Jer 13:20–27 as "pornoprophetics" and misogynist.[29] According to Robert Carroll and Ilse Müllner, however, such texts are not pornographic in an ordinary sense because they are neither historically nor currently a certain form of sexuality or used to arouse sexual fantasies.[30] Instead, Jer 13:20–27 aims at shocking its implicit audience, mostly men, who are called to identify with the negatively portrayed female figure.[31]

Recent studies on warfare in antiquity, authored by Cynthia Chapman, Rachel Magdalene, and Daniel Smith-Christopher, have demonstrated that a possible historical background for the sexual violence against the female city is the experience of Israelites as victims of Neo-Assyrian warfare, which included violence against men and sexual violence against

---

against dark-skinned people, see Madipoane Masenya (Ngwan'a Mphahlele), "'Can the Cushite Change His Skin...?' (Jer 13:23): Beating the Drums of African Biblical Hermeneutics," in *Congress Volume Stellenbosch 2016*, ed. Louis C. Jonker, Gideon R. Kotzé, and Christl M. Maier, VTSup 177 (Leiden: Brill, 2017), 285–301.

28. See the essay by Juliana Claassens in this volume.

29. See Athalya Brenner-Idan's essay in this volume.

30. See Robert Carroll, "Desire under the Terebinths: On Pornographic Representation in the Prophets—A Response," in *A Feminist Companion to the Latter Prophets*, ed. Athalya Brenner, FCB 8 (Sheffield: Sheffield Academic, 1995), 281–82; Ilse Müllner, "Prophetic Violence: The Marital Metaphor and Its Impact on Female and Male Readers," in Fischer, Schmid, and Williamson, *Prophetie in Israel*, 201.

31. Exum even calls this function of texts such as Jer 13 "a rhetorical strategy of abusing men verbally in the worst possible way" ("Ethics of Biblical Violence," 250).

women.³² According to Brad Kelle, "the violation of women as a metaphor fits the destruction of capital cities, for the stripping, penetration, exposure, and humiliation of the women is analogous to siege warfare, with its breaching of the wall, entrance through the gate, and so forth."³³ At the time of its authors, texts about the personified female city, on the one hand, characterize the experience of men and women and, on the other hand, blame the victims of violence by underlining their wrongdoings against their own deity. It is understandable that modern readers find this portrait of God as divine perpetrator cruel and unbearable. Postcolonial studies, however, have pointed out that in a situation of political and social oppression and of subjection to an imperial power, it is important for the oppressed to narrate their own history.³⁴ In order to preserve at least some agency and hope for a change of conditions, victims of imperial violence tend to name their own culpability instead of self-identifying as totally helpless and depicting the oppressors as omnipotent. Narrating Jerusalem's destruction as divine punishment for one's own transgressions, therefore, carries the hope that God will be more powerful than the human enemies and also be able to turn the fate of the city and its surviving population.

As the city is personified as a woman, and the victim is cast as a female character, this patriarchal perspective has to be critically assessed,³⁵ along with its irritating notion that the texts hold the victims of military violence

---

32. See Cynthia R. Chapman, *The Gendered Language of Warfare in the Israelite-Assyrian Encounter*, HSM 62 (Winona Lake, IN: Eisenbrauns, 2004); F. Rachel Magdalene, "Ancient Near Eastern Treaty-Curses and the Ultimate Texts of Terror: A Study of the Language of Divine Sexual Abuse in the Prophetic Corpus," in Brenner, *Feminist Companion to the Latter Prophets*, 326–52; Daniel L. Smith-Christopher, "Ezekiel in Abu Ghraib: Rereading Ezekiel 16:37-39 in the Context of Imperial Conquest," in *Ezekiel's Hierarchical World: Wrestling with a Tiered Reality*, ed. Stephen L. Cook and Corrine L. Patton, SymS 31 (Leiden: Brill, 2004), 141–57. For a proficient summary of previous research, see Ruth Poser, *Das Ezechielbuch als Trauma-Literatur*, VTSup 154 (Leiden: Brill, 2012), 169–248, and her essay in this volume.

33. Brad E. Kelle, "Wartime Rhetoric: Prophetic Metaphorization of Cities as Female," in *Writing and Reading War: Rhetoric, Gender, and Ethics in Biblical and Modern Contexts*, ed. Brad E. Kelle and Frank R. Ames, SymS 42 (Atlanta: Society of Biblical Literature, 2008), 104.

34. See Homi K. Bhabha, ed., *Narrating the Nation* (London: Routledge, 1990), 1–7; Bhabha, *The Location of Culture* (London: Routledge, 1994), 199–244.

35. See also Maria Häusl, *Bilder der Not: Weiblichkeits- und Geschlechtermetaphorik im Buch Jeremia*, HBS 37 (Freiburg: Herder, 2003), 166.

responsible for their own demise. These victims, however, are women and men, which means that the texts neither blame only women nor call for or justify violent acts against real women.

4.2. Foreign Cities: Tyre, Sidon, and Nineveh

The Phoenician harbor cities of Tyre and Sidon are characterized as wealthy female merchants in Isa 23, with their ships cruising the Mediterranean Sea up to Tarshish in southern Spain. The prophet denounces their trade relations as "whoring" (23:16–18), laments their pride (23:9) and the power of their rulers and merchants (23:8), and announces to them a fate equal to Jerusalem's—Sidon will be raped and find no rest (23:12), while Tyre will be forgotten for seventy years (23:15–17). The prophet Ezekiel predicts that Tyre will be besieged by Nebuchadnezzar (Ezek 26:7–14) and raises a dirge over the city, which is portrayed as a magnificent merchant ship that sinks into the sea (27:1–26). To Sidon, he prophesies her end by pestilence and sword (Ezek 28:21–23). The oracles against the nations in the books of Isaiah and Ezekiel concur in assigning the descent of the Phoenician trading cities to YHWH, Israel's God, who punishes their economic and political dominance, although neither Tyre nor Sidon is depicted as a direct opponent of Samaria or Jerusalem. Originally, these poems about the Phoenician cities probably commented on their demise or subjugation to the empires in order to highlight that YHWH is the lord of history. Sidon was conquered by the Assyrians in 677 BCE.[36] Tyre at times had to pay tribute to the Assyrians, Babylonians, and Persians, but, due to its location on an island, it was seized only in 333–332 BCE by Alexander the Great after a siege of seven months.[37] In the course of tradition, both texts were expanded with other motifs from the respective prophetic book and thus adjusted more closely to the prophecy of doom addressed to Jerusalem.

In contrast, Nineveh, the capital of the Neo-Assyrian Empire, represents a power inimical to both Israel and Judah. Nineveh's downfall is portrayed in the prophecy of Nahum (the name is derived from Hebrew נחם, "to console") by poetic images of terror. The city is counted among the

---

36. See Markus Saur, "Sidon," in *Das wissenschaftliche Bibellexikon im Internet*, ed. Michaela Bauks and Klaus Koenen (2015), https://tinyurl.com/SBL6016o.

37. See Markus Saur, "Tyrus," in *Das wissenschaftliche Bibellexikon im Internet*, ed. Michaela Bauks and Klaus Koenen (2011), https://tinyurl.com/SBL6016p.

enemies of YHWH (Nah 1:2) and characterized as a "city of bloodshed," in which treachery and violence abound (3:1); she is called "whore" and "mistress of sorcery" (3:4). In connecting images of military and sexual violence, Nah 3:4–7 describes the devastation and rape of the once-powerful city by YHWH. Actually, the Babylonians destroyed Nineveh in 612 BCE and thus set the seal on the end of the Neo-Assyrian Empire. In the context of ancient Near Eastern rhetoric and experience of war, the portrayal of YHWH as victorious perpetrator of sexual violence to Nineveh is neither novel nor perceived as unlawful, because the rape of a prostitute, unlike adultery, does not infringe the rights of another man.[38] Therefore, the psalm that is added in Nah 1:2–9 praises YHWH as a passionate and just God and interprets his actions as a message of comfort to Judah. From a modern perspective, however, such violence has to be judged as a war crime and massive violation of women's dignity. These violent imaginations of male victims of war in Judah are entirely inappropriate as metaphors depicting God. Following Baumann, the book of Nahum can be read today only as a text of lament that demonstrates the interweaving of systemic, military, and sexual violence and does not show any way out of violence.[39] The interpretation of these oracles against foreign cities as a message of comfort to Judah and Jerusalem, while discernible in the tradition and reception history, is inconceivable for modern readers.[40]

4.3 Babylon, the "Whore"

Babylon is mentioned 261 times in the Hebrew Bible, frequently in the title "the King of Babylon" and as abode of the exiles (Ezra 2:1; 5:12; Jer 39:9). The story about the building of Babylon's tower in Gen 11:1–9 relates the city's Hebrew name, בבל, with the verb בלל, "to confuse, to confound" (v. 9), as a divine judgment on human hubris. God destroys the mighty tower with which the people of Babylon aimed to "make a name" for themselves, and he confounds their language so that they are scattered.[41]

---

38. With Gerlinde Baumann, "Nahum: The Just God as Sexual Predator," in Schottroff and Wacker, *Feminist Biblical Interpretation*, 436.

39. See Baumann, "Nahum," 440.

40. For possible perspectives of healing for victims of military and sexual violence in biblical texts, see Ruth Poser's article in this volume.

41. For an interpretation of Gen 11:1–9 as polemics against the propaganda of the Neo-Assyrian Empire, see Christoph Uehlinger, *Weltreich und "eine Rede": Eine neue*

Jeremiah 51:13 describes Babylon as an affluent city on mighty waters; Isa 47:9–13 calls it a lady and a powerful city of knowledge, incantation, and astronomy. Isaiah 13:19–22 and Jer 50–51 unmask the striving for power of Daughter Babylon, the capital of the Neo-Babylonian Empire, and predict her utter devastation, as her army destroyed Jerusalem in 587 BCE (see also Ps 137:8).[42] Of these texts, Jer 50–51 raises the most serious allegations against Babylon and her king in a tangle of voices, war scenes, and forms of speech. Both chapters take up numerous motifs of the announcement of doom to Jerusalem in Jer 4–6, and also allude to the oracles against Babylon in Isa 13 and elsewhere. In portraying Babylon as a prototype of whoring and destruction, the author of Rev 17–18 draws from the plethora of motifs and charges in Jer 50–51 and announces the eschatological destruction of this famous city.

As Isa 47 continually addresses Babylon as a woman and adheres to her female personification, this text is chosen as an example of the city's characterization. Within the exilic-postexilic oracles of salvation in Isa 40–55, the chapter portrays the humiliation of the "young woman, Daughter Babylon" to slave status and offers a counterimage to the restitution of Lady Jerusalem, once abandoned and bereaved of children, to her royal dignity (Isa 54).

The speaker of Isa 47 is God, who in verse 3 announces his vengeance and is called גואל (v. 4), "redeemer." YHWH prophesies to Babylon the loss of her throne (v. 1) and the end of her status as גבירה (vv. 5, 7), "queen mother." She has to sit in the dust and work as a slave by grinding meal (v. 2). Named "Daughter Chaldea" (vv. 1, 5), she is summoned to wade through rivers and go into darkness. This situation and the verb גלה, "to strip, uncover," which is used three times and also means "to go into exile," announce to Babylon the fate of deportation and exile.[43] Like Jerusalem, she will experience widowhood and childlessness. For the Judean audience of this prophecy, Babylon's downfall signifies the end of their captivity.[44]

Deutung der sog. Turmbauerzählung (Gen 11,1–9), OBO 101 (Freiburg: Universitätsverlag, 1990).

42. Isaiah 21:9 raises a dirge over Babylon. For a detailed interpretation of texts about Babylon, see Ulrike Sals, *Die Biographie der "Hure Babylon": Studien zur Intertextualität der Babylon-Texte in der Bibel*, FAT 2/6 (Tübingen: Mohr Siebeck, 2004).

43. See Sals, *Biographie der "Hure Babylon,"* 303.

44. Sals, *Biographie der "Hure Babylon,"* 306. Ulrich Berges proposes a date

The conquest of the proud mistress Babylon is imagined in verses 2–3 as successive exposure of her body, which signifies a loss of status. The statement "your nakedness shall be uncovered, and your shame shall be seen" in verse 3a refers to sexual violence. The text further argues that YHWH brought about her loss of status and honor because Babylon did not show mercy to the deportees from Judah (v. 6) and believed that her own power would last forever (v. 7). She did not recognize that she would be YHWH's instrument only temporarily. The double citation of the female city's words, "I am, and there is no one besides me" (vv. 8, 10; see Zeph 2:15), emphasizes her claim to power. In Second Isaiah's prophecy, it also reminds readers of YHWH's self-declaration as the one and only deity (Isa 43:10, 13; 44:6; 45:5, 18; 48:12). Thus, Babylon is portrayed as an antagonist to Israel's God, who in the end disempowers her. Although her former pretentious words are cited again (vv. 7, 8, 10), she is silenced and, unlike Jerusalem, even unable to lament her fate.[45] Verses 11–15 mention, in retrospect, what formerly distinguished Babylon—wisdom and knowledge, incantation and the prediction of the future. Yet all these arts, the prophecy declares, will not prevent the fall of the famous city and will not save her.

On the one hand, this deconstruction of Babylon as the capital of imperial power takes up motifs of Second Isaiah's prophecy of salvation in order to emphasize the imminent fulfillment of the oracles of doom for Babylon in Isa 13:19–22 and 14:22–23.[46] On the other hand, it uses traditional metaphors of war, including images of sexual violence against the female city (see Jer 13; Ezek 16; 23). Isaiah 47 offers a fantasy of revenge, because Babylon's exposure and degradation are formulated in the form of a wish (v. 3), and the passage does not explicitly state the city's physical destruction. This feature probably takes account of the fact that Cyrus II did not destroy Babylon, as the priests of Marduk welcomed the foreign ruler to the city due to their opposition against the last Babylonian king, Nabonidus.[47] According to Isa 45:1–4, it is YHWH who summons Cyrus

---

around 520 BCE for the basic layer of Isa 46–48. See Berges, *Jesaja 40–48*, HThKAT (Freiburg: Herder, 2008), 480.

45. Sals, *Biographie der "Hure Babylon,"* 306, sees her loss of voice as the last and most brutal step of degradation.

46. See Berges, *Jesaja 40–48*, 487.

47. See Klaas R. Veenhof, *Geschichte des Alten Orients bis zur Zeit Alexanders des Großen*, trans. Helga Weippert, GAT 11 (Göttingen: Vandenhoeck & Ruprecht, 2001), 284–86; Berges, *Jesaja 40–48*, 376.

as liberator and puts an end to Babylon's reign.⁴⁸ Isaiah 47 thus underlines the inefficiency of the wisdom of Babylon and her gods.

From a feminist perspective, this announcement of doom to Babylon has to be probed like the one to Jerusalem, because it also victimizes the female city and depicts atrocities of war as a just punishment for human hubris and the will to exercise power.⁴⁹

5. Female Cities and Countries and Their Male God: A Patriarchal Construct

Feminist hermeneutics serves as a foundation and starting point for a critical reading of the female personification of cities and countries in prophetic literature. While there are only a few positive examples, among them the city as mother or daughter worthy of protection, negative characterizations of the city as "whoring" dominate, with regard to political alliances with the empires or to the veneration of other deities. The most frequent motif is the city's destruction, depicted by metaphors of exposure, degradation, and rape of the female figure. This motif is aimed at shocking the audience of the texts—and it appalls readers even today. These metaphors can be explained against the background of lived experiences of war, in which the people of Israel and Judah were most often the victims. In view of this cultural and historical origin, such an explanation of the metaphors may prevent modern female readers from identifying with the female victim and male readers from assuming the perspective of God and his prophet. No explanation, however, can fully eliminate the discomfort with the image of God as a violent perpetrator. For modern readers, these metaphors have to be interpreted as culture specific and time bound, as misleading and completely inappropriate for present-day characterizations of God. Therefore, the challenge for modern readers is to discover other images of God and to choose different modes of action in their interpersonal relations. Modern interpreters should articulately criticize these metaphors for their inherent misogyny and point out that

---

48. According to Berges, the text aims at portraying Israel's deity as well-known ruler of the world's history (*Jesaja 40–48*, 391–92).

49. Sals also points out the gender hierarchy inherent in the literary characters in Isa 14; 47 and their one-sided, misogynist interpretation (*Biographie der "Hure Babylon,"* 323–27).

the concepts of parenthood, marriage, and sexuality have changed in a fundamental way since biblical times.

In view of the above, it is important to point out that the genre most often used for the personification of cities and countries is the lament. If the sexual degradation and violent destruction of the city is presented in the form of a lament, modern interpreters should be aware that the texts express the trauma of destruction and the perspective of the victims. An easy identification of readers with the female figure would be even counterproductive.[50] Therefore, I propose that these laments about the devastation of a collective body, city or country, be interpreted as a critical countervoice against war and foreign rule, and that they be used as a starting point for continuous critique of dominant images of God and hierarchical gender relations.

Bibliography

Babylon—Mythos und Wahrheit: Eine Ausstellung der Staatlichen Museen zu Berlin, des Musée du Louvre und der Réunion des Musées Nationaux, Paris und des British Museum; London: Pergamonmuseum, Museumsinsel, 26. Juni–5. Oktober 2008. München: Hirmer, 2008.

Baumann, Gerlinde. "Nahum: The Just God as Sexual Predator." Pages 433–41 in *Feminist Biblical Interpretation: A Compendium of Critical Commentary on the Books of the Bible and Related Literature*. Edited by Luise Schottroff and Marie-Theres Wacker. Grand Rapids: Eerdmans, 2012.

———. *Love and Violence: Marriage as Metaphor for the Relationship between YHWH and Israel in the Prophetic Books*. Translated by Linda M. Maloney. Collegeville, MN: Liturgical Press, 2003.

Berges, Ulrich. *Jesaja 40–48*. HThKAT. Freiburg: Herder, 2008.

Beuken, Willem A. M. *Jesaja 28–39*. HThKAT. Freiburg: Herder, 2010.

Bhabha, Homi K. *The Location of Culture*. London: Routledge, 1994.

———, ed. *Narrating the Nation*. London: Routledge, 1990.

Black, Max. *Models and Metaphors: Studies in Language and Philosophy*. Ithaca, NY: Cornell University Press, 1962.

---

50. Similarly, Baumann, *Love and Violence*, 232.

Brenner, Athalya, and Fokkelien van Dijk-Hemmes. *On Gendering Texts: Female and Male Voices in the Hebrew Bible*. BibInt 1. Leiden: Brill, 1993.

Carroll, Robert. "Desire under the Terebinths: On Pornographic Representation in the Prophets—A Response." Pages 275–307 in *A Feminist Companion to the Latter Prophets*. Edited by Athalya Brenner. FCB 8. Sheffield: Sheffield Academic, 1995.

Chapman, Cynthia R. *The Gendered Language of Warfare in the Israelite-Assyrian Encounter*. HSM 62. Winona Lake, IN: Eisenbrauns, 2004.

Ehrensperger-Katz, Ingrid. "Stadt, Städte." Pages 198–205 in *Lexikon der christlichen Ikonographie*. Vol. 4. Edited by Engelbert Kirschbaum. Freiburg: Herder, 1972.

Emerton, John A. "The Historical Background of Isaiah 1:4–9." Pages 537–47 in *Studies on the Language and Literature of the Bible: Selected Works of J. A. Emerton*. Edited by Graham Davies and Robert P. Gordon. VTSup 165. Leiden: Brill, 2015.

Exum, J. Cheryl. "The Ethics of Biblical Violence against Women." Pages 248–71 in *The Bible in Ethics: The Second Sheffield Colloquium*. Edited by John W. Rogerson, M. Daniel Carroll R., and Margaret Davies. JSOTSup 207. Sheffield: Sheffield Academic, 1995.

Fischer, Irmtraud. "Isaiah: The Book of Female Metaphors." Pages 303–18 in *Feminist Biblical Interpretation: A Compendium of Critical Commentary on the Books of the Bible and Related Literature*. Edited by Luise Schottroff and Marie-Theres Wacker. Grand Rapids: Eerdmans, 2012.

Gidion, Anne. "Tochter Zion, freue dich—EG 13." Pages 291–93 in *Kirche klingt: 77 Lieder für das Kirchenjahr*. Edited by Jochen Arnold and Klaus-Martin Bresgott. Hannover: Lutherisches Verlagshaus, 2011.

Häusl, Maria. *Bilder der Not: Weiblichkeits- und Geschlechtermetaphorik im Buch Jeremia*. HBS 37. Freiburg: Herder, 2003.

Hardwig, Oswald G. *The Wartburg Hymnal*. Chicago: Wartburg, 1918.

Kaiser, Otto. *Der Prophet Jesaja: Kapitel 13–39*. ATD 18. Göttingen: Vandenhoeck & Ruprecht, 1973.

Kelle, Brad E. "Wartime Rhetoric: Prophetic Metaphorization of Cities as Female." Pages 95–112 in *Writing and Reading War: Rhetoric, Gender, and Ethics in Biblical and Modern Contexts*. Edited by Brad E. Kelle and Frank R. Ames. SymS 42. Atlanta: Society of Biblical Literature, 2008.

Magdalene, F. Rachel. "Ancient Near Eastern Treaty-Curses and the Ultimate Texts of Terror: A Study of the Language of Divine Sexual Abuse in the Prophetic Corpus." Pages 326–52 in *A Feminist Companion to the Latter Prophets*. Edited by Athalya Brenner. FCB 8. Sheffield: Sheffield Academic, 1995.

Maier, Christl M. "Body Space as Public Space: Jerusalem's Wounded Body in Lamentations." Pages 119–38 in *Constructions of Space 2: The Biblical City and Other Imagined Spaces*. Edited by Jon L. Berquist and Claudia V. Camp. LHBOTS 490. New York: T&T Clark, 2008.

———. *Daughter Zion, Mother Zion: Gender, Space, and the Sacred in Ancient Israel*. Minneapolis: Fortress, 2008.

———. "Feminist Interpretation of the Prophets." Pages 467–82 in *The Oxford Handbook of Prophets*. Edited by Carolyn J. Sharp. Oxford: Oxford University Press, 2016.

Masenya (Ngwan'a Mphahlele), Madipoane. "'Can the Cushite Change His Skin…?' (Jer 13:23): Beating the Drums of African Biblical Hermeneutics." Pages 285–301 in *Congress Volume Stellenbosch 2016*. Edited by Louis C. Jonker, Gideon R. Kotzé, and Christl M. Maier. VTSup 177. Leiden: Brill, 2017.

Meyer, Marion. "Anthropomorphe Bilder von Städten in der altgriechischen Kultur." Pages 169–78 in *Prophetie in Israel: Beiträge des Symposiums "Das Alte Testament und die Kultur der Moderne" anlässlich des 100. Geburtstags Gerhard von Rads*. Edited by Irmtraud Fischer, Konrad Schmid, and Hugh G. M. Williamson. Münster: LIT, 2003.

Müllner, Ilse. "Prophetic Violence: The Marital Metaphor and Its Impact on Female and Male Readers." Pages 199–204 in *Prophetie in Israel: Beiträge des Symposiums "Das Alte Testament und die Kultur der Moderne" anlässlich des 100. Geburtstags Gerhard von Rads*. Edited by Irmtraud Fischer, Konrad Schmid, and Hugh G. M. Williamson. Münster: LIT, 2003.

Otto, Eckart. "צִיּוֹן." *TDOT* 12:333–64.

Poser, Ruth. *Das Ezechielbuch als Trauma-Literatur*. VTSup 154. Leiden: Brill, 2012.

Richards, Ivor A. *The Philosophy of Rhetoric*. New York: Oxford University Press, 1993.

Ricoeur, Paul. *The Rule of Metaphor: Multi-disciplinary Studies of the Creation of Meaning in Language*. Translated by Robert Czerny. Toronto: University of Toronto Press, 1977.

Sals, Ulrike. *Die Biographie der "Hure Babylon": Studien zur Intertextualität der Babylon-Texte in der Bibel.* FAT 2/6. Tübingen: Mohr Siebeck, 2004.

Saur, Markus. "Sidon." In *Das wissenschaftliche Bibellexikon im Internet.* Edited by Michaela Bauks and Klaus Koenen. 2015. https://tinyurl.com/SBL6016o.

———. "Tyrus." In *Das wissenschaftliche Bibellexikon im Internet.* Edited by Michaela Bauks and Klaus Koenen. 2011. https://tinyurl.com/SBL6016p.

Schmid, Konrad. *Jesaja 1–23.* ZBK 19.1. Zürich: Theologischer Verlag, 2011.

Shields, Mary E. *Circumscribing the Prostitute: The Rhetorics of Intertextuality, Metaphor and Gender in Jeremiah 3.1–4.4.* JSOTSup 387. London: T&T Clark, 2004.

Smith-Christopher, Daniel. "Ezekiel in Abu Ghraib: Rereading Ezekiel 16:37–39 in the Context of Imperial Conquest." Pages 141–57 in *Ezekiel's Hierarchical World: Wrestling with a Tiered Reality.* Edited by Stephen L. Cook and Corrine L. Patton. SymS 31. Leiden: Brill, 2004.

Uehlinger, Christoph. *Weltreich und "eine Rede": Eine neue Deutung der sog. Turmbauerzählung (Gen 11,1–9).* OBO 101. Freiburg: Universitätsverlag, 1990.

Veenhof, Klaas R. *Geschichte des Alten Orients bis zur Zeit Alexanders des Großen.* Translated by Helga Weippert. GAT 11. Göttingen: Vandenhoeck & Ruprecht, 2001.

Weigel, Sigrid. *Topographien der Geschlechter: Kulturgeschichtliche Studien zur Literatur.* Reinbek bei Hamburg: Rowohlt, 1990.

Wischnowsky, Marc. *Tochter Zion: Aufnahme und Überwindung der Stadtklage in den Prophetenschriften des Alten Testaments.* WMANT 89. Neukirchen-Vluyn: Neukirchener, 2001.

The Marriage Metaphor in the Prophets: Some Gender Issues

Marta García Fernández

1. Introduction

The marriage metaphor used to express the relationship between God and Israel appears for the first time in Hos 1–3, and it is later developed by the greater prophets in Isa 54 and 62; Jer 2:2–4:4;[1] and Ezek 16 and 23. It is also found in wisdom literature but from a different perspective, as it does not express the alliance with YHWH as much as it expresses the relationship of absolute dedication that a disciple should have with Wisdom (Prov 1–9; 31:10–31; Sir 6:18–37; 14:20–15:10; 51:13–30).

The vast literature of the past forty years has shown a growing interest in this theme in the prophetic works and wisdom literature. But the focus of research over the years has changed. Until 1980, studies focused on God's action and love for Israel as the basis for the marriage metaphor. After the 1980s, however, the feminist approach began to put more emphasis on the main role of women, underlining the violent and sometimes pornographic character of marriage.[2] With the purpose of understanding the reason behind

---

I would like to thank Miguel de la Lastra Montalbán for his invaluable help in correcting the translation of this essay.

1. We also find other episodes with this symbolism in Jer 13:20–27; 31:31–34.

2. Six studies with a feminist slant are dedicated entirely to this theme: Nelly Stienstra, *YHWH Is the Husband of His People: Analysis of a Biblical Metaphor with Special Reference to Translation* (Kampen: Kok Pharos, 1993); Renita Weems, *Battered Love: Marriage, Sex, and Violence in the Hebrew Prophets*, OBT (Minneapolis: Fortress, 1995); Richtsje Abma, *Bonds of Love: Methodic Studies of Prophetic Texts with Marriage Imagery (Isaiah 50:1–3 and 54:1–10, Hosea 1–3, Jeremiah 2–3)*, SSN 40 (Amsterdam: Van Gorcum; Assen: Brill, 1999); Gerlinde Baumann, *Lieb und Gewalt: Die Ehe als Metapher für das Verhältinis JHWH, Israel in den Prophetenbüchern*, SBS

the punitive actions attributed to YHWH, current research is taking other paths—tracking the social situation of women and their status within the marriage that conforms to the laws that regulated the conjugal relationship.

2. The Use of the Marriage Metaphor:
Isaiah versus Hosea, Jeremiah, and Ezekiel

The literary device of metaphor is born from association and has as its basis a third element of comparison, which paradoxically remains hidden and appeals to the reader's intelligence. Deciphering it is fundamental to understanding the meaning and goal of its use. That said—and precisely because that third element remains hidden—we must be cautious not to simply transpose elements from biblical marriage to metaphorical marriage.[3] Taking into consideration the context where the metaphor is used may offer some clues that would help one escape from this hard-to-resolve impasse.

Traditionally, the appearance of the marriage metaphor is attributed to the prophet Hosea in the eighth century BCE. However, Hos 2:4–25 shows a certain correspondence with texts of a later dating (Jer 2:1–19; Ezek 16). Furthermore, Hos 1–3 itself alternates between denouncement and promise.[4] This is a typical juxtaposition of postexilic prophetism and an indication of the intense redactional work of these chapters.[5] In fact, in

---

185 (Stuttgart: Katholisches Bibelwerk, 2000); Teresa Solà, *Jahvè, espòs d'Israel: Poderosa metàfora profètica* (Barcelona: Claret, 2006); Sharon Moughtin-Mumby, *Sexual and Marital Metaphors in Hosea, Jeremiah, Isaiah, and Ezekiel*, OTM (Oxford: Oxford University Press, 2008). In addition to these studies—some of them are translated into Spanish, such as Renita J. Weems, *Amor maltratado: Matrimonio, sexo y violencia en los profetas hebreos*, CCM (Bilbao: Desclée du Brouwer, 1997)—other chapters or sections also focus on this theme in Spanish. See L. Alonso Schökel and José Luis Sicre Díaz, *Profetas: Comentario* (Madrid: Ediciones Cristiandad, 1980), 2:880; Mercedes Navarro Puerto, "La figura femenina en los libros de los profetas Amós y Oseas," in *De la ruina a la afirmación: El entorno del Reino de Israel en el siglo VIII a.C.*, ed. Santiago Ausín, ABE 33 (Estella: Editorial Verbo Divino, 1997), 193–218.

3. See Tikva Frymer-Kensky, *In the Wake of the Goddess: Women, Culture, and the Transformation of Pagan Myth* (Piscataway, NJ: Gorgias, 1982), 148–49; Hennie J. Marsman, *Women in Ugarit and Israel: Their Social and Religious Position in the Context of the Ancient Near East*, OtSt 49 (Leiden: Brill, 2003), 119.

4. Hos 1:2–9 (denouncement); 2:1–3 (promise); 2:4–15 (denouncement); 2:16–25 (promise); 3:1–3 (denouncement); 3:4–5 (promise).

5. See Bernard Renaud, "Genèse et unité rédactionnelle de Os 2," *RevScRel* 54 (1980): 1–20; Renaud, "Osée 1–3: analyse diachronique et lectura sinchronique, prob-

addition to Hos 1–3, the metaphor occurs mainly in texts with a postexilic framework (Isa 54; 62; Jer 2:2–4:4; Ezek 16; 23) in which the imagery of the new covenant predominates.[6] On the other hand, the use of the metaphor is not homogenous. Beyond the differences between the different prophets, the most remarkable is the positive characterization of the metaphor in Isaiah, which contrasts with the negative emphasis in the other prophets.

One indication of this is the presence of the root "to prostitute oneself" (זנה) or of the noun "prostitution" (זנונים). While this term occurs frequently in parts of Hosea, Jeremiah, and Ezekiel, where we see the spousal image, it is nonexistent in Isaiah.[7] Thus, although Isaiah speaks of Jerusalem as an abandoned and humiliated woman to symbolize the situation of the exile (Isa 54:1–6), it avoids marking her as an adulteress, and in this way the use of the image is associated with other semantic areas.[8] The other three prophets, in contrast, recreate—each in his own way—her almost innate tendency toward adultery.[9]

---

lèmes de méthode," *RevScRel* 57 (1983): 249–60; Walter Volges, "Diachronic and Syncronic Studies of Hos 1–3," *BZ* 28 (1984): 94–98. On postexilic prophetism, see Marta García Fernández, *Consolad, consolad a mi pueblo: El tema de la consolación en Deutero Isaías*, AnBib 181 (Rome: Gregorian & Biblical Press, 2018), 153 n. 151.

6. On the characteristics of the new covenant, see Angelo Borghino, *La "Nuova Alleanza" in Is 54; Analisi esegetico-teologica*, ST 118 (Rome: Gregorian & Biblical Press, 2005), 333–73.

7. In these chapters in Hosea, Jeremiah, and Ezekiel the verb זנה is found in Jer 2:20; 3:1, 3, 6, 8; Ezek 16:15, 16, 17, 26, 28 (2x), 30, 31, 33, 34, 35, 41; 23:3 (2x), 5, 19, 30, 43 (2x), 44; Hos 1:2 (2x); 2:7; 3:3. The plural noun זנונים is present in Ezek 23:11, 29; Hos 1:2 (2x); 2:4, 6. It appears only in a reference to Zion at the beginning in Isa 1:21, and in Isa 57:3 to refer to the Israelites as an adulterous generation.

8. The woman, identified with Zion, is found in a condition of shame and abandon (Isa 54:4–6). While in 54:4, her "youth" (עלומים) and "widowhood" (אלמנות) are marked by dishonor, as indicated by the semantic field of shame (חרפה, כלם, בוש, בשת), 54:6 presents the negative condition with the terminology of repudiation—"an abandoned woman" (אשה עזובה) whose "soul is afflicted" (עצובת רוח); the "woman of youth" (אשת נעורים) when she is "rejected" (מאס; see also Isa 60:15; 62:4). If Isa 54:4–6 highlights the Jerusalem-wife parallel, 54:1–3 centers on the Jerusalem-mother parallel and describes her negative situation with the adjectives "desolate" (שוממה) and "barren" (עקרה).

9. In this way, for example, Ezek 16:31–34 talks about an adultery without profit in which the woman not only does not obtain benefits but also has to pay in order to become a prostitute. This is an ironic way to ridicule tributes made to foreign nations in exchange for protection.

Hosea renders it as to "go after her lovers" (Hos 2:7, 9, 15),[10] while Jeremiah renders it as to "go far from the Lord," "walk after emptiness," or "rebelling" (Jer 2:4–8). However, this prophet is much more graphic when he ironically discusses female behavior.[11] If in Hosea she knew where she was going, Jeremiah signals that she will prostitute herself with any foreigner who passes by (Jer 2:24–25, 33, 36; see 3:1–2), and he also justifies it (Jer 2:20–35).[12] The prophet Ezekiel enriches this theme in a clear allegorization of the story (Ezek 16:15)—there is a time of idyllic love characterized by fidelity (Ezek 16:3–14 // Jer 2:2–3), followed by another marked by adultery (Ezek 16:15–34 // Jer 2:4–8). Forgetting the received gift—which is precisely what has conferred fame—becomes the reason for betrayal, named prostitution, which manifests itself in two ways—idolatry (Ezek 16:15–22) and alliance with foreign nations (Ezek 16:23–23).

Consequently, the image of God the husband is that of a man who, having been dishonored, rejects the wife and acts with vehemence against her,[13] moving his actions from desperation to win her back (Hos 2:8–9), to the severity of punishment (Ezek 16:37–41), to strong threats (Hos 2:5–6). Particularly, Ezek 23 has numerous extremely violent images. These include actions and threats such as mutilation (Ezek 23:25), public nudity, and the withdrawal of a husband's protection and goods (Ezek 16:8; Hos

---

10. While in Hosea there is a reference to the Baals as "lovers" or "partners" (Hos 2:7, 9, 12, 16–17), Jeremiah and Ezekiel allude to the foreign nations (Jer 22:10, 22; 30:14; Ezek 16:33, 36–37; 13:5, 9, 22).

11. For example, Jer 2:20–21 indicates that this "reliable stock" has converted into a "corrupt, wild vine," and in 2:23, she is called a "swift she-camel." God is presented as a "spring of living water," compared with the "broken cisterns" (2:13) of the towns where people go to drink (2:18) without satisfaction, since Israel is like a "dry throat" (2:25).

12. Although Jeremiah sees this aspect more as foolishness than evil and as the cause of an emerging behavior, Hosea also indicates that the root of this digression hinges on the confusion of believing that it is Baal who gives life (Hos 2:10, 15). This lack of understanding of where gifts come from (see Isa 1:2; Jer 2:6) has to do with forgetting, which is what perverts the gratitude of a relationship founded on reciprocal love (Deut 32:18; Jer 2:32; 3:21; Ezek 16:43).

13. In some cases, the formula of divorce is used—"because she is no longer my wife and I am not her husband" (Hos 2:4; Jer 2:9–10; see also Hos 1:9; 2:2, 25). See Mordechai A. Friedman, "Israel's Response in Hosea 2:17b: 'You Are My Husband,'" *JBL* 99 (1980): 199–204; Maria Dass, "The Divorce (?) Formula in Hos 2:4a," *ITS* 34 (1997): 56–88.

2:11–14), so that in the end the woman is left to die of thirst (Hos 2:5).[14] In this way, the God of life is shown as an anti-God who kills without compassion. Despite the severity of images used by the three prophets, they conclude this episode with the offer of a new covenant (Jer 2:9–19; 3:19–4:2; Ezek 16:44–63; Hos 2:16–25).

In Isaiah, on the other hand, it seems that it is the woman who is the offended party. In fact, throughout Second Isaiah, God must confront an implicit accusation that he has abandoned his duties.[15] It is in this way that one could read the inquisitorial question of Isa 50:1, "Where is your mother's certificate of divorce with which I sent her away?" which is in reality an argument of divine defense. Since Israel itself did not find the certificate of rejection, Israel is making up the divorce and its accusation of abandonment. God recognizes that he has been angered and infuriated, but it is circumstantial and lasts only for a short time compared to his eternal love (Isa 54:7–8).

Thus, Isa 54 draws a very different matrimonial imagery. She, far from being represented as an ignorant adulteress, is described using the categories of a suffering woman and in parallel to the servant of YHWH,[16]

---

14. This deals with the idea of withholding what allows the woman to live and what was part of the compromises acquired by the husband (see Exod 21:10). Hosea's idea of letting her die of thirst and turning her into a desert could be understood in this way, but the thirst could also allude to unsatisfied and unsatiated love (see Jer 2:24–25; 3:1–5). The absence of a relationship provokes sterility, and, because of this, she is as arid as a desert. Public nudity is mentioned in Hos 2:5.12; Jer 13:22, 26–27; Ezek 16:37, 39; 23:10, 26, 29. In addition to the law of counterbalance—because she was naked, now she is disrobed as a public humiliation (Lev 18:7)—the action can also be the prior step toward execution (see Ezek 16:37–41). In fact, capital punishment was the penalty for adultery (Lev 19:10–19; 20:10; Deut 22:22), as in Mesopotamic legislation (Laws of Eshnunna 28 = A II 34–37; B II 1–2). Unlike other laws in the ancient Near East, in the biblical laws that sanction adultery and incest, the prescribed punishment is identical for both the man and the woman. See Federico Lara Peinado, *Código de Hammurabi: Estudio preliminar, traducción y notas*, CP 23 (Madrid: Tecnos, 1986). For a list of laws governing sexual crimes, see Joaquin Sanmartín, *Códigos legales de tradición babilónica*, POr (Madrid: Editorial Trotta, 1999), 283.

15. García Fernández demonstrates this in ch. 4. See Fernández, *Consolad*, 175–233.

16. In fact, the second part of Deutero-Isaiah (Isa 49–55) is characterized by alternating between Servant and Zion: Servant (Isa 49:1–13)—Zion (Isa 49:14–50:3)—Servant (Isa 50:4–11)—Zion (Isa 51:1–52:12)—Servant (Isa 52:13–53:12)—Zion (Isa 54:1–17). See John F. A. Sawyer, "Daughter of Zion and Servant of the Lord in Isaiah:

to the point that it is from this suffering that salvation and children are conceived, not from prostitution but rather "servants" (עבדי יהוה; 54:17) and "disciples of the Lord" (למודי יהוה; 54:13). We therefore are not dealing with simple maternity but with qualified maternity in close connection to the paternity of the servant.[17]

In line with such a positive point of view, it is fitting that God the husband performs very different actions as to beautify Jerusalem (Isa 54:11–12), to reconstruct the inner parts of the heart (Isa 54:13–14), and to supply her with certain goods (Isa 54:11–17; 55:1–3). The expression in Isa 54:5, "for who marries you" (בעליך) is "your maker" (עשיך), is unique. And the act of salvation therefore comes with a creative connotation that makes someone capable of being in a relationship, specifically establishing a relationship as God's creature.[18] In this way, Isaiah inverts the metaphorical marriage imagery to depict a more positive vision of the woman-Jerusalem image.

3. Marriage Metaphor: In between Suitability and Uneasiness

Locating a metaphor in time helps us to understand its suitability. Therefore, admitting that the idea has its root in Hosea from the eighth century, we observe that the texts where it appears have a postexilic profile or, at least, they were rewritten from this point of view. What made this image the optimal one for describing the relationship with God during this period of crisis instead of other existing images such as father-son, king-vassal, patron-servant, or judge-accused?

In the first place, I agree with Angelo Borghino that the marriage typology underlines two aspects that are present in the relationship with

---

A Comparison," *JSOT* 44 (1989): 89–107. For descriptions using the categories of a suffering woman, see, e.g., in Isa 54:11: "not comforted" (לא נחמה), "afflicted" (עניה), and "lashed" (סערה); or in Isa 54:1, "desolate" (שוממה) and "barren" (עקרה).

17. See García Fernández, *Consolad*, 281–83. According to Borghino, there are three fundamental orientations—those who sustain a relationship between the servant and Zion, those who identify them, and those who see a parallel development in the two figures and consider both characters to be interchangeable (Borghino, *La "Nuova Alleanza,"* 396–97).

18. "Il nesso tra queste due espressioni dà risalto al fatto che l'azione di salvezza è creativa; nell'atto salvifico Yhwh ancora "crea" Israele, riportandolo, secondo la caratteristica propria dell'evento creatore, ad un essere in relazione" (Borghino, *La "Nuova Alleanza,"* 188–89).

God: equality and asymmetry.[19] The father-son link is also a profoundly affectionate one (Isa 1:2; Hos 11:1–4). However, the link is unequal in age and in the responsibilities of the father toward his offspring. The spousal relationship happens between equals because, despite having dissimilar commitments, there is a certain complementarity and parity in procreation and in family and work responsibilities.

Second, this inequality-similarity is also expressed in the fact that it is a free option mediated by a contract. While paternity-filiation is not chosen, marriage is an act of consent and agreement between two individuals called to unite themselves in one flesh but whose linkage—very different from a descendant's—is not genetic and could be dissolved through divorce.[20] Being a contract, noncompliance with what is established would have legal consequences. In this sense, the free acquisition of commitments is associated with the covenant (Exod 19:8; 24:3–7).[21] However, this disloyalty has other connotations when compared with the servant-patron. Given that mutual belonging is the essential element of the contracted alliance (Gen 2:24–25), exclusivity (Deut 6:4) and love (Deut 6:5) are two indispensable conditions of this relationship.[22]

---

19. See Borghino, *La "Nuova Alleanza,"* 195–96.

20. On the ability to choose one's partner in the ancient Middle East, see Marsman, *Women*, 49–73. With reference to divorce, generally the initiative came from the man. Mesopotamian laws, however, do consider certain cases in which women can take the initiative, because of abandonment or inappropriate conduct on the part of the husband (CH 141 = XX 33–59; CH 142 = XXX 60–XXXI, rev. VIII; CH 143 = XXXI 6–12). In cases in which the divorce was initiated by the man, he had to provide a reason (Deut 24:1–4), such as misappropriation of funds, injury against him, denial of the conjugal debt, or supposed infidelity. See Lara Peinado, *Código de Hammurabi*, LXXXVIII. And depending on the case, the dowry might have to be returned in its entirety or compensation was expected from the woman (CH 137 = XXIX 74 XXX, rev. VII 13; CH 138 = XXX 14–24; CH 139 = XXX 25–26; CH 140 = XX 25–29).

21. In Babylon, marriage was considered an adoption, since it dealt with a contract-transfer of a woman who until that point had been under the control of her father or her brother, to her husband; see Sanmartín, *Códigos*, 285. Additionally, the verb *to unite* (דבק), used in Gen 2:24, indicates more than an act—it is a link with someone marked by fidelity. Because of this, it is used to express the alliance. This fact again supports the association of the alliance with matrimonial imagery. See Gordon P. Hugenberger, *Marriage as a Covenant: A Study of Biblical Laws and Ethics Governing Marriage Developed from the Perspective of Malachi*, VTSup 52 (Leiden: Brill, 1994), 161–92.

22. Concerning Gen 2:24–25: In fact, in the discovery of Eve, Adam expresses his own identity: "he names the woman, but only could do so by naming himself

In this way, the metaphor is ideal for describing what happened during the exile and postexilic restoration. The suffering that Israel is experiencing is the consequence of breaking the commitment. Its posturing with the nations and with its gods is seen under the category of betrayal in the relationship (adultery), which is how Scripture understands sin, and not so much as the breaking of a rule. This produces emotional fissures that do not exist in other types of relationships and that give a lot of material to the prophets, who develop the image of a desperate God trying to recover a relationship or who is completely angered and dishonored and is punishing without piety. The divorce shows an open gulf of freedom, which turns into a drama, both because he might not forgive and because she might not want to return. This reconstruction of the love that once was is painful and slow, because it requires overcoming mutual rebukes and resistance, and also because it needs to be something new, since divorce was irreversible. Thus, it requires a new creative act, that is, a new covenant that is also expressed with a spousal tinge.

Having said that, with the exception of Deutero-Isaiah, whose plot is constructed on the tacit accusation that God has abandoned the people, in the rest of the prophets the same metaphor imposes the rules of the game—if God is always faithful, then the adulterer is the spouse. In

---

in the same act" ("nombra a la mujer, pero solo lo podía hacer nombrándose a sí mismo en el mismo acto"). See Paul Beauchamp, *El uno y el otro Testamento: Cumplir las Escrituras*, BAC Teología, EE 185 (Madrid: Biblioteca Autores Cristianos, 2015), 122. From that point, human language is born and will be crucial in the relationship between the two; "they will be one single flesh in the word" ("serán una sola carne en la palabra"; see Beauchamp, *El uno y el otro Testamento*, 125). This element contains an extra in its promise of unity since there would be no unity in flesh without unity in the word. See Carlos Granados García, *El camino del hombre por la mujer: El matrimonio en el Antiguo Testamento* (Estella: Editorial Verbo Divino, 2014), 39. On Deut 6:4, see Gianantonio Borgonovo, "Monogamia e monoteísmo alla radice del símbolo dell'amore sponsale nella tradizione dello jahvismo," in *Maschio e femmina li creò*, ed. Giovanni Angelini, Gianantonio Borgonovo, and Maurizio Chiodi (Milan: Glossa, 2008), 151–233. Exclusivity is linked to the ideal of monogamy, although practice may indicate otherwise, as shown in the patriarchal and monarchical stories. In some cases having secondary wives has its roots in Mesopotamian legislation, which was also, in theory, monogamous, but which allowed for this possibility in cases of sterility (see CH 145 = XXXI 28–42; CH 146 = XXXI 43–59; CH 147 = XXXI 60–64; CH 148 = XXXI 65–81; CH 149 = XXXII (rev IX) 1–9; CH 170 = XXXV 37–59; CH 171a = XXXV 60–77). Concerning Deut 6:5: Love poems give an account of this ideal toward which one is inclined (see Marsman, *Women*, 73–84).

addition, to the degrading humiliation inflicted on the woman, which is connected to the known problem of violence in the Old Testament, there is a certain unease with this imagery that is not calmed despite the numerous studies that have examined this issue. In my opinion, this vision wounds contemporary sensibilities, and particularly the female, because of the aggressive nature of the texts. It would be enough to understand that they are the product of a certain mentality and that, in addition to being highly symbolic, they respond to a worldview that is very different from ours. However, this type of answer is not fully satisfactory, and the reason should perhaps be sought in modern theory on metaphors.

In fact, current philology shows that, even though the formation of metaphors is a literary phenomenon, it surpasses linguistics itself. What is more, because our way of thinking is already metaphorical, metaphors form part of our daily lives, and our common language is full of them.[23] That said, the associative potential of a metaphor reveals not only that it is an expression or a way of understanding the world, but also that it is capable of generating thought and influencing the relationship that we maintain with this determined reality.[24] Thus, the metaphor "to charge with the responsibility" not only expresses our understanding of the responsibility as a charge but also predisposes us to experience that responsibility in such a way. In this way, life and language feed off one another.

This is where the problem arises. To a certain extent, it is understandable that ancient texts, which we also recognize as the word of God, carry with them a cultural gender burden. The problem resides in the fact that the metaphor is seen not only in the association that it creates, which is the product of a certain worldview, but also in its enormous persuasive capacity, which has the power to move a person emotionally. If in the previous example we said that this could cause a predisposition to view responsibility as a charge, in our own world it could continue to feed ideas that are embedded deeply in our social conscience, such as the asymmetrical

---

23. Current research has followed this trajectory. For example, Paul Ricoeur, *La métaphore vive: L'ordre métaphorique* (Paris: Routledge, 1975); Max Black, "More about Metaphor," in *Metaphors and Thought*, ed. Andrew Ortony (Cambridge: Cambridge University Press, 1979), 19–41; George Lakoff and Mark Turner, *Metaphors We Live By* (Chicago: University of Chicago Press, 1981); Eva F. Kittay, *Metaphor: Its Cognitive Force and Linguistic Structure* (Oxford: Clarendon, 1987).

24. See Julie Galambush, *Jerusalem in the Book of Ezekiel: The City as Yahweh's Wife*, SBLDS 130 (Atlanta: Society of Biblical Literature, 1992), 8–9.

relationship between men and women, gender violence, conditions of inferiority, and even submission by women.[25]

4. Conclusion: Some Light in the Darkness

The solution is not easily seen because the texts are what they are. Additionally, once a metaphor is created, it has its own life, meaning that it is impossible to control the reaction of a future reader. But precisely because a metaphor is not a mere substitution but rather a dynamic relationship with tension between the designated and the designating, there are infinite possibilities, and it is subject to change. In fact, Isaiah introduces new ideas to the initial imagery designated by Hosea, Jeremiah, and Ezekiel, producing a substantial modification in the meaning, since he inverts its use—from accusing Israel, it changes to accusing God.

However, this is not the only case in which there are apparent contradictions in the Scripture. Entering this internal dialogue maintained by the texts helps us to understand how, in innerbiblical reception, they were also responding to and putting this information into context. In this sense, it seems important to me to say that the Deutero-Isaiah relationship between the servant of YHWH and Jerusalem could be a vein that counteracts the image that is so tilted toward either her infidelity or his pardon. Certainly, Isa 54 shows a God-husband tilted toward Zion. Although this presentation, to a certain extent, corrects the violence of the other texts, it continues to be very polarized.

In my view, the suggestion by the same text that she is a suffering woman seems more potent—it is precisely her pain that produces the return of Israel and restores it as not only sons but servants and disciples. This could be a very valid path toward recovering her dignity. In fact, there is a very ancient tradition in respect to the literary genre of the

---

25. Ancient Mediterranean societies founded inequality between men and women based on biological indicators. In this way, while "men are warm and dense, women are cold, moist, and porous." This "excessive" nature, which needs to eliminate blood or become pregnant and nurse on a monthly basis, must be dominated. What is more, these corporeal markers are associated with personality traits such as feminine irrationality, which is compared to masculine rationality. See Elisa Estévez, *Las mujeres en los orígenes del cristianismo*, Que se sabe de ... 7 (Estella: Editorial Verbo Divino, 2012), 70–74.

lamentation of cities that takes root in the myth of the mother goddess.[26] This myth, in turn, responds to the question of the origin of life. Together with the explanation that we come from a couple, there is another that indicates "emergence."[27]

The idea of earth-mother-uterus is linked with the experience of giving birth (Gen 3:20) and is typical of the Paleolithic period.[28] In the Neolithic period, the move was from the goddess-earth to the god-heaven and from the god consort to the goddess consort. Furthermore, for some researchers, the goal of theogony in this period, in which there is a reversion to the goddess-mother, is to replace her with gods who, very different from her, place themselves on the other side of creation.[29] The ancient goddess begins to personify the chaos, which a masculine and celestial god must subdue. It is in this way that the death of Tiamat at the hand of Marduk is interpreted in the Enuma Elish.[30]

Although one could disagree with this view, it is clear that a great deal of effort has been put into exploring the origin of the metaphor but less into tracing its ultimate "origin," which is rooted in the association.[31] In my opinion, it is not enough to find the *Tertium comparationis*; one must understand it as a thread in the fabric of relationships that are rooted in a certain worldview. This is the only way to get to the nucleus of the association, which allows us to understand better why everything that has to do with the relationship between man and woman is dominated by the struggle between equality and asymmetry: a struggle that reflects the theogonic model turns into the anthropological narratives of

---

26. See Marta García Fernández, "El rostro materno de Dios en los textos bíblicos y orientales," *EstEcl* 89 (2014): 115–40.

27. I put "emergence" in quotation marks because it does not refer to the technical meaning of the term but to a model of representation that is cosmotheogonical in which the origin goes back not to a couple but to a unit that slowly differentiated itself and is generally linked to the myth of the mother-god.

28. In Mesopotamian tradition, Bēlet-ilī uses a figure of speech to personify a womb that procreates without competition from another divinity (Inūma ilū awīlum Old Babylonian I.iv.189–194).

29. See Anne Baring and Jules Cashford, *El mito de la diosa: Evolución de una imagen*, Siruela 38 (Madrid: Tapa blanda, 2005), 11–16, 182–208.

30. Baring and Cashford, *El mito de la diosa*, 321–50.

31. Borghino, *La Nuova Alleanza*, 192–96, presents a synthesis of the possibilities of the origin of the metaphor.

the differentiation of the sexes (Gen 1:27; 2:15–25)[32] and in turn affects law and society.[33]

Last, and to complete the idea of the marriage metaphor in which, according to Deutero-Isaiah, she is the agent, it would be necessary to delve deeper into Jerusalem's active role in the shared mission with God in favor of Israel. In fact, this aspect is also found in the metaphor's associative embryo. Thus, in order to tackle the task of having "to work" (עבד) and "to take care of" (שמר), Gen 2 indicates that the man finds himself alone. From verses 15–25, the story tries to compensate for this defect with the search for a "suitable helper" (עזר כנגדו; Gen 2:18). According to some experts, the expression not only should be understood in the sense of procreation or that the man has found his other half but should extend to the labor realm, which is one of the key points of the story.[34] With the creation of the woman, the expectations for humanity's agricultural vocation will be fulfilled,[35] which is, in turn, the mission that they share with God, since he was the first to plant a garden (Gen 2:5).

To a certain extent, the Greek term συνεργός, used in Paul's theology with the technical meaning of a male or female (since it is also used for

---

32. As Paul Beauchamp affirms, the "cosmology of differentiation" leads into an "anthropology of differentiation. See Beauchamp, *Création et separation: Étude exégetique du chapitre premier de la Genèse* (Paris: Cerf, 2005), 245–46.

33. The proceedings of a conference held at Brown University show that as history advances, there is a kind of involution and continuum in reference to social recognition and the presence of the woman. See Barbara S. Lesko, ed., *Women's Earliest Records: From Ancient Egypt and Western Asia*, BJS 166 (Atlanta: Scholars Press, 1989). There is an involution because, from what is deduced from the data, its social influence decreased from the third to the second millennium. See Frymer-Kensky, *In the Wake*, 70–80; Barbara S. Lesko, "Old Kingdom Egypt," in Lesko, *Women's Earliest Records*, 3; Rikvah Harris, "Independent Women in Ancient Mesopotamia?," in Lesko, *Women's Earliest Records*, 156; Marsman, *Women*, 44–45. There is a continuum, because some texts propose an "ontological" and legal equality (Gen 1:27), at least in theory (Exod 19:12; Lev 19:3; 20:9; Deut 5:16). See Carol Meyers, "Women and the Domestic Economy of Early Israel," in Lesko, *Women's Earliest Records*, 276.

34. See Gerhard Wallis, *Mein Freund hatte einen Weinberg: Aufsätze und Vorträge zum Alten Testament*, BEATAJ 23 (Frankfurt: Lang, 1994), 230–31; Bill T. Arnold, *Genesis*, NCB (Cambridge: Cambridge University Press, 2009), 60.

35. See J. A. Castro Lodeiro, "Venid y trabajad ¡Es tiempo de alabar! La vocación del hombre en los relatos de creación mesopotámicos y bíblicos" (diss., Facultad de Teología de Vitoria-Gasteiz, 2013), 166. This is a dissertation from which an excerpt was published in 2013.

women) collaborator (Rom 16:2; Phil 4:3), would be linked to the expression in Genesis, and it is well connected to Middle Eastern tradition. In fact, the female work and professions drawn in the iconography and in the Mesopotamian texts appear to be rich and surprising,[36] portraying an understanding of the relationship between man and woman that is simultaneously marked by equality and asymmetry. Perhaps digging deeper into the associative embryo of the metaphor from its own viewpoint and within that network of relationships would not only help to explain where this understanding originates but would also give us the hermeneutic clues for discovering new facets of this imagery in the texts and open new spaces for reflection.

Bibliography

Abma, Richtsje. *Bonds of Love: Methodic Studies of Prophetic Texts with Marriage Imagery (Isaiah 50:1–3 and 54:1–10, Hosea 1–3, Jeremiah 2–3)*. SNN 31. Amsterdam: Van Gorcum; Assen: Brill, 1999.

Arnold, Bill T. *Genesis*. NCB. Cambridge: Cambridge University Press, 2009.

Baring, Anne, and Jules Cashford. *El mito de la diosa: Evolución de una imagen*. Siruela 38. Madrid: Tapa blanda, 2005.

Baumann, Gerlinde. *Lieb und Gewalt: Die Ehe als Metapher für das Verhältinis JHWH, Israel in den Prophetenbüchern*. SBS 185. Stuttgart: Katholisches Bibelwerk, 2000.

Beauchamp, Paul. *Création et separation: Étude exégetique du chapitre premier de la Genèse*. Paris: Cerf, 2005.

———. *El uno y el otro Testamento: Cumplir las Escrituras*. BAC Teología. EE 185. Madrid: Biblioteca Autores Cristianos, 2015.

Black, Max. "More about Metaphor." Pages 19–41 in *Metaphors and Thought*. Edited by Andrew Ortony. Cambridge: Cambridge University Press, 1979.

Borghino, Angelo. *La "Nuova Alleanza" in Is 54: Analisi esegetico-teologica, Tesi Gregoriana*. ST 118. Rome: Gregorian & Biblical Press, 2005.

Borgonovo, Gianantonio. "Monogamia e monoteísmo alla radice del símbolo dell'amore sponsale nella tradizione dello jahvismo" Pages

---

36. Castro Lodeiro, "Venid y trabajad," 169.

151–233 in *Maschio e femmina li creò*. Edited by Giuseppe Angelini, Gianantonio Borgonovo, and Maurizio Chiodi. Milan: Glossa, 2008.

Castro Lodeiro, José A. "Venid y trabajad ¡Es tiempo de alabar! La vocación del hombre en los relatos de creación mesopotámicos y bíblicos. Sedes." Diss., Facultad de Teología de Vitoria-Gasteiz, 2013.

Dass, Maria. "The Divorce (?) Formula in Hos 2:4a." *ITS* 34 (1997): 56–88.

Estévez, Elisa. *Las mujeres en los orígenes del cristianismo Que se sabe de … 7*. Estella: Editorial Verbo Divino, 2012.

Friedman, Mordechai A. "Israel's Response in Hosea 2:17b: 'You Are My Husband.'" *JBL* 99 (1980): 199–204.

Frymer-Kensky, Tikva. *In the Wake of the Goddess: Women, Culture, and the Transformation of Pagan Myth*. Piscataway, NJ: Gorgias, 1992.

Galambush, Julie. *Jerusalem in the Book of Ezekiel: The City as Yahweh's Wife*. SBLDS 130. Atlanta: Society of Biblical Literature, 1992.

García Fernández, Marta. *Consolad, consolad a mi pueblo: El tema de la consolación en Deutero Isaías*. AnBib 181. Rome: Gregorian & Biblical Press, 2018.

———. "El rostro materno de Dios en los textos bíblicos y orientales." *EstEcl* 89 (2014): 115–40.

Granados García, Carlos. *El camino del hombre por la mujer: El matrimonio en el Antiguo Testamento*. Estella: Editorial Verbo Divino, 2014.

Harris, Rivkah. "Independent Women in Ancient Mesopotamia?" Page 156 in *Women's Earliest Records: From Ancient Egypt and Western Asia*. Edited by Barbara S. Lesko. BJS 166. Atlanta: Scholars Press, 1989.

Hugenberger, Gordon P. *Marriage as a Covenant: A Study of Biblical Laws and Ethics Governing Marriage Developed from the Perspective of Malachi*. VTSup 52. Leiden: Brill, 1994.

Kittay, Eva. F. *Metaphor: Its Cognitive Force and Linguistic Structure*. Oxford: Oxford University Press, 1987.

Lakoff, George, and Mark Turner. *Metaphors We Live By*. Chicago: University of Chicago Press, 1981.

Lara Peinado, Federico. *Código de Hammurabi: Estudio preliminar, traducción y notas*. CP 23. Madrid: Tecnos, 1986.

Lesko, Barbara S. "Old Kingdom Egypt." Page 3 in *Women's Earliest Records: From Ancient Egypt and Western Asia*. Edited by Barbara S. Lesko. BJS 166. Atlanta: Scholars Press, 1989.

———, ed. *Women's Earliest Records: From Ancient Egypt and Western Asia*. BJS 166. Atlanta: Scholars Press, 1989.

Marsman, Hennie. J. *Women in Ugarit and Israel: Their Social and Religious Position in the Context of the Ancient Near East*. OtSt 49. Leiden: Brill, 2003.

Meyers, Carol. "Women and the Domestic Economy of Early Israel." Pages 265-78 in *Women's Earliest Records: From Ancient Egypt and Western Asia*. Edited by Barbara S. Lesko. BJS 166. Atlanta: Scholars Press, 1989.

Moughtin-Mumby, Sharon. *Sexual and Marital Metaphors in Hosea, Jeremiah, Isaiah, and Ezekiel*. OTM. Oxford: Oxford University Press, 2008.

Navarro Puerto, Mercedes. "La figura femenina en los libros de los profetas Amós y Oseas." Pages 193-218 in *De la ruina a la afirmación: El entorno del Reino de Israel en el siglo VIII a.C*. Edited by Santiago Ausín. ABE 33. Estella: Editorial Verbo Divino, 1997.

Renaud, Bernard. "Genèse et unité rédactionnelle de Os 2." *RevScRel* 54 (1980): 1-20.

———. "Osée 1-3: Analyse diachronique et lectura sinchronique, problèmes de méthode." *RevScRel* 57 (1983): 249-60.

Ricoeur, Paul. *La métaphore vive: L'ordre métaphorique*. Paris: Routledge, 1975.

Sanmartín, Joaquín. *Códigos legales de tradición babilónica*. POr. Madrid: Editorial Trotta, 1999.

Sawyer, John F. A. "Daughter of Zion and Servant of the Lord in Isaiah: A Comparison." *JSOT* 44 (1989): 89-107.

Schökel, L. Alonso, and José Luis Sicre Díaz. *Profetas: Comentario*. Vol. 2. Madrid: Ediciones Cristiandad, 1980.

Solà, Teresa. *Jahvè, espòs d'Israel: Poderosa metàfora profètica*. Barcelona: Claret, 2006.

Stienstra, Nelly. *YHWH Is the Husband of His People: Analysis of a Biblical Metaphor with Special Reference to Translation*. Kampen: Kok Pharos, 1993.

Volges, Walter. "Diachronic and Syncronic Studies of Hos 1-3." *BZ* 28 (1984): 94-98.

Wallis, Gerhard. *Mein Freund hatte einen Weinberg: Aufsätze und Vorträge zum Alten Testament*. BEATAJ 23. Frankfurt: Lang, 1994.

Weems, Renita. *Amor maltratado: Matrimonio, sexo y violencia en los profetas hebreos*. CCM. Bilbao: Desclée du Brouwer, 1997.

———. *Battered Love: Marriage, Sex, and Violence in the Hebrew Prophets*. OBT. Minneapolis: Fortress, 1995.

Do the Prophets Have a Private Life?
Women as Literary and Redactional Tools

Benedetta Rossi

1. Introduction

Interest in the so-called private lives of the prophets can be traced back to two main interpretative trends of the nineteenth century, trends that persisted until the last two decades of the twentieth century. For a long time, the prophet—his person, his personality and history—were the principal focus of research in biblical prophecy. The unforgettable depiction of the prophets in prominent works such as Georg Ewald's *Propheten des Alten Bundes* heavily influenced biblical research on the topic.[1]

Against this backdrop of the focus on the prophet's life, a sharp distinction was drawn between the public life or ministry of the prophet and his private life. In the first part of his work *Prophetismus der Hebräer vollständig dargestellt*, August Knobel distinguishes the "Lebensweise der Propheten" ("way of life of the prophets") from a "Geschäft der Propheten" ("prophetic ministry").[2] The second paragraph of the "Lebensweise der Propheten" opens as follows: "The way of life of the prophets was the same as that of the rest of the population. They lived an orderly family life. They owned their own houses.... Numerous passages that mention their wives and sons confirm that they were married."[3]

---

1. See Georg H. A. Ewald, *Die Propheten des Alten Bundes: I–II* (Stuttgart: Krabbe, 1840–1841).

2. See August Knobel, *Der Prophetismus der Hebräer vollständig dargestellt* (Breslau: Max & Komp, 1837), 43.

3. "Die Lebenseinrichtung der Propheten war dieselbe, wie bei den Uebrigen. Sie lebten in einem geordneten Familienleben. So besassen sie eigene Häuser.... Dass

This assertion throws light on two important hermeneutical assumptions. First, the private life of biblical prophets has been interpreted by means of ideological categories as well as moral and social constructs typical of the modern middle class. Second, and consequently, marriage, women, children, and love affairs automatically were placed within the framework of the prophet's private life rather than in his public life and ministry as a prophet.

It seems likely, therefore, that the use of the adjective *private*, as well as the relegation of women and children to the so-called private life, depends heavily on ideological constructs and perceptions typical of nineteenth-century, middle-class, Christian male interpreters.[4] While focusing on the prophet as an individual, modern interpreters therefore ended up creatively recreating a so-called private life of the prophets, starting from the scanty evidence provided by the biblical texts.[5]

Against this background, this essay aims at reconsidering the so-called private life of the prophets from two interrelated perspectives. First, in a paradigm shift within current research on biblical prophecy, one finds a move from the prophet to the prophetic book, hence focusing on the prophetic books as traditional scribal literature (*Schriftgelehrte Traditionsliteratur*).[6] Second, owing to this focus on prophetic books, texts

---

sie veheirathet waren, lässt sich mit zahlreichen Stellen, wo ihrer Frauen und Söhne Erwähnung geschieht, nachweisen" (Knobel, *Prophetismus der Hebräer*, 43).

4. See in this regard Irmtraud Fischer, "Das Geschlecht als exegetisches Kriterium zu einer gender-fairen Interpretation der Erzeltern-Erzählungen," in *Studies in the Book of Genesis: Literature, Redaction and History*, ed. André Wénin, BETL 155 (Leuven: Peeters, 2001), 147–50; Fischer, *Gotteskünderinnen: Zur einer geschlechterfairen Deutung des Phänomens der Prophetie und der Prophetinnen in der Hebräischen Bibel* (Stuttgart: Kohlhammer, 2002), 193–94.

5. Typical examples of interpreters' productive imagination in reshaping the prophets' private lives are, for instance, Brooke P. Church, *The Private Lives of the Prophets and the Times in Which They Lived* (New York: Rinehart, 1953); Maurice D. Goldman, "Was Jeremiah Married?," *ABR* 2 (1952): 43–47; and the countless reconstructions of the love story between Hosea and Gomer with consequent apologetic interpretative efforts concerning moral issues. See in this regard the history of interpretation by Stephan Bitter, *Die Ehe des Propheten Hosea: Eine Auslegungsgeschichtliche Untersuchung*, GTA 3 (Göttingen: Vandenhoeck & Ruprecht, 1975); see also Brad E. Kelle, "Hosea 1–3 in Twentieth-Century Scholarship," *CBR* 7 (2009): 189–216.

6. See in this regard especially Uwe Becker, "Die Wiederentdeckung des Prophetenbuches. Tendenzen und Aufgaben der gegenwärtigen Prophetenforschung," *BTZ* 21 (2004): 30–60; Konrad Schmid, "Hintere Propheten (Nebiim)," in *Grundinforma-*

increasingly are being read without seeking to fill out narrative blanks or empty spaces.[7]

In this essay, a number of selected texts from the prophets (Isa 8:18; Ezek 24:16–18; Jer 16:1–4; Hos 1–3) will be examined in order to illustrate that the so-called private lives of the prophets does not allude to any prophetic privacy at all. On the contrary, the private lives of the prophets should be considered a literary construct that was constructed as an essential part of prophecy and the prophetic task. Occasionally, this goal is achieved by means of significant lexemes and clusters, or the prophetic life is coupled with the prophetic message through the redactional arrangement of the texts. Significant for the focus of this essay is what these texts all have in common—the intriguing role that women seem to play in this literary enterprise.

2. Isaiah 8:18: Lexical Clues for Interpreting the Private Lives of the Prophets

Isaiah 8:18 ("Behold, I and the children whom YHWH has given me are signs and portents in Israel from YHWH of hosts who dwells on Mount Zion") is the conclusion to the unit of Isa 8:1–18.[8] This concluding remark, uttered in the first person by the prophet, provides a significant interpretative key to Isaiah's so-called private life, which comes to the fore in 7:3 with the mention of Isaiah's son, Shear-Yashub (see also 8:1–4). Important lexical references connect Isa 8:18 to the larger context of Isa 7–8. For

---

tion Altes Testament, 4th ed., ed. Jan C. Gertz, UTB 2745 (Göttingen: Vandenhoeck & Ruprecht, 2010), 317–24.

7. See, in this regard, Fischer, Gotteskünderinnen, 203: "Bemüht man sich einmal, genau am Text zu bleiben, die erzählerischen Lücken zu thematisieren und sie nicht von vornherein fraglos phantasievoll zu füllen, so wird nicht nur Jesajas 'Privatleben' fraglich, sondern es zeigen sich weitere Leerstellen im Text."

8. See Hans Wildberger, *Jesaja: I Teilband Jesaja 1–12*, BKAT 10.1 (Neukirchen-Vluyn: Neukirchener Verlag, 1972), 343; Otto Kaiser, *Das Buch des Propheten Jesaja: Kapitel 1–12*, ATD 17 (Göttingen: Vandenhoeck & Ruprecht, 1981), 189; and, more recently, Willem A. M. Beuken, *Jesaja 1–12*, HThKAT (Freiburg: Herder, 2003), 214–15. While the separation of 8:16–18 from the previous 8:11–15 is commonly accepted, the relation between 8:16 and 8:17 is disputed—8:17 is sometimes considered a later addition. Convincing reasons for considering 8:16 as part of 8:16–18 are given by Beuken, *Jesaja 1–12*, 218–19, 230–31. Unless otherwise indicated, biblical translations are mine.

instance, the lexeme "children" (הילדים) hints at 7:14 and 8:3, while the noun "sign" (אות) refers back to 7:11 and 7:14 (with reference to "a child"), and 8:18 explains precisely the meaning and role of Isaiah's fatherhood and his children. They are "signs and wonders in Israel from YHWH of hosts" (ולמופתים בישראל מעם יהוה צבאות לאתות).

Hermann Gunkel describes a "sign" (אות) as "a thing, a process, an event by which one perceives, learns, or remembers something or discerns the credibility of a matter."[9] The semantic core of the lexeme אות seems to be its communicative nature and function. Occasionally, the cluster ל ("as") + אות ("sign") refers to a person; when this is the case, the person is either a prophet (Isa 8:18; 20:3; Ezek 14:8) or someone linked to a prophetic announcement (Isa 7:14). The cluster verb + ל + אות seems, therefore, to transfer the communicative force of a prophetic announcement to a person, the result being that this person turns out to embody the announcement itself. We are dealing, therefore, with a public function related to prophecy.

In Isa 8:18, not only the prophet Isaiah but also his children are given this role. Its public relevance is further highlighted by the contrast with the preceding verses (vv. 16–17). In Isa 8:16, the "testimony and the law" are bound and sealed—both the verbs צרר ("to bind") and חתם ("to seal") hint at a closure of the prophetic message, either metaphorical or actual.[10] By contrast, the nouns אות, "sign," and מופת, "wonder," allude to a visible and public communication. While the prophetic message is being closed (v. 16), its public role and function seem to be taken up by the prophet and his children.[11]

---

9. See Hermann Gunkel, *Genesis* (Macon, GA: Mercer University Press, 1997), 150. He further notes, "Such signs of perception, confirmation, and remembrance play a great role in antiquity which desired to have everything visible and comprehensible."

10. For the metaphorical meaning, see Wildberger, *Jesaja 1–12*, 347. On the other hand, Beuken underscores a possible concrete meaning of the action (*Jesaja 1–12*, 230–31). According to Kay Weißflog, the function of Isa 8:16–18 is to stress the authenticity of the prophet's announcements of judgment. See Weißflog,"*Zeichen und Sinnbilder": Die Kinder der Propheten Jesaja und Hosea*, ABG 36 (Leipzig: Evangelische Verlagsanstalt, 2001), 257.

11. According to Wildberger, the sealing of the prophetic message signifies that these words will remain unfulfilled for a long time; hence the need for signs to recall the promise hidden in the message (*Jesaja 1–12*, 346–47). Beuken ascribes to the children ("signs") the function of embodying the sealed message (*Jesaja 1–12*, 231).

What about the prophetess in Isa 8:3? Owing to the lack of lexical evidence for naming a wife according to her husband's role,[12] there is no reason to doubt her own role as a prophetess. At the same time, not a single piece of evidence that the prophetess is Isaiah's wife can be deduced either from terminology or from the context.

Regarding the meaning of the sentence ואקרב אל הנביאה, "I drew near to the prophetess" (Isa 8:3aα), Irmtraud Fischer does not consider a reference to sexual intercourse compelling. While the sequence of ואקרב אל הנביאה ("I drew near to the prophetess") and ותהר ותלד בן ("and she conceived and bore a son") in Isa 8:3a is typically and almost exclusively considered a "Tat-Folge-Zusammenhang" ("action-effect-connection"), Fischer shows another interpretative path. Although the phrase קרב ("to draw near") +אל ("toward") (referred to a woman) always implies physical proximity, a sexual connotation is not necessarily present, as shown, for instance, in Num 5:16, 25.[13] Moreover, the change of subject from a first-person singular (Isa 8:3aα) to a second-person singular feminine (Isa 8:3aβ) would be stressing the beginning of a new sequence of actions. As a result, the prophetess conceived and bore a son (Isa 8:3aβ), but it is not clear whether this was from Isaiah.

However, the following remarks can be made. First, in Num 5:16, 25, the verb קרב, "to draw near," has a causative nuance, conveyed by the *hiphil* form. Moreover, the goal of the movement (expressed by והקריב, "he shall bring near") is not the priest himself but rather YHWH (והעמדה לפני יהוה, "and set [her] before YHWH," Num 5:16), or the altar (אל המזבח, "to the altar," Num 5:25). In addition, textual evidence speaks against considering ותהר ותלד בן ("and she conceived and bore a son") in Isa 8:3aβ as the beginning of a new sequence of actions. In fact, 1QIsa[a] VII, 21 shows an empty space between ותהר ותלד בן ("and she conceived and bore a son," Isa 8:3aβ) and the following ויאומר יהוה אלי ("Then YHWH said to me," Isa 8:3b), suggesting, by contrast, a link between the former ואקרב אל הנביאה ("I drew near to the prophetess," Isa 8:3aα) and ותהר ותלד בן ("and she conceived and bore a son," Isa 8:3aβ).[14] Therefore, I do not see any compelling

---

12. Second Kings 4:1 identifies the wife of a prophet as one of the "wives of the sons of the prophets" (נשי בני הנביאים); conversely, in Ezek 24:18, the prophet only calls his wife "my wife" (אשתי). In this connection, see Fischer, *Gotteskünderinnen*, 196.

13. Fischer, *Gotteskünderinnen*, 196–97.

14. Donald W. Parry and Elisha Qimron, *The Great Isaiah Scroll (1QIsa[a]): A New Edition*, STDJ 32 (Leiden: Brill, 1999), 14–15.

reason to exclude reference to sexual intercourse in the sentence ואקרב אל הנביאה ("I drew near to the prophetess").[15]

If this is the case, the act of giving birth by the prophetess seems to aim at further enhancing the prophetic role of the child, born of a prophet and a prophetess.[16] Once her begetting function is fulfilled,[17] the prophetess completely disappears, as is shown already by Isa 8:18, that is, the following reference to Isaiah's sons.

To summarize, not only is a public and communicative role for Isaiah's sons hinted at by means of significant lexemes and clusters (see Isa 8:18), but also the prophetess, who is only mentioned in 8:3, comes to the fore as a literary tool aimed at emphasizing the prophetic authority and reliability of Maher-shalal-hash-baz, the son born of a prophet and a prophetess, by means of establishing a kind of prophetic lineage. The reproductive function, ascribed to the prophetess by Esther Fuchs,[18] seems to further serve the purpose of legitimizing "Maher" as a reliable means of prophetic communication.

3. Ezekiel 24:15–27: Ezekiel and His Wife (Or Did Ezekiel Have a Wife?)

In his 1897 commentary, Alfred Bertholet considers Ezek 24:15–27 one of the rare passages where the prophet gives word to his feelings, while referring to the wife as the delight of his eyes.[19] The prophet's innermost

---

15. Esther Fuchs goes further with this line of reasoning; according to her, "The נביאה emerges here as a sexual object and reproductive object that the prophet 'goes into' (קרב)." See Fuchs, "Prophecy and the Construction of Women," in *Feminist Companion to Prophets and Daniel*, ed. Athalya Brenner, FCB 2/8 (London: Sheffield Academic, 2001), 65.

16. Emphasizing the importance of prophets by exhibiting a prophetic ancestry, either fictitious or real, is not irrelevant in ancient cultures, as shown by Kim Beerden. See Beerden, *Worlds Full of Signs: Ancient Greek Divination in Context*, RGRW 176 (Leiden: Brill, 2013), 75–82. In particular, Beerden highlights the presence of five Greek mantic families, which claimed to descend from mythical mantic experts, e.g., from Melampos, Teiresias, or Kalchas. The reason is that "being part of a 'mantic family' was an ideal way to gain authority (the inheritance of knowledge was implied)" (76).

17. Fuchs ascribes to the prophetess in Isa 8:3 mere "uxorial and reproductive functions" ("Prophecy and the Construction," 65).

18. Fuchs, "Prophecy and the Construction," 65.

19. Alfred Bertholet, *Das Buch Hesekiel*, KHC 12 (Tübingen: Mohr Siebeck, 1897), 128: "Dass Hes. Sein Weib seiner Augen Lust nennt, ist eine der nicht zahlreichen Stellen, an denen er sein Gefühl zu Worte kommen lässt."

emotions continue to be given attention even by some contemporary scholars who sometimes tend to recreate the private life of a prophet by filling in the blanks within the text.[20] Following a different line of reasoning, I shall demonstrate that the allusion to Ezekiel's marriage results from textual and literary strategies that are aimed at stressing the public role of the prophet himself as a sign.

In Ezek 24:15–17, the prophet is told that he will be deprived (לקח√) of the "desire of your eyes" (את־מחמד עיניך), but that he should restrain from typical mourning rites. The expression "desire of one's eyes" points to a special bond with something desirable or precious.[21] This can refer to a person ("the beloved" in Song 5:16; "children" in Hos 9:16; or the object of the verb הרג, "to kill," in Lam 2:4), but also to precious things (1 Kgs 20:6; Lam 1:7–11), or even to the Jerusalem temple (Isa 64:10).[22] The expression is thus indeterminate and open to different interpretative possibilities.

Within the MT, Ezek 24:18c ("I did in the morning as I was commanded," ואעש בבקר כאשר צויתי), which expresses the conformity of the prophetic actions commanded by YHWH, allows the identification of the "desire of your eyes" only with Ezekiel's wife, whose death has been mentioned previously ("I spoke to the people in the morning; in the evening my wife died," Ezek 24:18ab).[23]

---

20. Reading Ezek 24:15–19 as a glimpse into the personal life of the prophet, Block writes about Ezekiel's wife: "She was not only witness to his prophetic service; while he performed his duties within his own house, his wife must have ministered to his needs." He further argues that the expression "delight of your eyes" "implies a felicitous marital relationship." See Daniel I. Block, *Ezekiel 1–24*, NICOT (Grand Rapids: Eerdmans, 1997).

21. According to Moshe Greenberg, it means "what you love to gaze on." See Greenberg, *Ezekiel 21–37: A New Translation with Introduction and Commentary*, AB 22 (New York: Doubleday, 1997), 507.

22. Moreover, as highlighted by Zimmerli, the phrase במגפה ("at a stroke," Ezek 24:16) does not usually point to individual punishment. On the contrary, it refers typically to collective and long-lasting plague and punishment, which follow transgression or rebellion (e.g., Num 14:17; 2 Sam 24:21, 25). See Walther Zimmerli, *Ezekiel 1: Chapters 1–24*, trans. Robert Clements, Hermeneia (Philadelphia: Fortress, 1979), 505.

23. As Pohlmann stresses, it is possible that the short announcement of 24:16–17 did not refer originally to the death of Ezekiel's wife. See Karl F. Pohlmann, *Das Buch des Propheten Hesekiel (Ezechiel): Kapitel 20–48* (Göttingen: Vandenhoeck & Ruprecht, 2001), 360. According to Greenberg, the prophet would have understood immediately that the term "delight of your eyes" referred to a person, but unless there were no children, he could not have known that it referred to his wife (*Ezekiel 21–37*, 507).

However, Ezekiel's wife does not seem to be the focus of the text, from both the literary and textual points of view. From a literary perspective, 24:18 is centered on the accomplishment of the divine command by the prophet (24:18c), which marks the prophetic response to the previous divine words while raising the subsequent question as well (24:19).

The issue at hand appears even more intriguing if considered through the lens of textual criticism.[24] Ezekiel 24:18, that is, the verse that allows the reader to imagine a private life for the prophet, shows an enthralling textual variant:

MT: ואדבר אל־העם בבקר ותמת אשתי בערב ואעש בבקר כאשר צויתי
I spoke to the people in the morning, and in the evening my wife died, and I did in the morning as I was commanded.

P967: και ελαλησα προς τον λαον το πρωι ον τροπον ενετειλατο μοι εσπερας και εποιησα το πρωι καθος επεταγη μοι.
I spoke to the people in the morning as I was ordered in the evening, and I did in the morning as I was commanded.

B: και ελαλησα προς τον λαον το πρωι ον τροπον ενετειλατο μοι εσπερας και εποιησα το πρωι καθος επεταγη μοι
I spoke to the people in the morning as I was ordered in the evening, and I did in the morning as I was commanded.

L^W: *et locutus sum ad populum mane quemadmodum mandauit mihi uespere et feci mane sicut imperatum est mihi.*
I spoke to the people in the morning as I was ordered in the evening, and I did in the morning as I was commanded.

L^s;[25] ... *mandauit mihi uespere et feci mane sicut imperatum est mihi.*
... I was ordered in the evening, and I did in the morning as I was commanded.

---

24. Johan Lust, "The Delight of Ezekiel's Eyes: Ez 24:15–24 in Hebrew and Greek," in *Tenth Congress of the International Organization for Septuagint and Cognate Studies: Oslo, 1998*, ed. Bernard A. Taylor, SCS 51 (Atlanta: Society of Biblical Literature, 2001), 1–26.

25. Although the first line of the verse is missing, the manuscript follows L^W here. See Alban Dold, *Neue St. Galler Vorhieronymianische Propheten-Fragmente: Der St. Galler Sammelhandschrift 1398b zugehörig*, TA 31 (Beuron: Beuroner Kunstverlag, 1940), 25–26.

The Greek text of P967[26] and Codex Vaticanus (B), as well as the Vetus Latina in Codex Wirceburgensis (L^w, and Fragmenta Sangallensia (L^s), do not mention the prophet's wife. Owing to the agreement of all the B witnesses, Joseph Ziegler prefers this particular reading.[27]

The difference between Ezek 24:18 MT and LXX, however, leads to the crucial question whether the LXX softened or the MT sharpened the text.[28] A clue about a possible answer can be found in verse 16cd.

MT: ולא תספד ולא תבכה ולא תבוא דמעתך
do not mourn or weep <u>nor shall any tear run down</u>.

LXX: ου μη κοπης ουδε μη κλαυσθης
do not mourn or weep.

While MT shows a sequence of three imperatives ("do not mourn or weep, *nor shall any tear run down*"), the LXX, by contrast, lacks any reference to the running down of tears ("do not mourn or weep"). According to Walther Zimmerli, the phrase ולא תבוא דמעתך ("nor shall any tear run down," v. 16d), which is deemed to be superfluous, marks a "transition … from a sphere of ritual lamentation to that of personal feeling."[29]

---

26. The codex of twenty-one leaves from the John Scheide Papyri Collection is considered to be part of a codex in the Chester Beatty collection of biblical papyri, containing Ezekiel and Esther and numbered by Rahlfs as P967. See Johnson Allan Chester, Henry Snyder Gehman, and Edmund Harris Kase, eds., *The John H. Scheide Biblical Papyri Ezekiel* (Princeton: Princeton University Press, 1938), 1–5. The importance of P967 for Ezekiel has recently been restated by Karl F. Pohlman. See Pohlman, "Ezekiel: New Directions and Current Debates," in *Ezekiel: Current Debates and Future Directions*, ed. William A. Tooman and Penelope Barter, FAT 112 (Tübingen: Mohr Siebeck, 2017), 8–9.

27. See Joseph Ziegler, ed., *Ezechiel*, SVTG 16.1 (Göttingen: Vandenhoeck & Ruprecht, 1977), 25–26. In this regard, see also Almut Hammerstaedt-Löhr et al., "Jezekiel. Ezechiel/Hesekiel," in *Psalmen bis Daniel*, vol. 2 of *Septuaginta Deutsch*, ed. Martin Karrer and Wolfgang Kraus (Stuttgart: Deutsche Bibelgesellschaft, 2011), 2928. According to these authors, it is not necessary to consider this MT expression "als ursprünglich."

28. Hammerstaedt-Löhr et al., "Jezekiel. Ezechiel/Hesekiel," 2928.

29. See Zimmerli, *Ezekiel 1*, 502. While explicitly picking up terminology from 24:17, the following sequence of gestures in 24:22–23 does not mention the flowing tears again. This could confirm Zimmerli's proposal. Hammerstaedt-Löhr et al. further add a stylistic note: MT interrupts the Parallelismus membrorum by the insertion of a third member ("Jezekiel. Ezechiel/Hesekiel," 2927).

Consequently, the reference to Ezekiel's wife's death (Ezek 24:18 MT), as well as the command about flowing tears (Ezek 24:16 MT), seems to pursue the same goal. The life of the prophet is being dramatized exponentially, first by introducing the death of his wife, who turns out to be identified by the reader with the earlier and vague phrase "delight of your eyes" (Ezek 24:15). Second, in light of this identification, the mention of tears in Ezek 24:16 provides an additional brief glimpse into the prophet's most intimate feelings.

The result of the abovementioned effort at dramatizing the private life of the prophet is further corroborated with the help of the following Ezek 24:19–24*. From the very beginning, a collective rereading of Ezekiel's gestures is stressed by means of the people's question in Ezek 24:19:[30] "And the people said to me: Will you not tell us [לנו] what these things that you are doing (mean) for us [לנו]?" While introducing the first explanation of the prophet's behavior, the question widens the meaning of his gestures (see the double לנו, "us/for us," in Ezek 24:19 MT).[31] In Ezek 24:20–21, the prophet interprets the divine words previously addressed to him and redirects them into a message addressed to the whole house of Israel. The report of the divine speech begins in Ezek 24:21 with the imperative "tell to the house of Israel" (אמר לבית ישראל), followed by the announcement of the desecration of YHWH's sanctuary, which is described as the "delight of your eyes."

In Ezek 24:22–23, the reported divine speech is interrupted, and the prophet directly addresses his interlocutors. By picking up lexemes and phraseology from Ezek 24:17, Ezekiel depicts his previous gestures as exemplary ones: "You shall do [עשה] as I have done [עשה]" (Ezek 24:22). Last, the cluster היה ("to be") +למופת לכם ("to you a sign," Ezek 24:24) highlights the public dimension of the prophet himself while simultaneously hinting at the communicative role of his person and actions.

---

30. In the light of Moses's speeches in the last triad of plagues (Exod 10:3–6; 11:4–8), Greenberg interprets the difference between 24:15–17 and 24:20–21 as a discrepancy between the "interior reception" of a message and its externalization. This phenomenon marks "both a closural change of pace and a heightening" (Greenberg, *Ezekiel 21–37*, 513–14).

31. The ancient versions (LXX, L^W, Syriac, and Targum) do not attest the second לנו, "for us" (הלא הגיד לנו מה אלה לנו, "will you not tell *us* what these things [mean] *for us*?" 24:19b), which is considered by Zimmerli an "erroneous repetition of the preceding" (*Ezekiel 1*, 503). In spite of his suggestion of emendation, the double לנו emphasizes the collective meaning of the prophetic gestures.

Thus, preceded by the allusion to Ezekiel's private life and intimate feelings, Ezek 24:19–24 gains an additional association. Not only do the prophetic gestures representatively foreshadow the dire fate of his addressees, as well as their future actions, but also the prophet himself, with his life and intimacy, turns out to embody the consequences of judgment—along with the prophetic actions, his intimate experience will be a sign.

In sum, Ezekiel's marriage as well as the allusions to his innermost feelings seem to be constructed by means of a tactical textual arrangement coupled with some literary devices (i.e., the strategic use of indeterminate terminology; collective rereading of Ezekiel's behavior). The so-called private life of the prophet, therefore, turns out to be a literary construct, created to enhance further the role of the prophet as a sign, and thus to be part of the public dimension of his prophetic ministry.

4. Jeremiah 16:1–4:
Jeremiah's So-Called Celibacy (Or Was Jeremiah Celibate?)

Jeremiah 16:1–4 has attracted the attention of interpreters owing to the awkwardness of the divine command to the prophet: "You shall not take a wife, nor shall you have sons or daughters in this place" (Jer 16:2). Against the backdrop of the focus on the prophetic persona, this command has been widely considered as one of a celibate way of life imposed on Jeremiah and subsequently assumed by him.[32] The aim of Jeremiah's so-called celibacy, a unique phenomenon within the Hebrew Bible, was to stress

---

32. The tendency to fill up blanks within the text results in different hypotheses about the circumstances that led to Jeremiah's celibacy. John Skinner interprets Jeremiah's renunciation of marriage in the light of Hosea: "What Hosea learned through the bitter experiences of his home life led Jeremiah early to renounce the hope of marriage." See Skinner, *Prophecy and Religion: Studies in the Life of Jeremiah* (Cambridge: Cambridge University Press, 1922), 22. According to Rudolph, Jeremiah's self-denial of marriage and family life is due to his engagement in the prophetic ministry: "die große Aufgabe verträgt keine Sorge um und Fürsorge für eine Familie." See Wilhelm Rudolph, *Jeremia*, 3rd ed., HAT 12 (Tübingen: Mohr Siebeck, 1968), 110–11. In this regard, Holladay also stresses the poignancy of Jeremiah's sacrifice in obeying the "permanent prohibition" against marrying and having children. See William Holladay, *Jeremiah 1: Chapters 1–25*, Hermeneia (Philadelphia: Fortress, 1986), 467–68. Carroll emblematically defines the focus on the prophetic persona as a "Skinnerian approach," with reference to John Skinner. See Robert P. Carroll, *From Chaos to Covenant: Prophecy in the Book of Jeremiah* (New York: Crossroad, 1981), 5–7.

his loneliness and increasing marginalization further.³³ Within this line of reasoning, Jer 16:1–9, both with regard to celibacy and to the following prohibitions to enter neither a house of mourning nor a joyful house, ended up being considered as prophetic symbolic actions.³⁴

The question here is whether the prohibition of Jer 16:1–4 actually deals with the prophetic persona and his intimate, private life,³⁵ and whether this can accordingly be considered a symbolic action. Interesting clues are suggested by three literary strategies at work within the text.

First, concerning the notion of *limitation* in Jer 16:2, the imperative not to take a wife or to have children is followed by the expression במקום הזה ("in this place"). Similar references occur in the following verse, 16:3 (במקום הזה, "in this place"; בארץ הזאת, "in this land"), 16:6 (בארץ הזאת, "in this land"), and 16:9 (מן המקום הזה, "from this place"). These references all aim at focusing on the place against which the coming judgement will be accomplished while, at the same time, providing a hint to a key issue within 16:1–9.

Against this background, the command addressed to the prophet in Jer 16:2 seems to be limited to a specific environment which is depicted as the target of an impending disaster.³⁶ Emphasis on the land as the background scenario to YHWH's prohibition is further emphasized in terms of 29:4–7. While, in 16:1–4, the prophet is forbidden to marry and have daughters and sons in the land, in 29:4–7, the land of exile is the right place to marry and have children.

Second, in terms of the effect of *intensification*, the prohibition of Jer 16:2—addressed to an individual—takes on an additional meaning in

---

33. See, among others, Arthur Weiser, *Das Buch Jeremia: Kapitel 1–25*, ATD 20 (Göttingen: Vandenhoeck & Ruprecht, 1976), 137–38; Pete A. R. Diamond, *The Confessions of Jeremiah in Context: Scenes from a Prophetic Drama* (Sheffield: Sheffield University Press, 1987), 164.

34. Georg Fohrer, "Die Gattung der Berichte über symbolische Handlungen der Propheten," *ZAW* 23 (1952): 101–20; Fohrer, *Die symbolische Handlungen der Propheten*, 2nd ed. (Stuttgart: Zwingli, 1968), 35–38; Weiser, *Jeremia 1–25*, 137; Kelvin G. Friebel, *Jeremiah's and Ezekiel's Sign-Acts: Rhetorical Nonverbal Communication*, JSOTSup 283 (Sheffield: Sheffield Academic, 1999), 82–99.

35. The question has already been addressed by Robert P. Carroll. See Carroll, *Jeremiah: A Commentary*, OTL (London: SCM, 1986), 341; see also Georg Fischer, *Jeremia 1–25*, HThKAT (Freiburg: Herder, 2005), 522.

36. Carroll, *Jeremiah*, 341.

16:3–4 by means of multiple lexical cross-references.³⁷ Thus, one finds that the root ילד, linked to the maternal generation (16:3c), refers back to 14:15; 15:9–10. Female imagery, as well as the generation of children in 16:2, seems, therefore, to recall previous depictions of the dire consequences of the catastrophe. In addition, 16:4 combines images and terminology that appear elsewhere in the book, such as the noun תחלאים ("diseases"), which occurs in 14:18 in the context of famine. One also finds that the combination of לא ("not") + ספד ("to be bewailed") and לא ("not") + קבר ("to be buried"), along with the phrase "to be as dung on the surface of the ground," occurs again in 25:33, in order to stress the worldwide catastrophe. Jeremiah 16:4b, considered by Winfried Thiel a secondary expansion, is identical to 8:2.³⁸ One thus finds that by means of multiple lexical cross-references, 16:4 seems to be arranged in such a way as to stress an intensification of the divine punishment. As a matter of fact, the prophetic life and persona come across as blurred, even while there appears to be a large-scale heightening of the sense of certain and widespread doom impending on the land.

Third, in terms of *redactional expansion*, Jer 16:10–13 should be considered a redactional addition to the earlier text of 16:1–9*,³⁹ which marks a distinct shift from a word addressed to the prophet (16:1) to a word directed to the whole people (16:10). By means of the rhetorical pattern of question and answer, 16:10–13 offers a further explanation of 16:1–9. What was originally a personal communication between YHWH and the prophet (16:2–4) turns out to be a message to be delivered to the people (see the reference "when you tell this people all these words" in 16:10). Furthermore, questions asked by the addressees of the prophetic message in 16:10 ("Why has the Lord pronounced all this great evil against us? What is our iniquity? What is the sin that we have committed against the

---

37. Cross-references between Jer 16:1–9 and chs. 14–15 are often recognized. See, e.g., Weiser, *Jeremia 1–25*, 137; Diamond, *Confessions of Jeremiah*, 164; Gianni Barbiero, *"Tu mi hai sedotto, Signore": Le confessioni di Geremia alla luce della sua vocazione profetica*, AnBib Studia 2 (Rome: Gregorian & Biblical Press, 2013), 106–8.

38. See Winfried Thiel, *Die deuteronomistische Redaktion von Jeremia 1–25*, WMANT 52 (Neukirchen-Vluyn: Neukirchener Verlag, 1973), 198, who considers Jer 16:4b a D expansion. Further lexical links are highlighted by Holladay, *Jeremiah 1*, 469–70; Fischer, *Jeremia 1–25*, 521–23.

39. See, in this regard, Thiel, *Jeremia 1–25*, 198; William McKane, *Jeremiah I: Introduction and Commentary on Jeremiah I–XXV*, ICC (Edinburgh: T&T Clark, 1986), 369–70; Carroll, *Jeremiah*, 342–43.

Lord our God?") provide an interpretative clue. They show, in fact, that the earlier 16:2–9 is essentially considered an expression of an impending and unavoidable judgment against the whole community.

Regarding the interpretation of the so-called celibacy, as well as the following prohibitions, as prophetic symbolic actions, it is evident that the text shows no interest in the accomplishment of the imperatives of 16:2. As a result, 16:1–4 can hardly be considered a symbolic action performed by the prophet.[40]

The above-mentioned literary strategies, along with the lack of a symbolic action, show that the command not to take a wife and not to have children (16:2) cannot be regarded as the imposition of a state of absolute and permanent celibacy on Jeremiah. In fact, this command is limited in space and related to judgment. By contrast, by means of redactional interventions (16:4b and especially 16:10–13), words addressed to the prophet are interpreted as part of a collective announcement of the punishment that will befall the people. In addition, the lack of reference to any fulfillment of YHWH's command suggests that the prohibition against marrying and having children remains de facto a divine message that does not necessarily involve the life of the prophet.

Jeremiah's so-called private life—connected with his marital status—seems, therefore, to turn out to be a literary construct with a rhetorical aim, stressing and widening the force of the announcement of judgment by suggesting an early involvement of the prophet in the impending disaster. In any case, as Robert Carroll clearly points out regarding the query about Jeremiah's marriage or celibacy, "The text does not permit us to answer such a question because it is not the unmediated record of somebody's life."[41]

5. Hosea 1–3: Building Up a Parallel

Hosea 1–3 has attracted interpreters' attention, especially on account of what seem to be pictures of the prophet's married life. This has ended in countless speculative reconstructions of Hosea's marriage and personal

---

40. See already Rudolph, *Jeremia*, 110; McKane, *Jeremiah I–XXV*, 363–64. As Carroll observes: "If vv. 1–2 do belong to the report of a symbolic action, then the account quickly moves from such a report to a series of statements about the people.... The unit shows no further interest in the symbolic nature of his behavior" (*Jeremiah*, 340).

41. Carroll, *Jeremiah*, 341.

love affairs, resulting in a special focus on the prophet's intimate feelings and experiences.[42] However, this interpretative effort leans, for the most part, on gaps in the biblical texts, which are filled by interpreters. By means of the following three steps, I shall highlight concisely how what seems to be an insight into the intimate life of the prophet turns out to be, rather, a redactional enterprise that aims at triggering a specific reader response.

In the first instance, the marriage between Hosea and Gomer does not seem to be the main interest of Hos 1:2–9*; rather, it functions primarily within 1:2–3 as an introduction.[43] Differently, the terminology as well as the development of the text concentrates mainly on the generation of the three children and their names.[44] Hosea 1:2–9 focuses, first, on transferring the character of prostitute from the mother ("woman of harlotry," אשת זנונים, 1:2a) to the children ("children of harlotry," ילדי זנונים, 1:2c).[45] Repetition of the root זנה (4x in 1:2) draws attention to prostitution, while occurrences of the root ילד (1:2, 3, 6, 8) and the verb הרה, "conceive" (1:3, 6, 8), emphasize the generational nature of this root. Another focal point of 1:2–9* concerns naming (1:4–5, 6be–7, 9). God orders the children to be given ominous names that clearly stress a rebellious attitude that mirrors their mother's prostitution.

Hosea 1:2–9* could be considered, thus, an etiology of the rebellious character of the children, for which only the mother is held responsible. A similar literary strategy, aiming at highlighting the innate rebellious character of Jerusalem with reference to her father and mother, can be observed also in Ezek 16:3 ("Your father was an Amorite, your mother an Hittite") and Ezek 16:45 ("Your mother was a Hittite and your father an Amorite").[46] The difference between these texts is that, in Hos 1:2–9*, only Gomer is held responsible. Hosea 2:1–3 provides further evidence.

---

42. See in this regard the overview by Kelle, "Hosea 1–3," 187–93.

43. Hans Walter Wolff, *Hosea*, Hermeneia (Philadelphia: Fortress, 1974), 10.

44. Regarding the relation of "children of harlotry" (Hos 1:2c) to the verb לקח ("take"), as well as interpretative problems related to the meaning of זנונים ("harlotry"), see Andreas Weider, *Ehemetaphorik im prophetischer Verkündigung: Hos 1–3 und seine Wirkungsgeschichte im Jeremiabuch: Ein Beitrag zum alttestamentliche Gottesbild*, FB 71 (Würzburg: Echter, 1993), 7–17.

45. See Wolff, *Hosea*, 13: "the children of both sexes possess the same character as their mother."

46. See Zimmerli, *Ezekiel 1*, 337–38; see also Ombretta Pettigiani, "Ma io ricorderò la mia alleanza con te": La procedura del rîb come chiave interpretativa di Ez 16, AnBib 207 (Rome: Gregorian & Biblical Press, 2015), 99–103.

Justification of the children is accomplished not only by changing their names but at the same time by eliminating any reference to maternal generation. This process is accomplished by means of a substitution—motherhood is replaced with divine fatherhood in 2:1d ("They will be called 'children of the living God,'" יאמר להם בני אל־חי), which is further emphasized by allusions to the promises to the patriarchs in Gen 15:5; 22:17; 32:13; and in Hos 1:2ab ("The number of the people of Israel shall be *like the sand of the sea, which cannot be measured or counted*," Hos 1:1ab).[47]

In the second instance, in Hos 1:9, divine words address a second-person plural: "for you [אתם] are not my people and I am not for you [לכם]." The third child of Hosea and Gomer is suddenly linked to a second-person plural, *you*, thus, producing a double effect. The second-person plural widens the recipients of the speech by referring not only to the prophet but rather to the whole of the people, and especially to Gomer's children, whose names mirror the fate of the people, who are now banished from the covenant.[48] On the other hand, the second-person plural (Hos 1:9) forms a bridge directly with 2:4, where the children are summoned to accuse their mother.[49]

Personal indexes (see Hos 1:9; 2:4), therefore, enable the reader to identify the mother who would be accused in Hos 2:4–25* with Gomer, that is, the mother of the child and children alluded to in 1:9. This identification is further achieved by means of lexical cross-references: "her harlotry" (זנוניה, 1:4) and "children of harlotry" (בני זנונים, 1:6) are links to the root זנה that in 1:2 characterizes Hosea's wife and her children. In addition, the reader can construct an additional comparison between Hosea and YHWH, who is depicted as husband in 2:4–25*.

Both comparisons, however, do not occur by chance. On the contrary, they seem to arise from the intention of the redactor who arranged Hos 1:2–9* on the lines of the earlier 2:4–25*. From a diachronic point of view, indeed, 2:4–25* presumably predates 1:2–9*, which seems to be composed

---

47. Wolff, *Hosea*, 26; Andrew A. Macintosh, *Hosea*, ICC (Edinburgh: T&T Clark, 1997), 35.

48. References to the covenant in Hos 1:9 are stressed by, among others, Wolff, *Hosea*, 21–22; Weider, *Ehemetaphorik im prophetischer Verkündigung*, 32–33; Macintosh, *Hosea*, 27–28.

49. Gale A. Yee, *Composition and Tradition in the Book of Hosea: A Redactional Critical Investigation*, SBLDS 102 (Atlanta: Scholars Press, 1987), 103.

in order to provide a narrative introduction, as well as an interpretative key to the following poetry.⁵⁰ The redactional connection between 1:2–9* and 2:4–25* is constructed not only by means of the indexical shift in 1:9 (preparing for 2:4–5) but also by means of references to the children of harlotry and to their mother, who is described as a prostitute. The repetition of the children's names in 2:24–25 seems to provide a conclusion to the whole redactional composition, which was constructed by joining together 1:2–9* and 2:24–25.⁵¹

In the third instance, the parallel between YHWH–Hosea and Israel/woman–Gomer remains defective, however. Indeed, Hos 1:2–9* does not include any reference to Gomer's adultery after the marriage,⁵² while in 2:4 the woman is being charged with both prostitution and adultery ("her adultery," נאפופיה, 2:4). Moreover, in 2:4–25*, her sexual behavior is punished by YHWH, who ends up taking her back again. Hosea 3:1–5, the latest addition to the whole complex of Hos 1–3, seems to be arranged so as to bring the overlap between the couple Hosea–Gomer and YHWH–Israel to completion.⁵³

Hosea 3:1–5 is a short first-person narrative in which the speaker is asked to love an adulterous woman. The passage can hardly be considered a doublet of 1:2–9*, especially owing to, first, the lack of any reference to adultery in 1:2–9*, and, second, the initial עוד ("again") in 3:1, which introduces a complementary redactional element rather than a doublet.

The complementary information provided by Hos 3:1–5 can be inferred from a lexical hinge; the root נאף in 3:1 refers back to 2:4 ("her adultery," נאפופיה). Moreover, the parallel between the action that is requested of the speaker of 3:1 ("go and love a woman who is loved by another man and is

---

50. See the analysis of Yee, *Composition and Tradition*, 101–4.
51. The further insertion of Hos 2:1–3, regarding the restoration of Hosea's children, corresponds to 2:24–25. In this regard, see Yee (*Composition*, 71–76, 88–90), who, however, considers 2:1 as the conclusion of 1:9 (*Composition*, 68–71).
52. If the reason given for the redactional framing of Hos 2:4–25* with 1:2–9* is right, the omission of any adulterous behavior on the part of Hosea's wife could be deliberate.
53. According to Yee, *Composition*, 129–30, Hos 3:1–5 achieves two main goals—the addition (1) "segregates the marriage tradition in Hos 1–2 from Hos 4–14" (129) and (2) locates 2:4–25*, the marriage between YHWH and Israel, within a narrative framework, thus giving to the marriage between YHWH and Israel a "prominent position." The statement that Hos 1–3 is the latest part of the book also comes from Yee (*Composition*, 60–64).

adulterous") and that of YHWH is now made explicit ("*as* YHWH loves the sons of Israel").⁵⁴ In addition, the limitation of sexual activity imposed on the adulterous woman in 3:3 recalls 2:8, 12–15, in which YHWH violently restricted the woman's behavior.⁵⁵

The root נאף, referring to the woman in Hos 3:1 and cross-referenced with 2:4 ("her adultery"), allows the reader to identify the woman of 3:1–5 with the woman of 2:4–25*, who, in turn, had been previously identified with Gomer (by means of the addition of 1:2–9*). Consequently, assuming the identification of the speaker in 3:1–5 with the prophet, the adulterous woman, whom he is asked to love, ends up corresponding to Gomer herself. The result is that Gomer, the woman of harlotry, turns out to be not only a harlot but also an adulterous wife, who is taken back again (after her adultery) by Hosea.

In conclusion, it seems that the love story between Hosea and Gomer, as well as the presumed insights into Hosea's private life, results essentially from the literary montage of different texts. The main objective of this redactional construction would be to create a correspondence between the prophetic announcement of Hos 2:4–25* and the prophet himself, whose vicissitudes are deemed to parallel and perhaps embody the content of 2:4–25*. If this is the case, the so-called private life is not actually private at all or a prophetic biography, but rather an explicit and deliberate parallel between the prophetic announcement and the prophet himself.

Within this literary montage, motherhood comes to the fore in Hos 1:2–9* in order to stress the transferring of negative maternal features to the children, leaving any paternal responsibility aside. Moreover, women, that is, Gomer, the harlot and the adulterous mother (2:4), as well as the beloved but adulterous woman (3:1), function as redactional linchpins between different texts. By means of these hinges, the creative reader is allowed to establish a so-called private life of Hosea, while at the same time constructing a mental story of his troubled marriage with Gomer.

---

54. The root אהב ("love/to love," 4x in Hos 3:1) provides additional references to 2:4–25*.

55. For an androcentric reception history regarding the woman's behavior in Hos 2:4–25*, see Yvonne Sherwood, "Boxing Gomer: Controlling the Deviant Woman in Hos 1–3," in *Feminist Companion to the Latter Prophets*, ed. Athalya Brenner, FCB 8 (Sheffield: Sheffield Academic, 1995), 101–25.

6. Conclusion

From the scant evidence about the so-called private lives of the prophets in the Hebrew Bible, we can conclude that, first, the distinction between private life and public life does not fit the biblical texts and narratives relevant to this topic. The so-called private life comes to the fore as an essential part of the prophetic ministry and public task. In fact, the so-called private life seems to have a political meaning (see Isa 8:1–4) or a public relevance in order to enhance the prophetic announcement (see Ezek 24:15–27; Jer 16:1–4). This can be expressed explicitly by terminology (e.g., clusters such as היה + ל + אות/מופת, "to be a sign"). Sometimes, however, allusions to the lives of the prophets result from a textual or redactional reworking that is aimed at paralleling the prophet and his announcement (see Ezek 24:15–27; Hos 1–3).

The so-called private life of the prophet, therefore, should be considered a literary product that highlights an important shift within prophetic literature—from the prophet as *subject* of prophecy (i.e., the prophet who prophesies by uttering prophecies) to the prophet as *object* of prophecy (i.e., narratives related to the prophet and his person, life, or relations)—that has become part of the prophetic books, and, consequently, of prophecy itself. While such a move in prophetic literature was taking place, not only were female prophets erased from the Latter Prophets,[56] but women also were employed as literary or redactional tools in the service of building up the private lives of male prophets while further emphasizing their relevance within the prophetic books.

Bibliography

Barbiero, Gianni. *"Tu mi hai sedotto, Signore": Le confessioni di Geremia alla luce della sua vocazione profetica.* AnBib Studia 2. Rome: Gregorian & Biblical Press, 2013.

Becker, Uwe. "Die Wiederentdeckung des Prophetenbuches. Tendenzen und Aufgaben der gegenwärtigen Prophetenforschung." *BTZ* 21 (2004): 30–60.

Beerden, Kim. *Worlds Full of Signs: Ancient Greek Divination in Context.* RGRW 176. Leiden: Brill, 2013.

---

56. Fuchs, "Prophecy."

Bertholet, Alfred. *Das Buch Hesekiel.* KHC 12. Tübingen: Mohr Siebeck, 1897.

Beuken, Willem A. M. *Jesaja 1–12.* HThKAT. Freiburg: Herder, 2003.

Bitter, Stephan. *Die Ehe des Propheten Hosea: Eine Auslegungsgeschichtliche Untersuchung.* GTA 3. Göttingen: Vandenhoeck & Ruprecht, 1975.

Block, Daniel I. *Ezekiel 1–24.* NICOT. Grand Rapids: Eerdmans, 1997.

Carroll, Robert P. *From Chaos to Covenant: Prophecy in the Book of Jeremiah.* New York: Crossroad, 1981.

———. *Jeremiah: A Commentary.* OTL. London: SCM, 1986.

Chester, Johnson Allan, Henry Snyder Gehman, and Edmund Harris Kase, eds. *The John H. Scheide Biblical Papyri Ezekiel.* Princeton: Princeton University Press, 1938.

Church, Brooke P. *The Private Lives of the Prophets and the Times in Which They Lived.* New York: Rinehart, 1953.

Diamond, Pete A. R. *The Confessions of Jeremiah in Context: Scenes from a Prophetic Drama.* Sheffield: Sheffield University Press, 1987.

Dold, Alban. *Neue St. Galler Vorhieronymianische Propheten-Fragmente: Der St. Galler Sammelhandschrift 1398b zugehörig.* TA 31. Beuron: Beuroner Kunstverlag, 1940.

Ewald, Georg H. A. *Die Propheten des Alten Bundes: I–II.* Stuttgart: Krabbe, 1840–1841.

Fischer, Georg. *Jeremia 1–25.* HThKAT. Freiburg: Herder, 2005.

Fischer, Irmtraud. "Das Geschlecht als exegetisches Kriterium zu einer gender-fairen Interpretation der Erzeltern-Erzählungen." Pages 147–50 in *Studies in the Book of Genesis: Literature, Redaction and History.* Edited by André Wénin. BETL 155. Leuven: Peeters, 2001.

———. *Gotteskünderinnen: Zur einer geschlechterfairen Deutung des Phänomens der Prophetie und der Prophetinnen in der Hebräischen Bibel.* Stuttgart: Kohlhammer, 2002.

Fohrer, Georg. "Die Gattung der Berichte über symbolische Handlungen der Propheten." *ZAW* 23 (1952): 101–20.

———. *Die symbolische Handlungen der Propheten.* 2nd ed. Stuttgart: Zwingli, 1968.

Friebel, Kelvin G. *Jeremiah's and Ezekiel's Sign-Acts: Rhetorical Nonverbal Communication.* JSOTSup 283. Sheffield: Sheffield Academic, 1999.

Fuchs, Esther. "Prophecy and the Construction of Women." Pages 54–69 in *Feminist Companion to Prophets and Daniel.* Edited by Athalya Brenner. FCB 2/8. London: Sheffield Academic, 2001.

Goldman, Maurice D. "Was Jeremiah Married?" *ABR* 2 (1952): 43–47.

Greenberg, Moshe. *Ezekiel 21–37: A New Translation with Introduction and Commentary*. AB 22. New York: Doubleday, 1997.
Gunkel, Hermann. *Genesis*. Macon, GA: Mercer University Press, 1997.
Hammerstaedt-Löhr, Almut, Michael Konkel, Hermut Löhr, and Knut Usener. "Jezekiel. Ezechiel / Hesekiel." Page 2928 in *Psalmen bis Daniel*. Vol. 2 of *Septuaginta Deutsch*. Edited by Martin Karrer and Kraus Wolfgang. Stuttgart: Deutsche Bibelgesellschaft, 2011.
Holladay, William. *Jeremiah 1: Chapters 1–25*. Hermeneia. Philadelphia: Fortress, 1986.
Kaiser, Otto. *Das Buch des Propheten Jesaja: Kapitel 1–12*. ATD 17. Göttingen: Vandenhoeck & Ruprecht, 1981.
Kelle, Brad E. "Hosea 1–3 in Twentieth-Century Scholarship." *CBR* 7 (2009): 189–216.
Knobel, August. *Der Prophetismus der Hebräer vollständig dargestellt*. Breslau: Max & Komp, 1837.
Lust, Johan. "The Delight of Ezekiel's Eyes: Ez 24:15–24 in Hebrew and Greek." Pages 1–26 in *Tenth Congress of the International Organization for Septuagint and Cognate Studies: Oslo, 1998*. Edited by Bernard A. Taylor. SCS 51. Atlanta: Society of Biblical Literature, 2001.
Macintosh, Andrew A. *Hosea*. ICC. Edinburgh: T&T Clark, 1997.
McKane, William. *Jeremiah I: Introduction and Commentary on Jeremiah I–XXV*. ICC. Edinburgh: T&T Clark, 1986.
Parry, Donald W., and Elisha Qimron. *The Great Isaiah Scroll (1QIsa^a): A New Edition*. STDJ 32. Leiden: Brill, 1999.
Pettigiani, Ombretta. *"Ma io ricorderò la mia alleanza con te": La procedura del rîb come chiave interpretativa di Ez 16*. AnBib 207. Rome: Gregorian & Biblical Press, 2015.
Pohlmann, Karl F. *Das Buch des Propheten Hesekiel (Ezechiel): Kapitel 20–48*. Göttingen: Vandenhoeck & Ruprecht, 2001.
———. "Ezekiel: New Directions and Current Debates." Pages 3–17 in *Ezekiel: Current Debates and Future Directions*. Edited by William A. Tooman and Penelope Barter. FAT 112. Tübingen: Mohr Siebeck, 2017.
Rudolph, Wilhelm. *Jeremia*. 3rd ed. HAT 12. Tübingen: Mohr Siebeck, 1968.
Schmid, Konrad. "Hintere Propheten (Nebiim)." Pages 317–24 in *Grundinformation Altes Testament*. 4th ed. Edited by Jan C. Gertz. UTB 2745. Göttingen: Vandenhoeck & Ruprecht, 2010.

Sherwood, Yvonne. "Boxing Gomer. Controlling the Deviant Woman in Hos 1–3." Pages 101–25 in *Feminist Companion to the Latter Prophets*. Edited by Athalya Brenner. FCB 8. Sheffield: Sheffield Academic, 1995.
Skinner, John. *Prophecy and Religion: Studies in the Life of Jeremiah*. Cambridge: Cambridge University Press, 1922.
Thiel, Winfried. *Die deuteronomistische Redaktion von Jeremia 1–25*. WMANT 52. Neukirchen-Vluyn: Neukirchener Verlag, 1973.
Weider, Andreas. *Ehemetaphorik im prophetischer Verkündigung: Hos 1–3 und seine Wirkungsgeschichte im Jeremiabuch; Ein Beitrag zum alttestamentliche Gottesbild*. FB 71. Würzburg: Echter, 1993.
Weiser, Arthur. *Das Buch Jeremia: Kapitel 1–25*. ATD 20. Göttingen: Vandenhoeck & Ruprecht, 1976.
Weißflog, Kay. *"Zeichen und Sinnbilder": Die Kinder der Propheten Jesaja und Hosea*. ABG 36. Leipzig: Evangelische Verlagsanstalt, 2001.
Wildberger, Hans. *Jesaja: I Teilband Jesaja 1–12*. BKAT 10.1. Neukirchen-Vluyn: Neukirchener Verlag, 1972.
Wolff, Hans Walter. *Hosea*. Hermeneia. Philadelphia: Fortress, 1974.
Yee, Gale A. *Composition and Tradition in the Book of Hosea: A Redactional Critical Investigation*. SBLDS 102. Atlanta: Scholars Press, 1987.
Ziegler, Joseph, ed. *Ezechiel*. SVTG 16.1. Göttingen: Vandenhoeck & Ruprecht, 1977.
Zimmerli, Walther. *Ezekiel 1: Chapters 1–24*. Translated by Robert Clements. Hermeneia. Philadelphia: Fortress, 1979.

Between Excruciating Pain and the Promise of New Life: Birth Imagery in the Prophets and Trauma Hermeneutics

L. Juliana Claassens

1. Introduction

Judah's experience in the context of military invasion, deportation, and exile at a number of crucial junctures in the prophetic books is expressed with the metaphor of a woman in labor. So the cries of giving birth resound amid the sights and sounds of war as this compelling metaphor is used in a number of prophetic texts to powerful rhetoric effect in order to capture the anguish and panic associated with military conquest. Scholars such as Claudia Bergmann and Katherine Pfisterer Darr have written extensively about the way in which this metaphor is used as an image of war, quite often to describe soldiers and, with much glee, enemy soldiers who have fallen in a state of panic.[1] For instance, in her essay, "We Have Seen the

---

1. Claudia Bergmann, "We Have Seen the Enemy, and He Is Only a 'She': The Portrayal of Warriors as Women," *CBQ* 69 (2007): 651–72; Katheryn Pfisterer Darr, "No Strength to Deliver: Bringing to Birth," in *Isaiah's Vision and the Family of God* (Louisville: Westminster John Knox, 1994), 205–24. See also her description of labor and birth imagery in the biblical traditions in the same book (100–109). Both these scholars have also written on the way the metaphor of a woman in labor is used to describe God in Isa 42:10–17 in conjunction with the more familiar metaphor of God as a mighty warrior. See Katheryn Pfisterer Darr, "Like Warrior, like Woman: Destruction and Deliverance in Isaiah 42:10–17," *CBQ* 49 (1987): 564–65; Katheryn Pfisterer Darr, "Two Unifying Female Images in the Book of Isaiah," in *Uncovering Ancient Stones: Essays in Memory of H. Niel Richardson*, ed. Lewis M. Hopfe (Winona Lake, IN: Eisenbrauns, 1994), 17–30; Claudia Bergmann, "'Like a Warrior' and 'Like a Woman Giving Birth: Expressing Divine Immanence and Transcendence in Isaiah 42:10–17," in *Bodies, Embodiment, and Theology of the Hebrew Bible*, ed. S. Tamar Kamionkowski

Enemy, and He Is Only a 'She,'" Bergmann considers those texts in which the metaphor of a woman in labor is utilized to shame enemy warriors in particular by portraying them as women in the midst of childbirth (e.g., Jer 50:37; 51:30; Nah 3:13).[2]

I myself have investigated the use of the woman in labor metaphor in the book of Jeremiah, showing how recent hermeneutical approaches such as feminist, postcolonial, and queer biblical interpretation in conjunction with trauma hermeneutics opens up new perspectives on the rhetorical significance of this metaphor in the book of Jeremiah.[3] Continuing with this line of inquiry, I briefly will focus in the first part of this essay on the valuable insights trauma hermeneutics may add to our understanding of the nature and significance of the woman-in-labor metaphor. Of particular interest for the purpose of this essay is the role of metaphors in the often-arduous process of recovering from severe trauma. In the second part of the essay, by way of illustration, I will introduce three instances of the woman-in-labor metaphor in three different prophetic books, namely, Jeremiah, Micah, and Isaiah, where one sees how the original metaphor, with its connotations of excruciating pain and despair associated with military invasion, has been reframed in such a way as to express the hope for restoration and new life.

2. Defining Trauma Hermeneutics

In recent years, trauma hermeneutics has become an increasingly important conversation partner in the study of the Hebrew Bible, reframing and reinvigorating biblical interpretation as scholars started to see the potential of trauma theory to offer insight into the human condition responsible for these texts.[4] Actually, much of Judah's history can be characterized as

---

and Wonil Kim (New York: T&T Clark, 2011), 38–56. See also Sarah Dille, *Mixing Metaphors: God as Mother and Father in Deutero-Isaiah*, JSOTSup 398 (London: T&T Clark, 2004), 41–73.

2. Bergmann, "We Have Seen the Enemy," 651.

3. L. Juliana Claassens, "Like a Woman in Labor: Gender, Queer, Postcolonial and Trauma Perspectives on Jeremiah," in *Prophecy and Power: Jeremiah in Feminist and Postcolonial Perspective*, ed. Christl M. Maier and Carolyn J. Sharp (London: Bloomsbury T&T Clark, 2013), 117–32; Claassens, "The Rhetorical Function of the Woman in Labor Metaphor in Jeremiah 30–31: Trauma, Gender and Postcolonial Perspectives," *JTSA* 150 (2014): 67–84.

4. For an important survey on the development as well as the impact of trauma hermeneutics on biblical studies, see the article by David G. Garber, "Trauma and

traumatic in nature, as the land repeatedly is invaded by one superpower after another. The survivors of these acts of organized violence were left to deal with the effects of these traumatic events as they continued to live in the shadow of the particular empire of the time, which included even more suffering under the heavy yoke of imperial rule.[5]

Given that many of the prophetic books emerged before, during, and in the aftermath of the Babylonian invasion and exile, they have benefited from being interpreted as trauma literature. According to Louis Stulman, prophetic books are elaborate artistic expressions that bear witness to devastating violence, moving "the worst of circumstances to a bearable distance" and elevating "the trauma of war from ground zero to the symbolic world of language." Similar to the outpouring of poetry, music, drama, art, and sermons that followed in the wake of 9/11—all of which had the intended goal of helping a traumatized people come to terms with the tragic events that they had experienced—prophetic literature created space for people to express their pain, to mourn, and ultimately to survive their ordeal.[6]

Elsewhere I have outlined in some detail the important role metaphors may play in the often difficult process of coming to terms with extreme trauma—in particular in moving from traumatic to narrative memories, which shows how the inexplicable has been introduced into some kind of interpretative framework that makes sense of the senseless.[7] For the purpose of this essay, the focus will be on the potential of trauma hermeneutics for offering new insight into the way the metaphor of a woman in labor may express the debilitating effects of severe trauma, as well as

---

Biblical Studies," *CBR* 14 (2015): 24–44. See also two recent collections of essays that include a very good representation of recent examples of trauma hermeneutics being used to read the Bible: Elizabeth Boase and Christopher G. Frechette, eds., *Bible through the Lens of Trauma*, SemeiaSt 86 (Atlanta: SBL Press, 2016); Eve-Marie Becker, Jan Dochhorn, and Else Holt, eds., *Trauma and Traumatization in Individual and Collective Dimensions: Insights from Biblical Studies and Beyond* (Göttingen: Vandenhoeck & Ruprecht, 2014). For an excellent treatment of trauma hermeneutics as applied to the book of Ezekiel, see Ruth Poser, *Das Ezechielbuch als Trauma-Literatur*, VTSup 154 (Leiden: Brill), 2012.

5. See Louis Stulman's reminder of Israel's traumatic past saying that one should not negate "the importance of its protracted history of war, exile, and diaspora" ("Reading the Bible as Trauma Literature: The Legacy of the Losers," *CBW* 34 [2014]: 3).

6. Stulman, "Reading the Bible," 7.

7. See L. Juliana Claassens, "From Traumatic to Narrative Memories: The Rhetorical Function of Birth Metaphors in Micah 4–5," *AcT* Supplement 26 (2018): 221–36.

highlighting a number of examples of where this metaphor is reframed in order to reflect Judah's hope for recovery.

3. The Metaphor of a Woman in Labor in the Context of Disaster

In her in-depth analysis of the childbirth metaphor in the Hebrew Bible against the backdrop of its ancient Near Eastern context, Bergmann shows how the metaphor of a woman in labor is used in a number of texts to capture the anguish that the Israelite warriors, as well as other members of the beleaguered society, are experiencing due to the life-threatening nature of an impending crisis that cannot be averted—just as birth cannot be stopped once it has started.[8] Building on Bergmann's argument, I propose that when read through a lens of trauma hermeneutics, and particularly considering the role of metaphor as outlined above, additional perspectives emerge that may enhance our understanding of the rhetorical function of the woman-in-labor metaphor in the Prophets.

First, the repeated occurrence of the woman-in-labor metaphor in the Prophets can be described as remnants of traumatic memories that exemplify the feeling of helplessness, panic, and despair experienced by the people of Judah during the most traumatic time, that of the Babylonian invasion and exile. Elsewhere, I have argued that in the book of Jeremiah quite a few of the instances of the woman-in-labor metaphor occur in the context of extreme trauma.[9] For instance, in Jer 4:31, the reference,

> For I heard a cry as of a woman in labor,
>   anguish as of one bringing forth her first child,
> the cry of daughter Zion gasping for breath,
>   stretching out her hands,
> "Woe is me! I am fainting before killers!"

is introduced in a context where disaster is said to overtake disaster (Jer 4:19).[10] It is a period when the entire land is devastated by the large-scale

---

8. Bergmann, "We Have Seen the Enemy," 651, 663. See the comprehensive survey of birth imagery in the Hebrew Bible as well as ancient Near Eastern texts in the articles by Bergmann, "Like a Warrior," 43–49, 53–54; Bergmann "We Have Seen the Enemy," 655–57.

9. Claassens, "Like a Woman in Labor," 119–20; Claassens, "Rhetorical Function," 68–74.

10. Unless otherwise noted, biblical translations follow the NRSV.

destruction brought about by the enemy from the north, resulting in a devastating loss of life and destruction of property, in addition to countless displaced and exiled persons.

These associations with the metaphor of a woman in labor derive from the reality of many women in a world before modern medicine who found themselves in a situation of life and death, with a high percentage of mothers dying in childbirth.[11] The thought of being trapped in endless labor and, in most texts if not all, with no baby to be born (see the specific reference in Isa 26:18 to giving birth to wind), captures something of the ongoing ordeal of the people of Judah, where there seems to be no hope for deliverance at all. In addition, the sense of powerlessness and an inability to do anything else while in the midst of labor, as well as, of course, the unbearable pain associated with childbirth in a world before pain medication or epidurals, seems to be well suited to express the experience of being severely traumatized by past and current events.[12]

Second, the woman-in-labor metaphor is one attempt by the prophets to integrate the traumatic memories of the terrifying violence into an interpretative framework that reframes the traumatic events and offers the victim some semblance of coherence amid the chaos in which the trauma victim had been hurled. Kathleen O'Connor writes as follow about the repetitive nature of dealing with traumatic memories: "Victims have to come to terms over and over again with catastrophe, to find language for the terrors, to re-enter and face fragmented memories, to overcome

---

11. Carol L. Meyers, *Discovering Eve: Ancient Israelite Women in Context* (New York: Oxford University Press, 1988), 112–13.

12. It has been argued that these perceptions regarding a woman in labor can be said to reflect a male perspective, stemming from the fact that men were absent and excluded from the act of giving birth. Thus, the male author remained fixated at the moment of the excruciating pain, conceivably mirroring the helplessness being felt by the fathers, brothers, uncles, and older sons when a woman found herself in labor. See Irmtraud Fischer, "Egalitär entworfen: Hierarchisch gelebt Zur Problematik des Geschlechterverhältnisses und einer genderfairen Anthropologie im Alten Testament," in *Der Mensch im alten Israel: Neue Forschungen zur alttestamentlichen Anthropologie*, ed. Bernd Janowski and Kathrin Liess, HBS 59 (Freiburg: Herder, 2009), 292; Bergmann, "Like a Warrior," 47. For a counter argument, see Hanne Løland, who problematizes the notion that the male perspectives regarding child birth always would be negative and the female perspective always positive. Løland, *Silent or Salient Gender? The Interpretation of Gendered God-Language in the Hebrew Bible, Exemplified in Isaiah 42, 46, and 49*, FAT 2/32 (Tübingen: Mohr Siebeck, 2008), 120.

numbness, to grieve deeply, to find stories to guide them through the void."[13] Moreover, the repetitive, stereotypical nature of the woman-in-labor metaphor is reminiscent of what Johan Anker describes as "frozen metaphors," according to which the various authors of the prophetic books fall back on some stereotypical way of trying to capture the traumatic circumstances in their respective contexts.[14] Even though this metaphor serves the function of expressing the worst feelings and emotions in a singular formulation, one also recognizes, in light of what has been argued before, that this attempt at saying the unsayable is limited and fragmented in nature, and moreover is reminiscent of recurring flashbacks and nightmares that can be quite debilitating to the individual seeking to survive the devastating ordeal.

For recovery to take place, though, these frozen metaphors of trauma have to be replaced by what Anker calls "metaphors of healing," which he describes as "more creative metaphors" that move individuals further along the process of transforming traumatic memories into narrative memories that manage to integrate past events and extract the poison of the traumatic memories.[15] In this regard, it is quite interesting that in a number of instances in the prophetic books outlined here (Jer 31:8–9; Isa 42:13–14; 66:6–9; Mic 4:9–5:3), the metaphor of a woman in labor is significantly altered to signal a time of hope and recovery in contrast to its more customary application.

4. Reframing the Metaphor of a Woman in Labor

4.1. Jeremiah 30–31

The first text in which the woman-in-labor metaphor is used twice in close proximity, first in a conventional fashion and then quite dramatically

---

13. Kathleen O'Connor, *Jeremiah: Pain and Promise* (Minneapolis: Fortress, 2011), 47.

14. Johan Anker, "Metaphors of Pain: The Use of Metaphors in Trauma Narrative with Reference to Fugitive Pieces," *Literator* 30.2 (2009): 66. See Fischer's position that these clichés reflect an androcentric perspective that erroneously views women in labor who do not give birth to a baby as a symbol of failure and panic (Isa 26:18; 33:11; 59:4). See Irmtraud Fischer, "Isaiah: The Book of Female Metaphors," in *Feminist Biblical Interpretation*, ed. Luise Schottroff and Marie-Theres Wacker (Grand Rapids: Eerdmans, 2012), 305.

15. Anker, "Metaphors of Pain," 66.

altered, is Jer 30–31, which forms part of what is called the little book of comfort (Jer 29–33).[16] As elsewhere in the book of Jeremiah (4:31; 6:24; 13:21; 22:23), in 30:6 the woman-in-labor metaphor is used to denote the extreme vulnerability that people experienced in the face of disaster when it is asked why strong men have become like women crouching in the excruciating pain associated with childbirth. Jeremiah 30:6 thus utilizes the connotations of pain and the inability to control one's circumstances, as well as the panic associated with the birthing process, to express something of the trauma effected by the Babylonian invasion and subsequent exile. In this text, though, one finds an explicit reference to the agony of the strong warrior-males (כל־גבר). By applying this metaphor to the strong men of the community, Jer 30:6 communicates, in even stronger terms, just how dire the situation is in which the people of Judah find themselves, for if the strong men are panicking and feeling utterly helpless, what chance do the rest of the population have?[17]

In Jer 31:8–9, though, the woman-in-labor metaphor is used for quite a different effect when this metaphor is introduced in the context of restoration and the promise of new life. Together with a group of mothers and disabled people, those in labor are included in a parade of seemingly vulnerable people called in verse 8 by God to lead the procession back home, so serving as evidence of God's new creation:

> See, I am going to bring them from the land of the north,
>   and gather them from the farthest parts of the earth,
> among them the blind and the lame,
>   those with child and those in labor, together;
>   a great company, they shall return here.
> With weeping they shall come,
>   and with consolations I will lead them back,
> I will let them walk by brooks of water,
>   in a straight path in which they shall not stumble;
> for I have become a father to Israel,
>   and Ephraim is my firstborn. (31:8–9)

---

16. This section offers a summary of a more extended argument found in my essay, Claassens, "Rhetorical Function," 68–74.

17. O'Connor, *Jeremiah*, 125. See also Angela Bauer, *Gender in Jeremiah*, StBibLit 5 (New York: Lang, 2003), 162.

That mothers are included with the women in labor bestows some very different connotations on this metaphor. It reminds the reader of the ultimate goal of labor—to bring new life into the world, which offers a sharp contrast to how this metaphor is used in 30:6, where the labor appeared to be futile. Therefore, even though this group may appear vulnerable, the mothers and the soon-to-be mothers hold the future in their hands.[18]

Moreover, in Jer 31:8, the act of including mothers together with women in labor also reminds the reader of the ultimate goal of labor: to give birth. In terms of trauma theory, the notion of birth is often used to denote the sense of a new beginning.[19] For the survivors of the Babylonian exile, the connotations of new life that are associated with the woman-in-labor metaphor in Jer 31 served as a creative means of conceptualizing their survival as a people—the notion of giving birth used to denote the future that God will give to the people in the land.

It is significant to see how the metaphor of a woman in labor is found in the context of restoration, as is evident in the repeated references that denote salvation in these particular chapters of Jeremiah. Throughout Jer 30–31, one finds references to God returning the people to the land (30:3, 10), saving the people (30:7), and gathering the people who were scattered (30:11; 31:10). God's salvation of the people is imaged in terms of God breaking the yoke from their necks (30:8), turning their mourning into joy (31:13), and restoring the health of the people (30:17).

In particular, the woman-in-labor metaphor in Jer 31 is transformed into a source of hope as the little scroll of consolation envisions a newly constituted community, including mothers and women in labor, that occurs in the context of God's liberative action of building and planting the people. A good example of this in 31:4–5 offers a sharp contrast to the exiles' experience of being uprooted and broken down. In this text, not only is the survival of the people imagined, in which the mothers and soon-to-be mothers play a central role, but also the land will be restored, yielding its fruit once more—its fertility matching the fertility envisioned by the reference to mothers and women in labor in 31:8.

Jeremiah 31:8–9 thus serves as a good example of how the woman-in-labor metaphor is transformed in order to transcend its original meaning, of which visible traces remain in the occurrence of the conventional use

---

18. O'Connor, *Jeremiah*, 106.
19. Flora Keshgegian, *Redeeming Memories: A Theology of Healing and Transformation* (Nashville: Abingdon, 2000), 64.

in Isa 30:6. In this creative application of the woman-in-labor metaphor, one finds that the women in labor are no longer hopeless and helpless but strong, active subjects who are marching to the future and who carry within them the promise of new life. In a great reversal, the strong men of 30:6 are called women in labor, only for the women in labor now to embrace a new kind of power, which signifies the power to give birth to a new generation who will return to the land and build up what was broken down, and plant what was uprooted.

4.2. Deutero- and Trito-Isaiah

A second prophetic book that offers some interesting examples of reframing the conventional understating of the metaphor of a woman in labor is Isaiah. In two texts that come from Deutero- and Trito-Isaiah, respectively, one finds some creative reapplications of the woman-in-labor metaphor as it speaks in new contexts.

Actually, in a number of texts in what is called First Isaiah, one sees how the metaphor of a woman in labor is used to express the traditional understanding of pain and anguish in the context of war and military invasion (see, e.g., Isa 13:8; 21:3). In this regard, 26:17–18 offers already a slight variation of the traditional application of the metaphor of the woman in labor. In a profound expression of the experience of communal suffering, the people liken themselves to pregnant women who are on the verge of giving birth. However, despite the extreme birthing pains, and notwithstanding the repeated reference to writhing (חול) that denotes the contractions associated with being in labor, all of this proves to be futile, as they lament: "We were pregnant, we writhed/labored [חלנו] like we were giving birth [ילדנו] to wind" (26:18). In this example of the woman-in-labor metaphor, the hopelessness of the situation in which the people of Judah find themselves is portrayed in terms of the absolute futility of the labor pains. No amount of contractions will yield new life—wind in this instance symbolizing "nothingness." As Sarah Dille writes, "All the pain and anguish of labor is for naught. The people are unable to accomplish anything; they are powerless."[20]

However, what is quite interesting about the occurrence of the woman-in-labor metaphor in the book of Isaiah is that two texts from

---

20. Dille, *Mixing Metaphors*, 63.

Deutero-Isaiah and Trito-Isaiah, respectively, reframe and challenge the conventional understanding of that metaphor as it also finds expression in Isa 26:18. These two texts that come from some later period underscore the ongoing process of sense making and dealing with a traumatic past.

Thus, in Isa 42:13–14, one sees how the metaphor of a woman in labor is applied to God when God in the first person exclaims:

> For a long time I have held my peace,
>   I have kept still and restrained myself;
> now I will cry out like a woman in labor,
>   I will gasp and pant.

What is quite distinctive about this occurrence of the woman-in-labor metaphor, besides being the only instance of this metaphor being used for God, is the introduction of the metaphor of a mighty warrior in the preceding verse when God is said to go "forth like a soldier, like a warrior he stirs up his fury; he cries out, he shouts aloud, he shows himself mighty against his foes" (Isa 42:13). By using these two paradoxical metaphors together to describe God, the traditional meaning of this metaphor is subverted by suppressing some of the more customary connotations of the woman-in-labor metaphor such as pain, panic, and vulnerability that we find in other occurrences of this metaphor in the prophetic literature.[21] In Isa 42:14, the element of crying out in pain that is typically found in the context of childbirth is elevated as this becomes a sign of breaking the silence that for a long time marked the people's experience of the divine.[22] Bergmann describes the dramatic change that has taken place in terms of the way this particular instance of the woman-in-labor metaphor functions in this text: "The metaphor of birth usually describes a person at the crossroads between life and death, but here YHWH is acting like a woman giving birth appears to be the beginning of something new."[23]

---

21. Fischer argues that in this text the metaphor is focused on the life-giving potential of childbirth instead of fixating on the associations of panic and excruciating pain ("Egalitär entworfen," 292). See also Løland, who argues that a "new context and a new target can create new salient features" (*Silent or Salient Gender?*, 123). As she writes: "Even through pain, fear, and struggle are salient both in a labor process and in our text, a woman in labor is not (only) powerless, and the simile does not picture a powerless God" (125).

22. Dille, *Mixing Metaphors*, 69.

23. Bergmann, "We Have Seen the Enemy," 661; see also Darr, "Like Warrior," 564.

This new understanding of the woman-in-labor metaphor is furthermore evident in terms of the motif of light and darkness that features prominently in this text. With reference to the proclamation by God in Isa 42:16, "I will turn the darkness before them into light," which follows closely after the woman-in-labor metaphor in 42:14, Dille observes that a central aspect of the birthing process is to move from darkness into the light. She writes: "If a child remains in the womb, it will die. It must move into the light to receive life. The release of the Israelite captives is thus implicitly a release from the womb to a successful birth and new life."[24]

It is thus evident that a few authors who have recently written on this text agree that the metaphor of a woman in labor is used for God in a distinctly different way from what has been the customary association with this metaphor, when it is transformed in such a way so as to express the hope for a new creation that is rooted in the belief in a God who makes all things new.[25]

Moreover, a second text from Trito-Isaiah continues this process of reinterpreting and reframing the traditional application of the woman-in-labor metaphor in earlier prophetic traditions. Isaiah 66:7–9 reinterprets in particular the notion of the labor process being futile in nature, as a way of describing the utter hopelessness of the situation, for example, in Isa 26:18, which states that even before her labor pains are due to start, Daughter Zion already has successfully given birth to her children.[26] What is unique about this text is that Godself is taking an active role in the delivery process, serving as the divine midwife, who is responsible for the birth and safely bringing the babies into the world:[27] "Shall I position for birth but not bring forth? Shall I who cause birth shut the womb?" (Isa 66:9). As in Isa 42:13–14, the focus in 66:6–9 falls on an active God who will act in a purposeful fashion to save the people of Jerusalem. Both of these texts from Deutero- and Trito-Isaiah thus speak clearly of transformation and a new creation. It appears that these texts are in direct conversation with those instances of the woman-in-labor metaphors that have been used both in earlier Isaianic traditions and elsewhere in the prophetic traditions

---

24. Dille, *Mixing Metaphors*, 70.
25. Dille, *Mixing Metaphors*, 71–72.
26. Darr, "No Strength to Deliver," 222.
27. L. Juliana Claassens, *Mourner, Mother, Midwife: Reimagining God's Liberating Presence* (Louisville: Westminster John Knox, 2012), 52–53.

to capture the people's anguish and despair due to one military onslaught after another.

Viewed in terms of trauma hermeneutics, one could argue that these two texts from Deutero- and Trito-Isaiah are good examples of how the traumatic memories captured in the woman-in-labor metaphor in earlier prophetic traditions are extracted and altered by introducing creative divine images that provide the necessary narrative framework to help the trauma survivors look at their traumatic past in a new way, thereby transforming a situation of death and despair into one of new life.

4.3. Micah 4–5

A final text in which the metaphor of a woman in labor is transformed in quite a significant fashion is Mic 4:9–5:3.[28] In her commentary on Micah in the Wisdom Commentary Series, Julia O'Brien reads this book as a product of the Persian period, which leads to my decision to treat this text last in this essay. Drawing on some compelling arguments by Ehud Ben Zvi and Oded Lipschits, O'Brien paints the context of Micah as one of impoverishment, crop failures, and heavy taxation under Persian imperial policies.[29] O'Brien imagines this community in duress as one "with members still scattered abroad, a society economically drained by support for war, and a Jerusalem without international standing."[30]

It is in this context of deprivation and suffering that one finds the longing for a different world as expressed in the vision in Mic 4–5, which imagines the exaltation of Daughter Jerusalem and her king.[31] Already in the opening verses in 4:1–7, one sees something of this desire for a restored city, with all the nations streaming to Jerusalem to worship God on his holy mountain. This vision is followed in 4:8–13 by a further promise of

---

28. An earlier version of this exposition on the birth imagery in Mic 4–5 appeared in Claassens, "From Traumatic to Narrative Memories."

29. Ehud Ben Zvi, *Micah*, FOTL 21B (Grand Rapids: Eerdmans, 2000), 9–10; Oded Lipschits, "Achaemenid Imperial Policy, Settlement Processes in Palestine, and the Status of Jerusalem in the Middle of the Fifth Century BCE," in *Judah and the Judeans in the Persian Period*, ed. Oded Lipschits and Manfred Oeming (Winona Lake, IN: Eisenbrauns, 2006), 19–52; Julia M. O'Brien, *Micah: Wisdom Commentary* (Collegeville, MN: Liturgical Press, 2015), xlix–liii.

30. O'Brien, *Micah*, 42.

31. O'Brien, *Micah*, 39–41.

restoring Daughter Zion to a position of honor and strength, in which the woman in labor metaphor plays a central role.

At first, it seems as if the woman in labor is used in its conventional sense as an image denoting panic and fear, when the female subject, Daughter Zion, cries out in anguish in Mic 4:9 about the absence of a king to deliver her. However, immediately following this customary application of this metaphor, we see how the metaphor is transformed in an unexpected manner in 4:10, as the woman who finds herself in the midst of labor emerges as a warrior who will go out of the city, where she will be delivered and redeemed by the liberator God. In an enactment of the holy-war tradition, Daughter Zion is said to be victorious over her enemies and promises to offer their spoils to her God. As O'Brien describes this portrayal of Daughter Zion in 4:13: "The newly empowered Daughter Zion is pictured with horns of iron and hooves of bronze, treading nations underfoot as it were grain on a threshing floor."[32]

In yet another important alteration of the metaphor of a woman in labor, in Mic 5:3 (MT 5:2), a woman is said to successfully give birth to a child—a text that, like Isa 7:14, has typically been associated with the birth of the Messiah in a little town in Bethlehem.[33] The birth of this child encapsulates the hope for a new ruler in the line of David to come, and it dramatically transforms the associations of despair, panic, and hopelessness in the way the metaphor of a woman in labor is used elsewhere in the prophetic traditions. By reframing the woman-in-labor metaphor in this unique way, the text in Mic 4–5 speaks of the hope of restoration and deliverance, and of a reinstatement of the kingship that will reverberate far beyond this original text.[34]

In this regard, the metaphor of a woman-in-labor-turned-warrior serves as a sign of Daughter Zion's empowerment. Dille, for instance, demonstrates how both Mic 4:9–10 and Isa 42:13–14 use the woman-in-labor metaphor to innovative effect by identifying the woman in labor also as a mighty warrior, which dramatically changes the meaning of the metaphor, from its original connotations of helplessness, panic, and

---

32. O'Brien, *Micah*, 50.

33. Erin Runions, *Changing Subjects: Gender, Nation and Future in Micah* (London: Sheffield Academic, 2001), 160.

34. See O'Brien's helpful exposition of the interpretation history of this text in the Christian tradition (*Micah*, 60–65).

anguish, to speak of deliverance and in particular emphasize the female subject's agency.[35]

This unexpected transformation of the metaphor from an image of distress to one that envisions a productive outcome is rooted in a call to the people of Zion to "writhe" (חול) and "bring forth" (גוח), thus, to actually *be* women in labor who are embracing the labor process in order to join in bringing about deliverance from the enemy.[36] In relation to trauma hermeneutics, this focus on giving back agency to the trauma victim and encouraging him or her to take action in a context of inaction can be considered a positive development. Viewed in this way, the occurrence of the woman-in-labor metaphor in Mic 4–5 seems to be a good example of reframing of a traumatic memory in such a way as to bring about a change of perception that may help the individual to reconstitute himself or herself.

However, on the other hand, this particular reinterpretation of the woman-in-labor metaphor in Mic 4–5, which fitted perfectly at the time of narration, also may serve as a warning that all narrative frameworks that form part of the recovery process are not equally healthy for all times. Actually, this particular reinterpretation of the woman-in-labor metaphor in Mic 4–5 can be considered problematic for a number of reasons. First, the association of violence, with Daughter Zion demolishing the nations and looting their possessions to honor God, ought to be troubling to the contemporary reader. This nationalistic inclination surrounding this text in today's world of an ever-increasing nationalist emphasis by many nations, which is too often rooted in a distinct concern for self-preservation, protecting borders, and building walls that might be quite dangerous, is already evident in the opening vision in Mic 4:1–7. This text, which finds a parallel in Isa 2:1–4 but, according to O'Brien, is much less universalistic in nature that its parallel text, underscores Micah's preoccupation with making Jerusalem great again.

Second, feminist scholars such as O'Brien have expressed concern about the gendered imagery used to describe Daughter Zion in Mic 4. In particular, O'Brien is troubled by the animalistic imagery used for the female subject, as Daughter Zion is portrayed as "a threshing heifer … pulveriz[ing] everything underfoot."[37] Moreover, as elsewhere in the prophetic literature, language of sexual violence is used to capture the sheer

---

35. Dille, *Mixing Metaphors*, 58, 65–66.
36. Dille, *Mixing Metaphors*, 65.
37. O'Brien, *Micah*, 51–52.

vulnerability of the city being invaded by enemy forces. Therefore, the reframing of the woman-in-labor metaphor in Mic 4 continues to occur in the context of the continuing victimization of the city, personified as a young woman, when a verb denoting sexual violence and coercion (חנף) is used in Mic 4:11 to describe Daughter Zion's ongoing experience of humiliation and the threat of being violated.[38]

5. Conclusion

In this essay, I have shown how in a number of prophetic texts the metaphor of a woman in labor has been reframed to communicate the hope for life beyond trauma. In this regard, trauma hermeneutics serves as a valuable conversation partner in considering the rhetorical significance of the woman-in-labor metaphor as the people of Judah found ways to deal with their traumatic past. We saw that central to individuals and groups moving beyond traumatic memories is the ability to offer creative alterations that speak of the prophets' ability to reframe the original metaphor in terms of a new narrative framework in order to help their audience cope with the traumatic events they had lived through. These reformulations, for instance in the book of Jeremiah, show signs that the prophetic tradition is dynamic in nature and continues to grow and change in the process of helping its audience to find new forms of understanding that may help them move beyond their painful past. This includes, especially in the examples found in Deutero- and Trito-Isaiah, thinking differently about God as dramatically new images of God capture their hope for a new beginning. In the example of Micah, though, this process of coming to terms with a traumatic past offers a word of warning that the new narrative frameworks utilized not perpetuate past injustices in terms of gender constructions, but also in terms of a turning-inward mentality at the cost of others, where the hope for restoration and deliverance of "us" is directly linked to the humiliation and destruction of the Other.

Bibliography

Anker, Johan. "Metaphors of Pain: The Use of Metaphors in Trauma Narrative with Reference to Fugitive Pieces." *Literator* 30.2 (2009): 49–68.

---

38. O'Brien, *Micah*, 49.

Bauer, Angela. *Gender in Jeremiah*. StBibLit 5. New York: Lang, 2003.

Becker, Eve-Marie, Jan Dochhorn, and Else Holt, eds. *Trauma and Traumatization in Individual and Collective Dimensions: Insights from Biblical Studies and Beyond*. Göttingen: Vandenhoeck & Ruprecht, 2014.

Ben Zvi, Ehud. *Micah*. FOTL 21B. Grand Rapids: Eerdmans, 2000.

Bergmann, Claudia. "'Like a Warrior' and 'Like a Woman Giving Birth: Expressing Divine Immanence and Transcendence in Isaiah 42:10–17." Pages 38–56 in *Bodies, Embodiment, and Theology of the Hebrew Bible*. Edited by S. Tamar Kamionkowski and Wonil Kim. New York: T&T Clark, 2011.

———. "We Have Seen the Enemy, and He Is Only a 'She': The Portrayal of Warriors as Women." *CBQ* 69 (2007): 651–72.

Boase, Elizabeth, and Christopher G. Frechette, eds. *Bible through the Lens of Trauma*. SemeiaSt 86. Atlanta: SBL Press, 2016.

Claassens, L. Juliana. "From Traumatic to Narrative Memories: The Rhetorical Function of Birth Metaphors in Micah 4–5." *AcT* Supplement 26 (2018): 221–36.

———. "Like a Woman in Labor: Gender, Queer, Postcolonial and Trauma Perspectives on Jeremiah." Pages 117–32 in *Prophecy and Power: Jeremiah in Feminist and Postcolonial Perspective*. Edited by Christl M. Maier and Carolyn J. Sharp. London: Bloomsbury T&T Clark, 2013.

———. *Mourner, Mother, Midwife: Reimagining God's Liberating Presence*. Louisville: Westminster John Knox, 2012.

———. "The Rhetorical Function of the Woman in Labor Metaphor in Jeremiah 30–31: Trauma, Gender and Postcolonial Perspectives." *JTSA* 150 (2014): 67–84.

Darr, Katheryn Pfisterer. "Like Warrior, like Woman: Destruction and Deliverance in Isaiah 42:10–17." *CBQ* 49 (1987): 564–65.

———. "No Strength to Deliver: Bringing to Birth." Pages 205–24 in *Isaiah's Vision and the Family of God*. Louisville: Westminster John Knox, 1994.

———. "Two Unifying Female Images in the Book of Isaiah." Pages 17–30 in *Uncovering Ancient Stones: Essays in Memory of H. Niel Richardson*. Edited by Lewis M. Hopfe. Winona Lake, IN: Eisenbrauns, 1994.

Dille, Sarah. *Mixing Metaphors: God as Mother and Father in Deutero-Isaiah*. JSOTSup 398. London: T&T Clark, 2004.

Fischer, Irmtraud. "Egalitär entworfen: Hierarchisch gelebt Zur Problematik des Geschlechterverhältnisses und einer genderfairen Anthropologie im Alten Testament." Pages 265–98 in *Der Mensch im alten Israel:*

Neue Forschungen zur alttestamentlichen Anthropologie. Edited by Bernd Janowski and Kathrin Liess. HBS 59. Freiburg: Herder, 2009.

———. "Isaiah: The Book of Female Metaphors." Pages 303–18 *in Feminist Biblical Interpretation.* Edited by Luise Schottroff and Marie-Theres Wacker. Grand Rapids: Eerdmans, 2012.

Garber, David G. "Trauma and Biblical Studies." *CBR* 14 (2015): 24–44.

Keshgegian, Flora. *Redeeming Memories: A Theology of Healing and Transformation.* Nashville: Abingdon, 2000.

Lipschits, Oded. "Achaemenid Imperial Policy, Settlement Processes in Palestine, and the Status of Jerusalem in the Middle of the Fifth Century BCE." Pages 19–52 *in Judah and the Judeans in the Persian Period.* Edited by Oded Lipshits and Manfred Oeming. Winona Lake, IN: Eisenbrauns, 2006.

Løland, Hanne. *Silent or Salient Gender? The Interpretation of Gendered God-Language in the Hebrew Bible, Exemplified in Isaiah 42, 46, and 49.* FAT 2/32. Tübingen: Mohr Siebeck, 2008.

Meyers, Carol L. *Discovering Eve: Ancient Israelite Women in Context.* New York: Oxford University Press, 1988.

O'Brien, Julia M. *Micah: Wisdom Commentary.* Collegeville, MN: Liturgical Press, 2015.

O'Connor, Kathleen. *Jeremiah: Pain and Promise.* Minneapolis: Fortress, 2011.

Poser, Ruth. *Das Ezechielbuch als Trauma-Literatur.* VTSup 154. Leiden: Brill, 2012.

Runions, Erin. *Changing Subjects: Gender, Nation and Future in Micah.* London: Sheffield Academic, 2001.

Stulman, Louis. "Reading the Bible as Trauma Literature: The Legacy of the Losers." *CBW* 34 (2014): 1–13.

Embodied Memories: Gender-Specific Aspects of Prophecy as Trauma Literature

Ruth Poser

1. Introduction

Paul Kim and Louis Stulman describe the prophetic writings as a "meditation on the horror of war."[1] The multiplicity of voices that these writings enfold is, as Stulman puts it, "not only set against the background of war, but it reenacts the ravages of war in poetry and artistic prose."[2]

I myself have investigated the book of Ezekiel as trauma literature. I hold that this book is a theological treatise of the besiegement, conquest, and destruction of Jerusalem at the beginning of the sixth century BCE and the related mass deportations of 597 and 587 BCE.[3] As Kathleen O'Connor and Stulman have explicated, for example, the book of Jeremiah

---

1. Louis Stulman and Hyun Chul Paul Kim, *You Are My People: An Introduction to Prophetic Literature* (Nashville: Abingdon, 2010), 6.

2. Louis Stulman, "Reflections on the Prose Sermons in the Book of Jeremiah: Duhm's and Mowinckel's Contributions to Contemporary Trauma Readings," in *Bible through the Lens of Trauma*, ed. Elizabeth Boase and Christopher G. Frechette, SemeiaSt 86 (Atlanta: SBL Press, 2016), 126.

3. See Ruth Poser, *Das Ezechielbuch als Trauma-Literatur*, VTSup 154 (Leiden: Brill, 2012). See also Daniel L. Smith-Christopher, *A Biblical Theology of Exile* (Minneapolis: Fortress, 2002); David G. Garber, "Traumatizing Ezekiel, the Exilic Prophet," in *Psychology and the Bible: A New Way to Read the Scriptures*, vol. 2, *From Genesis to Apocalyptic Vision*, ed. J. Harold Ellens and Wayne G. Rollins (Westport, CT: Praeger, 2004), 215–35; Brad E. Kelle, "Dealing with the Trauma of Defeat: The Rhetoric of the Devastation and Rejuvenation of Nature in Ezekiel," *JBL* 128 (2009): 469–90; Nancy R. Bowen, *Ezekiel* (Nashville: Abingdon, 2010).

also is a case in point.⁴ Stulman connects the Jeremiah texts to descriptions of trauma researcher Judith Herman and writes:

> These texts represent on multiple levels "an affiliation of the powerless." They are texts beset with events that "overwhelm the ordinary human adaptions of life," events that involve "threats to life or bodily integrity, or a close personal [or communal] encounter with violence and death," events that "confront human beings with the extremities of helplessness and terror, and evoke the responses of catastrophe."⁵

The book of Isaiah, specifically Isa 40–66, is also shaped by catastrophe, even though (or perhaps because) it does not narrate it explicitly. It contains both responses and revisions to the interpretations of the traumatic events of the beginning of the sixth century BCE in other biblical writings.⁶

It is notable that all the named writings contain a wide range of gendered and even sexualized metaphors.⁷ Again and again, the city of Jerusalem is depicted as God's wife, and other cities also are portrayed as women. Defeated soldiers are said to become womanish, and even God her- or himself is pictured once and again as a cheated husband, father, and warrior as well as, even if the references are scantier, a woman in labor, midwife, and mother.

---

4. See Kathleen M. O'Connor, *Jeremiah: Pain and Promise* (Minneapolis: Fortress, 2011); O'Connor, "How Trauma Studies Can Contribute to Old Testament Studies," in *Trauma and Traumatization in Individual and Collective Dimensions: Insights from Biblical Studies and Beyond*, ed. Eve-Marie Becker, Jan Dochhorn, and Else Holt (Göttingen: Vandenhoeck & Ruprecht, 2014), 210–22; Stulman, "Reflections."

5. Stulman, "Reflections," 126. See also Judith Herman, *Trauma and Recovery: The Aftermath of Violence—From Domestic Abuse to Political Terror*, rev. ed. (New York: Basic Books, 1997).

6. See Christopher G. Frechette, "Daughter Babylon Raped and Bereaved (Isaiah 47): Symbolic Violence and Meaning-Making in Recovery from Trauma," in Boase and Frechette, *Bible through the Lens*, 79.

7. In this essay, I focus on the books of Isaiah, Jeremiah, and Ezekiel. Nevertheless, traces of trauma are observable in nearly all the books of the Former and the Latter Prophets. Irmtraud Fischer also has investigated the book of Jonah as trauma narrative. See Fischer, "Jona: Prophet eines traumatisierten Volkes," in *Vom Leben umfangen: Ägypten, das Alte Testament und das Gespräch der Religionen, Gedenkschrift für Manfred Görg*, ed. Stefan Jakob Wimmer and Georg Gafus (Münster: Ugarit-Verlag, 2014), 33–41. Similarly, David Janzen analyses the Deuteronomistic History's narrative as trauma literature. See Janzen, *The Violent Gift: Trauma's Subversion of the Deuteronomistic History's Narrative*, OTL 561 (London: Bloomsbury, 2014).

Consequently, *which* traumas and, more importantly, *whose* traumas are pictured in the prophetic writings? What role does gender play in this context?

2. What Does *Trauma* Mean?

2.1. A Definition

In order to discuss the prophetic writings as trauma literature, the following definition provides a starting point. Trauma can be described as the "experience of a fundamental discrepancy between a threatening situation and an individual's possibilities for overcoming it. This experience is accompanied by feelings of helplessness, defenselessness, and abandonment and can permanently disrupt the person's understanding of the self and the world."[8] Hence, trauma is not an inherent element of an event or experience as such;[9] not everyone exposed to a potentially traumatizing event develops traumatic symptoms. Nevertheless, survivors of war, torture, and sexual violence are affected with particular frequency, as are those who have had to flee or been uprooted from their homelands. In general, we can assume that "the traumatizing effect of an event increases according to the size of the role that human beings play in bringing it about and the closeness of the relationship between perpetrator and victim."[10] Other factors include the degree of endangerment of one's own person and involvement in the event, exposure to injury and death, the frequency and duration of traumatic situations, and the resources available for overcoming the threat (resilience). Last, the response of the people in the victim's environment (or society in general) can also be decisive.

---

8. Gottfried Fischer and Peter Riedesser, *Lehrbuch der Psychotraumatologie*, 3rd ed. (München: Reinhardt, 2003), 82. Translation by Deborah L. Schneider, who translated my originally German essay: Ruth Poser, "No Words: The Book of Ezekiel as Trauma Literature and a Response to Exile," in Boase and Frechette, *Bible Through the Lens of Trauma*, 27–48). Except where otherwise noted, Schneider also translated all quotations in this article that were originally in German.

9. See Fischer and Riedesser, *Lehrbuch der Psychotraumatologie*, 62.

10. Peter Riedesser, "Belastende Kriegserfahrungen in der Kleinkindzeit," in *Kindheiten im Zweiten Weltkrieg: Kriegserfahrungen und deren Folgen aus psychohistorischer Perspektive*, ed. Hartmut Radebold, Gereon Heuft, and Insa Fooken (Weinheim: Juventa, 2006), 37.

Against this background, the historical events experienced by the inhabitants of Jerusalem and Judah at the beginning of the sixth century BCE are quite likely to have elicited trauma. Those affected by the siege experienced, as the books of Jeremiah and Ezekiel put it, famine, pestilence, and the sword (compare, e.g., Jer 16:4; Ezek 5:12), atrocities, torture, forms of sexual or sexualized violence, pillaging, and arson. Deportees had to endure a grueling march over hundreds of miles. They witnessed the weakening and death of fellow captives. Families were torn apart, and most exiles had no hope of ever returning home.[11]

If we take this background as factual and visualize it as a concrete reality, it becomes possible to read the prophetic writings engaging with this historical setting in a new light—as literary confrontations with the violence of war that men,[12] women, and children actually experienced, and as theological examples of trauma literature.

2.2. Language and Symptoms of Trauma

Traumatic events trigger a great variety of responses, but on closer examination many of them can be connected to two fundamental, contrary impulses: on the one hand, the violence that victims have suffered preoccupies them and constantly intrudes on their thoughts; on the other hand, victims try as hard as they can to ward off feelings of anxiety, pain, and helplessness, and to protect themselves from everything that is associated with the trauma. The term "intrusion symptoms" is used to describe situations in which victims relive the traumatic situation, which include intrusive thoughts, nightmares, and flashbacks. In contrast, "constriction symptoms" may manifest as psychological numbing, rigidity, and social withdrawal.[13]

This dialectic is closely linked to victims' inability to express what happened to them in symbolic language. They want to tell their stories—indeed, they must, in order to grasp the traumatic parts of their life histories—but they are often unable to do so because they lack words for

---

11. For more details, see Poser, *Ezechielbuch als Trauma-Literatur*, 121–248.

12. This essay refers to the gender/sex categories (e.g., men, women, male, female) present in the biblical text as a matter of convenience, not as a sign of acceptance of those categories.

13. See Fischer and Riedesser, *Lehrbuch der Psychotraumatologie*, 44–46.

their experiences. We have no language with which to express senseless violence, and perhaps no such language should exist.[14]

That so many victims of trauma are unable to tell the story of what happened to them, or find it extremely difficult to do so, leads to (further) symptoms. Trauma researcher Bessel van der Kolk sees the cause of this development in the particular nature of traumatic experiences: traumatic memories cannot be processed symbolically—a necessary step for "classifying them correctly and integrating them into [the individual's] other experiences." Instead of being processed like ordinary information, "they are first registered as feelings or affective states."[15] Van der Kolk, accordingly, assumes the existence of a trauma memory with specific processes for storing such incidents. In many cases, traumatic memories cannot be recalled as such; instead, they are largely reexperienced as affective states, in the form of visual images or physical sensations (embodied memories). These emotional and sensory states are characterized by their fragmentary nature and hence are difficult to express in words. Trauma victims are often unable to translate what they have suffered into a personal narrative. Nevertheless, the passage of time is less likely to distort traumatic memories than ordinary ones,[16] and certain internal and external stimuli can continue to trigger them for the rest of the victim's life. In such cases, they may surface (suddenly) or intrude on consciousness. When this happens, victims frequently experience the memories with the same degree of emotional force and sensory intensity as the original traumatic event.

In the context of trauma theory, the central goal in a recovery process is to reconstruct the traumatic event so that a patient can integrate a memory into his or her personal biography. The experience must be relived step by step—often an extremely painful process. The aim is not to "habituate [the patient] to anxiety and stress, as used to be assumed, but rather to 'neutralize' and modify the memory by creating a coherent personal narrative." Those affected should "be able to live with the traumatic

---

14. See Martina Kopf, *Trauma und Literatur: Das Nicht-Erzählbare erzählen—Assia Djebar und Yvonne Vera* (Frankfurt: Brandes & Apsel, 2005), 9–67.

15. Bessel A. van der Kolk, "Trauma and Memory," in *Traumatic Stress: The Effects of Overwhelming Experience on Mind, Body, and Society*, ed. Bessel A. van der Kolk, Alexander C. McFarlane, and Lars Weisaeth (New York: Guilford, 1996), 296.

16. See Fischer and Riedesser, *Lehrbuch der Psychotraumatologie*, 284–87.

memory without being handicapped by unresolved fears and distorted beliefs about themselves or the world."[17]

When victims embed the trauma in the framework of their own history, it acquires meaning for their identity, either explicitly or implicitly. Applying to both individual and collective experiences, survivors may interpret the traumatic experience in terms of fate, a catastrophe, a test, or as punishment or guilt, but also as a challenge or opportunity for growth.[18] Rationalizing a traumatic event in this manner has its problematic side, however, since, by making it possible to grasp an occurrence that was originally senseless, one can also render it banal.

3. How Trauma Becomes Literature

Anyone who attempts to turn individual or collective traumas into literature unavoidably enters the realm of paradox. On the one hand, massive eruptions of brutality resist expression; there are no words to represent these experiences. On the other hand, it is absolutely necessary to bear witness, to respond so that horror and violence do not have the last word. In recent years, scholars have occupied themselves increasingly with the question of how trauma is portrayed in literary texts and what kinds of narrative motifs and structures can appropriately serve this aim. The central dialectic of trauma as described by psychologists (see section 1.2 above) is also reflected in literary works on the subject. Stephan Freißmann notes that these works are characterized by certain strategies of repetition and indication of inexpressibility in the form of gaps.[19]

---

17. Martin Sack, "Narrative Arbeit im Kontext 'schonender Traumatherapie,'" in *Narrative Bewältigung von Trauma und Verlust*, ed. Carl Eduard Scheidt et al. (Stuttgart: Schattauer, 2015), 151.

18. See Carl Eduard Scheidt and Gabriele Lucius-Hoene, "Kategorisierung und narrative Bewältigung bindungsbezogener Traumaerfahrungen im Erwachsenenbindungsinterview," in Scheidt et al., *Narrative Bewältigung von Trauma*, 27. Individual and collective trauma differ considerably from each other, even if there might be similarities regarding the symptoms of an individual and of a community. See, e.g. Angela Kühner, *Kollektive Traumata—Annahmen, Argumente, Konzepte: Eine Bestandsaufnahme nach dem 11. September* (Berlin: Berghof Forschungszentrum, 2002), 58–63.

19. See Stephan Freißmann, "Trauma als Erzählstrategie" (thesis, University of Konstanz, 2005), 13, https://tinyurl.com/SBL6016q.

We observe the same strategies of repetition and omission or gaps in the book of Ezekiel. Ezekiel 4–24 can be read as recurring reenactment of the destruction of Jerusalem with increasingly violent imagery. Between chapters 24 and 25, at the point when the narrative reaches the siege of the city (24:1–2), God announces the end of the Judean capital one more time with the particularly gruesome image of a totally burned cooking pot (24:3–13). Exactly at that point, YHWH ceases to focus on "God's" city and turns attention to the surrounding nations (Ezek 25–32). The book never presents the annihilation of Jerusalem directly; rather, it is anticipated (Ezek 4–24) or mentioned as an occurrence in the past (33:21–22). In another sense, the events of 587 BCE are omitted in the book of Isaiah.[20]

According to Ronald Granofsky, the key technique of the modern trauma novel involves symbolization.[21] His study reflects two fundamental insights from psycho-traumatology—that the effect of traumatic situations is to destroy "the capacity to symbolize them and grasp their meaning," and that "trauma can only be assimilated by placing it in a symbolic sequence."[22] He observes further that the process of symbolization permits a confrontation with traumatic material with some degree of protection.[23] In the context of this literary symbolization process, most of the motifs involve, either directly or indirectly, biological functions or stages of development, such as birth, growth, eating, sexuality, and death. That seems to be immediately applicable to the metaphorical biographies in Ezek 16 and 23.

Regarding the motif of eating in literary treatments of trauma, Granofsky writes: "The 'perversion' of normal eating patterns, for example, in cannibalism, will often be a symbol for the dislocation effects of trauma both on an individual and a collective scale. In the trauma novel, certain kinds of eating may be symbolic of the necessity to assimilate raw experience, so to speak."[24] This, too, seems to hold true for the book of Ezekiel, which contains many scenes of aberrant eating—the prophet swallowing a scroll (2:8–3:3) or

---

20. On the exile as a void or gap in the book of Isaiah, see, e.g., Ulrich Berges, *Das Buch Jesaja: Komposition und Endgestalt* (Freiburg: Herder, 1998), 314–21.

21. See Ronald Granofsky, *The Trauma Novel: Contemporary Symbolic Depictions of Collective Disaster* (New York: Lang, 1995), 7.

22. Werner Bohleber, "Die Entwicklung der Traumatheorie in der Psychoanalyse," *Psyche* 9/10 (2000): 822–23; see also O'Connor, "Trauma Studies," 213–19.

23. See Granofsky, *Trauma Novel*, 6–7.

24. Granofsky, *Trauma Novel*, 14.

eating disgusting food (4:9–13), "cannibalism" (5:10), "consuming" fires (e.g. 15:4), and "devouring" famine (e.g., 7:15), as well as the already mentioned cooking pot (24:3–13). Not until Ezek 34 do eating and drinking gradually reacquire their role as sustenance for individuals and the community.[25]

The process of (re)symbolization is particularly evident in the book of Ezekiel with its use of the motif רוח, "air in motion—or breath, wind, spirit,"[26] which occurs fifty-two times. From the start, רוח appears as a powerful force, activating participants in the narrative and setting changes in motion. Up to Ezek 20, its nature is ambiguous—it moves the wheels of the throne (e.g., 1:12), but it can also be a windstorm that can bring down walls, signifying God's wrath (e.g., 13:11). At various points, it serves as a metaphor for deportation and captivity (e.g., 5:10). Furthermore, it may refer to the spirit of an individual, which can suffer harm or go astray (e.g., 11:5) but also be renewed (e.g., 11:19). After God proclaims that the news of the coming catastrophe will cause every spirit to grow faint (21:12), the term רוח does not occur again in a negative context—with one exception. This, however, represents the peak of its destructive potential (27:26). When רוח is used after Ezek 36:26, it functions as an unambiguously constructive source of energy that underlies and renews life, as 37:1–10 shows. It becomes a symbol for the life of Israel in the face of God and in the torah (37:14; 39:29; 42:20). The images of restoration recall רוח as an immense force that contains destructive potential but also is necessary for life. In this sense, רוח appears fitting for expressing the "secret of surviving" the catastrophe in a language close to the victims' bodily and religious experiences.[27]

While Helen Schüngel-Straumann assumes that the use of רוח as a feminine noun highlights "a background of wifelike experiences related to creation, coming to life, and giving birth,"[28] in my opinion, the grammati-

---

25. For a more detailed analysis of this motif, see Ruth Poser, "'Das Gericht geht durch den Magen': Die verschlungene Schriftrolle (Ez 2,8b–3,3) und andere Essensszenarien im Ezechielbuch," in *Essen und Trinken in der Bibel: Ein literarisches Festmahl für Rainer Kessler zum 65. Geburtstag*, ed. Michaela Geiger, Christl M. Maier, and Uta Schmidt (Gütersloh: Gütersloher Verlagshaus, 2009), 116–30.

26. For a more general discussion of רוח, see Rainer Albertz and Claus Westermann, "רוּחַ," *TLOT* 3:1202–20; Sven Tengström, "רוּחַ I–VI," *TDOT* 13:365–96.

27. For a more detailed analysis of the symbol רוח in Ezekiel, see Poser, *Ezechielbuch als Trauma-Literatur*, 543–66.

28. Helen Schüngel-Straumann, "Geist (AT)," in *Das wissenschaftliche Bibellexikon im Internet*, ed. Michaela Bauks and Klaus Koenen (2009), https://tinyurl.com/SBL6016r.

cal gender of the noun is secondary to this process of (re)symbolization. In the book of Ezekiel, רוח appears as a feminine noun often (e.g., 2:2; 17:10), but sometimes the grammatical gender is masculine (e.g., 27:26); and sometimes the word remains undefined, mainly when *God's* רוח is involved (e.g., 37:1). In this sense, רוח seems to be an inclusive or even a queer symbol, going beyond dichotomizing categories and even the book's gendered conceptions of God and human beings.

4. Siege Warfare as Gendered Warfare—and the Prophetic Writings

Even in antiquity, the conquest of cities and countries in war is deeply shaped by a mechanism that scholars refer to as the gendering of warfare. As Joshua Goldstein states, this mechanism includes mainly three aspects:

> *First*, and most strongly ... the toughening up of boys is found robustly across cultures, and by linking bravery and discipline in war to manhood—with shame as enforcement—many cultures use gender to motivate participation in combat. *Second* ... women actively reinforce—in various feminine war roles such as mothers, lovers, and nurses—men's tough, brave masculinity. *Third* ... male soldiers use gender to encode domination, feminizing enemies. Connected with this coding, but more elusive empirically, are the possible heightened ... sexuality of male soldiers, and the more intense exploitation of women's labor in wartime.[29]

For two reasons, the gendering of warfare might be even more effective in the context of (ancient) siege warfare. First, siege warfare involves the civilian population of a city or country—women, children, and older people—in a direct way. In his book *Ancient Siege Warfare* (1999), Paul Bentley Kern describes this as follows:

> Women and children were an essential part of siege warfare. Their presence threatened the notion of war as a contest between warriors, undermined the conventional standards of honor and prowess that governed ancient warfare, and paradoxically made war less restrained by creating a morally chaotic cityscape in which not only the walls collapsed but deeply rooted social and moral distinctions as well. We cannot

---

29. Joshua S. Goldstein, *War and Gender: How Gender Shapes the War System and Vice Versa* (Cambridge: Cambridge University Press, 2000), 406.

understand siege warfare without understanding the plight of women and children and the effect of their presence on war.[30]

Second, it must be considered that cities often were (and sometimes even are) presented as female entities. Consequently, the conquest and domination of a city in war is pictured as the violent conquest and domination of a woman. In siege warfare, real violence against a city as metaphorical woman merged into real violence against *real* women living in the city. Kern writes about this process thus:

> Rape was the ultimate violation of women, marking the complete possession of them by the soldiers who had taken possession of their city. From the phallic shape of the battering ram trying to penetrate the walls of a city to … soldiers pillaging and raping in a violated city was a logical progression. All warfare has a strong sexual undercurrent, but siege warfare was an explicit battle for sexual rights.… The raping that frequently followed the fall of a city starkly symbolized total victory in total war.[31]

In my opinion, texts such as Ezek 16 and 23 or Isa 47 cannot (and should not) be interpreted without strongly taking notice of the social background of ancient siege warfare and the gendering of warfare mechanisms. It is more than likely that rape of women was systematically applied as a weapon in ancient siege warfare, even though it is not mentioned in the inscriptions of the Assyrian kings or on the Assyrian palace reliefs, which fictionalize a wide range of wartime atrocities.[32]

In the Latter Prophets, wartime rape of women is referred to twice—in Isa 13:16 and Zech 14:2. Even the fact that these verses must be characterized as announcements of doom does not call into question that these announcements are experience based, as Lam 5:11 might indicate. Biblical narratives such as Gen 34; Judg 19; and 2 Sam 13 also reflect a knowledge of the correlation between sexual and wartime violence. According

---

30. Paul Bentley Kern, *Ancient Siege Warfare* (Bloomington: Indiana University Press, 1999), 4.

31. Kern, *Siege Warfare*, 81. See also Brad E. Kelle, "Wartime Rhetoric: Prophetic Metaphorization of Cities as Female," in *Writing and Reading War: Rhetoric, Gender, and Ethics in Biblical and Modern Contexts*, ed. Brad E. Kelle, Frank Ritchel Ames, and Jacob L. Wright, SymS 42 (Atlanta: Society of Biblical Literature, 2008), 104.

32. See Angelika Berlejung, "Gewalt ins Bild gesetzt. Kriegsdarstellungen auf neuassyrischen Palastreliefs," *BK* 60 (2005): 205–11.

to Alice Keefe (and similar to, e.g., Ezek 16; 23), in these narratives, the woman's body, disrupted by sexual violence, functions as a metonymy for the social body, for the society devastated by war.[33] We thus may assume that the war crime of rape, on the one hand, was perceived as a breach of taboo and "a nightmare representing the collapse of human culture," but, on the other hand, constituted "the most common atrocity against noncombatants in siege warfare."[34]

At the same time, there are strong indications that even men—civilians and, probably more often, male soldiers defending the city—were affected by sexual and sexualized violence and humiliation by the intruding army. This, too, is attributable to the mechanisms of gendered warfare by which *all* members of the defeated army are feminized, while the members of the prevailing army prove (or are proven) to be "real men." The sources are quite silent in this respect also; but in Sennacherib's report of his military campaigns, there is an explicit hint at genital mutilation: "(Their) testicles I cut off, and tore out their privates like the seeds of cucumbers" (*ARAB* 2.127). A similar image might be implied in some texts of the Saul-David narratives (e.g., 1 Sam 18:11, 25–27; 19:10; 20:33; 24:5; 26:7–8).[35]

Several times defeated male soldiers are compared with or even designated as women (Isa 19:16; Jer 50:37; 51:30; Nah 3:13). In Jer 50:37, we read: "A sword against her [that is, Chaldea's] horses and against her chariots, and against all the foreign troops in her midst, that they may become women!"[36] Corrine Patton does not read these latter references as merely figurative but argues,

> Although the practice of emasculation may not have been routinely performed, I expect it was common enough to be a real fear for any male who was captured in battle. Even postexilic texts such as Isa 56:3–5 speak of the inclusion into restored temple worship of those who had been emasculated. Apparently, mutilation of male genitals had been widespread enough for it to be of concern to those seeking restoration.[37]

---

33. See Alice A. Keefe, "Rapes of Women/Wars of Men," *Semeia* 61 (1993): 79–97.
34. Kern, *Siege Warfare*, 83.
35. See also Tracy M. Lemos, "Shame and Mutilation of Enemies in the Hebrew Bible," *JBL* 125 (2006): 225–41; Moshe Greenberg, *Ezekiel 21–37: A New Translation with Introduction and Commentary*, AB 22A (New York: Doubleday, 1997), 661–62.
36. Unless otherwise indicated, biblical translations follow the ESV (2016).
37. Corrine L. Patton, "'Should Our Sister Be Treated Like a Whore?': A Response to Feminist Critiques of Ezekiel 23," in *The Book of Ezekiel: Theological and Anthropo-*

In the Assyrian reliefs, the topic of feminization of the defeated also is quite prominent. Not only are the vanquished persons often pictured naked, but

> the naked enemy male is almost always positioned such that his genitalia face the viewer, and in many cases are also within the gaze of the Assyrian king. Corresponding to the written boast of having pierced or bored through the enemy, the naked soldier is often depicted visually being penetrated by a weapon, sometimes in a clearly sexual way.[38]

As a last example of the gendering of warfare, I want to highlight the Hebrew root גלה, which has quite many references in the Latter Prophets. In its different modifications, the word has a wide range of connotations. The original meaning might be "to uncover something or even somebody,"[39] but the nouns גולה and גלות denote "war captivity," and what is more, גולה has become a technical term for the Babylonian captivity of the Judeans. In combination with the object ערוה ("nakedness"), which often denotes the female genitalia, גלה points to "illegal" sexual intercourse (Lev 18; 20), and it can also be suggestive of rape, as in Ezek 22:10, where ענה is used as a byword for גלה. The uncovering expressed by גלה can also refer to an unmasking of guilt, as in Lam 2:14, or to the baring of a city's foundations in the context of war, as in Ezek 13:14. In Ezek 16:36–37, which is an announcement to the city of Jerusalem, the references to גלה as well as ערוה converge.

According to Daniel Smith-Christopher, this metaphor of stripping is drawn from the practice of stripping prisoners of war in Neo-Assyrian and Neo-Babylonian military practice.[40] He points to Isa 20, where the

---

logical Perspectives, ed. Margaret S. Odell and John T. Strong, SymS 9 (Atlanta: Society of Biblical Literature, 2000), 235.

38. Cynthia R. Chapman, "Sculpted Warriors: Sexuality and the Sacred in the Depiction of Warfare in the Assyrian Palace Reliefs and in Ezekiel 23:14–17," *ld* 1 (2007), 10, https://tinyurl.com/SBL6016s. A matching example of such a relief can be found in Poser, *Ezechielbuch als Trauma-Literatur*, 182 (fig. 3).

39. Yet, compare Claus Westermann and Rainer Albertz, who hold that there is no good cause "für die Annahme zweier verschiedener Wurzeln גלה; denn wie sich Auswanderung oder Verbannung als Entblößung des Landes verstehen läßt, der Ausdruck des Enthüllens, Entblößens also die Grundbedeutung von גלה sein könnte … so kann man auch umgekehrt argumentieren." See Westermann and Albertz, "גלה," *THAT* 1:419.

40. See Daniel L. Smith-Christopher, "Ezekiel in Abu Ghraib: Rereading Ezekiel 16:37–39 in the Context of Imperial Conquest," in *Ezekiel's Hierarchical World:*

prophet is said to have wandered naked for three years, which symbolizes war captivity. He also calls attention to the fact that, in the Assyrian reliefs, only male prisoners are pictured completely stripped, whereas female prisoners are never portrayed as completely naked. Instead, "the bronze gates of Shalmaneser III (858–824 BCE) from Balawat clearly depict Assyrian soldiers leading away captive women raising the front of their skirts."[41]

This seems to be a good parallel to Isa 47:2–3, a text that prefigures the decline of "daughter Babylon" in a manner reflecting the ruin of Jerusalem in Ezek 16; 23, and other texts:[42] "Take the millstones and grind flour, put off [גלה] your veil, strip off your robe, uncover [גלה] your legs, pass through the rivers. Your nakedness [ערוה] shall be uncovered [גלה], and your disgrace [חרפה][43] shall be seen."

5. Prophetic Texts Reflecting Traumatic Guilt and Shame

Psycho-traumatology reveals that many victims of trauma struggle with guilt and shame; often, this adds to the difficulty of talking about what they suffered (see section 1.2 above). If family members and friends have been murdered, some even feel guilty about having survived. Although there is no objective reason for them to blame themselves, occasionally survivors will accuse themselves instead of the perpetrator. Such an assumption of guilt after trauma is often connected with the fact "that it can be easier to maintain one's mental balance if one was guilty rather than completely helpless."[44]

In my opinion, this background of traumatic guilt plays an important role in the prophetic writings, the following aspects being most crucial: (1)

Wrestling with a Tiered Reality, ed. Stephen L. Cook and Corrine L. Patton, SymS 31 (Atlanta: Society of Biblical Literature, 2004), 141–57.

41. David Vanderhooft, *The Neo-Babylonian Empire and Babylon in the Latter Prophets* (Atlanta: Scholars Press, 1999), 182 (cited in Smith-Christopher, "Ezekiel in Abu Ghraib," 152). The matching examples from the reliefs can be found in Poser, *Ezechielbuch als Trauma-Literatur*, 192.

42. An interpretation of Isa 47 against the background of psycho-traumatology is presented by Frechette ("Daughter Babylon").

43. Nowhere else in the Hebrew Bible does the noun חרפה denote female genitalia. In Isa 47:3, the term might have been chosen in order to enlarge the meaning with regard to sociopolitical implications and to charge what is to be said with ambiguity. Concerning the root חרף, compare also Ernst Kutsch, "חרף II," *TDOT* 5:209–15.

44. Kühner, *Traumata*, 32.

the catastrophe occurs—as the texts put it—because there is no other way to expunge Israel's guilt; and (2) YHWH is the perpetrator. It is YHWH alone who is responsible for the people's exile, not the Babylonians, who only act(ed) as YHWH's tool. The assumption of guilt enables a powerless Israel to take the initiative and act effectively. If Israel follows God's commandments in the future, this will help ensure that no similar catastrophe ever occurs again. Assigning the role of perpetrator to God removes the terrible events from the sphere of human volition and earthly contingency, and it preserves the idea of YHWH as a deity of immense power. Or, as David Carr puts it in his book *Holy Resilience*:

> Such self-blame offered Israel a way to see itself as empowered in an otherwise helpless situation.... "For many who suffer deeply, the only thing that frightens them more than the idea that God is punishing them is the idea that God is not in charge at all." For some, such self-blame can be corrosive, undermining their faith. But for others the idea of a powerful God, even a judging God, can be reassuring. At least there is a chance to change one's behavior and be saved. Things can look quite different if the world is totally devoid of God. Then one is truly subject to its most powerful forces, even if they are brutally tyrannical.[45]

Ultimately, the burden of guilt ascribed to Israel not only establishes the basis to overcome the people's traumatic powerlessness, but also makes it possible for God to survive as their deity even after the catastrophe of exile.

But these justifications come at a price; one is left, on the one hand, with an image of God that seems violent or even sadistic, and, on the other hand, with a massive blaming-the-victim syndrome. On a metaphorical level, the roles of offender and victim are dualistically gendered—we mainly find (cities and countries as) female personifications, which are, due to their would-be extreme sinfulness, exposed to extreme violence on the part of men/God (see, e.g., Isa 1:21–31; 47; Jer 2–6; 13:20–27; Ezek 16; 23; Nah 3:1–7). The reference to female and male bodies naturally marked by the necessity to sin and, accordingly, to punish, makes it difficult to deconstruct or even "queer" the imagery—even though the male elites of Judah and Jerusalem are to be seen as implicit addressees of the

---

45. David M. Carr, *Holy Resilience: The Bible's Traumatic Origins* (New Haven: Yale University Press, 2014), 32–33; see also O'Connor, "Trauma Studies," 215–17.

texts.[46] Recently Brad Kelle has pointed out that the prophetic imagery of sexual/sexualized violence against women is found only in the context of the devastation of cities and countries, metaphorized as harlots, or as women committing adultery. For this, the (discursive) strategy of feminization and the knowledge of sexual/sexualized wartime atrocities are most crucial (see §3 above).[47]

The connection between female gender and sin, uncleanness, and moral wrongness manifesting itself on the surface of the debated texts is partly suspended within the progression of the prophetic narratives,[48] especially when the restoration of Jerusalem/Daughter Zion comes into view. However, the strategies developed in the prophetic books in this respect are quite different, the distinctions between Isaiah and Ezekiel being most impressive.[49]

In the book of Isaiah, namely, in Isa 54:5–8 (see 62:4–5), the recovery of the relationship between God and Jerusalem is (re-)fictionalized as heterosexual love affair, the time of catastrophe being defined as a stage of God's wrathful pullback from the bonds of marriage, which are now installed as perennial. But in Isa 40–66, Zion comes to the fore not only as a beloved woman but also as queen, respectively, as crown in God's

---

46. See, for example, Ilse Müllner, "Prophetic Violence: The Marital Metaphor and Its Impact on Female and Male Readers," in *Prophetie in Israel*, ed. Irmtraud Fischer, Konrad Schmid, and Hugh G. M. Williamson (Münster: LIT, 2003), 202–4; Jaqueline E. Lapsley, "The Proliferation of Grotesque Bodies in Ezekiel: The Case of Ezekiel 23," in *Ezekiel: Current Debates and Future Directions*, ed. William A. Tooman and Penelope Barter, FAT 112 (Tübingen: Mohr Siebeck, 2017), 382–86. On the difficulty of deconstructing or queering the imagery, see S. Tamar Kamionkowski, *Gender Reversal and Cosmic Chaos: A Study on the Book of Ezekiel*, JSOTSup 368 (Sheffield: Sheffield Academic, 2003); Deryn Guest, *Beyond Feminist Biblical Studies* (Sheffield: Sheffield Phoenix, 2012), 77–117 (ch. 3: "Genderqueer Analysis of the Pornoprophetic Debate").

47. See Kelle, "Wartime Rhetoric."

48. Smaller fractures are to be found within the texts themselves, e.g., Jer 13:23–24, where the addressee changes from *city-wife* (feminine singular) to a group (masculine plural), or Ezek 16:41, where quite immediately the "houses" of the city-wife are said to be burned. Yet compare also Ulrike Sals, *Die Biographie der "Hure Babylon": Studien zur Intertextualität der Babylon-Texte in der Bibel*, FAT 2/6 (Tübingen: Mohr Siebeck, 2004), 319.

49. Another strategy is found in the book of Jeremiah. Here, a restoration of the broken family seems to be looming while the gendered and sexualized role of the city-wife remains vacant (Jer 3:10–13; see O'Connor, *Pain*, 40).

hand (62:1–5), and as mother of many children (54:1–4; 66:7–11). What is more, she is accompanied by the glittering (male) figure of the servant of God.[50] The violent downfall and the horrors of destruction of the city-wife Jerusalem are conveyed to the city-wife Babylon—the latter has to descend from the throne and is uncovered (47:1–3; see §3 above), while the former is to accede to the throne, to be crowned and solemnly clothed and decorated (52:1–2). The accusation in Isa 57:6–13 fictionalizes Jerusalem once again in the image of a whoring woman,[51] and once again even the metaphor of God as cheated husband is hinted at in this context. But what carries more weight in Isa 40–66 is the innovative presentation of God in female roles—YHWH features as woman in labor (42:14), midwife (66:9), and (co)mother (46:3–4; 49:15; 66:13).[52] Overall, in Second and Third Isaiah, the (dual) gendered connotations are not abandoned but are multiplied.

The outcome of the book of Ezekiel is completely different—it seems that in Ezekiel's restorative passages (Ezek 33–48), the gendered images are deliberately omitted, even though restoration starts off with the actual human bodies that have been violated and injured (see, more importantly, 11:19–20; 36:26–27; 37:1–14).[53] The images of the city-wife are limited to the contexts of wartime destruction, the new city, which is designed as a text-based space in Ezek 40–48, does not even share the name with the historical city of Jerusalem (see 48:35). In this regard, Julie Galambush notes:

> Ezekiel's vision in chaps 40–48 of the new temple city completes the cycle of the city's defilement, destruction, and restoration. The God who left in rage returns in triumph, and the city is renewed and recreated. Only Jerusalem, the chastened and forgiven wife, is absent from the scene. The new city is described as inanimate stone, and its private parts bear no reminders of their former, sexual signification. Yahweh's proph-

---

50. See Christl M. Maier, *Daughter Zion, Mother Zion: Gender, Space, and the Sacred in Ancient Israel* (Minneapolis: Fortress, 2008), 163.

51. See Maier, *Daughter Zion, Mother Zion*, 183–86.

52. Maier, *Daughter Zion, Mother Zion*, 201–5. See also Irmtraud Fischer, "Das Buch Jesaja: Das Buch der weiblichen Metaphern," in *Kompendium Feministische Bibelauslegung*, ed. Luise Schottroff and Marie-Theres Wacker (Gütersloh: Gütersloher Verlagshaus, 1998), 246–57.

53. See Ruth Huppert, *Israel steht auf: Eine Studie zu Bedeutung und Funktion von Ez 37,1–14 im Buch Ezechiel* (Berlin: LIT, 2016), 223–60. Huppert reinterprets Ezek 37:1–14 as counternarrative to Ezek 16.

ecy that, having been purified, Jerusalem would never open her mouth again (16:63) is fulfilled, albeit ironically. She does not open her mouth because, no longer portrayed as a woman, she cannot. The restored city is faithful, but only because the elimination of the city's female persona has made infidelity impossible.[54]

I agree with these observations but would like to go one step further. It is, at any rate, notable that those passages that indicate future prospects for Israel not only eliminate "the female" but *totally* abstain from gender-specific metaphors. With the warriors of Gog who are disarmed and disempowered, hegemonic masculinity, omnipotence, and warmongering are obliterated (see 39:1–21). Even YHWH him-/herself no longer acts out as a (jealous and angry) husband but performs the quite different (and ungendered) roles of a shepherd (e.g., 34:11–16), a city builder (e.g., 36:33–36), and a gardener (e.g., 36:8–9). Even the deity, which proliferates his/her people, appears (as well as the people themselves) as gender- and sexless (e.g., 36:10–12; 37–38), which is totally different from the book of Isaiah. In sum, the so-called marital metaphor has served its function within the unbearable horrors of Ezek 16 and 23.

What is not yet conceivable, even in the more positive sections of this book, is the destigmatization of the victims; except in the second part of the book of Isaiah, the book of Ezekiel seems to be bound by the traumatic catastrophe beyond its narration. While it is true that even the latter enfolds the ideas of a future remission, reacceptance, and renewal of the covenant between YHWH and Israel (e.g., 16:60–63; 37:23–28), the former declares Israel's sin forgiven, quite from the outset (see Isa 40:1–2).

This is even more obvious considering the issue of shame. Referring to the book of Isaiah, Eric Ortlund writes, "When YHWH perfectly, gloriously restores and reverses the desolation of exile, there will be no shame for Lady Zion, but only glorious beauty which is publicly recognized (Isaiah 54)."[55] The same seems to hold true for the figure of the servant, since Israel's deity always rallies around the people (50:7; see 49:23).

---

54. Julie Galambush, *Jerusalem in the Book of Ezekiel: The City as Yahweh's Wife*, SBLDS 130 (Atlanta: Scholars Press, 1992), 147–48.

55. Eric Ortlund, "Shame in Restoration in Ezekiel," *SEJ* 2 (2011): 1–17, https://tinyurl.com/SBL6016t. On the topic of shame in the book of Isaiah, see Johanna Stiebert, *The Construction of Shame in the Hebrew Bible: The Prophetic Contribution*, JSOTSup 346 (Sheffield: Sheffield Academic, 2002), 87–109.

The book of Ezekiel, however, holds onto the sensation of shame even (and in particular) for a *recreated* Israel (see 16:59–63; 20:43–44; 36:31–32; 39:26; 43:10–11; 44:9–14). While it is announced that God's people will no longer be embarrassed and humiliated by the nations (36:6, 30), Israel itself is *not* imagined as falling short of shame. In my opinion, this peculiarity is best explained against the background of psycho-traumatology,[56] particularly since the models of a Mediterranean shame society, with specifically gendered forms of shame or of specific patterns of shame and honor, have proved to be hardly applicable to the texts of the Hebrew Bible. As the prophetic writings do not so much reflect the social structures of everyday life but rather mirror the reversal of social values in times of emergencies, and because shame phenomena in the Hebrew Bible are closely tied to bodily deterioration, it can be assumed that most of the shame language in the prophetic writings (as well as in the Psalms) hints at traumatic shame.[57] This concept refers to a (feeling of) shame, specifically humiliation, which arises when the protecting somatic barriers of a human being are transgressed or even pulled over by intruding violence.[58]

In this regard, the ubiquity of shame in the book of Ezekiel mirrors the catastrophe's gravity—and might also be a hint that (parts of) this biblical

---

56. E.g., Ortlund, "Shame in Restoration"; Tobias Häner, "Reading Ezekiel 36:16–38 in Light of the Book: Observations on the Remembrance and Shame after Restoration (36:31–32) in a Synchronic Perspective," in Tooman and Barter, *Ezekiel*, 323–44. See also Stiebert, *Construction of Shame*, 129–62; Poser, *Ezechielbuch als Trauma-Literatur*, 517–41.

57. See Stephan Marks, *Scham: Die tabuisierte Emotion* (Düsseldorf: Patmos 2007), 29–33. For the medical and psychological dimensions, see also Terry F. Taylor, "The Influence of Shame on Post-trauma Disorders: Have We Failed to See the Obvious?," *EJP* 6 (2015), https://tinyurl.com/SBL6016u. On shame phenomena in the Hebrew Bible, see Matthew J. Lynch, "Neglected Physical Dimensions of 'Shame'-Terminology in the Hebrew Bible," *Bib* 91 (2010): 499–517. On reversal in emergencies, see Stiebert, *Construction of Shame*, 95–96.

58. The term *intruding violence* does not only refer to sexual/sexualized violence but can equally be related to the impaling (חלל in Hebrew) of war victims with a sword, a phenomenon (also) quite present in the book of Ezekiel. See David G. Garber, "A Vocabulary of Trauma in the Exilic Writings," in *Interpreting Exile: Displacement and Deportation in Biblical and Modern Contexts*, ed. Brad E. Kelle, Frank Richtel Ames, and Jacob L. Wright (Atlanta: Society of Biblical Literature, 2011), 309–22; Lapsley, "Proliferation of Grotesque Bodies."

writing might have emerged relatively close to the date of 587 BCE.[59] A thorough recovery from the wounds that the horrors of war have inflicted seems to be unthinkable, even in the long run. What remains is a glimmer of hope—that all that is traumatic is saved (and, maybe, rescinded in the everlasting relationship between Israel and YHWH).[60]

6. Conclusion

What then can be concluded from this short overview of some aspects of the prophetic writings as a "meditation on the horror of war," in which I have tried to combine insights from traumatology, social history, and literary theory? Quite often, it has been assumed that the prophets, in this case Ezekiel, stare at the events of 587 BCE with a male and voyeuristic gaze (if not a sadistic gaze or a gaze that glorifies violence). Smith-Christopher, however, explains that it is more of an imperial than a male gaze, which permeates the imagery of gendered warfare in the prophetic texts. Regarding Ezekiel, he explains:

> While the language of Ezekiel could be read to primarily buttress a male/female hierarchy within exilic Israelite communities … this is not the only way to read many of the images of Ezekiel 16. Given the context of war and exile, it must also be asked whether Ezekiel's imagery more basically reveals the impact of a degrading imperial hierarchy on himself and his fellow exiles. Indeed, this other "hierarchy" that consists of military defeat and engendered humiliation in the ancient Near Eastern context may well raise serious questions about how "normative" any discussion of male/female relations could possibly be in the book of Ezekiel.[61]

I think this is true—and even more so, as the books of Isaiah, Jeremiah, and Ezekiel show that they really have in mind that war, even ancient siege warfare, is traumatizing for everybody, regardless of gender, age, class, and so on (e.g., Jer 6:11; Ezek 9:6; 24:21). In my opinion, against a background of literary trauma theory, the metaphorization of the besieged, conquered, and ruined city as woman and wife proves to be quite queer—queer in that

---

59. See Poser, *Ezechielbuch als Trauma-Literatur*, 668–72; O'Connor, "Trauma Studies," 220.

60. See Ortlund, "Shame in Restoration," 4: "It [the shame in restoration] is 'private' in the sense of existing only in relation to YHWH."

61. Smith-Christopher, "Ezekiel in Abu Ghraib," 157.

it compounds different genders, individual and collective aspects, reality and symbol, experiences and the explanation of experiences. By this, the (nevertheless dangerous) metaphorization offers a passably safe space for all the victims of war and their wounds, making those wounds visible, appreciable, attestable, mournable, and nameable.

Recently, Viola Rüdele has brought into conversation the extremely bodily imagery[62] of Ezek 16 and 23 and the wounds as well as the vulnerability these chapters reflect with Judith Butler's political essays presented in the anthology *Precarious Life: The Politics of Mourning and Violence* (2004). Rüdele holds that texts such as Ezek 16 and 23 and their embodied memories challenge us to renew our theological and even political thinking, envisioning the vulnerability of all life.[63] Or, as Butler puts it in the preface of her work:

> That we are vulnerable, that others are vulnerable, that we are subject to death due to the whim of others are reasonable grounds for anxiety and grief. But it is less reasonable that the experiences of vulnerability and loss directly induce military violence and revenge. There are other ways out. If we are interested to stop the spiral of violence and to look for less violent consequences we should be eager to ask which political possibilities might develop from grief—beyond the call for war.[64]

Bibliography

Albertz, Rainer, and Claus Westermann. "רוח." *TLOT* 3:1202–20.

Berges, Ulrich. *Das Buch Jesaja: Komposition und Endgestalt*. Freiburg: Herder, 1998.

---

62. Lapsley looks at the bodily imagery of Ezek 23 with reference to the idea of the grotesque and points out, "Through his grotesque imagery, through the pierced bodies and profaned temple [Ezekiel] exorcises the demonic, the human sin, and through the work of pain, seeks to forge a new, God-centered identity. Even as one must take issue with Ezekiel's method, one can also appreciate that this is the hardest theological work there is: he brings a word of hope to a traumatized people even as he himself is among those traumatized" ("Proliferation of Grotesque Bodies," 389).

63. See Viola Kristin Rüdele, "Die Verwundbarkeit des Körpers als Perspektive, Ezechiel 16 und 23 zu verstehen," *Id* 1 (2018), https://tinyurl.com/SBL6016v.

64. Judith Butler, *Gefährdetes Leben: Politische Essays* (Frankfurt: Suhrkamp, 2012), 7 (my translation). The cited sentences are found only in the foreword of the German edition of Butler's work.

Berlejung, Angelika. "Gewalt ins Bild gesetzt. Kriegsdarstellungen auf neuassyrischen Palastreliefs." *BK* 60 (2005): 205–11.

Bohleber, Werner. "Die Entwicklung der Traumatheorie in der Psychoanalyse." *Psyche* 9/10 (2000): 797–839.

Bowen, Nancy R. *Ezekiel*. Nashville: Abingdon, 2010.

Butler, Judith. *Gefährdetes Leben: Politische Essays*. Frankfurt: Suhrkamp, 2012.

Carr, David M. *Holy Resilience: The Bible's Traumatic Origins*. New Haven: Yale University Press, 2014.

Chapman, Cynthia R. "Sculpted Warriors: Sexuality and the Sacred in the Depiction of Warfare in the Assyrian Palace Reliefs and in Ezekiel 23:14–17." *Id* 1 (2007). https://tinyurl.com/SBL6016s.

Fischer, Gottfried, and Peter Riedesser. *Lehrbuch der Psychotraumatologie*. 3rd ed. München: Reinhardt, 2003.

Fischer, Irmtraud. "Das Buch Jesaja: Das Buch der weiblichen Metaphern." Pages 246–57 in *Kompendium Feministische Bibelauslegung*. Edited by Luise Schottroff and Marie-Theres Wacker. Gütersloh: Gütersloher Verlagshaus, 1998.

———. "Jona: Prophet eines traumatisierten Volkes." Pages 33–41 in *Vom Leben umfangen: Ägypten, das Alte Testament und das Gespräch der Religionen, Gedenkschrift für Manfred Görg*. Edited by Stefan Jakob Wimmer and Georg Gafus. Münster: Ugarit-Verlag, 2014.

Frechette, Christopher G. "Daughter Babylon Raped and Bereaved (Isaiah 47): Symbolic Violence and Meaning-Making in Recovery from Trauma." Pages 67–83 in *Bible through the Lens of Trauma*. Edited by Elizabeth Boase and Christopher G. Frechette. SemeiaSt 86. Atlanta: SBL Press, 2016.

Freißmann, Stephan. "Trauma als Erzählstrategie." Thesis, University of Konstanz, 2005. https://tinyurl.com/SBL6016q.

Galambush, Julie. *Jerusalem in the Book of Ezekiel: The City as Yahweh's Wife*. SBLDS 130. Atlanta: Scholars Press, 1992.

Garber, David G. "Traumatizing Ezekiel, the Exilic Prophet." Pages 215–35 in *Psychology and the Bible: A New Way to Read the Scriptures*. Vol. 2, *From Genesis to Apocalyptic Vision*. Edited by J. Harold Ellens and Wayne G. Rollins. Westport, CT: Praeger, 2004.

———. "A Vocabulary of Trauma in the Exilic Writings." Pages 309–22 in *Interpreting Exile: Displacement and Deportation in Biblical and Modern Contexts*. Edited by Brad E. Kelle, Frank Richtel Ames, and Jacob L. Wright. SymS 42. Atlanta: Society of Biblical Literature, 2011.

Goldstein, Joshua S. *War and Gender: How Gender Shapes the War System and Vice Versa*. Cambridge: Cambridge University Press, 2000.

Granofsky, Ronald. *The Trauma Novel: Contemporary Symbolic Depictions of Collective Disaster*. New York: Lang, 1995.

Greenberg, Moshe. *Ezekiel 21–37: A New Translation with Introduction and Commentary*. AB 22A. New York: Doubleday, 1997.

Guest, Deryn. *Beyond Feminist Biblical Studies*. Sheffield: Sheffield Phoenix, 2012.

Häner, Tobias. "Reading Ezekiel 36.16–38 in Light of the Book: Observations on the Remembrance and Shame after Restoration (36.31–32) in a Synchronic Perspective." Pages 323–44 in *Ezekiel: Current Debates and Future Directions*. Edited by William A. Tooman and Penelope Barter. FAT 112. Tübingen: Mohr Siebeck, 2017.

Herman, Judith. *Trauma and Recovery: The Aftermath of Violence—From Domestic Abuse to Political Terror*. Rev. ed. New York: Basic Books, 1997.

Huppert, Ruth. *Israel steht auf: Eine Studie zu Bedeutung und Funktion von Ez 37,1–14 im Buch Ezechiel*. Berlin: LIT, 2016.

Janzen, David. *The Violent Gift: Trauma's Subversion of the Deuteronomistic History's Narrative*. OTL 561. London: Bloomsbury, 2014.

Kamionkowski, S. Tamar. *Gender Reversal and Cosmic Chaos: A Study on the Book of Ezekiel*. JSOTSup 368. Sheffield: Sheffield Academic, 2003.

Keefe, Alice A. "Rapes of Women/Wars of Men." *Semeia* 61 (1993): 79–97.

Kelle, Brad E. "Dealing with the Trauma of Defeat: The Rhetoric of the Devastation and Rejuvenation of Nature in Ezekiel." *JBL* 128 (2009): 469–90.

———. "Wartime Rhetoric: Prophetic Metaphorization of Cities as Female." Pages 95–111 in *Writing and Reading War: Rhetoric, Gender, and Ethics in Biblical and Modern Contexts*. Edited by Brad E. Kelle, Frank Richtel Ames, and Jacob L. Wright. SymS 42. Atlanta: Society of Biblical Literature, 2008.

Kern, Paul Bentley. *Ancient Siege Warfare*. Bloomington: Indiana University Press, 1999.

Kolk, Bessel A. van der. "Trauma and Memory." Pages 279–302 in *Traumatic Stress: The Effects of Overwhelming Experience on Mind, Body, and Society*. Edited by Bessel A. van der Kolk, Alexander C. McFarlane, and Lars Weisaeth. New York: Guilford, 1996.

Kopf, Martina. *Trauma und Literatur: Das Nicht-Erzählbare erzählen—Assia Djebar und Yvonne Vera*. Frankfurt: Brandes & Apsel, 2005.

Kühner, Angela. *Kollektive Traumata—Annahmen, Argumente, Konzepte: Eine Bestandsaufnahme nach dem 11. September*. Berlin: Berghof Forschungszentrum, 2002.

Kutsch, Ernst. "חרף II." *TDOT* 5:209–15.

Lapsley, Jacqueline E. "The Proliferation of Grotesque Bodies in Ezekiel: The Case of Ezekiel 23." Pages 377–90 in *Ezekiel: Current Debates and Future Directions*. Edited by William A. Tooman and Penelope Barter. FAT 112. Tübingen: Mohr Siebeck, 2017.

Lemos, Tracy. M. "Shame and Mutilation of Enemies in the Hebrew Bible." *JBL* 125 (2006): 225–41.

Lynch, Matthew J. "Neglected Physical Dimensions of 'Shame'-Terminology in the Hebrew Bible." *Bib* 91 (2010): 499–517.

Maier, Christl M. *Daughter Zion, Mother Zion: Gender, Space, and the Sacred in Ancient Israel*. Minneapolis: Fortress, 2008.

Marks, Stephan. *Scham: Die tabuisierte Emotion*. Düsseldorf: Patmos, 2007.

Müllner, Ilse. "Prophetic Violence: The Marital Metaphor and Its Impact on Female and Male Readers." Pages 199–204 in *Prophetie in Israel*. Edited by Irmtraud Fischer, Konrad Schmid, and Hugh G. M. Williamson. Münster: LIT, 2003.

O'Connor, Kathleen M. "How Trauma Studies Can Contribute to Old Testament Studies." Pages 210–22 in *Trauma and Traumatization in Individual and Collective Dimensions: Insights from Biblical Studies and Beyond*. Edited by Eve-Marie Becker, Jan Dochhorn, and Else Holt. Göttingen: Vandenhoeck & Ruprecht, 2014.

———. *Jeremiah: Pain and Promise*. Minneapolis: Fortress, 2011.

Ortlund, Eric. "Shame in Restoration in Ezekiel." *SEJ* 2 (2011): 1–17. https://tinyurl.com/SBL6016t.

Patton, Corrine L. "'Should Our Sister Be Treated Like a Whore?': A Response to Feminist Critiques of Ezekiel 23." Pages 221–38 in *The Book of Ezekiel: Theological and Anthropological Perspectives*. Edited by Margaret S. Odell and John T. Strong. SymS 9. Atlanta: Society of Biblical Literature, 2000.

Poser, Ruth. *Das Ezechielbuch als Trauma-Literatur*. VTSup 154. Leiden: Brill, 2012.

———. "'Das Gericht geht durch den Magen': Die verschlungene Schriftrolle (Ez 2, 8b 3, 3) und andere Essensszenarien im Ezechielbuch." Pages 116–30 in *Essen und Trinken in der Bibel: Ein literarisches Festmahl für Rainer Kessler zum 65. Geburtstag*. Edited by Michaela

Geiger, Christl M. Maier, and Uta Schmidt. Gütersloh: Gütersloher Verlagshaus, 2009.

———. "No Words: The Book of Ezekiel as Trauma Literature and a Response to Exile." Pages 27–48 in *Bible through the Lens of Trauma*. Edited by Elisabeth Boase and Christopher G. Frechette. SemeiaSt 86. Atlanta: SBL Press, 2016.

Riedesser, Peter. "Belastende Kriegserfahrungen in der Kleinkindzeit." Pages 37–50 in *Kindheiten im Zweiten Weltkrieg: Kriegserfahrungen und deren Folgen aus psychohistorischer Perspektive*. Edited by Hartmut Radebold, Gereon Heuft, and Insa Fooken. Weinheim: Juventa, 2006.

Rüdele, Viola Kristin. "Die Verwundbarkeit des Körpers als Perspektive, Ezechiel 16 und 23 zu verstehen." *ld* 1 (2018). https://tinyurl.com/SBL6016v.

Sack, Martin. "Narrative Arbeit im Kontext 'schonender Traumatherapie.'" Pages 150–60 in *Narrative Bewältigung von Trauma und Verlust*. Edited by Carl Eduard Scheidt, Gabriele Lucius-Hoene, Anja Stukenbrock, and Elisabeth Waller. Stuttgart: Schattauer, 2015.

Sals, Ulrike. *Die Biographie der "Hure Babylon": Studien zur Intertextualität der Babylon-Texte in der Bibel*. FAT 2/6. Tübingen: Mohr Siebeck, 2004.

Scheidt, Carl Eduard, and Gabriele Lucius-Hoene. "Kategorisierung und narrative Bewältigung bindungsbezogener Traumaerfahrungen im Erwachsenenbindungs Interview." Pages 26–38 in *Narrative Bewältigung von Trauma und Verlust*. Edited by Carl Eduard Scheidt, Gabriele Lucius-Hoene, Anja Stukenbrock, and Elisabeth Waller. Stuttgart: Schattauer, 2015.

Schüngel-Straumann, Helen. "Geist (AT)." In *Das wissenschaftliche Bibellexikon im Internet*. Edited by Michaela Bauks and Klaus Koenen. 2009. https://tinyurl.com/SBL6016r.

Smith-Christopher, Daniel L. *A Biblical Theology of Exile*. Minneapolis: Fortress, 2002.

———. "Ezekiel in Abu Ghraib: Rereading Ezekiel 16:37–39 in the Context of Imperial Conquest." Pages 141–57 in *Ezekiel's Hierarchical World: Wrestling with a Tiered Reality*. Edited by Stephen L. Cook and Corrine L. Patton. SymS 31. Atlanta: Society of Biblical Literature, 2004.

Stiebert, Johanna. *The Construction of Shame in the Hebrew Bible: The Prophetic Contribution*. JSOTSup 346. Sheffield: Sheffield Academic, 2002.

Stulman, Louis. "Reflections on the Prose Sermons in the Book of Jeremiah: Duhm's and Mowinckel's Contributions to Contemporary Trauma Readings." Pages 125–39 in *Bible through the Lens of Trauma*. Edited by Elizabeth Boase and Christopher G. Frechette. SemeiaSt 86. Atlanta: SBL Press, 2016.

Stulman, Louis, and Hyun Chul Paul Kim. *You Are My People: An Introduction to Prophetic Literature*. Nashville: Abingdon, 2010.

Taylor, Terry F. "The Influence of Shame on Post-trauma Disorders: Have We Failed to See the Obvious?" *EJP* 6 (2015). https://tinyurl.com/SBL6016u.

Tengström, Sven. "רוּחַ I–VI." *TDOT* 13:365–96.

Vanderhooft, David. *The Neo-Babylonian Empire and Babylon in the Latter Prophets*. Atlanta: Scholars Press, 1999.

Westermann, Claus, and Rainer Albertz. "גלה." *THAT* 1:418–26.

Pornoprophetics Revisited, Decades Later

Athalya Brenner-Idan

1. To Begin With

Over twenty years ago, the article "On Prophetic Propaganda and the Politics of 'Love': The Case of Jeremiah" appeared in *A Feminist Companion to the Latter Prophets* (1995).[1] After thinking and talking and writing about this topic for many years, I published this article, together with three others, under the heading "On the Pornoprophetics of Sexual Violence."[2] Articles by the late Fokkelien van Dijk-Hemmes, the late Robert Carroll, Pamela Gordon and Harold Washington, and Rachel Magdalene also grappled with the question widely discussed by feminist critics in the late 1980s and early 1990s: How can one cope with the images of the Israel/Judah or Samaria/Jerusalem communities that are blatantly shamed, described as sexual deviants, punished—all in the name of monotheistic prophetic ideology?[3]

---

1. Athalya Brenner, "On Prophetic Propaganda and the Politics of 'Love': The Case of Jeremiah," in *A Feminist Companion to the Latter Prophets*, ed. Athalya Brenner, FCB 8 (Sheffield: Sheffield Academic, 1995), 256–74.

2. Athalya Brenner, "On the Pornoprophetics of Sexual Violence," in Brenner, *Feminist Companion to the Latter Prophets*, 243–352.

3. Fokkelien van Dijk-Hemmes, "The Metaphorization of Woman in Prophetic Speech: An Analysis of Ezekiel 23," in Brenner, *Feminist Companion to the Latter Prophets*, 244–55; Robert Carroll, "Desire under the Terebinths: On Pornographic Representation in the Prophets—A Response," in Brenner, *Feminist Companion to the Latter Prophets*, 275–307; Pamela Gordon and Harold C. Washington, "Rape as a Military Metaphor in the Hebrew Bible," in Brenner, *Feminist Companion to the Latter Prophets*, 308–25; F. Rachel Magdalene, "Ancient Near Eastern Treaty Curses and the Ultimate Texts of Terror: A Study of the Language of Divine Sexual Abuse in the Prophetic Corpus," in Brenner, *Feminist Companion to the Latter Prophets*, 326–52.

In that 1995 *Feminist Companion to the Latter Prophets* essay, I read Jer 2 and 5, in conjunction with Ezek 16 and 23 and Hos 1–3, as propaganda literature. That reading was performed in conversation with a 1950s pornographic novel attributed to a French woman, *The Story of O*, which charts the passage of an independent young woman to a sex slave to her male master/lover, then to his friends and all men, with her consent and approval. In reading these portrayals together, pornographic representation was defined as a visual or verbal means for arousing sexual desire and for using it for gender control; and the features, functions, and causes of pornography were described. In that essay, I emphasized how male supremacy, greater female exposure in vision or word, violence, and lack of consent were considered important elements of the definition. My conclusion of this exercise was more or less as follows.

The religious propaganda of the so-called "prophetic 'love' metaphor" abuses and shames female sexuality, although, to be sure, it attacks male sexuality too. I do not know whether a *historical* person named Jeremiah (or Hosea or Ezekiel) was responsible for such sexualized passages that bear their name as authors in our canon. Hence, the metaphor should not be dismissed on the grounds that "he," the prophet, was unfortunately motivated by "his" own personal circumstances with "his" wife or "wives," or female partners. Instead, I would like to point out that whoever composed these passages perceived men, God, women, and gender relations in a certain way. That vision, that male fantasy of desire, presupposes a complementary fantasy of female desire. The fantasy is not just simply erotic. It is a pornographic fantasy, and so is its presentation—it *is* pornographic. As an F/f (Female/feminine, biologically and as culturally gendered, respectively) bible reader, I can resist the fantasy by exposing it, by criticism, by reflection.[4] But within the present cultural system, then and even now, I do so at my own peril. I was raised and educated to comply with that male fantasy and to adopt it as my very own. Like other F/f readers, I may deconstruct myself at times; the temptation to reciprocate this M/m (Male/Masculine, biological as well as culturally gendered) fantasy, even to appropriate it, may still be there. Awareness helps, but the ideological odds are against me. And against you.

Have my efforts to become an F reader been successful? How was I, now that my response to the "prophetic 'love' metaphor" was out in the

---

4. Throughout this essay, I refer to *bible* (initial lowercase) rather than *Bible*.

open, to respond to its literary mirror image across cultures and centuries, *The Story of O*, ostensibly written from an F/f viewpoint? I had two alternatives. The one is to identify with O, for her fantasy is, at least to a certain extent, my fantasy too, acquired by the gendered socialization process I have undergone myself. The other option was and is to rebel against the myth of female masochism and female sexual objectification. I can, and so can you, refuse the recommendation/urgent demand to achieve female selfhood by submission to male rule at the price of female sexual independence and even female minimal agency. I can say, and so can you: This is carrying things too far, this subordination of F/f fantasy to M/m fantasy. I do not want, and you may not want either, to be negated in order to join the symbolic male order. I am no prude; I can tolerate, sometimes enjoy, pornographic representations up to a point. But I cannot ignore the gendering effect most pornographic presentations have for persons who belong to the same anatomical sex as I do.

Returning to the pornoprophetic passages now, decades later. How am I, how are you, to respond to the biblical prophetic propaganda that depicts Judah and Jerusalem and Samaria and Israel as an objectified spouse, an animalized it-woman? This propaganda cleverly constructs a stereotype: EveryWoman, especially EveryWife, is potentially a sexual deviant and should therefore be tightly controlled. By males, of course. Wife abuse and rape should, of course, be directly linked to the worldview that makes such prophetic propaganda acceptable.

Religio-political propaganda can lead to wholesale rape of women—read the news about Bosnia, about Da'esh, about Yazidi women in Iraq, about Boko Haram in Nigeria, about Rohingya in Myanmar. In all these cases, large-scale rape of females is used as a military and ideological weapon in what are defined at least partly as religious wars. So, once more, I, and you, have two alternatives with regard to the prophets' religious war, as expressed in the "love" metaphor. The one is to identify with the biblical male author's viewpoint, which is presented as God's viewpoint. The other option is to resist the kind of religious pornography, the rape by speech and written letter, that is characteristic of this husband-wife metaphor. We can object to the social roles such descriptions imply, whether consciously or otherwise, for persons gendered as F/f.

Toward the end of her analysis of pornography, Jessica Benjamin writes: "The same psychological issues run through both political and erotic forms of domination, for they both embody denial of the other subject."[5] The fight for religious domination, be it morally just or otherwise, undoubtedly belongs to the category of political domination. This, at the very least, is the bottom line.

2. And Further

In the previous section I have referred to my previous work, updating it slightly, at length because, basically, my position has not changed. I still read those chapters with a shudder. I still view them as religious propaganda that utilizes pornography as a kick: for education? For pulling authority? What I would like to do, nevertheless, is to add some considerations for strengthening this reading and for buttressing it some more, including some highlighting and specification. Moreover, nowadays I read those passages not as pornography but as *hard porn*—not the equivalent of a euphemistically termed "adult" film or *soft porn*, but as the equivalent of a violent, deadly *snuff porn*. That, in civilized societies, is punishable by law, especially when it involves underage or nonconsenting persons. In what follows, I will highlight four themes that demonstrate developments in my thinking on this topic.

3. Religion and the Erotic

Eroticism is part and parcel of religiosity, I guess since religion cannot escape human corporeality or embodiment; this is no news. This is true for Judaism—from the pornoprophetic metaphor to the postbiblical allegorical interpretation of the Song of Songs as a divine-human love hi/story to Qabalah and Shekinah definitions. This is true, inter alia, also for Christian mysticism and the troubled Christian vision of human sexuality and the reservation of the erotic pleasure proper to the cultic realm, as evidenced both by sexual denial, that is, celibacy, as well as the directing of erotic pleasure to the divine. Also to be mentioned here is the development of the veneration of Mary not only as a mother but as a sexualized woman; all one needs to do is to look at European art about her.[6] In both Judaism

---

5. Jessica Benjamin, *The Bonds of Love: Psychoanalysis, Feminism and the Problem of Domination* (Toronto: Random House, 1988), 66.

6. In this connection, it is worthwhile to mention that, in some instances of the so-called metaphysical poetry, an abusive divine/human male-to-male relationship is sought, clad in sexual and marriage language. See below.

and Christianity, although it is different in Islam, eroticism is highly present this way or another. Need I state that eroticism is sexual and is not only sexuality? Eros/desire may be spiritual as well as corporeal. On the other hand, it is superficial to claim that human sexuality is "only a metaphor" for divine love or for human love of the divine. When the two are confused, and sexual violence in word or deed enters the text or picture, so does pornography. When both need to be regulated by someone, or some class, or some gender, force has to be introduced. The customary social hierarchy, be it divine-human or male-female, is reinforced by shocking means.

4. Violence

Had I written my original statement later, I probably would have emphasized even more the violence of the images introduced. In the prophetic texts, female images are exposed, naked and raped. They are raped and exposed by their loving, authoritative husband(s). Do we condone wife beating, wife rape, date rape, in our society? Even if a wife or partner has been actually or imaginatively unfaithful? Do we still subscribe to the notion of *crime passionelle* as deserving punishment for a sexual transgressor in the punisher's eyes? This is a rhetorical question. If we do not, we should reject such images, complete with the righteous and punishing male image. It is good to remember that rape is about domination and hierarchy, more so than about sexual desire. Much more. A fantasy of desire that has force at its core cannot be forgiven even if it is biblical.

5. Heterosexuality and Fixity of Roles

It should be emphasized again and again that, ostensibly, the biblical texts reflect a heterosexual prophetic fantasy, from a heterosexual male viewpoint. But not quite: as has been noticed widely, the divine is identified as the superior male. By identifying the "woman" as the metaphorical audience, in the context of the male community, a certain gender reversal is added to the picture. The metaphorical woman is now a feminized male. In the biblical text, "s/he" is silent. Now, as transgendered in the text, would s/he respond to the prophetic harangue as John Donne does?

> Batter my heart, three-person'd God, for you
> As yet but knock, breathe, shine, and seek to mend;
> That I may rise and stand, o'erthrow me, and bend

> Your force to break, blow, burn, and make me new.
> I, like an usurp'd town to another due,
> Labor to admit you, but oh, to no end;
> Reason, your viceroy in me, me should defend,
> But is captiv'd, and proves weak or untrue.
> Yet dearly I love you, and would be lov'd fain,
> But am betroth'd unto your enemy
> Divorce me, untie or break that knot again,
> Take me to you, imprison me, for I,
> Except you enthrall me, never shall be free,
> Nor ever chaste, except you ravish me.[7]

This sonnet accepts, nay, invites divine violence on the male self in terms of sexual language. Nowadays, this male-male invitation should carry more weight than in past analysis. To boot: a queer reading, or "queer-defined" reading, to adapt a term from Deryn Guest,[8] should emphasize that the hierarchical vision of the metaphor moves beyond heterosexual signification—and so does its significance for our lives with the bible.

Moreover, the metaphor's gender roles are fixed. Eternally so. The female/feminized partner is always to blame, always to be punished. The male/superior/divine partner is always just, strong, violent, and authoritative. Unlike in life, no exchange of position ever occurs—the wife image never gets to punish her tormentor; indeed, "she" is seldom allowed to talk in self-defense. The male/divine image is presented as victim, judge, accuser, and executor: "he" is not naked or described as naked; his spouse is.

In recent years, masculinities and gay and queer studies are applied to the Hebrew bible with great energy and insight by, among others, Ken Stone; Teresa Hornsby; Hornsby and Guest; Hornsby and Stone; Guest; Martti Nissinen; Ovidiu Creanga; Stephen Moore; and Meir Bar Mymon.[9]

---

7. John Donne, "Holy Sonnet 14" (1633), https://tinyurl.com/SBL6016w.

8. Deryn Guest, *When Deborah Met Jael: Lesbian Biblical Hermeneutics* (London: SCM, 2005). Guest struggles with defining *lesbian* and finally settles for "lesbian-defined."

9. A good introduction to this field is Bjorn Krondorfer, ed., *Men and Musculinities in Christianity and Judaism: A Critical Reader* (London: SCM, 2009). Especially relevant are parts 4–5 there (pp. 163–331), with reprinted and original articles by Boyarin, Burrus, and Stone, among others. See Ken Stone, *Practicing Safer Texts: Food, Sex and Bible in Queer Perspective* (London: T&T Clark, 2005); Stone, ed., *Queer Commentary and the Hebrew Bible* (Sheffield: Sheffield Academic, 2001);

Some results of these research endeavors are already forthcoming. The literary figure Ezekiel (and, to a certain extent, Samson), for instance, is depicted as a runner-up or mirror image of the ultimate alpha male, who is Yhwh. This image of masculinity is rigid and nonchangeable. If you, M/m, want to imitate it, your qualities too will be immutable and indisputable. Masculinities studies certainly offer other images of males—as crying, mothering, showing empathy rather than cruelty. Following such lines of reasoning shows us that the prophetic metaphor is devastating not only for F/f audiences (listeners or readers) but also for M/m audiences. Add to this the feminization of the male target audience, as argued above. Add to this the possible reception by LGBTQ audiences, then and now. So, nowadays, this pornographic image will be even more painful. And even more thought provoking, in view of present discourse on human sexual behavior.

6. Pornoprophetics and BDSM

The pornoprophetic fantasy can now be nuanced further, which would have not been possible decades ago. It is in fact a representation of what is now known as BDSM: *B*ondage, *D*ominance, *S*ubmission, *S*adism, and *M*asochism. In this fantasy of sexual desire, S/M relationships are enacted, or acted out, to satisfy the desire of the participants. This behavioral phenomenon is well documented in visual media, literature, and newspapers of the present time.

BDSM is not my personal cup of tea, among other things because it a priori entails the exercise of deliberate physical violence. However, three things are routinely stressed by BDSM participants. First, the partners

---

Teresa Hornsby, "Ezekiel," in The *Queer Bible Commentary*, ed. Deryn Guest et al. (London: SCM, 2011), 412–26; Hornsby and Deryn Guest, eds., *Transgender, Intersex, and Biblical Interpretation*, SemeiaSt (Atlanta: SBL Press, 2016); Hornsby and Stone, eds., *Bible Trouble: Queer Reading at the Boundaries of Biblical Scholarship* (Atlanta: Society of Biblical Literature, 2011); Guest, *When Deborah Met Jael*; Martti Nissinen, *Homoeroticism in the Biblical World: A Historical Perspective* (Minneapolis: Fortress, 2004); Ovidiu Creanga and Peter-Ben Smit, eds., *Biblical Masculinities Forgrounded* (Sheffield: Sheffield Phoenix, 2014); Stephen D. Moore, *God's Beauty Parlor and Other Queer Spaces in and around the Bible* (Stanford: Stanford University Press, 2001), especially part 2; Meir Bar Mymon, "This Season You'll Be Wearing God," in *Joshua and Judges*, ed. Athalya Brenner and Gale A. Yee, TC (Minneapolis: Fortress, 2013), 191–208.

enter into the situation consciously and knowingly—or so they imagine. Second, there is a mutual contract as to what the partners to this series of sexual games can do in the line of violence and exerting force, without crossing agreed boundaries. And third, positions of dominance and submission may change by mutual consent—in other words, such positions are fluid rather than rigidly fixed as a matter of basic structure. Supposedly, an enactment of BDSM is a performance between two or more consenting adults. Nevertheless, it is a dangerous performance that can easily get out of bounds, and as such falls into the category of unsafe sex. Its representation can be defined as pornography, that is, a picture of a certain sexual fantasy that is far from equal for participating partners and does contain socially imbalanced exposure and violence.

In biblical studies, several scholars have recently analyzed biblical texts in terms of BDSM. Roland Boer, Moore, and Moore and Virginia Burrus apply the notion of unsafe sex to the holy grail of feminist biblical criticism's favorite object, Song of Songs.[10] Lori Rowlett writes similarly about Samson and Delilah.[11] Emma England considers the story of Judith and Holofernes in that light.[12] These scholars raise the possibility that, indeed, unsafe sex—for the literary participants, but also for their audiences—has traces in various biblical texts, or, at the very least, can be understood as such by contemporary readers. Indeed, most of us would have little hesitation in evaluating the Samson-Delilah encounter as a BDSM game gone wrong (for Samson), with all the teasing back-and-forth in Judg 16; some would even consider Holofernes's submission to Judith's pretense as a knowing maneuver, unfortunately for him. Note, in passing, that the violent perpetrator in both stories is a female figure. However, fewer readers would consent to find such traces in the Song of Songs. And fewer still in the pornoprophetic metaphor.

---

10. Roland Boer, "Night Sprinkle(s): Pornography and the Song of Songs," in *Knockin' on Heaven's Door: The Bible and Popular Culture* (London: Routledge, 1999), 53–70; Stephen Moore, "The Song of Songs in the History of Sexuality," in Moore, *God's Beauty Parlor*, 21–88; Virginia Burrus and Stephen D. Moore, "Unsafe Sex: Feminism, Pornography, and the Song of Songs," *BibInt* 11 (2003): 24–52.

11. Lori Rowlett, "Violent Femmes and S/M: Queering Samson and Delilah," in Stone, *Queer Commentary*, 106–15.

12. Emma E. England, "Second Thoughts on Female Terrorists and More: A Self-Response," in *A Feminist Companion to Tobit and Judith*, ed. Athalya Brenner-Idan and Helen Efthiamides-Keith, FCB 2/20 (London: Bloomsbury T&T Clark, 2015), 259–61.

Nevertheless, I would like to suggest that the so-called "love metaphor" bears similarities to a BDSM situation. The metaphor is based on a condition of knowledge: a contract, a covenant—so the "male" partner claims. Punishment and reward systems have been set up. And things went too far. However, as things progressed, the "female" partner withdrew "her" consent. As a result, the partner will punish her and hold her to the conditions of the game, whether she wants to or not.

It follows, for me, that if I could read the pornoprophetic metaphor years ago in BDSM terms, I would define it even more radically. I would say that this is a BDSM situation when one party, after much foreplay and play, withdrew "her" consent. The other party refused to accept the withdrawal and submitted "her" to the original terms. A representation of "his" desire is served to us to adopt as the only fantasy of dominion that is legitimate.

7. Shaming

Much has been said and discussed in recent years about social shaming, especially body shaming, on social networks. Think about Facebook or TikTok. Stories of children's suicide and the destruction of adult reputation—especially of female persons—abound. Think of it. Would you agree with virtual body shaming? Would you allow it as a pedagogical device, for whatever lofty purpose? How would you react if it were applied to you or yours? Is the shaming exposure of some biblical verses in, say, Ezek 16 and 23 different, less or more visual, less or more pornographic, less damaging, than posting a teenage girl's naked image on a social network, and without her consent? In our culture, such postings are known as pedophilia at best, and punishable by law. Similarly, nonconsensual publishing of naked adults—mostly women—on social networks is considered illegal.

Yet this is exactly what is happening in those prophetic texts—the equivalent of publishing photographs of a naked women (and oversized male sexual organs), having sexual copulation, being beaten, being tortured. I would say, if you empathize with Mother/Daughter Zion in Lamentations, when this is done to her, why not empathize with Daughter Jerusalem/Samaria in Ezekiel or Jeremiah or Hosea?[13] In Lamentations, at

---

13. It is perhaps worthwhile to repeat that the latent incest contents of defining a partner, albeit a metaphorical literary partner, as a "daughter" as well as "wife" and "mother of children," cannot be overlooked. It goes over and beyond the usual biblical

the very least, "she" gets to speak directly, unlike the sporadic embedded speech she has in the prophetic "metaphor."[14]

8. What to Do with the Discomfort? #MeToo

It is terribly uncomfortable to even consider biblical literature as pornographic literature—yes, even for a secularist like me, and especially if you define yourself as a member of a faith community.

So, first and foremost, let us remember the following. The bible is a wonderful library, or book if you wish. But not everything in it is wonderful. It has slavery, rape, eye-for-eye punishment, corporeal punishment, genocide, and many more contemporarily unacceptable features, all presented as divinely decreed. If you accept those as invalid for our place and times, with or without the excuse of older times, older cultures, please consider doing the same for the notion that the so-called prophets are not above using descriptions of sexual relations of a certain kind, that is, pornography, to advance their case.

This essay is written at the very end of 2017; 2017 will be remembered as the year of the #MeToo outbreak, when numerous women (and some men) came forward with their own voices, and at times faces and names, recounting their own experience of sexual harassment on a spectrum from nonconsensual touch to rape mostly by white, influential men. The men publicly accused are mostly from media, politics, entertainment, and even the judicial system. Several come also from religious institutions. The #MeToo movement started in the United States, but has since spread to Europe and beyond. It is, basically, a shaming in reverse, a call for social reckoning by the victims against the perpetrators, with all the implications involved.

Judged in the light of the #MeToo call to action, the "prophetic love metaphor" looks like a one-sided gendered call for sexual abuse and even rape more than before. Ask yourself, candidly: Would I tolerate such a

---

and ancient Near Eastern custom of referring to cities, spaces and ethnical units as "daughters." But this is a topic for another discussion.

14. See Archie C. C. Lee, "Reading Daughter Zion and Lady Meng: Tears, Protests and Female Voices," in *The Five Scrolls*, ed. Athalya Brenner-Idan, Archie C. C. Lee, and Gale A. Yee, TC (London: Bloomsbury T&T Clark, 2018), 159–73; Athalya Brenner-Idan, "Lamentations as Musical Performances, Its Origins and Life Occasions: Some Reflections," in Brenner-Idan, Lee, and Yee, *Five Scrolls*, 159–85.

biblical call if advanced in today's public life, even if or especially if it delineates a program against women who disagree with male dominion? If and when it contains graphic sexual images that humiliate females but may arouse the desire of m/M, would I regard such a call as religiously and socially acceptable? Or would I view it as a pornographic distortion of reality, my reality as well as ancient reality?

The scholarly and social bible experience, may we quietly remind ourselves, is not only about theorizing "the bible as it was" or its far-removed historical reception; it is also, and perhaps principally, about assessing how it has shaped and still determines our lives, to this day, in all types of monotheistic-style and therefore male-dominated communities.

Bibliography

Bar Mymon, Meir. "This Season You'll Be Wearing God." Pages 191–208 in *Joshua and Judges*. Edited by Athalya Brenner and Gale A. Yee. TC. Minneapolis: Fortress, 2013.

Benjamin, Jessica. *The Bonds of Love: Psychoanalysis, Feminism and the Problem of Domination*. Toronto: Random House, 1988.

Boer, Roland. "Night Sprinkle(s): Pornography and the Song of Songs." Pages 53–70 in *Knockin' on Heaven's Door: The Bible and Popular Culture*. London: Routledge, 1999.

Brenner, Athalya. "On Prophetic Propaganda and the Politics of 'Love': The Case of Jeremiah." Pages 256–74 in *A Feminist Companion to the Latter Prophets*. FCB 8. Edited by Athalya Brenner. Sheffield: Sheffield Academic, 1995.

———. "On the Pornoprophetics of Sexual Violence." Pages 243–352 in *A Feminist Companion to the Latter Prophets*. Edited by Athalya Brenner. FCB 8. Sheffield: Sheffield Academic, 1995.

Brenner-Idan, Athalya. "Lamentations as Musical Performances, Its Origins and Life Occasions: Some Reflections." Pages 174–85 in *The Five Scrolls*. Edited by Athalya Brenner-Idan, Archie C. C. Lee, and Gale A. Yee. TC. London: Bloomsbury T&T Clark, 2018.

Burrus, Virginia, and Stephen D. Moore. "Unsafe Sex: Feminism, Pornography, and the Song of Songs." *BibInt* 11 (2003): 24–52.

Carroll, Robert. "Desire under the Terebinths: On Pornographic Representation in the Prophets—A Response." Pages 275–307 in *A Feminist Companion to the Latter Prophets*. Edited by Athalya Brenner. FCB 8. Sheffield: Sheffield Academic, 1995.

Creanga, Ovidiu Creanga, and Peter-Ben Smit, eds. *Biblical Masculinities Foregrounded*. Sheffield: Sheffield Phoenix, 2014.

Dijk-Hemmes, Fokkelien van. "The Metaphorization of Woman in Prophetic Speech: An Analysis of Ezekiel 23." Pages 244–55 in *A Feminist Companion to the Latter Prophets*. Edited by Athalya Brenner. FCB 8. Sheffield: Sheffield Academic, 1995.

Donne, John. "Holy Sonnet 14." 1633. https://tinyurl.com/SBL6016w.

England, Emma E. "Second Thoughts on Female Terrorists and More: A Self-Response." Pages 259–61 in *A Feminist Companion to Tobit and Judith*. Edited by Athalya Brenner-Idan with Helen Efthiamides-Keith. FCB 2/20. London: Bloomsbury T&T Clark, 2015.

Gordon, Pamela, and Harold C. Washington. "Rape as a Military Metaphor in the Hebrew Bible." Pages 308–25 in *A Feminist Companion to the Latter Prophets*. Edited by Athalya Brenner. FCB 8. Sheffield: Sheffield Academic, 1995.

Guest, Deryn. *When Deborah Met Jael: Lesbian Biblical Hermeneutics*. London: SCM, 2005.

Hornsby, Teresa. "Ezekiel." Pages 412–26 in *The Queer Bible Commentary*. Edited by Deryn Guest, Rita E. Goss, Mona West, and Thomas Bohache. London: SCM, 2011.

Hornsby, Teresa J., and Deryn Guest, eds. *Transgender, Intersex, and Biblical Interpretation*. SemeiaSt. Atlanta: SBL Press, 2016.

Hornsby, Teresa J., and Ken Stone, eds. *Bible Trouble: Queer Reading at the Boundaries of Biblical Scholarship*. Atlanta: Society of Biblical Literature, 2011.

Krondorfer, Bjorn, ed. *Men and Masculinities in Christianity and Judaism: A Critical Reader*. London: SCM, 2009.

Lee, Archie C. C. "Reading Daughter Zion and Lady Meng: Tears, Protests and Female Voices." Pages 159–73 in *The Five Scrolls*. Edited by Athalya Brenner-Idan, Archie C. C. Lee, and Gale A. Yee. TC. London: Bloomsbury T&T Clark, 2018.

Magdalene, F. Rachel. "Ancient Near Eastern Treaty Curses and the Ultimate Texts of Terror: A Study of the Language of Divine Sexual Abuse in the Prophetic Corpus." Pages 326–52 in *A Feminist Companion to the Latter Prophets*. Edited by Athalya Brenner. FCB 8. Sheffield: Sheffield Academic, 1995.

Moore, Stephen D. *God's Beauty Parlor and Other Queer Spaces in and around the Bible*. Stanford: Stanford University Press, 2001.

Nissinen, Marti. *Homoeroticism in the Biblical World: A Historical Perspective.* Minneapolis: Fortress, 2004.
Rowlett, Lori. "Violent Femmes and S/M: Queering Samson and Delilah." Pages 106–15 in *Queer Commentary and the Hebrew Bible.* Edited by Ken Stone. Sheffield: Sheffield Academic, 2001.
Stone, Ken. *Practicing Safer Texts: Food, Sex and Bible in Queer Perspective.* London: T&T Clark, 2005.
———, ed. *Queer Commentary and the Hebrew Bible.* Sheffield: Sheffield Academic, 2001.

The Meaning of the Female Presence in Messianic Texts within the Corpus of the Nevi'im

Ombretta Pettigiani

1. Messianism in General and Recent Trends

On the delimitation of the textual sphere, I refer here exclusively to the Latter Prophets, adhering to the way in which the Hebrew Bible defines them: Isaiah, Jeremiah, Ezekiel, and the Twelve (thus excluding Daniel). With this clarification, and in order to identify the presence of the feminine in the messianic oracles, we must establish which oracles can be defined as such. The task is not simple, since the very concept of messianism is widely debated.

In undertaking the study of this subject (referring only to biblical studies and not, more generally, to the messianic expectations that still concern the faith of Israel), one notices a rather particular situation: messianism was a topic that very much interested exegetes from the late nineteenth century to the mid-twentieth century.[1] Later, there was a period of decline in interest, with a gradual revival in the 1980s and an upsurge of studies in the new millennium. However, the way we speak of messianism in recent studies is very different from what was previously adopted. We can say that current research moves in three directions:

---

1. Brigg's and Mowinckel's works remain a landmark on the subject. See Charles Augustus Briggs, *Messianic Prophecy: The Prediction of the Fulfilment of Redemption through the Messiah* (Edinburgh: T&T Clark, 1886); Sigmund Mowinckel, *He That Cometh: The Messiah Concept in the Old Testament and Later Judaism* (Grand Rapids: Eerdmans, 2005).

1. the study of messianism within Judaism in a broad sense, with special reference to what is called Middle Judaism;[2]
2. the clarification of the relationship between messianism and regal ideology within the Hebrew Bible;[3]
3. the in-depth examination of the differences between the Hebrew text and the Greek LXX Septuagint, with a more explicit affirmation of the latter's messianic expectation.[4]

Within this field of research, we are witnessing the study of messianism in its historical evolution in an attempt to trace its development both in biblical texts and in coeval literature.[5]

Last, we sometimes find attempts that seem to defend the Hebrew Bible as a whole as messianic because of a general discredit of the idea of messianism.[6] At the same time, there is an effort to clarify the concept of messianism. In short, it seems we have two parallel lines:

1. those who see the Messiah as a figure linked to expectations of restoration of the house of David, understood substantially in an eschatological sense, and that therefore underline the link with the royal context, as well as a late birth of the messianic idea;[7]

---

2. See, e.g., Paolo Collini, *Messianismo: Indice concettuale del Medio Giudaismo 3* (Magnano: Qiqajon, 2009).

3. See for example the work of Adela Yarbro Collins and John Joseph Collins, *King and Messiah as Son of God: Divine, Human, and Angelic Messianic Figures in Biblical and Related Literature* (Grand Rapids: Eerdmans, 2008).

4. See, in this regard, important studies such as Johan Lust, *Messianism and the Septuagint: Collected Essays*, BETL 178 (Leuven: Peeters, 2004); Rodrigo F. De Sousa, *Eschatology and Messianism in LXX Isaiah 1–12*, LHBOTS 516 (New York: T&T Clark, 2010); Abi Tomba Ngunga, *Messianism in the Old Greek of Isaiah: An Intertextual Analysis*, FRLANT 245 (Göttingen: Vandenhoeck & Ruprecht, 2013).

5. Antti Laato, *A Star Is Rising: The Historical Development of the Old Testament Royal Ideology and the Rise of the Jewish Messianic Expectations* (Atlanta: Scholars Press, 1997).

6. See Michael Rydelnik, *The Messianic Hope: Is the Hebrew Bible Really Messianic?* (Nashville: B&H, 2010). On the general idea of messianism, see Enzo Cortese, "Come sbloccare l'attuale esegesi Messianica," in *Il tempo della fine: Messianismo ed escatologia nel messaggio profetico*, ed. Enzo Cortese, SBFA 76 (Milan: Terra Santa, 2010), 53–64.

7. See, e.g., Heskett, who states, "Our definition of a Messiah requires that a person or persons offer a solution in extraordinary way to activate and restore within

2. those who adopt a broader concept of messianism, not necessarily linked to the monarchy or postexile.[8]

What emerges from all this is that the question of different types of messianic expectations is already attested within Judaism and is not, therefore, a matter that can be limited to the relationship between Judaism and Christianity.[9]

Although it is not easy to move within this forest of opinions and perspectives and the different overlapping problems, it is necessary to arrive at a broad definition of the concept of messianism, one that is broad enough to embrace a plurality of attestations and phenomena. Among recent authors, Abi Toba Ngunga seems to be on the right path in compiling the work of authors who preceded him. He affirms that on his part the concept "is used with reference to the hope of an individual figure with a substantial mission to launch a new period of redemption."[10]

2. Messianic Texts: How Many and Which Ones?

Having arrived at an indicative definition of messianism, we shall try to delimit the texts that can be defined as messianic, in order to trace the presence or absence of the feminine in them. An initial review of works by various authors and all the texts that were considered messianic by more than one scholar reveals, surprisingly, that the texts are much more numerous than we could have imagined (Isa 4:2; 7:10–17; 8:8–10; 8:23–9:6; 11:1–10; 16:4b–5; 32:1–8; 41:8–13; 42:1–9; 49:1–13; 50:4–11;

---

this world the promise made to David after the monarchy has ended." Randall Heskett, *Messianism within the Scriptural Scroll of Isaiah*, LHBOTS 456 (New York: T&T Clark, 2007), 3.

8. Barton thoroughly discusses the presence of a deep-seated problem—some definitions are too narrow and therefore limiting, while others are too broad (e.g., every real charismatic or simply expected leader) and so not useful for research. See John Barton, "The Messiah in the Old Testament Theology," in *King and Messiah in Israel and the Ancient Near East: Proceedings of the Oxford Old Testament Seminar*, ed. John Day, JSOTSup 270 (Sheffield: Sheffield Academic, 1998), 365–79.

9. See Jacob Neusner, *Judaisms and Their Messiahs at the Turn of the Christian Era* (Cambridge: Cambridge University Press, 1987); John J. Collins, *The Scepter and the Star: Messianism in Light of the Dead Sea Scrolls*, 2nd ed. (Grand Rapids: Eerdmans, 2010).

10. Ngunga, *Messianism in the Old Greek*, 17.

52:13-53:12; 55:3-5; 61:1-3; Jer 17:19-27; 22:1-5; 23:1-4; 30:8-11, 18-22; 33:14-26; Ezek 17:22-24; 34:1-34; 37:15-28; 40-48; Hos 2:1-3; 3:4-5; Amos 9:11-15; Mic 2:12-13; 5:1-5; Hag 2:20-23; Zech 2:14-15; 3:1-10; 6:9-15; 9:9-10; 11:4-14; 12:9-14; 13:7-9). This has enabled us to understand why many scholars choose to adopt selective criteria in tracing these texts. However, even this approach can lead to extreme positions.[11]

After broadly following the history of research and evaluated the findings, we have selected our texts based on the definition adopted, namely, Isa 7:10-17; 8:23-9:6; 11:1-10; 32:1-8; 42:1-9; 49:1-13; 50:4-11; 52:13-53:12; 61:1-3; Jer 23:1-4; 33:14 to 26; Ezek 34:23-25; *37:15-28*; Amos 9:11-15; *Mic 2:12-13*; 5:1-5; *Zech 2:14-15*; 9:9-10; 12:9-14; 13:7-9.[12]

3. Messianism and the Feminine

Having identified the texts to be examined, we can now probe them for any occurrence of the feminine. However, this next step is difficult to take because the feminine presence is hidden in the folds of the texts and is not at all directly visible—the Messiah is thought of as masculine.

However, by carefully studying the biblical passages, I have come to the conclusion that the feminine component is more present than what appears at first glance, both in the quantity and quality of the evidence. From a strictly quantitative point of view, it appears that out of a total of twenty texts, in as many as six of them one would find references to feminine presence (Isa 7:1-10; 49:1-13; Mic 5:1-5; Zech 2:14-15; 9:9-10; 12:9-13).[13]

From the qualitative point of view, it manifests itself in two highly significant places that should be properly investigated—origin and destination. Origin—because it is clearly from the feminine component that messianic characters come. Destination—because it is toward a person thought of as feminine that the Messiah carries out his mission.

---

11. Fitzmyer, for example, reaches a conclusion that makes any research on messianism in subsequent prophets impossible, since no excerpt, after being examined, is considered messianic. He only "saves" Dan 9:24-27, which, however, does not belong to the Latter Prophets, according to Jewish tradition. See Joseph Fitzmyer, *The One Who Is to Come* (Grand Rapids: Eerdmans, 2007).

12. Texts marked in italics may, in my opinion, be considered messianic to a greater degree of certainty than others.

13. A special case must be made for Isa 32:1-8. We shall return to this point.

The feminine presence is therefore the place of departure and arrival of the task that the Messiah is to perform. Can it be proved? Certainly, through a meticulous reading of the passages. The first element is probably better known, but I think that often it is not sufficiently reflected in the fullness of its meaning: the Messiah comes from a woman.

3.1. From a Woman

Let us start from a simple observation: the authors could have simply avoided any reference to the mother of the Messiah, conception, birth. On the other hand, in various texts, it is explicitly the relationship between "the one who will come," or who is sent on a particular mission, and the mother, the womb, the one from whom this messianic figure comes. This is not an isolated phenomenon, and thus one we might consider accidental, but rather one that clearly recurs in at least two texts considered strongly messianic, namely, Isa 7: 10–17 and 49:1–6. These are very different and greatly studied pericopes. Therefore, we do not claim to provide a detailed exegetical study; nevertheless, we think it useful to make some observations.

3.1.1. Isa 7:10–17

The case of Isa 7 is certainly the most complicated and intriguing. The identification of the young woman and her child, as well as the textual problems concerning verse 14 and the use that the New Testament makes of this text (Matt 1:23), have inspired a great deal of research.[14] I will just mention here the textual question connected with the act of naming the child. While clearly only a woman can be expected to conceive and give birth, and while the utterance refers to a man, this should be understood in an ironic or metaphorical sense;[15] the act of bestowing the name belongs, within the biblical tradition, to both the father and the mother.

---

14. For a study of the text as messianic, see Antti J. Laato, *Who Is Immanuel? The Rise and the Foundering of Isaiah's Messianic Expectations* (Åbo: Åbo Academy Press, 1988), 117–63.

15. We think of Moses's protest in Num 11:12 and Isa 26:17–18, where a "we" that represents the people is compared to a woman in labor; while in their suffering they are similar, this is not in the final outcome. In Isa 33:11, the subject is in second-person masculine plural, and, again, the image is that of a stillbirth.

In the LXX the task is assigned to Ahaz (καὶ καλέσεις, "you will call").[16] Not so, however, in the MT, where the woman who conceives and gives birth is also the one to name her child.[17] A different situation is found in 1QIsa[a], which instead reports וקרא, and therefore places the Lord as the subject of action, since אדני is the only previous masculine noun.[18] In this case, it seems that the Hebrew language tradition has deliberately excluded Ahaz from such a task, attributing it either to God himself (Qumran) or to his mother (MT and Aleppo), probably due to the totally unseemly position of this king—unable to faithfully keep up his relationship with God, he is deprived of his gifts and paternal prerogatives. In fact, the MT here emphasizes the role of women, reconnecting the עלמה to women who find themselves at the onset of Israel's history. They are above all the matriarchs Leah and Rachel, in the famous story of their struggle to give Jacob children, and who take it on themselves to give their children significant names for the history they are living through (see Gen 29–30; 35).[19] In Isa 7:14, we are dealing precisely with a name that declares the sense of history and the inappropriateness of the fear that is getting the best of King Ahaz.

It is therefore the young woman who assumes the task of naming the Messiah, a name that specifies his mission and defines it as a tangible sign of the presence of YHWH amid his people. It is her voice that God uses to reveal his identity and to tell Israel how to stand before him. It is her

---

16. The LXX therefore implies that Ahaz is the child's father, which is never directly affirmed. In the story of the birth of Christ, Matthew places on Joseph the burden of naming him (Matt 1:24), while Luke assigns this task to his mother (Luke 1:31).

17. See also the Aleppo Codex; see Moshe H. Goshen-Gottstein, *The Book of Isaiah*, HUBP (Jerusalem: Magnes, 1995). It is certainly possible to take the final *t*- as a second-person masculine singular and that therefore the LXX effectively offers the best understanding of the text, though the vowelizing does not go in that direction. See Otto Kaiser, *Isaia (capp. 1–12)*, AT 17 (Brescia: Paideia, 1998), 202, 205, 213, 225.

18. See Eugene C. Ulrich, ed., *The Biblical Qumran Scrolls: Transcriptions and Textual Variants; Isaiah–Twelve Minor Prophets* (Leiden: Brill, 2013), 2:343.

19. Other women who name their children are Eve (Gen 4:25); Lot's two daughters (Gen 19:37–38); the wife of Judah (Gen 38:4–5); the Pharaoh's daughter in the case of Moses (Exod 2:10), whose situation is, however, particular (she is not a Hebrew woman, and there is no father to refer to in the story); Samson's mother (Judg 13:24); Hannah and Samuel (1 Sam 1:20); and Eli's daughter-in-law, at the point of death (1 Sam 4:21). On the birth stories, see Timothy Finlay, *The Birth Report Genre in the Hebrew Bible*, FAT 2/12 (Tübingen: Mohr Siebeck, 2005); Irmtraud Fischer, *Die Erzeltern Israels: Feministisch-theologische Studien zu Genesis 12–36* (Berlin: de Gruyter, 1994).

voice as a woman who, in contrast to the king's silence, affirms the trust in Adonai, who acts and does not abandon Israel. The woman and the Messiah are therefore deeply allied in this text, and she not only gives birth to him but also acts in a position of authority over him—giving him his name, that is, telling him who he is.

3.1.2. Isaiah 49:1–6

In the second Servant Song, the messianic figure that is placed before us is quite different—an adult man, sent on a mission of proclamation to all peoples.[20]

However, in introducing the servant, reference is made to his origin, and insistent reference to his origin "from the womb" (twice in v. 1 and once in v. 5). His mother is also expressly mentioned again in verse 1, ממעי אמי.

The first thing that the servant says about himself is, יהוה מבטן קראני ממעי אמי הזכיר שמי. He speaks and tells of another (Adonai), who called him and gave him his name. The action of pronouncing his name is now attributed directly to God; what in Isa 7 his mother did (MT) is done here by God himself (as in 1QIsa ͣ), assuming a role that, in the image evoked, can in all likelihood be called paternal. But what this does is to highlight a very close collaboration between God and the woman. He calls him, pronouncing his name, but does so by way of her body. God and the woman both take center stage at this point of defining the servant's identity and mission. Hence, the woman is depicted as a place where God acts; in her the voice of YHWH resounds, calling and registering the name of the servant, and her womb becomes the space not only of the stupendous rise of his physical life but also of the even more prodigious encounter with a voice that defines his identity.

---

20. I take the Servant Songs as messianic texts referring, in this sense, to the Christian tradition. Nonetheless, I consider it excessive to maintain that the Hebrew tradition has never considered them messianic and that there is no room for such an interpretation. It rather adopts different perspectives. See Antti J. Laato, *Who Is the Servant of the Lord? Jewish and Christian Interpretations on Isaiah 53 from Antiquity to the Middle Ages*, SRB 4 (Åbo: Åbo Academy University Press, 2012), 280. See also Joel E. Rembaum, "The Development of a Jewish Exegetical Tradition Regarding Isaiah 53," *HTR* 75 (1982): 289–311. The author shows, for example, how rabbinical Judaism considered this text messianic and offered a different interpretation only from the Middle Ages (291–93).

Once again, we come up against an unnecessary fact—her mention could have been avoided; the choice could have been made to call the prophet-servant after his birth. Instead, the author chooses the mother-womb element in order to emphasize the anteriority of this call with respect to anything else—not from his birth but before his birth; not when the servant sees the light but when all is still darkness. There are evident links between this text and Jer 1:5, where the prophet is likewise chosen in a moment of absolute anteriority. While this marks a belonging to God that could not be thought of in more radical terms, what must be noted is that it is precisely the woman who is the only other agent who has a vital relationship with the unborn child.

The womb therefore takes on a special value because there God himself "forms" (יצר, v. 5) and, from there, confers his mission. Of great interest is the symbolic value that the image of the uterus acquires; the womb is an unattainable place, closed, secret, and, at the same time, necessarily open, communicating with the outside (to allow both conception and birth). It is here that the mission-identity is defined, within that double matrix, which is the will/word of God and the gift of the mother's flesh.

In this light, it appears significant that the servant is led by God, in continuity with the image of verse 1, to relive an experience very similar to that of the womb. In fact, in verse 2, he is hidden in the shadow of the hand of God and placed in his quiver, as in other places of preparation for his task, to later be flung into his mission (like a sword or an arrow). Hence, YHWH himself becomes a kind of "womb" for his servant and assumes traits very much like a mother's.

This kind of identification process between God and mother proceeds in the subsequent literary unit by maintaining a close relationship of continuity with the Servant Song, in which Isaiah states that God "pronounces" the name of his servant by using a phrase constructed with *hiphil* of the verb זכר. But the issue of remembrance-forgetfulness that appears elusively in verse 1 receives an important development in Isa 49:14–26, where the focus shifts to Jerusalem. Zion complains of being abandoned and neglected (verbs עזב and שכח) by the Lord, but its complaint is answered with the assurance of a perennial and indelible memory. Significantly, this assurance is made by identifying God with the mother figure. If, in Isa 49:1, 5, God was like a father and acted from within the womb of the woman, calling his son by name and, in preparing him for his mission, had taken on maternal traits, now, in Isa 49:14–15, he identifies himself completely with those mothers who cannot help but be moved for their children (the בטן, "womb," substantive returns, v. 15) and who could only with difficulty forget them.[21]

3.2. The Special Case of Micah 5:1–5

The Mic 5:2 text, like Isa 7:14, also refers to a woman in labor (יולדה). Here the story is much less developed, and the role of the woman less detailed. But here also the significant element is time—the moment that God chooses to manifest his favorable intervention is connected to a birth. The end of oppression, their ordeal in the hands of their enemies, is defined by the childbearing by this anonymous woman. It is a time that is not specified (we do not know whether the woman is pregnant and only a few months must elapse before the end of oppression), yet we know that salvation has to do with Bethlehem and with a birth.

The childbirth image is employed mainly in reference to three ideas: In the first instance, it evokes the passage through a time of suffering. Second, it serves to establish a date of termination: the child cannot remain in his mother's womb forever but must necessarily come to light. Finally, it is connected to novelty—a new human comes into being, capable of bringing with him the novelty that God wants to introduce into the history of his people.

For all these reasons, the image appears appropriate for declaring the end of a crisis period and the start of a new phase whose outlines cannot be predicted precisely.[22]

Nonetheless, if we wonder who the woman in labor is, and if we here refer to the mother of a child whose birth is imminent (as in Isa 7), we must recognize that, in terms of the textual references established by the book, the woman refers emphatically to Zion and must be identified with it.[23] There are several reasons for affirming this position. We find the same

---

21. On the image of God as mother in this text, see Hanne Løland, *Silent or Salient Gender? The Interpretation of Gendered God-Language in the Hebrew Bible, Exemplified in Isaiah 42, 46 and 49*, FAT 32 (Tübingen: Mohr Siebeck, 2008), 161–92.

22. See Claudia D. Bergmann, *Childbirth as a Metaphor for Crisis: Evidence from the Ancient Near East, the Hebrew Bible, and 1QH XI, 1–18*, BZAW 328 (Berlin: de Gruyter, 2008).

23. This is also the interpretation by Francis I. Andersen and David Noel Freedman, *Micah: A New Translation with Introduction and Commentary*, AB 24E (New

beginning with ואתה in Mic 4:8 (opening of the section) and here, in Mic 5:1. Moreover, the name of the place to which it is addressed follows—Jerusalem (in 4:8), referred to with an unusual expression, מגדל־עדר, and Bethlehem (in 5:1). In addition, one immediately afterward finds that there appears the image of a birth in Mic 4:9–10 and 5:2 (speaking of יולדה). Finally, both texts refer to someone who will rule the land, using the root משל; Mic 4:8 speaks of the return of the ממשלה of Jerusalem, Mic 5:2 of the coming of מושל from Bethlehem.

If we then read the two texts in juxtaposition, we are led to a somewhat different interpretation from the one in Mic 5:2, which speaks of a royal woman and the birth of her child.[24] The first text clearly deals with Jerusalem, which is suffering the pains of childbirth and therefore is preparing to go into exile. The second one affirms that the new leader will come from Bethlehem; but first, the children of Israel will be under the control of others (under the rule of their enemies) until the woman has given birth. Now, the only woman who must give birth, in the text, is Jerusalem,[25] which thus undergoes and overcomes its ordeal.

Therefore, the Messiah comes to sanction a time of pain that has ended and not so much to end it. He comes to rule after the return of the sons of Israel; he comes to restore peace after the childbirth and the subsequent salvation that God himself performs. It is significant that Jerusalem's birth pangs were primarily because of the lack of rulers capable of carrying out their task (4:9); the new ruler comes to prevent the recurrence of those pangs.

If this interpretation is correct, the woman who gives birth then would not be the one from whom the Messiah comes, as might seem at first glance,[26] but rather, Zion, for whom the Messiah comes.

In the next section, we will find that the book of Zechariah moves along a similar line.

York: Doubleday, 2000), 469–70; Daniel L. Smith-Christopher, *Micah: A Commentary*, OTL (Louisville: Westminster John Knox, 2015), 167.

24. Mays already took this diretion in his commentary: "The 'birth' is the end of that term of 'labour' when all the remaining dispersion return to Israel." See James Luther Mays, *Micah: A Commentary*, OTL (London: SCM, 1980), 116–17.

25. The identification with Bethlehem is not permitted by the MT, which associates the place with masculine pronouns.

26. He comes from Bethlehem, but the image of birth is not used in reference to this city.

3.3. Toward a Woman: Zechariah 9:9–10

While the Messiah's origin from a woman appears quite clear in several texts (though, in our opinion, little recognized in scope), it is less clear that at times the recipient of the Messiah's action is thought of as a female subject. In Mic 5:2, as we have seen, the fact must be understood from the context, while in Zech 2:14–15 and 9: 9–10, the occurrence is explicit. For reasons of space and because of the difficulties that the text of Zech 2:14–15 presents in terms of whether it is messianic, I choose to consider here only Zech 9:9–10.

The verses under examination follow a declaration of protection from the Lord, who in turn appears after the description of the demolition of a series of enemy cities. God therefore guards his people by freeing them from those who stood against them and placing himself as sentinel (Zech 9:1–8).

The feminine presence begins to appear already in verses 2–5, in which all the cities mentioned are described as female subjects.[27] There are two facts to consider here—the first, a grammatical one, is that the noun עיר is female; the second is the tendency to metaphorize cities as women, so that they also take on in a certain sense female roles (mother, bride or daughter).[28]

In verse 9, we arrive in Jerusalem, which is urged to rejoice. The text is very beautiful, constructed according to the typical Hebrew parallelism—two imperatives (feminine singular) and two toponyms linked to "daughter," which indicate the same city.

3.3.1. The Role of the Daughter of Zion

The female metaphorization of the city implies that it can assume, as we said, different roles and therefore invites the reader to identify which is more relevant in each case.

---

27. Gaza is actually said to be in the throes of labor (verb חיל), and so also is Ekron.
28. There are numerous studies on the topic, but only two more recent ones are cited here. See Christl M. Maier, *Daughter Zion, Mother Zion: Gender, Space, and the Sacred in Ancient Israel* (Minneapolis: Fortress, 2008); Maier, "Daughter Zion as Queen and the Iconography of the Female City," in *Images and Prophecy in the Eastern Mediterranean*, ed. Martti Nissinen and Charles Carter, FRLANT 233 (Göttingen: Vandenhoeck & Ruprecht, 2009), 147–62.

Here Zion appears as a young woman. According to Carol Meyers and Eric Meyers, the use of the term *daughter* indicates an unmarried woman still dependent on her parents, with particular reference to her father.²⁹ In our opinion, this connotation is difficult to establish, because YHWH does not seem to perform a paternal task here (as the authors maintain), nor is such a task assigned to the king, who immediately appears. In fact, the image continues to indicate the coming of a king, "your king," who moves directly toward her. The encounter is therefore between a young woman and her sovereign. Can we maintain that the image is of a spousal character? Various elements lead in this direction.

The texts most similar to ours can be found in Isa 49:18 and 60:4–5, which speak of the coming of the peoples to Jerusalem. The same verb, בוא, is used, followed by לך, and the city is personified as a woman; in both cases she is a bride and a mother.³⁰ Nevertheless, the images make it difficult to define in a totally precise way the relationships between the characters, and on the contrary they seem to deliberately confuse the reader with an overload of possibilities. Isaiah 49 is particularly complex. First, the Lord assumes a maternal role toward the city (vv. 14–16). Then she is adorned with those who return (from exile?), like a bride (but it is not specified whose). Last, the maternity image returns, but this time it is attributed to Jerusalem in connection to its inhabitants.

Even in Zech 9:9, the situation is complex, or at least triangular. Jerusalem is placed before its king, but behind the scenes it is possible to detect the presence of the Lord, who saves the king himself and appears in verse 10 as the subject of the verb והכרתי. The authors report a split between YHWH and the Messiah-King, along with a certain overlap between the two.³¹

---

29. Carol L. Meyers and Eric M. Meyers, *Zechariah 9–14: A New Translation with Introduction and Commentary*, AB 25C (New York: Doubleday 1993), 121. For a discussion of the meaning of the expression, see Michael H. Floyd, "Welcome Back, Daughter of Zion!," *CBQ* 70 (2008): 484–504.

30. In Isa 49:18, we have the expression ותקשרים ככלה, whereas Isa 60:4–5 speaks of the sons and daughters of Jerusalem. At the same time, the text emphasizes the strong link between the city and the Lord (60:14), which, in our opinion, implies, though not made explicit, a spousal relationship with YHWH.

31. Collins, in his study of Zech 9:9, notes that the first part of 9:9 leads in one direction (prophetic proclamation of the coming of the Lord), while, the second disorients the reader by introducing the figure of the humble king. See Terry Collins,

What can we say then about the relationships between the characters, in light of the brief observations made?

On the one hand, the text shows a rite of enthronement, with the king coming to rule over the city, on the other, the metaphorization of Jerusalem as a young woman who rejoices alludes to royal nuptials. In this case, Jerusalem is implicitly depicted as the bride-queen (see Isa 62:1–5). What is striking is the double invitation to rejoice, which we could associate with the double declaration of joy in Song 1:4, when the heroine is introduced by King Solomon in the literary fiction produced by the Song in his chambers.[32]

We also note the numerous elements of contact between Zech 9:9 and Ps 45, defined as a royal epithalamium—the use of the term *daughter* to address the girl (see v. 11); the movement of one toward the other (vv. 14–15; in this case, she is the one who goes toward him); the repeated presence of the joy motif (בשמחת וגיל, v. 16).

In this context, the task of Zion-Jerusalem is to rejoice. Nothing else is required of her, except, very insistently, this. This point is interesting because it places Zech 9:9–10 within that series of prophetic texts that completely redeem the city-woman, who often draws on herself accusations and threats by the same prophets. But now her task is the joy of welcoming him who comes to her; he chooses her, but she is also called on to choose him.

3.3.2. "Behold, Your King Comes to You"

If her joy derives from the fact that the king approaches her, at this point his characteristics and mode of approach are described. The first two adjectives that describe him are "just" (צדיק) and "saved" (ונושע). The task of exercising justice is typically regal and does not stir amazement. However, the second term is debated, generally amended, or translated in the active voice, as does the LXX Septuagint (σώζων, "victorious"). We agree with the commentators who read the MT without modifying it[33] and interpret the

---

"The Literary Contexts of Zechariah 9:9," in *The Book of Zechariah and Its Influence*, ed. Christopher M. Tuckett (Aldershot, UK: Ashgate, 2003), 37.

32. See verb הביאני in Song 1:4 in my forthcoming article in *RivBib*.

33. See Meyers and Meyers, *Zechariah 9–14*, 126–27; Paul L. Redditt, *Zechariah 9–14*, IECOT (Stuttgart: Kohlhammer, 2012), 35, 44; Mirko Montaguti, *Costruire dialogando: Mt 21–27 e Zc 9–14 tra intertestualità e pragmatica*, AnBib 218 (Rome:

niphal as a sign of the divine action toward his Messiah: YHWH is he who saves his messenger, guards him, and rules the world through his action. In this sense, it appears significant that the Messiah is the one who, first of all, experiences the salvation of God and is made a mediator for others.

Verse 9b proceeds with the indication of the mount, the donkey, on which he appears, which is also a subject of differing interpretations: some say that it was typical of kings to show themselves riding a donkey, while others emphasize the gap between this choice and the more obvious one of coming with signs of power and therefore on horseback.³⁴ It seems to us more reasonable to grasp here the difference with respect to the common expectations, especially because of the context, that is, which further indicates the disappearance of carts and horses (v. 10).

In fact, verse 10 brusquely changes subject and presents a first-person singular that cannot coincide with the king, who until now has been spoken of in the third person. The commentators believe that YHWH himself declares his action to remove all war mounts and all kinds of weapons from the kingdom of Judah and that of Israel (summarily indicated by Ephraim and Jerusalem).

This interpretation of the text allows us to focus on the synergy between YHWH and his king, and shows the progressive assignment of the Lord's duties to his Messiah:

- והכרתי: the Lord removes the chariots and the horses;
- ונכרתה קשת: the bow of war is broken, but it is not said by whom;
- ודבר שלום: the king-Messiah announces peace to the nations;
- in the end, it is stated that "his dominion" (the king's) extends vastly.

If this is the type of king that Jerusalem welcomes, what can we say about her? It is clear that the action of the Messiah is essentially thought of as an action that brings peace and that the woman-city is the place where this peace is first and foremost achieved. Jerusalem is therefore the one

---

Gregorian & Biblical Press, 2016), 97; Mark J. Boda, *The Book of Zechariah*, NICOT (Grand Rapids: Eerdmans, 2016), 566–68. Petersen translates it instead in the attive, following the LXX. See David L. Petersen, *Zechariah 9–14 and Malachi: A Commentary*, OTL (London: SCM, 1995), 55. Besides, for the author, the figure of the king is not messianic or individual, but rather corporative.

34. See Boda's observations on this (*Book of Zechariah*, 569–70).

(female) who welcomes the Messiah, who experiences the establishment of his peace, and who becomes the point of radiating this good to all nations. Once again, the feminine presence is, primarily, a space of welcoming openness (without her the Messiah could not accomplish his project), as well as a larger-scale resurgence of his mission.

3.3.3. "As for You …"

But the text does not end here. The following unit (Zech 9:11–17) continues to refer to a female subject. Although there is no consensus either on delimiting the oracle or on its internal structuring, the authors observe that what we have is a precise desire for connection through the use of the feminine pronoun.[35] Verse 11 continues with a very clear "thou" feminine singular (גַּם־אַתְּ), and with the suffix of second-person feminine singular connected to the following nouns. It is not specified whom this "thou" refers to, but the only reasonable possibility is that it continues to indicate the female character mentioned so far, namely, Zion-Jerusalem.

It is therefore in reference to the woman-city that the text is constructed in a rich way—the initial phrase remains suspended and, at the same time, emphasized; the "thine" (feminine singular) alliance motif is emphasized without specifying who the contracting parties are (but hinting that they will be Zion and YHWH), and the image of the blood that recalls a series of other texts in an alliance context is introduced.[36] It is therefore clearly an act by God to liberate prisoners and an invitation to return home, to the citadel.[37] Last, in verse 13, the warlike imagery appears—Judah, Ephraim, and Zion themselves are the weapons that YHWH will use against his enemies.

There remains a certain tension in the text. On the one hand, there is an announcement of joy for Zion that is linked to the reason for the king's coming and the establishment of peace; on the other, this peace is a

---

35. This matters nonetheless only for 9:11–13, which function as a transition.

36. In particular, note Exod 24; Ezek 16. Meyers and Meyers note the relationship between Zech 9:11 and Ezek 16, referring, above all, to the last part of the pericope (Ezek 16:61–62; Meyers and Meyers, *Zechariah 9–14*, 140). In our opinion, however, the strong reference to blood should rather indicate the initial events in Jerusalem, in Ezek 16:6–9.

37. Here, a *hapax* is used, which is in agreement with "daughter of Zion" (see Boda, *Book of Zechariah*, 580–81).

precondition for a war that the Lord commands. In this battle, Zion does not remain on the sidelines but is used by YHWH as a weapon, together with Judah and Ephraim. In particular, she is described as the "sword," just as it is in the mouth of the Lord's servant (Isa 49:2).

The Messiah, therefore, is born of a woman and together performs his work in relation to a female figure, namely, Zion—to state the acceptance of the Messiah by his people, it seems necessary to resort to a female figure. We might wonder whether a male figure would not have perhaps been sufficiently credible. In fact, it is the city as "woman" that welcomes him with joy.

It also happens, in a rather curious way, that it is not the Messiah-king who fights for her, but she who becomes a powerful weapon in the hands of YHWH, the only one who actually wages war. Are we to acknowledge even a combative side of the woman whom the Messiah addresses? This seems to be a fact that should not be ignored (see also Mic 4:13–14).

4. Other Roles of the Feminine

Last, if we ask ourselves about other possible roles of the feminine in the messianic oracles, we believe we can identify two texts—Isa 32:9–14 and Zech 12:9–13. In both cases, the women assume a penitential attitude in a situation of suffering, in reference to a character with messianic traits.

Isaiah 32 is made up of three small units: (1) verses 1–8: a king who will reign and princes who will reign, according to justice;[38] (2) verses 9–14: women invited to tremble, to listen and to beat their breasts; (3) verses 15–20: an extraordinary outpouring of the spirit and a general transformation of the country from desert to garden, with tones typical of a messianic era.[39]

Verses 9–14, placed at the center, express a strongly negative opinion of the women involved—proud, confiding (evidently in someone other than the Lord). However, it must also be noted that it is only to them that the prophet turns. They are invited to listen to his voice, to lend an ear. They are called on to take up the signs of mourning, recognizing in advance the

---

38. This is the text that is considered messianic, but it must be read in correlation with what follows.

39. On the history of the composition of Isa 32, see Gary Stansell, "Isaiah 32: Creative Redaction in the Isaian Tradition," in *SBL 1983 Seminar Papers*, ed. Kent H. Richards, SBLSP 22 (Chico, CA: Scholars Press, 1983), 1–12.

gravity of the evil that is about to befall their country. This fact, of course, can be interpreted in various ways. It may be assumed that the males are not named because they do not need conversion. Nevertheless, verses 6–7 do not endorse such a hypothesis at all, as they deal with men who are swindlers and fools, and describe their wicked behavior in detail.

Thus, the appeal to women can be understood as a way of highlighting their role in the promised change. If the combination of the units makes sense, it is indeed that, thanks to their repentance, a breath from above can at last reach the whole people. The Hebrew conjunction עד, which opens the following unit (v. 15), indicates that their attitude must last "until" the promised era of peace appears. It therefore arises as a kind of premise needed for this advent.

A similar thing happens in Zech 12:9–13, where the weeping is an attitude that involves Jerusalem and the whole country (וספדה הארץ). All the families of Israel are saddened by the death of the "pierced one," but the role of women is reported separately (five times). Certainly, this manner of highlighting women separately is a rhetorical device to construct a poetically well-structured text and refers, concretely, to the typical task of lamenters in funeral rites. Nevertheless, this insistence on the role of women at least poses a question about their importance at this juncture: Is it perhaps that women have an especially greater ability to understand this kind of event? The text does not say so, but its insistence on the female presence at least leaves the question open.

5. Conclusion

The path we have taken has allowed us first of all to reflect on the different meanings of messianism in the history of research and contemporary exegesis, and to identify a series of texts that, after careful consideration, we have defined as messianic.

We have tried to investigate the feminine presence in the selected biblical texts. We have thus noted that, beyond an apparent concealment, female figures are actually very much present at key points and strategic positions of the story of the Messiah himself. In fact, two places are marked by the appearance of women in relation to the Messiah: the moment of his origin (Isa 7; 49) and the aim of his mission (Mic 5; Zech 9).

The Messiah cannot reach his people except through a woman, and it is she, the mother, who has the responsibility of issuing his name, that is, his identity and mission. But it is also at the people, thought of in a feminine form (Zion-Jerusalem), that the Messiah's mission is aimed. It is a mission of liberation and salvation, a mission of peace, whose only adequate sentiment of response toward such an undertaking is joy. In all this, the female attitude is never seen as passive but, on the contrary, it is constantly described as the most appropriate activity in relation to what takes place.

Women are recognized as having a special aptitude for involving themselves, through the most appropriate sentiments, in the events of Israel that concern the Messiah, either by identifying the people as a whole with a female figure (as in Zech 9) or by emphasizing the female element of the people when this is the case (especially when the required behavior is an expression of repentance or pain, as in Isa 32; Zech 12).

Therefore, if the Messiah is thought of as masculine, he cannot disregard significant feminine presence—and this, of course, affects everyone.

Bibliography

Andersen, Francis I., and David Noel Freedman. *Micah: A New Translation with Introduction and Commentary*. AB 24E. New York: Doubleday, 2000.

Barton, John. "The Messiah in the Old Testament Theology." Pages 365–79 in *King and Messiah in Israel and the Ancient Near East: Proceedings of the Oxford Old Testament Seminar*. Edited by John Day. JSOTSup 270. Sheffield: Sheffield Academic, 1998.

Bergmann, Claudia D. *Childbirth as a Metaphor for Crisis: Evidence from the Ancient Near East, the Hebrew Bible, and 1QH XI, 1–18*. BZAW 328. Berlin: de Gruyter, 2008.

Boda, Mark J. *The Book of Zechariah*. NICOT. Grand Rapids: Eerdmans, 2016.

Briggs, Charles Augustus. *Messianic Prophecy: The Prediction of the Fulfilment of Redemption through the Messiah*. Edinburgh: T&T Clark, 1886.

Collini, Paolo, *Messianismo: Indice concettuale del Medio Giudaismo 3*. Magnano: Qiqajon, 2009.

Collins, John J. *The Scepter and the Star: Messianism in Light of the Dead Sea Scrolls*. 2nd ed. Grand Rapids: Eerdmans, 2010.

Collins, Terry. "The Literary Contexts of Zechariah 9:9." Pages 29–40 in *The Book of Zechariah and Its Influence*. Edited by Christopher M. Tuckett. Aldershot, UK: Ashgate, 2003.

Cortese, Enzo. "Come sbloccare l'attuale esegesi Messianica." Pages 53–64 in *Il tempo della fine: Messianismo ed escatologia nel messaggio profetico*. Edited by Enzo Cortese. SBFA 76. Milano: Terra Santa, 2010.

De Sousa, Rodrigo F. *Eschatology and Messianism in LXX Isaiah 1–12*. LHBOTS 516. New York: T&T Clark, 2010.

Finlay, Timothy. *The Birth Report Genre in the Hebrew Bible*. FAT 2/12. Tübingen: Mohr Siebeck, 2005.

Fischer, Irmtraud. *Die Erzeltern Israels: Feministisch-theologische Studien zu Genesis 12–36*. Berlin: de Gruyter, 1994.

Fitzmyer, Joseph. *The One Who Is to Come*. Grand Rapids: Eerdmans, 2007.

Floyd, Michael H. "Welcome Back, Daughter of Zion!" *CBQ* 70 (2008): 484–504.

Goshen-Gottstein, Moshe H.. *The Book of Isaiah*. HUBP. Jerusalem: Magnes, 1995.

Heskett, Randall. *Messianism within the Scriptural Scroll of Isaiah*. LHBOTS 456. New York: T&T Clark, 2007.

Kaiser, Otto. *Isaia (capp. 1–12)*. AT 17. Brescia: Paideia, 1998.

Laato, Antti J. *A Star Is Rising: The Historical Development of the Old Testament Royal Ideology and the Rise of the Jewish Messianic Expectations*. Atlanta: Scholars Press, 1997.

———. *Who Is Immanuel? The Rise and the Foundering of Isaiah's Messianic Expectations*. Åbo: Åbo Academy Press, 1988.

———. *Who Is the Servant of the Lord? Jewish and Christian Interpretations on Isaiah 53 from Antiquity to the Middle Ages*. SRB 4. Åbo: Åbo Academy University Press, 2012.

Løland, Hanne. *Silent or Salient Gender? The Interpretation of Gendered God-Language in the Hebrew Bible, Exemplified in Isaiah 42, 46 and 49*. FAT 32. Tübingen: Mohr Siebeck, 2008.

Lust, Johan. *Messianism and the Septuagint. Collected Essays*. BETL 178. Leuven: Peeters, 2004.

Maier, Christl M. "Daughter Zion as Queen and the Iconography of the Female City." Pages 147–62 in *Images and Prophecy in the Eastern Mediterranean*. Edited by Martti Nissinen and Charles Carter. FRLANT 233. Göttingen: Vandenhoeck & Ruprecht, 2009.

———. *Daughter Zion, Mother Zion: Gender, Space, and the Sacred in Ancient Israel*. Minneapolis: Fortress, 2008.

Mays, James Luther. *Micah: A Commentary*. OTL. London: SCM, 1980.

Meyers, Carol L., and Eric M. Meyers. *Zechariah 9–14: A New Translation with Introduction and Commentary.* AB 25C. New York: Doubleday, 1993.

Montaguti, Mirko. *Costruire dialogando: Mt 21–27 e Zc 9–14 tra intertestualità e pragmatica.* AnBib 218. Rome: Gregorian & Biblical Press, 2016.

Mowinckel, Sigmund. *He That Cometh: The Messiah Concept in the Old Testament and Later Judaism.* Grand Rapids: Eerdmans, 2005.

Neusner, Jacob. *Judaisms and Their Messiahs at the Turn of the Christian Era.* Cambridge: Cambridge University Press, 1987.

Ngunga, Abi Tomba. *Messianism in the Old Greek of Isaiah: An Intertextual Analysis.* FRLANT 245. Göttingen: Vandenhoeck & Ruprecht, 2013.

Petersen, David L. *Zechariah 9–14 and Malachi: A Commentary.* OTL. London: SCM, 1995.

Redditt, Paul L. *Zechariah 9–14.* IECOT. Stuttgart: Kohlhammer, 2012.

Rembaum, Joel E. "The Development of a Jewish Exegetical Tradition Regarding Isaiah 53." *HTR* 75 (1982): 289–311.

Rydelnik, Michael. *The Messianic Hope: Is the Hebrew Bible Really Messianic?* Nashville: B&H, 2010.

Smith-Christopher, Daniel L. *Micah: A Commentary.* OTL. Louisville: Westminster John Knox, 2015.

Stansell, Gary. "Isaiah 32: Creative Redaction in the Isaian Tradition." Pages 1–12 in *SBL 1983 Seminar Papers.* Edited by Kent H. Richards. SBLSP 22. Chico, CA: Scholars Press, 1983.

Ulrich, Eugene C., ed. *The Biblical Qumran Scrolls: Transcriptions and Textual Variants; Isaiah–Twelve Minor Prophets.* Vol. 2. Leiden: Brill, 2013.

Yarbro Collins, Adela, and John J. Collins. *King and Messiah as Son of God: Divine, Human, and Angelic Messianic Figures in Biblical and Related Literature.* Grand Rapids: Eerdmans, 2008.

The Never-Ending Search for God's Feminine Side: Feminine Aspects in the God-Image of the Prophets

Hanne Løland Levinson

1. Introduction

The feminine side of the image of God in the prophets is a topic I have worked on for a long time and that so far has resulted in my doctoral dissertation in 2007 and my first book in 2008.[1] But that was more than ten years ago. What do I have to say about this topic today? Is there anything more to add to this discussion? In her study *Menstruation and Childbirth in the Bible*, Tarja Philip writes, "The female features of God have already been discussed in research."[2] Obviously she is right; female features of God have been on the agenda not only in Hebrew Bible research but also in religious studies and theological discourses since the early 1970s, as well as in the synagogue and in the church. This fact alone, though, does not mean that the discussion is exhausted. Whether there is more to say—or not— about the feminine side of God depends on whether we have achieved what we set out to do, whether we reached our goals.[3] I propose that we have not. The goals of the search for the feminine side of God were two-

---

1. Hanne Løland, *Silent or Salient Gender? The Interpretation of Gendered God-Language in the Hebrew Bible, Exemplified in Isaiah 42, 46 and 49*, FAT 2/32 (Tübingen: Mohr Siebeck, 2008). This book provides the basis for much of the present essay, which also aims to update the discussion by reflecting the changes of the past ten years.

2. Tarja S. Philip, *Menstruation and Childbirth in the Bible: Fertility and Impurity*, StBibLit 88 (New York: Lang, 2006), 101.

3. *We* is used here as a loose reference to the collective of scholars who have taken part in the search for the feminine side of God.

fold: documentation and change.[4] While we have done a good job with the documentation, the desire for change does not seem to have been met. I will return to both of these claims later, but first a few clarifying remarks.

2. Clarifying Remarks: What Are We Searching For?

It is beyond the scope of this essay to provide an overview of every occurrence of feminine images of God in the Prophets or a review of the scholarly contributions to this field.[5] What I will do here, based on my own work and teaching experiences, is to reflect on where we are today compared to where we set out from. I want to draw our attention to some important achievements that we have made, as well as to what seems to be missing, both intellectually and culturally.

The search for God's feminine side is part of the larger discussion on God and gender, or more precisely, the gender *of* God. This discussion has been ongoing for a long time in different research traditions, theological disciplines, and also in religious communities, hence the title of this article, "The Never-Ending Search for God's Feminine Side." Questioning the dominant male/masculine image of God has been one of the main feminist concerns in theological and religious discourses since Mary Daly wrote in 1973, "If God is male, then the male is God."[6]

Hebrew Bible scholars have primarily taken two different approaches in the search for God's feminine side. One approach, the one that I (and

---

4. Not every scholar working on questions about the feminine aspects of God has change as a goal. Change is a contemporary theological goal, the desire to change the god-language of today. See below.

5. For an overview of the field until 2007, see Løland, *Silent or Salient Gender*. For research in the last ten years, the articles to the individual prophetic books in both the *Women's Bible Commentary* and *Feminist Biblical Interpretation* are a good starting point. See Carol A. Newsom, Sharon H. Ringe, and Jacqueline E. Lapsley, eds., *Women's Bible Commentary*, 3rd ed. (Louisville: Westminster John Knox, 2012); Luise Schottroff and Marie-Theres Wacker, eds., *Feminist Biblical Interpretation: A Compendium of Critical Commentary on the Books of the Bible and Related Literature* (Grand Rapids: Eerdmans, 2012). See also Irmtraud Fischer, "Las Imágens De Dios Tras La Adopción Del Monoteísmo: Ninguna Imagen Iconográfica, Pero Miles De Imágenes Verbales," in *Los Rostros De Dios: Imágens y experiencias de lo divino en la Biblia*, ed. Carmen Bernabé Ubieta (Estalla: Editorial Verbo Divino, 2013), 167–80.

6. Mary Daly, *Beyond God the Father: Toward a Philosophy of Women's Liberation* (Boston: Beacon, 1973), 19.

several others) have focused on and will discuss here, is the study of the imagery or language used for God in biblical texts, "the god-language" of the Hebrew Bible. Another approach has been to search for YHWH's feminine traits, especially for the understanding of YHWH's gender in the context of the broader landscape of gods and goddesses of the ancient Near East.[7] This second line of research we could label "a search for the missing goddess." Raphael Patai, as early as 1967, argued that beside the Hebrew God there has always been the Hebrew Goddess.[8] This would, of course, imply that the Hebrew God, YHWH, was understood as a male deity, and Patai is not the only one who draws this conclusion.[9]

Our focus here is not really on the gender of God but on the gendered language for God. The term *god-language* emphasizes that we are working with language and texts, and that the images or concepts of God that are constructed when reading these texts are embedded in language. This does not mean that the god-language is isolated from the broader context. Silvia Schroer, in an earlier volume of The Bible and Women series, formulates it thus: "Each metaphor in a psalm ... evoked a world of ideas that was sustained by myths, cult, mental images, and literary metaphors. It is anachronistic to postulate 'pure' metaphors, namely figures of speech that would not reactivate the mythological-imaginary background."[10]

The question in my research is not whether God was or is male or female but simply how the deity, the god, of ancient Israel, YHWH, is portrayed in the prophetic literature and how the readers or listeners of these texts might have imagined this god.[11] No discussion about God is simple, though, and discussion of the language with which the prophet constructed

---

7. See Løland, *Silent or Salient Gender*, 4–20.

8. Raphael Patai, *The Hebrew Goddess* (New York: KTAV, 1967). The search for a missing Hebrew goddess overlaps partly with a growing interest in goddesses in general and the so-called goddess movement.

9. Prominent examples are Mark Smith, *The Early History of God: Yahweh and Other Deities in Ancient Israel* (San Francisco: HarperSanFrancisco, 1990); Athalya Brenner, "The Hebrew God and His Female Complements," in *The Feminist Companion to Mythology*, ed. Carolyne Larrington (London: Pandora, 1992), 48–62.

10. Silvia Schroer, "Ancient Near Eastern Pictures as Keys to Biblical Metaphors," in *The Writings and Later Wisdom Books*, ed. Christl M. Maier and Nuria Calduch-Benages, BW 3 (Atlanta: SBL Press, 2014), 133.

11. Whether it is in fact possible to refer to God with our language or whether "God" as such exists are questions we, of course, cannot answer in an academic context, and I do not set out to say anything about God as such.

his or her image of God is not simple either. It is even less simple when it comes to contemporary discussion of what language we should use today to talk of God, because images have power, as does language.

The Prophets here refers to the Latter Prophets, and my examples will come mainly from Isa 40–66. This said, most of what is stated here applies to god-language in general. The expression *feminine aspects* refers to the fact that most of the god-language is gendered male or female. I will return to these identifications later. With these clarifications done, let us return to my proposition that we have not achieved what we set out to do. One reason for this claim concerns my reading of the scholarly literature; another stems from my experiences in the classroom. I will start with the latter because, from the students' thoughts and reactions, we can determine whether we actually have achieved any changes over the last decades.

3. Classroom Experiences: Lack of Change

> As a mother comforts her child, so I will comfort you; you shall be comforted in Jerusalem. (Isa 66:13)[12]

"What is God portrayed as in this text?" I asked my class in Oslo some years ago. "A father!" the answer came without hesitation. "Are you sure?" I replied. The student responded, more hesitantly this time, "A parent?" He was not technically wrong in his second reply—a mother is a parent, but what part of the phrase "as a mother comforts her child" does not clearly paint an image of a mother, a woman, a female, who comforts her child? That the Hebrew text reads somewhat differently from most English and German translations, as well as the Norwegian translation that we read in class, could be a topic for discussion for Hebrew Bible scholars, but that was beyond the undergraduate student's basic comprehension.[13] He read and then revised the reference "as a mother comforts her child" into "as a father God will comfort you."

I taught in Norway for twelve years before I moved to the United States to take up a position at the University of Minnesota. Much is different in the United States. However, teaching gendered god-language in 2017

---

12. All translations are from the NRSV unless otherwise noted.
13. The point of comparison in the Hebrew text is actually not between the comforter and God but rather between the one who is being comforted by God and a man who is comforted by his mother.

in Minnesota is not so different from what it was in Norway in the early 2000s—something that confirms my suspicion that we have not made as much progress as we thought we had. Two notions became clear in both contexts: that female god-language (possibly) gives women a sense of value that male god-language cannot, and that women (may) have problems (for different reasons) connecting with a male God. Again, these notions can be questioned, but they still represent some women's experiences and were reflected in my classroom. None of the responses in my 2017 class in Minnesota went in the direction of the Norwegian student. There was no attempt to reinterpret, for example, the image of God as midwife (in Ps 22) as a male image. In other words, the female imagery for God in the Psalms was recognized as female, and the students embraced it as such.

Of course, we cannot expect a direct relationship between identifying or documenting feminine god-language in the Hebrew Bible and an immediate radical change in religious communities and doctrines today. The Hebrew Bible does not present Judaism or Christianity; it reflects the religious thinking of certain elite, male-dominated groups in ancient Israel. Nonetheless, the Hebrew Bible continues to be an important source for theologizing in both Judaism and Christianity.

4. Metaphorical Language, or the Duck Test

If it looks like a metaphor, reads like a metaphor, and quacks like a metaphor, then it probably is a metaphor. I do not think we can overestimate the importance of contemporary metaphor theory in the search for the feminine side of God. Of course, we have known for a long time that the biblical authors spoke of God in the form of metaphors. When the prophets depict God as saying, "I will devour them like a lion" (Hos 13:8), or "Is there any god besides me? There is no other rock" (Isa 44:8), we see these as metaphorical utterances and not literary descriptions of God. But contemporary metaphor theory, and cognitive linguistics in particular, has given us a vocabulary with which to describe the god-language, identifying its sources, and to come closer to an understanding of how the metaphorical utterances work.[14] In the words of Janet Soskice, "Metaphor is that figure

---

14. See Løland, *Silent or Salient Gender*, 31–56. See also Mary Therese DesCamp and Eve E. Sweetser, "Metaphors for God: Why and How Do Our Choices Matter for Humans? The Application of Contemporary Cognitive Linguistics Research to the Debate on God and Metaphor," *PP* 53 (2005): 207–38.

of speech whereby we speak about one thing in terms which are seen to be suggestive to another."[15] God is thus talked of in language and in concepts that are usually used in other contexts.[16]

There are typically two elements or thoughts in a metaphor, often referred to as *source* and *target*, or *source domain* and *target domain*. Target is the one that is talked about. The target of all god-language is constant—God. The source domains vary a lot, though. In Hos 13:8, the source domain is a lion; in Isa 44:8, it is a rock. The Hebrew Bible authors use anthropomorphic ("shepherd" in Isa 40:11, "woman in labor" in Isa 42:14, and "husband" in Isa 54:6), zoomorphic ("mother bear," "lion," and "leopard" in Hos 13:8), and physiomorphic ("rock" in Isa 44:8 and "dwelling place" in Ps 90:1) source domains for God. God is talked of as human, animal, or nature. It is generally understood that the meaning of a metaphor is to be found in the interaction between the source and the target or in the blend that is created when the source and the target interact. The blend is new, and the metaphor thus creates something that is not limited to either source or target.[17] The metaphor constructs a new image of God.

Metaphors are one way of talking about God; another is through comparisons or similes. In recent debates, some scholars have argued that metaphors and similes are not merely two different linguistic expressions but that using one or the other implies a conceptual difference. I have argued elsewhere that there is no cognitive difference between a metaphor and a simile, even though they are linguistically different,[18] so I will not dwell on this point here but only mention that, in the Hebrew Bible, we find several examples of a source domain used for God in both similes and metaphors. For instance, in Isa 63:16, one reads: "For you are our father,

---

15. Janet Martin Soskice, *Metaphor and Religious Language* (Oxford: Oxford University Press, 1985), 15.

16. Note that DesCamp and Sweetser emphasize that metaphor is not a matter of language but that "human beings use metaphors to conceptualize one mental domain in terms of another" ("Metaphors for God," 215).

17. For an introduction to blending theory, see Gilles Fauconnier and Mark Turner, *The Way We Think: Conceptual Blending and the Mind's Hidden Complexities* (New York: Basic Books, 2002).

18. See Løland, *Silent or Salient Gender*, 47–51. This discussion is especially pointed in terms of the liturgical debate on god-language. During the 2010 debate about the revision of the liturgy in the Church of Norway, many participants argued that one could not include prayers to "God our Mother" in the liturgy, but rather prayers formulated in similes: "God is like a mother …"

though Abraham does not know us and Israel does not acknowledge us; you, O Lord, are our father." Here "Lord (or God) our father" is formulated in a metaphorical utterance, whereas in Ps 103:13, "father" is used in a simile: "As a father has compassion for his children, so the Lord has compassion for those who fear him." The source domain "father" and the target "God" are brought together in an interaction in both the metaphor and the simile. In both cases, there is an invitation to the reader to relate the two domains to each other. In both examples, God is a father and God is not literally a father. In both similes and metaphors, there is a tension between "is" and "is not."[19]

The emphasis on god-language as metaphorical language has also made it clear that we cannot treat one category of god-language as fundamentally different or more descriptive than another, because there are no subcategories of metaphors. If God our mother is a metaphor, then God our father is a metaphor as well.[20] This brings us to the discussion of gendered metaphors.

5. Gendered Metaphors

"Feminine imagery for God is more prevalent in the Old Testament than we usually acknowledge."[21] This statement was made by Phyllis Trible already in 1973. Until the 1970s, there was hardly any acknowledgment of the feminine imagery or language for God in the Hebrew Bible. From the 1970s and 1980s and onward, there has been a continuing production of literature on the topic. We have done well in documenting the presence of female god-language in the Hebrew Bible; not only specialized literature but also exegetical commentaries and even study Bibles often acknowledge the presence of female language in a text (or the possibility of reading the language as female). I have been working on Num 11 for another project, and for this text the *HarperCollins Study Bible* comments:

---

19. Paul Ricoeur, *The Rule of Metaphor: Multi-disciplinary Studies of the Creation of Meaning in Language*, trans. Robert Czerny with Kathleen McLaughlin and John Costello (London: Routledge & Kegan Paul, 1978).

20. I am aware of the theological claim sometimes made that "Father" in "God the Father" is a name, not a metaphor, but this view cannot be defended on linguistic grounds. See also DesCamp and Sweetser, "Metaphors for God," 213–14.

21. Phyllis Trible, "Depatriarchalizing in Biblical Interpretation," *JAAR* 41 (1973): 32.

"The female imagery used here … is unusual, but not unique."[22] I consulted the study Bible here, first of all, because it is a more common source of information for students than the vast corpora of scholarly literature. Moreover, if female metaphors are recognized in study Bibles, it shows that the scholarly work we have done has also been picked up in more mainstream research. Today, no (serious) Hebrew Bible scholar will question the occurrence of female god-language in the biblical material. How he or she understands this imagery may vary, though.

Gendered language is language that awakens associations to gender and constructs ideas of gender for the reader.[23] Female god-language is language that constructs ideas of female gender. Gender must thus be part of the source domain if metaphorical language should be identified as gendered language.[24] Gender can be either explicitly or implicitly present in the source language. Father, king, and husband all refer to a male person, and male biological gender (sex) is therefore explicitly present not only in the source but also in the metaphorical statements "God is father," "God is King," and "God is husband." When gender is part of the social constructions of what is male or female, masculine or feminine, gender is implicit in the source. In ancient Israel, only women were midwives. But this profession is not biologically exclusive; men can also perform the role of midwives, and this is thus an example of a sociocultural construction. When God is portrayed as a midwife (e.g., Ps 22:10), it is a role indirectly marked for female gender and therefore an example of feminine gendered god-language. A source domain can also be nongendered, which could mean no associations to gender, or the source can be gender ambiguous, and thus the markers can indicate either male or female gender.

Our understanding of gender has changed dramatically since the 1970s and especially over the past couple of decades; therefore, the above-mentioned categories are not without problems. They are binary and heteronormative and can be questioned based on current theories of

---

22. Jo Ann Hackett, "Introduction and Notes to Numbers," in *The HarperCollins Study Bible: New Revised Standard Version, Including the Apocryphal/Deuterocanonical Books*, ed. Harold W. Attridge, Wayne A. Meeks, and Jouette M. Bassler (San Francisco: HarperSanFrancisco, 2006), 214.

23. *Gender* is used here in an inclusive way and not limited to gender as in the gender/sex distinction.

24. For a more thorough discussion of gendered language, see Løland, *Silent or Salient Gender*, 75–90.

gender fluidity. More and more scholars, including myself, would argue with Judith Butler that not only gender but also sex is a social construction, and that gender is something we perform.[25] Corrine Carvalho raises the thoughtful question "Whose gendered language for God?" in a recent article titled with that very question.[26] Her concern is first and foremost contemporary in nature, that is, "how this more recent research [on gender fluidity] can or should affect a biblically based theology of gender in contemporary churches."[27] However, she and other Hebrew Bible scholars have shown that gender can be understood as fluid also in some of the biblical material.[28] This said, I think it is still fair to claim that "biblical cultures rest firmly on a binary foundation," and one of these binary foundations is gender/sex.[29] Male/female and man/woman are the primary categories of gender/sex in the biblical material, and for the purpose of documentation we need categories that are in line with the material. This does not mean that we should not question these binary categories and challenge them when we formulate god-language today, but that is another task to take on after the documentation.

I argued in my book *Silent or Salient Gender* that it is not enough to document whether gender, in this case female gender, is part of the source domain of god-language. This simply leaves us with an observation that the Hebrew Bible has a handful of female metaphors for God against a multitude of male metaphors. Then what? We also have to ask whether the gender is of significance (is salient) and whether it contributes to the construction of the concept of God in the concrete texts. Elizabeth Johnson argues: "If it is not meant that God is male when masculine imagery is

---

25. Judith Butler, *Gender Trouble: Feminism and the Subversion of Identity* (New York: Routledge, 1990).
26. Corrine L. Carvalho, "Whose Gendered Language of God?," *CurTM* 43 (2016): 12–16.
27. Carvalho, "Whose Gendered Language," 12.
28. Examples include Corrine L. Carvalho, "Sex and the Single Prophet: Marital Status and Gender in Jeremiah and Ezekiel," in *Prophets Male and Female: Gender and Prophecy in the Hebrew Bible, the Eastern Mediterranean, and the Ancient Near East*, ed. Jonathan Stökl and Corrine L. Carvalho, AIL 15 (Atlanta: Society of Biblical Literature, 2013), 237–67; Tamar S. Kamionkowski, *Gender Reversal and Cosmic Chaos: A Study on the Book of Ezekiel*, JSOTSup 368 (London: Sheffield Academic, 2003).
29. Kamionkowski, *Gender Reversal*, 3–4. This assumption has been questioned; see Carvalho ("Whose Gendered Language," 12–16).

used, why the objection when female images are introduced?"³⁰ In other words, the gender of the god-language does not gender "God as such," according to Johnson, and thus there should be no hesitation in using female language. This is an important, thought-provoking question, but, again, we are not focusing on God as such. Our concern is whether the gendered god-language constructed a gendered image of God for the readers and listeners of the ancient texts, and my claim is that it did, and often a highly gendered image. The gendered language often constructed an image or concept of God as male, and at other times constructed an image of God as female, as we will see shortly.

6. Female God-Language in Second Isaiah

Second Isaiah is different from the rest of the Bible when it comes to its use of female god-language.³¹ Irmtraud Fischer titled her chapter on Isaiah in *Feminist Biblical Interpretation* "Isaiah: The Book of Female Metaphors," and Mayer Gruber claims that we find "a whole series of maternal expressions applied to the LORD in Isa 40–66 … the like of which do not occur anywhere else in the Hebrew Bible."³² In my work on Second Isaiah, it is also evident that, in these texts, God is not only conceptualized as female but also often imagined with a body, a female body.³³ Let us consider

---

30. Elizabeth A. Johnson, *She Who Is: The Mystery of God in Feminist Theological Discourse* (New York: Crossroad, 1997), 34.

31. This is a claim made over and again in the literature on female god-language, but I have not seen any statistics that actually support the claim. This spring semester (2017), I had two students working for me as part of a new Dean's Freshman Research & Creative Scholars Program at the University of Minnesota. The assignment I gave them was to read the Prophetic Books and highlight every reference to or description of God, every verb with God as a subject, and every body part assigned to God. Next, our joint effort was to determine how these activities and descriptions were gendered. Further work is needed, but there is no doubt that Second Isaiah has the most occurrences of female god-language. I am grateful for the work of Cassidy Drummond and Lena Figlear, and for the work done by my research assistant Maximilian Beyendorff on this project as well as the editorial work on this article.

32. Irmtraud Fischer, "Isaiah: The Book of Female Metaphors," in Schottroff and Wacker, *Feminist Biblical Interpretation*, 303–18; Mayer I. Gruber, "The Motherhood of God in Second Isaiah," *RB* 90 (1983): 351–59.

33. In recent years, several studies on the embodiment of God in the HB have been published. Some important works are Esther J. Hamori, *"When Gods Were Men": The Embodied God in Biblical and Near Eastern Literature* (Berlin: de Gruyter, 2008);

some examples:[34] "I have been silent for a long time, I have kept still and restrained myself. Like a woman in labor I will cry out, I will gasp and pant at the same time" (Isa 42:14, my translation).

In Isa 42:14, YHWH is in travail. YHWH is crying out in labor pains. The salient feature here is not the outcome of the birth; it is not the baby but the process of labor, with all its implications, that is emphasized. Birth is a powerful force, but it also entails pain, struggle, and screaming. The woman-in-labor simile is explicitly marked for female sex, and YHWH is conceptualized as a female subject. The image also implies a notion of pain and anguish as part of the image of God, which is maybe even more striking to the contemporary reader than the female imagery. YHWH is like a woman in labor.

> Listen to me, house of Jacob and all the remnant of the house of Israel.
> You who have been carried since the time of pregnancy
> you who have been lifted up at birth
> Until old age I am, and until gray hair I will bear.
> I have made and I will carry, and I will sustain and I will save.
> (Isa 46:3–4, my translation)

Isaiah 46:3–4 can be read as a story—a child is carried from the womb, carried during the pregnancy. Here the text clearly describes also the outcome of the birth. The baby is lifted out of the birth canal at birth. The child is Israel; the one who carries is YHWH. YHWH is said to have a womb (בטן), the only reference to God's womb in the entire Hebrew Bible. YHWH is depicted as a pregnant woman. The image shifts as YHWH also acts as the midwife who lifts up the child at birth. The child grows up and

---

Benjamin D. Sommer, *The Bodies of God and the World of Ancient Israel* (Cambridge: Cambridge University Press, 2009); Andreas Wagner, ed., *Göttliche Körper—göttliche Gefühle. Was leisten anthropomorphe und anthropopathische Götterkonzepte im Alten Orient und Alten Testament?*, OBO 270 (Fribourg: Universitätsverlag, 2014); Mark Smith, "The Three Bodies of God in the Hebrew Bible," *JBL* 134 (2015): 471–88. On the question of God's body and gender, see the works of Gerlinde Baumann, "Das göttliche Geschlecht: YHWHs Körper und die Gender-Frage," in *Körperkonzepte im Ersten Testament—Aspekte einer Feministischen Anthropologie*, ed. Hedwig-Jahnow-Forschungsprojekt (Stuttgart: Kohlhammer, 2003), 220–50; Christl Maier, "Körperliche und emotionale Aspekte JHWHs aus Genderperspektive," in Wagner, *Göttliche Körper–göttliche Gefühle*, 171–89.

34. For a thorough discussion of the following text examples, see Løland, *Silent or Salient Gender*, part 2.

is still carried, it gets old, and it is carried and sustained, even when its hair turns gray.

Another striking image for YHWH is found in Isa 49:14–15, where YHWH is depicted as a nursing mother: "But Zion said, 'YHWH has abandoned me, the Lord has forgotten me.' Can a woman forget her suckling child, a compassionate mother, the child of her womb? Even if these could forget I cannot forget you" (Isa 49:14–15, my translation). Isaiah 49:14–15 can be read as a disputation. Zion is accusing YHWH, her husband, of having abandoned her. YHWH tries to repudiate this accusation by arguing that *she* cannot forget Zion, like nursing mothers cannot forget their children. In this text, YHWH is both the husband and the mother, and we have one of several examples where male and female metaphors are used together, either in contrast or as comparison. To convince Zion of YHWH's incapability of forgetting, the strongest bond known is set forth—the bodily connection between a mother and her suckling child. YHWH is a woman who cannot forget her suckling child.

The female language in these examples is connected to the process of giving birth or to being a mother, and the images are as a result distinctly connected to the female body. This association has been understood by some as quite limiting and even negative.[35] It is clear that in many ways, the female language for YHWH does draw on very limited source domains—those of motherhood, birth giving, and midwifery—but we cannot forget that these were highly valued roles in ancient Israel, and this was one of the main realms of female experiences. This brings us to one more important notion of god-language as metaphorical language and my concluding remarks.

7. Conclusion: Language as Experience and the Desire for Change

Tryggve Mettinger once made the following statement with regard to god-language: "These symbols speak of God but do so in terms of categories drawn from the world of human experience."[36] We are not talking here of sectarian or even religious experiences but about everyday human experiences. The Hebrew Bible's authors thought about God based on their life

---

35. See Rhiannon Graybill, "Yahweh as Maternal Vampire in Second Isaiah: Reading from Violence to Fluid Possibility with Luce Irigaray," *JFSR* 33 (2017): 17.

36. Tryggve N. D. Mettinger, *In Search of God: The Meaning and Message of the Everlasting Names*, trans. Frederick H. Cryer (Philadelphia: Fortress, 1988), 1.

experiences, and so do we. This is also the reason for our criticisms of the god-language in Jewish-Christian tradition. Since most if not the entire Bible was formulated by men, and the traditions have been dominated by men, the god-language used in the Hebrew Bible reflects mostly men's experiences, while women's experiences have had very little influence on the formulation of the god-language. We are left with a diminished god-language, and a diminished god-language constructs a limited, and limiting, image of God.

We here return to the goal of change, outlined in the beginning of this essay, that is, the desire to change contemporary god-language and with that how *we* imagine God. One way to avoid a diminished god-language and an all-male image of God is by using a multitude of metaphors. By using several different metaphors for God, we would reflect a wider range of experiences and include more people's life experiences in the formulation of our god-language and, at the same time, we would maintain the idea that the god-language is not literal descriptions for God. Several scholars have argued that this is exactly what we find in the Hebrew Bible and especially in Second Isaiah. For example, Marc Zvi Brettler and Maria Häusl show how Second Isaiah underlines the incomparability of God (that God is not like anything or anyone) and, at the same time, uses multiple and often contradicting metaphors for God.[37] To maintain the idea that God is not like anyone or anything else, it seems necessary to use a wide variety of metaphors that also include contradictory metaphors. Juliana Claassens emphasizes how listening to all voices, including the minority voices of female god-language, in the Hebrew Bible can help us create a more inclusive god-language.[38] To me, this is a project of deconstructing and constructing. The documentation of female god-language and the multitude of metaphors for God in the Hebrew Bible give us the tools necessary

---

37. Marc Zvi Brettler, "Incompatible Metaphors for YHWH in Isaiah 40–66," *JSOT* 18 (1998): 97–120; Maria Häusl, "'Mit wem wollt ihr mich vergleichen?' Gottesbilder und Geschlechterperspektive in Jes 40–55," in *Glaube in der Welt von heute: Theologie und Kirche nach dem Zweiten Vatikanischen Konzil; Für Elmar Klinger*, ed. Thomas Franz and Hanjo Sauter (Würzburg: Echter, 2006), 2:127–38.

38. L Juliana Claassens, "Rupturing God-Language: The Metaphor of God as Midwife in Psalm 22," in *Engaging the Bible in a Gendered World: An Introduction to Feminist Biblical Interpretation in Honor of Katherine Doob Sakenfeld*, ed. Linda Day and Carolyn Pressler (Louisville: Westminster John Knox, 2006), 166–75. She develops the idea of the minority voice with the help of Bakhtin.

to deconstruct the all-male image of God in the Jewish-Christian tradition and give us the opportunity to construct a new image of God.

Mary Therese DesCamp and Eve Sweetser have noted that "how we speak of God clearly shapes how we think of God, and of God and humans."[39] My student Abby formulates this statement in the following way: "Having examples of female god-language is important to young girls growing up and knowing that they are valued for who they are."[40] That young women, like Abby, still experience this in 2017, that all too often young girls are *not* valued for who they are, suggests that there is more work to be done in the search for the feminine side of God.

Bibliography

Baumann, Gerlinde. "Das göttliche Geschlecht: YHWHs Körper und die Gender-Frage." Pages 220–50 in *Körperkonzepte im Ersten Testament—Aspekte einer feministischen Anthropologie*. Edited by the Hedwig-Jahnow-Forschungsprojekt. Stuttgart: Kohlhammer, 2003.

Brenner, Athalya. "The Hebrew God and His Female Complements." Pages 48–62 in *The Feminist Companion to Mythology*. Edited by Carolyne Larrington. London: Pandora, 1992.

Brettler, Marc Zvi. "Incompatible Metaphors for YHWH in Isaiah 40–66." *JSOT* 18 (1998): 97–120.

Butler, Judith. *Gender Trouble: Feminism and the Subversion of Identity*. New York: Routledge, 1990.

Carvalho, Corrine L. "Sex and the Single Prophet: Marital Status and Gender in Jeremiah and Ezekiel." Pages 237–67 in *Prophets Male and Female: Gender and Prophecy in the Hebrew Bible, the Eastern Mediterranean, and the Ancient Near East*. Edited by Jonathan Stökl and Corrine L. Carvalho. AIL 15. Atlanta: Society of Biblical Literature, 2013.

———. "Whose Gendered Language of God?" *CurTM* 43 (2016): 12–16.

Claassens, L. Juliana. "Rupturing God-Language: The Metaphor of God as Midwife in Psalm 22." Pages 166–75 in *Engaging the Bible in a Gendered World: An Introduction to Feminist Biblical Interpretation in Honor of Katherine Doob Sakenfeld*. Edited by Linda Day and Carolyn Pressler. Louisville: Westminster John Knox, 2006.

---

39. DesCamp and Sweetser, "Metaphors for God," 236.

40. Abby Resch was a student in my Women, Gender and the Hebrew Bible class at the University of Minnesota, spring semester 2017. Quote used with permission.

Daly, Mary. *Beyond God the Father: Toward a Philosophy of Women's Liberation*. Boston: Beacon, 1973.
DesCamp, Mary Therese, and Eve E. Sweetser. "Metaphors for God: Why and How Do Our Choices Matter for Humans? The Application of Contemporary Cognitive Linguistics Research to the Debate on God and Metaphor." *PP* 53 (2005): 207–38.
Fauconnier, Gilles, and Mark Turner. *The Way We Think: Conceptual Blending and the Mind's Hidden Complexities*. New York: Basic Books, 2002.
Fischer, Irmtraud. "Isaiah: The Book of Female Metaphors." Pages 303–18 in *Feminist Biblical Interpretation: A Compendium of Critical Commentary on the Books of the Bible and Related Literature*. Edited by Luise Schottroff and Marie-Theres Wacker. Grand Rapids: Eerdmans, 2012.
———. "Las Imágens De Dios Tras La Adopción Del Monoteísmo: Ninguna Imagen Iconográfica, Pero Miles de Imágenes Verbales." Pages 167–80 in *Los Rostros De Dios: Imágens y experiencias de lo divino en la Biblia*. Edited by Carmen Bernabé Ubieta. Estalla: Editorial Verbo Divino, 2013.
Graybill, Rhiannon. "Yahweh as Maternal Vampire in Second Isaiah: Reading from Violence to Fluid Possibility with Luce Irigaray." *JFSR* 33 (2017): 9–25.
Gruber, Mayer I. "The Motherhood of God in Second Isaiah." *RB* 90 (1983): 351–59.
Hackett, Jo Ann. "Introduction and Notes to Numbers." Pages 194–254 in *The HarperCollins Study Bible: New Revised Standard Version, including the Apocryphal/Deuterocanonical Books*. Edited by Harold W. Attridge, Wayne A. Meeks, and Jouette M. Bassler. San Francisco: HarperSanFrancisco, 2006.
Hamori, Esther J. *"When Gods Were Men": The Embodied God in Biblical and Near Eastern Literature*. Berlin: de Gruyter, 2008.
Häusl, Maria. "'Mit wem wollt ihr mich vergleichen?' Gottesbilder und Geschlechterperspektive in Jes 40–55." Pages 127–38 in *Glaube in der Welt von heute: Theologie und Kirche nach dem Zweiten Vatikanischen Konzil; Für Elmar Klinger*. Vol. 2. Edited by Thomas Franz and Hanjo Sauter. Würzburg: Echter, 2006.
Johnson, Elizabeth A. *She Who Is: The Mystery of God in Feminist Theological Discourse*. New York: Crossroad, 1997.

Kamionkowski, Tamar S. *Gender Reversal and Cosmic Chaos: A Study on the Book of Ezekiel*. JSOTSup 368. London: Sheffield Academic, 2003.

Løland, Hanne. *Silent or Salient Gender? The Interpretation of Gendered God-Language in the Hebrew Bible, Exemplified in Isaiah 42, 46 and 49*. FAT 2/32. Tübingen: Mohr Siebeck, 2008.

Maier, Christl M. "Körperliche und emotionale Aspekte JHWHs aus Genderperspektive." Pages 171–89 in *Göttliche Körper—göttliche Gefühle: Was leisten anthropomorphe und anthropopathische Götterkonzepte im Alten Orient und Alten Testament?* Edited by Andreas Wagner. OBO 270. Fribourg: Universitätsverlag, 2014.

Mettinger, Tryggve N. D. *In Search of God: The Meaning and Message of the Everlasting Names*. Translated by Frederick H. Cryer. Philadelphia: Fortress, 1988.

Newsom, Carol A., Sharon H. Ringe, and Jacqueline E. Lapsley, eds. *Women's Bible Commentary*. 3rd ed. Louisville: Westminster John Knox, 2012.

Patai, Raphael. *The Hebrew Goddess*. New York: KTAV, 1967.

Philip, Tarja S. *Menstruation and Childbirth in the Bible: Fertility and Impurity*. StBibLit 88. New York: Lang, 2006.

Ricoeur, Paul. *The Rule of Metaphor: Multi-disciplinary Studies of the Creation of Meaning in Language*. Translated by Robert Czerny with Kathleen McLaughlin and John Costello. London: Routledge & Kegan Paul, 1978.

Schottroff, Luise, and Marie-Theres Wacker, eds. *Feminist Biblical Interpretation: A Compendium of Critical Commentary on the Books of the Bible and Related Literature*. Edited by Martin Rumscheidt. Grand Rapids: Eerdmans, 2012.

Schroer, Silvia. "Ancient Near Eastern Pictures as Keys to Biblical Metaphors." Pages 129–64 in *The Writings and Later Wisdom Books*. Edited by Christl M. Maier and Nuria Calduch-Benages. BW 1.3. Atlanta: SBL Press, 2014.

Smith, Mark. *The Early History of God: Yahweh and Other Deities in Ancient Israel*. San Francisco: HarperSanFrancisco, 1990.

———. "The Three Bodies of God in the Hebrew Bible." *JBL* 134 (2015): 471–88.

Sommer, Benjamin D. *The Bodies of God and the World of Ancient Israel*. Cambridge: Cambridge University Press, 2009.

Soskice, Janet Martin. *Metaphor and Religious Language*. Oxford: Oxford University Press, 1985.

Trible, Phyllis. "Depatriarchalizing in Biblical Interpretation." *JAAR* 41 (1973): 30–48.

Wagner, Andreas, ed. *Göttliche Körper—göttliche Gefühle: Was leisten anthropomorphe und anthropopathische Götterkonzepte im Alten Orient und Alten Testament?* OBO 270. Fribourg: Universitätsverlag, 2014.

Contributors

Michaela Bauks is Professor of Old Testament and Religious History at the Institute for Protestant Theology at the University of Koblenz-Landau.

Athalya Brenner-Idan is Professor Emeritus of Hebrew Bible/Old Testament at the University of Amsterdam and Extraordinary Visiting Professor at the Department of Old and New Testament, Faculty of Theology, Stellenbosch University, South Africa.

Ora Brison is a postdoctoral fellow at the Department of Biblical Studies, Tel Aviv University.

L. Juliana Claassens is Professor of Old Testament at the Department of Old and New Testament and head of the Gender Unit, Faculty of Theology, Stellenbosch University, South Africa.

Marta García Fernández is associate professor at the Departamento of Sacred Scripture and Church History at the Pontifical University of Comillas, Madrid.

Maria Häusl is Professor of Biblical Theology at the Institute for Catholic Theology of the Dresden University of Technology.

Rainer Kessler is Professor Emeritus of Old Testament at the Faculty of Protestant Theology of the Philipps-Universität Marburg.

Nancy C. Lee is Professor of Religious Studies (Hebrew Bible) at the Department of Religious Studies at Elmhurst College, Elmhurst, Illinois, and Extraordinary Visiting Professor in the Department of Old and New Testament, Faculty of Theology, Stellenbosch University.

Hanne Løland Levinson is associate professor at the Department of Classical and Near Eastern Studies at the University of Minnesota.

Christl M. Maier is Professor of Old Testament at the Faculty of Protestant Theology of the Philipps-Universität Marburg and Extraordinary Visiting Professor in the Department of Old and New Testament, Faculty of Theology, Stellenbosch University.

Ilse Müllner is Professor of Biblical Theology at the Institute for Catholic Theology of the University of Kassel.

Martti Nissinen is Professor of Old Testament Studies at the Theological Faculty of the University of Helsinki.

Ombretta Pettigiani teaches Scripture at the Istituto Teologico di Assisi.

Ruth Poser is a lecturer in distance learning of the Protestant Church in Central Germany.

Benedetta Rossi is a lecturer at the Pontifical Biblical Institute, Rome.

Silvia Schroer is Professor of Old Testament at the Theological Faculty of the University of Bern.

Omer Sergi is a lecturer at the Department of Archeology and Ancient Near Eastern Cultures, Tel Aviv University.

Ancient Sources Index

Hebrew Bible/Old Testament

Genesis
- 1:27 — 288
- 2 — 288
- 2:5 — 288
- 2:18 — 288
- 2:24 — 283
- 2:15–25 — 288
- 2:24–25 — 283
- 3:20 — 49, 287
- 4:25 — 378
- 11:1–9 — 268–69
- 12–36 — 378
- 15:5 — 308
- 16:4 — 242
- 16:8–9 — 242
- 19 — 173, 185, 203
- 19:5 — 185
- 19:37–38 — 378
- 22:17 — 308
- 24:19–34 — 178
- 24:64 — 178
- 29–30 — 378
- 31:19–35 — 204
- 32–33 — 28
- 32:13 — 308
- 34 — 159, 342
- 35 — 378
- 36 — 264
- 38:4–5 — 378
- 44:5–16 — 4

Exodus
- 2:10 — 378
- 3:1–5 — 141
- 7:10 — 113
- 7:11 — 112, 115
- 10:3–6 — 302
- 11:4–8 — 302
- 15 — 146
- 15:1 — 180–81
- 15:20 — 6, 53, 92
- 15:21 — 96, 180–81
- 19:8 — 283
- 19:12 — 288
- 21:10 — 281
- 22:15 — 116
- 22:16 — 116
- 22:17–18 — 115
- 24 — 387
- 24:3–7 — 283
- 34:15–16 — 123
- 38:8 — 51, 101

Leviticus
- 16–27 — 181
- 17:7 — 123
- 18 — 203, 344
- 18:7 — 281
- 18:18 — 236
- 18:25 — 188
- 19:3 — 288
- 19:10–19 — 281
- 20 — 203, 344
- 20:5–6 — 123
- 20:9 — 288
- 20:10 — 281
- 20:27 — 115, 136
- 21:9 — 120

Ancient Sources Index

Leviticus (cont.)
27:28	181
27:28–29	182
27:29	182

Numbers
5:16	297
5:25	297
11	399
11:12	377
12	96, 101
12:2	96
12:6–8	96
13–14	175
14:17	299
14:45	175
21:1–3	181
21:2–3	181
21:3	174
21:4–5	180
21:23–30	180
26:33	173
27:1–11	173, 179
27:36	179
31	189
31:15–18	189
36:11	173

Deuteronomy
1:22–40	175
1:44	175
5	6
5:16	288
5:22–33	5
6:4	283–84
6:5	283
13:13–19	188
13:16	187
16:17–18:22	4
17:16	217
17:16–20	240
17:18–20	94
17:20	148
18	6, 112
18:9–14	136
18:9–22	4
18:10	124
18:10–11	112, 115
18:10–14	4
18:11	5, 120
18:14–15	113
18:14b–22	5
18:15	5
18:15–18	5
18:15–22	94
18:18	5
18:19	5
21:10	168
21:14	169
21:22–23	168
22:5	188
22:22	281
24:1–4	283
31:16	123
32:18	280

Joshua
2	173, 179
2:1–3	161
2:4–7	161
2:9–11	161
2:12–13	161
2:15	68
6	173, 179, 181
6:21	187
6:25	161
10:28–39	187
11:11–14	187
11:21–22	175
14:6–15	175
15	178
15:12	176
15:13–14	175
15:13–19	173–74
15:15–19	175
15:18	177–78
15:15–20	174
15:20–63	176
16:1–6	179
17:3–4	173

19:4	175	4:14	95, 164
		4:16	187
Judges		4:17	165
1	173, 176, 184, 189–90	4:17–22	68, 142
1–12	180	4:21	178
1:1–20	175	5	142, 145, 176
1:1–2:5	174	5:1	143
1:3	175, 179	5:2–6	142–43
1:8	187	5:4–6	143
1:10–15	173–74, 176	5:6	120
1:10–20	174	5:6–7	165
1:12	176	5:7	95, 142–43
1:14	176, 178	5:8	142
1:14 LXX A	177	5:9–12a	142
1:14 LXX B	177	5:12	95, 142
1:15	176	5:13–19	142
1:16–17	178	5:20–31	142
1:17	175, 181, 187	5:24	165
1:19	175	5:25	120
1:20	175	5:26	142
1:21	175	5:27	165, 185
1:22–36	175	5:28–30	68
1:25	187	5:30	165
2:6	175	5:31	142
2:6–9	175	6–8	186
2:11	175	8:4–21	28
2:11–12	175	8:27	123
2:14–16	175	9:50–57	165
2:17	123	10:6	175
2:18–19	175	10:6–7	180
3–16	176	10:8	180
3:7	175	10:17–11:11	180
3:7–11	175	11	173, 182–84, 186, 188
3:12–12:15	176	11:1	180
4	95, 141, 145–46, 165	11:17–18	180
4–5	29, 94, 114, 116, 120, 164, 173	11:19–24	180
4:1–3	141, 146	11:23–24	180
4:1–9	164	11:25	180
4:1–5:31	140	11:27	180
4:4	92, 95	11:29	180
4:4–5	94, 140, 146	11:29–40	158, 180
4:5	95	11:30–31	180
4:6	95, 141	11:30–40	180, 182
4:9	141, 164	11:31	158
4:12–17	142	11:34	53, 68, 180

Ancient Sources Index

Judges (cont.)

11:35–36	181	21	28, 173, 184
11:36	182	21:1–5	187
11:37–40	182	21:6	187
11:39	158, 182–83	21:10–14	187
12:1–4	180	21:11	187
12:6	180	21:12	188
13:24	378	21:13–14	190
14	173	21:15–23	188
14:5–9	60	21:20–24	190
14:19	60	21:21	188
15:15	60	21:25	185, 189
16	173, 366		
16:4–22	166	1 Samuel	
16:5	166	1–4	26
16:18	166	1–12	186
16:19	60	1–14	25–26
16:30	60	1:2	167
17	173	1:5–6	167, 170
17–18	113	1:6	167
17–21	176, 184, 190	1:8	167
18:27	187	1:12–15	167
19	158–59, 185, 342	1:15	167
19–21	184, 186, 190	2:1–2	139
19:1	159, 185, 189	2:1–10	167
19:1–2	158, 185	2:3	140
19:3–9	185	2:4	167
19:9–10	158	2:5	167
19:22–27	185	2:6	168
19:23–30	185	2:8	168
19:24–25	158	2:12–36	198
19:26–27	158	2:21	167
19:27	68, 158	2:22	51, 53
19:29	158	2:27	120
20	184	2:30–31	197
20–21	173, 187	2:30–36	197
20:4–7	186	3	198
20:5	188	4:21	378
20:8–26	186	8	208
20:23	188	8:13	237
20:37	187	8:14–15	236
20:38–40	188	9–10	16, 26
20:40	186–87	9–14	13–14, 27, 31
20:47	186, 188	9–2 Sam 5	13, 15, 36
20:48	186–87	9:1	32
		9:1–10	16, 24

9:7	117	17:12	35
9:19–20	113	17:23	31
9:19–24	137	17:52	31
10:17–27	24	17:58	34
11	26	18	202–3
11:1	28	18–19	34–35, 203–4
11:1–15	24–25	18:1	162
11:3	28	18:2	34, 203
11:5	28	18:6	180
11:7	186	18:6–7	53
11:9–11	28	18:7	200
11:15	25, 32	18:11	343
13–14	24–26, 32	18:16	162
13–15	208	18:17	34
13–2 Kgs 12	15	18:18	35, 203
13:4–6	20, 32	18:20	162–63, 202
13:5–6	29	18:20–29	240
13:7b–15	26	18:23	203
13:14	29	18:25–27	58, 343
13:17–18	29	18:26	203
13:19–22	29	18:27	162–63, 203
13:20	29	18:28	162
14	199	19	202, 248
14:22–24	32	19:10	343
14:31	29	19:11–17	162, 240
14:32–35	26	19:12	68
14:39	188	20	162
14:41–42	113	20:33	343
14:44	188	21:11	31
14:46–51	26	21:12	200
14:46–52	26	21:13	31
14:47	32, 199	23–26	31
14:49	238, 240	23:2	35
14:49–51	202	23:4	35
15–16	162	24:5	343
15–2 Sam 5	27	25	204, 206
15:23	117	25:3	163
16	205	25:19	163
16–2 Sam 5	13–14, 30–31, 36	25:23	178
16:14–21	239	25:25	163
16:14–23	30	25:28	163, 206
16:17–19	30	25:28–31	205
16:21	239	25:36–38	163
17:2	32	25:39–42	163
17:4	31	25:32	205

1 Samuel (cont.)		5	31
25:44	162–63, 202, 240	5:1	35
26:7–8	343	5:1–2	34–35
27	31	5:1–3	30, 35
27–2 Sam 1	30	5:6	36
27:2–4	31	5:7	261
27:3	164	5:13–15	240
27:11	31	5:13–16	199
27:12	35	5:19	35
28	116, 120, 136, 200	5:23–24	35
28:3	117	6	202, 248
28:3–25	117, 120	6:16	68, 162–63, 203, 215
28:7	118	6:16–23	202, 240
28:7–20	114	6:20	163
28:8	118	6:20–23	162, 203, 215
28:10	4	6:21	204
29–30	31	6:23	202
29:5	200	7	163, 198–99, 206
30:5	164	7:5	199
31	26–27	7:11	199
31–2 Sam 1	30	7:11–16	209
31:1	29	7:13	199
31:1–13	26	7:16	199, 206
31:10	29	7:24	199
31:12	28	7:25	199
31:13	28	7:26	199
		7:29	199
2 Samuel		9	204
1–22	159	10–20	220
2:1–4	30, 35–36	11	206–10
2:4–5	28	11–12	206
2:2	164, 206	11:1	207
3	203, 214	11:3	240
3:2–5	240	11:5	208
3:3	164, 206	11:21	165
3:3–5	199	11:26	208
3:6–11	215	11:27	208
3:7	215, 241	12	208, 211
3:8	27	12:8	240
3:12–16	162	12:11	240
3:13	163	12:12	214
3:13–14	240	12:24	208, 240
3:13–16	202	13	159, 211, 238, 342
3:14	58, 163	13–20	15
4:4	237	13:3	221

13:12	212	1:33	25
13:12–18	185	1:39	25
13:13	212	2	201, 211, 214, 216, 229, 243
13:17–20	68	2:12–46	243
13:18	238	2:13–19	240
13:20	212–13	2:13–25	210, 215
13:23–27	212	2:17	239
14	101, 200	2:18–22	243
14–22	166	2:19	211, 243
14:1–24	238	3	218
15:14	241	3–12	15
15:16	213	3:1	217, 240
16:20–23	213	5–7	240
16:21	213–14, 241	5:3	242
16:22	241	7:8	217, 236, 240
19:6	240	9:16	240, 249
19:36	238	9:24	217, 236, 238, 240
20	66, 101, 165, 200	10	200
20:3	213, 236, 241	10:22	258
20:14–20	65	10:26–29	218
20:14–22	165	11	218
20:16	165	11:1	218, 240
21	198, 215	11:1–3	217
21:1	170, 198	11:1–4	241
21:1–14	215, 219	11:3	241
21:8	168, 202, 204, 240	11:5	264
21:8–11	241	11:7	264
21:10	215	11:19	242
21:12	28	12:25	28
22:1–51	140	14:21	244
24	215	14:31	244
24:21	299	15:2	244
24:25	299	15:5	208
		15:8	246
1 Kings		15:10	244
1	206, 209, 216, 229, 248	15:13	242, 244, 249
1–2	15, 206, 209–10, 220, 240	16:8–20	160
1–14	209	16:24	20
1:1–4	239	16:31	121, 159, 241
1:4	216, 239	16:31–34	248
1:10	209	17:10–16	113
1:11	209	18–24	113
1:11–31	209, 240	18:4	121, 159, 248
1:13	209	18:4–19	241
1:19	209	18:13	121, 159

1 Kings (cont.)		19:21	258
18:19	121, 159	20:18	236
19:1	241	21:1	245
19:1–2	159	21:6	4, 112
19:21	136	21:19	245
20:3	240	22–23	94
20:6	299	22:3–20	93, 147
21	160	22:4	55
21:5–25	241	22:12	246
21:25	160	22:12–20	116
22:42	244	22:14	92, 246
		22:14–20	114, 147, 238
2 Kings		22:15	147–48
2:9–12	144	22:15–20	148
2:10–11	144	22:16	148
2:12	144	22:18–20	149
2:13	144	22:20	149
2:13–18	144	23:2	94
2:20–22	144	23:7	249
3:4	21	23:24	264
4:1	297	23:29–30	149
4:23	181	23:31	245
7:11–12	235	23:36	245
8:17–18	244	24:8	245
8:18	244, 248	24:12	236, 245
8:26	160, 241, 244, 248	24:15	240, 245
9:7	159	24:18	245
9:7–37	241		
9:20–29	160	1 Chronicles	
9:22	116, 121, 248	1	264
9:30	68, 233	2:16	221
9:30–37	160	2:49	173
9:31	233	3:1–4	240
9:32	236, 247	3:5	240
10:13	242	3:5–9	240
11	160, 241, 244	3:10	246
11:2	237–38	4:30	175
11:20	161	10:12	28
12:2	244	10:13	118
14:2	244	14:3	240
15:2	244	15:29	240
15:33	244	21:1	177
16:2	244	25:1–7	136
18–20	262	25:5–6	101
18:2	245	26:1–19	55

Ancient Sources Index

33:6	113	2:11	235
34:20–28	116	2:13	235
		2:14	235–36
2 Chronicles		2:15	236
8:11	240		
11:18–21	241	Job	
11:20–22	244	2:3	177
13:21	241		
15:16	242, 244	Psalms	
18:2	177	8:5	203
21:6	244	9:15	258
21:12–19	240	22	397, 405
22:2	244	22:10	400
22:11	237–38	45	385
23:19	54	45:9	238
24:3	241	45:10	238, 241
29:1	245	45:11	385
34	94	45:13	258
34:22–28	147	45:14–15	235, 385
34:22	92	45:16	385
35:25	238	48:8	258
		51:2	240
Ezra		58:6	120
2:1	268	68:24–26	53
2:55	237	90:1	398
2:57	237	103:13	399
2:65	237	114:12	52
5:1–2	92	123:2	242
5:12	268	137:8	258, 269
6:14	92	147:10	61
9:11	92		
		Proverbs	
Nehemiah		1	65
2:6	241	1–9	277
6:5–9	92	2:17	264
6:14	92, 135	8	65
9:26	92	9:13	120
9:30	92	9:14	61
9:32	92	30:23	242
13:26	218, 241	31:3–5	240
		31:10	120
Esther		31:10–31	277
2:3	235–36		
2:8	236	Ecclesiastes	
2:9	235	2:7	237

Ancient Sources Index

Ecclesiastes (cont.)
2:8	238

Song of Songs
1:4	385
5:16	299

Isaiah
1	263
1–8	93
1–12	295–96, 374
1–23	262
1–39	263
1:2	280, 283
1:4–9	262
1:7–8	261
1:8	258
1:21	279
1:21–31	346
1:29	50
2:1–4	328
2:6	124
2:16	258
3:1–15	8
3:12	245
3:16–4:1	8
4:2	375
5	140
6	93
6:6–7	141
7	377, 379, 381, 389
7–8	295
7:1–10	376
7:3	295
7:10–17	375–77
7:11	296
7:14	137, 296, 327, 377–78, 381
8:1–4	93, 295, 311
8:1–18	295
8:3	2, 92–93, 116, 135, 296–98
8:3–4	137
8:8–10	375
8:11–15	295
8:16	295–96
8:16–17	137, 296
8:16–18	295–96
8:17	295
8:18	137, 295–96, 298
8:23–9:6	375–76
10:32	258
11:1–10	375–76
13	269
13:8	265, 323
13:16	342
13:19–22	269–70
14	271
14:22–23	270
16	93
16:1	258
16:4–5	375
19:16	343
20	344
20:3	296
21:3	323
21:6	150
21:9	269
22:4	259, 263
22:15	238
23	267
23:1	258
23:8	267
23:9	267
23:10	258
23:12	258, 267
23:15–17	267
23:16–18	267
24:2	242
26:17–18	323, 377
26:18	319–20, 323–25
28–39	263
30:6	323
32	388, 390
32:1–8	375–76, 388
32:6–7	389
32:9–14	388
32:15	389
32:15–20	388
33:11	320, 377
36–39	262–63
37	263

Reference	Page(s)
37:21	123
37:22–23	262
37:22	258
40	151, 263
40–48	270–71
40–55	151, 269, 405
40–66	151, 334, 347–48, 396, 402, 405
40:1–2	349
40:6–7	151
40:9	151
40:11	398
41:8–13	375
42	319, 381, 393
42:1–9	375–76
42:10–17	315
42:11	177
42:13	324
42:13–14	320, 324–25, 327
42:14	324–25, 348, 398, 403
42:14–16	151
42:16	325
43:10	270
43:13	270
44:6	270
44:8	397–98
45:1–4	270
45:5	270
45:18	270
46	270, 319, 381, 393
46–48	270
46:3–4	348, 403
47	269–71, 342, 345–46
47:1	123, 258, 269
47:1–3	348
47:1–15	117, 123–25
47:2	269
47:2–3	125, 270, 345
47:3	63, 269–70, 345
47:5	242, 258, 269
47:6	270
47:7	242, 269–70
47:8	270
47:9	120, 124
47:9–13	123, 269
47:10	270
47:11–15	270
47:12	124
47:13	125
48:12	270
49	319, 381, 384, 389, 393
49–55	281
49:1	380
49:1–6	377, 379
49:1–13	281, 375–76
49:2	388
49:5	380
49:9	152
49:13–21	151
49:14	263
49:14–15	380, 404
49:14–16	384
49:14–26	380
49:14–50:3	281
49:15	263, 348
49:18	384
49:21	263
49:23	241, 349
50:1	281
50:1–3	277
50:4–11	281, 375–76
50:7	349
51:1–52:12	281
51:17–20	263
51:23	263
52:1–2	348
52:2	258, 263
52:8	150
52:13–53:12	376
53	379
54	269, 277, 286, 349
54:1	263, 282
54:1–3	279
54:1–4	348
54:1–6	279
54:1–10	277
54:1–17	281
54:4	263, 279, 320
54:4–6	279
54:5–8	347

Isaiah (cont.)

54:5	282
54:6	263, 279, 398
54:7–8	281
54:11	282
54:11–12	282
54:11–17	282
54:13	282
54:13–14	282
54:17	282
54	279
55:1–3	282
55:3–5	376
56:3–5	343
57:3	117, 123–24, 279
57:3–13	123
57:5	50
57:6–13	348
57:9	124
60:4–5	384
60:14	384
60:15	279
61:1–3	376
62	277, 279
62:1–5	348, 385
62:4	279
62:4–5	347
62:11	258
63:16	398
64:10	299
66:3	264
66:6–9	320, 325
66:7–9	325
66:7–11	348
66:9	325, 348
66:13	348, 396

Jeremiah

1–25	304–5
1:1	380
1:2	380
1:5	380
2	9, 360
2–3	277
2–6	346
2:1–19	278
2:2	123
2:2–3	280
2:2–4:4	277, 279
2:4–8	280
2:6	280
2:9–10	280
2:9–19	281
2:13	280
2:18	280
2:20	50, 123, 279
2:20–21	280
2:20–35	280
2:23	280
2:24–25	280
2:25	280
2:32	280
2:33	280
2:36	280
3–9	259
3:1	279
3:1–2	280
3:1–5	281
3:1–13	123
3:1–4:4	260
3:2	61
3:3	279
3:4	264
3:6	50, 279
3:8	279
3:10	322
3:10–13	347
3:19–4:2	281
3:21	280
4–6	269
4:1	264
4:14–18	263
4:30–31	263
4:31	258, 318, 321
5	9, 360
5:1–6	263
6:1–8	263
6:2	258
6:11	351
6:17	150

6:23	258	22:26	242, 245
6:24	265, 321	23:1–4	376
7	57	24:1	242
7:30	264	25:33	305
8:2	305	26	376
9	65	26:22	246
9:21	68	27:9	112, 124
13	264–65, 270	29–33	321
13:18	242, 245, 263	29:2	242, 245
13:20–21	264	29:4–7	304
13:20–27	263, 264–65, 277, 346	30–31	316, 320–22
13:21	264–65, 321	30:3	322
13:22	63, 264–65, 281	30:6	265, 321–22
13:23	265	30:7	322
13:23–24	347	30:8	322
13:24	264–65	30:8–11	376
13:25	264	30:11	322
13:26	264–65	30:14	280
13:26–27	281	30:17	322
13:27	264	30:18–22	376
14:8	305	31	322
14:15	305	31:4	259
15:9–10	305	31:4–5	322
16:1	305	31:8	322
16:1–4	295, 303–4, 306, 311	31:8–9	321–22
16:1–9	304–5	31:10	322
16:2	303–6	31:13	322
16:2–4	305	31:21	259
16:2–9	306	31:31–34	277
16:3	304–5	33:14	376
16:3–4	305	33:14–26	376
16:4	305–6, 336	36:12	246
16:6	304	38:22	238
16:9	304	38:22–23	240
16:10	305	39:9	268
16:10–13	305–6	41:10	238
16:14–15	305	43:6	238
17:19–27	376	44	57
18:13	259	44:15–19	57
18:18	5	46:11	259
20:9	141	48:18	258
22:1–5	376	46:19	259
22:10	280	46:24	259, 265
22:22	280	50–51	269
22:23	321	50:37	316, 343

Ancient Sources Index

Jeremiah (cont.)		11:5	340
50:42	258	11:19	340
50:43	265	11:19–20	348
51:13	269	13	97, 117, 149
51:30	316, 343	13:1–16	97, 118
51:33	258	13:2–3	149
		13:5	280
Lamentations		13:6	149
1–2	258	13:9	280
1:6	258	13:10	149
1:7–11	299	13:11	340
1:15	259	13:14	344
2–4	259	13:17	5, 92, 118, 149
2:1	258	13:17–23	2, 96–97, 101, 114, 116, 118, 149
2:2	259		
2:4	258	13:18–22	149
2:5	259	13:19	117
2:8	258	13:22	280
2:10	258	13:23	97, 149
2:13	258	14:8	296
2:14	344	15:4	340
2:15	258	16	9, 61, 270, 277, 279, 339, 342–43, 345–46, 348–49, 351–52, 360, 367, 387
2:18	258		
4:21	259		
4:22	258–59	16:3–14	280, 307
5:11	342	16:6–9	387
		16:8	280
Ezekiel		16:15	279–80
1:4	141	16:15–22	280
1:12	340	16:15–34	280
1:27	141	16:16	279
2:2	341	16:17	279
2:8–3:3	339	16:23–23	280
3:17	150	16:26	279
4–24	339	16:28	279
4:9–13	340	16:30	279
5:10	340	16:31	279
5:11	264	16:31–34	279
5:12	336	16:33	279–80
7:15	340	16:34	279
7:20	264	16:35	279
8:3–6	51	16:36–37	280, 344
8:7–11	48	16:37	125, 281
8:14	51	16:37–39	266, 344
9:6	351	16:37–41	280–81

16:39	281	24:16	299, 302
16:41	279, 347	24:16–18	295
16:43	280	24:17	302
16:44–63	281	24:18	297, 299–302
16:45	307	24:19	300, 302
16:59–63	350	24:19–24	302–3
16:60–63	349	24:20–21	302
16:61–62	387	24:21	351
16:63	349	24:22	302
17:10	341	24:22–23	302
17:22–24	376	24:24	302
19	242, 245–46	25	339
20	340	25–32	339
20:43–44	350	26:7–14	267
21–37	299, 302, 343	27:1–26	267
21:12	340	27:26	340–41
22:10	344	28:21–23	267
23	9, 270, 277, 279–80, 339, 342–43, 345–347, 349, 352, 359–60, 367	33–48	348
		33:1–6	150
23:3	279	33:21–22	339
23:5	279	34	340
23:5–7	61	34:1–34	376
23:10	281	34:11–16	349
23:11	279	34:23–25	376
23:12	61	36:6	350
23:14–15	48	36:8–9	349
23:14–16	61	36:10–12	349
23:14–17	60, 344	36:16–38	350
23:19	279	36:26	340
23:23	61	36:26–27	348
23:25	280	36:30	350
23:26	281	36:31–32	350
23:29	63, 279, 281	36:33–36	349
23:30	279	37–38	349
23:41	61	37:1	341
23:43	279	37:1–10	340
23:44	279	37:1–14	348
24	339	37:14	340
24:1–2	339	37:15–28	376
24:3–13	339–40	37:23–28	349
24:15	302	39:1–21	349
24:15–17	299, 302	39:26	350
24:15–19	299	39:29	340
24:15–24	300	40–48	348, 376
24:15–27	298, 311	42:20	340

Ezekiel (cont.)
- 43:10–11 — 350
- 44:9–11 — 55
- 44:9–14 — 350
- 48:35 — 348

Daniel
- 2:2 — 115
- 2:15 — 115
- 9:24–27 — 376
- 11:31 — 264

Hosea
- 1–2 — 309
- 1–3 — 9, 264, 377–79, 294–95, 306–7, 309–11, 360
- 1:1 — 308
- 1:2 — (2x)
- 1:2–3 — 307
- 1:2–9 — 93, 278, 307–10
- XXXX — 279, 307–8
- 1:2 — 307–8
- 1:3 — 307
- 1:4 — 308
- 1:4–5 — 307
- 1:6 — 307–8
- 1:6–7 — 307
- 1:8 — 307
- 1:9 — 280, 307–9
- 2:1 — 308–9
- 2:1–3 — 278, 307, 309, 376
- 2:2 — 280
- 2:4 — 123, 279–80, 308–10
- 2:4–5 — 309
- 2:4–15 — 278, 308–10
- 2:4–25 — 278
- 2:5 — 125, 281
- 2:5–6 — 280
- 2:6 — 279
- 2:7 — 279–80
- 2:8 — 310
- 2:8–9 — 280
- 2:9 — 279–80
- 2:10 — 280
- 2:11–14 — 281
- 2:12 — 125, 280
- 2:12–15 — 310
- 2:15 — 280
- 2:16–17 — 280
- 2:16–25 — 278, 281
- 2:17 — 280
- 2:18–22 — 123
- 2:25 — 280
- 3:1 — 309–10
- 3:1–3 — 278
- 3:1–5 — 309–10
- 3:3 — 279, 310
- 3:4–5 — 278, 376
- 4 — 49
- 4–14 — 309
- 4:12–13 — 123
- 4:12–14 — 8
- 9:8 — 150
- 9:16 — 299
- 11 — 49
- 11:1–4 — 283
- 13:8 — 397–98

Joel
- 1 — 152
- 1:1 — 152
- 2 — 152
- 2:28–29 — 152
- 3 — 101, 152
- 3:1 — 2

Amos
- 4:3 — 235
- 5:2 — 259
- 8:1–2 — 150
- 8:3 — 238
- 9:11–15 — 376

Micah
- 1:13 — 258
- 2:8–11 — 8
- 2:12–13 — 376
- 3:11 — 117
- 4 — 329
- 4–5 — 317, 326–28

4:1–7	326, 328	Zechariah	
4:8	258, 382	2:11	258
4:8–13	326	2:14	258
4:9	327, 382	2:14–15	376, 383
4:9–10	265, 327, 382	2:15	270
4:9–5:3	320, 326	3:1–10	376
4:10	258, 327	3:14	258
4:11	63, 329	6:9–15	376
4:13	258, 327	9	389–90
4:13–14	388	9–14	384–87
5	389	9:1–8	383
5:1	382	9:2–5	383
5:1–5	376, 381	9:9	255, 258, 383–86
5:2	381–83	9:9–10	376, 383, 385
5:3 (MT 5:2)	327	9:10	384, 386
5:11–13	123	9:11	387
5:12–14	125	9:11–17	387
6	150	9:13	387
6:4	96, 150	11:4–14	376
7	150–51	12	390
7:1–10	150	12:5–6	264
7:4	150	12:9–13	376, 388–89
7:5–6	150	12:9–14	376
7:7	150	13:7–9	376
7:8–10	150	14:2	342
7:10	151		
		Malachi	
Nahum		2:10–16	8
1:2	268	3:5	115
1:2–9	268	3:23–24	3
2–3	125		
3	117	Deuterocanonical Works	
3:1	268		
3:1–7	346	Judith	
3:4	113, 123, 125, 268	9:11	61
3:4–7	268		
3:5	63	2 Esdras	
3:13	316, 343	16:14	92
Habakkuk		Sirach	
2:1	150	6:18–37	277
		14:20–15:10	277
Haggai		24:23–33	4
2:20–23	376	51:13–30	277

New Testament

Matthew
1	161
1:6–7	161
1:23	377
1:24	378
11:14	
14:6	54
16:14	3
17:10–13	3
21–27	385

Mark
6:15	
6:22	54
8:28	3

Luke
1:17	3
1:31	378
2:36–38	135
9:19	3

Acts
2:17–18	152

Romans
16:2	289

Philippians
4:3	289

Revelation
2:20	122
17–18	269
21:10–23	257

Early Jewish Works

b. Meg.
14a	136, 140
14b	148

b. Sanh.
67a	128

b. Sotah
12b	136

m. Sanhedrin
6:4	128

y. Sanh.
6:6	128

Ancient Near Eastern Texts

Inūma ilū awīlum
I.iv.189–194	287

ARAB
2.127	343

Modern Authors Index

Abma, Richtsje	277	Barton, John	375
Abusch, Tzvi	111	Bassler, Jouette M.	400
Ackerman, Susan	76, 96, 120, 145, 230	Bauer, Angela	321
Adams, Matthew J.	18	Bauks, Michaela	7, 158, 180, 184, 203, 215, 267, 340
Ahuis, Ferdinand	220		
Akkermans, Peter M. M. G.	16	Baumann, Gerlinde	63, 260, 268, 272, 277, 403
Albertz, Rainer	340		
Albright, William F.	19	Beauchamp, Paul	284, 288
Allen, Spencer L.	79	Bechmann, Ulrike	179
Alpi, Frédéric	99	Becker, Eve-Marie	317, 334
Alter, Robert	162	Becker, Uwe	195, 294
Ames, Frank R.	266, 342, 350	Becking, Bob	94
Amit, Yaira	14	Beerden, Kim	298
Andersen, Francis I.	381	Ben-Barak, Zafrira	230
Andreasen, Niels-Erik A.	229	Benjamin, Jessica	361–62
Angelini, Giovanni	284	Berges, Ulrich	339, 269–71
Anker, Johan	320	Bergmann, Claudia D.	315–16, 318–19, 324, 381
Annus, Amar	113		
Anthonioz, Stéphanie	122	Berlejung, Angelika	62, 342
Arnold, Bill T.	288	Bernett, Monika	51
Arnold, Jochen	255	Berquist, Jon L.	258
Asher-Greve, Julia M.	60	Berthelot, Katell	94–95
Atkinson, Clarissa W.	144	Bertholet, Alfred	298
Attridge, Harold W.	400	Beuken, Willem A. M.	263, 295–96
Augustin, Matthias	239	Beyendorff, Maximilian	402
Auld, Graeme	24–26, 28	Bezzel, Hannes	14, 24–26, 195
Ausín, Santiago	278	Bhabha, Homi K.	266
Aviram, Joseph	22	Bickel, Susanne	52
Bachmann, Mercedes G.	6, 135	Biran, Avraham	22
Bal, Mieke	140, 178	Bitter, Stephan	294
Barbiero, Gianni	305	Black, Max	256, 285
Baring, Anne	287	Block, Daniel I.	299
Barstad, Hans M.	94	Blum, Erhard	28
Barter, Penelope	301, 347, 350	Boase, Elizabeth	317, 333–34
Barthélemy, Dominique	178	Boda, Mark J.	386

Boer, Roland	366	Chester, Johnson A.	301
Bohak, Gideon	111	Chiodi, Maurizio	284
Bohleber, Werner	339	Church, Brooke P.	294
Borghino, Angelo	279, 282–83, 287	Claassens, L. Juliana	9, 152, 265, 316–18, 321, 325–26, 405
Borgonovo, Gianantonio	284		
Bottéro, Jean	111	Clements, Ronald E.	119
Bowen, Nancy R.	94, 97, 118–19, 149, 333	Clines, David J. A.	158, 163, 201
		Cohen, Chaim	115
Boyarin, Daniel	364	Collini, Paolo	374
Braulik, Georg	194	Collins, Adela Y.	374
Breithaupt, Fritz	196	Collins, John J.	374–75
Brekelmans, Christianus	25		
Brenner (Brenner-Idan), Athalya	9, 95–96, 112, 114, 118, 121, 123, 136–38, 142, 230–32, 260, 265, 298, 310, 359, 365–66, 368, 395	Collins, Terry	384
		Cook, Stephen L.	266, 345
		Cortese, Enzo	374
		Costello, John	399
Bresgott, Klaus-Martin	255	Creanga, Ovidiu	364–65
Brettler, Marc Z.	405	Cross, Frank M.	124, 202
Briggs, Charles A.	373	Crüsemann, Frank	231, 236
Brison, Ora	4, 95, 114, 116, 118, 120, 136–37, 142	Cryer, Frederick H.	111, 404
		Culley, Robert C.	25
Brockmüller, Katrin	175	Curvers, Hans H.	16
Bryce, Trevor R.	16	Czerny, Ernst	19
Buber, Martin	215	Czerny, Robert	256, 399
Buchanan, Constance H.	144	Daly, Mary	394
Bunnens, Guy	16	Darr, Katheryn P.	315, 324–25
Bürki, Micaël	79	Dass, Maria	280
Burns, Rita J.	138	Davies, Graham	262
Burrus, Virginia	364, 366	Davies, Margaret	260
Butler, Judith	252, 401	Davies, Philip R.	94
Butting, Klara	3, 136, 138, 141, 145, 147	Day, John	76, 375
Cahill, Jane	21	Day, Linda	405
Calduch-Benages, Nuria	47, 395	Day, Peggy L.	122
Camp, Claudia V.	258	De Sousa, Rodrigo F.	374
Campbell, Anthony F.	24–26	DeMaris, Richard E.	203
Campbell, Edward F.	18–19	Denning-Bolle, Sara J.	119
Carol L. Meyers	319	DesCamp, Mary T.	397–99, 406
Carr, David M.	346	Diamond, Pete A. R.	304–5
Carroll, Robert P.	92, 265, 303–6, 359	Díaz, José L. S.	278
Carroll R., M. Daniel	260	Dietrich, Walter	13–14, 24–25, 27, 29, 31, 35, 65, 166, 186, 194, 219
Carter, Charles E.	94, 383		
Carvalho, Corrine L.	75–77, 83, 401	Dijk-Hemmes, Fokkelien van	138, 260, 359
Cashford, Jules	287		
Chapman, Cynthia R.	58, 266, 344	Dille, Sarah	316, 323–25, 328
Charpin, Dominique	79–80	Dochhorn, Jan	317, 334

Dold, Alban 300
Donne, John 364
Donner, Herbert 229
Dozeman, Thomas B. 28
Drummond, Cassidy 402
Dube, Musa W. 162
Durand, Jean-Marie 25, 79, 81, 230
Dutcher-Walls, Patricia 121
Ebach, Ruth 1
Edelman, Diana V. 25, 27, 122
Edenburg, Cynthia 195
Efthimiadis-Keith, Helen 232, 366
Ehrensperger-Katz, Ingrid 257
Ehrlich, Carl S. 25
Eisen, Ute E. 196–97
El Azhary Sonbol, Amira 135
Ellens, J. Harold 333
Emerton, John A. 262
England, Emma E. 366
Eskenazi, Tamara C. 158, 163, 201–2
Estévez, Elisa 286
Evans, Craig E. 28
Ewald, Georg H. A. 293
Exum, J. Cheryl 145, 158, 201, 260, 265
Fauconnier, Gilles 398
Fernández, Marta G. 7, 279, 281–82, 287
Fewell, Danna N. 145
Figlear, Lena 402
Fink, Amir S. 233
Finkelstein, Israel 14–15, 17–23, 27- 29, 47, 76, 92–94, 96, 101, 112, 116, 121, 127, 233
Finlay, Timothy 378
Fischer, Andrea 207, 210
Fischer, Georg 304–5
Fischer, Gottfried 335–37
Fischer, Irmtraud 1, 3–4, 6, 8, 135–36, 138–39, 141, 147, 163–64, 186, 195–96, 200, 204–5, 210, 217–19, 238, 257, 262–63, 265, 294–95, 297, 319–20, 324, 334, 347–48, 378, 394, 402
Fishbane, Michael 111–12, 119–20
Fishbane, Simcha 128
Fitzmyer, Joseph 376
Fleming, Daniel 20, 34
Fleming, Erin E. 215
Flower, Michael A. 77
Floyd, Michael H. 92, 384
Fohrer, Georg 304
Fooken, Insa 335
Foucault, Michel 221
Frahm, Eckart 90
Franklin, Norma 20
Franz, Thomas 405
Frechette, Christopher G. 317, 333–34, 345
Freedman, David N. 381
Freißmann, Stephan 338
Frevel, Christian 194, 196, 230, 247
Friebel, Kelvin G. 304
Friedl, Corinna 240
Friedman, Mordechai A. 280
Fritschel, Ann L. 114, 119, 126
Frymer- Kensky, Tikva 278, 288
Fuchs, Esther 298, 311
Gadot, Yuval 18–20, 23
Gafney, Wilda C. 76, 93–94, 96, 101, 116, 136, 138, 140
Gafus, Georg 334
Galambush, Julie 123, 126, 285, 349
Galor, Katharina 180–81
Garber, David G. 316, 333, 350
García, Carlos G. 284
Garnier, Claudia 215
Gaß, Erasmus 28
Gehman, Henry S. 301
Geiger, Michaela 340
Gerber, Christine 196
Gertz, Jan C. 295
Gidion, Anne 255
Goitein, Shlomo D. 138
Goldingay, John 151
Goldman, Maurice D. 294
Goldstein, Joshua S. 341
Goodman, Nelson 6
Gordon, Pamela 359
Gordon, Robert P. 262
Goshen-Gottstein, Moshe H. 378
Grabbe, Lester L. 20, 75, 111, 113

Granofsky, Ronald	339	Hopfe, Lewis M.	315
Graybill, Rhiannon	404	Hornsby, Teresa	364–65
Green, Albert R. W.	113	Horwitz, Liora	23, 29
Greenberg, Moshe	119, 299, 302, 343	Hossfeld, Frank-Lothar	210
Grønbæk, Hans J.	27, 31	Hübner, Ulrich	14
Groß, Walter	28, 158, 175–76, 178, 180, 182, 185–86, 188	Huffmon, Herbert B.	113
		Hugenberger, Gordon P.	283
Gruber, Mayer I.	150–51, 402	Hühn, Peter	195
Guest, Deryn	347, 364–65	Hulster, Izaak de	16, 27
Guinan, Ann K.	85	Huppert, Ruth	348
Gunkel, Hermann	296	Hurvitz, Avi	115
Gunn, David M.	145	Hutton, Jeremy M.	28
Haak, Robert D.	92	Ihromi	229
Hackett, Jo Ann	144, 400	Jannidis, Fotis	195
Haex, Odette M.C.	16	Janowski, Bernd	3, 62, 196, 220–21, 319
Halbertal, Mosheh	197	Jansson, Patrik	97
Halpern, Baruch	20	Janzen, David	334
Hammerstaedt-Löhr, Almut	301	Jaques, Margaret	65
Hamori, Esther J.	76, 80, 92–97, 100–101, 114–16, 119, 123, 127, 136, 139, 147, 149, 181, 402	Jeffers, Ann	111–12, 115, 120
		Jobling, David	25
		Jochum-Bortfeld, Carsten	231, 236
Handel, Georg F.	255	Johnson, Elizabeth A.	401–2
Handy, Lowell K.	94, 101	Jonker, Louis C.	265
Häner, Tobias	350	Josephus, Flavius	261
Harding, James E.	203	Jost, Renate	174, 230, 243, 247
Hardwig, Oswald G.	255	Kaiser, Otto	14, 24–26, 263, 295, 378
Harris, Rivkah	288	Kajava, Mika	77
Hartenstein, Friedhelm	215	Kamionkowski, S. Tamar	315, 347, 401
Hartenstein, Judith	181	Kannada, Dolores G.	182
Hasel, Michael G.	33	Karrer, Martin	177, 301
Häusl, Maria	8, 196, 201, 214, 216, 221, 229, 236, 238–39, 243, 266, 405	Kase, Edmund H.	301
		Kauz, Sophie	233
Heeßel, Nils P.	90	Keefe, Alice A.	343
Hentschel, Georg	209, 218	Keel, Othmar	49, 51, 53, 55, 61–62, 64, 66–67
Herman, Judith	334		
Hertog, Cornelius G. den	14, 177	Kelle, Brad E.	266, 294, 307, 333, 342, 347, 350
Heskett, Randall	374–75		
Heuft, Gereon	335	Kern, Paul B.	341–43
Heym, Stefan	210	Keshgegian, Flora	322
Hieke, Thomas	181	Kessler, Rainer	7, 96, 136, 148, 174, 198
Hitchcock, Louise	23, 29	Kiesow, Anna C.	230, 232, 236–37, 239, 242–43, 246
Holladay, William	303, 305		
Holloway, Steven W.	90	Killbrew, Anne E.	21
Holmes, Stephen	197	Kim, Hyun C. P.	333
Holt, Else	317, 334	Kim, Wonil	316

Modern Authors Index

Kipfer, Sara 197, 221
Kirschbaum, Engelbert 257
Kittay, Eva F. 285
Kleiman, Assaf 19
Klein, Jacob 115–16, 128
Knauf, Ernst A. 34, 93, 209
Knobel, August 293–94
Knoppers, Gary N. 13
Koch, Ido 32
Koch, Klaus 3
Koenen, Klaus 267, 340
Kolk, Bessel A. van der 337
Kopf, Martina 337
Korpel, Maijo C. A. 119, 232–33
Kotzé, Gideon R. 265
Kratz, Reinhard G. 14–15, 24–26, 31
Kraus, Wolfgang 177, 301
Krondorfer, Bjorn 364
Küchler, Max 49, 64
Kühner, Angela 338, 345
Kunz, Andreas 193, 200
Kupitz, Yaakov S. 94–95
Kutsch, Ernst 345
Laato, Antti 374, 377, 379
Lakoff, George 285
Lamphere, Louise 116
Lampinen, Antti 77
Langlois, Michael 25
Lanoir, Corinne 174, 178–79
Lapsley, Jacqueline E. 149, 152, 347, 350, 352, 394
Lastra Montalbán, Miguel de la 277
Lavender-Fagan, Teresa 111
Lederman, Zvi 18
Lee, Archie C. C. 118, 137, 368
Lee, Nancy C. 6, 136, 140, 144, 146, 150–51
Lee, Sharon 17
Lehmann, Gunnar 23, 30–31
Lemaire, André 116
Lemos, Tracy M. 343
Lesko, Barbara S. 288
Leuenberger, M 1
Levinson, Hanne L. 7, 151
Levy, Janet 231
Levy, Thomas 17
Lewis, Theodore J. 112, 124
Liess, Kathrin 203, 215, 319
Lipschits, Obed 18, 21, 32, 326
Lloyd, Jeffrey B. 119
Lodeiro, J. A. Castro 288–89
Lohr, Joel N. 28
Løland, Hanne 319, 324, 381, 393–95, 397–98, 400, 403
Loretz, Oswald 167
Luchsinger, Jürg 222
Lucius-Hoene, Gabriele 338
Lust, Johan 25, 300, 374
Lynch, Matthew J. 350
Macintosh, Andrew A. 308
Maeir, Aren M. 23, 29, 31
Magdalene, F. Rachel 266, 359
Maier, Christl M. 7, 47, 51, 65, 256–60, 265, 316, 340, 348, 383, 395, 403
Malamat, Abraham 235
Maloney, Linda M. 260
Marjanen, Antti 77
Marks, Stephan 350
Marsman, Hennie J. 232–33, 278, 283–84, 288
Masenya (Ngwan'a Mphahlele), Madipoane 265
Mathys, Hans P. 222
Maul, Stefan M. 90
Maurey, Yossi 233
Maurizio, Lisa 77
Mays, James L. 382
Mazar, Amihai 17, 21
Mazzoni, Stefania 16
McCarter, P. Kyle 24–26
McConville, J. Gordon 13
McEvenue, Steve 151
McFarlane, Alexander C. 337
McKane, William 305–6
McLaughlin, Kathleen 399
Meeks, Wayne A. 400
Melville, Sarah C. 214
Merlo, Paolo 79
Mettinger, Tryggve N. D. 404
Metzler, Luise 168–69, 219, 241

Meyer, Marion 257
Meyers, Carol L. 116, 127, 138–39, 231, 288, 384–85, 387
Meyers, Eric M. 384–85, 387
Miescher, Elisabeth C. 218
Miles, Margaret R. 144
Milgrom, Jacob 113, 235
Mirkam, Nivi 18
Molin, Georg 229
Montaguti, Mirko 385
Moore, Stephen D. 364–66
Moughtin-Mumby, Sharon 278
Mowinckel, Sigmund 373
Müller, Christoph G. 197
Müller, Hans-Peter 180
Müller, Monika C. 239
Müllner, Ilse 8, 51, 159, 186, 188, 194, 196–97, 199, 211, 222, 231, 236, 265, 347
Münger, Stefan 14, 27, 29, 52
Mymon, Meir B. 364–65
Na'aman, Nadav 14–15, 20–21, 24–27, 31–32, 35–36
Nauman, Thomas 13
Navarro Puerto, Mercedes 6, 47, 135, 139, 278
Nelson, Harold H. 58
Nelson, Sarah M. 231
Neusner, Jacob 375
Newsom, Carol A. 149, 152, 394
Newsome, James 151
Ngan, Lai L. E. 193, 195
Ngunga, Abi T. 375
Niditch, Susan 146, 176, 178–79, 183–85, 188–89
Niehr, Herbert 16
Niemann, Hermann Michael 20, 23, 30–31, 239
Nissinen, Martti 364, 383
Nissinen, Martti 4–5, 49, 76, 78, 83, 88, 90–92, 94, 97–98, 100, 113
Noth, Martin 28
O'Brien, Julia M. 326–29
O'Connor, Kathleen M. 320–22, 334, 339, 346–47, 351

Odell, Margaret S. 344
Oeming, Manfred 16, 27
Oeming, Manfred 326
Olmo Lete, Gregorio del 79
Olyan, Saul M. 25, 112
Ortlund, Eric 349–51
Ortony, Andrew 285
Otto, Eckart 261
Overholt, Thomas W. 75
Pakkala, Juha 195
Parpola, Simo 87–88, 91, 100
Parry, Donald W. 297
Patai, Raphael 395
Patton, Corrine L. 266, 343, 345
Paul, Shalom M. 115
Payne, David 151
Paz, Sarit 53, 180–81
Peinado, Federico L. 281, 283
Peled, Ilan 83
Petersen, David L. 28, 386
Pettigiani, Ombretta 3, 307
Philip, Tarja S. 393
Pithan, Annebelle 49
Poethig, Eunice B. 138, 144–45
Pohlmann, Karl F. 299, 301
Polaschegg, Andrea 210
Porter, Ann 33–34
Poser, Ruth 9, 65, 266, 268, 317, 333, 335–36, 340, 344–45, 350–51
Pressler, Carolyn 405
Pury, Albert de 28
Qimron, Elisha 297
Qualbrink, Andrea 49
Radebold, Hartmut 335
Rake, Mareike 174
Ramsey, Bronk 17
Ranke, Friedrich H. 255
Rapp, Ursula 96
Rechenmacher, Hans 237, 246
Redditt, Paul L. 385
Rehm, Ellen 233–34
Rembaum, Joel E. 379
Renaud, Bernard 278
Resch, Abby 406
Richards, Ivor 256

Modern Authors Index 437

Ricoeur, Paul 7, 256, 285, 399
Riede, Peter 203, 215
Riedesser, Peter 335–37
Ringe, Sharon H. 149, 152, 394
Robin, Christian 233
Rogerson, John W. 260
Rollins, Wayne G. 333
Rollston, Christopher 233
Römer, Thomas 25, 28, 79, 94, 203, 233
Rosa, Hartmut 196
Rosaldo, Michelle Z. 116, 127
Rosen, Baruch 18
Rosenberg, Joel 220
Rossi, Benedetta 6
Rost, Leonhard 207
Rowe, Jonathan Y. 203
Rowlett, Lori 366
Rüdele, Viola K. 352
Rudolph, Wilhelm 303, 306
Runions, Erin 327
Rütersworden, Udo 148, 238
Rydelnik, Michael 374
Sack, Martin 338
Sader, Helen 16
Saggs, Henry 118–19
Sals, Ulrike 269–71, 347
Sanmartín, Joaquin 281, 283
Sasson, Jack 180–81
Saur, Markus 222, 267
Sauter, Hanjo 405
Sawyer, John F. A. 281
Schäfer-Lichtenberger, Christa 206
Scheidt, Carl E. 338
Scheuer, Blaženka 94
Schmid, Konrad 28, 257, 262, 265, 294, 347
Schmidt, Ludwig 24–25, 27
Schmidt, Uta 157, 160, 167, 340
Schmitt, Rüdiger 111–12, 121, 183
Schneider, Deborah L. 335
Schnocks, Johannes 215–16
Schökel, L. Alonso 278
Scholz, Susanne 193
Schottroff, Luise 8, 186, 229, 262, 268, 320, 348, 394

Schroer, Silvia 7, 47, 49, 51–53, 55–56, 60–61, 65–66, 166, 229, 238, 257, 395
Schüngel-Straumann, Helen 340
Schwartz, Glenn M. 16
Schwienhorst-Schönberger, Ludger 210
Scurlock, Jo Ann 119
Sefati, Yitschak 115–16, 128
Segovia, Fernando F. 122
Sergi, Omer 6, 15–16, 18–22, 27–28, 30–32
Shargent, Karla G. 193
Sharp, Carolyn J. 260, 316
Sherwood, Yvonne 310
Shields, Mary E. 260
Sicre, José L. 161
Simon, Uriel 118
Siquans, Agnethe 1
Sjöberg, Michael 184
Skinner, John 303
Smelik, Klaas A. D. 34
Smit, Peter-Ben 365
Smith, Mark 395, 403
Smith-Christopher, Daniel L. 266, 333, 344–45, 351, 382
Snell, Daniel C. 214
Soggin, J. Alberto 174, 178
Solà, Teresa 278
Solvang, Elna K. 214, 221, 231, 234–38, 242
Sommer, Benjamin D. 403
Soskice, Janet M. 398
Spanier, Ktizah 230
Spieckermann, Hermann 5–6, 15
Spiering-Schomborg, Nele 196
Spina, Frank A. 113
Stager, Lawrence E. 20
Standhartinger, Angela 196
Stansell, Gary 203, 388
Staubli, Thomas 53, 233, 236
Stegemann, Wolfgang 203
Steiner, Margaret L. 21
Steiner, Till M. 209–10
Stiebert, Johanna 349–50
Stienstra, Nelly 277

Stjerna, Kirsi 75
Stoebe, Hans J. 24–25
Stökl, Jonathan 75–79, 81, 83, 87, 91, 97, 149, 401
Stolz, Fritz 24–26, 31
Stone, Bebb W. 151
Stone, Ken 198, 364–65
Strawn, Brent A. 94
Strohmaier, Alexandra 196
Strong, John T. 344
Stulman, Louis 317, 333–34
Suchanek-Seitz, Barbara 239, 243
Svärd, Saana 83, 89–90, 197, 201, 207, 214, 217–18, 221, 229, 231, 236, 240–41
Sweeney, Deborah 60
Sweetser, Eve E. 397–99, 406
Szanton, Nahshon 22–23
Szuchman, Jeffrey 34
Taschl-Erber, Andrea 6, 47
Taylor, Bernard A. 300
Taylor, Terry F. 350
Teppo, Saana 91, 238
Tervanotko, Hanna 76, 96
Thiel, Winfried 305
Thöne, Yvonne S. 51
Tiemeyer, Lena-Sofia 151
Timm, Stefan 219
Toffolo, Michael B. 17
Tolbert, Mary A. 122
Tooman, William A. 301, 347, 350
Toorn, Karel van der 112, 119–20
Trible, Phyllis 158, 184–86, 399
Tuckett, Christopher M. 385
Turner, Mark 285, 398
Ubieta, Carmen B. 394
Uehlinger, Christoph 49, 64, 268
Ulrich, Eugene C. 92, 378
Uro, Risto 91
Ussishkin, David 20
Uziel, Joe 22–23
Van Der Steen, Evelin J. 18, 33–34
Van Oorschot, Jürgen 221
Van Seters, John 31
Vanderhooft, David 345

Vaughn, Andrew G. 21
Veenhof, Klaas R. 270
Veijola, Timmo 31
Ventura, Agnès G. 83
Vermeulen, Karolien 125
Volges, Walter 279
Vos, Cor de 177
Wacker, Marie-Theres 8, 49, 186, 229, 262, 268, 320, 348, 394
Wagner, Andreas 221, 403
Wallis, Gerhard 288
Washington, Harold C. 359
Watson, Wilfred G. E. 119
Weems, Renita J. 94, 277–78
Weider, Andreas 307–8
Weidner, Daniel 210
Weidner, Ernst 234
Weigel, Sigrid 256
Weingart, Kristin 34
Weippert, Helga 270
Weippert, Manfred 78, 87, 91, 219
Weisaeth, Lars 337
Weiser, Artur 30, 304–5
Weißflog, Kay 296
Wellhausen, Julius 24, 26
Wénin, André 294
Westbrook, April D. 212–14, 220
Westermann, Claus 340
White, Marsha C. 25–26
Wildberger, Hans 295–96
Wilhelm, Gernot 231
Willi, Thomas 222
Williamson, Hugh G. M. 20, 76, 92–95, 257, 265, 347
Willi-Plein, Inna 34–35, 204, 219–21
Willmes, Bernd 197
Wimmer, Stefan J. 334
Winter, Urs 55, 57, 61
Wischer, Mariele 49
Wischnowsky, Marc 258–59
Wolff, Hans W. 307–8
Wright, David P. 235
Wright, Jacob L. 14, 26–28, 342, 350
Wright, John W. 55
Wyatt, Nicolas 119

Yee, Gale A.   95, 114, 142, 145, 308–9, 365, 368
Zakovitch, Yair   165
Zenger, Erich   194
Zertal, Adam   18
Ziegler, Joseph   301
Ziegler, Nele   80
Zimmerli, Walther   118–19, 299, 301–2, 307
Zsolnay, Ilona   83
Zvi, Ehud Ben   122, 326